THE NATIONAL UNDERWRITER COMPANY
a division of ALM Media, LLC

PRACTICAL GUIDE TO MERGERS, ACQUISITIONS AND BUSINESS SALES

Joseph B. Darby III, J.D.

Buying and selling a business is a challenging process that involves rituals and interactions often similar to that of a couple's courtship. And while many business courtships end in an economic marriage, others fail. Many unsuccessful business negotiations could have made sense, but floundered, because negotiations went badly awry at some crucial point.

Concise and easy to understand, ***Practical Guide to Mergers, Acquisitions and Business Sales*** not only helps readers truly grasp the tax consequences of buying or selling a business, but also carefully examines the art of successfully closing major business transactions through a solid understanding of the tax ramifications of the deal.

Drawing on a vast 30 years of experience, author **Joseph B. Darby III**—a business and transactional tax law expert—incorporates insightful, real-life examples throughout his coverage of buying and selling of all forms of business entities, including: Sole Proprietorships; Partnerships; S Corporations; C Corporations; Limited Liability Companies, Professional Corporations; and more.

Broad in scope, with numerous citations to the IRS Code, rulings, and regulations, this resource covers:

- how tax aspects of the sale of a business can influence negotiations, both in a positive and negative way
- the areas for "give and take" in any negotiation of tax liability for the sale of a business
- strategies related to Installment Sales, Contingent Payments, Goodwill, Consulting Agreements with prior owners, and other methods that can be introduced into a business acquisition
- common pitfalls in the negotiation process, including the overlooking of critical tax issues

A must-have for financial advisors, lawyers, CPAs, or any professional involved in advising clients on the buying and selling of a business, ***Practical Guide to Mergers, Acquisitions and Business Sales*** succeeds in its mission of teaching its readers how to pare the tax costs of transactions to the absolute minimum, as well as how tax liabilities can be negotiating tools for buying or selling a business.

For customer service questions or to place additional orders, please call 1-800-543-0874.

Related Titles Also Available:

Tax Facts on Investments
Tax Facts on Individuals & Small Business
The Tools & Techniques of Financial Planning
Takeovers & Freezeouts
Negotiated Acquisitions of Companies, Subsidiaries and Divisions
Acquisitions Under the Hart-Scott-Rodino Antitrust Improvements Act
REITs: Mergers and Acquisitions
Savings Institutions: Mergers, Acquisitions and Conversions

Second Edition

PRACTICAL GUIDE TO MERGERS, ACQUISITIONS AND BUSINESS SALES

- C Corporations • S Corporations • Partnerships
- Limited Liability Companies • Sole Proprietorships

Joseph B. Darby III, J.D.

ISBN: 978-1-945424-51-9
Library of Congress Control Number: 2017943284

published by
THE NATIONAL UNDERWRITER COMPANY

The National Underwriter Company
A Division of ALM Media, LLC
4157 Olympic Blvd. Ste. 225
Erlanger, KY 41018

Second Edition

Printed in the United States of America

ABOUT THE NATIONAL UNDERWRITER COMPANY

a division of ALM Media, LLC

For over 110 years, The National Underwriter Company, *a division of ALM Media, LLC* has been the first in line with the targeted tax, insurance, and financial planning information you need to make critical business decisions. Boasting nearly a century of expert experience, our reputable Editors are dedicated to putting accurate and relevant information right at your fingertips. With *Tax Facts, Tools & Techniques, National Underwriter Advanced Markets, Field Guide, FC&S®, FC&S Legal* and other resources available in print, eBook, CD, and online, you can be assured that as the industry evolves National Underwriter will be at the forefront with the thorough and easy-to-use resources you rely on for success.

Update Service Notification

This National Underwriter Company publication is regularly updated to include coverage of developments and changes that affect the content. If you did not purchase this publication directly from The National Underwriter Company, *a division of ALM Media, LLC* and you want to receive these important updates sent on a 30-day review basis and billed separately, please contact us at (800) 543-0874. Or you can mail your request with your name, company, address, and the title of the book to:

The National Underwriter Company
a division of ALM Media, LLC
4157 Olympic Boulevard
Suite 225
Erlanger, KY 41018

If you purchased this publication from The National Underwriter Company, *a division of ALM Media, LLC*, directly, you have already been registered for the update service.

Contact Information

To order any National Underwriter Company title, please

- call 1-800-543-0874, 8-6 ET Monday – Thursday and 8 to 5 ET Friday
- online bookstore at www.nationalunderwriter.com, or
- mail to Orders Department, The National Underwriter Company, *a division of ALM Media, LLC*, 4157 Olympic Blvd., Ste. 225, Erlanger, KY 41018

To my father, Joseph B. Darby, Jr., who taught me to write, and my brother, Leslie F. Darby, who inspired me to do so.

Finally, to my mother, Eleanor Daley Darby, for all the books she read to me when I was young and for reading – or at least solemnly claiming to have read – this book.

PREFACE

I decided to write this book a few years ago when I went to find it in my law firm library and it wasn't there.

What I was looking for, specifically, was a practical book on buying and selling companies that provided a fast, insightful education on a wide range of common (and not-so-common) tax and business issues.

The emphasis in this book is on "practical." Business acquisitions are both fast- paced and complicated, and often there simply is not time to do scholarly research on every theoretical tax issue that presents itself in the course of a transaction. This is not to say that negotiators should ignore the nuances of tax law—far from it. Rather, this book recognizes that in a high-pressure negotiating environment, where major decisions are being made in real time, one can't always know the complete answer right away, but should always know enough to ask the right questions.

The goal of this book, therefore, is to provide people negotiating real deals— tax lawyers, business lawyers, accountants, and even clients—with the tools they need to gain a fast, reasonably complete understanding of the crucial tax and business issues. In brief, the goal is to explain relatively complicated matters in a manner that is both efficient and sufficient.

There are, to be sure, other, longer, more dismal tomes covering many of these topics—indeed, when there is time, I consult them myself. This book, however, is written to be a practical first resource to answer questions ranging from "Should I make a 338(h)(10) election?" to "How can I use an ESOP to finance an acquisition?" to "Is it better to buy stock or assets?"

Of course, when the topic is as sophisticated and dense as merger and acquisition transactions, even a practical guide is going to address some inherently complicated topics. However, my hope is that this book will demystify some of the more mysterious elements of the Internal Revenue Code and, in turn, will "de-confuse" certain subjects that readers might otherwise find inherently confusing.

Someone once observed that any reasonably intelligent person can explain a complicated topic and make it sound complicated: What is far harder is to explain a complicated topic and make it sound simple.

In writing this book I was motivated by the desire to find a better, simpler way to describe how the Internal Revenue Code applies to the buying and selling of businesses. Hopefully, in a significant and useful way, I have achieved that goal.

Joseph B. Darby III
January 2006

ABOUT THE AUTHOR

Joseph B. Darby III is a partner in Sullivan & Worcester's Boston office, focusing his practice on business and transactional tax law. Mr. Darby advises a wide variety of corporations and high-net-worth individuals on tax and legal aspects of business and real estate activities and represents these taxpayers before federal and state taxing authorities. He also works with high-net-worth individuals and business owners to organize their personal income tax and estate planning affairs in order to maximize wealth preservation and minimize tax on transfers to family members, charities and other recipients. This is accomplished through the use of the latest sophisticated estate planning strategies, including family limited partnerships, installment sales to defective grantor trusts, the formation of family charitable foundations, and other similar techniques.

Mr. Darby has represented and advised numerous public and private companies, as well as private equity and venture capital firms, on investment and acquisition transactions and on the disposition of business interests, in transactions ranging from early-stage investments in high-tech startups to acquisitions and sales of mature, late-stage companies and publicly traded corporations.

Another focus in Mr. Darby's practice is the taxation of intellectual property, including tax aspects related to the development, licensing and exploitation of intellectual property rights, the migration of valuable intellectual property to offshore jurisdictions and the tax-efficient sale of intellectual property rights.

Mr. Darby has extensive experience in the areas of structuring mergers, acquisitions, business sales, and related business transactions. He teaches graduate-level courses on the buying and selling of businesses at Boston University School of Law in the Graduate Tax Program and at Bentley University McCallum Graduate School of Business in the Masters of Taxation Program.

Mr. Darby has been the recipient of numerous journalism and writing awards, and has authored two books and more than 1,000 articles published in such diverse publications as *The Tax Lawyer, Worth Magazine, Venture Capital Magazine, Banker & Tradesman, Mass High Tech, Hemispheres Magazine, Contract Professional, Trusts & Estates Magazine, The Boston Globe, The Boston Herald, The Boston Business Journal* and *The Boston Phoenix*. Mr. Darby is a frequent contributor to the World Trade Executive family of publications, including *Practical International Tax Strategies, Practical European Tax Strategies*, and *Practical US Tax Strategies*, and is a member of the editorial and advisory board of *World Trade Executive*.

Mr. Darby served as a member of the Board of Assessors for the Town of Watertown from 1993-2011, and has served as pro bono legal and tax counsel to a variety of Boston-area charitable organizations. He is a former president of the Boston Police Foundation (2008-2012) and is currently president of the Watertown Police Foundation, an organization he founded in April 2013 to help Watertown recover from the violent events that led to the capture of the Marathon bombing suspects.

Mr. Darby is the editor of the Tax & Sports Update.

ABOUT THE PUBLISHER

Kelly B. Maheu, J.D., is Vice President in charge of the Practical Insights Division of ALM Media, which produces National Underwriter's professional publications. Kelly has been with National Underwriter since 2006, and has served as the Managing Director of National Underwriter's Professional Publishing Division as well as performing editorial, content acquisition, and product development roles.

Prior to joining The National Underwriter Company, Kelly worked in the legal and insurance fields for LexisNexis®, Progressive Insurance, and a Cincinnati insurance defense litigation firm.

Kelly has edited and contributed to numerous books and publications including the *Personal Auto Insurance Policy Coverage Guide, Cyberliability and Insurance, The National Underwriter Sales Essentials Series*, and *The Tools & Techniques of Risk Management for Financial Planners*.

Kelly earned her law degree from The University of Cincinnati College of Law and holds a BA from Miami University, Ohio, with a double major in English/Journalism and Psychology.

ABOUT THE MANAGING EDITOR

Richard H. Cline, J.D., is the Manager, Tax and Insurance Content for the Practical Insights Division at The National Underwriter Company. He is responsible for both the print and online versions of Tax Facts as well as developing new tax products for our customers.

Richard joined the company in 2013 but has over twenty-five years of tax editing and publishing experience. Prior to joining our team, Richard worked for Lexis-Nexis, CCH, Inc., and PricewaterhouseCoopers.

He has a B.S. degree from Franklin and Marshall College in Lancaster, Pennsylvania, and earned his law degree from Tulane University in New Orleans, Louisiana.

ABOUT THE EDITOR

Jason Gilbert, J.D., M.A., is an assistant editor with the Practical Insights Division of The National Underwriter Company, a division of ALM Media, LLC. He edits and develops publications related to tax and insurance products, including titles in the *Advisor's Guide* and the *Tools & Techniques* series of investment and planning products. He also develops content for National Underwriter's other financial services publications and online products. He has worked on insurance and tax publications for more than nine years.

Jason has been a practicing attorney for more than a dozen years in the areas of criminal defense, products liability, and regulatory enforcement actions. Prior to joining National Underwriter, his experience in the insurance and tax fields has included work as a Westlaw contributor for Thomson Reuters and a tax advisor and social media contributor for Intuit. He is an honors graduate from Wright State University and holds a J.D. from the University Of Cincinnati College Of Law as well as a master's degree in Economics from Miami University in Ohio.

EDITORIAL SERVICES

Connie L. Jump, Senior Manager, Editorial Operations

TABLE OF CONTENTS

BASIC CONSIDERATIONS IN BUYING OR SELLING A BUSINESS

CHAPTER 1

OVERVIEW

This book is about the tax aspects of buying and selling a business—but, inevitably, it is also about the special art of closing a major business transaction successfully.

Selling a business is a challenging process. It involves rituals and interactions that are sometimes eerily similar to the courtship dynamic between a human couple that begins dating, gets engaged, and eventually marries. There is an early period of curiosity, a period of exploration and discovery, a point of infatuation when the courting relationship becomes serious, and often a rocky period when the relationship seems likely to fall apart. There are frequently family members (or at least minority shareholders) dead set against the union, and sometimes a competing suitor waiting in the wings. And finally, despite all the obstacles and travails, through hard work and perseverance the business marriage is successfully consummated.

Or not. While many business courtships end in an economic marriage, plenty of others fail, for a variety of reasons. Often, if a business deal does not satisfy rigorous business logic, it eventually becomes apparent to one or both parties. This can be viewed as a "successful" conclusion in the sense that the right outcome is achieved. But plenty of other unsuccessful business negotiations are "could haves" and "should haves"—transactions that made sense, or could have made sense, but ultimately floundered because negotiations went badly awry at some crucial point.

Practical experience shows that tax issues are often the major source of missteps in a business mating dance. Not surprisingly, the parties can get well into a negotiation before they get into a serious tax-structuring discussion. After all, you have to decide if you like each other before you start to talk about marriage. At that point, however, and to the shock and dismay of one or both sides, it can become apparent for the first time that the two parties have been operating on tax assumptions that are either fundamentally different or wrong, or both. A business deal needs to maintain a certain forward momentum to completion. An abrupt change in prevailing tax assumptions can throw a negotiation off so badly that sometimes it never recovers. This is especially true when the parties have expended a significant amount of time and effort negotiating a transaction based on a flawed tax framework. Sometimes, too much effort and energy has been expended reaching now meaningless compromises, and the parties are unable or unwilling to start the courting ritual over again.

For example, I once received an emergency telephone call from a partner who was at another law firm closing a merger in which we represented the Target. In fact, the transaction was already "closed" as far as all the participating parties were concerned. However, after all of the documents were signed, the attorney (prudently, if belatedly) decided to run the transaction past me so that I could "bless it". (Being a tax attorney is sometimes akin to being a minister or rabbi.) The transaction was supposed to be a "reverse triangular merger" qualifying as a "tax-free reorganization". However, the proposed transaction, which involved the acquisition of our client's corporation through a merger into a second-tier subsidiary (a sub of a sub), did not satisfy the technical requirements to be a tax-free reorganization. It is okay to merge a target corporation into a first-tier sub in a reverse-triangular merger, but not into a second-tier sub. I had to tell the attorney (and a roomful of other people listening on the speaker phone) that the deal they had just negotiated for three months and thought was closed, based on the assumption that it was tax free, was in fact a fully taxable transaction.

The parties tore up the documents and tried to rework the deal but were unable to renegotiate a satisfactory new arrangement. Eventually they called the business wedding off. Worse than that, some of them decided I had "killed" the deal. This is an occupational hazard for a tax attorney.

This situation is repeated with depressing regularity in merger and acquisition (M&A) transactions. Another time, just as I arrived at work one morning, one of my partners pulled me into a conference room and asked if I would take a quick look at a deal that was about to close and "bless it". Fifteen people were in the conference room for the signing, and it turned out that my firm's primary role was to provide the conference room (and coffee) for the closing. Nonetheless, my partner, to his credit, wanted a quick final review of a transaction that was supposed to be "tax free" to our client. This deal was another reverse triangular merger and, once again, I could see almost immediately that the transaction was in fact going to be taxable. The reason this time was that the transaction provided 50 percent cash and 50 percent stock to the target shareholders, which is okay in a forward triangular merger, but not in a reverse triangular merger.

I quietly pulled my partner into the hallway outside the conference room and told him my concerns. It turned out that our client had been relying (it sounds idiotic just to say it) on the tax attorney for the *other* side to structure the transaction, even though our client was the one seeking the tax-free treatment. After we explained the situation to our client, he insisted that we call the tax attorney for the other side immediately (he was conspicuously absent at the closing). I will never forget the tax attorney's response after I explained the situation: "I merely told your client the transaction was structured as a reverse triangular merger. I *never* said it was going to be tax free!" The discussion, and the deal, degenerated from there.

Unfortunately, there are a myriad of examples of negotiations that go on for weeks and months—even actually close—before the parties discover that the tax assumptions underlying their deal have been wrong. Trust me; you never want to be in the position I have been in—explaining to a room full of people that, because they made fundamental mistakes of tax law, all their work has been a complete waste of time and the negotiations they thought were over need to start over, almost from scratch.

THE ROLE OF GOVERNMENTS (AND TAXES) IN AN ACQUISITION

Every merger and acquisition transaction has a buyer (Buyer), also referred to as an "Acquirer", and a seller (Seller), also referred to as a "Target". There are also two other parties with a major economic stake in the transaction: the federal government and (usually at least one) state government.

The Internal Revenue Code (the "Code") is more than just the law of the land; it is a sophisticated partnership agreement between the U.S. government and every U.S. person. This partnership is one of the most technically complex arrangements imaginable, but the basic thrust is actually easy to summarize. The U.S. government is your mandatory partner in all economic and business endeavors. For the most part it is a very uncongenial and ungenerous partner. The government is quick to claim a share of profits in the good years, but far less willing to share losses in the bad years. For example, if you generate a loss or, even worse, if you have losses from capital transactions, the government is slow to help mitigate the burden. Net operating losses (NOLs) can be carried back only two years, which means that the government keeps its taxes from the good years (subject to the two-year carryback) and offers only a prospective form of relief—your losses translate into a benefit if, and only if, you return to profitability in the future. Capital losses cannot be carried back at all. With limited exceptions, they can only be used against future capital gains. It is, in short, a very asymmetrical and unfair partnership.

It gets worse. Your "partner" has the right to change the partnership arrangement at any time, without your consent, and even make these changes retroactively. You may not like the partnership (or your partner), but there isn't much you can do about it. You are bound by the pact until you die or emigrate.[1]

The role of a tax attorney advising on an acquisition transaction is to make everyone aware that there are two silent partners in the room at all times and that the Buyer and Seller have a common interest in cutting the silent partners out of the deal—or, at least, cutting them as small a slice of the economic pie as possible. The good news is that such conduct on your part is both ethical and expected. In the immortal words of Judge Learned Hand, "Any one may so arrange his affairs that his taxes shall be as low as possible; he is not bound to choose the pattern which will best pay the Treasury; there is not even a patriotic duty to increase one's taxes."

The Code may be an unequal and unfair partnership, but it does have the considerable redeeming virtue of being known or knowable—which is to say you can read it carefully and organize your affairs accordingly. If the Code permits a method of reducing, deferring, or avoiding taxes, you may exploit it. If there is a way to shave the tax costs from a transaction, the parties are free to employ it. The purpose and mission of this book is to teach people how to pare the tax costs of a transaction to the absolute minimum, within the boundaries of ethical and appropriate tax reporting.

BASIC DECISIONS IN PLANNING THE SALE OF A BUSINESS

It is an axiom of tax planning that "corporations do not pay taxes, people pay taxes". This observation reflects the fact that individuals are ultimately the persons who pay taxes, no matter how complex the corporate structure may be. In this same vein, it is individuals who ultimately own and sell businesses. These individuals invariably want legal advice on how to minimize the taxes ultimately borne by them, as individuals, when a sale, exchange, or other transfer of an incorporated business takes place. For Sellers, the operative question is, "How can I get the most money and/or value after paying the required taxes"? For Buyers, it is the equivalent query: "How do I pay the least amount possible after taking into account tax benefits from the purchase"?

In analyzing and structuring an acquisition transaction from a tax perspective, it is natural to assume that both the Buyer and Seller will want to evaluate the projected results based on a present-value, after-tax basis. Any tax analysis of a transaction structure must take into consideration tax consequences to both the Seller and Buyer. To the extent that the tax consequences of a transaction stretch beyond the current tax year (as they almost always do), the Buyer and Seller will need to use present-value concepts to put a price tag on the deferred aspects of the transaction (from deferred payments to the tax benefits of long-term depreciation or amortization). This involves making a variety of assumptions about future tax rates, and about the appropriate interest rate to use in a present-value computation. These projections about future economic conditions and events are necessarily of a squishy nature and, like all forays into the dismal science, must be done with trepidation—but, in all events, must be done.

Although the purchase and sale of a business is an unavoidably complicated transaction, the fundamental tax objectives are actually easy to articulate. There are three basic decisions that the parties need to make:

1. Is the transaction going to be tax-free or taxable?
2. If it will be taxable, is the Buyer going to purchase stock (equity) or assets?
3. Is the purchase price going to be paid entirely up front, or is some portion (or all) of it going to be paid on a deferred basis?

The three decisions are easy to identify, but far less easy to make. These choices are often nuanced and complex. There is often no clear or correct answer. In structuring acquisition transactions, the famous dictum is this: "The rule of thumb is there is no rule of thumb." Each of these three seemingly simple questions requires a sophisticated analytical answer, and the correct choice is usually the accretion of many small and nuanced decisions.

DECIDING WHETHER A SALE SHOULD BE TAXABLE OR TAX-FREE

The first decision that Buyers and Sellers have to make is whether to structure the transaction as a "taxable" or a "tax-free" transaction. I can assure you that, described in this manner, and without more information, every client wants to hear all about the "tax-free" option first.

"Tax-free" and partially tax-free transactions are discussed in considerable detail at various points in this book. The fundamental characteristic of such transactions is that the owners of the Target are swapping their Target equity for equity in another, larger entity that is almost certain to be controlled by someone else. The immediate concern, therefore, is whether the owners of the Target want to give up control of their business in exchange for a minority position in a larger, combined business. As a practical matter, the answer to this question usually turns on the degree to which the new equity interests can later be sold or liquidated at the unilateral discretion of the former Target owners.

In some cases, such as when the Acquirer is a publicly traded corporation and the post-transaction equity is (or shortly will be) readily marketable, the Target owners will be interested, even eager, to participate in a tax-free or partially tax-free transaction. However, if the equity of the Acquirer is not highly liquid, the owners or Target may be reluctant to pursue a tax-free transaction. Reasons why an individual might opt for a taxable instead of a tax-free transaction include the following:

1. The consideration received in a tax-free reorganization consists predominantly or entirely of stock in a different corporation. Such stock may be relatively unattractive to an individual for the following reasons: (1) the stock may be subject to restrictions on transferability, whether imposed by securities laws or through a buy-sell agreement; (2) even if the stock is not subject to restrictions on resale, the stock may be difficult to sell; (3) even if a buyer for the stock can be found, the stock may have to be sold at a significant minority and marketability discount; (4) the stockholder may lack meaningful control or input in the operation of the reorganized corporate entity; and (5) ultimately, stock is not cash and therefore is subject both to greater economic risk and lesser liquidity than cash.

2. The total tax cost of a "taxable" transaction may not be unduly onerous. For example, even a "C" corporation may have sufficient tax basis in its assets or sufficient net operating losses to make a sale of corporate assets relatively inexpensive in terms of tax costs, and the shareholders may have a sufficient basis in their stock to avoid having to incur a substantial "double tax" cost. Alternatively, shareholders may be able to negotiate a structure for the transaction that involves a sale of stock at favorable capital gains rates or may be able to negotiate employment agreements, consulting agreements, and noncompetition agreements that reduce the amount of double taxation involved in the transaction.

DECIDING WHETHER A SALE SHOULD BE OF BUSINESS ASSETS OR EQUITY

Taxable acquisitions can usually be divided into two basic categories: (1) a sale of the business assets or (2) a sale of the business equity.

In the case of a C corporation, a frequently stated "truism" about taxable acquisitions is that a Buyer wants to buy assets while a Seller wants to sell stock. The problem with this simplistic formulation is that obviously both of these objectives cannot be met; otherwise, no business acquisition would ever be completed. True, a Buyer may be looking to buy assets rather than the stock of a corporation because the Buyer would like to get a step-up in the tax basis of depreciable and amortizable assets and would also like to avoid the Seller's legal liabilities that would accompany a stock purchase. Also true, the Seller would in theory like to sell Target stock and pay a single tax at capital gains rates. However, the truism conspicuously omits the factor that ultimately makes it possible to bridge the differences between Buyer and Seller: the price!

The tax consequences to a Buyer and Seller can vary dramatically between an asset sale and an equity sale. However, both types of sales can be valued in terms of money, and the comparative attractiveness of one acquisition structure versus another can be determined on an after-tax, present-value analysis. The Seller wants to receive the greatest possible after-tax return, after taking into account all tax costs and time-value-of-money considerations, and the Buyer wants to pay the lowest true cost, after taking into account all tax costs and time-value-of-money considerations. Figuring out a structure that gets the Seller a high enough after-tax return, and costs the Buyer a low enough after-tax purchase price, while meeting all the other objectives and interests of the parties, is the art of negotiating the deal.

A Buyer is often willing to pay a premium for an asset sale because the Buyer gets the operating business free and clear of its legal history and obtains a step-up in tax basis that can almost always be depreciated, amortized, or otherwise deducted, thereby reducing the after-tax cost of the acquisition. Conversely, a Buyer of corporate stock gets little or no tax benefit as a result of the purchase because the tax basis is "trapped" in the acquired stock. Note that this "wasted" tax basis problem is a major issue when the Target is a C corporation, but is usually solvable if the Target is an S corporation or a limited liability company (LLC). An election under Code section 338 can help turn outside stock basis into inside depreciable basis, but as a practical matter, the circumstances where this proves advantageous are limited.

In certain situations, a Buyer may actually prefer to buy the stock of the Target. For example, a Buyer will often take the "risk" of buying stock if the Target has valuable contractual or franchise rights that could terminate on an asset sale or if the selling shareholder is willing to take a sufficiently lower price to make the overall transaction attractive.

The short answer, therefore, is that there is no short answer or rule of thumb for determining which alternative is better. The Buyer and the Seller each have specific and often unique business objectives and tax attributes that can affect their willingness to structure a transaction one way or the other. For example, a Buyer that runs chronic tax losses or has large NOLs will not put much value in additional tax deductions, and may prefer a stock purchase if the asking price is lower. In a similar vein, a Seller with large NOLs may be entirely content to sell assets at a higher price, since the NOLs may eliminate the detrimental aspects of double taxation.

Each Buyer and Seller must evaluate both a stock sale and an asset sale in light of its own specific tax situation, and then determine the value of each alternative acquisition structure using a present-value, after-tax analysis.

PAYMENT NOW VERSUS PAYMENT LATER

The third major structuring issue is whether some or all of the purchase price will be paid on a deferred basis. The answer, as always, depends on the unique circumstances of the Buyer and Seller. For example, a Buyer with limited access to capital, or otherwise in need of financing from the Seller, may be willing to pay a higher price for the right to make payments over time (referred to as an "installment sale"). Likewise, a Seller in need of immediate cash may be willing to take a lower price as an "inverse premium" for immediate liquidity.

Generally, a Buyer often has in mind the not-too-subtle objective that the Target business ultimately "pays for itself", meaning that an ideal arrangement is an installment sale structured such that the Target business will generate the cash needed to fund the purchase price, and the Buyer never has to pay any money out of its own pocket (or, at least, not much and not for long). A typical Seller, by contrast, usually wants to pocket as much cash up front as possible, but will agree to an installment sale if the transaction offers enough upfront cash and enough backend reward.

An important subset of installment sales is the category of contingent payment transactions (often labeled an "earn out"). Most parties will privately agree that there is no accurate way to determine the true value of an ongoing business, if by "true value" one means the value that the business proves to have in the hands of the Buyer. Obviously, a business is valued based on its ability to generate profits going forward, and the Buyer would naturally be willing to pay more if it knew for certain that the profits would reach certain desired levels. A common way to address the fundamental uncertainty about future performance is to set the purchase price for the business using a "base" of guaranteed payments (which component is usually paid entirely up front, although a portion of the base payment may be deferred) plus an additional, contingent payment that is based on the actual performance of the business after the sale. Often, this contingent portion of the purchase price is based on objective performance factors, such as gross or net earnings of the business in the hands of the Buyer—hence, the term "earn out".

The fundamental logic and fairness of an earn out is underscored by the fact that, in many cases, the selling individuals remain as employees of the Target after the transaction closes, and thus to a meaningful extent "control their fate". Earn outs are very popular because both parties like the self-correcting quality of an earn out pricing mechanism—the Seller is happy to receive more, and the Buyer is happy to pay more if the business produces the hoped-for success. On the other hand, earn outs reduce the importance of due diligence and guess work on the Buyer's part by automatically adjusting for risk—if the business turns out to be worth less, the purchase price is automatically adjusted downward. Earn outs are in effect an "agreement to agree" or, stated another way, an agreement to reach a final decision on purchase price at a point in time in the future, after the actual operating results of the business in the hands of the Buyer are known.

CHAPTER ENDNOTE

1. Just to add insult to tax injury, the very act of expatriating is (or can be) a further taxable event if your average annual net income tax for the five years ending before the date of expatriation or your net worth exceed specified levels. See IRC Sec. 877A.

TAX CHARACTERISTICS OF THE MOST POPULAR BUSINESS ENTITIES

CHAPTER 2

OVERVIEW

The choice of business entity is perhaps the single most important tax factor in structuring acquisition transactions. When a business is founded as a C corporation, it is often hard to achieve optimum tax results later on. A popular metaphor (at least in Boston) is to compare a C corporation to a lobster trap; it is easy to get into, but hard to get out of. This metaphor illustrates that once business assets are placed in a C corporation, they can generally be extracted or separated only at great tax cost and/or complexity.

Some of the tax disadvantages of a C corporation can be ameliorated by subsequently electing S status, but the best tax strategy is to be a "pass-through" entity from the outset—either an S corporation, a partnership (including a multi-member limited liability company (LLC)), or a sole proprietorship (including a single member LLC).

Unfortunately, choosing the right business entity is largely moot by the time one must address the acquisition of the Target business. If the Target is an LLC or a "pure" S corporation (the term sometimes used to describe an S corporation that has no C corporation history or was converted to S status more than five years previously), then one can generally structure the acquisition to give the Seller a single level of capital gains tax *and* give the Buyer a step-up in tax basis in the acquired assets. This is as good as it gets in an acquisition transaction—tax nirvana.

On the other hand, if the Target is a C corporation, one must approach the transaction quite differently. The basic strategy is to minimize the amount paid directly to the C corporation and to maximize the payments outside the corporation (e.g., by maximizing employment contracts for owner-employees, offering consulting contracts, non-compete agreements, and/or purchasing personal goodwill). C corporation transactions are generally tougher to negotiate because the tax burdens are significantly higher. There are, however, a few circumstances when C corporation status allows special tax benefits (notably Code sections 1045 and 1202).

BRIEF TAX HISTORY OF BUSINESS ENTITIES

Given the significant disparities in tax treatment among the various business entities, it is useful to look at a brief history of how parties have structured acquisition transactions and then look at each of the most popular business entities in greater detail. Until 1986, the most popular legal vehicles for operating a closely-held business were, in rough order of popularity and importance, the following:

1. C corporation
2. S corporation
3. Limited partnership
4. General partnership
5. Sole proprietorship

Comment: Actually, the number of sole proprietorships always has been large, but, because a sole proprietorship lacks limited liability protection, most businesses convert into a limited liability vehicle once a business reaches a certain size or risk profile.

Prior to 1986, the Code allowed the assets of a C corporation to be sold or distributed for a single level of tax at capital gain tax rates. (See, for example, Code sections 331, 333, and 337 under the Internal Revenue Code of 1954.) However, the Tax Reform Act of 1986 (P.L. 99-514) (TRA-86) repealed the so-called "General Utilities Doctrine", as well as Code section 333, and generally provided, with some limited transition relief, that all C corporations were subject to double taxation on a sale of assets. This continues to be the rule to the present day.

At approximately the same time, the LLC came into vogue. The first LLC statute was enacted by Wyoming in 1977, and the second by Florida in 1982, but because it was unclear how these new-fangled entities would be taxed under federal law, they remained largely overlooked until 1988 when the IRS, in Rev. Rul. 88-76,[1] ruled that a properly structured Wyoming LLC would be treated as a partnership for federal income tax purposes. Following Rev. Rul. 88-76, states began to adopt LLC statutes, and the trend quickly turned into a stampede. Today, all fifty states and the District of Columbia have some form of LLC statute.

In 1996, the IRS issued "check-the-box" regulations, which represented a huge—perhaps even revolutionary—change in federal income tax principles because they allow an LLC to elect to be taxed as a partnership regardless of its legal structure and characteristics. The regulations also provide that a single member LLC will be taxed as a sole proprietorship, not as a corporation, even though it also provides limited liability to the sole owner.

Today, a ranking of the business entities chosen for operating a business (as distinct from owning real estate) would probably be as follows:

1. S corporation
2. LLC (both partnership and sole proprietorship)
3. C corporation
4. Limited liability partnership (LLP)
5. Limited partnership
6. General partnership

By contrast, if the business activity consists entirely or substantially of holding real estate for use in a trade or business or for leasing, the LLC is probably the most popular vehicle, the limited partnership second, and the S corporation is probably a distant third (and probably inappropriate) vehicle.

However, as businesses grow, both S corporations and LLCs are often converted into C corporations at two key junctures:

1. When venture capital or other equity investors put cash into a business and require, as a condition of investment, that the entity be converted into a C corporation that can issue them preferred stock.

2. When the business "goes public" by registering its securities, in which case Code section 7704 generally requires that a publicly traded partnership be taxed as a C corporation.

C CORPORATION

A C corporation is a separate taxpayer for federal income tax purposes. Its income is subject to tax at the corporate level, at special corporate tax rates.[2] Corporate distributions to shareholders may, depending on the circumstances, be characterized as distributions of earnings and profits and thus taxable as dividends, as a "tax-free" return of capital, or as a distribution triggering capital gains to shareholders.[3]

Since the repeal of the General Utilities Doctrine by TRA-86, the so-called "double taxation" of corporate income has discouraged the use of C corporations and encouraged the use of "pass-through entities", particularly S corporations and LLCs taxable as partnerships. However, the C corporation is the business vehicle of choice in two common situations: (1) when investors demand a preferred class of equity, and (2) when a corporation becomes publicly traded. Some older businesses continue to operate as C corporations for reasons best ascribed to inertia.

A C corporation has the following tax and business characteristics:

1. It is possible to contribute appreciated assets to a C corporation tax-free under Code section 351, but it usually works best at the time of formation and can be difficult and tricky to accomplish later on. Code section 351 is not as flexible as the corresponding partnership tax provision, Code section 721.

2. The corporation provides limited liability to shareholders.

3. A C corporation does not pass through income or losses to its shareholders; instead, income is taxed at the corporate level, at special corporate rates.[4]

4. A C corporation is subject to unique and complex taxes, including the accumulated earnings tax,[5] personal holding company tax,[6] and the corporate alternative minimum tax.[7] Closely-held C corporations are also subject to the passive-loss rules[8] and at-risk rules.[9]

5. Liquidations of C corporations are taxed at both the corporate and shareholder levels, creating a so-called "double tax" on liquidation.[10]

6. On a sale of assets, the C corporation pays tax on income and gain at the corporate level. There is no preferential tax rate for capital gains recognized by a corporation. Shareholders do not get a step-up in tax basis in their shares as a result of corporate gain recognition.

7. Money and other property distributed to shareholders by a C corporation following an asset sale is taxed as a dividend or, if the corporation has adopted a plan of liquidation, as capital gain (i.e., as if the corporation were purchasing stock from its shareholders).

8. After a C corporation sells substantially all of its assets, it is likely to be a personal holding company (PHC) until it liquidates.

9. If there is a sale of corporate stock, the selling shareholders get capital gains tax treatment. If the shareholder is an individual, the shareholder will enjoy the preferential individual tax rate on capital gains. The Buyer will enjoy a step-up in tax basis in the shares, but this may not be terribly valuable because the tax basis cannot be amortized or depreciated and will be utilized—if at all—only upon a sale or liquidation of the Target corporation.

10. Upon the purchase of corporate stock, the purchaser can elect, under Code section 338, to intentionally trigger a taxable transaction equivalent to the Target corporation selling assets to itself. This strategy makes sense in a few limited circumstances (discussed in Chapter 12) but is not generally beneficial.

11. A C corporation can participate in a tax-free reorganization under Code section 368, including mergers, consolidations, and divisive reorganizations. As will be discussed in detail in Chapter 7, tax-free reorganizations are generally appropriate only in specific circumstances, but if those circumstances exist (e.g., the Acquirer is a publicly traded corporation), the availability of Code section 368 can be a huge advantage.

S CORPORATION

An S corporation is a pass-through entity, which means that corporate income is generally not subject to taxation at the entity level. Because an S corporation and a C corporation have identical corporate characteristics, the decision to elect S status and to conform with the S corporation eligibility requirements is driven solely by federal (and sometimes state) income tax considerations. An S corporation is attractive to taxpayers seeking a pass-through entity, but this generally favorable tax treatment brings with it significant restrictions. An S corporation can be a relatively rigid and inflexible operating vehicle, with substantial limitations on the number of its shareholders, classes of stock, and qualifications for shareholder status.

An S corporation has the following tax and business characteristics:

1. It is possible to contribute appreciated assets to an S corporation tax-free under Code section 351, but it usually works best only at the time of formation and can be difficult and tricky to accomplish tax-free later on. This provision is not as flexible as the corresponding provision that applies to LLCs, Code section 721.

2. An S corporation provides limited liability to shareholders.

3. The S corporation is a pass-through entity. S corporation items of income, gain, loss, deduction, and credit are not subject to tax at the corporate level but instead are taxed to the shareholders.[11]

4. S corporation income and gain is taxed one time at the shareholder level, at individual tax rates.

However, if the S corporation was formerly a C corporation, it may be subject to the "sting taxes" under Code sections 1374 and 1375. Code section 1374 is basically a kind of recapture tax that tracks and taxes the "built-in gain" as measured at the time when a C corporation converts to S status. The tax is applied at the maximum corporate tax rate to built-in gain recognized during the first five years following conversion. It is designed to prevent C corporations from avoiding the double-tax on asset sales through the expedient of a belated conversion to S status. An S corporation is also subject to a sting tax under Code section 1375, which is the S corporation analog to the personal holding company tax. Shareholders are subject to the passive activity loss rules,[12] the at-risk rules,[13] and sometimes onerous tax basis rules.

5. There are significant limitations on structuring an S corporation. An S corporation must comply with the requirements for electing S status set forth in Code section 1361. An S corporation cannot have more than 100 shareholders or more than one class of stock. An S corporation's shareholders can only be individuals, estates, or certain qualified trusts or exempt organizations; no nonresident aliens can be shareholders.

6. The liquidation of an S corporation is a taxable event, the equivalent of a disposition of the corporate assets at fair market value[14] and produces the equivalent of a "single" tax on gains in most cases. There are special rules that can affect a liquidation and dissolution, particularly Code section 1374, but generally a liquidating S corporation that has always been an S corporation should be subject to the equivalent of one level of tax (as contrasted with the "double" tax on liquidation of a C corporation).

7. On a sale of assets, the S corporation generally recognizes capital gain at the corporate level, which passes out to shareholders (as reported on Schedule K-1), and, if the shareholders are individuals, is taxed at the preferential capital gains tax rate for individuals. Shareholders in turn get a step-up in tax basis in their shares as a result of the corporate gain recognition.[15]

8. A distribution of appreciated property by an S corporation is treated as a sale or exchange[16] and triggers tax at what is usually the capital gains tax rate (subject to recapture rules under Code section 1245) for most S corporation assets. In turn, there is a step-up of outside basis, so the net tax consequence is a single level of tax, again most likely at capital gains rates. A distribution of cash following a sale will usually be a return of tax basis under Code section 1368 (tax free). However, such a distribution can generate dividend treatment in cases where the distribution is deemed to be from C corporation earnings and profits (E&P).[17] If a distribution exceeds a shareholder's outside tax basis in the S corporation stock, it can produce capital gains.

9. After an S corporation with accumulated E&P from a prior C corporation year sells substantially all of its assets, it is likely to be subject to both Code section 1362(d)(3) and Code section 1375. Both Code provisions penalize a corporation that has retained E&P and more than 25 percent passive income (e.g., a corporation with investment assets but no substantial operating business). There is a *strong* incentive to liquidate an S corporation before the end of three years (at which time its S status will terminate), or distribute the E&P as a dividend.

10. If there is a sale of S corporation stock, the selling shareholders get capital gains tax treatment. If they are individuals, they will enjoy the preferential individual tax rate on capital gains. Absent a Code section 338(h)(10) election or Code section 336(e) election, Buyers will enjoy a step-up in tax basis in the shares, but this may not be terribly valuable because it cannot be amortized or depreciated.

11. Upon the purchase of S corporation stock, a corporate Buyer and the selling shareholders can jointly elect, under Code section 338(h)(10), to treat the transaction for federal income tax purposes as the equivalent of the Target corporation selling assets rather than as a stock sale.[18] This election, unlike the normal 338 election, is extremely beneficial. Sellers generally get a single level of capital gains tax, and Buyers get stepped-up basis in assets that can be depreciated. A similar election can be made under Code section 336(e). These elections are discussed in detail in Chapter 12.

12. An S corporation, like a C corporation, can participate in tax-free reorganizations under

Code section 368. As will be discussed in detail in Chapter 7, tax-free reorganizations are generally appropriate only in specific circumstances, but if those circumstances exist (e.g., the Acquirer is a publicly traded corporation), the availability of Code section 368 can be a major advantage.

LLCS/GENERAL PARTNERSHIPS/LIMITED LIABILITY PARTNERSHIPS/ LIMITED PARTNERSHIPS

LLCs, general partnerships, limited liability partnerships, and limited partnerships are each treated (absent an election to be treated as a corporation) as a partnership for federal income tax purposes and can therefore enjoy the tax advantages of partnership taxation under Subchapter K of the Code.

The glaring drawback of a general partnership is that it does not have limited liability for any of its partners. Instead, each general partner has unlimited personal liability for the liabilities and obligations of the partnership. Moreover, each general partner typically has the authority, under the general partnership laws of most or all states, to make legally binding commitments on behalf of the partnership, which in turn can become legal obligations and liabilities of the other general partners, even if those general partners did not personally know about or consent to the transaction. In general, the lack of limited liability, coupled with the authority of each partner to make binding commitments on behalf of the partnership, makes the general partnership a very unattractive vehicle in many or most business situations. A general partnership comprised of five equal partners has been described, sardonically, as an arrangement whereby each partner has "20 percent of the upside and 100 percent of the downside".

The LLP statutes vary, sometimes considerably, from state to state, but as a general characterization (at the risk of oversimplification), the LLP is basically a general partnership that has filed a special election with the state of formation to obtain whatever limited liability protection is afforded by that state's LLP statute. The LLP may provide less comprehensive liability protection than an LLC, and sometimes requires a general partnership style of management, whereby each partner has the ability to legally bind the partnership, the ability to terminate the partnership on withdrawal, and to otherwise play a role in the affairs and management of the entity that may not be suitable if a more centralized and hierarchical form of business is preferred (as is often the case). An LLC typically can provide all the benefits and do everything that an LLP can do, but the converse is not the case because an LLP is a less flexible vehicle from a management and business perspective. Nonetheless, LLPs are popular in certain situations.

A limited partnership combines limited liability for its limited partners with the tax advantages of a partnership. A limited partner must have at least one general partner with unlimited liability; however, this problem can be ameliorated by using a corporate general partner to limit and control liability risks. The main drawback is that a limited partnership has always been an awkward vehicle for operating a business. The advent of the LLC has put the limited partnership into eclipse because an LLC is basically a more flexible, functional version of a limited partnership.

An LLC is a non-corporate entity, usually with two or more members (although an increasing number of states allow a single member LLC), formed pursuant to the statutory provisions of a state. A key characteristic of the LLC is that the members have limited liability, similar to corporate shareholders, regardless of their involvement in management. An LLC can be treated for federal income tax purposes as either a partnership or a corporation, depending on the "check-the-box" rules.

Some states tax LLCs as a corporation, or otherwise impose an entity-level tax, even though it qualifies as a partnership for federal income tax purposes.

An LLC taxable as a partnership (the default tax status in the absense of an election to the contrary) is extremely flexible in most operational respects. Its operating agreement can, within certain relatively broad parameters, define on a contractual basis almost any type of management structure, operational arrangement, and economic sharing of profits, losses, and risks that the members may want. An LLC taxed as a partnership will enjoy all of the corresponding income tax advantages, including the ability to create a single level of taxation at the partner level and the ability to make sophisticated allocations of profits and losses.

Entities taxed as partnerships have the following tax and business characteristics:

1. Generally, there is no gain or loss on formation.[19] However, special rules under Code sections 721(b), 707(a)(2), and 704(c) can cause

a property contribution to a partnership to be characterized as a taxable sale or exchange.

2. The key disadvantage of a general partnership is the unlimited personal liability of all partners. The LLP offers limited liability, but sometimes the liability protection is limited (e.g., to professional malpractice). The limited partnership requires at least one general partner with unlimited liability and is an awkward vehicle from an operating standpoint. The LLC is by far the best partnership vehicle. It provides flexible management and limited liability for all members.

3. Items of income, gain, loss, deduction, and credit are subject to tax one time at the partner level. A partnership may, subject to relatively complicated regulations, provide for special allocations of partnership items.

4. The partners are subject to the at-risk rules[20] and the passive loss rules.[21]

5. Generally there is no gain or loss upon either the liquidation of the partnership or the distribution of partnership property to a partner, except to the extent money or marketable securities are distributed in excess of the partner's tax basis in his or her partnership interest.[22] This is often a huge advantage over a C corporation (double tax on liquidation) and an S corporation (equivalent of a single tax on liquidation in most cases).

6. On a sale of assets, the partnership generally recognizes capital gain at the partnership level, and that gain is passed out to partners (as reported on Schedule K-1). If the partners are individuals, the gain is taxed at the preferential capital gains tax rate for individuals.

7. After a partnership sells substantially all of its assets, there are no equivalent penalty taxes to the PHC tax for C corporations or the Code sections 1362(d)(3) and 1375 problems for S corporations.

8. If there is a sale of a partnership interest, each selling partner generally gets capital gains tax treatment (except to the extent the partnership holds "hot assets" under Code section 751). If the Seller is an individual, the Seller will enjoy the preferential individual tax rate on capital gains. Meanwhile, the Buyer will enjoy a step-up in tax basis in the acquired interest, and can (and almost always will) elect to have the inside basis of the partnership assets "stepped-up" to match the outside tax basis.[23] Unlike Code section 338(h)(10) or Code section 336(e), this "step-up" election does not require the cooperation and consent of the Seller.

9. Partnership entities, including LLCs, are not eligible to participate in a tax-free reorganization under Code section 368. Partnership status can be a drawback if an Acquirer shows up offering a lucrative tax-free reorganization acquisition structure.

COMPARING C CORPORATIONS, S CORPORATIONS, AND LLCS

Since the repeal of the General Utilities Doctrine in 1986, federal income tax law has strongly encouraged the use of pass-through entities, notably S corporations and LLCs, and discouraged the use of C corporations. Income is taxed once when earned by a C corporation and a second time when distributed to the corporation's shareholders. In addition, pass-through entities have the advantage of passing out losses to equity owners (subject to limitations imposed by the passive activity loss rules, at-risk rules, and tax-basis rules), which can be particularly valuable in the early years of a business or investment activity, when losses frequently occur.

On the other hand, for smaller C corporations it is sometimes possible to "mimic" pass-through tax status, especially where the business activity involves primarily the rendering of services (e.g., an advertising agency, architectural firm, or law firm). Basically, the "pass through" tax characteristics are achieved through payment of compensation and bonuses that minimize or eliminate the corporate-level tax. It may be possible in the appropriate circumstance to structure the acquisition of a C corporation so that a large portion of the total consideration is paid to an individual owner (e.g., by allocating the consideration to a consulting agreement, to a covenant not to compete, or possibly to a purchase of personal goodwill) and thus avoid or reduce double taxation. In short, a relatively small C corporation can sometimes overcome the inherent disadvantages of C status through aggressive allocation mechanisms. A large C corporation, on the other hand, has difficulty avoiding the tax disadvantages of C status.

Between an S corporation and a partnership (usually an LLC), the partnership has certain key tax advantages, including:

1. A partner can contribute appreciated property under Code section 721 tax-free after the formation of the partnership without meeting the control requirements of Code section 351.

2. A partner can increase outside tax basis under Code section 752 by guaranteeing partnership liabilities. By contrast, shareholders cannot increase their outside basis by guaranteeing S corporation liabilities.

3. A partnership can liquidate and distribute its appreciated assets tax-free in most cases under Code section 731.

In addition, a partnership allows the maximum flexibility in allocating income and tax attributes between and among the participants. By contrast, an S corporation has very rigid allocation and distribution rules based on the requirement that the S corporation have a single class of stock.

The single greatest drawback of an LLC is that it is not as "user friendly" as a corporation. In general, ordinary business people seem to understand instinctively how an S corporation (or a C corporation) works, but seem to misunderstand completely how an LLC works. A modern partnership agreement designed to comply with the safe harbors in the Code section 704 regulations is an incomprehensible document, even to most lawyers. There is a virtue in simplicity, even if it is at the cost of flexibility, and one must weigh this tradeoff in deciding whether to utilize an LLC.

One other notable drawback of an LLC is that it cannot participate in a tax-free reorganization under Code section 368. This is no problem whatsoever if the Acquirer offers a cash acquisition, and/or if the Acquirer's stock is not of interest to the Target owners. However, if a publicly traded corporation shows up offering a stock-for-stock reorganization transaction (as happened frequently at the height of the dot.com boom, though far less frequently in most normal market situations), the Target will wish it were a corporation.

Comment: An S corporation can enjoy both pass-through taxation and eligibility to participate in a reorganization.

When parties choose an S corporation as the appropriate business vehicle, their choice is almost always driven by the combination of (1) tax advantages as compared to a C corporation, (2) simplicity as compared to an LLC, and/or (3) eligibility to participate in a reorganization transaction. However, having adopted the S corporation form for these reasons, taxpayers and their advisors then typically spend large amounts of time trying to make the S corporation as flexible as possible (i.e., basically, they try to make it operate like a C corporation with S corporation tax attributes). There are a variety of interesting mechanisms that taxpayers have developed over the years in order to circumvent the fairly rigid and mechanical S corporation rules and thus meet the needs of real-world business deals.

CASE STUDIES FOR CHOICE OF BUSINESS ENTITY

The blue jeans, accountant, natural business deal and "crystal ball" rules can be helpful in analyzing what type of business entity is best for a client.

The Blue Jeans Rule

Two young men, Adam and Bart, decide to form a business to sell and repair high-tech bicycles. Both are experienced in the service end of the business, but neither has ever owned or operated a business. They have moderate but not extensive educational backgrounds, and they plan to keep their own books. They are worried about liability risk in case a customer is hurt on the premises (there are lots of sharp gears in a bike shop) and also if any bike repair is done defectively (bike crashes are surprisingly dangerous). They view their relationship as a "50-50 partnership". They show up at the first meeting wearing blue jeans.

Practice Point: The blue jeans rule suggests that clients who are not interested in conforming to the suit-and-tie world probably belong in an S corporation. Note that this rule can encompass highly educated software programmers as well as low-tech bicycle shop owners. The issue is to put the clients into a vehicle that is intuitively easy to operate. This particular business is viewed as a "50-50" deal by the participants, and neither is putting in a large amount of money compared to the other, so the rigid "straight up" allocations of an S corporation are entirely appropriate. As advisor, you want these clients focusing on their business, not on the complexities of tax allocations, and an S corporation is the right fit.

The Accountant Rule

Carson, Drew, Evelyn, and Frank want to establish a sophisticated investment banking entity that will offer investment banking services to select clients. Carson and Drew anticipate developing numerous ideas and spinning them off into separate ventures, with each new venture seeking separate funding from whatever investors are interested. They anticipate offering interests to employees over time, but intend to hold onto the equity themselves for the time being. Carson, Drew, Evelyn, and Frank have, in typical investment banker style, developed an extremely complicated formula for allocating business profits among themselves. They show up at the first meeting wearing suits and ties. They bring their accountant with them.

Practice Point: The accountant rule says that if the clients bring an accountant to the first meeting it means that (1) the deal is probably complicated and (2) they have someone who can deal with the complexity. In general, partnership taxation is very confusing, and perhaps the simple but telling measure of its complexity is the LLC operating agreement, which can be 40 pages or more in length and virtually unreadable by anyone but a tax lawyer. However, if there is someone who can manage the accounting work, then an LLC is spectacularly flexible and can accommodate almost any permissible transaction. In this case, the clients can form an LLC and allocate profits according to whatever complicated formula they choose. They can in the future issue profits interests to employees without triggering tax consequences. At any future time, if a corporation is a better alternative, they can very likely incorporate without tax consequences.

The Natural Business Deal Rule

There is such a thing in this world as the "natural business deal". If business deals grew on trees in sun-dappled orchards, fertilized by 100 percent organic ingredients, they would look something like this: The money person and the idea person meet in the shade of the orchard and form the natural business deal. The money person provides funding in money or money's worth, and the idea person provides the Idea for a grand and glorious new business. The idea person is typically young, energetic, bubbling with enthusiasm, and broke. The money person is often older (though not always), far less energetic, and loaded (with financial resources).

The deal itself almost invariably follows the following "natural" blueprint: The money person contributes money, the idea person contributes the Idea, and together they set up and begin operating the new business. The two parties agree that the first priority of the business is to earn and repay the money person if full for the contributed funds (often with an agreed "interest" or "priority return" on the contributed capital until repaid), and then the parties will split all profits going forward on a 50-50 basis. The details can of course vary. For example, the idea person will probably want a modest salary or income on which to live until the money person is fully repaid the capital contribution. Alternatively some of the early profits can go to the idea person. The back end split may be different than 50-50, or may be 50-50 up to a specified return, and then adjust to 60-40 or 80-20. There can be lots of variations in the natural business deal, but in the end the transaction adheres surprisingly closely to the parameters described above.

As it turns out, the natural business deal fits very poorly into an S corporation but fits beautifully – dare we say "naturally" – into an LLC taxable as a partnership.

It is possible to "crowbar" the natural business deal into an S corporation – indeed, because of the desire to operate with pass-through taxation, the natural business deal by default was set up using S corporations until the advent of the LLC in the 1990s – but it was always a difficult and awkward fit. An S corporation has the following problems housing and hosting the natural business deal. First, the idea person is supposed to receive 50 percent of the equity ownership in the business, but the issuance of stock in a corporation in exchange for services creates immediate adverse tax consequences (income with no cash to pay the tax) under Code section 83.

The "solution" in the pre-LLC era was to have the idea person form the S corporation, wait as long as possible (often not very long) and then have the money person invest as a first round of investor financing. However, since the investment arrangement was often anticipated in advance, there was always a concern that the IRS would treat the steps as a single transaction and whack the idea person with a hefty tax bill. That left the idea person with stock in the start-up business, a significant tax liability, and no cash to pay the tax. Rest assured that the money person was almost always unenthusiastic about using the recently contributed funds to pay the idea person's taxes.

Then there was the considerable issue of giving the money person a priority allocation of profits and distributions until the contributed capital was repaid. S corporations require pro-rata allocations, and so it was not possible simply to allocate the profits disproportionately. One "solution" was to have the money person lend the funds to the S corporation – except that the money person was now the creditor and had the ability – sometimes later exercised – to foreclose on the business and take away the Idea and the business.

Another "solution" was to give the idea person stock options at low strike prices to acquire 50 percent of the S corporation stock, which options became exercisable after the company earned and distributed the original capital back to the money person. The problem was that by the time the options became exercisable the S corporation was profitable and the income tax problem under Code section 83 again reared its ugly head – significant tax liabilities coupled with illiquid stock (and no cash to pay the taxes due).

Still another problem with using an S corporation was the "Oops! I made a mistake" problem, when the money person decided early on that the "Idea" was in fact merely a lower case "idea" and that the business model was unpromising. Once the money went into the S corporation, and the idea person owned 50 percent of the stock, that meant that on an early termination and liquidation the idea person was entitled to 50 percent of the distributions (because money person and ideal person both received a single class of common stock, and so liquidation preferences were not permitted).

All in all, the S corporation was far from the natural home for the natural business deal.

Enter the LLC. The LLC has in fact turned out to be a perfect habitat for the natural business deal. First, the issuance of a 50 percent profits interest in the entity to the idea person is a non-taxable event under Code section 83, thanks to case law and Rev. Proc. 93-27 and subsequent IRS authority on the issuance of "profits interests" in a partnership.

Second, the maintenance of capital accounts meant that if the money person wanted to pull the plug on the business venture early in time and get back all (or most) of the invested capital, the parties could easily engineer that result. In particular, under partnership tax rules the money person could get back all (or at least the remaining amount) of the money, the idea person could get the Idea back, and they could then go their separate ways.

Third, partnership tax law makes it easy to make priority distributions of cash to the money person until the initial capital is returned (possibly with a preferred return on top of it) and then divide the profits going forward as provided in the agreement (e.g. 50-50). The LLC operating agreement will need to address federal income tax on profits, with mandatory tax distributions to cover taxes, but as a practical matter the asymmetrical distributions anticipated by the natural business deal fit easily into partnership taxation, even as they create enormous problems under S corporation tax rules.

For these reasons, a natural business deal, where there are both money people and the idea/services people are coming together to form the business, fits well into an LLC and not well at all into an S corporation.

The "Crystal Ball" Rule

Greg and Helen are entrepreneurs who think they can do a roll-up of high-tech bicycle businesses and eventually take the business public. They are even bigger know-it-alls than their investment bankers, Carson, Drew, Evelyn, and Frank, LLC. Greg and Helen come to the meeting with their investment bankers, with their accountant, and also with the blue jeans-wearing Adam and Bart, whose S corporation Greg and Helen want to acquire in order to start their roll-up business. Greg and Helen confidently announce that they have already figured out that they should be a C corporation from the outset, since they will likely issue preferred stock to investors along the way, and in all events will be going public in the next few years.

Practice Point: Don't take legal advice from clients; give it. Greg and Helen should form a pass-through entity unless and until there is a good reason to use a different type of business entity. The point is, you never know which way the business path will lead next, which makes flexibility valuable.

The typical analysis in this situation is to avoid C corporation status and instead to compare LLC versus S corporation at the start up. An LLC can do most or all of what Greg and Helen want to do, and can still maintain flexibility. They can, for example, purchase the assets of the S corporation from Adam and Bart and operate in the highly flexible form of an LLC until their business develops further. Another factor is determining when they *really* think they will be going public. This requires a crystal ball to peer into the future, or, failing that (which is always), making the best educated judgment.

There are at least two possible transactions that could arise down the road, often with little warning, that could make Greg and Helen prefer to be an S corporation. First, when an LLC converts to corporate status, the one-year holding period requirement of the equity for Rule 144 purposes begins only on the incorporation date, with no tacking or credit for prior LLC periods. An initial public offering (IPO) usually takes time to complete, and there is usually a lock-up agreement (typically for 180 days) for existing shareholders, but sometimes the Rule 144 waiting period causes clients to rush into corporate status (sometimes prematurely).

The second is if a corporate acquirer suddenly appears and offers to engage in a tax-free reorganization, offering publicly traded stock in exchange for the Target. In that circumstance, it may be ideal if the Target can participate in a tax-free reorganization, which is available to an S corporation but not an LLC.There are also situations, albeit less common, where a founder might well prefer to form the business as a C corporation, such as when the business owner is likely to seek the benefits of Code sections 1045 and 1202, discussed in detail in Chapter 19. Those two provisions both require that the stockholder hold the stock in a C corporation for substantially all the stockholder's holding period.

What is the right answer? Just look in the crystal ball and see what the future brings, and the answer is easy. However, if your crystal ball is not working just now, then you have to make an educated guess. Usually, opting for flexibility (meaning an LLC) is the better long-term choice. However, if you are worried about being second-guessed, S corporation status is the low-risk alternative.

HYPOTHETICAL SITUATIONS ILLUSTRATING HOW THE CHOICE OF ENTITY AFFECTS NET AFTER-TAX INCOME

The following are a series of hypothetical situations illustrating the comparative tax consequences of various transactions when conducted by a C corporation, an S corporation, or an entity taxable as a partnership (including an LLC).

Hypothetical Situation #1—Comparison of Entities—Annual Taxable Income

This hypothetical explores the consequences of operating a business that generates $1 million of earnings from business operations per year.

The projections simplify the analysis by assuming that a C corporation is subject to a combined federal and state income tax rate of 40 percent; that all individual owners of a C corporation, S corporation, or LLC are subject to a combined federal and state income tax rate of 38 percent (this rate assumes a 35-percent federal income tax rate, a five-percent state tax rate, and a deduction of state taxes on Schedule A of the federal return); and that all individual owners of a C corporation, S corporation, or LLC are subject to a combined federal and state tax rate of 20 percent on long-term capital gains and qualified dividend income.

C corporation tax consequences. The C corporation is subject to tax on the $1 million at the corporate level and pays $400,000 of income tax. A subsequent distribution of the net earnings and profits of $600,000 as a dividend would, in turn, result in qualified dividend income at the shareholder level, and would trigger additional tax at a rate of 20 percent, or $120,000 of additional tax. The net after-tax distribution to C corporation shareholders, therefore, is $480,000.

S corporation tax consequences. The S corporation is not subject to tax at the corporate level on its income (assuming Code section 1374 is inapplicable). Instead, shareholders are taxed on their share of the income. The $1 million of income is taxed to shareholders at a 38-percent tax rate and results in $380,000 of income tax, leaving the shareholders with net after-tax income of $620,000.

Figure 2.1

Annual business income			$1,000,000
C corporation combined federal and state tax rate			40%
Individual seller's combined tax bracket (federal and state) for ordinary income (OI)			38%
Individual seller's combined tax bracket (federal and state) for long-term capital gain (LTCG)			20%
Individual seller's combined tax bracket (federal and state) for dividends			20%
	C Corporation	*S Corporation*	*LLC*
Business income	$1,000,000.00	$1,000,000.00	$1,000,000.00
Entity-level tax	$400,000.00	$0.00	$0.00
Net distribution	$600,000.00	$1,000,000.00	$1,000,000.00
Owner-level tax (assumes individual owner)	$120,000.00	$380,000.00	$380,000.00
Net after-tax income to individual owner	$480,000.00	$620,000.00	$620,000.00

LLC tax consequences. LLC members have the same "pass through" tax treatment as S corporation shareholders. It is assumed that no member is subject to self-employment tax on the member's share of the LLC's income. Like S corporation shareholders, LLC members are left with net after-tax income of $620,000.

Practice Point: Hypothetical Situation #1 demonstrates the basic proposition that, as an on-going operating entity, a C corporation can generate significantly higher tax costs than an S corporation or an LLC. To be sure, many small C corporations "mimic" pass-through status by paying much or all of their income to shareholder-employees as compensation, thereby reducing or eliminating the corporate-level tax. However, this strategy is available mainly to small corporations and is not apposite to a sale of business assets.

Hypothetical Situation #2—Comparison of Entities—Annual Taxable Income with Capital Gain

Hypothetical Situation #2 starts with the same assumptions as Hypothetical Situation #1, but further assumes that $500,000 out of the $1 million of annual revenue is LTCG.

C corporation tax consequences. The C corporation is subject to tax on the $1 million at the corporate level and pays $400,000 of income tax. Note that there is no preferential tax rate for LTCG recognized by a C corporation. A subsequent distribution of the net earnings and profits of $600,000 would, as in Hypothetical Situation #1, result in qualified dividend income for the shareholders and would trigger an additional tax of $120,000 (20% × $600,000 = $120,000). The net after-tax distribution to C corporation shareholders, therefore, is again $480,000.

S corporation tax consequences. The S corporation is not subject to tax at the corporate level on its income (assuming Code section 1374 is inapplicable). Instead, shareholders are taxed on their share of the income, which has the same character in the hands of the shareholders as it had for the corporation. Therefore, the $1 million is treated as $500,000 of ordinary income, taxed to shareholders at a 38-percent rate of tax, and $500,000 of LTCG, taxed to shareholders at a 20-percent rate of tax. The amount of tax paid by shareholders on the $1 million is $290,000 [($500,000 × 38%) + ($500,000 × 20%) = $190,000 + $100,000 = $290,000]. The shareholders' net after-tax income is $710,000.

LLC tax consequences. LLC members enjoy the same "pass through" tax treatment as S corporation shareholders. The $500,000 of ordinary income and $500,000 of LTCG will be taxed to members, who will have to pay the same amount of tax as S corporation shareholders. Like S corporation shareholders, members will be left with $710,000 of net after-tax income.

Figure 2.2

Total annual business income			$1,000,000
Portion of LTCG in annual business income			$500,000
C corporation combined federal and state tax rate			40%
Individual seller's combined tax bracket (federal and state) for OI			38%
Individual seller's combined tax bracket (federal and state) for LTCG			20%
Individual seller's combined tax bracket (federal and state) for dividends			20%
	C Corporation	*S Corporation*	*LLC*
Business income (BI)	$1,000,000.00	$1,000,000.00	$1,000,000.00
LTCG portion of BI	$500,000.00	$500,000.00	$500,000.00
Entity-level tax	$400,000.00	$0.00	$0.00
Net distribution	$600,000.00	$1,000,000.00	$1,000,000.00
Owner-level tax (assumes individual owner)	$120,000.00	$290,000.00	$290,000.00
Net after-tax income to individual owner	$480,000.00	$710,000.00	$710,000.00

Note: Hypothetical Situation #2 assumes approximately 40 percent combined federal and state tax on a C corporation. It assumes individual tax rate on OI of 38 percent and on LTCG of 20 percent. It assumes half of all income is ordinary income and half is LTCG.

Hypothetical Situation #3—Comparison of Entities—Annual Taxable Income with Corporate Payments to Owner-Employees

This Hypothetical Situation illustrates the ability of a C corporation to reduce or eliminate its corporate-level tax liabilities by paying out profits as compensation to owner-employees (assuming that such payments constitute "reasonable compensation" under the applicable standards of Code section 162).

This Hypothetical Situation assumes that a C corporation with $1 million of earnings pays $600,000 of its profits as compensation to owner-employees, that the corporation distributes its remaining income to the shareholders as a dividend, and that the owner-employees and corporation have to pay a combined two-percent FICA tax (added to the employees' tax) on the compensation (a rate that probably underestimates the true tax costs of converting C corporation income to compensation).

Based on these assumptions, the C corporation pays an income tax of $160,000 ($400,000 × 40% = $160,000), and the owner-employees pay $288,000 [($600,000 × 40%) + ($240,000 × 20%) = $240,000 + $48,000 = $288,000], which leaves shareholders with $552,000 ($1 million – ($160,000 + $288,000) = $552,000), which exceeds the $480,000 of net after-tax benefit in Hypothetical Situations #1 and #2.

The S corporation and LLC continue to enjoy a far better after-tax result (i.e., $620,000 in Hypothetical Situation #1).

Hypothetical Situation #4—Comparison of Entities—Sale of Assets (All LTCG)

Hypothetical Situation #4 assumes a proposed sale of business assets for $10 million and resulting in recognition of $10 million in LTCG.

C corporation tax consequences. The C corporation is subject to tax on the $10 million at the corporate level, and, because there is no preferential LTCG tax rate, pays an estimated $4 million of income tax. A subsequent distribution of the net earnings and profits of $6 million would, in turn, result in LTCG at the shareholder level, and would trigger additional tax at a rate of 20 percent, or $1.2 million of additional tax. The net after-tax amount received by C corporation shareholders, therefore, is $4.8 million.

S corporation tax consequences. Assuming the S corporation is not subject to the Code section 1374 built-in gains tax, all income and gain is distributed to its shareholders, pro-rata in accordance with their share ownership, and retaining the same character as in the hands of the S corporation. The $10 million of LTCG is

Figure 2.3

Total annual business income			$1,000,000
Portion of LTCG in annual business income			$0
C corporation combined federal and state tax rate			40%
Individual owner's combined tax bracket (federal and state) for OI			38%
Individual owner's combined tax bracket (federal and state) for LTCG			20%
Individual owner's combined tax bracket (federal and state) for dividends			20%
Individual owner's compensation tax (including SS tax)			40%
	C Corporation	*S Corporation*	*LLC*
Business income (BI)	$1,000,000.00	$1,000,000.00	$1,000,000.00
LTCG portion of BI	$0.00	$0.00	$0.00
Deduction for compensation to owner-employee	–$600,000.00	$0.00	$0.00
Net entity level income	$400,000.00	$1,000,000.00	$1,000,000.00
Entity-level tax	$160,000.00	$0.00	$0.00
Net distribution to owners	$240,000.00	$1,000,000.00	$1,000,000.00
Owner-level tax (assumes individual owner)	$48,000.00	$380,000.00	$380,000.00
Net distribution after tax	$192,000.00	$620,000.00	$620,000.00
Owner-level compensation income	$600,000.00		
Owner-level tax on compensation	$240,000.00		
Net compensation after tax	$360,000.00		
Total net after-tax income to individual owner	$552,000.00	$620,000.00	$620,000.00

Note: Hypothetical Situation #3 assumes approximately 40 percent combined federal and state tax on a C corporation. It assumes individual tax rate on OI of 38 percent, on compensation (including SS) is 40 percent, and on LTCG of 20 percent.

taxed at the shareholder level at a 20-percent rate of tax, which results in $2 million of income tax and leaves the shareholders with net after-tax income of $8 million.

LLC tax consequences. LLC members have the same "pass through" tax treatment as S corporation shareholders. Therefore, they would pay $2 million in income taxes and would be left with net after-tax income of $8 million.

Hypothetical Situation #5—Comparison of Entities—Sale of Assets (LTCG and OI)

Hypothetical Situation #5 assumes that a sale of assets will produce an estimated $9.5 million of LTCG and $500,000 of ordinary income (e.g., recapture income or some other form of OI recognized on a disposition of assets).

Under this modification of the assumed facts, the C corporation continues to have the exact same tax consequences as in Hypothetical Situation #4, since the C corporation pays the same tax rate and same tax whether the taxable income is ordinary income or capital gain. (Note, however, that the character occasionally matters, such as if the C corporation has long-term capital loss (LTCL) carried over from a recent prior year.) Thus, the projections again show net after-tax income of $4.8 million.

For the S corporation and LLC, by contrast, converting a portion of the sales proceeds to ordinary income causes that portion of the income to be taxed at the personal income tax rate for ordinary income (assumed to be 38 percent) and thus produces an after-tax income of $7.91 million ($9,500,000 × 20% = $1,900,000; $500,000 × 38% = $190,000; $10,000,000 – $1,900,000 – $190,000 = $7,910,000) instead of the $8 million projected in Hypothetical Situation #4.

Figure 2.4

Total gain on sale			$10,000,000
Portion of gain reported on LTCG			$10,000,000
C corporation combined federal and state tax rate			40%
Individual seller's combined tax bracket (federal and state) for OI			38%
Individual seller's combined tax bracket (federal and state) for LTCG			20%
Individual seller's combined tax bracket (federal and state) for dividends			20%
	C Corporation	*S Corporation*	*LLC*
Gain on sale	$10,000,000.00	$10,000,000.00	$10,000,000.00
LTCG portion of gain	$10,000,000.00	$10,000,000.00	$10,000,000.00
Entity-level tax	$4,000,000.00	$0.00	$0.00
Net distribution	$6,000,000.00	$10,000,000.00	$10,000,000.00
Owner-level tax (assumes individual owner)	$1,200,000.00	$2,000,000.00	$2,000,000.00
Net after-tax income to individual owner	$4,800,000.00	$8,000,000.00	$8,000,000.00
Note: Hypothetical Situation #4 assumes approximately 40 percent combined federal and state tax on a C corporation. It assumes individual tax rate on OI of 38 percent and on LTCG of 20 percent. It assumes identified portion of gain is LTCG.			

Practice Point: As Hypothetical Situation #1 demonstrates, the S corporation and LLC are more tax efficient than a C corporation even if *all* the income is ordinary income. However, when most or all of the income is LTCG, as is almost always the case in a sale of business assets, the difference between the double-tax regime of a C corporation and the single-level shareholder tax (and, most importantly, the availability of preferential LTCG tax rates) imposed in the case of a pass-through entity makes both the S corporation and LLC dramatically more tax efficient.

Figure 2.5

Total gain on sale			$10,000,000
Portion of gain reported on LTCG			$9,500,000
C corporation combined federal and state tax rate			40%
Individual seller's combined tax bracket (federal and state) for OI			38%
Individual seller's combined tax bracket (federal and state) for LTCG			20%
Individual seller's combined tax bracket (federal and state) for dividends			20%
	C Corporation	*S Corporation*	*LLC*
Gain on sale	$10,000,000.00	$10,000,000.00	$10,000,000.00
LTCG portion of gain	$9,500,000.00	$9,500,000.00	$9,500,000.00
Entity-level tax	$4,000,000.00	$0.00	$0.00
Net distribution	$6,000,000.00	$10,000,000.00	$10,000,000.00
Owner-level tax (assumes individual owner)	$1,200,000.00	$2,090,000.00	$2,090,000.00
Net after-tax income to individual owner	$4,800,000.00	$7,910,000.00	$7,910,000.00
Note: Hypothetical Situation #5 assumes approximately 40 percent combined federal and state tax on a C corporation. It assumes individual tax rate on OI of 38 percent and on LTCG of 20 percent. It assumes identified portion of gain is LTCG.			

CHAPTER ENDNOTES

1. 1988-2 CB 360.
2. IRC Sec. 11.
3. IRC Sec. 301(c).
4. IRC Sec. 11.
5. IRC Secs. 531-537.
6. IRC Secs. 541-547.
7. IRC Secs. 53 and 55-59.
8. IRC Sec. 469.
9. IRC Sec. 465.
10. See IRC Secs. 331 and 336.
11. IRC Sec. 1366.
12. IRC Sec. 469.
13. IRC Sec. 465.
14. IRC Sec. 336(a).
15. IRC Sec. 1367.
16. IRC Sec. 311(b).
17. IRC Sec. 1368 ordering rules.
18. Reg. § 1.338(h)(10)-1(c).
19. IRC Sec. 721(a).
20. IRC Sec. 469.
21. IRC Sec. 465.
22. IRC Sec. 731.
23. IRC Sec. 743.

TAX ASPECTS OF BUYING AND SELLING A SOLE PROPRIETORSHIP—PURCHASE PRICE ALLOCATION

CHAPTER 3

OVERVIEW

The sale of a sole proprietorship business is the "vanilla" fact pattern for a sale of business assets. In turn, the tax issues raised in a proprietorship asset sale can be used to build a basic understanding of the tax aspects of more complicated asset sales by other entities. We will assume in this chapter that the Target is a "sole proprietorship", i.e., a business with a single individual owner reporting all tax aspects of the business, including the sale transaction, on Schedule C to Form 1040. A "sole proprietorship" asset sale includes the sale by an individual member of his entire interest in a single-member LLC.[1]

Individuals, unlike corporations, enjoy a preferential tax rate on long term capital gains. Compare Code section 1 to Code section 11. As a result, the important tax issues raised by the sale of a sole proprietorship generally involve the character of the assets being sold and, in turn, the character of the income or gain recognized by the Seller (i.e., ordinary income, ordinary loss, capital gain, and/or capital loss). By contrast, as we will examine in Chapter 4 and succeeding chapters of this book, in the case of a sale of corporate assets, the important tax structuring issues usually turn on how the various payments are allocated among the asset purchase price, consulting or compensation payments, noncompete payments, and possibly the purchase of individual goodwill.

The importance of generating capital gain in an asset sale is in direct proportion to the differential between ordinary income tax rates and capital gains tax rates. Immediately after the Tax Reform Act of 1986 (P.L. 99-514), ordinary income and capital gains were (briefly) subject to an equal tax rate, which was intentionally designed to eliminate the tax planning contortions that arise because of a tax rate differential. Needless to say, that policy—while perhaps laudable—was quickly eviscerated. At the moment, the maximum capital gains tax rate is 20 percent, while the maximum ordinary income rate is nearly double that, currently 39.6 percent.[2] Thus, there is currently a huge benefit to generating capital gain rather than ordinary income on a sale of assets.

The timing of income and/or gain recognition, and therefore of income taxation, turns on whether a particular transaction constitutes a "sale or exchange".[2] Remarkably enough, the term "sale or exchange" is not defined in the Code or in any regulations. As a practical matter, it is usually relatively obvious whether a transaction constitutes a sale or exchange. However, there are certain circumstances in which the parties may wish to avoid sale or exchange treatment, or, alternatively, where the parties may want to make sure that they achieve it (usually to assure capital gain treatment). For example, whether a transaction constitutes a "lease" of property or a "sale" of property often turns on the economic substance of the transaction. It is frequently possible to structure a lease or a license arrangement so that it qualifies as a sale or exchange transaction, especially when the parties are motivated by substantial tax savings.

An important exception to the broad scope of sale or exchange rules is that a transaction resulting from the termination or cancellation of an obligation may not be considered a sale or exchange.[3]

TAX CLASSIFICATION OF BUSINESS ASSETS BY SELLER—DESPERATELY SEEKING CAPITAL GAINS

To understand how the sale of a business asset is taxed, it is necessary to understand how the asset is classified for tax purposes.

Capital Asset Defined

The term "capital asset" is defined in Code section 1221. Interestingly enough, a capital asset is technically defined by exception rather than inclusion (meaning that a capital asset is anything that is *not* excluded from the definition of capital asset). Under Code section 1221(a), assets excluded from capital gain characterization, and, therefore, characterized (with a few notable exceptions, such as Code section 1221(a)(2)) as "ordinary assets" generating ordinary income on sale, include the following (enumerated to conform to Code section 1221(a)):

(1) stock in trade of the taxpayer or other property of a kind which would properly be included in the inventory of the taxpayer if on hand at the close of the taxable year, or property held by the taxpayer primarily for sale to customers in the ordinary course of his trade or business;[4]

(2) property, used in his trade or business, of a character which is subject to the allowance for depreciation provided in section 167, or real property used in his trade or business;[5]

(3) a copyright, a literary, musical, or artistic composition, a letter or memorandum, or similar property, held by—

(A) a taxpayer whose personal efforts created such property,

(B) in the case of a letter, memorandum, or similar property, a taxpayer for whom such property was prepared or produced, or

(C) a taxpayer in whose hands the basis of such property is determined, for purposes of determining gain from a sale or exchange, in whole or part by reference to the basis of such property in the hands of a taxpayer described in subparagraph (A) or (B);[6]

(4) accounts or notes receivable acquired in the ordinary course of trade or business for services rendered or from the sale of property described in paragraph (1);[7]

(5) a publication of the United States Government (including the Congressional Record) which is received from the United States Government or any agency thereof, other than by purchase at the price at which it is offered for sale to the public, and which is held by—

(A) a taxpayer who so received such publication, or

(B) a taxpayer in whose hands the basis of such publication is determined, for purposes of determining gain from a sale or exchange, in whole or in part by reference to the basis of such publication in the hands of a taxpayer described in subparagraph (A);[8]

(6) any commodities derivative financial instrument held by a commodities derivatives dealer, unless—

(A) it is established to the satisfaction of the Secretary that such instrument has no connection to the activities of such dealer as a dealer, and

(B) such instrument is clearly identified in such dealer's records as being described in subparagraph (A) before the close of the day on which it was acquired, originated, or entered into (or such other time as the Secretary may by regulations prescribe);[9]

(7) any hedging transaction which is clearly identified as such before the close of the day on which it was acquired, originated, or entered into (or such other time as the Secretary may by regulations prescribe); or[10]

(8) supplies of a type regularly used or consumed by the taxpayer in the ordinary course of a trade or business of the taxpayer.[11]

In general, and at the risk of over simplification, "ordinary assets" are those in the nature of inventory, accounts receivable acquired in connection with the sale of inventory, and similar types of interests and assets that represent the stock in trade or inventory of a business.[12] Depreciable property used in a trade or business (i.e., property subject to the allowance for depreciation under Code section 167) is excluded from the definition of capital asset by Code section 1221(a)(2), but will nonetheless generally enjoy the tax benefits of long-term capital-gain treatment so long as the property is held for more than one year. See below.

Code Section 1231 Property

Perhaps the single most important category of business assets is property governed by the exception in Code section 1221(a)(2), which will be referred to herein as "Code section 1231 property". In general, Code section 1231 property is property used in the trade or business of a character which is subject to the allowance for depreciation provided in Code section 167, held for more than one year, and also real property used in the trade or business, held for more than one year. Although Code section 1231 property is not, technically, a capital asset, it actually has attributes that can sometimes be even ***better*** than those of a capital asset, namely capital gain/ ordinary loss treatment on a sale.

In keeping with the notion that Code section 1231 represents a special category of capital asset, Code section 1231 intentionally excludes from Code section 1231 treatment some appropriate and obvious types of business property (generally categories conforming to the exclusions from capital asset treatment under Code section 1221(a)), including the following:[13]

1. Property of a kind that properly would be includible in the taxpayer's inventory if on hand at the close of the tax year.
2. Property held primarily for sale to customers in the ordinary course of the taxpayer's trade or business.
3. A copyright, literary, musical, or artistic composition, characterized as an ordinary income asset under Code section 1221(a)(3).
4. A publication of the U.S. government that is received from the U.S. government, or any agency of the U.S. government, other than by purchase at a price at which it is offered for sale to the public and that is held by a taxpayer described in Code section 1221(a)(5).

Comment: Property that would otherwise be Code section 1231 property except that it is not held for more one year is neither a Code section 1231 asset nor a capital asset (because of Code section 1221(a)(2)) and therefore, by process of elimination, is an "ordinary" asset, producing ordinary gain or loss on disposition.

Code section 1231 property has distinctive tax attributes. To the extent Code section 1231 gains exceed Code section 1231 losses, the net gain is characterized as long term capital gain. On the other hand, to the extent that Code section 1231 losses exceed Code section 1231 gains, the loss is characterized as an ordinary loss. As a result, gains enjoy potentially preferential capital gains tax treatment (if the business gains are ultimately taxed to an individual), and losses are characterized as ordinary losses, and thus avoid the very onerous limitations on the utilization of capital losses imposed by Code sections 1211 and 1212.

Example 1: Xavier, an individual, owns through a single member LLC depreciable real property used in a trade or business and subject to the allowance of depreciation under Code section 167. This real estate has been held for several years and has been depreciated on a straight-line basis over the applicable thirty-nine-year recovery period. The original tax basis of $450,000 has, as a result of depreciation, been reduced to $400,000. In addition, the business has depreciable machinery and equipment, which was purchased for $200,000 and now has a tax basis of $96,000. Assume that Xavier can sell the real estate to one purchaser for $600,000 and can sell the equipment, at a loss, for $50,000. Based on these facts, Xavier would recognize a $200,000 Code section 1231 gain on the sale of the real estate, and a $46,000 Code section 1231 loss on the equipment. These two transactions would be offset, and Xavier would recognize a net gain of $154,000, which would be characterized as capital gain, and as long term capital gain since the real estate has been held for more than one year.

Example 2: The same facts as above, except the real estate is sold for $420,000, producing a $20,000 gain. On these facts, the $46,000 loss from the sale of the equipment will offset the $20,000 gain and produce a $26,000 Code section 1231 loss, which will be an ordinary loss. This loss, in turn, can be used to offset other income of Xavier (subject to Code section 469 passive activity loss limitations and possibly other limitations).

Code Section 1245 Property

A special category of business asset is what is known as "Section 1245 property". This category of property becomes important when gain is recognized from the disposition of certain depreciable property governed by Code section 1245 and causes all or a portion of such gain to be taxed as ordinary income. section 1245 property is defined in Code section 1245(a)(3) and generally includes any property which is or has been property of a character subject to allowance for depreciation provided in Code section 167 and which falls into one of the following categories: (1) personal property; (2) other property (not including a building or its structural components), but only if such other property is tangible property that has been depreciated or amortized while used for certain (relatively common) business purposes; or (3) certain other specialized kinds of real property which are beyond the scope of this book.[14] Basically, at the risk of oversimplification, Code section 1245 property typically consists of non-real estate personal property subject to the allowance for depreciation that has previously been depreciated while being used in the taxpayer's trade or business.

The policy rationale underlying Code section 1245 is that a taxpayer has received amortization or depreciation deductions that have sheltered ordinary income of a business, and has enjoyed the accelerated depreciation methods permitted by the Code. (In general, tax depreciation and tax amortization are usually more accelerated than the corresponding financial or book amortization and depreciation.) The theory is that to the extent the taxpayer enjoys the depreciation benefits as an offset against ordinary income, but then sells the business asset for an amount greater than the remaining tax basis in the property, the taxpayer should "give back" the tax benefit of the prior "ordinary" deduction (i.e., a depreciation deduction that offsets ordinary income) by recognizing ordinary income. (Code section 1245 can be viewed as a very specific, codified version of the tax benefit rule.) Therefore, Code section 1245 basically "recaptures", as ordinary income, gain on the sale of previously depreciated or previously amortized assets, but only up to the point that all prior depreciation or amortization deductions have been fully recaptured.

Technically, Code section 1245 operates in the following manner:

Figure 3.1

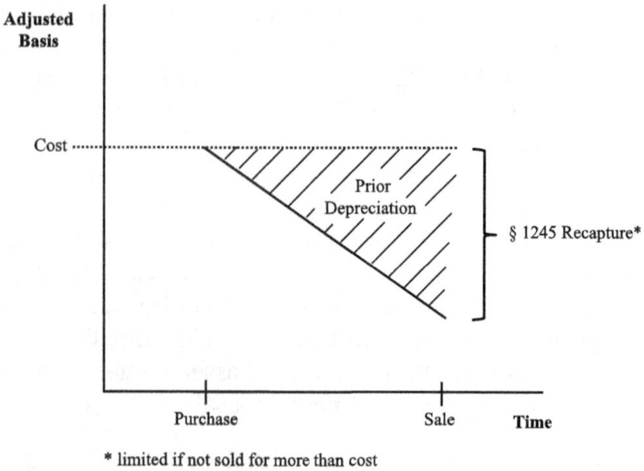

The amount of gain subject to "recapture" as ordinary income under Code section 1245(a)(1) is computed by subtracting the taxpayer's current adjusted tax basis in the property from the least of the following three amounts: (1) the recomputed basis in the property (essentially the original tax basis in the property before any depreciation was claimed), (2) in the case of a sale, exchange, or involuntary conversion of the property, the amount realized from such transaction, or (3) in the case of any property disposition other than by sale, exchange, or involuntary conversion, the fair market value of the property. The first category represents all depreciation claimed to date on the property, and is sometimes called the "depreciation limitation". The second category represents the amount of gain realized on the sale, exchange, or involuntary conversion of the property, and is sometimes called the "gain limitation". The third category applies only to those (relatively uncommon) transactions that do not constitute a sale, exchange, or involuntary conversion (e.g., if a corporation sells an asset to a shareholder for below fair-market value).

In any property transaction that qualifies under the Code as a sale, exchange, or involuntary conversion (i.e., the vast majority of transactions), the amount of Section 1245 recapture income will be the lesser of (1) the gain realized on the sale or (2) all depreciation ever claimed with respect to the property. Thus, any Section 1245 property that is sold at a gain (i.e., for more than its current tax basis) will generate ordinary (recapture) income, with the maximum amount of such recapture income being the full amount of depreciation previously claimed with respect to the property. If Section 1245 property is sold for more than its original purchase price (unlikely, but possible, for most non-real estate business assets), the gain on the sale for the amount excess of the original purchase price is not subject to recapture and thus generates conventional capital gain.

The following examples are from Reg. § 1.1245-1(b)(2):

Figure 3.2

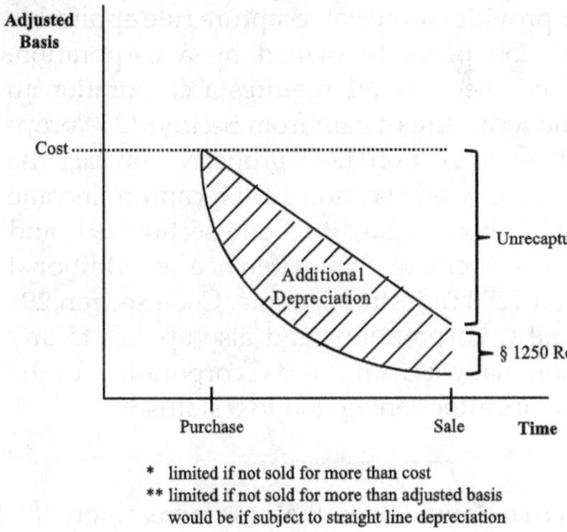

Example (1). On January 1, 1964, Brown purchases section 1245 property for use in his manufacturing business. The property has a basis for depreciation of $3,300. After taking depreciation deductions of $1,300 (the amount allowable), Brown realizes after selling expenses the amount of $2,900 upon sale of the property on January 1, 1969. Brown's gain is $900 ($2,900 amount realized minus $2,000 adjusted basis). Since the amount realized upon disposition of the property ($2,900) is lower than its recomputed basis ($3,300, i.e., $2,000 adjusted basis plus $1,300 in depreciation deductions), the entire gain is treated as ordinary income under section 1245(a)(1) and not as gain from the sale or exchange of property described in section 1231.

Example (2). Assume the same facts as in example (1) except that Brown exchanges the section 1245 property for land which has a fair market value of $3,700, thereby realizing a gain of $1,700 (the $3,700 amount realized minus $2,000 adjusted basis). Since the recomputed basis of the property ($3,300) is lower than the amount realized upon its disposition ($3,700), the excess of recomputed basis over adjusted basis, or $1,300, is treated as ordinary income under section 1245(a)(1). The remaining $400 of the gain may be treated as gain from the sale or exchange of property described in section 1231.

Code Section 1250 Property

Depreciable real estate is generally not subject to Code section 1245 (there are a few special exceptions under Code section 1245(a)(3)), and instead is subject to the rather peculiar rules set forth under Code section 1250. In general, Code section 1250 was originally created as a corresponding "recapture" provision for real estate, and in fact served that function for many years. As with Section 1245 property, gain recognized on a disposition of Section 1250 property is subject to recapture based on the least of three amounts: (1) "additional depreciation", (2) in the case of a sale, exchange, or involuntary conversion of the property, the amount realized from such transaction over the adjusted basis of such property, or (3) in the case of any property disposition other than by sale, exchange, or involuntary conversion, the fair market value of the property over the adjusted basis of such property.[15] In turn, "additional depreciation" means, in the case of property held for more than one year, depreciation adjustments only to the extent they exceed depreciation under the straight line method of adjustment.[16]

Since the MACRS system of depreciation went into effect under Code section 168 in 1987, the practical effect has been that there is no "additional depreciation" and hence no Section 1250 recapture income on a sale of depreciable real estate placed in service after 1986. Meanwhile, property placed in service under earlier, more accelerated depreciation or cost recovery systems before 1987 continue (for the moment) to have small but dwindling amounts of "additional depreciation".

Although a sale of depreciable real estate is increasingly unlikely to generate Section 1250 recapture income, such a sale by a noncorporate taxpayer is very likely to trigger Section 1250 recapture income's "evil twin" called "unrecaptured Section 1250 gain", which is a special category of long-term capital gain generally taxed at a 25-percent tax rate.[17] "Unrecaptured Section 1250 gain" is technically defined as the excess (if any) of (1) the amount of long-term capital gain (not otherwise treated as ordinary income) which would be treated as ordinary income if Code section 1250(b)(1) included all depreciation and the applicable percentage under Code section 1250(a) were 100 percent, over (2) the excess (if any) of so-called 28-percent rate losses (defined in Code section 1(h)(4)(B)) over 28-percent rate gains (defined in Code section 1(h)(4)(A)).[18] A further limitation with respect to Section 1231 property applies such that the amount described in (1) from sales, exchanges, and conversions described in Code section 1231(a)(3)(A) (i.e., Section 1231 gain) for any tax year shall not exceed the net Section 1231 gain (as defined in Code section 1231(c)(3)) for such year.[19]

Assuming for the moment that on a sale of depreciable real estate held for more than one year, there are no excess 28-percent rate losses (frequently the case), there are no offsetting Section 1231 losses (could well be the case), and the real estate is sold for greater than its original purchase price (almost always the case), then this means the "unrecaptured Section 1250 gain" is simply a computation, essentially identical to the computation of Section 1245 recapture income, that causes all long-term gain on such sale attributable to depreciation deductions (other than any amounts treated as Section 1250 recapture income) to be taxed at a special rate of 25 percent.[20] Practically speaking, since all depreciable real estate placed in service after 1987 has been depreciated on a straight-line basis under the MACRS system,[21] any sale of such property at a gain will never generate recapture income taxable at ordinary rates but will always generate "unrecaptured Section 1250 gain" taxable at a special 25-percent rate. Thus, Code section 1250 in practice is actually not a "recapture" rule but rather an "unrecapture" rule!

> ***Practice Point:*** Be aware that when computing the actual tax rate on unrecaptured Section 1250 gain, the special 25-percent tax rate is subject to the many additional adjustments and modifications that apply as part of the computation of the maximum capital gains tax rate under Code section 1(h). (The capital gains tax rate for individuals may seem intuitive and easy until to you read Code section 1(h)—which is one of the most astonishing complicated provisions in the entire Code!) Depending on whether there are other capital losses, and whether the taxable income is above certain thresholds, the actual effective tax rate could be well below 25 percent.

Any gain on a sale of real estate in excess of all prior depreciation deductions will not be "unrecaptured" gain and instead will be conventional capital gain (i.e., subject generally to a 15-percent tax rate if held more than one year).

Meanwhile, in the case of a corporate taxpayer, Code section 291 provides a special recapture rule applicable to Section 1250 property owned by a corporation. Basically, Code section 291 requires a corporation to calculate the recapture of gain from Section 1250 property as if it were Section 1245 property, subtract the actual amount of Code section 1250 recapture income determined without regard to Code section 291, and then add 20 percent of this difference as additional Code section 1250 recapture income. Code section 291 applies to all C corporations and also applies to any S corporation that was formerly a C corporation for the first three years after conversion to S status.[22]

> ***Practice Point:*** Given that it is increasingly rare for a sale of depreciable real estate to generate any recapture income whatsoever under Code section 1250, Code section 291 interacts with Code section 1250 to create a *de facto* "20 percent" depreciation recapture rule for real estate held by corporations. However, the policy purpose for this provision is far from clear. First, holding real estate in a C corporation is almost, by definition, a dumb idea, as the discussion in Chapter 4 will amply demonstrate, and so arguably no C corporation should ever do it under any circumstances. Second, since there is no favorable capital gains tax rate applicable to C corporations, the recharacterization of capital gains as ordinary income has only limited practical effect, e.g., capital gain could be used to offset capital losses while ordinary income could not, but otherwise the tax rate is the same. Meanwhile, the three-year rule applicable to S corporations that were formerly C corporations dates back to 1982, and at that time corresponded to the three-year recognition period for the "built-in gains tax" under Code section 1374. The fact that this provision has never been updated probably speaks volumes about how little relevance Code section 291 has at the present time.

The following examples illustrate the application of Code sections 1250 and 291:

Example 3: Isabelle Darby, a sole proprietor, acquires land and a building for use in her trade of business. The purchase price of the property is $450,000, of which $60,000 is allocated to nondepreciable land, and the remainder, $390,000, is allocated to the building. The building is depreciated on a straight line basis over thirty-nine years, producing MACRS deductions of $10,000 per year. At the end of five years, after claiming $50,000 of depreciation deductions, Isabelle sells the property for $500,000. The sale price is allocated by the parties such that $60,000 is allocated to land and $450,000 to the building. Isabelle's adjusted tax basis in the property at the time of sale is $400,000, of which $60,000 is allocated to the land and $340,000 to the building. Isabelle recognizes gain of $100,000 on the sale. Because the property has been depreciated using the straight line method, there will be no recapture income under Code section 1250; however, there will be unrecaptured Section 1250 gain. The amount of unrecaptured Section 1250 gain is the lesser of the gain limitation [amount realized on sale minus adjusted basis in property ($500,000 – $400,000 = $100,000)] or the depreciation limitation [recomputed basis (i.e., original basis) minus adjusted basis ($390,000 – $340,000 = $50,000], and so the unrecaptured Section 1250 gain in this case is $50,000. Such gain will be subject to the special 25-percent tax rate under Code section 1(h) (but also subject to the numerous computational modifications required by Code section 1(h)). The gain in excess of unrecaptured Section 1250 gain will be taxed at "normal" capital gains rates.

Example 4: Assume the same facts as Example 3 except that the owner of the business is a C corporation. There is no Section 1250 recapture in this case, because the property has been depreciated using the straight-line method. However, under Code section 291, the corporation must calculate the recapture of gain from its Section 1250 property as if it were Section 1245 property, subtract the actual amount of Code section 1250 recapture income determined without regard to Code section 291 (i.e., zero), and multiply the difference by 20 percent. Thus the product ($50,000 – 0 = $50,000; $50,000 × 20% = $10,000), or $10,000, will be characterized as ordinary income by Code section 291, and the balance, or $40,000, will be characterized as long-term capital gain. There is no difference in tax rate for a C corporation, but the recharacterization could affect the ability of the C corporation to utilize capital losses from other transactions.

Land

Land used in a trade or business, like depreciable real estate or depreciable tangible property, is classified as a Code section 1231 asset and not, technically, as a capital asset.[23] While depreciable personalty and depreciable realty are subject to the recapture rules described above under Code sections 1245 and 1250, land is not subject to depreciation or amortization, and therefore will never generate recapture income on sale under these provisions. It will, however, generate capital gain/ordinary loss treatment if held for more than one year.[24]

Leases

A lease, whether of personal property or realty, is considered a Code section 1231 asset. Therefore, gain or loss recognized on a transfer of the lease will be characterized under that Code section. In general, the character of the lease is governed by the character of the underlying property: Thus, a lease of tangible personal property that would be classified as Section 1245 property is itself treated as Section 1245 property.[25] As a practical matter, a lessee will have recapture income on the transfer of a leasehold only if there is an improvement or other attribute that the lessee can directly depreciate or amortize. Payment of rent is not considered depreciation or amortization that generates ordinary recapture income to the lessee if the lease is later sold.[26] A lease of real estate under current tax rules requires the lessee to amortize over thirty-nine years any improvements made in the leasehold, regardless of the term of the lease.[27] Therefore, there will not be any recapture under Code section 1250 on the transfer or sale of a real estate lease by the lessee/leaseholder, but there could be unrecaptured Section 1250 gain.[28]

Patents

Patents are subject to favorable tax treatment under the Code. Basically, there are two ways that a patent transfer can be eligible for capital gains treatment: (1) if the transfer meets the requirements of Code section 1235, or (2) if the transfer otherwise qualifies as a sale of a capital asset (or of Section 1231 property) under the well-developed body of case law in this area.[29]

Code section 1235 applies only to patents. It generally provides for capital gains treatment if all requirements of that provision are met. The key requirements of Code section 1235 include (1) the property transferred must be a "patent", which includes a U.S. patent, any foreign patent granting rights, and general rights to a patentable product even if there is no patent application on file at the time of the transfer; (2) the transfer must be by a "holder", which is defined to mean an individual (not a corporation) who either created the patent or acquired his or her interest in exchange for consideration paid to a patent creator before the invention was reduced to practice; and (3) the "holder" must transfer "all substantial rights", or an undivided interest in such rights, including all claims or inventions which exist and have value at the time of the transfer.

For individual transferors not meeting requirements of Code section 1235 and for corporate transferors, it is still possible for a patent transfer to qualify as a "sale" of an asset producing long-term gain under a large body of case law governing this area. Generally, to enjoy capital gain treatment, a transferor must transfer the exclusive right to "make, use, and vend" the patented invention. While case law generally requires that the transferor transfer all substantial rights and applies many of the same principles as Code section 1235 in determining whether a sale has occurred, there are some potentially important distinctions. For example, case law has permitted sale treatment where the assignment of rights under the patent covered only a specified geographical portion of the United States.[30] Similarly, field of use fragmentation may also be eligible for capital gains treatment under case law.[31]

Copyrights

Gain or loss on the sale or other disposition of a copyright by a taxpayer whose personal efforts created such property is defined by the Code to be "ordinary income" because such copyrights are expressly excluded from both the definition of a capital asset and from treatment as Section 1231 property.[32] Likewise, any person who is a transferee of a copyright and who determines his basis in the copyright in whole or in part by reference to the tax basis in the hands of the transferor (for example, a donee who receives an interest in a copyright as a gift from a relative) will also have ordinary gain treatment.[33]

However, there is a narrow exception to this ban on capital gain treatment for self-created musical works.[34] Thanks to the lobbying efforts of NASI (a songwriting industry group in Nashville, Tennessee), taxpayers may elect at the time of sale to treat self-created musical works as capital assets to recognize capital gain instead of ordinary income.[35]

On the other hand, a party purchasing a copyright (or an interest in a copyright) is not subject to the Code section 1221(a)(3) exclusion or the Code section 1231(b)(1)(C) exclusion, and therefore will generally be eligible to treat the copyright interest as a Code section 1231 asset (assuming it is used in a trade or business) or as a capital asset under Code section 1221 (if it is not used in a trade or business). However, even for an acquired copyright, several factors can affect whether a subsequent sale of the copyright will generate ordinary income or capital gain. First, to the extent that the copyright is depreciated or amortized, as would often be the case, the copyright will be intangible personal property under Code section 1245 and thus will be subject to the recapture provisions of that Code section. Moreover, to the extent that a copyright is sold for gain in excess of the depreciation limitation under Code section 1245, there remains a significant potential obstacle to enjoying capital gain treatment. In general, Code section 1231(b)(1) defines "property used in a trade or business" to include depreciable property held for more than one year. However, Code section 1231(b)(1)(B) excludes from the definition of "property used in a trade or business" any property primarily held by the taxpayer for sale to customers in the ordinary course of the taxpayer's trade or business. The question, therefore, is whether the copyright is covered by the general rule in Code section 1231(b)(1) or by the exclusion in (b)(1)(B). At the risk of simplifying some very complicated case law, this is generally a question of fact that ultimately turns on the intentions and conduct of the taxpayer.

Franchises, Trademarks, and Trade Names[36]

Franchises, trademarks, and trade names are governed by their own special provision, Code section 1253, which is unique and markedly different from the rules applied to patents under Code section 1235. Basically, Code section 1253 allows capital gain treatment on a sale of a franchise, trademark, or trade name, but ***only*** under relatively limited and stringent circumstances. For example, Code section 1253(a) denies capital gain treatment on a transfer of a franchise, trademark, or trade name "if the transferor retains any significant power, right, or continuing interest with respect to the subject matter of the franchise, trademark, or trade name".

> ***Comment:*** Code section 1253(a) is clearly aimed at franchisors, who are in the business of selling franchise rights, and whose business activity is viewed as essentially sales of intangible property rights in the ordinary course of business.

Code section 1253(b)(2) provides that the term "significant power, right, or continuing interest" includes, but is not limited to, the following rights with respect to the interest transferred:

- A right to disapprove any assignment of such interest, or any part thereof.
- A right to terminate at will.
- A right to prescribe the standards of quality of products used or sold, or of services furnished, and of the equipment and facilities used to promote such products or services.
- A right to require that the transferee sell or advertise only products or services of the transferor.
- A right to require that the transferee purchase substantially all of its supplies and equipment from the transferor.
- A right to payments contingent on the productivity, use, or disposition of the subject matter of the interest transferred, if such payments constitute a substantial element under the transfer agreement.

In addition to precluding capital gain treatment if any significant right is retained, Code section 1253 expressly precludes capital gain treatment (and thus effectively mandates ordinary income treatment), *even if all rights in the asset are transferred*, to the extent that any amounts received by the transferor are contingent upon the productivity, use, or disposition of the franchise, trademark, or trade name transferred.[37] Thus, the most rational and logical way for a Buyer and Seller to measure the value of a trade name or franchise, namely by making contingent "earn-out" payments based on productivity and use, will not generate capital gains under Code section 1253, but rather will generate ordinary income to a Seller. Therefore, the only way to enjoy solely capital gain as a Seller of an asset governed by Code section 1253 is to sell all rights in the asset in exchange for a fixed payment amount (i.e., an amount not contingent on productivity, use, or disposition).

> ***Practice Point:*** The practical effect of these Code section 1253 rules is that a franchisor, which generally retains rights in the applicable intangible asset, will never be eligible for capital gain treatment on a sale, but a franchisee that later sells the franchise business (meaning a sale all of franchisee's rights for a fixed (noncontingent) amount) likely will enjoy capital gain treatment.

Code Section 197 Intangibles

Code section 197 was enacted in 1993 to apply consistent tax rules to a purchase of intangible business assets, which is a category of assets that has grown increasingly important in the modern economy. Interestingly, Code section 197 itself addresses only the tax treatment of intangible assets in the hands of the Buyer, and does not address the tax character or treatment of these assets in the hands of a Seller. Instead, one must look to case law and other general authority for the Seller's tax consequences.

In general, most or all of the Code section 197 intangibles will be treated as Code section 1231 property in the hands of the Seller because they are business assets, often in the nature of goodwill. Goodwill has long been recognized to be a capital asset.[38] Note that Code section 197 intangibles are intangible personal property and thus are subject to the recapture rules under Code section 1245 to the extent such assets have enjoyed amortization under Code section 197 prior to the sale. Code section 197 is discussed in great detail in Chapter 11.

Covenant Not-to-Compete

A payment under a covenant not-to-compete has historically been treated as ordinary income to the recipient.[39] The payee (usually but not always an individual) takes the payments into income under the payee's method of accounting (e.g., as received in the case of individuals on the cash method of accounting). This is true even if the payment by the payer is governed by Code section 197 and is amortized by the payer over fifteen years.

Although the tax conclusion that noncompete payments are ordinary income to the recipient is well established, the underlying theoretical basis is more than a little murky. From the earliest cases, it was generally argued—and assumed—that since selling one's skills and abilities was a form of ordinary income, the negative covenant of agreeing not to sell these skills and abilities was the equivalent of affirmative personal services, and hence taxable as ordinary income.[40] On the other hand, it is equally well established that despite the theory that noncompete payments are in the nature of compensation for services, the payments are not considered earned income subject to FICA or self-employment taxes.[41] As will be discussed in much greater detail in Chapter 17, the author believes that a very creditable argument can be made that a covenant not-to-compete is, in fact, a contractual mechanism to transfer personal goodwill. More importantly, there may be an ability to allocate some portion of the purchase price in an acquisition transaction to a transfer of the personal goodwill of the key business individual.

For a more detailed discussion of Code section 197, see Chapter 11.

Trade Secrets, Know-How, and Other Knowledge-Based Intangibles

Various informational or knowledge-based intangible assets, such as trade secrets, know-how, and the like, are often transferred in connection with the sale of a business. The sale or exchange of such assets can usually result in capital gain treatment, based on one of several different sections of the Code.

The first is under Code section 1235, which provides capital gain treatment on the sale of a patent by an individual inventor or other holder. It is not necessary that the patent or the patent application for the invention be in existence if the requirements of Code section 1235 are otherwise met.[42] Therefore, if the trade secret, know-how, or other knowledge-based intangible is "patentable", the taxpayer may be able to claim the benefits of Code section 1235, even if no patent has been issued or even applied for.

Even if a trade secret or know-how does not qualify for capital gain treatment under Code section 1235, the intangible assets will very likely fall within the definition of a capital asset under Code section 1221, or within the definition of property used in a trade or business for purposes of Code section 1231. Trade secrets and other know-how created by the Seller, through research or other development, are generally either capital assets or Section 1231 property in the hands of the Seller. Note that, since expenses incurred in creating the asset are often currently deductible, either under Code section 162 or under Code section 174, this means that the asset typically has a "zero" tax basis, and so the entire amount of the sales price allocated to the asset results in capital gain. A trade secret is usually considered a Code section 1221 asset because it is not subject to the allowance for depreciation or amortization (usually because the useful life cannot be reasonably estimated). In the fairly unusual case that a trade secret or know-how has a reasonably estimated useful life, then the asset is subject to depreciation or amortization under Code section 167, and the property will then fall into the category of Code section 1231 property used in a trade or business.

Comment: Code section 1221 is usually a more attractive alternative to the Seller than Code section 1231 because there is no recapture of prior deductions on a Code section 1221 asset. For example, research expenditures deducted under Code section 174 are not required to be recaptured as ordinary income on a subsequent sale of the property, even under the tax benefit rule.[43] Code section 1231 property, on the other hand, is subject to statutory recapture rules under Code section 1245, to the extent that prior depreciation or amortization deductions have been claimed. See Code section 197(f)(7), which treats Code section 197 amortization deductions as Code section 167 deductions, including for purposes of Code section 1245.

Goodwill, Going Concern Value, Customer Based Intangibles, Supplier Based Intangibles, and Business Information

Goodwill, going concern value, customer based, and supplier based intangibles, business information, customer lists, and all similar assets can fall under the general category of "business goodwill" and basically represent the operational value of an existing on-going business. Economically speaking, goodwill, work force in place, and other specific intangible business assets (which might be viewed as individual sticks within the larger bundle of business goodwill) are the attributes that make a business worth more than the sum of its individual parts.

Many intangible assets, in the nature of goodwill, have been treated as capital assets, including customer lists.[44]

Most business assets of this nature will have "zero" tax basis because the cost of creating these assets is typically deductible on a current basis under Code section 162 or possibly Code section 174. Most of these assets will be considered capital assets under Code section 1221. However, a notable exception has arisen under a fairly voluminous case law, relating to service contracts, which is discussed below.

To the extent that the costs of creating going concern value or certain intangible assets are subject to being capitalized and amortized under Code section 167 or Code section 195, the assets will be considered Code section 1231 assets, and depreciation deductions will eventually be subject to recapture under Code section 1245.

Comment: As this discussion should make obvious, there is a huge benefit to deducting asset-creation expenses currently under Code section 162 or Code section 174, rather than capitalizing them, because the taxpayer not only enjoys the full tax benefit of a deduction immediately, but avoids later recapture income, taxed at ordinary income rates.[45]

Governmental Licenses, Permits, and Contract Rights and Benefits

Rights granted, or otherwise acquired from or through another party, including governmental licenses, governmental permits, and contractual rights, often have a crucial and central value in the operation of a business. Obviously, many businesses can be operated only with a governmental license, including a liquor store, a television station, or a taxi business. In other cases, a specific permit may allow a company to do everything from building a building to disposing of waste under an environmental regulation.

Although the category of governmental licenses and permits is voluminous and diverse, all of these intangible assets, at core, generally fall within the definition of a Code section 197 intangible asset, which expressly includes "any license, permit, or other right granted by a governmental unit or any agency or instrumentality thereof".[46]

In a typical circumstance, the taxpayer may spend little or no money in applying for a permit, but to the extent that there are legal fees or other costs related to obtaining the license or permit, such costs are generally capitalized under Code section 263 if they result in enjoyment of a benefit beyond the current tax year. Not surprisingly, taxpayers often aggressively take the position that the expenditures to acquire a license or permit are ordinary and necessary business expenses deductible under Code section 162. At the risk of simplifying a rather convoluted and complicated area of case law, the general rule is that expenses incurred in obtaining a license or permit should usually be capitalized.

Assuming the cost of obtaining a license must be capitalized and amortized over fifteen years under Code section 197, the asset will be considered a Code section 1231 asset and will be subject to depreciation recapture under Code section 1245 upon disposition.

Nongovernmental contract rights are not expressly governed by Code section 197, particularly if they are "self-created" assets that have not been purchased from another party, and the characterization of such assets has been surprisingly complicated. On one hand, some contractual rights, such as a right to obtain shelf space in a store, have been viewed as amortizable Code section 1231 assets, while most self-created customer lists or other similar intangible assets are typically considered non-amortizable Code section 1221 capital assets.

On the other hand, where the asset in question can be viewed as a right to earn or receive future income of an ordinary nature, the IRS often argues, with frequent success, that the sale of the asset should generate ordinary income rather than capital gains. For example, various kinds of service contracts, such as agency contracts, requirements contracts, management contracts, and the like, have been held to generate ordinary income on sale. To the extent that there is a reconcilable theory in these cases (sometimes a bit of a stretch!), the theory appears to be that an intangible asset that represents an interest in property is a capital asset, while an intangible asset that represents the right to receive or earn income may be viewed as an "ordinary asset".[47]

SELLER'S HOLDING PERIOD FOR PROPERTY

A selling individual taxpayer seeking to enjoy favorable long-term capital-gains tax rates must satisfy a one-year holding requirement.[48] At the risk of simplifying some of the nuances of Code section 1223, defining the "holding period of property", the general rule is that the holding period of property begins at the time that the taxpayer purchases or acquires the property in a taxable sale or exchange.[49] For property acquired in a nontaxable transaction, such as stock acquired through a contribution of appreciated assets to a corporation in a nonrecognition transaction under Code section 351, the general rule is that the holding period of the new property includes (is "tacked" onto) the taxpayer's holding period with respect to the earlier property, to the extent the earlier property was either a capital asset or a Section 1231 asset.[50]

The holding period rules tend to be relatively intuitive, but it is useful to note one important exception, which is that there is no tacking of the holding period for a contribution of inventory or other ordinary assets to a corporation under Code section 351.[51]

DETERMINING AMOUNT OF SELLER'S GAIN OR LOSS

Computing Realized Gain

Gain or loss on the sale or exchange of property is measured by the difference between the amount realized in the sale and the adjusted tax basis of the property.[52] The statutory definition of "amount realized" includes:[53]

1. the amount of money received;
2. the fair market value of other property received; and
3. the amount of real property taxes allocable to the Seller if such taxes are paid by the Buyer.

In addition, the amount realized will include any liabilities that are assumed by the purchaser. If property is transferred subject to a liability, the amount of such liability constitutes part of the amount realized by the Seller. This is true even if the Seller is not personally liable on the debt, and even if the Buyer does not personally assume the liability.[54]

Tax Basis

The adjusted tax basis is the original cost of the property increased by expenses related to the property and properly capitalized, and decreased by losses and allowable depreciation.[55]

Deferral of Recognition

The Code has a strong bias in favor of taxation (big surprise there), and so gain or loss is generally recognized on any sale or exchange of property, as of the date of the transaction, unless there is a specific Code provision that permits either deferral or nonrecognition.[56] Perhaps the most commonly used "deferral" provision is Code section 453, which allows installment sale reporting of a sale transaction where the consideration will be paid in cash, but at a later time.

Nonrecognition Provisions

The most common nonrecognition provisions are very well-known:

1. Code section 1031, providing general nonrecognition of gain in "like-kind" exchanges (but subject to some very complicated boot rules).
2. Code section 351 (tax-free contributions of property to a corporation under qualifying circumstances).
3. Code section 721 (tax-free contributions of property to a partnership under qualifying circumstances).
4. Code section 368 (generally providing nonrecognition for transactions qualifying as corporate "reorganizations").
5. Code section 1033 (allowing nonrecognition on an involuntary conversion or theft of property where the insurance or other proceeds are reinvested within specified periods of time).

ALLOCATION OF PURCHASE PRICE TO ACQUIRED ASSETS—CODE SECTION 1060

Overview

Naturally, a selling sole proprietor generally seeks capital gains treatment, rather than ordinary income treatment, on a sale of business assets and thus will be happy to allocate each marginal dollar of purchase price to a capital asset (or a Code section 1231 asset that generates capital gain) rather than to an ordinary asset. The Buyer, on the other hand, would naturally like to deduct or depreciate the purchase price as rapidly as possible, and accordingly would prefer to allocate purchase price to items (such as consulting payments) that can be deducted immediately, or, in the alternative, to items that are deductible over shorter periods of time (such as five-year depreciation of tangible assets) rather than over longer periods of time (such as fifteen-year amortization of intangible assets). This is all common sense.

As a practical matter, there are inherent tensions between the objectives of the Buyer and the objectives of the Seller. That is why every business negotiation is unique; it turns on the respective tolerances and appetites of each party based on the party's particular tax and financial circumstances. This tension will be evaluated in great depth in Chapter 6, but, for the moment, it is sufficient to note that the parties can generally fashion between themselves an arrangement that maximizes the aggregate after-tax benefit to the Seller and to the Buyer. The final agreement is generally achieved by shaving the tax costs of the deal (meaning the taxes paid to the federal and/or state governments) as thinly as possible. This is called good tax planning.

Given of the known objectives of the Buyer and Seller, it would obviously be advantageous for both parties in some circumstances to allocate an excessive and unreasonable amount of purchase price to certain (tax-favored) assets and away from certain other (less tax-favored) assets if this were allowed. However, the IRS figured out this allocation game early on, and as a result Congress enacted Code section 1060, which is designed to prevent (or at least put a limit on) aggressive tax allocation strategies. The goal in enacting Code section 1060 was to allocate purchase price in a rational economic manner, based on the so-called "residual method". The residual method is nothing more complex than a set of rules whereby the aggregate purchase price of a business is allocated in a logical economic progression, from the most easily valued assets (cash being the most easy-to-value asset), and descending in order of valuation ease until the remaining amount (the so-called "residual amount") is allocated to the assets with the most difficult and imponderable value, namely business goodwill.

Code section 1060(a) provides that in the case of any "applicable asset acquisition", the parties must allocate the purchase price among the acquired assets in the same manner as under Code section 338(b)(5). These allocation rules will then be binding for purposes of determining both (1) the transferee's basis in such assets and (2) the gain or loss of the transferor with respect to such acquisition.[57] If, in connection with an applicable asset acquisition, the transferee and transferor agree in writing as to the allocation of any consideration, or as to the fair-market value of any assets, such agreement shall be binding on both the transferee and transferor unless the IRS determines that such allocation (or fair-market value) is not appropriate.[58]

Transactions Subject to Code Section 1060

An "applicable asset acquisition" means any transfer (whether directly or indirectly) (1) of assets which constitute trade or business and (2) with respect to which the transferee's basis in such assets is determined wholly by reference to the consideration paid for such assets.[59] An "applicable asset acquisition" includes a transaction with respect to which Code section 1031 applies to a portion of the assets transferred.[60] The Regulations state that an applicable asset acquisition exists if the assets transferred constitute a trade or business in the hands of *either* the Seller or the purchaser.[61]

Residual Method Defined

For purposes of determining the Seller's amount realized for each of the assets sold in an applicable asset acquisition, the Seller allocates consideration to all the assets sold by using the residual method under Reg. § § 1.338-6 and 1.338-7 (substituting consideration for aggregate deemed sale price (ADSP)). The residual method under those regulations also is used to determine the purchaser's basis in each of the assets purchased in an applicable asset acquisition, except that consideration is substituted for adjusted grossed-up basis (AGUB).[62] (ADSP and AGUB are described more fully in Chapter 12 as part of the discussion of Code section 338 elections.) In general, the residual method allocates the consideration paid in an applicable asset acquisition in sequential order to seven classes of assets, designated as Class I assets, Class II assets, Class III assets, Class IV assets, Class V assets, Class VI assets, and then the residual amount to Class VII assets. The definition of each of the seven asset classes is as follows:

1. Class I assets are cash and general deposit accounts (including savings and checking accounts) other than certificates of deposit held in banks, savings and loan associations, and other depository institutions.[63]

2. Class II assets are actively traded personal property within the meaning of Code section 1092(d)(1) and Reg. § 1.1092(d)-1 (determined without regard to Code section 1092(d)(3)). In addition, Class II assets include certificates of deposit and foreign currency, even if they are not actively traded personal property. Examples of Class II assets include U.S. government securities and publicly traded stock.[64]

3. Class III assets are assets that the taxpayer marks to market at least annually for federal income tax purposes and debt instruments (including accounts receivable).[65]

4. Class IV assets are stock in trade of the taxpayer or other property of a kind that would properly be included in the inventory of a taxpayer if on hand at the close of the tax year, or property held by the taxpayer primarily for sale to customers in the ordinary course of its trade or business.[66]

5. Class V assets are all assets other than Class I, II, III, IV, VI, and VII assets.[67]

6. Class VI assets are all Code section 197 intangibles, as defined in Code section 197, except goodwill and going concern value.[68]

7. Class VII assets are goodwill and going concern value (whether or not the goodwill and going concern value qualifies as a Code section 197 intangible).[69]

Residual Method Allocations

The amount of consideration allocated to an asset other than a Class VII asset cannot exceed the fair-market value of that asset at the beginning of the day after the acquisition date.[70] The result of the residual method is that the portion of the purchase price not allocated to assets in Classes I, II, III, IV, V, and VI is allocated to the Class VII assets.

Reporting Requirements on the Sale of Assets

One of the requirements of Code section 1060 is that the parties to the transaction must negotiate the purchase price allocation, and report it consistently, on Form 8594. This requirement is designed to prevent the IRS from getting "whip-sawed", the term used to describe the practice where the Buyer and the Seller would allocate the same purchase price in very different ways, each to its own maximum advantage. The IRS imposed significant reporting requirements on an applicable asset acquisition for the very reason that there historically has been so much maneuvering and aggressive planning in the allocation of purchase price.

The Buyer and the Seller each must report information concerning the amount of consideration in the transaction and its allocation among the assets transferred, and they must also report information concerning subsequent adjustments to consideration.[71] In particular, Buyer and Seller must each file asset acquisition statements on Form 8594 with their income tax returns or returns of income for the tax year including the first date assets are sold pursuant to an applicable asset acquisition.[72] This reporting requirement applies to all applicable asset acquisitions.[73]

When an increase or decrease in consideration is taken into account after the close of the first tax year that includes the first date assets are sold in an applicable asset acquisition, the seller and the purchaser each must file a supplemental asset acquisition statement on Form 8594 with the income tax return or return of income for the tax year in which the increase (or decrease) is properly taken into account.[74]

Furthermore, the IRS has statutory authority (not exercised in the most recent regulations) to issue information reporting requirements for any 10-percent shareholder in the Target who enters into an employment contract, covenant not-to-compete, royalty or lease agreement, or other agreement with the transferee.[75]

Naturally, a purpose of requiring both the Buyer and the Seller to file a Form 8594 is so that the IRS can compare the allocations by parties on the opposite sides of the same transaction. Accordingly, it is common to include as part of the purchase and sale agreement a stipulation of the allocations between the parties and a covenant to report the transaction consistently. As a practical matter, both parties have an interest in reducing the risk of an IRS audit. If the Buyer and the Seller agree in writing concerning the allocation of purchase price or otherwise agree to the fair-market value of any of the assets sold, the agreement is binding on the parties for federal tax purposes unless the IRS determines that such allocations (or fair-market values) are not appropriate.[76]

Tax Windfall Agreements

The allocations agreed to by Buyer and Seller are always subject to challenge by the IRS.[77] In many cases, an IRS reallocation may inure to the benefit of one party and cause substantial detriment to the other. In all events, the parties typically negotiate the final form of a transaction with certain expectations concerning the tax consequences, which expectations may or may not be borne out in an IRS audit. Accordingly, it is not unusual to include a tax windfall agreement as part of a transaction. Such an agreement is designed to share the risk and/or mitigate the financial consequences of an unexpected (but not unanticipated) IRS challenge.

However, be aware that significant concerns have been raised about whether a tax windfall agreement is enforceable or whether it is against public policy because it may encourage aggressive tax reporting.

Purchase Price Allocation Strategies

The Buyer's tax basis in the assets purchased from the Seller equals the portion of the purchase price allocated to each such asset.[78] Naturally, the Buyer would like to allocate as much of the purchase price as possible to the assets that are likely to generate the fastest return (using present-value principles) on the available tax basis. Therefore, Buyers generally like to allocate as much of the purchase price as feasible to inventory (the tax basis is effectively recovered on the sale of the inventory), capital equipment (the tax basis is recovered through depreciation), and consulting or employment agreements (these amounts are generally deductible as paid). Noncompete agreements were once a favorite asset for assignment of residual purchase price because the tax basis was generally amortized over the period of the noncompete agreement; however, such an allocation is far less desirable today because such payments must now be amortized over fifteen years, pursuant to Code section 197. Goodwill formerly was the pariah of purchased assets prior to 1993 because it was not amortizable or deductible in any way. Now it is also subject to fifteen-year amortization under Code section 197, making it certainly better than before, but still not a terribly attractive alternative.

Constraints on Allocation Strategies

As a practical matter, the Buyer and the Seller usually have a common interest in allocating as much of the purchase price as possible to Code section 1231 assets and inventory. However, because there are standard valuation methodologies for most kinds of real and personal property, it is often difficult to overstate the value of such property dramatically. Allocating purchase price to consulting or wage agreements is the new area that offers the greatest amount of flexibility, but, realistically, the IRS can be expected to view such allocations with skepticism unless the amounts meet the IRS's definition of reasonable compensation. (Not coincidentally, reasonable compensation is always one of the "hot button" audit issues for the IRS.)

Note that both consulting and wage agreements will cause the income stream to be subject to either FICA or self-employment taxes. Therefore, there is always an extra tax cost with regard to such income. Noncompete payments are considered not to be subject to social security taxes (although the authority for this reporting position is surprisingly scarce).[79] Therefore, noncompete payments are modestly more attractive to the payee than wages or consulting payments but, as noted above, are generally unattractive to the payor because of the fifteen-year amortization rule under Code section 197. Wages, consulting payments, and noncompete payments are all taxed as ordinary income to the recipient. For authority on noncompete payments as ordinary income to a seller, see *J.A. Patterson*.[80]

Noncompete Payments as a Form of Individual Goodwill

An argument can be made that a noncompete payment is really in the nature of the purchase of an individual person's "goodwill". This, in turn, begs the question of who owns the "goodwill" of a business operated through a C corporation by a talented and well-regarded individual. A strong argument can be made that in the case of an accounting practice, the "goodwill" of the business does not belong to the corporation but rather to the individual accountant.[81] After all, if the accountant sells his or her corporation, but does not enter into a noncompetition agreement with the purchaser, the purchaser has probably gotten very little for his or her money. Indeed, it is not unusual in the sale of an accounting practice, or similar business, to see as much as 80 percent of the total consideration allocated to the noncompete payment payable to the predominant shareholder.

Can a Noncompete Payment Be Characterized as a Capital Gain Asset?

Given that a noncompete payment is essentially a mechanism for purchasing the goodwill of an individual (e.g., in the case of an accountant, the payment compensates the accountant for foregoing his or her right to utilize the longstanding business relationships that he or she has developed over the years), the question is whether this could be characterized as a capital asset. Clearly, the individual goodwill of the accountant in this situation is essentially identical to the goodwill of the corporation through which the accounting practice was conducted. Under current tax law, the corporate goodwill is considered a capital asset, while the noncompete payments to the individual are considered ordinary income.[82]

However, as will be discussed in Chapter 17, the author believes a reasonable position can be taken that the individual goodwill of the accountant is a distinct capital asset that can be sold in connection with the sale of an accounting business.

Summary

As a practical matter, even under the residual method, there is an opportunity for the Buyer and Seller to negotiate allocations among various items, including goodwill, covenants not-to-compete, and/or consulting payments to a selling individual. In addition, as discussed more fully in Chapter 17, it also may be possible to bifurcate goodwill into that owned by the company/business and that owned by the individual owners.

TAX CONSEQUENCES FOR BUYER—SEEKING MAXIMUM TAX BENEFIT

Allocation Tension between Seller and Buyer

Naturally, the allocation strategies in a sale of a sole proprietorship focus on the tension between the Seller wanting capital gain and the Buyer wanting to accelerate tax deductions. As we will explore in great detail in Chapter 6, it is generally appropriate to analyze the tax consequences of an allocation structure on a present-value, after-tax basis to determine the "true" costs and benefits enjoyed by each party.

In general, if the Buyer is acquiring the assets for use in a similar business (which is far and away the most common situation), the assets will usually have a tax character identical to the character of the assets in the hands of the Seller. For example, Section 1231 property in the hands of the Seller will, in virtually all sale circumstances, continue to be Section 1231 property in the hands of the Buyer, assuming the Buyer continues in the same line of business as the Seller. In turn, purchase price allocated to Section 1231 property will be subject to depreciation or amortization, which in turn means that Code sections 1245 and 1250 recapture will be a potential issue in the future when and if such property is resold.

As a practical matter, Code section 1231 property will generally be depreciated over a five-year period if it is a tangible asset, and over a fifteen-year period if it is an intangible asset. A creator of various types of intangible assets, such as customer-based or supplier-based intangible assets, may be able to characterize the assets as Code section 1221 capital gain assets, but, in the hands of a Buyer, they will still usually be Code section 197 intangibles, and thus subject to fifteen-year amortization. Depreciable nonresidential real estate is depreciated over thirty-nine years; land, meanwhile, will be nondepreciable Code section 1231 property in the hands of the purchaser.

The Buyer, naturally, subject to Code section 1060, will want to allocate as much of the purchase price as possible to either consulting payments (deductible immediately when paid), cash or cash equivalent assets (the tax basis is returned immediately or when the asset is utilized), inventory (depending on the inventory accounting method, the purchase price is effectively recovered when the inventory is sold, under the first-in first-out (FIFO) method), and five-year tangible property (cost recovery over five years is much better than amortization over fifteen years, which is the amortization period for all Code section 197 intangibles, including noncompete payments connected with the acquisition of the business).

However, there are some specific assets that can (or are certain to) have a different tax character in the hands of the Buyer than in the hands of the Seller.

Patents

A patent purchased in connection with an acquisition of a business or a substantial interest therein is governed by Code section 197. Therefore, the purchase price allocated to such patents is capitalized and amortized over fifteen years.[83] This is true regardless of the remaining useful life of the patent. On the other hand, a "separately acquired" patent (i.e., one not purchased in connection with the acquisition of a business) is exempted from these rules by Code section 197(e)(4)(C); instead, a separately acquired patent will generally be characterized as Code section 1231 property and will be capitalized and amortized, under Code section 167, over the remaining useful life of the patent. As a practical matter, the IRS generally allows the purchaser of a separately acquired patent to recover tax basis using the income forecast method.[84]

Copyrights

A copyright in the hands of the original creator whose personal efforts created such property is defined as an ordinary asset, by virtue of its exclusion from the definitions of capital asset and Code section 1231 property.[85] By contrast, the character of a copyright purchased by an unrelated party depends on whether it is acquired in connection with the acquisition of a business or a substantial interest therein or is "separately acquired". If purchased as part of a business acquisition, the copyright will be subject to Code section 197, and the purchase price will amortized ratably over fifteen years.[86] If the copyright is separately acquired, the purchase price will be capitalized and depreciated under Code section 167.[87] As with patents, the IRS and the courts have generally favored the use of the income forecast method to amortize the costs of a copyright.[88]

Other Code Section 197 Intangibles

Code section 197 provides the general rule that all intangible property acquired by a Buyer that falls within the definition of "Section 197 intangibles" will all be amortized ratably over a fifteen-year period. Code section 197 intangibles include, in addition to patents and copyrights acquired in connection with a business acquisition, such diverse forms of intellectual or intangible property as goodwill, noncompete payments entered into in connection with the acquisition of a business, work force in place, information base, know-how, any customer-based intangible, any supplier-based intangible, and any license, permit, or other rights granted by a governmental unit or agency, any franchise, trademark, or trade name. See Chapter 11 for a detailed discussion of Code section 197.

Covenant Not-to-Compete

A noncompete agreement can be entered into in a variety of business contexts, but one of the most prominent situations is when a business is sold. The Buyer clearly wants to make sure that the Seller, including all the key individuals who own and/or are employed by the Seller, agrees not to compete with the Buyer's newly acquired business. This type of noncompete agreement is usually intended to cover a relatively substantial period of time after the sale. Code section 197 specifically requires fifteen-year amortization for noncompete agreements "entered into in connection with the acquisition (directly or indirectly) of an interest in a trade or business or substantial portion thereof".

Comment: Noncompete agreements that are not entered into in connection with an acquisition are subject to a very different set of rules. For example, noncompete agreements are increasingly frequent between an employer and key employees when the employer wants to prevent the employee from quitting and immediately competing in a manner that expropriates the confidential and proprietary assets of the employer. Such noncompete agreements, to the extent they call for payments by the employer to the employee (among other reasons, so that the employer can enforce the agreement) are ordinary income to the recipient upon receipt[89] and are amortizable by the employer ratably over the term of the noncompete.[90]

Service Contracts

When a Buyer acquires various service contracts that permit the Buyer to perform services for a third party, the proper accounting appears to be that the Buyer should capitalize its costs over the life of the contract, and recover the purchase price ratably against the income charged to the client for the services. However, the tax characterization of service contracts, both by Buyer and Seller, is one of the most murky and complicated areas of federal income tax law and is discussed in greater detail in Chapter 17.

Franchise, Trademark, or Trade Name

Trademark, trade name, and franchise rights are subject to the unique rules of Code section 1253, which are generally hostile to taxpayers and embody two basic tax policies: (1) it is difficult for a Seller of these rights to get capital gain treatment unless all rights are transferred and the transferor does not retain any significant power, right, or continuing interest, and (2) post-transfer payments by Buyer to Seller that are contingent on productivity, use or disposition of the transferred rights will be treated as ordinary income to the Seller.[91] In addition, on the Buyer side of the ledger, payments for such rights will be capitalizable by the Buyer *unless* they qualify as contingent serial payments.[92] In order to be a contingent serial payment, the payment must meet the following three criteria: (1) it must be contingent on the productivity, use, or disposition of the franchise or related rights; (2) it must be part of a series of payments that are payable not less frequently than annually through the entire term of the transfer agreement; and (3) the payments must be either "substantially equal in amount" or "payable under a fixed formula.[93] Payments that do not fall within this relatively rigid and stringent definition in Code section 1253(d)(1) are capitalized and amortized over a fifteen-year period under Code section 197.[94]

CASE STUDY OF A SALE OF A SOLE PROPRIETORSHIP

Assume that Tina Talent makes scented candles, which she initially sold to friends and eventually turned into a more-than-cottage business. Assume also that Tina operates as a sole proprietorship.

One day Tina receives the proverbial offer she can't refuse from Candle Conglomerate, to whom she decides to sell her entire business for a lump sum payment of $2,000,000.

Tina's business assets include the following:

1. A certain amount of cash on hand ($10,000).
2. Accounts receivable from stores that buy her candles ($100,000).
3. An inventory of existing candles (valued at $120,000 on the books).
4. An inventory of materials that she can use to make candles (valued at $30,000).
5. Certain prepaid expenses of the business (worth $5,000).
6. Various machinery and other property, generally of a depreciable nature, used in the business (original tax basis $80,000, depreciated down to $20,000).
7. A building on a small parcel of land owned by Tina and used as a business location to manufacture her candles (purchase price of the property was $450,000 with $390,000 allocated to depreciable real estate and $60,000 allocated to land. After approximately five years of straight-line depreciation, the tax basis is now reduced to $400,000 of which $340,000 is allocated to depreciable real estate and $60,000 to land).
8. A lease of an adjoining parcel of land, which Tina leased several years ago when her business outgrew the original business location.
9. Various methods, techniques, know-how, and trade secrets that she has developed in making the candles.
10. A patent that she filed with the USPTO, claiming rights in her special proprietary candle-making technology.
11. Copyrights owned by Tina to various (generally bad) inspirational poems that she includes in the packages with her candles.
12. The goodwill of the business, including the right to certain trade names and trademarks she has developed over time.
13. A covenant not-to-compete given by Tina to Candle Conglomerate. Tina agrees not to compete in the candle business for a period of five years.
14. An explicit agreement never to start a new business using her name or in any way using her name in a manner that would harm the value of the business acquired by Candle Conglomerate.

Practical Overview of Tax Issues Raised by Various Assets in the Case Study

Cash. In almost any asset sale (and the sale of a proprietorship business is a pure asset sale), the Seller keeps the cash on hand. Moreover, to the extent that cash is ever transferred, it is almost always transferred at face value. Therefore, the purchase price equals the cash value, producing no gain or loss. Amazingly enough, in the extraordinarily unlikely event that an allocation of purchase price to cash that is greater than or less than the face value of the cash (this would likely occur only if someone lit one of Tina's candles and then smoked something else), the sale of cash would be treated as a sale of a capital asset that causes recognition of capital gain or loss.[95] The logic behind this case law is almost unassailable: capital is, indeed, a capital asset!

Accounts receivable. Accounts receivable, notes receivable, and any equivalent assets acquired by Tina in the ordinary course of business are defined by Code section 1221(a)(4) as excluded from the category of capital assets, and therefore are ordinary assets. Since Tina has an inventory, her business is required to use the accrual method of accounting, and her accounts receivable will have a tax basis equal to the income "booked" at the time of the sale. If the accounts receivable are sold to the Buyer at a discount to tax basis (often the case), an ordinary loss will be recognized.[96] By contrast, if Tina were the owner of a different type of business that was allowed to be on the cash method of accounting, (e.g., a service business), there would be no accrued tax basis with respect to the receivables, and any proceeds allocated to the acquisition of receivables would produce ordinary income pursuant to Code section 1221(a)(4).

> ***Comment:*** As a practical matter, valuing the accounts receivable in an acquisition transaction is a huge headache for both sides because the Seller wants to be paid the full face value of the receivables, and the Buyer is very leery about whether the receivables are, in fact, fully collectable (and is afraid that the accounts receivable may in fact be worth far less than their face amount). On the other hand, a Buyer of a business often wants to acquire the self-sustaining "cash flow" of the existing business, especially if the Buyer is buying the business on the installment method and/or needs the cash flow from receivables in the short term as operating revenue. Ultimately, both parties would like to collect the receivables as fully as possible and in an orderly fashion.

There are several possible solutions to this challenge, with different tax consequences:

1. One easy answer is for the Seller to keep the receivables, collect them himself or herself, and thereby avoid the accounts receivable pricing issue entirely. However, business considerations may preclude this solution. The Buyer may want to use the cash flow, and both the Buyer and the Seller may be leery of having two parties trying to collect receivables from the same customer base at the same time (Seller collecting the "old" receivables and Buyer the newly generated post-sale receivables).

2. The Seller can transfer the accounts receivable to the Buyer, and the Buyer can then collect the money and remit it, as collected, back to the Seller, with the expectation that there will be a "true up" before the end of the tax year, i.e., setting the purchase price after the fact to equal the amounts actually collected. This works well if the sale occurs in January, so that the accounts receivable can be collected and the purchase price adjusted and reconciled over a period of the next 11 months, but it doesn't work as well for a sale in December.

3. The Buyer can negotiate a satisfactory discount (e.g., a 20 percent discount from face value), so that both the Buyer and Seller will live with the consequences of collection. This is a "logical" solution, but rarely happens.

4. The Seller can make a contingent or installment sale of the accounts receivable to the Buyer, bearing in mind that this asset is not eligible for tax deferral under Code section 453 because the asset being sold is an ordinary asset and not a capital gain asset. See the discussion of installment sales in Chapter 10.

There is no "right" answer to this problem, and it is usually worked out between the parties in a manner that allows the Buyer to collect the money on behalf of the Seller, while the Seller retains all or substantially all the risk of noncollection.

Inventories. Stock in trade, inventories, and other property held for sale to customers in the ordinary course of business are not capital assets.[97] Therefore, gain or loss on the sale of inventory will be ordinary rather than capital. This is true even though the inventory is sold as a bulk asset.[98]

As a practical matter, inventories are always subject to the uniform capitalization rules under Code section 263A, and it is ***extremely*** common for the parties to allocate to the inventory a purchase amount that is exactly equal to the capitalized cost of the inventory, meaning that the Seller recognizes exactly zero gain or loss.

Prepaid expenses. Prepaid expenses, which can range from prepaid insurance premiums to prepaid rent and other similar amounts, should be treated as a Code section 1231 asset. The fair market value of these assets, like cash, is likely to be the un-amortized amount of the prepayment, possibly adjusted (although not necessarily) by a time/value of money factor. If the purchase price allocated to the prepaid item is greater than or less than the "tax basis" in the asset, the transaction should have capital gain/ordinary loss consequences to the Seller, like every other Code section 1231 asset. If the prepaid item has already been expensed or deducted, there should be recapture of the deduction (probably as ordinary income) under the tax benefit rule.[99]

Depreciable equipment. Depreciable tangible property held for more than one year is a Code section 1231 asset, subject to capital gains/ordinary loss treatment. However, as a practical matter, most depreciable/tangible property (e.g., computers, office equipment, etc.) is also subject to Code section 1245 recapture. Because equipment of this type is rarely sold for an amount greater than its original purchase price, all of the amount allocated to the depreciable tangible property in excess of its tax basis will be ordinary recapture income. In general, the Seller is averse to recognizing ordinary recapture income more than the Buyer is interested in the benefits of five-year depreciation. Therefore, not surprisingly, the allocation of purchase price to depreciable equipment is often exactly equal to adjusted tax basis, and the parties look to other assets to create a favorable tax arbitrage.

Depreciable real estate. Depreciable real estate is likewise a Code section 1231 asset, and is subject to recapture rules under Code section 1250, and also the special 25-percent capital gains tax rate on unrecaptured Section 1250 gain.[100] Because depreciable nonresidential real estate is currently depreciated on a straight-line basis over thirty-nine years, recapture under Code section 1250 will generally be zero, but gain attributable to prior depreciation deductions will be subject to the special 25-percent tax rate. The portion of the real estate attributable to land (as opposed to depreciable improvements) is likewise Code section 1231 property. The land cannot be depreciated, and therefore would never be subject to recapture provisions.

Because a Buyer naturally has little interest in thirty-nine-year depreciation when there are many other intangible assets that can be amortized over fifteen years, logic and self-interest suggest that the Seller and Buyer will naturally gravitate toward increasing the allocation to intangible assets, and away from real estate. Of course, real property is a Class V asset under Code section 1060, and therefore is subject to a price allocation based on fair market value. Although fair market value is always in the eye of the beholder, it places realistic constraints on how aggressively one can "low ball" the real estate allocation.

Lease of adjacent property. A lease is a Code section 1231 asset, and any gain or loss on the transfer or resale of the lease will be characterized under that provision. An issue to keep in mind is whether the lease property has improvements by the "lessee" that potentially will be subject to recapture under Code section 1245 (for tangible property) or Code section 1250 (for fixtures or improvements to the real estate). Note that since a purchaser of a lease would, among other things, assume the obligations to make payments under the lease, the value assignable to the acquisition of the lease would, in substance, represent the difference between the current market rent for this space and the amount of the rent obligations under the lease. If the lease has built-in value, e.g., because rents have increased for comparable space since the lease was signed, the Buyer will pay a premium for the lease, and the Seller will recognize capital gain (subject to any recapture income for depreciated leasehold improvements). Conversely, if the rental market has declined since the lease was signed, the Buyer will probably assume the lease only at a discount, and the Seller should enjoy an ordinary (Code section 1231) loss.

Know-how and trade secrets. Know-how and trade secrets are generally either Code section 1221 or Code section 1231 assets, depending on whether the assets have a reasonably ascertainable useful life or are otherwise subject to amortization or depreciation. The amounts allocated to the acquisition of these assets will create capital gain to the Seller (subject to Code section 1245 recapture if the assets are Code section 1231 assets previously depreciated or amortized) and will be Code section 197 intangibles to the Buyer.

Patents. Patents are subject to special rules under Code section 1235, which generally states that an inventor of a patent can sell all rights to the patent and treat the gain as gain from the sale of a capital asset. This is in striking contrast to copyrights, artistic creations, and similar properties, which, in the hands of their creator, generate ordinary income on sale.[101]

In any event, patents used in carrying on a trade or business are Code section 1231 assets.[102] In the present case, Tina is the inventor of the patent and is selling all rights in it. However, the patent also independently qualifies as a Code section 1231 asset and is clearly eligible for capital gain treatment under applicable case law even if Code section 1235 is not applicable for any reason.

Poems copyrighted by Seller. The gain or loss on the disposition of a copyright by the creator is ordinary income because copyrights sold by their creator are excluded from both capital gain treatment[103] and Code section 1231 property treatment.[104] In the present case, Tina will recognize ordinary income for any portion of the purchase price allocated to the poems. This being said, Tina may well decide either not to sell the poems as part of the transaction, or to agree with the Buyer to allocate a minimal purchase price to the poems. The facts support this allocation, since Tina's poetry is not admired as much as her candles.

Goodwill of business. The goodwill of a business is conventionally a capital asset.[105] As we will see in Chapter 4 in the discussion of corporate goodwill, the goodwill of a company may or may not be separable from the goodwill belonging to one or more individual owners who participate in the business. Making the separation between individual and business goodwill in the case of a sole proprietorship is even more complicated and difficult. As we will discuss more fully, it seems entirely possible to identify a "goodwill" component belonging to the business (e.g., a going concern value or going business value of the enterprise) and goodwill belonging to the individual owner (in this case, Tina's right to use her own name as she chooses, exploit her business contacts, and so forth). Practically speaking, the separation of individual goodwill and business goodwill does not make much difference in the sale of an unincorporated business because, however allocated, the "goodwill" is a capital asset, subject to capital gains rates at the individual level. However, this allocation issue will make a huge difference when the business assets are held in a C corporation, which is discussed more fully in Chapter 4.

Covenants not-to-compete. Payments received by a Seller in consideration for a covenant not-to-compete are characterized as ordinary income to the recipient. The history of this, however, is more than a little complicated. There is case authority indicating that a noncompete payment is ordinary income,[106] and the IRS took this position in Rev. Rul. 69-643.[107] Interestingly, the IRS in the mid-1960s wrestled with the question of whether some portion of a noncompete payment might be construed as a capital asset,[108] and it eventually opted for the blanket rule set forth in Rev. Rul. 69-643. As will be discussed more fully below, a noncompetition agreement has, among its inherent qualities, an agreement by an individual not to use the person's own relationships, contacts, and business experience—in short, it transfers the equivalent of the "goodwill" owned by the individual. As is explored later in Chapter 17, it may be entirely possible, when a business is sold, to divide the general concept of goodwill into three parts:

1. The goodwill of the business (which, in the case of a C corporation, is owned by the corporation).
2. A noncompete payment and/or consulting payment, which is in the nature of ordinary income to the selling individual.
3. Possibly a separate component of goodwill, in the nature of a capital asset, belonging to the individual owner of the business.

Allocation Strategies for the Case Study: Two Alternatives

The preceding material examined and discussed the various tax and allocation issues that can arise with respect to each of the assets identified in the case study. The following are two alternative allocation approaches that could be applied to the sale by Tina of her assets to Candle Conglomerate, including a comparison of the relative tax costs to Tina of each alternative.

Alternative 1. This alternative assumes that the parties have agreed to an aggregate purchase price of $2,000,000, which (somewhat artificially) is assumed to be allocable with some flexibility between and among the assets being sold by the Seller. (*Note:* What makes it artificial is the fact that if the tax allocations penalize the Seller too much, the Seller will naturally demand an increase in the proposed purchase price, i.e., $2,000,000 is a starting point, but not a fixed amount, in a "real negotiation".) We have assumed, for purposes of this example, that the aggregate (combined federal and state) tax bracket of the Seller is 40 percent for ordinary income and 20 percent for capital gains. This takes into account both federal and state taxation and assumes a relatively "high" state tax rate.

In Alternative 1, the purchase price is allocated to the assets as follows:

Cash—$10,000

Accounts receivable—$100,000

Inventory—$130,000

Materials—$30,000

Prepaid expenses—$5,000

Depreciated machinery—$30,000

Depreciable real estate—$440,000

Nondepreciable land—$80,000

Lease of an adjoining parcel—$20,000 (a premium paid by the Buyer to assume the lease)

Trade secrets and know-how—$100,000

Patents—$200,000

Copyrights—$25,000

Trademarks—$25,000

Noncompete—$300,000

Goodwill—$505,000 (the "residual" amount from $2,000,000, after all the other allocations, pursuant to Code section 1060)

The allocations in Alternative 1 are designed to highlight several important issues:

- *Cash.* Cash is almost always sold for exactly the value of cash. More realistically, cash would not be put in the deal at all. The Seller would simply keep the cash and reduce the purchase price on a dollar-for-dollar basis.

- *Accounts receivable.* It is very common to sell the accounts receivable for an amount exactly equal to the tax basis in the accounts receivable (which is typically the face amount).

- *Inventory.* Alternative 1 anticipates that the inventory will be sold at a $10,000 "premium". The point is to demonstrate that inventory (like accounts receivable) sold at a premium creates ordinary income, which is always a very unattractive allocation from the Seller's perspective.

- *Materials.* The materials used in manufacturing inventory are typically sold at their tax basis (no more and no less).

- *Prepaid expenses.* This is effectively the equivalent of "cash" and is usually sold at exactly face value (possibly with some type of time value adjustment, but not usually).

- *Depreciated machinery.* The point here is that any "premium" paid above the Seller's tax basis will be ordinary recapture income under Code section 1245. Therefore, the parties will typically assign a fair market value exactly equal to the tax basis, unless the resulting price is absurd. (If the tax basis in the machinery is "0", but it has undeniable value, the parties will try to assign a nominal purchase price and have a correspondingly nominal amount of ordinary recapture income.)

- *Depreciable real estate.* For depreciable real estate, Alternative 1 assumes that the purchase price is $440,000 with a tax basis of $340,000, and the Seller recognizes $100,000 of long term capital gain. Real estate is subject to Code section 1250 recapture, but because the property has been depreciated on a straight-line basis of thirty-nine years, there is no recapture; however, the special 25-percent tax rate will apply to unrecaptured Section 1250 gain. Note that the Buyer is not especially eager to allocate purchase price to thirty-nine-year property, and would much rather have it allocated to something that can be recovered over a much shorter period (even fifteen years looks good compared to thirty-nine years).

- *Nondepreciable land.* The purchase price allocation to nondepreciable land is set, rather artificially for illustrative purposes, at $80,000, so that there is a capital gain attributable to the land of $20,000. However, since nondepreciable land has no depreciation benefit to the Buyer, the parties are even less likely to allocate "extra" purchase price to nondepreciable real estate than to depreciable real estate.

The Seller and Buyer can be trusted to figure out that there is more benefit to themselves, and less benefit to the government, if the purchase price is allocated to an asset that generates the same capital gain to the Seller, but allows the Buyer to enjoy fifteen-year amortization.

- *The lease of adjoining parcel.* Alternative 1 assumes that a premium is being paid by the Buyer to acquire the assignment of a favorable lease (i.e., a lease below current market value). Note that, realistically, it is unlikely that a Seller can assign a leasehold because landlords typically require permission for an assignment and are quick to ensure that any value is either shared with or allocated entirely to the landlord. A "sale" of a lease would generate capital gain to the Seller under Code section 1231, and the purchase price would be amortized over the remaining life of the lease by the Buyer.
- *Trade secrets.* Trade secrets are generally intangible Code section 1231 assets. They generate long-term capital gain to the Seller and are amortizable over fifteen years by the Buyer under Code section 197.
- *Patents.* Patents generate long-term capital gain to the Seller (assuming that either Code section 1235 or Code sections 1221 and 1231 apply). In the hands of the Buyer, the purchase price of a patent typically would be amortizable over fifteen years under Code section 197.
- *Copyrights.* Because copyrights are ordinary assets under Code section 1221(a)(3), the Seller recognizes ordinary income. The Buyer would amortize this purchase price over fifteen years under Code section 197. Because the Seller has a substantial detriment, and the Buyer has no significant advantage, to an allocation to copyright assets, the parties will likely find little or no value to the copyrights in this case study.
- *Trademarks.* Trademarks, when all rights are transferred, generate capital gain to the Seller[109] and are amortizable by the Buyer over fifteen years.[110]
- *Noncompete.* A noncompete payment paid in the context of a purchase of assets would be ordinary income to Tina, but would be amortizable by the Buyer over fifteen years under Code section 197. This is not an optimal category for shaving down the tax costs.
- *Goodwill.* Goodwill is a capital asset to the Seller and is amortizable over fifteen years by the Buyer.

Figure 3.3 summarizes the tax consequences of using Alternative 1 to allocate the purchase price. Note that the estimated total tax owed by the Seller would be $336,800.

Alternative 2. Alternative 2 shows a more "appropriate" allocation of purchase price in the same deal. Basically, the parties will start by allocating purchase price to assets such as cash, accounts receivable, inventory, and materials so that the purchase price exactly matches the tax basis of the assets in the hands of the Seller. This allocation strategy means that the Seller recovers his tax basis (tax free), and the Buyer gets a tax basis that is recoverable over a reasonably rapid period of time. A Seller will generally balk if any more is allocated to these assets because it would result in ordinary income in the case of accounts receivable, inventory, and materials.

Depreciable machinery is likewise allocated a purchase price exactly equal to its tax basis of $20,000 to avoid ordinary income (Code section 1245 recapture) to the Seller.

Depreciable real estate is allocated a purchase price of $450,000, and nondepreciable real estate is allocated a purchase price of $60,000, which was the original purchase price in the hands of the Seller. The reason for this allocation is to allocate (with a straight face) the lowest feasible amount to depreciable real estate. Generally, the Seller is satisfied to allocate the "unused" purchase price to other capital assets, while the Buyer has no interest in allocating a single dollar more than necessary to depreciable real estate (thirty-nine years) or to nondepreciable land (no depreciation whatsoever).

The lease of the adjoining parcel is one area where the Seller gets capital gain. Because the Buyer can amortize the purchase price over the remaining life of the lease (typically shorter than fifteen years), this may be a good place to allocate an appropriate amount or even a "premium".

Trade secrets and patents frequently generate capital gain on a sale to the Seller and are amortizable over fifteen years (or possibly a shorter period of time if

Figure 3.3

Alternative 1	
Aggregate Purchase Price	$2,000,000
Seller's Combined Tax Bracket (Fed and State) for OI	40%
Seller's Combined Tax Bracket (Fed and State) for LTCG	20%
Seller's Combined Tax Bracket (Fed and State) for Unrecaptured	
Section 1250 Gain	30%

Asset	*Tax Basis*	*FMV (Or at least Price Allocated to Asset!)*	*Original Depreciable Basis*	*Ordinary or Recapture Income*	*LTCG Gain to Seller*
Cash	$10,000.00	$10,000.00		$0.00	$0.00
Accounts receivable	$100,000.00	$100,000.00			
Inventory	$120,000.00	$130,000.00		$10,000.00	
Materials	$30,000.00	$30,000.00			
Prepaid-expenses	$5,000.00	$5,000.00			
Depreciated machinery	$20,000.00	$30,000.00	$80,000.00	$10,000.00	$0.00
Depreciable real estate	$340,000.00	$440,000.00	$390,000.00	$0.00	$100,000.00
Nondepreciable land	$60,000.00	$80,000.00			$20,000.00
Lease of adjoining parcel	$0.00	$20,000.00			$20,000.00
Trade secrets and know-how	$0.00	$100,000.00	$0.00		$100,000.00
Patent	$0.00	$200,000.00			$200,000.00
Copyrights	$0.00	$25,000.00		$25,000.00	
Trademarks	$1,000.00	$25,000.00			$24,000.00
Noncompete		$300,000.00		$300,000.00	$0.00
Compensation		$0.00		$0.00	
Total other than goodwill		$1,495,000.00			
Goodwill	$0.00	$505,000.00			$505,000.00
Totals	*$686,000.00*	*$2,000,000.00*		*$345,000.00*	*$969,000.00*
OI Taxed at 40%				$138,000.00	
LTCG at 20%					$183,800.00
Unrecaptured Section 1250 gain at 30%					$15,000.00
Total Tax					$336,800.00

the patent will expire in less than fifteen years) by the Buyer. This is a generally good place for the Seller and Buyer to agree to allocate purchase price. In Alternative 2, $200,000 of the purchase price (vs. $100,000 for Alternative 1) is allocated to trade secrets and know-how, and $300,000 (vs. $200,000 for Alternative 1) is allocated to the patent.

Copyrights are very deleterious to the Seller (ordinary income is recognized because the Seller in this case is the creator of the copyrighted material), and the Buyer has to amortize the amount over fifteen years (which is no better than many of the other assets under Code section 197). Therefore, it would not be surprising to find that the copyright had "little" value allocated to it. In Alternative 2, $1.00 (vs. $25,000 for Alternative 1) of the purchase price is allocated to the copyrights.

Trademarks are a capital asset, like trade secrets and patents, and would generate capital gain to the Seller and would be amortizable over fifteen years to the Buyer. Because the trademark rules on "earn out" payments are so Seller-unfriendly, it would usually make sense to allocate any earn out payments to the value of other assets in the deal—although query whether the IRS will respect such an allocation. Alternative 2 allocates the same amount of the purchase price to trademarks as Alternative 1. A noncompete payment is ordinary income to the Seller and amortizable over fifteen years by the Buyer—not a very attractive combination from a tax perspective. By contrast, "consulting payments", payable over three years, would also be ordinary income to the Seller (and would be subject to social security/self-employment tax, which may result in a higher tax cost to the payee than a noncompete payment), but would be deductible immediately by the Buyer when paid (much better than fifteen-year amortization under Code section 197). Alternative 2 allocates $50,000 (vs. $300,000 for Alternative 1) of the purchase price to the non-compete agreement.

Figure 3.4

Alternative 2	
Aggregate Purchase Price	$2,000,000
Seller's Combined Tax Bracket (Fed and State) for OI	40%
Seller's Combined Tax Bracket (Fed and State) for LTCG	20%
Seller's Combined Tax Bracket (Fed and State) for Unrecaptured	
Section 1250 Gain	30%

FMV (Or at least Price Allocated Asset	*Original Depreciable Tax Basis*	*Ordinary or Recapture to Asset!)*	*LTCG Gain Basis*	*Income*	*to Seller*
Cash	$10,000.00	$10,000.00		$0.00	$0.00
Accounts receivable	$100,000.00	$100,000.00			
Inventory	$120,000.00	$120,000.00			
Materials	$30,000.00	$30,000.00			
Prepaid expenses	$5,000.00	$5,000.00			
Depreciated machinery	$20,000.00	$20,000.00	$80,000.00	$0.00	$0.00
Depreciable real estate	$340,000.00	$440,000.00	$390,000.00	$0.00	$100,000.00
Nondepreciable land	$60,000.00	$60,000.00			$0.00
Lease of adjoining parcel	$0.00	$20,000.00			$20,000.00
Trade secrets and know-how	$0.00	$200,000.00	$0.00		$200,000.00
Patent	$0.00	$300,000.00			$300,000.00
Copyrights	$0.00	$1.00		$1.00	
Trademarks	$1,000.00	$25,000.00			$24,000.00
Noncompete		$50,000.00		$50,000.00	$0.00
Compensation		$0.00		$0.00	
Total other than goodwill		$1,380,001.00			
Goodwill	$0.00	$619,999.00			$619,999.00
Totals	*$686,000.00*	*$2,000,000.00*		*$50,001.00*	*$1,263,999.00*
OI Taxed at 40%				$20,000.40	
LTCG at 20%					$242,799.80
Unrecaptured Section 1250 gain at 30%					$15,000.00
Total Tax					$277,800

The residual goodwill allocation in Alternative 2 is $609,999.00.

Figure 3.4 summarizes the tax consequences of Alternative 2. Note that simply by making a more tax efficient allocation of the purchase price the total amount of taxes paid by the Seller would be $277,800.20 for a tax savings of $58,999.80 over Alternative 1.

The parties can push the envelope even further should they so choose with the corresponding risk that the IRS will come in and do its own allocation on audit!

CHAPTER ENDNOTES

1. See Rev. Rul. 99-5, 1999-1 CB 434.
2. IRC Sec. 1001. However, this book uses the 15 percent capital gains rate and 35 percent ordinary income rate for illustrations.
3. See IRC Sec. 108(e)(5).
4. IRC Sec. 1221(a)(1).
5. IRC Sec. 1221(a)(2).
6. IRC Sec. 1221 (a)(3). But see IRC Sec. 1221(b)(3) (self-created musical work exception, at the election of the taxpayer).
7. IRC Sec. 1221(a)(4).
8. IRC Sec. 1221(a)(5).
9. IRC Sec. 1221(a)(6).
10. IRC Sec. 1221(a)(7).
11. IRC Sec. 1221(a)(8).
12. See also IRC Sec. 751, discussed in Chapter 9, providing a comparable rule for "hot assets" held by partnerships.
13. See IRC Sec. 1231(b)(1).
14. IRC Sec. 1245(a)(3) provides the exact definition of "Section 1245 property".
15. IRC Sec. 1250(a)(1).
16. IRC Sec. 1250(b)(1).
17. IRC Sec. 1(h)(1)(E) and 1(h)(6).
18. IRC Sec. 1(h)(6)(A).
19. IRC Sec. 1(h)(6)(B).
20. IRC Sec. 1(h)(1)(D).
21. IRC Sec. 168.
22. IRC Sec. 1363(b)(4).
23. IRC Secs. 1231(b)(1) and 1221(a)(2).
24. IRC Sec. 1231(a).
25. See Reg. § 1.1245-3(a)(2).
26. See Reg. § 1.1245-2(a)(3).
27. Treas. Reg. § 1.167-4(a).
28. See Chapter 3.
29. See Chapter 20.
30. *V.A. Marco*, 25 TC 544, (1955), acq.
31. *Merck & Co. v. Smith*, 261 F.2d 162 (1958).
32. IRC Secs. 1221(a)(3) and 1231(b)(1)(C).
33. IRC Secs. 1221(a)(3)(C) and 1231(b)(1)(C).
34. IRC Sec. 1221(b)(3).
35. Treas. Reg. § 1.1221-3(b).
36. See also Chapter 20.
37. IRC Sec. 1253(c).
38. *M.L Killian*, 314 F.2d 852 (5th Circuit, 1963).
39. *Ullman v. Comm.*, 264 F.2d 305 (1995).
40. Compare *T.L. Cox*, 71 F.2d 987 (1934), with *D.H. Ullman*, 29 TC 129 (1957).
41. See *A.G. Furman, III*, 602 F.Supp. 444 (1984). See *A. Molasky*, 897 F.2d 334 (1990).
42. Reg. § 1.1235-2(a).
43. Rev. Rul. 85-186, 1985-2, CB 84.
44. *Hillside Dairy Company*, 3 TCM 174, Dec. 174, Dec. 13773 (M) (1944); secret processes, E.I. *Duy Pont de Nemours and Company*, 153 Ct.Cls. 274, 288 F.2d 904; a license to do business, *M Nachman*, 191 F.2d 934 (1951).; franchises, *Gr. Gowdey Estate*, CA-4, 307 F.2d 816 (1962).; *V.H. Moberg*, 305 F.2d 800. (1962).
45. Rev. Rul. 85-186, 1985-2 CB 84.
46. IRC Sec. 197 (d)(1)(D).
47. See *Maryland Coal and Coke Company*, DC Pa., 225 F.Supp. 854, (1961) aff'd per curiam, 350 F.2d 293 (1965).
48. See IRC Secs. 1222 and 1231; but see IRC Sec. 1235, with a rare and notable exception to the one-year holding requirement.
49. IRC Secs. 1012 and 1223(1).
50. IRC Sec. 1223(1).
51. IRC Sec. 1223(1); see Rev. Rul. 85-164, 1985-2 CB 117.
52. IRC Sec. 1001(a).
53. IRC Sec. 1001(b).
54. *B.B. Crane*, S.Ct., 331 US 1, 67 S.Ct. 1047.
55. IRC Secs. 1011, 1012, and 1016.
56. IRC Sec. 1001(c).
57. IRC Sec. 1060.
58. IRC Sec. 1060.
59. IRC Sec. 1060(c).
60. *Id.*
61. Reg. § 1.1060-1(b)(1).
62. Reg. § 1.1060-1(c)(2).
63. Reg. § 1.338-6(b)(1).
64. Reg. § 1.338-6(b)(2)(ii).
65. Reg. § 1.338-6(b)(2)(iii).
66. Reg. § 1.338-6(b)(2)(iv).
67. Reg. § 1.338-6(b)(2)(v).
68. Reg. § 1.338-6(b)(2)(vi).
69. Reg. § 1.338-6(b)(2)(vii).
70. Reg. § 1.338-6(c)(1).
71. Reg. § 1.1060-1(e).
72. Reg. § 1.1060-1(e)(1)(ii)(A).
73. *Id.*

74. Reg. § 1.1060-1(e)(1)(ii)(B).
75. IRC Sec. 1060(e)(1).
76. IRC Sec. 1060(a).
77. IRC Sec. 1060(a).
78. IRC Sec. 1060(a)(1); Reg. § 1.1060-1 (c)(2).
79. See note 39 *supra*.
80. 810 F.2d 562 (1987).; Rev. Rul. 69-643, 1969-2 CB 10.
81. See Chapter 17 and the *Norwell* case discussed in this chapter.
82. Rev. Rul. 69-643, 1969-2 CB 10.
83. IRC Sec. 197(d)(1)(C)(iii).
84. Rev. Rul. 79-285, 1979-2 CB 91.
85. IRC Secs. 1221(a)(3) and 1231(b)(1)(C).
86. IRC Sec. 197(d)(1)(C)(iii).
87. IRC Sec. 197(e)(4)(C).
88. Rev. Rul. 79-285, 1979-2 CB 91.
89. *Warren L. Baker, Jr.*, 338 F.3d 789 (2003).; Rev. Rul. 69-643, 1969-2 CB 10.
90. See, e.g., *Warsaw Photographic Associates, Inc.*, 84 TC 21, (1985).
91. IRC Sec. 1253(a) and (c).
92. IRC Sec. 1253(d).
93. IRC Sec. 1253(d)(1).
94. IRC Secs. 1253(d)(2) and 197(d)(1)(F).
95. *A.F. Williams*, 152 F.2d 570 (1946).
96. Reg. § 1.1221-1(d).
97. IRC Sec. 1221(a)(1).
98. *Grace Brothers, Inc.*, CA-9, 49-1 USTC ¶ 9181, 173 F.2d 170.
99. See IRC Sec. 111.
100. See Chapter 3.
101. See IRC Sec. 1221(a)(3).
102. See IRC Secs. 1231(b)(1) and 1221(a)(2).
103. IRC Sec. 1221(a)(3).
104. IRC Sec. 1231(b)(1)(C).
105. See *M.L. Killian*, 314 F.2d 852 (1963).
106. *C.C. Hamlin Trust*, 209 F.2d 761 (1954); *Warren L. Baker, Jr.*, 338 F.3d 789 (2003).
107. 1969-2 CB 10.
108. Rev. Rul. 65-180, 1965-2 CB 279.
109. IRC Sec. 1253.
110. IRC Sec. 197.

STRUCTURING A SALE OF CORPORATE ASSETS

CHAPTER 4

OVERVIEW

Chapter 1 observed that in structuring business acquisition transactions, the parties must address and answer three basic questions: (1) Will it be taxable or tax free? (2) Will it be a sale of equity or a sale of assets? (3) Will there be any deferred payments?

In addressing the first question, the parties in a large majority of corporate business acquisitions choose fully taxable transactions. Even among the so-called "tax-free" acquisition transactions, there is often a significant amount of taxable income or gain recognized by the Sellers. The reason for this is obvious: Sellers generally want all or a significant portion of the consideration paid in cash or in other highly liquid assets. In turn, while tax law may be complex in most respects, one simple rule of thumb generally prevails: cash = tax liabilities.

One situation where the owners of a Target will accept (and in many cases will eagerly seek) an entirely "tax-free" transaction is if the Acquirer's stock is publicly traded, especially if the Selling Shareholders are either being given registration rights or, at worst, will be able to sell the stock in the public markets (or to an accredited investor) in compliance with SEC Rule 144, within a reasonable period of time after the closing. Alternatively, Selling Shareholders will consider a tax-free reorganization even if the Acquirer's stock is not publicly traded so long as there is a clear and reliable exit strategy—which might include "put" rights or similar rights to liquidate the investment in an orderly manner. Generally, Selling Shareholders will explore a tax-free transaction only if there is a clear liquidation mechanism.

Conversely, if the stock of the Acquirer corporation is closely held, especially if it lacks any prospect of becoming a registered security in the short or intermediate term, owners of a Target corporation are reluctant to trade ownership and control of a successful business (why, after all, is it a Target corporation in the first place?) in exchange for a minority interest in an illiquid stock where the ability to unlock the economic value of the stock is entirely controlled by others.

Chapters 4 through 6 explore the various mechanisms for implementing a taxable sale of a C corporation business. This chapter focuses on an asset sale by a C corporation and builds on the information developed in Chapter 3, which addressed the tax aspects of an asset sale by a sole proprietorship. As will become clear, a Buyer of assets experiences the exact same tax consequences whether the Seller is a sole proprietorship or a C corporation (or, for that matter, any other entity). Therefore, the discussion in Chapter 3 is directly relevant in understanding and evaluating the Buyer's tax issues. However, the tax issues facing the Seller are quite different. A selling C corporation is subject to so-called "double taxation" (i.e., it is taxed a first time at the corporate level on income and gain from the sale transaction, and then a second time at the shareholder level on distributions, including liquidating distributions, from the corporation). Naturally, avoiding or at least mitigating the effects of double taxation is the driving factor in a C corporation asset sale. Indeed, precisely because the tax consequences of an asset sale are so dramatically different when the Seller is a C corporation, it leads, in turn, to major differences in the allocation strategies and in the negotiation itself.

Avoiding or minimizing double taxation in a C corporation asset sale leads, inevitably, to various "outside the corporation" tax planning strategies, most notably the strategy of paying some portion of the "purchase price" in the form of consulting, noncompete, or other payments to the individual owners of the Target. The ability to implement this strategy will vary widely, depending on the configuration of the Target and its owners, but generally the parties will want to explore carefully whether they can avoid, or at least minimize, double taxation for their mutual benefit.

A directly related issue is the role of the Target's individual owners in the post-acquisition business. In the modern economy, few businesses are valuable solely because of the real and tangible assets. And, when an Acquirer purchases intangible assets, ranging from goodwill to intellectual property, the value of those assets is often intimately related to the personal talents of individuals who work for the Target, especially those employed in upper management. Thus, the logical desire to pay significant salary and consulting payments to key individuals often dovetails nicely with the desire to avoid double taxation.

Although compensation strategies often make sense to both parties, a limiting factor is the fact that the individuals who founded and manage a business often have a difficult time, and sometimes an impossible time, running their old business while taking orders from a new boss. Indeed, the "generic" acquisition strategy usually calls for the founding owners to enter into a noncompete agreement with the Acquirer, to participate as consultants or employees after the acquisition for a short period of time, and then to exit gracefully (hopefully leaving voluntarily, rather than with a push out the door) within a period of one to three years.

By contrast, a far more common recipe for success is for the non-owner senior management (i.e., the key employees who worked for the prior owners) to assume the senior management roles and to work successfully with the Acquirer. This is in part because the senior employees do not have ego or other reasons that might prevent them from easily taking orders, and in part because these senior employees are often more valued by the new owners, precisely because they have the skills to manage the newly acquired business. The pragmatic observation is that key employees are often more valuable to a new owner than to an existing one, and this leads to a favorable synergy, including stock options, respect, autonomy, and promotion.

The remainder of the chapter explores the tax aspects of acquiring assets from a C corporation. Chapter 5 looks at the tax aspects of acquiring the stock of a C corporation, instead of purchasing a business and its assets. Chapter 6 examines how to compare the tax consequences of an asset sale to a stock sale, and in particular examines how to formulate an effective acquisition structure that meets the needs of both Buyer and Seller.

ALLOCATION STRATEGIES ON A SALE OF C CORPORATION ASSETS

The tax consequences to the Buyer in an asset acquisition are discussed in substantial detail in Chapter 3, but a brief review is in order. The Buyer's natural objective in any acquisition transaction is to pay as low a price as possible. Generally, this is achieved if the Buyer can deduct and write off the acquisition costs as quickly as possible. However, most of the purchased assets will need to be either depreciated or amortized over the relatively lengthy periods established by the Code. Although it may be possible to use Code section 1060 to play some allocation games at the margin, this usually does not present a major opportunity for tax savings.

> ***Example 1:*** The Buyer might want to "inflate" the price allocated to five-year depreciable assets and correspondingly reduce the amounts allocated to fifteen-year amortizable assets, in order to claim more of the depreciation/amortization deductions earlier in time. This proposal would benefit the Buyer and would not harm a C corporation Seller because, even though an allocation of "extra" purchase price to tangible property is likely to trigger Code section 1245 recapture, a C corporation Seller is generally indifferent because there is no preferential tax rate for a C corporation on capital gains. (If the Seller's gain is passed through to an individual taxpayer, by contrast, there will likely be great resistance to such an allocation because it increases ordinary income (taxed at up to a 35-percent federal rate) and decreases capital gain (taxed at up to a 20- percent federal rate).) Even if both parties are in agreement, however, there are significant constraints on this type of allocation gamesmanship, including standardized "bluebook" valuations for many types of business assets. (*Note:* The allocation rules under Code section 1060 are discussed in detail in Chapter 3.)

The tax consequences to the Seller are dominated by two factors: (1) double taxation and (2) the absence of a preferential long-term capital gains tax rate for C corporations. Compared to a sale of assets by a sole proprietorship, a sale of assets by a C corporation costs two-to-three times the amount of federal income tax liability on the exact same purchase price allocation.

Example 2: Assume a Target business is "worth" $10 million to the Buyer, and the Buyer insists on structuring the transaction as an asset acquisition for nontax reasons (e.g., the Buyer does not want to do a stock purchase and assume the existing liabilities of the Target). Assume the Seller has the following simplified asset structure:

Asset Description	*Original Purchase Price*	*Tax Basis*	*Fair Market Value*
Desks, chairs, furniture, computer equipment, and other Code section 1245 property	$800,000	$500,000	$500,000
Inventory	$1,500,000	$1,500,000	$1,500,000
Goodwill and going concern value	$0	$0	$8,000,000

If the business described in Example 2, above, is operated as a single member LLC (a sole proprietorship for federal income tax purposes), its assets are sold for $10 million in cash, and the purchase price is allocated according to the fair market values shown above, the selling sole proprietor, an individual, will recognize $8 million of long-term capital gain from the sale of the goodwill, which is a capital asset in the hands of the seller. Assuming a combined federal and state income tax rate on long-term capital gains of 20 percent, the Seller would pay $1.6 million of tax ($8,000,000 × 20%) and enjoy after-tax proceeds of $8.4 million.

If the business in Example 2 is instead operated through a C corporation, the sale of assets is taxed first at the corporate level at what we will assume is a 40-percent combined federal and state corporate income tax rate, so that on $8 million of long-term capital gain the C corporation would pay $3.2 million in federal income taxes ($8,000,000 × 40%). If we assume that the corporation then liquidates and distributes all of its after-tax cash of $6,800,000 ($10 million in proceeds minus taxes of $3.2 million), we assume the outside basis of the shareholder in the C corporation stock is $300,000, and we assume a combined federal and state income tax rate on long-term capital gains is 20 percent, the distribution of $6.8 million will result in $6.5 million of gain recognized by the shareholder ($6.8 million minus tax basis of $300,000), which produces an additional $1.3 million of tax liability ($6.5 million of gain multiplied by the tax rate of 20 percent). After paying this second level of tax, the shareholder enjoys after-tax proceeds of $5.5 million (the $6.8 million cash distribution minus $1.3 million in shareholder-level taxes). Thus, comparing two asset-acquisition transactions that have identical tax consequences to the Buyer, the net after-tax benefit to the Seller is $8.4 million for a sale by a sole proprietorship and $5.5 million for a sale by a C corporation. In effect, the sole proprietorship would pay $1.6 million in total taxes in this example, while the C corporation and the shareholder together would pay $4.5 million in total taxes. In this example (not far-fetched by any means) double taxation not only "doubles" but actually triples the tax cost!

Tax Strategies in the Allocation of Purchase Price

One of the obvious and irresistible structuring strategies in a C corporation asset sale is to explore ways to allocate part of the "purchase price" to consulting payments, or wages, paid to the individuals who own and/or manage the Target C corporation. For the Buyer, this strategy is attractive because (reasonable) consulting payments and wages can be deducted immediately, rather than being capitalized and amortized over fifteen years (the amortization period for an allocation of purchase price to "goodwill" or to a noncompete agreement). Meanwhile, for the individual-payee on the other side of the table, such an allocation produces ordinary income, which is not attractive compared to paying a one-time capital gains tax but is usually more attractive than allocating the payment to a purchase of corporate goodwill (subject to double taxation) and usually only slightly worse than allocating the payment to noncompete payments (noncompete payments are taxed as ordinary income to the recipient, and thus are taxed at the same income-tax rates as consulting payments; however, noncompete payments are not subject to self-employment taxes).[1] The point is that both Seller and Buyer can enjoy a more favorable after-tax benefit if part of the total acquisition price is allocated to what might be called "personal" payments.

Example 3: Start with the same facts as in Example 2, where the Buyer pays $10 million to purchase business assets, with $8 million of the acquisition price allocated to Code section 197 intangibles (for the goodwill and going concern value), which amount is capitalized and amortized by the Buyer over fifteen years; $1.5 million allocated to inventory; and $500,000 allocated to tangible property that will be depreciated over five years. The question is, how much would the Seller and Buyer benefit, respectively, if the parties could plausibly support an allocation of $1 million to a consulting payment to Nancy, the sole owner of Target C corporation and reduce to $7 million the amount allocated to goodwill and going concern value.

The first part of the exercise is to calculate the net present-value after-tax consequences to the Buyer and Seller of allocating the "last" $1 million of purchase price to goodwill. Since the Target has zero basis in its goodwill assets and is subject to a 35-percent federal income tax rate (and assuming, artificially, no state income taxes), the Target pays an incremental $350,000 of corporate-level federal income tax if the "last" $1 million is allocated to goodwill. When the Target is subsequently liquidated, distributing after-tax proceeds to its shareholders (and assuming a tax rate of 15 percent at the shareholder level on this distribution), the shareholders would receive an incremental distribution of $650,000 and pay $97,500 in additional capital gains taxes ($650,000 × 15%), netting $552,500 of after-tax proceeds on the "last" $1 million.

The Buyer, meanwhile, would capitalize its "last" $1 million of purchase price as part of its tax basis in Code section 197 intangibles, and would amortize the $1 million ratably over fifteen years. This means that over fifteen years the tax savings to the Buyer, assuming the Buyer is taxed at a 35-percent tax rate, would be $350,000. However, because the recovery of tax basis is stretched over fifteen years, a reasonable approximation of the present value of those tax savings might be roughly half of the gross tax savings (equivalent to an annual discount rate of slightly more than 10 percent). Therefore, the Buyer's net present-value tax savings might be valued at approximately 50 percent of $350,000, or $175,000. (As we will explore in far more detail in Chapter 6, this present value analysis is ultimately driven by the economic assumptions defined by the Buyer.) Based on these assumptions, the net present-value after-tax cost to the Buyer of spending the "last" $1 million on goodwill would be approximately $825,000 on an after-tax basis.

Example 4: Assume the same facts as in Example 2, except that the parties agree to pay Nancy, the sole shareholder of the Target, a "reasonable" consulting payment of $1 million, which, to simplify the calculations, we will assume can all be paid and deducted in the first year of the acquisition. Assume that ordinary income earned by Nancy is subject to a 35-percent federal tax rate and no state income tax. For Nancy, receiving a $1 million compensatory payment directly, which payment is taxed at a 35-percent individual federal income tax rate, would result in $650,000 of after-tax income. By comparison, if the $1 million were paid to the Target and subjected to double taxation (i.e., taxed at a rate of 35 percent on the $1 million, then 15 percent on the remaining $650,000), the net after-tax benefit to Nancy would be $552,500. Therefore, characterizing $1 million of the $10 million "purchase price" as consulting payments to Nancy would give Nancy a net after-tax federal income-tax benefit of $97,500 (the difference between $650,000 and $552,500).

Comment: Even this "simple" example creates additional complications because a consulting payment will cause Nancy to owe self-employment (SE) taxes on net income from her consulting activities, which SE tax is currently imposed at a rate of 15.3 percent up to the OASD maximum (an amount indexed each year that is $127,200 for 2017 and 2.9 percent on all amounts above the OASD maximum (with an additional tax of 39.6.9 percent on incomes over $200,000, for a single person, in 2017, thus increasing tax to 3.8 percent), but further adjusted by a credit for OASD payments on behalf of the individual for the year from other sources (e.g., social security taxes paid on W-2 wages). As a tax-planning shorthand, most tax planners estimate an additional three percent SE tax cost for large consulting payments. This would reduce the after-tax benefit by approximately $30,000 (the approximate tax cost of an estimated three percent multiplied by $1 million) but would still leave Nancy with an after-tax benefit in the range of $67,500 ($97,500 minus $30,000).

For the Buyer, meanwhile, deducting the $1 million consulting payment in the first year is far better than capitalizing and amortizing ratably over fifteen years. By making the allocation to a consulting payment, the Buyer saves approximately 35 percent of $1 million, or $350,000, in the first year, compared to an estimated value of $175,000 in net present-value tax benefits if the $1 million payment is amortized ratably over fifteen years. Therefore, the estimated net present value, after-tax benefit to the Buyer of shifting from goodwill to consulting payments is $175,000 ($350,000 minus $175,000).

In summary, both the Seller and Buyer benefit significantly from a reallocation of purchase price from the purchase of goodwill to a consulting payment to the principal employee-shareholder of the corporation. Ignoring SE tax and state tax adjustments, the Seller enjoys an extra $97,500 in present-value after-tax proceeds, while the Buyer saves $175,000 in present-value after-tax purchase price.

Example 5: Assume the same facts as in Example 4, except that instead of allocating $1 million to a consulting payment to Nancy, the parties agree that Nancy will receive a one-time noncompete payment of $1 million, to be paid at the closing. Since the noncompete payment arises in connection with the acquisition of a trade or business, the Buyer is required by Code section 197(d)(1)(E) to treat the noncompete payment as a Section 197 intangible and amortize the $1 million payment ratably over fifteen years. Thus, the Buyer receives no after-tax benefit from allocating $1 million to a noncompete payment compared to an allocation of the $1 million to goodwill, and enjoys far less after-tax benefit compared to an allocation of the $1 million to consulting payments, as shown in Example 4. However, as a practical matter, a typical Buyer will want to make a substantial allocation to a noncompete payment for nontax reasons, namely, to put some economic leverage into the noncompete agreement. Therefore, although there is no tax difference to the Buyer between an allocation to goodwill and an allocation to a noncompete, the Buyer may consider it more desirable for nontax reasons.

Meanwhile, the Seller will have a modest preference toward receiving noncompete payments as compared to consulting payments because the Seller (meaning Nancy) will thus be able to avoid the SE tax on noncompete payments. For example, assuming Nancy has W-2 wages from other sources that exceed the OASD maximum, the tax savings to Nancy of a noncompete payment compared to a consulting payment would be to avoid the 3.8 percent HI component of the SE tax, a savings of $38,000 on a $1 million payment.

As these examples demonstrate, moving incremental payments from goodwill to consulting and noncompete payments has an overall tax advantage. They also address important nontax issues in the transaction as well (because the Buyer usually wants the leverage to pay noncompete payments over a period of years to ensure good behavior by the Seller and the related individuals).

The rule of thumb in acquisition tax planning is that the Buyer wants to deduct more money earlier—unless, of course, the opposite is true. This is an intentionally ironic comment designed to highlight the fact that a "typical" Buyer usually wants to "front load" the deductions—but only if and to the extent that the deductions offset income at high federal tax rates. For example, an individual sole proprietor who purchases a small going concern may actually prefer to spread the deductions over a period of years and use them against income in later years to offset income in the highest marginal tax brackets, rather than "clump" all the deductions into a single year and thereby shelter income at the lowest tax brackets.

Allocation of Purchase Price under Code Section 1060

The technical aspects of Code section 1060 and the "residual method" are discussed in detail in Chapter 3, but a brief review is in order. Code section 1060(a) provides that in the case of any "applicable asset acquisition", the parties must allocate the purchase price among the acquired assets in the same manner as amounts are allocated to assets under Code section 338(b)(5). These allocation rules are binding for purposes of determining both (1) the transferee's basis in such assets and (2) the gain or loss of the transferor with respect to such acquisition.[2] If, in connection with an applicable asset acquisition, the transferee and transferor agree in writing as to the allocation of any consideration, or as to the fair-market value of any assets, such agreement shall be binding on both the transferee and transferor unless the IRS determines that such allocation (or fair-market value) is not appropriate.[3] Obviously, all allocation planning starts with a clear and defensible agreement between the Buyer and Seller as to the appropriate values to be placed on the various assets and allocations.

As previously noted, there is a common and often irresistible urge to allocate "purchase price" either to "personal" payments, such as consulting payments, wages, and/or noncompete payments, or to what might be called "parallel" payments—payments to the Seller or an individual related to the Seller that produce a tax favored result for both parties. For example, it is not unusual for the principal individual owner of the Seller to also own and lease to the Seller the real estate used as the Seller's principal place of business. Often, a Buyer will agree to lease these premises pursuant to a new, long-term lease that offers an advantageous economic return for the principal owner of the Seller, as lessor, and permits the Buyer to deduct, as paid, the "enhanced" rent payments. Likewise, the individual owner of the Seller may have other rights, ranging from ownership interests in patents to rights in web addresses or trademark that can be the basis of a favorable "parallel payment" allocation.

SPECIFIC TAX CONSEQUENCES TO C CORPORATION SELLER UPON SALE OF ASSETS

A selling C corporation realizes gain or loss on the sale of its assets equal to the difference between the purchase price allocated to each asset and the corporation's tax basis in such assets. The tax character of such gain or loss will vary depending on the nature and class of the assets, and can be ordinary income or loss, capital gain or loss, or, in the case of Code section 1231 property, capital gain or ordinary loss. The tax character of assets is discussed extensively in Chapter 3.

The selling C corporation may also recognize so-called "recapture income" on the sale of an asset, all or a portion of which may be taxed as ordinary income under Code section 1245 (applicable to gain from dispositions of certain depreciable personal property) and Code section 1250 and Code section 291 (applicable to gain from dispositions of certain depreciable real property). These rules are discussed in detail in Chapter 3.

An important aspect in a C corporation asset sale is that because a selling C corporation does not enjoy an advantageous tax rate on capital gains, an allocation that changes the characterization of the sales proceeds from ordinary income to capital gain does not lower the applicable tax rate.[4] However, a C corporation generally seeks to avoid a capital loss because it can deduct losses from sales or exchanges of capital assets only to the extent of gains from such sales or ex-changes.[5] A corporation that has a net capital loss for any year can generally carry back such capital loss to each of the three preceding tax years and may carry such loss forward to each of the five succeeding tax years.[6] The entire amount of net capital loss for any tax year is carried to the earliest of the tax years to which such loss may be carried and must be used in such year to the extent of the net capital gain in such year; any remaining carryback loss is then carried forward to the next oldest tax year.[7]

Obviously, a corporation selling assets must be mindful of the extent to which it may incur capital losses and the degree to which such losses can be utilized. Note, however, that under Code section 1231, if the losses attributable to the sale or exchange of property used in the corporation's trade or business exceed the gains recognized on the sale of such property, the resulting loss for the year is characterized as ordinary loss rather than capital loss.[8] Thus, a corporation will generally recognize net capital losses *only* from sales of assets *not* used in the corporation's trade or business. This should usually be relatively easy to avoid.

Example 6: Assume Zella's Zeroes, Inc., a C corporation, is experiencing economic problems and is selling its assets on an expedited basis in order to raise cash quickly. Zella's Zeroes, Inc. has the following assets that it is able to sell to other competitors in the industry:

1. Relatively new manufacturing equipment, purchased for $1 million, with a current tax basis of $800,000, which it can sell for $700,000 and recognize a $100,000 loss.

2. An inventory of products manufactured (cost of goods) for $250,000, which Zella's Zeroes, Inc. can sell for $200,000 and recognize a $50,000 loss.

3. A building and land that Zella's Zeroes, Inc. no longer needs because of its business contraction. The real estate was purchased for $2.5 million, with $2 million allocated to the building and $500,000 to the land. The real estate has been held for more than one year and has a remaining depreciable tax basis of $1.9 million allocable to the building, and a remaining tax basis of $500,000 allocable to the land. Zella's Zeroes, Inc. can sell the real estate quickly for $2.2 million and generate a $200,000 loss.

4. Stocks, bonds, and similar investment assets, which were originally purchased by Zella's Zeroes, Inc. for $500,000 but which have dropped in market value to $400,000 and could be sold currently for a $100,000 loss.

Discussion of Example 6:

1. Because the manufacturing equipment is a Code section 1231 asset, its sale for $700,000 ($800,000 of tax basis) would produce a $100,000 Code section 1231 loss, which is deductible first against any Code section 1231 gains, and then is treated as an ordinary loss.

2. Because inventory is an ordinary asset (*not* a Code section 1231 asset), its sale for $200,000 (tax basis of $250,000) would generate a $50,000 ordinary loss not subject to the Code section 1231 offset rules.

3. The building and land are likewise Code section 1231 assets because they are currently being used in the trade or business (even though that use will soon become redundant). Sale of the building and land for $2.2 million would generate a $200,000 Code section 1231 loss; the difference between the remaining tax basis in the real estate, $2.4 million, and the sales price of $2.2 million.

4. Zella's Zeroes, Inc.'s investment assets, such as stocks and bonds, are capital assets in its hands, their sale would generate a capital loss of $100,000. Note that if the investment assets were not readily tradable on a public exchange, it might be possible to "push" various allocations subject to capital gain and loss because the selling corporation generally does not want to have a capital loss. However, this valuation strategy would be far more difficult to justify with publicly traded assets. On the other hand, if the corporation had no prospect of being able to use its capital loss (e.g., because it was not a $100,000 capital loss, but $10,000,000 capital loss), the apportionment of purchase price might become more important.

In summary, the tax planning for the selling C Corporation must recognize two basic issues. First, because ordinary income and capital gain are both taxed at the same corporate tax rate, there is often little incentive for *Seller* to allocate income and gains between competing assets. Second, because ordinary losses, capital losses, and Code section 1231 losses have differing benefits and limitations, allocations in a loss situation may actually be more important than on the gain side!

Comment: Selling Code section 1231 property at a gain does *not* automatically solve the problem of offsetting capital losses because the Code section 1231 gain and loss are first offset against each other before being apportioned to offsetting other capital gain or loss.

For federal income tax purposes, a C corporation selling its assets can generally offset income or gain by using net operating losses (NOLs) or capital losses from prior years to reduce the income or gain recognized from the sale of its assets. NOLs are defined in Code section 172 and generally can be carried back two tax years and forward for twenty tax years. A distressed business with significant NOLs and/or capital losses may be able to use these losses to reduce or avoid gain on an asset sale. This strategy may be especially attractive since Code section 382 imposes significant limitations on the right of a Purchaser to utilize losses of a Target corporation arising before the acquisition date. These Code section 382 limitations are discussed in greater detail in Chapter 13. NOLs can also make it economically attractive for a Buyer to make a Code section 338 election, although generally the NOLs would need to be relatively large in comparison to the amount of gain triggered by the Code section 338 election.

Immediately after the sale of some or all of its corporate assets, a selling C corporation is likely to have a high percentage of investment assets and also a large amount of accumulated earnings and profits relative to the size of any remaining business activities. As a result, the corporation may be subject to the Accumulated Earnings (AE) Tax under Code section 531 *et seq.* or, even more likely, subject to the Personal Holding Company (PHC) Tax under Code section 541 *et seq.* unless the selling C corporation is liquidated in the year of the asset sale. However, as a practical matter, even though it may be subject to ongoing AE tax or PHC tax, the question is whether a C corporation, after it sells off most or all of its business assets, should be liquidated and thereby inflict the second level of the dreaded double taxation, or whether it should stay in existence and manage the AE tax/PHC tax liabilities.[9]

This question is especially germane if the C corporation stock is owned primarily by one or two elderly individuals and actuarial projections indicate that, because of the step-up in tax basis on the death of a shareholder under Code section 1014, the heirs may be able to avoid the second level of "double taxation" (i.e., the tax imposed at the shareholder level). This is an interesting but complicated issue to address, but basically some older shareholders (and sometimes not-so-older shareholders) prefer to keep a C corporation alive after it sells its business assets and then use appropriate management strategies to deal with the AE tax and the PHC tax. The AE tax and the PHC tax both require careful planning to avoid unexpected and surprisingly large tax costs. Some examples of management strategies are discussed below.

If the selling C corporation liquidates immediately following the sale of all or substantially all of its assets, the corporation frequently will be distributing entirely cash (or mostly cash) to the shareholders and probably will not recognize any significant additional income at the corporate level. Be aware, however, that if the corporation distributes any retained assets that have a fair-market value in excess of the corporation's tax basis, the distribution will trigger further recognition of income at the corporate level under Code sections 311(b) or 336(a). Such a liquidation will, of course, also generate tax consequences to the corporation's shareholders, as described below.

TAX CONSEQUENCES OF SELLING C CORPORATION'S SHAREHOLDERS

Immediately after a sale of corporate assets, the selling corporation's shareholders are usually in a situation that is commonly described as a Hobson's Choice.

Literary Aside: Hobson ran a stable during the 17th Century in Cambridge, England, and rented horses to customers. To prevent customers from overusing his best horses, Hobson put all his horses in order and gave the customer a choice of taking the next horse in line or no horse at all. A Hobson's Choice has come to mean, in the common vernacular, a choice between two unpalatable alternatives, but, in fact, its precise and true meaning is captured in the phrase "take it or leave it". A choice between two unpalatable alternatives is more nearly reflected in the biblical story of "Balaam's Ass".

The stockholders of the selling C corporation must decide whether to liquidate the corporation and thereby trigger a second level of taxation contemporaneous with the asset sale transaction or whether to leave the proceeds from the sale at the corporate level and attempt to wrestle with the AE tax, PHC tax, and/or corporate alternative minimum tax (AMT).

Before discussing the various post-sale tax strategies, however, a brief explanation of the AE tax and PHC tax is necessary.

Accumulated Earnings (AE) Tax

The AE tax[10] is a tax at the corporate level on C corporations formed for the purpose of avoiding income tax with respect to shareholders by permitting earnings and profits to accumulate instead of being divided or distributed. The purpose of the tax is to compel distributions of corporate profits not needed for conduct of the business.

The AE tax is imposed at a rate of 15 percent on "accumulated taxable income".[11] Accumulated taxable income is taxable income with certain adjustments specified in Code section 535(b), and reduced by dividends paid and by the greater of (1) $250,000 ($150,000 for some personal service companies) or (2) amounts retained for reasonable business needs minus net capital gains.[12] The AE tax is in addition to any income taxes the corporation may have already paid on the taxable income, i.e., it is a second tax on a modified version of after-tax income. Significantly, the AE tax is imposed on the current year's taxable income, even though it is triggered by an excess accumulation of profits from prior years. Indeed, an important planning strategy for the AE tax exploits the fact that tax-exempt interest income is not "taxable income" and thus is not included in the calculation of accumulated taxable income.[13]

Comment: AE tax is imposed because of wrongful intent to avoid income tax. What's more, the burden of proof concerning this wrongful intent is borne by the taxpayer if the IRS provides a notice to the taxpayer prior to mailing the notice of deficiency.[14] The taxpayer then has an opportunity to make a submission, in which case the burden would be moved back to the IRS.[15] As a practical matter, however, the burden of proof is probably not a major factor, and the fundamental issue will be whether the objective facts suggest a wrongful intent.

Unreasonable accumulation results when retained earnings and profits are in excess of reasonable business needs.[16] Reasonable business needs are those that a prudent businessman would consider necessary for maintenance of the current business of the corporation and the reasonably anticipated future needs.[17] Examples of qualifying needs that have been recognized in Regulation § 1.537-2(b) and case law include:

1. Replacement of plant or business expansion.

2. Working capital needs, but the determination of working capital needs has produced extensive litigation. Formulas used by the IRS in audit proceedings to determine working capital needs may be found in the IRS Agents Manual.

3. Acquisition of another business.

4. Retirement of corporate debt.

Personal Holding Company Tax

The PHC tax is a second, alternative penalty tax that applies a 15-percent tax at the corporate level to closely-held C corporations that have too much passive income. In contrast to the AE tax, which is based on subjective intent, the PHC tax is driven strictly by objective mathematical tests. Significantly, if a corporation is a personal holding company subject to the PHC tax, it is not subject to the AE tax.[18]

The PHC tax is imposed at a 15-percent tax rate on every personal holding company with undistributed personal holding company income. A "personal holding company" is a C corporation that meets both of the following two tests:[19]

1. ***Stock Ownership Test.*** At any time during the last half of the tax year more than 50 percent in value of the stock is owned by five or fewer individuals. (Under Code section 544, elaborate and distinctive ownership attribution rules apply).

2. ***Passive Income Test.*** At least 60 percent of the adjusted ordinary gross income (AOGI) for the year consists of PHC income. AOGI is defined in Code section 543(b)(2) as, roughly, gross income less gains from sales of capital assets and Section 1231 property, and making special adjustments for certain rents, royalties, and interest payments.

"Personal holding company income", in turn, means the portion of the AOGI that consists of the following (generally passive) types of income: (1) dividends, interest, royalties, and annuities, (2) rents, (3) mineral, oil, and gas royalties, (4) copyright royalties, (5) film rents, (6) compensation for the use of corporate property by a 25-percent or more shareholder, and (7) personal service contracts.

A corporation can avoid the PHC tax by "flunking" either the Stock Ownership Test or the Passive Income Test. (Caution: Be aware that this may merely throw the corporation into the AE tax.) Assuming a corporation is closely held, it can still avoid the PHC tax by structuring its activities such that PHC income does not exceed 60 percent of AOGI.

Planning Point: One strategy to reduce or avoid PHC tax exposure is for the corporation to invest in government obligations that generate tax-exempt interest income, since tax-exempt interest is excluded from both AOGI and from PHC income in applying the 60-percent test.[20] Another idea is to acquire "good" income (i.e., non-PHC income) by investing in a partnership conducting an active business, based on the fact that a partner is deemed engaged in the business of the partnership and thus can treat the allocable share of partnership income as "good" income. Note that since AOGI is a *gross* income test, a relatively modest share of the gross income of the partnership may push the corporation below the 60-percent threshold for the PHC tax. Alternatively, the corporation can distribute sufficient dividends to reduce or eliminate the "undistributed PHC income" upon which the tax is assessed.[21]

Managing the PHC Tax and AE Tax Exposure of a Post-Sale C Corporation

A C corporation that has sold all or substantially all of its assets can, of course, liquidate and distribute all its assets to shareholders, thereby triggering a second level of tax. Alternatively, the shareholder(s) of the C corporation may decide that it is more advantageous to keep the C corporation alive, even though it may be subject to the PHC tax or AE tax, because such taxes are either manageable or less costly overall than the tax triggered by a corporate liquidation.

Example 7: Assume that Zander Zorro, Inc., a C corporation, sells all its assets for $16.6 million and that after paying federal and state income taxes of approximately 40 percent, the net after-tax amount realized on the transaction is $10 million. Assume that Alex, the sole shareholder of Zander Zorro, Inc., is an eighty-five-year-old man with zero tax basis in his stock. Assume further that Zander Zorro, Inc. has $10 million of retained earnings and profits (which means that if the corporation's cash assets are distributed in a nonliquidating distribution, the distribution will be taxable as a dividend). On these facts, a distribution/ liquidation, even at the relatively preferential dividend and capital gain rates of 15 percent (and assuming another five percent state level tax), would result in taxes of $2 million and reduce the post-liquidation, after-tax assets from $10 million to $8 million.

On the other hand, if Zander Zorro, Inc. anticipated that it could enjoy a 10-percent annual investment return on taxable investments and a five-percent tax-exempt return on investments (the assumed investment rates of return are chosen for mathematical convenience rather than current market accuracy), the selling shareholder, Alex, may conclude that it is better to keep the $10 million in net, after-tax sale proceeds at the corporate level, and invest these proceeds, subject to the PHC tax, rather than liquidate Zander Zorro, Inc. and pay the immediate $2 million in additional distribution/ liquidation taxes. The analysis suggests that the selling shareholder, at age eighty-five, will be better off to hold the corporate stock until his death, after which his estate will enjoy a step-up in tax basis. The analysis is as follows:

Scenario 7A: The $10 million is invested at the corporate level at a 10-percent investment return and generates $1 million of interest income, which, if taxed at a combined 40-percent corporate-level tax rate (the approximate effective combined rate for federal and state taxes, after taking into account deductibility of state taxes), would leave $600,000 of after-tax income. This $600,000 is then either distributed in a dividend distribution, taxable at 20 percent (based on a 15-percent federal tax and probably about a five-percent state tax), or is subject to the PHC tax (also a 15-percent corporate level tax, but there probably is no similar state penalty tax). This means that the shareholder's net after-tax amount is $480,000 per year in the case of a dividend or $510,000 in the case of assets retained by the corporation and subject to the PHC tax.

Scenario 7B: By contrast, if there had previously been a taxable liquidating distribution by the corporation of $10 million in net after-tax proceeds, the eighty-five-year-old shareholder would have held $8 million in post-liquidation cash, which he could personally invest at a 10-percent return, subject to approximately a 40-percent individual-level income tax. The shareholder would gross $800,000 of income ($8 million invested at 10 percent) and net $480,000 in after tax proceeds after paying $320,000 in taxes ($800,000 × 40%). This net after-tax return is approximately equal to the after-tax return anticipated in Scenario 7A. This comparative analysis is sensitive, of course, to the actual tax rates (both federal and state) applicable to the individual, but the general conclusion that can be drawn is that at the very least, the PHC tax disadvantage of keeping the corporation in existence is greatly if not entirely offset by the $2 million in extra corporate assets that would result from keeping the C corporation alive as a PHC and avoiding the immediate second level of tax that would be triggered by a liquidating distribution.

Estate Planning Benefit: If the sole shareholder dies, say, at the age of ninety, five years after implementing the PHC tax strategy (and assuming all current income of the PHC has been distributed as a dividend in each of the intervening five years), the decedent's stock will enjoy a step up in basis under Code section 1014 and will therefore be valued at $10 million in the gross estate of the decedent (assuming no capital appreciation in the assets held in the corporation). Zander Zorro, Inc. can thereafter be liquidated at that time, and, assuming the corporate assets continue to be worth exactly $10 million (something that is not going to be exactly correct, but may be approximately correct, especially if the investments are generally in bonds and the interest rates have not varied substantially in the intervening five years), there would be no gain to either the C corporation or its shareholders on liquidation of the corporation under Code section 336 and, likewise, no gain at the shareholder level, since the estate would now have $10 million of tax basis in the corporate stock and would receive a distribution of $10 million of assets.

Comment: The outside basis issue is automatically self-correcting. If the assets of the corporation appreciate in the intervening period between the sale of the business and the shareholder's death, the tax basis of the shares under Code section 1014 will be adjusted accordingly. However, if there is appreciation in the investment assets over the five-year period between sale of the assets by Zander Zorro, Inc. and the death of Alex, there will be some additional gain recognition at the corporate level on the sale and/or distribution of the assets under Code section 336(a)/311(b) principles.

Although this example is somewhat simplified in its assumptions, it illustrates the fact that even if the C corporation is subject to the PHC tax on its investment earnings, the net PHC tax (in light of the dividend tax rate of 15 percent) is relatively modest, and is basically dwarfed by the combined benefits of avoiding capital gain on liquidation of the corporation, coupled with the step-up in tax basis under Code section 1014.

Comment: This assumes that the estate tax remains a significant factor in the future and is not in fact abolished, and that the step-up in basis under Code section 1014 is not altered. Assume for the sake of simplicity that the estate tax on Alex's gross estate is imposed at a 50-percent tax rate and that the incremental value of the Zander Zorro, Inc. stock, and also the $8 million in cash assets, would be subject to this estate tax rate. After paying estate tax, the estate would be better off with $10 million in full-basis corporate stock (worth an after-estate-tax net of $5 million after paying a 50-percent estate tax) than with $8 million in cash (worth $4 million after paying the estate tax).

Scenario 7C: This is the same set of facts, except that the PHC invests in tax-exempt obligations, which produce income that is excluded from the computation of AOGI, and thus is not subject to current PHC tax. Under this scenario, $8 million invested by an individual at a five-percent tax-free return would generate $400,000 of tax-exempt income in each year. At the corporate level, meanwhile, $10 million invested at a five-percent tax-exempt return would generate $500,000 of tax exempt income, not subject to either ordinary income tax nor to the PHC penalty tax.

Comment: Depending on the nature of the tax-exempt obligations, the tax-exempt income may be a tax preference for the corporate alternative minimum tax pursuant to Code section 56(g), but in principle this alternative could potentially produce results that are even more favorable than the taxable investments described in Scenarios A and B.

Under this set of assumptions, over a period of five years the PHC would actually earn and retain more tax-exempt income than the shareholder because the corporation would be investing $10 million while the shareholder would be investing $8 million. Then, on the death of the shareholder, there would be a full step-up in tax basis of the stock to fair market value. Thus, for example, if Zander Zorro, Inc. started with $10 million and earned $500,000 in tax exempt income per year for five years, then, ignoring compounding of interest on reinvested interest, the corporation would have $12.5 million of assets ($10 million plus 5 × $500,000), and the fair market value of the stock in the hands of the estate would be stepped up to $12.5 million. This would ensure that the corporation would have substantially greater after-death value than the assets would have, after liquidation taxes, in the hands of the shareholder, and the after-tax advantage or "spread" would actually increase rather than decrease over the intervening years.

Converting to S Status as a Possible Alternative

Note that the PHC tax dilemma described in the preceding paragraphs does not exist for an S corporation that has always been an S corporation. In particular, the AE tax, the PHC tax, and the corporate AMT are all imposed solely on C corporations. Note, however, that an S corporation with former C corporation earnings and profits (this can occur if a corporation elects S status after previously operating as a C corporation) has the S corporation version of this dilemma. In particular, if an S corporation has Subchapter C earnings and profits and if more than 25 percent of that S corporation's gross receipts for a tax year constitute "passive investment income", as defined in Code section 1362(d)(3)(D) (likely to occur after the sale of all a corporation's business assets), the S corporation (1) will be subject to the so-called "sting tax" under Code section 1375 and (2) will lose its eligibility for S status after three such consecutive years under Code section 1362(d)(3). For an S corporation facing this dilemma, the solution may be for the S corporation to distribute out all of its prior C corporation earnings and profits as a taxable dividend, in which case neither Code section 1375 nor Code section 1362(d)(3) will apply. Since the capital gains tax rates and the tax rates on dividends are now the same, distributing a dividend can be a good "solution" to these problems.

Liquidating the C Corporation

If the shareholders of a C corporation elect to liquidate the corporation, the corporation itself will recognize taxable gain or loss pursuant to Code section 336(a) in amounts equal to the difference between the fair-market value of its assets and its tax basis in each such asset at the time of the liquidating distribution. (However, if a corporation has just sold substantially all of its assets for cash, the corporation's tax basis in its cash assets is likely to be almost exactly equal to the fair-market values of such assets. Therefore, the amount of gain recognized at the corporate level may be minimal.) In addition, there is a second tax recognition event at the shareholder level, and each shareholder will recognize capital gain or loss measured by the difference between the value of the distributed assets received and the share-holder's tax basis in the stock.[22] Long-term capital gains are currently taxed to individuals at a maximum 15-percent federal tax rate. Capital losses can be used by individuals to offset capital gains, and an additional $3,000 may be deducted each year against other income.[23] Any remaining capital losses recognized by such individual shareholders are carried forward to future years.[24]

HYPOTHETICAL SITUATIONS ILLUSTRATING HOW TO STRUCTURE A TAXABLE SALE OF ASSETS

The following are hypothetical situations designed to illustrate some of the important mathematical and computational elements of a taxable sale of assets by a C corporation.

Hypothetical Situation #1

Hypothetical Situation #1 is designed to provide a "baseline" for purposes of comparison. Hypothetical Situation #1 assumes that a Buyer seeks to purchase the assets of a C corporation for exactly $10 million. It assumes that the discount rate that the Buyer will use to evaluate deferred tax benefits and other time-value-of-money issues is 10 percent. With respect to tax rates, Hypothetical Situation #1 assumes a combined tax rate on corporate income of 40 percent (combining federal and state income taxes, and allowing a federal deduction for state taxes paid), a combined individual (state and federal) tax rate of 40 percent, and a combined individual (state and federal) long-term capital-gains tax rate of 20 percent. These are approximations, of course, but they are also the approximations that are commonly used by tax planners and forecasters in 2017.

Hypothetical Situation #1 assumes that the Seller will keep all its cash. Therefore, the $10 million purchase price is allocated to the following assets:

1. *Accounts receivable*. Seller is assumed to have accounts receivable with an original purchase price (i.e., face amount) of $400,000 and a

current tax basis of $400,000. It is assumed that the fair market value of these assets is also $400,000.

2. *Inventory*. It is assumed that the original purchase price (cost of acquiring or creating inventory) is $600,000, the current tax basis is $600,000, and the current fair market value is $600,000.

3. *Depreciable assets* (property such as desks, chairs, equipment, and any similar property used in the business). It is assumed that the original purchase price is $1,250,000, the current tax basis is $500,000 (reduced by $750,000 of depreciation deductions that previously have been claimed), and the current fair market value is $500,000, the same as the tax basis in such assets.

4. *Section 197 intangibles*. Hypothetical Situation #1 assumes the Seller has patents, trademarks, copyrights, software products, and various other Section 197 intangibles (excluding goodwill), with a total cost basis of $0 and a current fair market value of $2.5 million.

5. *Consulting and noncompete payments*. Hypothetical Situation #1 assumes that the parties will allocate some significant portion of the purchase price to individual payments for consulting services and noncompete covenants. Hypothetical Situation #1 assumes that the consulting payments will be $1.5 million, and the noncompete payments will total $500,000.

6. *Goodwill*. Goodwill is allocated the "residual" amount after allocating the rest of the $10 million purchase price to the other assets. In this example, goodwill is $4 million. It is assumed that the goodwill has no current tax basis.

Seller tax consequences. As the table demonstrates, based on these facts the Seller (a C corporation) will

Figure 4.1 summarizes the tax consequences of this proposed transaction:

Basic Tax Assumptions			
Aggregate purchase price of assets			$10,000,000.00
Assumed discounting rate			10.00%
Combined corporate tax rate			40.00%
Combined individual tax rate			40.00%
Combined individual long-term capital gain (LTCG) rate			20.00%
Approximated SE tax			3.00%
C Corporation Assets	*Original Purchase Price*	*Current Tax Basis*	*Current Fair Market Value*
A/R (Class III assets)	$400,000.00	$400,000.00	$400,000.00
Inventory (Class IV assets)	$600,000.00	$600,000.00	$600,000.00
Depreciable assets (Class V)	$1,250,000.00	$500,000.00	$500,000.00
Various Section 197 intangibles (excluding goodwill)	$0.00	$0.00	$2,500,000.00
Consulting ($500,000/yr. for 3 yrs.)			$1,500,000.00
Noncompete			$500,000.00
Non-goodwill total			$6,000,000.00
Goodwill	$0.00	$0.00	$4,000,000.00
Total	$2,250,000.00	$1,500,000.00	$10,000,000.00

Figure 4.1 (cont'd)

Tax Consequences to Selling C Corporation	
Corporation	***Asset Sale***
Purchase price	$8,000,000.00
Asset tax basis	$1,500,000.00
Net income or gain	$6,500,000.00
NOL	$0.00
Net taxable gain	$6,500,000.00
Tax (40%)	$2,600,000.00
Liquidating distribution	$5,400,000.00

Tax Consequences to Shareholders on C Corporation Liquidation	
Compensation to Shareholder	$1,500,000.00
Combined income and SE tax on comp (43%)	$645,000.00
Net compensation	$855,000.00
Noncompete payment	$500,000.00
Tax (40%)	$200,000.00
Net after-tax noncompete	$300,000.00
Distribution/payment	$5,400,000.00
Aggregate tax basis in stock	$100,000.00
Taxable gain	$5,300,000.00
Tax (20%)	$1,060,000.00
Net distribution to shareholders	$4,340,000.00
Total after tax benefit	$5,495,000.00

Tax Consequences to Buyer Asset Purchase

YEAR*	**1**	**2**	**3**	**4**	**5**	**6**
A/R	$400,000.00					
Depreciation	$100,000.00	$160,000.00	$96,000.00	$57,600.00	$57,600.00	$28,800.00
Inventory	$600,000.00					
Section 197 Intangibles	$166,666.67	$166,666.67	$166,666.67	$166,666.67	$166,666.67	$166,666.67
Consulting	$500,000.00	$500,000.00	$500,000.00			
Noncompete	$33,333.33	$33,333.33	$33,333.33	$33,333.33	$33,333.33	$33,333.33
Goodwill	$266,666.67	$266,666.67	$266,666.67	$266,666.67	$266,666.67	$266,666.67
Total annual tax deductions	$2,066,666.67	$1,126,666.67	$1,062,666.67	$524,266.67	$524,266.67	$495,466.67
Tax savings	$826,666.67	$450,666.67	$425,066.67	$209,706.67	$209,706.67	$198,186.67
Present value of tax savings	$751,515.15	$372,451.79	$319,358.88	$143,232.48	$130,211.34	$111,871.21
Total PV benefit	$2,435,460.35					
Total payments	$10,000,000.00					
Net after-tax cost	$7,564,539.65					

*This page shows the early years of a fifteen-year period, and shows total PV benefit for all fifteen years.

receive $8 million on the sale of its assets, while $2 million will be paid directly to the individual owners as consulting ($1,500,000) and noncompete ($500,000) payments. Because Seller has a total of $1.5 million of tax basis in its assets, it would have $6.5 million of net income or gain. Because there is no preferential corporate capital gains rate, the entire amount would be taxed at a combined 40-percent tax rate, producing $2.6 million of corporate-level tax. Therefore there will be $5.4 million in liquidating distributions (or dividends) from the Seller C corporation to its shareholders.

The owner-employees of Seller will receive compensation payments of $1.5 million. The Hypothetical Situation does not attempt (at this point in time) to factor in time-value-of-money considerations, but it does apply a 40-percent income tax rate and a three-percent SE tax (it does not attempt to adjust for the relatively minor effect of being able to deduct 1/2 of the SE tax when calculating adjusted gross income). The 43-percent effective tax rate on the $1.5 million produces $645,000 of tax. Accordingly, after-tax compensation amounts to $855,000.

The $500,000 in noncompete payments are subject to a tax rate of 40 percent, producing after-tax income of $300,000.

The third element of the tax analysis is the liquidating distribution of $5.4 million. Hypothetical Situation #1 assumes that the shareholders might have a $100,000 tax basis in their stock. This will produce a taxable gain of $5.3 million, and, assuming a tax rate to the shareholders on LTCG of 20 percent, the tax amount is $1,060,000. Therefore, the net distribution to the shareholders on an after-tax basis is $4,340,000.

The total after-tax amount enjoyed by shareholders is the sum of the after-tax compensation payment, the after-tax noncompete payment, and the after-tax distribution, a total of $5,495,000.

Buyer tax consequences. For the Buyer, the tax benefits are broken out to show the years in which various depreciation deductions are claimed. This analysis takes into account the present value of deferred tax benefits, using a 10-percent discount rate.

1. *Accounts receivable*. The Hypothetical Situation assumes that the $400,000 allocated to accounts receivable is recovered in the first year because receivables are typically collected in 30-180 days, and most or all are thus either collected or in serious risk of noncollection within one year.
2. *Inventory*. Inventory is one of the more interesting issues to discuss, but the spreadsheet assumes that the $600,000 paid for inventory is recovered by the Buyer in the first year, in part because if the inventory is not purchased then the Buyer would have to expend $600,000 almost immediately to build up the necessary inventory.
3. *Depreciable property*. The Class V assets are depreciated over five years (which, because of the mid-year convention used under Code section 168, means the deductions are spread over six tax years).
4. *Code section 197 intangibles*. Code section 197 intangibles are amortized ratably over fifteen years.
5. *Consulting and noncompete payments*. The consulting payments are deducted as paid, ratably over each of the first three years. The noncompete payments are subject to a fifteen-year amortization under Code section 197(d)(1)(E), as a covenant not to compete entered into in connection with the acquisition of an interest in a trade or business.
6. *Goodwill*. Goodwill is subject to fifteen-year amortization under Code section 197(d)(1)(A).

Although one can discuss and possibly debate whether one should treat expenditures to purchase accounts receivable and expenditures to purchase inventory as "deductions" producing "tax savings" in the first year, the spreadsheet assumes $10 million of tax expenditures, producing a "gross" tax savings of $4 million (at a 40-percent tax rate). Applying a present value analysis based on when these deductions are enjoyed by the Buyer, as shown on the spreadsheet, the net deemed tax savings of the proposed purchase price allocation is $2,435,460.35. Therefore, the after-tax cost of the purchase to the Buyer in Hypothetical Situation #1 is $7,564,539.65 ($10,000,000 paid minus the present-value of the tax savings, or $2,435,460.35).

Comment: Calculations of this sort produce amounts determined to the "penny". However, these calculations should not be viewed as "precise", even though they are "exact", because they simply represent the computationally precise results that come from using very approximate assumptions.

As a practical matter, the lesson one can discern from this Hypothetical Situation #1 is that the aggregate effective tax rate imposed on the Seller, based on the transactional structure and allocation and other assumptions described above, is about 45 percent, and thus leaves the Seller with a net present-value, after-tax benefit of about $5.5 million. Meanwhile, the Buyer enjoys approximately $2.5 million of present-value after-tax benefits and thus has a present-value, after-tax cost to acquire the assets in the range of $7.5 million.

Hypothetical Situation #2

Hypothetical Situation #2 is based on the same transactional structure as Hypothetical Situation #1, but demonstrates the consequences when various allocations are adjusted or modified. Hypothetical Situation #2 basically reverses the respective amounts allocated to consulting payments and to noncompete payments, by allocating $500,000 to consulting and $1.5 million to noncompete payments, to demonstrate and measure the effect.

Hypothetical Situation #2 demonstrates that the after-tax cost to the Buyer increases from $7,554,000 to $7,693,000, or an increase in estimated after-tax costs of approximately $140,000. Meanwhile, Hypothetical Situation #2 assumes that the owner-employee of the Seller is only saving an approximated three percent on the SE tax, and so the Seller Group's after-tax benefit adjusts upward by just $30,000 (to $5,525,000 from $5,495,000). This all makes intuitive sense because consulting payments are deducted by the Buyer as paid, while noncompete payments are amortized over fifteen years. Therefore, this reallocation logically results in a fairly substantial detriment to the Buyer ($1 million is going from deductible currently as paid to capitalized and amortized over fifteen years), while the Seller Group enjoys a very small reduction in the tax rate, from 43 percent to 40 percent, which reflects the approximate tax savings to the owner-employees of the Seller from being able to avoid the SE tax on $1 million of otherwise ordinary income. In substance, reallocating payment amounts from consulting payments to noncompete payments under these assumed facts substantially reduces the after-tax benefits to the Buyer, while providing a

Figure 4.2 summarizes the financial consequences of this transaction:

Basic Tax Assumptions			
Aggregate purchase price of assets			$10,000,000.00
Assumed discounting rate			10.00%
Combined corporate tax rate			40.00%
Combined individual tax rate			40.00%
Combined individual LTCG rate			20.00%
Approximated SE tax			3.00%
C Corporation Assets	*Original Purchase Price*	*Current Tax Basis*	*Current Fair Market Value*
A/R (Class III assets)	$400,000.00	$400,000.00	$400,000.00
Inventory (Class IV assets)	$600,000.00	$600,000.00	$600,000.00
Depreciable assets (Class V)	$1,250,000.00	$500,000.00	$500,000.00
Various Section 197 intangibles (excluding goodwill)	$0.00	$0.00	$2,500,000.00
Consulting ($166,666.67/yr. for 3 yrs.)			$500,000.00
Noncompete			$1,500,000.00
Non-goodwill total			$6,000,000.00
Goodwill	$0.00	$0.00	$4,000,000.00
Total	$2,250,000.00	$1,500,000.00	$10,000,000.00

Figure 4.2 (cont'd)

Tax Consequences to Selling C Corporation	
Corporation	***Asset Sale***
Purchase price	$8,000,000.00
Asset tax basis	$1,500,000.00
Net income or gain	$6,500,000.00
NOL	$0.00
Net taxable gain	$6,500,000.00
Tax (40%)	$2,600,000.00
Liquidating distribution	$5,400,000.00
Tax Consequences to Shareholders on C Corporation Liquidation	
Compensation to shareholder	$500,000.00
Combined income and SE tax on comp (43%)	$215,000.00
Net compensation	$285,000.00
Noncompete payment	$1,500,000.00
Tax (40%)	$600,000.00
Net after-tax noncompete	$900,000.00
Distribution/payment	$5,400,000.00
Aggregate tax basis in stock	$100,000.00
Taxable gain	$5,300,000.00
Tax (20%)	$1,060,000.00
Net distribution to shareholders	$4,340,000.00
Total after tax benefit	$5,525,000.00

Tax Consequences to Buyer Asset Purchase					
YEAR*	**1**	**2**	**3**	**4**	**5**
A/R	$400,000.00				
Depreciation	$100,000.00	$160,000.00	$96,000.00	$57,600.00	$57,600.00
Inventory	$600,000.00				
Section 197 intangibles	$166,666.67	$166,666.67	$166,666.67	$166,666.67	$166,666.67
Consulting	$166,666.67	$166,666.67	$166,666.67		
Noncompete	$100,000.00	$100,000.00	$100,000.00	$100,000.00	$100,000.00
Goodwill	$266,666.67	$266,666.67	$266,666.67	$266,666.67	$266,666.67
Total annual tax deductions	$1,800,000.00	$860,000.00	$796,000.00	$590,933.33	$590,933.33
Tax savings	$720,000.00	$344,000.00	$318,400.00	$236,373.33	$236,373.33
Present value of tax savings	$654,545.45	$284,297.52	$239,218.63	$161,446.17	$146,769.24
Total PV benefit	$2,306,708.87				
Total payments	$10,000,000.00				
Net after-tax cost	$7,693,291.13				

*This page shows the early years of a fifteen-year period, and shows total PV benefit for all fifteen years.

minimal benefit to the Seller Group. The net change is that the Buyer pays a lot more in after-tax purchase price in order for the Seller to enjoy a very modest benefit. The big winner in this scenario is the IRS which, on a present-value-after-tax basis, gains $140,000 from the Buyer and gives back $30,000 to the Seller, for a net gain of $110,000.

Comment: If the Seller's consulting payments were subject to full SE tax (including a 15.3-percent tax aggregate tax rate imposed on self-employment income up to the OASD maximum amount, which was $127,500 of net self-employment income in 2017), the tax savings to the Seller would be equal to 15.3 percent on the first $127,500, or approximately $19,500. Therefore, depending on how the consulting payments were structured (e.g., consulting payments paid over several years could potentially subject the owner-employees of the Seller to the full SE tax up to the OASD maximum amount in each of those years), the tax savings to the Seller Group from such a reallocation can become far more significant than the three-percent savings shown in Hypothetical Situation #2. In fact, in smaller transactions where the annual consulting payments are modest (e.g., at or below the $127,500 annual amount subject to the maximum SE tax rate of 15.3 percent), the reallocation of purchase price from consulting payments to noncompete payments may make more sense. However, because there is always a significant detriment to Buyer in capitalizing and amortizing expenses over fifteen years, it is a relatively specific and unusual situation where this type of "reallocation" would result in a net tax savings between the Buyer and Seller Group.

Hypothetical Situation #3

Hypothetical Situation #3 assumes that the discounting rate is set at 15 percent, rather than at 10 percent, and illustrates the fact that the Buyer (or the decision-makers for the Buyer) can sometimes place a relatively low value on tax deductions ten to fifteen years down

Figure 4.3 summarizes the financial consequences of this transaction:

Basic Tax Assumptions			
Aggregate purchase price of assets			$10,000,000.00
Assumed discounting rate			15.00%
Combined corporate tax rate			40.00%
Combined individual tax rate			40.00%
Combined individual LTCG rate			20.00%
Approximated SE tax			3.00%
C Corporation Assets	*Original Purchase Price*	*Current Tax Basis*	*Current Fair Market Value*
A/R (Class III assets)	$400,000.00	$400,000.00	$400,000.00
Inventory (Class IV assets)	$600,000.00	$600,000.00	$600,000.00
Depreciable assets (Class V)	$1,250,000.00	$500,000.00	$500,000.00
Various Section 197 intangibles (excluding goodwill)	$0.00	$0.00	$2,500,000.00
Consulting ($500,000/yr. for 3 yrs.)			$1,500,000.00
Noncompete			$500,000.00
Non-goodwill total			$6,000,000.00
Goodwill	$0.00	$0.00	$4,000,000.00
Total	$2,250,000.00	$1,500,000.00	$10,000,000.00

Figure 4.3 (cont'd)

Tax Consequences to Selling C Corporation	
Corporation	***Asset Sale***
Purchase price	$8,000,000.00
Asset tax basis	$1,500,000.00
Net income or gain	$6,500,000.00
NOL	$0.00
Net taxable gain	$6,500,000.00
Tax (40%)	$2,600,000.00
Liquidating distribution	$5,400,000.00
Tax Consequences to Shareholders on C Corporation Liquidation	
Compensation to shareholder	$1,500,000.00
Combined income and SE tax on comp (43%)	$645,000.00
Net compensation	$855,000.00
Noncompete payment	$500,000.00
Tax (40%)	$200,000.00
Net after-tax noncompete	$300,000.00
Distribution/payment	$5,400,000.00
Aggregate tax basis in stock	$100,000.00
Taxable gain	$5,300,000.00
Tax (20%)	$1,060,000.00
Net distribution to shareholders	$4,340,000.00
Total after tax benefit	$5,495,000.00

Tax Consequences to Buyer Asset Purchase

YEAR*	1	2	3	4	5
A/R	$400,000.00				
Depreciation	$100,000.00	$160,000.00	$96,000.00	$57,600.00	$57,600.00
Inventory	$600,000.00				
Section 197 intangibles	$166,666.67	$166,666.67	$166,666.67	$166,666.67	$166,666.67
Consulting	$500,000.00	$500,000.00	$500,000.00		
Noncompete	$33,333.33	$33,333.33	$33,333.33	$33,333.33	$33,333.33
Goodwill	$266,666.67	$266,666.67	$266,666.67	$266,666.67	$266,666.67
Total annual tax deductions	$2,066,666.67	$1,126,666.67	$1,062,666.67	$524,266.67	$524,266.67
Tax savings	$826,666.67	$450,666.67	$425,066.67	$209,706.67	$209,706.67
Present value of tax savings	$718,840.58	$340,768.75	$279,488.23	$119,900.47	$104,261.28
Total PV benefit	$2,034,013.18				
Total payments	$10,000,000.00				
Net after-tax cost	$7,965,986.82				

*This page shows the early years of a fifteen-year period, and shows total PV benefit for all fifteen years.

the road, and in effect may look at the "horizon" of the transaction as merely the next five to seven years.

This Hypothetical Situation #3 shows that compared to Hypothetical Situation #1, the present value of the aggregate tax savings drops from approximately $2,435,000 to $2,034,000, or a drop of more than $400,000 in the "value" of these deferred tax savings for the Buyer.

Comment: In the author's experience, the CFO of an acquiring company once insisted on using an 18-percent discounting rate for determining the present value of future tax benefits in an acquisition by his company. His explanation— candidly disarming but also revealing—was that "I don't expect to be here five years from now, so why should I care about tax deductions in the year 2030?" The point is that present value assumptions of a Buyer and Seller are ultimately unique and personal, and, in many deals, will diverge significantly, and perhaps even dramatically, because the Buyer and the Seller have very different interests and objectives, including how they value (and present value) deferred tax benefits.

Comment: A higher discount rate could also be used by the Buyer as a means for reflecting risk as to whether the Buyer will continue to be a profitable taxpayer and thus able to utilize future tax benefits. In particular, if a Buyer has concerns about the ability to generate net taxable income in each of the next fifteen years (which is a prerequisite for enjoying deferred tax deductions), a mechanism that takes this concern into account could be a higher discount rate.

Hypothetical Situation #4

Hypothetical Situation #4 illustrates the strategy of "pushing the envelope" to try and enhance the tax benefits to both parties. The parties will treat the depreciable assets as having a fair market value of $1 million,

Figure 4.4 summarizes the financial consequences of this transaction:

Basic Tax Assumptions			
Aggregate purchase price of assets			$10,000,000.00
Assumed discounting rate			10.00%
Combined corporate tax rate			40.00%
Combined individual tax rate			40.00%
Combined individual LTCG rate			20.00%
Approximated SE tax			3.00%
C Corporation Assets	*Original Purchase Price*	*Current Tax Basis*	*Current Fair Market Value*
A/R (Class III assets)	$400,000.00	$400,000.00	$400,000.00
Inventory (Class IV assets)	$600,000.00	$600,000.00	$600,000.00
Depreciable assets (Class V)	$1,250,000.00	$500,000.00	$1,000,000.00
Various Section 197 intangibles (excluding goodwill)	$0.00	$0.00	$2,500,000.00
Consulting ($1,000,000/yr. for 3 yrs.)			$3,000,000.00
Noncompete			$500,000.00
Non-goodwill total			$8,000,000.00
Goodwill	$0.00	$0.00	$2,000,000.00
Total	$2,250,000.00	$1,500,000.00	$10,000,000.00

Figure 4.4 (cont'd)

Tax Consequences to Selling C Corporation	
Corporation	***Asset Sale***
Purchase price	$6,500,000.00
Asset tax basis	$1,500,000.00
Net income or gain	$5,000,000.00
NOL	$0.00
Net taxable gain	$5,000,000.00
Tax (40%)	$2,000,000.00
Liquidating distribution	$4,500,000.00
Tax Consequences to Shareholders on C Corporation Liquidation	
Compensation to shareholder	$3,000,000.00
Combined income and SE tax on comp (43%)	$1,290,000.00
Net compensation	$1,710,000.00
Noncompete payment	$500,000.00
Tax (40%)	$200,000.00
Net after-tax noncompete	$300,000.00
Distribution/payment	$4,500,000.00
Aggregate tax basis in stock	$100,000.00
Taxable gain	$4,400,000.00
Tax (20%)	$880,000.00
Net distribution to shareholders	$3,620,000.00
Total after tax benefit	$5,630,000.00

Tax Consequences to Buyer Asset Purchase

YEAR*	1	2	3	4	5
A/R	$400,000.00				
Depreciation	$200,000.00	$200,000.00	$200,000.00	$200,000.00	$200,000.00
Inventory	$600,000.00				
Section 197 Intangibles	$166,666.67	$166,666.67	$166,666.67	$166,666.67	$166,666.67
Consulting	$1,000,000.00	$1,000,000.00	$1,000,000.00		
Noncompete	$33,333.33	$33,333.33	$33,333.33	$33,333.33	$33,333.33
Goodwill	$266,666.67	$266,666.67	$266,666.67	$266,666.67	$266,666.67
Total annual tax deductions	$2,666,666.67	$1,666,666.67	$1,666,666.67	$666,666.67	$666,666.67
Tax savings	$1,066,666.67	$666,666.67	$666,666.67	$266,666.67	$266,666.67
Present value of tax savings	$969,696.97	$550,964.19	$500,876.53	$182,136.92	$165,579.02
Total PV benefit	$3,126,599.52				
Total payments	$10,000,000.00				
Net after-tax cost	$6,873,400.48				

*This page shows the early years of a fifteen-year period, and shows total PV benefit for all fifteen years.

rather than assigning the current tax basis of $500,000. (This reallocation will help the Buyer by permitting it to depreciate an extra $500,000 of the purchase price over five years rather than fifteen years.) The parties also aggressively push money from goodwill to consulting payments, by doubling the consulting payment to $3 million, payable $1 million per year over three years.

As one would expect, both parties come out ahead by aggressively pushing these mutually beneficial allocations. The after-tax benefit to the Seller increases to $5,630,000, an after-tax increase in benefits of $135,000, while the Buyer reduces its after-tax cost to $6,873,000, an after-tax reduction of almost $700,000.

Comments on Hypothetical Situation #4. Pushing an extra $500,000 of the purchase price from goodwill to Class V assets increases the benefit to the Buyer by allowing the Buyer more to depreciate over a five-year period instead of a fifteen-year period. Meanwhile, because the Seller is a C corporation and has no tax rate advantage between ordinary income and capital gain (other than foregoing the relatively limited benefit of being able to offset capital gains against capital losses), the Seller does not increase its tax liabilities as a result of the Code section 1245 recapture income being characterized as ordinary income rather than capital gain.

Likewise, pushing payments from goodwill to consulting payments has a favorable impact on the Buyer because consulting payments can be deducted currently instead of being amortized ratably over fifteen years under Code section 197 and it also reduces the Seller's tax costs significantly by eliminating double taxation on the payments (the reallocated amount is taxed a single time at an estimated 43-percent rate).

The purpose of this reallocation exercise, of course, is not to assert that aggressive allocations are defensible (all allocations have to ultimately be defended as "reasonable" for tax purposes), but rather to show the obvious mathematical and computational benefits of making allocations to certain categories of assets and away from others.

Summary

These Hypothetical Situations demonstrate some of the fundamental allocation strategies in an asset sale, which can be summarized as follows:

- The Buyer usually benefits from being able to write off deductions right away (e.g., as compensation or consulting payments) and thereby avoid the substantial deferral of benefit resulting from an allocation to goodwill (amortizable over fifteen years).

- When the Seller is a C corporation, the Seller Group benefits from an allocation to compensation or consulting because it avoids double taxation of the income.

- A reallocation of purchase price to property depreciable over five years instead of fifteen years benefits the Buyer quite significantly and makes no difference to the Seller. A selling C corporation does not care whether it has ordinary income (including recapture income in this case under Code section 1245) or capital gain because both are taxed at the same rate.

- Valuations are always subject to a requirement of reasonableness, and to the accuracy-related penalties of the Code, which the IRS has indicated will be enforced with increased vigor in the future. However, within the range of discretionary valuation allocations (and the fair market value of any asset, other than perhaps publicly traded assets or commodities, is always to some degree a judgment call), it obviously makes a difference how purchase price is allocated within the permissible boundaries of Code section 1060.

CHAPTER ENDNOTES

1. See discussion in Chapter 3.
2. IRC Sec. 1060.
3. Reg. § 1.1060-1(c)(3).
4. Compare IRC Sec. 11 with IRC Sec. 1(h).
5. IRC Sec. 1211(a).
6. IRC Sec. 1212(a)(1).
7. *Id.*
8. IRC Sec. 1231(a)(2).
9. See also the further discussion of this issue below and in Chapter 14.
10. IRC Secs. 531-537.
11. IRC Sec. 531.
12. IRC Sec. 535(a).
13. Rev. Rul. 70-497, 1970-2 CB 128.

14. IRC Sec. 534(b).
15. IRC Sec. 534(c).
16. IRC Secs. 535(c) and 537.
17. Reg. § 1.537-1(a).
18. IRC Sec. 532(b)(1).
19. IRC Sec. 542(a).
20. IRS Letter Ruling 8706022.
21. IRC Sec. 545(a).
22. IRC Sec. 331.
23. IRC Sec. 1211(b).
24. IRC Sec. 1212(b).

TAXABLE PURCHASES OF C CORPORATION STOCK

CHAPTER 5

OVERVIEW

Chapter 4 examined the tax and other business consequences of acquiring a business through the purchase of a Target C corporation's assets.

Chapter 5 now explores the alternative structure of acquiring the business by purchasing all of the Target C corporation's stock. A stock purchase may be chosen over an asset purchase because of a variety of common transaction factors, including the following:

1. First, the "numbers" (i.e., the present-value, after-tax analysis) may suggest that the optimum structure for both parties is a stock sale (at an appropriately adjusted price) rather than an asset sale. In particular, the shareholders of the Target may find that double taxation on a sale of the Target's assets produces a lower after-tax benefit than a stock sale, even if the stock purchase price offered the Buyer is lower than the offered price for an asset purchase.

2. Second, the Sellers and/or Buyers may bring special tax attributes to the table that make a stock sale attractive. For example, the shareholders of the Target may have huge capital losses that militate in favor of maximum capital gains, or a Target may have large net operating losses (NOLs) that can be used to obtain a step-up in basis through a Code section 338 election.

3. Third, the Target may have contracts or other valuable property rights that cannot be assigned or transferred easily without the consent of a third party, but which can be acquired without third-party consent as part of a stock purchase.

4. Fourth, the "purchase price" for the Target may include significant payments directly to an individual owner of the Target, such as consulting or noncompete payments. This combination, coupled with a lower stock price, may provide the best overall arrangement for the parties.

In general, when an acquisition is structured as a stock purchase, the stock is almost always classified as a capital asset in the hands of the selling shareholders under Code section 1221. Moreover, if stock has been held by the Target shareholders for more than one year (almost always the case for at least some shareholders), the gains are taxed at a maximum federal capital gains tax rate of 15 percent (20 percent for certain high-income taxpayers). The Target itself does not recognize income or gain on a stock purchase transaction. The Buyer, meanwhile, allocates the purchase price (and the resulting tax basis) to the Target stock, and generally (subject to certain elections under Code section 338 discussed below) such a purchase structure does not allow the Buyer to increase the tax basis in the Target's underlying business assets. In most cases, a Buyer generally would prefer to have tax basis in the Target's assets rather than in the Target stock, but this "general" observation is always subject to the caveat that the Buyer, in the end, wants to acquire the Target for the lowest present-value, after-tax purchase price. Therefore, a Buyer will choose a stock purchase over an asset purchase if the "price is right".

As purely a nontax, risk-avoidance measure, the Buyer will often want to acquire the Target's business without also acquiring the historic operating liabilities of the Target, a stock acquisition is often unattractive because it brings with it the risks of the Target's prior operating history. However, as previously noted, there can be business reasons why a Buyer might strongly prefer to purchase stock rather than assets. For example, a stock purchase may permit the Buyer to avoid the often protracted process of obtaining third-party consent for the sale of the Target's assets (e.g., from a customer of the Target with whom the Target has a lucrative contract that requires the consent of both parties to be assigned) or to avoid triggering adverse contract clauses (e.g., cancellation of franchise agreements, favorable leases, or borrowings on favorable lending terms). Also, a Seller may be willing to take a sufficiently lower price for a sale of stock (e.g., because the transaction is taxed once at capital gains tax rates) that it more than compensates the Buyer for the combined effects of additional risks and/or loss of tax benefits.

Another factor, of which the author is increasingly aware, is that Buyers often find the process of transferring and retitling business assets to be slow, onerous, and expensive. For example, in an asset sale, not only are there valuable contract rights and other rights that may require third-party consents, but even the pedestrian process of completing a title transfer of conventional assets can be expensive and time consuming. A Target that engages in the construction business, for example, may have dozens or even hundreds of vehicles that need to be registered and transferred at the registry of motor vehicles. Governmental operating rights, or grandfathered environmental or zoning rights, or a host of other (generally nontax) business factors can also militate in favor of an "easy" stock acquisition.

The beauty of a stock purchase is that it is simple to implement; the drawback, of course, is that the parties must negotiate (often in painstaking detail) the allocation of risk with respect to existing Target liabilities, both known and unknown. A Buyer will generally require a significant "hold back" or indemnification escrow as a form of security against undisclosed risks. However, the author is aware of Buyers who have reached the conclusion that the combination of a good due diligence process, coupled with a strong indemnity provision and a substantial hold back of purchase price through an indemnity escrow, is the fastest, easiest way to get a "good" deal done. (A "good" deal in this context is one where, as it turns out, there was no material additional undisclosed liability. This is, unfortunately, something that is usually known only in hindsight.)

There is always significant tension between the interests of the Buyer and Seller in an acquisition transaction, and resolving that tension successfully is called a negotiation. Figuring out how best to structure a transaction—and whether it can be done at all under terms acceptable to both sides—is the art of getting a deal closed.

There can be special circumstances where a sale of stock by the Seller is treated other than as a capital gains transaction. These include transactions involving a Seller who makes a market in the stock being sold, and sales of so-called "Section 306 stock". These special circumstances are discussed later in this chapter.

As we examined in detail in Chapter 4, an acquisition of C corporation assets, especially from a closely held C corporation, inexorably leads to structuring payments directly to the Target owners. Likewise, a stock purchase where the Target is a closely held C corporation owned by individuals active in the business can favor direct payments to these individuals. These payments can include consulting payments, wages, and noncompete payments (sometimes referred to in this book as "personal payments"), but can also include such things as rent payments for the leasing of real estate retained by the Target owners, payments for the rental or licensing of other property used in or related to the acquired business, and various other payment arrangements that allow the acquirer to make a payment to the individual owners of the Target (sometimes referred to in this book as "parallel payments").

The tax characteristic of personal payments and parallel payments is that they may permit an individual owner of a C corporation to receive a direct payment (usually, but not always, in a form categorized as ordinary income) subject to a tax rate that is higher than capital gains but lower than the double taxation imposed on C corporation income or gain, while allowing the Buyer to enjoy a tax deduction or other tax benefit more valuable to the Buyer than tax basis in the Target assets or the Target stock.

> ***Example 1:*** The Buyer is willing to pay \$1 million in after-tax money for a business that involves the rendering of personal services (e.g., a consulting business). Assume the Target business has a single shareholder who is the principal manager and employee of the business and who has been operating the consulting business through a C corporation. If the Buyer purchases stock of the Target corporation and views the resulting tax basis in the stock as having almost zero present value (a not-unreasonable conclusion), the purchase price would be \$1 million (because the Buyer enjoys zero tax benefits,

he or she will not pay more than $1 million). Meanwhile, assuming the Seller has held the stock for more than one year and thus will have to pay an effective capital gains tax rate of 15 percent (assuming no state income taxes), the Seller nets $850,000.

Example 2: Assuming that the Buyer can justify a substantial allocation of purchase price to consulting payments to the principal individual owning the Target (a very likely scenario in the sale of a consulting business), it might be possible to allocate $350,000 to an acquisition of the Target stock and $1 million to consulting payments or wages paid over the first two years to the sole owner of the Target. Assume that the Buyer is in the 35-percent tax bracket for federal income tax purposes (and no state taxes) and can deduct $1 million of consulting payments in the first two years. Ignoring for the moment the time-value-of-money adjustments, the Buyer will save the effective federal income tax rate of 35 percent multiplied by the $1 million in deductible consulting or wage payments, which would represent $350,000 in tax savings. Thus, after paying $1,350,000 to acquire the Target, and enjoying $350,000 in tax benefits, the Buyer's net after-tax cost would be $1 million, as it was in Example 1.

The Target owner, meanwhile, receives $1 million of consulting payments for his services and $350,000 for the Target stock. Assuming the Target owner is subject to a 35-percent federal income tax rate on the consulting income, this results in after-tax income to the Target owner of $650,000. Assuming the $350,000 paid for the stock is taxed at a 15-percent long-term capital gains tax rate, the tax is $52,500, and the after-tax gain on the stock sale is $297,500 (i.e., $350,000 – $52,500). Therefore, the net after-tax benefit to the owner of the Target in Example 2 is $650,000 + $297,500 = $947,500. Clearly, this is better than the $850,000 after-tax amount in Example 1. Moreover, the Target owner also might have NOLs or active business losses that could reduce or offset the $1 million in consulting payments. In addition, the Target owner is now engaged in a consulting business that can often "absorb" various business costs and expenses, such as travel, entertainment, automobiles, and so forth.

The comparison of the tax results between Example 1 and Example 2 illustrates what is sometimes a shocking epiphany to parties structuring taxable trans-actions—ordinary income can be better for Sellers than capital gain! Everyone assumes that the selling shareholders "want" capital gain, but in fact the principal beneficiary of a capital gains transaction is the IRS.

Illustration: Assume the Buyer and selling shareholders are both in the same tax bracket for federal income tax purposes (e.g., 35 percent). Assume first that the Buyer purchases stock of the Target and selling shareholders are paid $1 million, subject to long-term capital gains (15 percent) to the Sellers, and producing no significant tax benefit to the Buyer. The IRS comes out ahead by $150,000 ($1,000,000 × 15 percent). As an alternative, assume the same parties can justify an allocation of $1 million to reasonable consulting payments. The Sellers will pay tax on $1 million at ordinary income tax rates, but the Buyer will now have a current tax deduction of $1 million, and will save in current taxes approximately the same amount that the Sellers will owe (each will own, or save, respectively, 35 percent × $1,000,000). Thus, the IRS ends up "net zero", with $350,000 in additional taxes from the Seller, but $350,000 in lower taxes paid by the Buyer. Obviously, if the IRS is taking $150,000 less in net taxes from the two parties, it stands to reason that the parties can figure out how to structure their transaction to mutually benefit from this net reduction in taxes.

The "sharing" of tax benefits by the parties to an acquisition transaction is an interesting and curious exercise that deserves a brief discussion. In the real world, parties often strike an initial arrangement, such as Example 1, and then later identify a better alternative, such as Example 2. If the parties have come to view Example 1 as "the deal", the parties will often agree to "split" the additional tax savings of a better arrangement between them.

Example 2 produces more after-tax benefit to the Target owner and no additional cost to the Buyer. This is because the parties have figured out how to cut the allocation to the third (albeit invisible) party to the deal, the federal government. However, as a deal progresses, it is not unusual for one party to propose a better alternative and for the other party to expect "something" in return, whether in cash, tax savings, tax benefits (a form of cash), or in kind.

Conversely, if the better tax-planning alternative is on the table from the outset, the tax benefits are less likely to be the subject of "splitting" by the parties. To illustrate, if the selling shareholders propose Example 2 at or near the outset of negotiations, the Buyer may (or may not) accept the proposal. If the Buyer accepts the proposal, the Buyer is less likely to expect a "share" of the tax savings because there is no standard against which to measure the "new" proposal, (i.e., there is no Example 1). In general (at least in the author's experience), the longer Example 1 is on the table as the structuring paradigm for the transaction, and the later Example 2 is broached as an alternative, the more likely the tax savings will be split between the parties.

SUMMARY OF TAX CONSEQUENCES TO STOCK SELLER

In a taxable stock purchase, the shareholders of the Target have a taxable disposition under Code section 1001 and will "realize" an amount equal to the difference between what is realized from the sale over the adjusted tax basis provided in Code section 1011. The amount realized from the sale is the sum of any money received plus the fair market value of any property (other than money) received.[1] The amount "recognized" on such a sale will be the amount "realized" under the foregoing rules, unless nonrecognition treatment of some or all of the transaction is provided elsewhere in the Code.[2]

To the extent the sale transaction is eligible for reporting on the installment method, gain or loss attributable to any installment payment in a tax year will be determined under Code section 453.[3] A sale of corporate stock can generally be reported on the installment method except if (1) the promissory notes received by the Seller are demand notes or are readily tradable or (2) the Target stock is traded on an established securities market.[4] However, if the transaction involves a large installment sale (generally a sale where the principal of the installment note exceeds $5 million), the deferred tax amount is subject to a current "interest" charge determined annually under Code section 453A. If the sales price (the amount realized) is contingent or is fixed and determined by events after the close of the tax year of sale, the transaction will also be governed by the rules under Code section 453 applicable to contingent payment arrangements. These installment sale rules are discussed in detail in Chapter 10.

In connection with an installment sale of eligible (nonpublicly traded) stock, if the Buyer pays part of the consideration in nonpublicly traded notes that do not state adequate interest under the rules established under Code section 1274, the installment sale will be further modified by the related original issue discount (OID) rules, which generally discount and re-determine the principal amount of the note to reflect an increase in the interest rate (to the minimum interest rate permitted under Code section 1274(d)) and a corresponding decrease in principal amount. These recomputed interest and principal amounts will then be used to determine the amounts of interest (or OID) and the amounts of principal (subject to installment reporting under the applicable rules) deemed paid by the Buyer and recognized by the selling shareholders in each year.

Shares of stock, whether or not publicly traded, will generally be a capital asset in the hands of the selling shareholders, pursuant to Code section 1221, unless the stock is considered an inventory asset in the hands of the Seller (i.e., because the Seller is engaged in the trade or business of making a market in the stock). As noted above, the capital gain tax rates imposed on individuals (currently a maximum of 20 percent) compare favorably to the tax rates imposed on other categories of income, including the double taxation that would apply to an asset sale by a C corporation. (However, as noted above, capital gains to the selling shareholders often produces little or no tax benefit to the Buyer, and may, in the aggregate, produce a worse tax result than a different acquisition structure providing greater benefits to the Buyer.)

Obviously, a stock purchase can involve, as part of the larger transaction, personal payments or parallel payments to a shareholder in the capacity as an employee, director, and/or owner of other property used by or related to the corporate business and owned individually by such person. Thus, even though a stock purchase is nominally the acquisition of the entire business of the corporation, there can be other categories of payments among which the "total consideration" for the acquisition can be allocated.

Code section 306 contains special anti-abuse rules that address so-called preferred stock bailouts. A preferred stock bailout occurs when a shareholder receives a tax-free stock distribution of preferred stock, which is then sold. Code section 306 views this combination of transactions as the equivalent of a dividend, and therefore characterizes the sale of "Section 306 stock" as dividend income to the extent the amount would have been a dividend if the distributing corporation had distributed cash equal to the fair market value of the Section 306 stock. The Code section 306 provisions do not apply if the shareholder sells all of his or her stock, including the Section 306 stock, in the same transaction to an unrelated shareholder.[5] Therefore, Code section 306 generally does not raise problems in a sale of an entire business to an unrelated purchaser. Because under current law, dividends are taxed at the same rate (15 percent) as long-term capital gains, the adverse consequences of Section 306 stock have been greatly reduced (for the moment). Be aware, however, that dividend treatment could still potentially raise withholding tax issues under Code section 1441 for a sale by a non-U.S. taxpayer.

TAX CONSEQUENCES TO THE TARGET CORPORATION

The Buyer (or the Buyer in conjunction with the selling shareholder(s)), can make an election under Code section 338 under certain circumstances to structure a business acquisition as a purchase of stock for corporate purposes but to treat the transaction for federal income tax purposes as a sale of assets to a newly formed corporation occurring either immediately prior to the sale of the Target to the Buyer (in the case of a Code section 338(h)(10) election) or immediately after the sale (in the case of a regular Section 338 election). The requirements, mechanics and strategies of making such elections are discussed in Chapter 12.

Except in the case of an election under Code section 338, the Target itself does not recognize gain or loss on a sale of stock by its shareholders, and the Target's tax basis in its assets remains the same before and after the stock purchase. Likewise, the Target's other tax attributes remain the same as before the acquisition, including such corporate-level tax items or attributes as earnings and profits, tax credits, NOLs, and capital loss carryforwards. However, there are a number of Code provisions that if triggered by the factual circumstances surrounding the stock sale, can limit the Target's ability to use its net operating losses, capital loss carryforwards, and tax credit carryforwards following the stock purchase. The provisions that can limit the tax attributes of the post-acquisition Target include Code sections 269, 382, and 383, discussed briefly below and in great detail in Chapter 13.

SUMMARY OF TAX CONSEQUENCES TO THE STOCK BUYER

Buyer's Tax Basis in the Target

In the absence of an election under Code section 338 (discussed in detail in Chapter 12), the Buyer generally takes a tax basis in purchased stock equal to the "cost" of the property (i.e., the purchase price paid).[6] The Target retains its existing tax basis in its own assets and likewise retains its other tax attributes, including earnings and profits, tax credits, NOLs, capital loss carryforwards, and other corporate-level attributes. The purchase price paid for stock is often very easy to determine, although payment of part or all of the consideration on a deferred basis using the installment method can sometimes result in purchase-price adjustments under the installment sale rules and/or the OID rules.[7] By contrast, the purchase price/tax basis computations when there is a Code section 338 election, particularly a Code section 338(h)(10) election, are infamously complicated and are discussed in detail in Chapter 12.

Post-Acquisition Liquidation of the Target by the Corporate Acquirer: Code sections 332 and 337

The general rule is that a complete liquidation of a corporation is taxable at two levels: (1) at the level of the liquidating corporation, as a disposition of assets at fair market value (Code section 336(a)) and (2) at the shareholder level, as the equivalent of a sale or exchange of the shareholder's stock in exchange for the liquidating proceeds.[8] However, several Code provisions combine to override this general rule, in specific circumstances, to permit a parent corporation, including in some cases the new corporate parent of a newly acquired Target corporation, to liquidate a subsidiary corporation without triggering tax recognition.[9] Together, these provisions allow a corporate parent to unwind or "reverse" on a tax-free basis a prior tax-free contribution of assets to a subsidiary corporation under Code section 351. In most cases, these provisions are also available to an Acquiring Corporation, subject to limitations under Code section 269(b), discussed below.

Code Section 332

Code section 332(a) provides the very broad general statement that "[n]o gain or loss shall be recognized on the receipt by a corporation of property distributed in complete liquidation of another corporation". However, Code section 332(b) requires that all of the following must be present for nonrecognition treatment:

1. The corporation receiving the liquidating distribution must be the owner of stock (of the liquidating corporation) meeting the requirements of Code section 1504(a)(2) (the parent must own stock that possesses at least 80 percent of the total voting power of the liquidating corporation's stock and that has a value equal to at least 80 percent of the total value of the liquidating corporation's stock; a parent meeting this criteria is sometimes referred to as an "80-80 corporation").

2. The liquidating corporation must cancel or redeem all of its stock.

3. The transfer and distribution of all property must occur within the specified statutory time periods.

Carryover Tax Basis under Code Sections 332 and 334(b)(1)

Code section 334(b)(1) provides that if property is received by a corporate distributee in a distribution in a complete liquidation to which Code section 332 applies, the tax basis of the distributed property in the hands of the distributee will be the same as it would be in the hands of the transferor; except that the tax basis in the hands of the distributee will be the fair market value of the distributed property at the time of the distribution if either (1) gain or loss is recognized by the transferor on the distribution, or (2) the transferor is a foreign corporation, the distributee is a domestic corporation, and the distributee's adjusted basis in the property distributed exceeds the fair market value of the property.[10] This general rule means that an 80-80 corporation's tax basis in the subsidiary is eliminated and essentially thrown away, which can be particularly detrimental if the tax basis in the stock is relatively high because of a recent acquisition.

Example 3: Assume the Acquirer purchases all the stock of the Target for $1 million, assume the assets of the Target were worth $1 million of fair market value on the acquisition date, and assume that the Target's tax basis in its assets was $200,000. Assume further that, shortly after the acquisition, and before a liquidation of the Target, the fair market value of the Target's assets is decreased, due to market fluctuations in value, to $900,000. Pursuant to a Section 332 liquidation of the Target, the Acquirer would not recognize a $100,000 loss (even though stock with $1 million of tax basis is being surrendered for assets with a fair market value of $900,000) but instead the Acquirer would hold the assets of the Target after the liquidating distribution with a carryover tax basis of $200,000 (i.e., the tax basis of the property in the hands of the liquidating subsidiary). On a subsequent sale of those assets (assuming no further fluctuations in value) for $900,000, the Acquirer would recognize $700,000 of gain. Thus, the difference in tax basis between the $1 million paid by the Acquirer for the stock of the Target, and the $200,000 carryover tax basis from Target following the Section 332 liquidation, or $800,000 of tax basis, disappears permanently.

Example 4: Assume the same facts as in Example 3, except that the Acquirer purchases the Target stock at what turns out to be a bargain price of $1 million, the Target has $1.3 million of tax basis in its assets, and its assets have a fair market value of $1.2 million. On a prompt Section 332 liquidation immediately after the acquisition (at a time when there has been no change in the fair market value of Target's assets), the Acquirer would succeed to the $1.3 million of tax basis in the property in the hands of the transferor (i.e., the liquidating Target). Thus, on these facts, the Acquirer, having paid $1 million for a Target with assets worth $1.2 million, not only will avoid the $200,000 of built-in gain but will also have a tax loss of $100,000 if the Target assets are sold immediately following the liquidation.[11]

Stuck with Code Section 332 Treatment

As these two examples illustrate, the combination of Code sections 332, 334(b), and 337(a) (stating that no gain or loss is recognized by the liquidating corporation on the distribution of property to an 80-80 corporation in a complete liquidation governed by Code section 332) is that the acquisition price paid by an Acquirer is basically disregarded, and the Acquirer takes the tax basis of the

Target (together with the Target's other tax attributes, thanks to Code section 381). Where, as is often the case, an Acquirer has paid fair market value to purchase stock of a Target with low tax basis in its assets, the results are often both unfair and unavoidable.

Code section 332 is not on its face an elective provision; hence it applies even if the Acquirer, the Target, or both would prefer not to have it apply. As will be examined below and in greater detail in Chapter 12, one remedy for this situation is for the 80-80 parent to make an election under Code section 338 and gain the benefit of higher tax basis at the price of a self-inflicted hypothetical sale. However, as the Tax Court has pointed out, although Code section 332 is mandatory on its face, a smart parent corporation (or savvy Acquirer) can also structure the transaction to fail the pre-conditions for Code section 332, and thus convert the liquidation into a fully taxable transaction.[12]

Liquidating Distribution Governed by Code Section 332 Is Nonetheless Taxable to Minority Shareholders

It is possible to have a Code section 332 liquidation where the "parent" owns the requisite amount of stock to be an 80-80 corporation but does not own all the stock of the subsidiary. In that case, the shareholders other than the 80-80 corporation will not be eligible for tax-free distribution treatment under Code section 332 and will recognize taxable gain (or loss) on the liquidating distribution. In addition, as discussed below, the liquidating corporation will likewise be taxable on any property distributed by it to any shareholders other than the 80-80 corporation.[13]

Example 5: Subsidiary is owned 90 percent by the parent (which satisfies the 80-80 test) and 10 percent by minority shareholders. Subsidiary distributes to the parent assets worth $900,000 with a tax basis of $900,000, and distributes to the minority shareholders assets worth $100,000 with a tax basis of zero. The result is tax recognition of $100,000 of gain by the liquidating corporation, with respect to the assets distributed to the minority shareholders, pursuant to Code section 336(a), and recognition of gain by the shareholders, equal to the difference between the fair market value of the assets received and their tax basis in their Target shares, pursuant to Code section 331.

Example 6: Assume the same facts as Example 5, except that by rearranging the assets distributed to its shareholders, the Target now distributes assets with a fair market value of $900,000 and a tax basis of $800,000 to the parent, and assets with a fair market value of $100,000 and a tax basis of $100,000 to the minority shareholders. The assets distributed to the 80-80 parent do not trigger any tax to either the distributing corporation or to the parent. The assets distributed to the minority shareholders trigger taxable gain at both levels, but there is no gain to the distributing corporation because tax basis is equal to fair market value.

Example 7: Assume the same facts as Example 5, except that the Target distributes property to the parent with a fair market value of $900,000 and with a tax basis of $750,000, and distributes property to the minority shareholders with a fair market value of $100,000 and a tax basis of $150,000. On these facts, the loss realized by the subsidiary on the distribution to the minority shareholders is not recognized because of the application of Code section 336(d)(3). In addition, the minority shareholders will recognize gain or loss equal to the difference between their tax basis in their stock and the fair market value of the distributed assets, pursuant to Code sections 331(a) and 1001, and, since the distribution will trigger recognition of gain or loss on receipt, the new tax basis of the assets in the hands of the minority shareholders will be set at the fair market value, or $100,000. Thus, in this example, the "extra" tax basis of $50,000 in the assets distributed to the minority shareholders is essentially thrown away.

Carryover of Target Tax Attributes and Limitations on Use of Certain Tax Attributes by the Target

In the absence of a Code section 338 election, upon on a Code section 332 liquidation by an Acquirer that is an 80-80 parent corporation, the parent corporation will, in addition to the carryover of tax basis under Code section 334(b), also succeed to the liquidating subsidiary's other tax attributes pursuant to Code section 381(a)(1). However, Code section 381 itself contains a number of "anti-abuse" limitations on the use of tax attributes from a Target by an Acquirer, and is supplemented by Code sections 269, 382, and 383 with respect to various tax items.

Limitations on the Acquiring Corporation's Use of Tax Attributes: Code Sections 269, 382 and 383

As previously noted, a stock purchase of 100 percent of Target stock without a Code section 338 election results in the Acquirer owning the Target with the Target's tax history fully intact. In addition, Code section 332, on its face, permits an acquisition and prompt liquidation of a newly acquired subsidiary, thereby passing the Target assets tax-free to the Acquirer, including all of the Target's tax attributes under Code section 381. However, the Code contains a number of "anti-abuse" provisions that are designed to limit the trafficking in losses and so-called "loss corporations", including Code sections 269 and 382/383. At the risk of over simplification, Code section 269 provides a "subjective" intent test that bars or limits the use of tax attributes in situations where an acquisition is deemed to be motivated by an intent to evade or avoid income tax. Code sections 382 and 383, by contrast, provide an objective (albeit wildly complicated) set of rules that bar the use of net operating losses, tax credit carryforwards, and capital loss carryforwards from a Target Corporation if there is a transfer of 50 percent or more of the Target shares within specified time periods. These Code sections, and the various technical requirements and planning considerations that they raise, are discussed briefly below and in much greater detail in Chapter 13.

Code Sections 382 and 383

In most cases the analysis of limitation on use of Target tax attributes starts with Code sections 382 and 383 because these are mechanical "objective" tests that can be applied to produce a certain result (albeit through a complicated set of computations). These provisions are triggered if there is a change in ownership of the Target that is more than 50 percent within a three-year period. If triggered, these provisions generally impose an annual limit on the ability of the Target to use NOLs, tax credits, and capital loss carryforwards. The limitation in each year is generally equal to a specified rate (the long-term tax-exempt bond rate) multiplied by the fair market value of the Target stock immediately before the ownership change. The limitation applies not only to actual NOLs but also to "built in" losses (i.e., where the Target has tax basis in assets significantly above the fair market value of those assets). In addition, if the Target does not meet a continuity of business enterprise test for two years after the ownership change, use of the Target's tax attributes is disallowed entirely. These issues are addressed in depth in Chapter 13.

Code Section 269

Code section 269(a) applies to an acquisition of stock of a corporation (or an acquisition of assets where the tax attributes carry over) where "the principal purpose for which such acquisition was made is evasion or avoidance of [f]ederal income tax by securing the benefit of a deduction, credit or other allowance which such [acquirer] would not otherwise enjoy. . . "If Code section 269 applies, the IRS is given authority to disallow the deduction, credit, or other allowance.

Code section 269(b) expressly addresses a stock purchase by one corporation of another corporation where an election could have been made under Code section 338 but was not, and within two years of the acquisition date the Target corporation is liquidated (presumably under Code section 332) and the principal purpose of such liquidation is the evasion or avoidance of federal income tax. Again, the IRS is empowered to deny the acquiring corporation the benefit of a deduction, credit, or other allowance.

Code section 269 overlaps substantially with Code section 382 in many cases, and, by virtue of the very existence of Code section 382, an Acquirer is not likely to have the requisite wrongful "intent" when Code section 382, by mechanical application, severely limits use of most important tax attributes. Nonetheless, as will be examined in Chapter 13, Code section 269 can apply in some circumstances where Code section 382 will not (e.g., because Code section 382 requires more than a 50-percent ownership change, while Code section 269 requires only a 50-percent change in control measured by vote or value). Thus, Code section 269 will apply, for example, to an acquisition by a 50-50 joint venture where one of the two joint venturers is a new investor, where Code section 382 will not apply on those facts.

Code Section 338 Election

If the Buyer is a corporation and purchases an amount of stock of the Target that gives the Buyer 80-percent control of the Target within a 12-month period, the Buyer can unilaterally elect under Code section 338 to treat the Target as if the Target had sold its assets at their fair-market value in a hypothetical sale to a new corporation.

A Code section 338 election generally results in the Target (or a corporation into which the Target is liquidated) obtaining tax basis in the Target's assets generally equal to the sum of (1) the aggregate purchase price paid by the Buyer for the Target's stock plus (2) the liabilities of the Target.[14] However, this step-up in the tax basis comes at the tax cost of causing the Target to recognize immediate taxable gain on the deemed hypothetical sale transaction. In effect, a Code section 338 election allows the Buyer to first purchase the stock of the Target, and then treat the Target as if, once the Target's stock is in the Buyer's hands, the Target's assets were then sold in a fully taxable asset sale to a new corporation also controlled by the Buyer. The Target recognizes taxable gain, but the deemed "new" acquirer (which is the Target, and so the Target is essentially selling assets to itself) now holds those assets with a stepped-up tax basis as a result of the deemed sale transaction.

The technical requirements of Code section 338, and some of the strategies involved in a Code section 338 election, are discussed more extensively in Chapter 12.

When a Code Section 338 Election Makes Sense

If the Target is a C corporation,[15] a Code section 338 election (including a Code section 338(h)(10) election) generally is advantageous only in certain specific and relatively limited circumstances:

1. The Target has an NOL that is both allowable and sufficient in amount to offset any corporate-level income or gain attributable to the Code section 338 hypothetical sale.

2. The Target is a subsidiary filing consolidated returns with one or more other corporations that have NOLs sufficient to offset the Target's gain on the hypothetical sale.

3. The Target is a subsidiary filing consolidated returns with (or as a division of) a larger corporation owning assets not being sold to the Acquiring Corporation, and this parent corporation's gain on selling the Target's assets would not be materially greater than its gain on selling the Target's stock.

The Code section 338 election must be made by the fifteenth day of the ninth month beginning after the month in which 80-percent control is acquired.

Tax Basis Allocation Rules under Code Section 338

Regulations under Code section 338 provide the rules for allocating tax basis among the assets of a Target when a Code section 338 election is made. These rules should be familiar: They are the purchase price allocation rules adopted by Code section 1060.[16]

Code Section 338(h)(10) Elections

An interesting and increasingly common variation on the Section 338 election is the Section 338(h)(10) election, which allows a Buyer and Seller, where each is an affiliated group of corporations, to elect jointly to treat a sale of Target stock as if the Target has sold its assets to a newly formed corporation while still owned by the selling group, followed by a deemed liquidation of the Target. Thus, the parties can use this alternative election to provide a step-up in the "inside" tax basis of the Target's assets as part of the acquisition by the Buyer, but can cause the corresponding income and gain from the deemed sale transaction to be reported by the Seller group rather than the Buyer group. In effect, the difference between a Section 338 election and a Section 338(h)(10) election is when, exactly, in time the fully taxable hypothetical sale of assets by the Target is deemed to occur: in the case of a Section 338 election, the deemed sale takes place after the Buyer has acquired the the Target stock, and the Buyer's corporate group must bear the tax costs of the deemed sale; in the case of a Section 338(h)(10) election, the hypothetical sale of assets by the Target is deemed to occur before the purchase of the Target stock by the Buyer, and therefore the tax consequences and costs associated with the deemed asset sale are borne by the Seller group instead of the Buyer group.

When Code Section 338(h)(10) Elections Make Sense

This election can be advantageous in specific, limited circumstances, such as when the selling consolidated group has NOLs that can shelter gain from the deemed asset sale. It is also extremely common to see a Section 338(h)(10) election where the target corporation is an

S corporation, because the election permits an Acquirer to purchase the stock of the Target S corporation, but, by virtue of the 338(h)(10) election, treat the transaction for federal income tax purposes as a sale of assets by the Target to a new corporation owned by the Buyer. This has the extremely attractive consequence of giving the Buyer a step-up in basis in the Target assets, and usually produces approximately the same amount of long-term capital gain to the selling S corporation shareholders.

As will be explored more fully in Chapter 12, a stock purchase coupled with a Section 338(h)(10) election can produce dramatically different tax results than a stock sale would otherwise produce. Indeed, because a Section 338(h)(10) election can often produce a far more favorable result to the Buyer, at what can sometimes be a small increase in tax cost to the Seller, it is not uncommon to have an agreement between the Buyer and the Seller whereby the Buyer agrees to make additional payments to the Seller to cover some or all of the additional tax liability resulting to the shareholders of a Target S corporation as a result of a Section 338(h)(10) election.

Noncompete Payments and Code Section 197

Code section 197 is a central aspect of an asset sale but is usually of minor relevance to a stock sale. However, the one area where it does come directly into play is in connection with noncompete payments made by an Acquirer to an individual owner or employee of the Target. Code section 197(d)(1)(E) states that a noncompete covenant entered into in connection with the acquisition (directly or indirectly) of an interest in a trade or business (or a substantial portion thereof) is a Section 197 intangible and must be capitalized and amortized over fifteen years by the Acquirer. The payments are, of course, ordinary income to the recipient whether or not subject to Code section 197 treatment.

Noncompete payments are often paid over time, and are sometimes contingent in amount. In general, for purposes of applying any provision of the Code to a person who is making a payment that is capitalized and amortized under Code section 197 (this would include noncompete payments), the capitalized (and amortized) amount is determined by treating all such payments as payable under a debt instrument given in consideration for the sale or exchange of the applicable Section 197 intangible.[17] Thus, if noncompete payments are paid as a fixed annual payment over several years, and assuming the payments are viewed as a reasonable purchase price for the noncompete covenants, then the regulations indicate that the payment stream should be treated as a debt instrument and then discounted to determine the applicable capitalizable (and amortizable) amount.

That said, the Regulations, Reg. § 1.197-2(k), Example 6, provide the following, rather confusing example:

Example (6). Acquisition and amortization of covenant not to compete. (i) As part of the acquisition of a trade or business from C, B and C enter into an agreement containing a covenant not to compete. Under this agreement, C agrees that it will not compete with the business acquired by B within a prescribed geographical territory for a period of three years after the date on which the business is sold to B. In exchange for this agreement, B agrees to pay C $90,000 per year for each year in the term of the agreement. The agreement further provides that, in the event of a breach by C of his obligations under the agreement, B may terminate the agreement, cease making any of the payments due thereafter, and pursue any other legal or equitable remedies available under applicable law. The amounts payable to C under the agreement are not contingent payments for purposes of § 1.1275-4. The present fair market value of B's rights under the agreement is $225,000. The aggregate consideration paid excluding any amount treated as interest or original issue discount under applicable provisions of the Internal Revenue Code, for all assets acquired in the transaction (including the covenant not to compete) exceeds the sum of the amount of Class I assets and the aggregate fair market value of all Class II, Class III, Class IV, Class V, and Class VI assets by $50,000.[18]

(ii) Because the covenant is acquired in an applicable asset acquisition (within the meaning of section 1060(c)), paragraph (f)(4)(ii) of this section applies and the basis of B in the covenant is determined pursuant to section 1060(a) and the regulations thereunder. Under §§ 1.1060-1(c)(2) and 1.338-6(c)(1), B's basis in the covenant cannot exceed its fair market value. Thus, B's basis in the covenant immediately after the acquisition is $225,000. This basis is amortized ratably over the fifteen-year period beginning on the first day of the month in which the agreement is entered into. All of the remaining consideration after allocation to the covenant and other Class VI assets, ($50,000) is allocated to Class VII assets (goodwill and going concern value).[19]

Example 6 may stand for the proposition that if an acquirer pays the selling business owner $90,000 per year for a three-year noncompete agreement (apparently a total of $270,000), such payments are not contingent, and the present fair market value of such payments is $225,000 (which phrase may be intended to mean the calculation of "present value" using market interest rates for discounting purposes), then the amortizable basis in the covenant is $225,000. (Presumably, the difference of $45,000 should then treated as imputed interest or OID under Code sections 483 and 1274, although the example is not clear on this latter issue.) However, Example 6 may simply stand for the proposition (confused by an IRS math error) that the amortizable basis in a covenant not to compete cannot exceed its fair market value, and that any excess value is allocated (under the example) to goodwill. (If so, such difference would appear to be $45,000 rather than the $50,000 amount used in the example.)

In all events, treating deferred payments to acquire a Section 197 intangible as a debt instrument is consistent with other provisions of the Code (see Chapter 10), and would actually benefit an acquirer to the extent that a portion of the payment is being characterized as interest or OID (presumably currently deductible) rather than as capitalized basis.

Contingent noncompete payments, meanwhile, are added to the amortizable tax basis of the covenant in the first month in which each such contingent payment becomes a fixed obligation, and are then amortized ratably over the remainder of the fifteen-year period.[20] The amount added to amortizable tax basis is determined in the same manner that the principal payment amount is determined on contingent amounts payable under a debt instrument given in consideration for the Section 197 intangible.[21] Any portion of a contingent payment not added to amortizable tax basis would likewise presumably be treated as imputed interest or OID.

Comment: The regulations that characterize deferred payments for a Section 197 intangible as a "debt instrument" given for such intangible (and thus triggering the imputed interest and OID rules), specifically provide that such rules apply "to a person making payments" and thus rather conspicuously suggest that such rules may not apply to the payee of such payments. Practically speaking, in the case of noncompete payments, the payee is likely to report the payments as ordinary income according to the payee's method of accounting (e.g., in the year received, in the case of an individual on the cash method), and thus, even if the OID rules were deemed applicable to the payee, in most cases there would not be a material change in tax consequence. See Chapter 17 for a further discussion of the tax treatment of noncompete payments.

HYPOTHETICAL SITUATIONS ILLUSTRATING THE TAX CONSEQUENCES OF A STOCK PURCHASE TRANSACTION

The following are a series of sequentially related hypothetical situations that illustrate some of the important tax consequences for a business acquisition transaction structured as a taxable stock purchase. The "baseline" hypothetical will be identical to the hypothetical facts used in hypothetical Situation #1 at the end of Chapter 4. In particular, we will assume that a Buyer is now interested in purchasing the stock of the Target, a C corporation, for exactly $10 million.

Comment: As we will examine in Chapter 6, a rational Buyer would not be likely to offer the exact same purchase price in an asset acquisition as in a stock acquisition because a stock acquisition provides less advantageous tax benefits to the Buyer, but confers dramatically more favorable tax benefits to the selling shareholders. Therefore, a "rational" negotiation would reflect these factors, both of which would tend to drive down the price in a stock acquisition compared to the price offered by the Buyer in an asset acquisition.

These hypothetical situations generally assume (unless expressly stated to the contrary) that the discount rate is 10 percent per annum, the combined (federal and state) corporate tax rate is approximately 40 percent, the combined (federal and state) individual tax rate on ordinary income is 40 percent, and the combined (federal and state) individual tax rate on long-term capital gains (federal and state) is 20 percent. We will again assume that a three-percent additional tax is a reasonable approximation of the self-employment tax on consulting/wage payments to an individual shareholder/employee for consulting payments or salary paid in connection with the acquisition of the business.

Hypothetical Situation #1

Hypothetical Situation #1 assumes that the Buyer and Seller agree to an allocation of $8 million to the purchase of the stock, $1.5 million to consulting payments (payable $500,000 per year for three years) to the principal shareholder, and a $500,000 noncompete payment also to the principal shareholder.

In Hypothetical Situation #1, the Target corporation uses the accrual method of accounting and holds the following assets:

1. *Accounts receivable.* It has an accounts receivable of $400,000 with a tax basis of $400,000.
2. *Inventory.* Target company has inventory with a tax basis of $600,000 and a current fair market value of $600,000.

Figure 5.1 summarizes the financial consequences of this transaction:

Basic Tax Assumptions			
Aggregate purchase price of assets			$10,000,000.00
Assumed discounting rate			10.00%
Combined corporate tax rate			40.00%
Combined individual tax rate			40.00%
Combined individual long-term capital gains (LTCG) rate			20.00%
Approximated self-employment (SE) tax			3.00%
C Corporation Assets	***Original Purchase***	***Current Tax Basis***	***Current Fair Market Value***
Accounts receivable (Class III assets)	$400,000.00	$400,000.00	$400,000.00
Inventory (Class IV assets)	$600,000.00	$600,000.00	$600,000.00
Depreciable assets (Class V)	$1,250,000.00	$500,000.00	$500,000.00
Various Section 197 intangibles (excluding goodwill)	$0.00	$0.00	$2,500,000.00
Consulting ($500,000/yr. for 3 yrs.)			$1,500,000.00
Noncompete			$500,000.00
Non-goodwill total			$6,000,000.00
Goodwill	$0.00	$0.00	$4,000,000.00
Total	$2,250,000.00	$1,500,000.00	$10,000,000.00
Tax Consequences to Selling C Corporation Corporation			***Stock Sale***
Purchase price			$0.00
Asset tax basis			$1,500,000.00
Net income or gain			$0.00
NOL			$0.00
Net taxable gain			$0.00
Tax (40%)			$0.00
Liquidating distribution			$0.00

Figure 5.1 (cont'd)

Tax Consequences to Shareholders on C Corporation Liquidation	
Compensation to shareholder	$1,500,000.00
Combined income and SE tax on comp (43%)	$645,000.00
Net compensation	$855,000.00
Noncompete payment	$500,000.00
Tax (40%)	$200,000.00
Net after-tax noncompete	$300,000.00
Stock purchase price	$8,000,000.00
Aggregate tax basis in stock	$100,000.00
Taxable gain	$7,900,000.00
Tax (20%)	$1,580,000.00
After-tax proceeds of stock sale	$6,420,000.00
Total after tax benefits to shareholders	$7,575,000.00

Tax Consequences to Buyer Asset Purchase					
YEAR*	1	2	3	4	5
A/R	$400,000.00				
Depreciation	$200,000.00	$200,000.00	$100,000.00		
Inventory	$600,000.00				
Section 197 intangibles	$0.00	$0.00	$0.00	$0.00	$0.00
Consulting	$500,000.00	$500,000.00	$500,000.00		
Noncompete	$33,333.33	$33,333.33	$33,333.33	$33,333.33	$33,333.33
Goodwill	$0.00	$0.00	$0.00	$0.00	$0.00
Total annual tax deductions	$1,733,333.33	$733,333.33	$633,333.33	$33,333.33	$33,333.33
Tax savings	$693,333.33	$293,333.33	$253,333.33	$13,333.33	$13,333.33
Present value of tax savings	$630,303.03	$242,424.24	$190,333.08	$9,106.85	$8,278.95
Total PV benefit	$1,131,316.72				
Total payments	$10,000,000.00				
Net after-tax cost	$8,868,683.28				

*This page shows the early years of a fifteen-year period, and shows total PV benefit for all fifteen years.

3. *Depreciable assets.* It holds depreciable assets with an original purchase price of $1,250,000 and a current tax basis of $500,000 which assets are assigned a current fair market value of $500,000.

4. *Intangible assets.* There are Code section 197 intangibles worth $2.5 million.

5. *Consulting and noncompete payments.* The parties agree to a $1.5 million consulting payment ($500,000 a year for three years), and a noncompete of $500,000.

6. *Goodwill.* If this were structured as an asset sale, the rest of the value, $4 million, would be allocated to goodwill.

Comment: Because this is a stock purchase, there is no step up in the tax basis of the Target's assets upon the purchase of the stock for $8 million.

The tax basis of the Target's assets remains $1.5 million before and after the stock sale, of which $400,000 is allocated to accounts receivable, $600,000 to inventory, and $500,000 to Class V depreciable assets that are partially depreciated, and will continue to be depreciated.

Tax Consequences to Seller Group. The consulting payments to the owner-employee of $1.5 million will be subject to tax at an estimated 40-percent individual tax rate and, for purposes of Hypothetical Situation #1, it is assumed that the SE tax on such consulting payments will be approximately an additional three percent "add on" of tax. (*Note:* The SE tax would in fact be significantly higher if the payee had no other earned income subject to SE tax or Social Security in the years in question.) Accordingly, using a 43-percent estimated tax rate for the combined effects of income and SE tax, the income tax on $1.5 million of consulting payments would be $645,000, and the net compensation would be $855,000, without taking into account time-value-of-money.

The noncompete payment of $500,000 would be subject to tax at ordinary income tax rates, but not to SE tax. Assuming a 40-percent tax rate, $300,000 would be the net after-tax payment.

The stock purchase price of $8 million paid to the selling shareholders, assuming a $100,000 tax basis in the target company stock in the hands of such shareholders, would result in a taxable gain of $7.9 million and, assuming an LTCG tax rate of 20 percent, the tax amount would $1,580,000. Thus, the after-tax proceeds attributable to the stock sale would be $6,420,000.

The total after-tax benefits to the shareholders in Hypothetical Situation #1 (combining after-tax compensation payments, the after-tax noncompete payment, and after-tax stock proceeds) is $7,575,000.

Tax Consequences to Buyer Group. For the Buyer, meanwhile, the tax benefits arising from the stock purchase are somewhat improved by the fact that $1.5 million is allocated to consulting payments, paid ratably over the first three years, and $500,000 is allocated to the noncompete. In addition, the Target corporation itself has $1.5 million of tax basis in its assets and, for the reasons described in Chapter 4, it is reasonable to treat the tax basis in the accounts receivable and in the inventory as if such assets were enjoyed by the Acquirer in the first tax year (because the Acquirer, if it did not spend this money in connection with the acquisition, would have to spend the same amount of money in the first year to acquire inventory and to replace the accounts receivable with a cash equivalent).

The depreciation schedule for the remaining $500,000 of tax basis in the Class V assets would, of course, depend on the respective remaining depreciation lives of these assets. The spreadsheet somewhat arbitrarily approximates the remaining depreciation on this $500,000 by assigning to $200,000 of depreciation to year one, $200,000 to year two, and $100,000 to year three. This is intended to reflect the fact that assets acquired through a stock sale do not get treated as placed in service and amortized over a five-year period, but rather complete their depreciation periods as if there had not been a change in ownership. Accordingly, for the existing assets, on average, there would probably be approximately three years left of depreciation, and the spreadsheet attempts to approximate that result. Again, it is not important that the numbers be precise so long as they reasonably approximate the estimated tax consequences, especially for purposes of comparison and illustration between and among these hypothetical situations.

Based on these assumptions, the Buyer actually extracts about $3.5 million of tax basis and corresponding tax benefits from this transaction, $1.5 million representing the tax basis of the Target corporation in its assets, with an additional $2 million being allocated between the consulting and noncompete payments to the individual shareholders of the Target. As will be illustrated in the next hypothetical situation, the allocation related to the stock purchase and to consulting and noncompete payments helps the Buyer to the detriment of the Seller, and the negotiation becomes an exercise in finding the right balance between Buyer and Seller. The net result in Hypothetical Situation #1 is that the after-tax cost to the Buyer is estimated at approximately $8,868,683.[22]

Comment: Again, one derives very precise numbers based on computations that start with very approximate estimates, so one should use these amounts as estimated approximations.

Hypothetical Situation #2

Hypothetical Situation #2 switches the consulting and noncompete payments so that the consulting payment is reduced to $500,000 and the noncompete payment is increased to $1.5 million. This modification

Figure 5.2 summarizes the financial consequences of this transaction:

Basic Tax Assumptions			
Aggregate purchase price of assets			$10,000,000.00
Assumed discounting rate			10.00%
Combined corporate tax rate			40.00%
Combined individual tax rate			40.00%
Combined individual LTCG rate			20.00%
Approximated SE tax			3.00%
C Corporation Assets	***Original Purchase Price***	***Current Tax Basis***	***Current Fair Market Value***
A/R (Class III assets)	$400,000.00	$400,000.00	$400,000.00
Inventory (Class IV assets)	$600,000.00	$600,000.00	$600,000.00
Depreciable assets (Class V)	$1,250,000.00	$500,000.00	$500,000.00
Various Section 197 intangibles (excluding goodwill)	$0.00	$0.00	$2,500,000.00
Consulting ($166,666.66/yr. for 3 yrs.)			$500,000.00
Noncompete			$1,500,000.00
Non-goodwill total			$6,000,000.00
Goodwill	$0.00	$0.00	$4,000,000.00
Total	$2,250,000.00	$1,500,000.00	$10,000,000.00
Tax Consequences to Selling C Corporation			
Corporation			***Asset Sale***
Purchase price			$0.00
Asset tax basis			$1,500,000.00
Net income or gain			$0.00
NOL			$0.00
Net taxable gain			$0.00
Tax (40%)			$0.00
Liquidating distribution			$0.00
Tax Consequences to Shareholders on C Corporation Liquidation			
Compensation to shareholder			$500,000.00
Combined income and SE tax on comp (43%)			$215,000.00
Net compensation			$285,000.00
Noncompete payment			$1,500,000.00
Tax (40%)			$600,000.00
Net after-tax noncompete			$900,000.00
Stock purchase price			$8,000,000.00
Aggregate tax basis in stock			$100,000.00
Taxable gain			$7,900,000.00
Tax (20%)			$1,580,000.00
Net distribution to shareholders			$6,420,000.00
Total after tax benefit			$7,605,000.00

Figure 5.2 (cont'd)

Tax Consequences to Buyer Asset Purchase					
YEAR*	1	2	3	4	5
A/R	$400,000.00				
Depreciation	$200,000.00	$200,000.00	$100,000.00	$0.00	$0.00
Inventory	$600,000.00				
Section 197 intangibles	$0.00	$0.00	$0.00	$0.00	$0.00
Consulting	$166,666.67	$166,666.67	$166,666.67		
Noncompete	$100,000.00	$100,000.00	$100,000.00	$100,000.00	$100,000.00
Goodwill	$0.00	$0.00	$0.00	$0.00	$0.00
Total annual tax deductions	$1,466,666.67	$466,666.67	$366,666.67	$100,000.00	$100,000.00
Tax savings	$586,666.67	$186,666.67	$146,666.67	$40,000.00	$40,000.00
Present value of tax savings	$533,333.33	$154,269.97	$110,192.84	$27,320.54	$24,836.85
Total PV benefit	$1,002,565.24				
Total payments	$10,000,000.00				
Net after-tax cost	$8,997,434.76				

*This page shows the early years of a fifteen-year period, and shows total PV benefit for all fifteen years.

produced a very significant result in Chapter 4 in the Hypothetical Situation #2 related to an asset sale, and the purpose is to do a similar comparison to a stock sale. The assumptions remain the same as in Hypothetical Situation #1.

As happened in Hypothetical Situation #2 in Chapter 4, the reallocation of $1,000,000 from consulting payments to noncompete payments results in a very modest projected tax benefit to the selling shareholder, increasing the after-tax benefit by $30,000. (As noted in Chapter 4, Hypothetical Situation #2, the reallocation allows a selling shareholder to avoid SE tax, and in some cases (especially smaller transactions) the reduction in SE tax may be more than three percent.)

Meanwhile, the after-tax cost to the Buyer is increased quite significantly, to $8,997,000 from $8,868,000. It would cost approximately $130,000 of additional tax to the Buyer in order to give the Seller an additional $30,000 of tax benefit.

Hypothetical Situation #3

Hypothetical Situation #3 is the same as Hypothetical Situation #1 except that the discount rate is set at 15 percent rather than 10 percent, reflecting the fact that the Buyer places less value on deductions ten or fifteen years down the road.

Figure 5.3 summarizes the financial consequences of this transaction:

Basic Tax Assumptions			
Aggregate purchase price of assets			$10,000,000.00
Assumed discounting rate			15.00%
Combined corporate tax rate			40.00%
Combined individual tax rate			40.00%
Combined individual LTCG rate			20.00%
Approximated SE tax			3.00%
C Corporation Assets	***Original Purchase Price***	***Current Tax Basis***	***Current Fair Market Value***
A/R (Class III assets)	$400,000.00	$400,000.00	$400,000.00
Inventory (Class IV assets)	$600,000.00	$600,000.00	$600,000.00
Depreciable assets (Class V)	$1,250,000.00	$500,000.00	$500,000.00
Various Section 197 intangibles (excluding goodwill)	$0.00	$0.00	$2,500,000.00
Consulting ($500,000/yr. for 3 yrs.)			$1,500,000.00
Noncompete			$500,000.00
Non-goodwill total			$6,000,000.00
Goodwill	$0.00	$0.00	$4,000,000.00
Total	$2,250,000.00	$1,500,000.00	$10,000,000.00
Tax Consequences to Selling C Corporation			
Corporation			***Asset Sale***
Purchase price			$0.00
Asset tax basis			$1,500,000.00
Net income or gain			$0.00
NOL			$0.00
Net taxable gain			$0.00
Tax (40%)			$0.00
Liquidating distribution			$0.00
Tax Consequences to Shareholders on C Corporation Liquidation			
Compensation to shareholder			$1,500,000.00
Combined income and SE tax on comp (43%)			$645,000.00
Net compensation			$855,000.00
Noncompete payment			$500,000.00
Tax (40%)			$200,000.00
Net after-tax noncompete			$300,000.00
Stock purchase price			$8,000,000.00
Aggregate tax basis in stock			$100,000.00
Taxable gain			$7,900,000.00
Tax (20%)			$1,580,000.00
Net distribution to shareholders			$6,420,000.00
Total after tax benefit			$7,575,000.00

Figure 5.3 (cont'd)

Tax Consequences to Buyer Asset Purchase					
YEAR*	**1**	**2**	**3**	**4**	**5**
A/R	$400,000.00				
Depreciation	$200,000.00	$200,000.00	$100,000.00		
Inventory	$600,000.00				
Section 197 Intangibles	$0.00	$0.00	$0.00	$0.00	$0.00
Consulting	$500,000.00	$500,000.00	$500,000.00		
Noncompete	$33,333.33	$33,333.33	$33,333.33	$33,333.33	$33,333.33
Goodwill	$0.00	$0.00	$0.00	$0.00	$0.00
Total annual tax deductions	$1,733,333.33	$733,333.33	$633,333.33	$33,333.33	$33,333.33
Tax savings	$693,333.33	$293,333.33	$253,333.33	$13,333.33	$13,333.33
Present value of tax savings	$602,898.55	$221,802.14	$166,570.78	$7,623.38	$6,629.02
Total PV benefit	$1,038,793.41				
Total payments	$10,000,000.00				
Net after-tax cost	$8,961,206.59				

*This page shows the early years of a fifteen-year period, and shows total PV benefit for all fifteen years.

On these facts, the net after-tax cost to the Buyer is increased to $8,961,206.59, reflecting the corresponding reduction in the present value of the Buyer's tax benefits. Note that in contrast to the asset purchase agreement, where a higher discount rate dramatically increased the after-tax cost to the Buyer, this is less true in a stock purchase precisely because relatively little of the tax benefit extends out for any appreciable period of time. In fact, the only tax benefit in the hypothetical that extends beyond the third tax year is the noncompete payment of $500,000, which is assumed to be amortized ratably over a fifteen-year period starting in year one.

Hypothetical Situation #4

This is designed to illustrate that if more of the purchase price is allocated to the noncompete payments and the discount rate is increased, there is a corresponding "double effect". It is assumed that the discount rate is 15 percent, the consulting payments total $500,000, and the noncompete payments total $1,500,000.

Not only are more of the tax benefits deferred, but they are also valued even less in the eyes of the Buyer. As with most exercises in tax planning and tax allocation in an acquisition context, this is intuitive and "makes sense", but it is always interesting and instructive to see how much of a difference it actually makes in practice by running the hypothetical numbers. On this basis, the net after-tax purchase price is increased to $9,109,706.74, which is about a magnitude of $100,000 greater in after-tax cost than the projected after-tax cost to the Buyer in Hypothetical Situations #2 and #3. On the other hand, in comparison to a $10 million deal, it represents about one percent of the total acquisition price, so it is not "huge".

Figure 5.4 summarizes the financial consequences of this transaction:

Basic Tax Assumptions			
Aggregate purchase price of assets			$10,000,000.00
Assumed discounting rate			15.00%
Combined corporate tax rate			40.00%
Combined individual tax rate			40.00%
Combined individual LTCG rate			20.00%
Approximated SE tax			3.00%
C Corporation Assets	***Original Purchase Price***	***Current Tax Basis***	***Current Fair Market Value***
A/R (Class III assets)	$400,000.00	$400,000.00	$400,000.00
Inventory (Class IV assets)	$600,000.00	$600,000.00	$600,000.00
Depreciable assets (Class V)	$1,250,000.00	$500,000.00	$500,000.00
Various Section 197 intangibles (excluding goodwill)	$0.00	$0.00	$2,500,000.00
Consulting ($166,666.66/yr. for 3 yrs.)			$500,000.00
Noncompete			$1,500,000.00
Non-goodwill total			$6,000,000.00
Goodwill	$0.00	$0.00	$4,000,000.00
Total	$2,250,000.00	$1,500,000.00	$10,000,000.00
Tax Consequences to Selling C Corporation			
Corporation			***Asset Sale***
Purchase price			$0.00
Asset tax basis			$1,500,000.00
Net income or gain			$0.00
NOL			$0.00
Net taxable gain			$0.00
Tax (40%)			$0.00
Liquidating distribution			$0.00
Tax Consequences to Shareholders on C Corporation Liquidation			
Compensation to shareholder			$500,000.00
Combined income and SE tax on comp (43%)			$215,000.00
Net compensation			$285,000.00
Noncompete payment			$1,500,000.00
Tax (40%)			$600,000.00
Net after-tax noncompete			$900,000.00
Stock purchase price			$8,000,000.00
Aggregate tax basis in stock			$100,000.00
Taxable gain			$7,900,000.00
Tax (20%)			$1,580,000.00
Net distribution to shareholders			$6,420,000.00
Total after tax benefit			$7,605,000.00

Figure 5.4 (cont'd)

Tax Consequences to Buyer Asset Purchase					
YEAR*	1	2	3	4	5
A/R	$400,000.00				
Depreciation	$200,000.00	$200,000.00	$100,000.00	$0.00	$0.00
Inventory	$600,000.00				
Section 197 Intangibles	$0.00	$0.00	$0.00	$0.00	$0.00
Consulting	$166,666.67	$166,666.67	$166,666.67		
Noncompete	$100,000.00	$100,000.00	$100,000.00	$100,000.00	$100,000.00
Goodwill	$0.00	$0.00	$0.00	$0.00	$0.00
Total annual tax deductions	$1,466,666.67	$466,666.67	$366,666.67	$100,000.00	$100,000.00
Tax savings	$586,666.67	$186,666.67	$146,666.67	$40,000.00	$40,000.00
Present value of tax savings	$510,144.93	$141,146.82	$96,435.71	$22,870.13	$19,887.07
Total PV benefit	$890,293.26				
Total payments	$10,000,000.00				
Net after-tax cost	$9,109,706.74				

*This page shows the early years of a fifteen-year period, and shows total PV benefit for all fifteen years.

Hypothetical Situation #5

Hypothetical Situation #5 is comprised of the same facts as Hypothetical Situation #1 except that no money is allocated to consulting and noncompete payments, and the entire $10 million is treated as the acquisition price for the stock. This means that all the purchase price is treated as long-term capital gain taxed at the long-term capital gains rates to the Seller, while the Buyer gets no tax benefits whatsoever in the acquisition.

> ***Comment:*** An always interesting issue to discuss is what economic value one should place on tax basis in the stock of a Target corporation acquired by another corporation. As previously discussed in this chapter, Code section 332 has the nasty effect of making that tax basis disappear—unless, of course, a Section 338 election is made.

The results in Hypothetical Situation #5 demonstrate that the Target shareholders get a very attractive after-tax return on a $10 million sale of $8,020,000, reflecting the fact that 20-percent tax is imposed on $9.9 million of long-term gain. (The hypothetical again assumes that the Target shareholders have $100,000 of tax basis in the stock.) The Buyer, meanwhile, enjoys only the tax benefits attributable to acquiring the Target corporation's existing tax basis in its assets. The hypothetical does anticipate that the $400,000 of tax basis in the accounts receivable, and the $600,000 of tax basis in the inventory can be viewed as a tax benefit enjoyed by the Buyer in the first year. However, the total present value of the tax benefits is approximately $500,000, and so the net after-tax cost to the Buyer under Hypothetical Situation #5 is estimated to be approximately $9.5 million.

Figure 5.5 summarizes the financial consequences of this transaction:

Basic Tax Assumptions			
Aggregate purchase price of assets			$10,000,000.00
Assumed discounting rate			10.00%
Combined corporate tax rate			40.00%
Combined individual tax rate			40.00%
Combined individual LTCG rate			20.00%
Approximated SE tax			3.00%
C Corporation Assets	*Original Purchase Price*	*Current Tax Basis*	*Current Fair Market Value*
Accounts receivable (Class III assets)	$400,000.00	$400,000.00	$400,000.00
Inventory (Class IV assets)	$600,000.00	$600,000.00	$600,000.00
Depreciable assets (Class V)	$1,250,000.00	$500,000.00	$500,000.00
Various Section 197 intangibles (excluding goodwill)	$0.00	$0.00	$2,500,000.00
Consulting ($0/yr. for 3 yrs.)			$0.00
Noncompete			$0.00
Non-goodwill total			$4,000,000.00
Goodwill	$0.00	$0.00	$6,000,000.00
Total	$2,250,000.00	$1,500,000.00	$10,000,000.00
Tax Consequences to Selling C Corporation			
Corporation			*Stock Sale*
Purchase price			$0.00
Asset tax basis			$1,500,000.00
Net income or gain			$0.00
NOL			$0.00
Net taxable gain			$0.00
Tax (40%)			$0.00
Liquidating distribution			$0.00
Tax Consequences to Shareholders on C Corporation Liquidation			
Compensation to shareholder			$0.00
Combined income and SE tax on comp (43%)			$0.00
Net compensation			$0.00
Noncompete payment			$0.00
Tax (40%)			$0.00
Net after-tax noncompete			$0.00
Stock purchase price			$10,000,000.00
Aggregate tax basis in stock			$100,000.00
Taxable gain			$9,900,000.00
Tax (20%)			$1,980,000.00
After-tax proceeds of stock sale			$8,020,000.00
Total after tax benefits to shareholders			$8,020,000.00

Figure 5.5 (cont'd)

Tax Consequences to Buyer Asset Purchase				
YEAR*	1	2	3	4
A/R	$400,000.00			
Depreciation	$200,000.00	$200,000.00	$100,000.00	
Inventory	$600,000.00			
Section 197 intangibles	$0.00	$0.00	$0.00	$0.00
Consulting	$0.00	$0.00	$0.00	
Noncompete	$0.00	$0.00	$0.00	$0.00
Goodwill	$0.00	$0.00	$0.00	$0.00
Total annual tax deductions	$1,200,000.00	$200,000.00	$100,000.00	$0.00
Tax savings	$480,000.00	$80,000.00	$40,000.00	$0.00
Present value of tax savings	$436,363.64	$66,115.70	$30,052.59	$0.00
Total PV benefit	$532,531.93			
Total payments	$10,000,000.00			
Net after-tax cost	$9,467,468.07			

*This page shows the early years of a fifteen-year period, and shows total PV benefit for all fifteen years.

Hypothetical Situation #6

Hypothetical Situation #6 is the same as Hypothetical Situation #5, except that the Buyer elects to make a Code section 338 election, causing the Target, immediately following its acquisition by the Buyer, to be treated as if it had sold its assets to itself in a hypothetical sale transaction that was fully taxable to the Target corporation. The entire $10 million purchase price is being allocated to the Target stock, and no portion of the purchase price is being allocated to either consulting or noncompete payments.

Hypothetical Situation #6 shows that, at the corporate level, there is a deemed purchase of the assets for $10 million, which is allocated among Target assets with an existing tax basis of $1.5 million, and therefore generating $8.5 million of corporate level gain taxed at an estimated 40-percent tax rate. This results in an estimated tax of $3.4 million, due and payable by the Target corporation in the first year. In addition, the Buyer has paid $10 million out-of-pocket, so the total acquisition cost to the Buyer is stock purchase price of $10 million plus the tax cost of the Code section 338 election, or a total of $13.4 million. The Buyer, as a consequence, now enjoys substantially better tax benefits since the assets now have tax basis totaling $10 million. However, under these assumptions, most or all of this enhanced purchase price is allocated to goodwill (which is allocated $6 million of residual value, assuming there are no consulting or noncompete payments). Therefore, the total present value tax benefit of this transaction is about $2,242,000. As this exercise demonstrates, the Buyer, including the cost of the Section 338 election, pays a total of $13.4 million (including taxes), gets back $2,242,333 of benefits, and ends up with a net after-tax cost of $11,157,667.

The point of this exercise is to demonstrate a Section 338 election does not make a lot of sense in "normal" circumstances because the Buyer will pay (1) the purchase price for the Target stock plus (2) the full tax cost of the deemed asset sale triggered by the Section 338 election, and then get back corresponding tax benefits spread over a period of up to fifteen years.

Figure 5.6 summarizes the financial consequences of this transaction:

Basic Tax Assumptions			
Aggregate purchase price of assets			$10,000,000.00
Assumed discounting rate			10.00%
Combined corporate tax rate			40.00%
Combined individual tax rate			40.00%
Combined individual LTCG rate			20.00%
Approximated SE tax			3.00%
C Corporation Assets	***Original Purchase Price***	***Current Tax Basis***	***Current Fair Market Value***
Accounts receivable (Class III assets)	$400,000.00	$400,000.00	$400,000.00
Inventory (Class IV assets)	$600,000.00	$600,000.00	$600,000.00
Depreciable assets (Class V)	$1,250,000.00	$500,000.00	$500,000.00
Various Section 197 intangibles (excluding goodwill)	$0.00	$0.00	$2,500,000.00
Consulting ($0/yr. for 3 yrs.)			$0.00
Noncompete			$0.00
Non-goodwill total			$4,000,000.00
Goodwill	$0.00	$0.00	$6,000,000.00
Total	$2,250,000.00	$1,500,000.00	$10,000,000.00
Tax Consequences to Selling C Corporation on 338 Election			
Corporation			***Stock Sale***
Purchase price			$10,000,000.00
Asset tax basis			$1,500,000.00
Net income or gain			$8,500,000.00
NOL			$0.00
Net taxable gain			$8,500,000.00
Tax (40%)			$3,400,000.00
Tax Consequences to Shareholders on C Corporation Liquidation			
Compensation to shareholder			$0.00
Combined income and SE tax on comp (43%)			$0.00
Net compensation			$0.00
Noncompete payment			$0.00
Tax (40%)			$0.00
Net after-tax noncompete			$0.00
Stock purchase price			$10,000,000.00
Aggregate tax basis in stock			$100,000.00
Taxable gain			$9,900,000.00
Tax (20%)			$1,980,000.00
After-tax proceeds of stock sale			$8,020,000.00
Total after tax benefits to shareholders			$8,020,000.00

Figure 5.6 (cont'd)

Tax Consequences to Buyer Asset Purchase					
YEAR*	1	2	3	4	5
A/R	$400,000.00				
Depreciation	$100,000.00	$160,000.00	$96,000.00	$57,600.00	$57,600.00
Inventory	$600,000.00				
Section 197 intangibles	$166,666.67	$166,666.67	$166,666.67	$166,666.67	$166,666.67
Consulting	$0.00	$0.00	$0.00		
Noncompete	$0.00	$0.00	$0.00	$0.00	$0.00
Goodwill	$400,000.00	$400,000.00	$400,000.00	$400,000.00	$400,000.00
Total annual tax deductions	$1,666,666.67	$726,666.67	$662,666.67	$624,266.67	$624,266.67
Tax savings	$666,666.67	$290,666.67	$265,066.67	$249,706.67	$249,706.67
Present value of tax savings	$606,060.61	$240,220.39	$199,148.51	$170,553.01	$155,048.19
Total PV benefit	$2,242,333.14				
Total stock purchase price	$10,000,000.00				
Tax cost of Section 338 election	$3,400,000.00				
Total acquisition cost to buyer	$13,400,000.00				
Net after-tax cost	$11,157,666.86				

*This page shows the early years of a fifteen-year period, and shows total PV benefit for all fifteen years.

CHAPTER ENDNOTES

1. IRC Sec. 1001(b).
2. IRC Sec. 1001(c).
3. IRC Sec. 1001(d).
4. IRC Sec. 453(k)(2).
5. IRC Sec. 306(b)(1).
6. IRC Sec. 1012.
7. Chapter 10.
8. IRC Sec. 331 (a).
9. IRC Secs. 332, 334(b), 337, and 381.
10. IRC Sec. 334(b)(1).
11. The loss on recognition would be subject to the limitation on built-in losses under IRC Sec. 382. See Chapter 13.
12. *H. K. Porter Co.*, 87 TC 689, Dec. 43,405 (1986).
13. IRC Secs. 336(a) and 337(a).
14. Reg. § 1.338-5(b)(1).
15. 15 An S corporation that makes a qualified stock purchase of a Target can also make an IRC Sec. 338 election. Reg. § 1.1361-4.
16. Reg. § 1.338-6.
17. Reg. § 1.197-2(f)(3)(iv)(B)(1).
18. § 1.338-6(b) for rules for determining the assets in each class.
19. § § 1.1060- 1T(c)(2) and 1.338-6T(b).
20. Reg. § 1.197-2(f)(2)(i).
21. Reg. § 1.197-2(f)(2)(iii).
22. The spreadsheet treats compensation paid in years 2 and 3 as subject to present-value discounting, which is erroneous since the consulting payments will not be paid until the year of deduction. However, the distortion is modest and the author opts for simplicity over exactness.

CHOOSING BETWEEN AN ASSET SALE AND A STOCK SALE

CHAPTER 6

OVERVIEW

The structuring of taxable corporate acquisitions has proven, not surprisingly, to be very sensitive to federal income tax law and, in some cases, to state tax law. This chapter continues to assume that the Target is a C corporation. The following is a brief review of factors that will affect the structuring decision:

1. A sale of C corporation assets is subject to double taxation, first at the corporate level at (generally high) corporate tax rates, and second at the shareholder level at (generally lower) individual rates.

2. Individual shareholders, by contrast, can potentially sell their stock in the Target and enjoy favorable long-term capital-gains tax rates.

3. The Buyer in an asset acquisition enjoys a step-up in tax basis in the assets, and most or all of the acquired assets will be depreciable or amortizable under either Code section 167 or 197.

4. The Buyer in a stock acquisition, absent a Section 338 election, has the purchase price allocated to the stock. The resulting tax basis is not amortizable or depreciable and will be utilized, if at all, only when the stock is sold at a future date.

5. Payments by the Acquirer to individual owners/employees of the Seller for salary, consulting, noncompete, and other purposes can help address both business and tax objectives in the transaction. In particular, consulting payments are ordinary income to the consultant, but immediately deductible by the payor. This may be an efficient tax strategy in a variety of contexts that will be explored in this chapter.

As a brief historical note, the federal income tax law before 1986 was very favorable to a sale of C corporation assets followed immediately thereafter by a liquidation. Under the so-called General Utilities Doctrine,[1] embodied in the pre-1986 version of Code section 337, if a C corporation sold its assets and then liquidated within twelve months, the transaction would generally result in only a single level of federal income tax assessed at the shareholder level at capital gains tax rates.

The Tax Reform Act of 1986 (TRA-86) drastically altered the taxation of an asset sale by a C corporation. Under the post-1986 scheme, both a sale of corporate assets, followed by a liquidation, and the liquidation of a C corporation, followed by a sale of its assets, will trigger double taxation. The first level of tax is at the corporate level. A sale of assets by the C corporation is a taxable disposition, and a liquidating distribution of assets is treated, under Code section 336(a), as the equivalent of a sale or exchange of such assets. In both cases the corporation recognizes gain or loss measured by the difference between the fair-market value of the distributed assets and the corporation's tax basis in the assets on the date of the applicable transaction. Since the seller is a C corporation, the gain is taxed at normal corporate tax rates, with no preferential rate accorded to capital gains. The second level of tax is at the shareholder level and triggers capital gain or loss to each shareholder equal to the difference between the fair-market value of the property (including cash) received by the shareholder in the liquidating distribution compared to the shareholder's basis in the corporate stock.

After 1986 and before August 11, 1993, a typical mechanism used by taxpayers to mitigate double taxation was to couple a sale of corporate assets with a consulting agreement and/or noncompete agreement that effectively allocated a significant portion of the total consideration to the purchase of services (or of noncompetition) from the selling shareholder rather than to the purchase of assets from the company. Such a structure was particularly attractive in cases where the corporate assets were comprised primarily of going concern value and goodwill. Corporate goodwill before August 11, 1993, was a non-amortizable asset in the hands of the Buyer, and was subject to double taxation on the part of the Seller (assuming a subsequent corporate liquidation). Therefore, neither the Buyer nor the Seller was eager to allocate any significant amount of the purchase price to goodwill. Rather, both the Buyer and the Seller had a substantial tax incentive to allocate purchase price to consulting agreements and noncompete agreements.

ALLOCATION STRATEGIES FOLLOWING THE 1993 TAX ACT

The Omnibus Budget Reconciliation Act of 1993 (the "1993 Tax Act") (P.L. 103-66) had a major impact on the structuring of taxable C corporation acquisitions, and it defines the planning landscape today. The two biggest changes were (1) the enactment of Code section 197 (see Chapter 11) which today mandates fifteen-year amortization for the portion of the purchase price allocated to most "intangible" assets, including both goodwill and noncompete payments; and (2) a substantial increase in the tax-rate differential for individual taxpayers between ordinary income and capital gains. This latter factor became even more significant when the long-term capital gains tax rate for individuals was reduced to 20 percent in 1997, and then to just 15 percent in 2003 (and then, after 2012, back to a maximum LTCG rate of 20 percent plus a 3.8 percent Net Investment Income Tax (NIIT), or a combined rate of 23.8 percent).

Today, individuals are taxed on ordinary income at a nominal rate of up to 39.6 percent (the effective tax rate is higher at some income levels, due to various phase-outs), and individual capital gains and dividends are generally taxed at a maximum federal rate of 23.8 percent (including NIIT). This tax differential, not surprisingly, has had a major impact on structuring acquisition transactions, as individuals seek to take advantage of the very favorable tax rates that apply to capital gains and, for the moment, to dividends.

C corporations are taxed for federal income tax purposes at graduated rates, with a nominal maximum rate of 35 percent. Due to various phase out and recapture rules, the federal corporate income tax is imposed on the taxable income of a C corporation at the following rates under Code section 11(b), taking into account the various rate adjustments:

Taxable Income	*Rate*
$0–50,000	15%
$50,000–75,000	25%
$75,000–100,000	34%
$100,000–335,000	39%
$335,000–$10,000,000	34%
$10,000,000–$15,000,000	35%
$15,000,000–$18,333,333	38%
More than $18,333,333	35%

Comment: Capital gains are taxed to a C corporation at regular corporate rates. There is no corporate capital gains preference, which means that long-term capital gains are taxed at roughly double (or more) the rate if the Seller is a C corporation than if the Seller is an individual or a pass-through entity (e.g., an S corporation, partnership, LLC, or sole proprietorship).

A C corporation is also subject to a variety of other, generally unpalatable tax regimes, some of which can play an important part in an asset sale by a C corporation or in its aftermath.

1. In the case of a "qualified personal service corporation," the taxable income is assessed at a flat 35-percent rate from the first dollar (i.e., there is no graduation of rates).[2]

2. There is a corporate alternative minimum tax that is imposed on alternative minimum taxable income at a flat rate of 20 percent.[3]

3. C corporations are also subject to the personal holding company (PHC) tax imposed under Code section 541 *et seq.*, and the accumulated

earnings tax imposed under Code section 531 *et seq.*

Code section 197, enacted in 1993, eliminated the dramatically different tax consequences that arose between allocating purchase price to corporate goodwill versus noncompete payments by making both goodwill and noncompete payments amortizable over a fifteen-year period. Thus, a Buyer has no economic incentive to allocate purchase price to one over the other. However, a Seller may prefer to allocate purchase price to one over the other. For example, the sole owner of a Target C corporation in an asset sale would prefer to be paid personally for a noncompete covenant (taxable at an estimated 40 percent for federal and state taxes combined) rather than allocate purchase price to goodwill and run the gain through the double tax regime of a corporate asset sale.

By contrast, an owner of an S corporation will probably prefer the opposite allocation, namely allocating purchase price to goodwill (a capital asset) so that the gain passes through to the shareholder as long-term capital gain (taxable at a maximum federal rate of 23.8 percent) rather than to personal noncompete payments (taxable at individual rates of up to 39.6 percent). See Chapter 8, which discusses acquisitions of S corporations.

Another significant factor is that, as between noncompete payments and consulting/employment payments, the Buyer now has a strong tax incentive to characterize a larger portion of the purchase price as consulting payments, which gives the Buyer an immediate deduction in the year of payment (for a cash basis payor) or accrual (for an accrual basis payor). This deduction is, of course, subject to limitations on reasonable compensation for the services actually rendered. A payee, by contrast, may have a modest preference for such payments to be characterized as noncompete payments (which are not subject to self-employment tax) rather than as consulting payments (subject to self-employment tax). A more comprehensive discussion of these issues is found in Chapter 17.

CHOOSING BETWEEN AN ASSET SALE AND A STOCK SALE—THE "RATIONAL" NEGOTIATION BASED ON PRESENT-VALUE ANALYSIS

A "rational" negotiation of a business acquisition should evaluate the respective transaction structures based on the present-value, after-tax benefits and costs to the Buyer and Seller. In particular, one must compare the present-value, after-tax cost to the Buyer, and the present-value, after-tax benefit to the Seller, of both an asset sale and a stock sale, in order to put some parameters on the negotiating process. When the Target is a C corporation, what makes the process distinctive is that one must take into account the complexities of double taxation, and the specific tax characteristics of both the Buyer and Seller, plus the myriad unique rules that apply to a C corporation acquisition. As we will see in subsequent chapters, the acquisition structure when the Target is an S corporation or an LLC is often so obvious as to merit little or no discussion. By contrast, when the Target is a C corporation, the parties can expect to engage in complicated gyrations—gyrations that can threaten the balance and stability of the negotiations and the deal—as the parties grapple with the heavy toll of corporate double taxation.

Observation: Conventional wisdom is that a target shareholder will prefer to sell the target stock and a purchaser will prefer to purchase the target's assets. What's wrong with this statement? The answer is obvious: The price is missing! Specifically, this often-repeated kernel of "wisdom" assumes that a Buyer will offer the same price to purchase stock or purchase assets—an assumption that is, to put it bluntly, palpably and provably wrong. In fact, the correct statement would be the following: "A target shareholder wants to maximize how much he or she receives, and a purchaser wants to minimize how much he or she pays, determined on a present value, after-tax basis." The difference in tax rules and tax rates makes this a complicated analysis, but the fundamental principal is simple: The parties want to cut a deal that maximizes their own respective benefits while giving the thinnest slice of the tax pie possible to the government(s).

In Chapters 4 and 5, we examined the tax consequences to the Buyer and Seller of an asset purchase and a stock purchase. However, in this chapter, we must take two very different and complicated alternatives and decide which one is better for both parties. In Chapters 4 and 5, the discussion focused on how to take a particular assumed payment amount and allocate it among various alternatives to observe the effect on both the Buyer and Seller. However, in the real world, the biggest "variable" between the Buyer and Seller can often be the purchase price: The Buyer will propose to pay less for a stock sale (because the Buyer takes on the risk of the existing business and enjoys little or no tax benefit from a stock purchase), and the Seller will be willing to entertain less for a stock sale provided that the after-tax benefit is better. To compare one transaction structure to another, one must do a present value analysis for both the proposed asset acquisition and stock acquisition alternatives and see which one works out better for the parties.

***Example 1:** Asset sale by the Target for $10 million.* Example 1 analyzes the tax consequences of an asset sale. Assume the following facts (which should now be relatively familiar): The Buyer offers to purchase the assets of the Target for $8 million, and offers to pay $1.5 million in consulting payments and $500,000 in noncompete payments to the sole shareholder/key employee. The discounting rate in this example is 10 percent, and the tax rates (including both federal and state income tax liabilities) are estimated to be a combined rate of 40 percent on corporate income, 40 percent on individual ordinary income, 20 percent on individual LTCG, and three percent as an approximation of self-employment (SE) tax. The Target is going to keep or distribute its cash prior to the sale transaction. The Acquirer is going put purchase the following assets:

1. *Accounts receivable.* These have a face value, tax basis, and fair market value all equal to $400,000.
2. *Inventory.* The inventory has a tax basis and fair market value of $600,000.
3. *Depreciable (Class V) assets.* These were originally purchased for $1,250,000 and have $500,000 of remaining tax basis. Fair market value is assumed to equal current tax basis of $500,000. Most or all the assets are assumed to be five-year property under Code section 168, with approximately three tax years of depreciation remaining. (This last assumption is based on the fact that assets are purchased and placed in service continuously in an on-going business. An actual balance sheet of assets, and the depreciation schedule related to those assets, can be extremely detailed, but in the end the results are prosaic—namely, how much depreciation is available in each year if the transaction is a stock sale. Therefore, the approximation proposed above is sufficient for purposes of this exercise.)
4. *Intangible assets.* This assumes the Code section 197 intangibles (excluding goodwill) have zero tax basis and an FMV of $2.5 million.
5. *Consulting and noncompete payments.* It is assumed that $2 million is allocated to "personal" payments to owner-employees of the Target, divided $1.5 million to consulting ($500,000/year for three years) and $500,000 for a noncompete covenant.
6. *Goodwill.* Determined using the residual method, the goodwill is valued at $4 million in Example 1.

Seller-side tax consequences of asset sale. On the Seller side, the C corporation would sell its assets with $1.5 million of tax basis for $8 million, would recognize $6.5 million of taxable gain, and at an assumed 40-percent (federal and state) tax rate, would pay approximately $2.6 million in tax. The remaining $5.4 million in cash proceeds would be distributed to its shareholders.

At the Target shareholder level, the shareholders would receive a $5.4 million liquidating distribution. Because they are assumed to have $100,000 of tax basis in the Target stock, their taxable gain would be $5.3 million. Assuming a combined (federal and state) LTCG tax rate of 20 percent, the tax is $1,060,000, and the after-tax distribution amount is $4,340,000.

The Target shareholders are paid $1.5 million in consulting payments and pay an estimated 43 percent in combined federal and state income tax and SE tax, or $645,000 (ignoring any time value of money issues), leaving $855,000 after such taxes. The $500,000 noncompete payment is subject to an estimated 40 percent income tax (federal and state), or $200,000 of tax, leaving $300,000 of after-tax income.

Adding the after-tax amounts from the three categories of payments described above, the Target shareholders are projected to receive $5,495,000 in after-tax proceeds from $10 million of payments structured in the manner described above.

Figure 6.1 summarizes the tax consequences of an asset sale:

Basic Tax Assumptions			
Aggregate purchase price of assets			$10,000,000.00
Assumed discounting rate			10.00%
Combined corporate tax rate			40.00%
Combined individual tax rate			40.00%
Combined individual LTCG rate			20.00%
Approximated SE tax			3.00%
C Corporation Assets	***Original Purchase Price***	***Current Tax Basis***	***Current Fair Market Value***
A/R (Class III assets)	$400,000.00	$400,000.00	$400,000.00
Inventory (Class IV assets)	$600,000.00	$600,000.00	$600,000.00
Depreciable assets (Class V)	$1,250,000.00	$500,000.00	$500,000.00
Various Section 197 intangibles (excluding goodwill)	$0.00	$0.00	$2,500,000.00
Consulting ($500,000/yr. for 3 yrs.)			$1,500,000.00
Noncompete			$500,000.00
Non-goodwill total			$6,000,000.00
Goodwill	$0.00	$0.00	$4,000,000.00
Total	$2,250,000.00	$1,500,000.00	$10,000,000.00
Tax Consequences to Selling C Corporation			
Corporation			***Asset Sale***
Purchase price			$8,000,000.00
Asset tax basis			$1,500,000.00
Net income or gain			$6,500,000.00
NOL			$0.00
Net taxable gain			$6,500,000.00
Tax (40%)			$2,600,000.00
Liquidating distribution			$5,400,000.00
Tax Consequences to Shareholders on C Corporation Liquidation			
Compensation to Shareholder			$1,500,000.00
Combined income and SE tax on comp (43%)			$645,000.00
Net compensation			$855,000.00
Noncompete payment			$500,000.00
Tax (40%)			$200,000.00
Net after-tax noncompete			$300,000.00
Distribution/payment			$5,400,000.00

Figure 6.1 (cont'd)

Aggregate tax basis in stock	$100,000.00
Taxable gain	$5,300,000.00
Tax (20%)	$1,060,000.00
Net distribution to shareholders	$4,340,000.00
Total after tax benefit	$5,495,000.00

Tax Consequences to Buyer Asset Purchase

YEAR	1	2	3	4	5	6	7
A/R	$400,000.00						
Depreciation	$100,000.00	$160,000.00	$96,000.00	$57,600.00	$57,600.00	$28,800.00	
Inventory	$600,000.00						
Section 197 intangibles	$166,666.67	$166,666.67	$166,666.67	$166,666.67	$166,666.67	$166,666.67	$166,666.67
Consulting	$500,000.00	$500,000.00	$500,000.00				
Noncompete	$33,333.33	$33,333.33	$33,333.33	$33,333.33	$33,333.33	$33,333.33	$33,333.33
Goodwill	$266,666.67	$266,666.67	$266,666.67	$266,666.67	$266,666.67	$266,666.67	$266,666.67
Total annual tax deductions	$2,066,666.67	$1,126,666.67	$1,062,666.67	$524,266.67	$524,266.67	$495,466.67	$466,666.67
Tax savings	$826,666.67	$450,666.67	$425,066.67	$209,706.67	$209,706.67	$198,186.67	$186,666.67
Present value of tax savings	$751,515.15	$372,451.79	$319,358.88	$143,232.48	$130,211.34	$111,871.21	$95,789.52
Total PV benefit	$2,435,460.35						
Total payments	$10,000,000.00						
Net after-tax cost	$7,564,539.65						

YEAR	8	9	10	11	12	13	14	15
A/R								
Depreciation								
Inventory								
Section 197 intangibles	$166,666.67	$166,666.67	$166,666.67	$166,666.67	$166,666.67	$166,666.67	$166,666.67	$166,666.67
Consulting								
Noncompete	$33,333.33	$33,333.33	$33,333.33	$33,333.33	$33,333.33	$33,333.33	$33,333.33	$33,333.33
Goodwill	$266,666.67	$266,666.67	$266,666.67	$266,666.67	$266,666.67	$266,666.67	$266,666.67	$266,666.67
Total annual tax deductions	$466,666.67	$466,666.67	$466,666.67	$466,666.67	$466,666.67	$466,666.67	$466,666.67	$466,666.67
Tax savings	$186,666.67	$186,666.67	$186,666.67	$186,666.67	$186,666.67	$186,666.67	$186,666.67	$186,666.67
Present value of tax savings	$87,081.38	$79,164.89	$71,968.08	$65,425.53	$59,477.75	$54,070.68	$49,155.17	$44,686.52
Total PV benefit								
Total payments								
Net after-tax cost								

Buyer-side tax consequences of asset sale. The Buyer allocates its $10 million of payments as described above. In order to place a value on various economic and tax benefits, a spreadsheet is constructed showing the various assets or categories to which payments are allocated, and the resulting year-by-year benefits over the next fifteen years.

Accounts receivable and inventory, allocated a total of $1 million of purchase price, and are arguably enjoyed in the first year because these expenses would need to be replaced by operating capital of the Buyer immediately.

The purchase price of Class V assets is capitalized and depreciated over the MACRS period permitted for five-year property, resulting in deductions, mostly front-loaded, over the first six tax years.

Consulting payments are paid $500,000 a year for three years. One can question whether these payments should be "discounted" in Years 1, 2, and 3 since the payments are not made until the year in which the deduction is claimed. However, because the discounting formula is relatively benign in the first few years, these payments are included with all other tax deductions and subjected to a present value discount. (Technically, one can argue that each annual consulting payment should be discounted for one and only one year, since consulting payments for each year are made throughout that particular tax year, and are not claimed until the tax return is filed the following April 15. Readers are welcome and encouraged to make such refinements as they deem appropriate.)

Noncompete payments are capitalized and amortized over fifteen years under Code section 197. Note that this example assumes the $500,000 noncompete payment is paid in full in year one, and thus is amortized ratably over fifteen years. If noncompete payments in connection with an acquisition are paid in whole or in part after the year of sale, the payment amount is not added to amortizable tax basis until the year such payment is made, and it is then amortized ratably over the remaining portion of the fifteen-year amortization schedule. Thus, not only are noncompete payments stretched out over fifteen years, but payments made after the first year are in effect further "backloaded" by amortizing the payment amount ratably over the remainder of the fifteen-year term.

Goodwill is likewise amortized ratably over fifteen years. The later years of the chart show that the discounting of present value grows increasingly pronounced with each passing year.

The spreadsheet shows $10 million of expenditures over fifteen years, and, at a 40-percent assumed tax rate for the Acquirer in each year, gross tax savings of $4 million. Applying present value discounts at a 10-percent discounting rate, this $4 million in gross tax savings translates into $2,435,460.35 in net present-value tax benefits. Therefore, evaluated on an after-tax, present-value basis, the estimated cost of the acquisition to the Buyer in this example is $7,564,539.65. This is an estimate and approximation, but it does provide a reasonably good measurement of the estimated tax benefits and total net cost.

Example 2: *Sale of Target stock for $7 million.* In this example, the Seller Group approaches the Acquirer and asks the Acquirer to make an alternative acquisition offer based on the assumption that the transaction will be structured as a stock purchase. The Seller's motive is to take advantage of the low long-term capital gains tax rate that would apply to a stock sale. The Seller expects the Acquirer to offer a lower amount, but would like to know what this amount might be in order to do a direct after-tax comparison of benefits.

On the facts known thus far, based on Example 1, the Acquirer would have a theoretical "indifference point" where the stock purchase price is the Acquirer's approximation of the $7,564,539.65 after-tax cost calculated in Example 1. Stated differently, the Acquirer will likely view a stock purchase as "dead money" with no reasonably anticipated tax benefit within the foreseeable future, and hence the Acquirer will be willing to pay no more than the after-tax, present value cost of the asset sale. Any price higher than this indifference point would be *worse* to the Acquirer than the proposed asset sale. However, any price lower than this indifference point would produce a *better* present-value, after-tax benefit to the Acquirer. The Acquirer would have to weigh the "risk cost" of buying the Target's stock instead of choosing a "risk-free" asset acquisition. On the other hand, if the stock acquisition requires a lower payment, it may be attractive to the Acquirer because a stock purchase is often mechanically easier to implement. A transfer of shares of stock is easy

Figure 6.2 summarizes the tax analysis of the parties with respect to this offer:

Basic Tax Assumptions			
Proposed purchase price of target stock			$7,000,000.00
Assumed discounting rate			10.00%
Combined corporate tax rate			40.00%
Combined individual tax rate			40.00%
Combined individual LTCG rate			20.00%
Approximated SE tax			3.00%
C Corporation Assets	***Original Purchase Price***	***Current Tax Basis***	***Current Fair Market Value***
A/R (Class III assets)	$400,000.00	$400,000.00	$400,000.00
Inventory (Class IV assets)	$600,000.00	$600,000.00	$600,000.00
Depreciable assets (Class V)	$1,250,000.00	$500,000.00	$500,000.00
Various Section 197 intangibles (excluding goodwill)	$0.00	$0.00	$2,500,000.00
Consulting ($0/yr. for 3 yrs.)	$0.00	$0.00	$0.00
Noncompete	$0.00	$0.00	$0.00
Non-goodwill total			$4,000,000.00
Goodwill	$0.00	$0.00	$3,000,000.00
Total	$2,250,000.00	$1,500,000.00	$7,000,000.00
Tax Consequences to Target on Stock Sale			
Corporation			***Stock Sale***
Purchase price			$0.00
Asset tax basis			$1,500,000.00
Net income or gain			$0.00
NOL			$0.00
Net taxable gain			$0.00
Tax (40%)			$0.00
Liquidating distribution			$0.00
Tax Consequences to Target Shareholders on Stock Sale			
Compensation to shareholder			$0.00
Combined income and SE tax on comp (43%)			$0.00
Net compensation			$0.00
Noncompete payment			$0.00
Tax (40%)			$0.00
Net after-tax noncompete			$0.00
Stock purchase price			$7,000,000.00

Figure 6.2 (cont'd)

Aggregate tax basis in stock							$100,000.00
Taxable gain							$6,900,000.00
Tax (20%)							$1,380,000.00
After-tax proceeds of stock sale							$5,620,000.00
Total after tax benefits to shareholders							$5,620,000.00
Tax Consequences to Buyer Stock Purchase							
YEAR	**1**	**2**	**3**	**4**	**5**	**6**	**7**
A/R	$400,000.00						
Depreciation	$200,000.00	$200,000.00	$100,000.00				
Inventory	$600,000.00						
Section 197 intangibles	$0	$0.00	$0.00	$0.00	$0.00	$0.00	$0.00
Consulting	$0.00	$0.00	$0.00				
Noncompete	$0.00	$0.00	$0.00	$0.00	$0.00	$0.00	$0.00
Goodwill	$0.00	$0.00	$0.00	$0.00	$0.00	$0.00	$0.00
Total annual tax deductions	$1,200,000.00	$200,000.00	$100,000.00	$0.00	$0.00	$0.00	$0.00
Tax savings	$480,000.00	$80,000.00	$40,000.00	$0.00	$0.00	$0.00	$0.00
Present value of tax savings	$436,363.64	$66,115.70	$30,052.59	$0.00	$0.00	$0.00	$0.00
Total PV benefit	$532,531.93						
Total payments	$7,000,000.00						
Net after-tax cost	$6,467,468.07						

YEAR	**8**	**9**	**10**	**11**	**12**	**13**	**14**	**15**
A/R								
Depreciation								
Inventory								
Section 197 intangibles	$0.00	$0.00	$0.00	$0.00	$0.00	$0.00	$0.00	$0.00
Consulting								
Noncompete	$0.00	$0.00	$0.00	$0.00	$0.00	$0.00	$0.00	$0.00
Goodwill	$0.00	$0.00	$0.00	$0.00	$0.00	$0.00	$0.00	$0.00
Total annual tax deductions	$0.00	$0.00	$0.00	$0.00	$0.00	$0.00	$0.00	$0.00
Tax savings	$0.00	$0.00	$0.00	$0.00	$0.00	$0.00	$0.00	$0.00
Present value of tax savings	$0.00	$0.00	$0.00	$0.00	$0.00	$0.00	$0.00	$0.00
Total PV benefit								
Total payments								
Net after-tax cost								

to document (although it is often harder to negotiate precisely because the Acquirer wants as much information as possible about the risks the Acquirer is assuming through a stock purchase).

Based on these factors, assume that the Acquirer comes back and offers to buy the Target stock for $7 million, with half of the purchase price held in an escrow account for three years to protect against undisclosed risks. Because the escrow account issues are discussed in detail in Chapter 10, we will not dwell on them in this chapter. Assume the parties both view this as a $7 million offer to purchase only shares of the Target.

Seller-side tax consequences of stock sale. Under Example 1, the Seller's estimated after-tax benefit from a $10 million transaction, structured as an $8 million asset sale coupled with a $1.5 million consulting agreement and a $500,000 noncompete agreement, was projected to be approximately $5,495,000.

On a sale of stock for $7 million, by contrast, assuming Target shareholders have $100,000 of tax basis in their Target stock, the selling shareholder(s) would recognize $6.9 million of LTCG. Assuming an estimated 20-percent aggregate federal and state income tax on long-term capital gains, and, assuming the Target stock has been held by the shareholders for more than one year, the shareholders would pay $1,380,000 of capital gains tax ($6,900,000 × 20%), leaving an after-tax benefit of $5,620,000. This is clearly better to the Target shareholders than the after-tax benefit of the proposed asset sale in Example 1, by an estimated $125,000 ($5,620,000 compared to $5,495,000).

Buyer-side tax consequences of stock sale. The Acquirer, meanwhile, acquires the stock of the Target and, absent a Code section 338 election, will not enjoy any step-up in the tax basis of the Target assets as a result of the purchase. As noted above in Chapter 5, a subsequent liquidation of the Target into the Acquirer under Code section 332 is a nonrecognition transaction and does not produce any basis step-up in the Target assets either.

However, the Acquirer does inherent and enjoy the Target's existing tax basis in its assets, which is $1.5 million, and which is treated as enjoyed or recovered by the Target in the manner shown on the spreadsheet.

Based on the calculations shown, the Acquirer has lowered its estimated after-tax acquisition cost from $7,564,539.65 to $6,467,468.07, a net present-value, after-tax savings to the Acquirer of over $1 million.

Comment: Thus far, based on the particular facts in this hypothetical transaction, a stock sale costs the Acquirer less and gives the Target shareholders more on an after-tax present-value basis.

Also, note that the calculations in Example 2 give zero value to the tax basis in the Target stock after the purchase by the Acquirer. Obviously, such tax basis does not have a lot of value to the Acquirer, but one can argue that is has some value (e.g., when and if the Acquirer decides to sell its Target stock to another unrelated party years in the future). Therefore, readers might consider whether to account for the $7 million of purchase basis as part of this exercise as well.

Example 3: *Sale of stock for $8 million.* The Seller considers the benefits of the structure described in Example 2 and decides to make a counter offer to the Buyer. The Seller has done its own internal calculations, and the Seller takes note of the fact that the Buyer is getting a significant tax benefit from the $1.5 million of tax basis in the Target's assets. The Seller therefore proposes that the Buyer boost the stock purchase price to $8 million, up from $7 million.

Seller-side tax consequences of stock sale. On a sale of Target stock for $8 million, assuming Target shareholders have $100,000 of tax basis in their stock, the selling shareholder(s) would recognize $7.9 million of LTCG. Assuming an estimated 20-percent aggregate federal and state income tax on long-term capital gains and assuming the Target stock has been held by the shareholders for more than one year, the shareholders would pay $1,580,000 of capital gains tax ($7,900,000 × 20 percent), leaving an after-tax benefit of $6,420,000. This improves the Target shareholders' after-tax benefit, compared to Example 2, by an estimated $800,000 ($6,420,000 compared to $5,620,000). This result makes obvious sense, since an additional $1 million is being paid to the Seller, subject to an assumed LTCG tax rate of 20 percent.

Buyer-side tax consequences of stock sale. The Buyer, meanwhile, sees its after-tax acquisition cost

Figure 6.3 summarizes how the buyer and seller would analyze this proposal:

Basic Tax Assumptions			
Proposed purchase price of target stock			$8,000,000.00
Assumed discounting rate			10.00%
Combined corporate tax rate			40.00%
Combined individual tax rate			40.00%
Combined individual LTCG rate			20.00%
Approximated SE tax			3.00%
C Corporation Assets	***Original Purchase Price***	***Current Tax Basis***	***Current Fair Market Value***
Accounts receivable (Class III assets)	$400,000.00	$400,000.00	$400,000.00
Inventory (Class IV assets)	$600,000.00	$600,000.00	$600,000.00
Depreciable assets (Class V)	$1,250,000.00	$500,000.00	$500,000.00
Various Section 197 intangibles (excluding goodwill)	$0.00	$0.00	$2,500,000.00
Consulting ($0/yr. for 3 yrs.)	$0.00	$0.00	$0.00
Noncompete	$0.00	$0.00	$0.00
Non-goodwill total			$4,000,000.00
Goodwill	$0.00	$0.00	$4,000,000.00
Total	$2,250,000.00	$1,500,000.00	$8,000,000.00
Tax Consequences to Selling C Corporation			
Corporation			***Stock Sales***
Purchase price			$0.00
Asset tax basis			$1,500,000.00
Net income or gain			$0.00
NOL			$0.00
Net taxable gain			$0.00
Tax (40%)			$0.00
Liquidating distribution			$0.00
Tax Consequences to Shareholders on C Corporation Liquidation			
Compensation to shareholder			$0.00
Combined income and SE tax on comp (43%)			$0.00
Net compensation			$0.00
Noncompete payment			$0.00
Tax (40%)			$0.00
Net after-tax noncompete			$0.00
Stock purchase price			$8,000,000.00

Figure 6.3 (cont'd)

Aggregate tax basis in stock	$100,000.00
Taxable gain	$7,900,000.00
Tax (20%)	$1,580,000.00
After-tax proceeds of stock sale	$6,420,000.00
Total after tax benefits to shareholders	$6,420,000.00

Tax Consequences to Buyer Stock Purchase

YEAR	1	2	3	4	5	6	7
A/R	$400,000.00						
Depreciation	$200,000.00	$200,000.00	$100,000.00				
Inventory	$600,000.00						
Section 197 intangibles	$0.00	$0.00	$0.00	$0.00	$0.00	$0.00	$0.00
Consulting	$0.00	$0.00	$0.00				
Noncompete	$0.00	$0.00	$0.00	$0.00	$0.00	$0.00	$0.00
Goodwill	$0.00	$0.00	$0.00	$0.00	$0.00	$0.00	$0.00
Total annual tax deductions	$1,200,000.00	$200,000.00	$100,000.00	$0.00	$0.00	$0.00	$0.00
Tax savings	$480,000.00	$80,000.00	$40,000.00	$0.00	$0.00	$0.00	$0.00
Present value of tax savings	$436,363.64	$66,115.70	$30,052.59	$0.00	$0.00	$0.00	$0.00
Total PV benefit	$532,531.93						
Total payments	$8,000,000.00						
Net after-tax cost	$7,467,468.07						

YEAR	8	9	10	11	12	13	14	15
A/R								
Depreciation								
Inventory								
Section 197 intangibles	$0.00	$0.00	$0.00	$0.00	$0.00	$0.00	$0.00	$0.00
Consulting								
Noncompete	$0.00	$0.00	$0.00	$0.00	$0.00	$0.00	$0.00	$0.00
Goodwill	$0.00	$0.00	$0.00	$0.00	$0.00	$0.00	$0.00	$0.00
Total annual tax deductions	$0.00	$0.00	$0.00	$0.00	$0.00	$0.00	$0.00	$0.00
Tax savings	$0.00	$0.00	$0.00	$0.00	$0.00	$0.00	$0.00	$0.00
Present value of tax savings	$0.00	$0.00	$0.00	$0.00	$0.00	$0.00	$0.00	$0.00
Total PV benefit								
Total payments								
Net after-tax cost								

increase by exactly $1 million, reflecting the fact that the additional $1 million of purchase price is allocated to tax basis in the Target stock, which tax basis is valued at or near zero by the Buyer. The Buyer's estimated after-tax cost, $7,467,468.07, is still approximately $97,000 less than the Buyer's estimated present-value, after-tax cost of $7,564,539.65 in Example 1. However, the spread has narrowed considerably, and the Buyer may perceive the reduction as now being too small to compensate the Buyer for the added risks inherent in a stock acquisition.

Comment: Practically speaking, the adjustment proposed by the Seller in Example 3 is clearly not very "tax efficient" because the Buyer must incur $1 million in additional after-tax cost in order to transfer $800,000 of after-tax benefit to the Seller. The big winners in this proposed strategy are the federal and state governments—they end up with an estimated $200,000 of additional tax revenues compared to Example 2 on an after-tax, present-value basis.

Example 4: *Sale of stock for $6.8 million plus $1.2 million in consulting and noncompete payments.* The Buyer responds to the Seller with a counteroffer and proposes that instead of adding an extra $1 million of purchase price to the stock, the Buyer will add $1 million of extra payments, but will now allocate the $8 million of payments as follows: $900,000 to consulting payments, payable $300,000 a year over three years; $300,000 to a noncompete payment paid in the first year; and the balance of $6.8 million allocated to the stock purchase.

This "reallocation" or adjustment of purchase price to include personal payments to the key Target shareholder(s) creates $1.2 million of consulting and noncompete income to the Seller group, generally taxed at 40-43 percent, but also creates corresponding tax deductions to the Buyer, with the consulting payments deductible as paid over the first three years following the acquisition, and with the $300,000 noncompete payment amortized ratably over fifteen years. These allocations to personal payments produce results for the Acquirer that are significantly better results than "dead" money spent on a stock acquisition.

The respective consequences to each side would be as follows:

Seller-side tax consequences. The Target shareholders would have an estimated after-tax, present value benefit from the proposal, combining the stock sale, the consulting payments, and the noncompete payment, that totals $6,153,000. Compared to the projected present-value, after-tax benefit in Example 3, the Target shareholders' net benefit has decreased by $267,000 (from $6,420,000 to $6,153,000). On the other hand, the Target shareholders are still looking at a much better after-tax return than in Example 1 ($5,495,000) and Example 2 ($5,620,000).

Buyer-side tax consequences. The Buyer, meanwhile, has decreased its after-tax, present-value cost by approximately $360,000 (from $7,467,468.07 to $7,108,197.19, according to the overly precise calculations). Clearly, converting $1.2 million of the total acquisition payment from stock purchase to consulting/noncompete payments reduces the tax costs in the transaction by a magnitude of approximately $100,000. (Sellers pay $267,000 more in taxes, while Buyer projects $360,000 in present-value tax savings).

Comment: Again, although it is usually counterintuitive, structuring an acquisition transaction as a stock purchase to give the Target shareholders LTCG can actually be a poor tax strategy. In particular, a stock sale generating LTCG to a Seller also results in "dead" tax basis to a Buyer, and so is a poor tax result for the parties collectively and a great result for the federal and state taxing authorities, because the Seller pays and estimated 20-percent combined capital gains taxes, while the Buyer's investment produces little or no future tax savings.

By contrast, moving the money away from a stock purchase and toward deductible categories is less beneficial to the taxing authorities because the added tax costs borne by the Seller (generally income taxed at ordinary income tax rates) are almost entirely offset (except for present value considerations) by the tax deductions enjoyed by the Buyer. In particular, $100 of LTCG on a stock sale should generate $20 of tax with

Figure 6.4 summarizes the financial consequences for this proposed transaction:

Basic Tax Assumptions			
Aggregate purchase price of business			$8,000,000.00
Assumed discounting rate			10.00%
Combined corporate tax rate			40.00%
Combined individual tax rate			40.00%
Combined individual LTCG rate			20.00%
Approximated SE tax			3.00%
C Corporation Assets	***Original Purchase Price***	***Current Tax Basis***	***Current Fair Market Value***
Accounts receivable (Class III assets)	$400,000.00	$400,000.00	$400,000.00
Inventory (Class IV assets)	$600,000.00	$600,000.00	$600,000.00
Depreciable assets (Class V)	$1,250,000.00	$500,000.00	$500,000.00
Various Section 197 intangibles (excluding goodwill)	$0.00	$0.00	$2,500,000.00
Consulting ($300,000/yr. for 3 yrs.)			$900,000.00
Noncompete			$300,000.00
Non-goodwill total			$5,200,000.00
Goodwill	$0.00	$0.00	$2,800,000.00
Total	$2,250,000.00	$1,500,000.00	$8,000,000.00
Tax Consequences to Selling C Corporation			
Corporation			***Stock Sale***
Purchase price			$0.00
Asset tax basis			$1,500,000.00
Net income or gain			$0.00
NOL			$0.00
Net taxable gain			$0.00
Tax (40%)			$0.00
Liquidating distribution			$0.00
Tax Consequences to Shareholders on C Corporation Liquidation			
Compensation to shareholder			$900,000.00
Combined income and SE tax on comp (43%)			$387,000.00
Net compensation			$513,000.00
Noncompete payment			$300,000.00
Tax (40%)			$120,000.00
Net after-tax noncompete			$180,000.00
Stock purchase price			$6,800,000.00

Figure 6.4 (cont'd)

Aggregate tax basis in stock							$100,000.00
Taxable gain							$6,700,000.00
Tax (20%)							$1,340,000.00
After-tax proceeds of stock sale							$5,460,000.00
Total after tax benefits to shareholders							$6,153,000.00
Tax Consequences to Buyer Stock Purchase							
YEAR	**1**	**2**	**3**	**4**	**5**	**6**	**7**
A/R	$400,000.00						
Depreciation	$200,000.00	$200,000.00	$100,000.00				
Inventory	$600,000.00						
Section 197 intangibles	$0.00	$0.00	$0.00	$0.00	$0.00	$0.00	$0.00
Consulting	$300,000.00	$300,000.00	$300,000.00				
Noncompete	$20,000.00	$20,000.00	$20,000.00	$20,000.00	$20,000.00	$20,000.00	$20,000.00
Goodwill	$0.00	$0.00	$0.00	$0.00	$0.00	$0.00	$0.00
Total annual tax deductions	$1,520,000.00	$520,000.00	$420,000.00	$20,000.00	$20,000.00	$20,000.00	$20,000.00
Tax savings	$608,000.00	$208,000.00	$168,000.00	$8,000.00	$8,000.00	$8,000.00	$8,000.00
Present value of tax savings	$552,727.27	$171,900.83	$126,220.89	$5,464.11	$4,967.37	$4,515.79	$4,105.26
Total PV benefit	$891,802.81						
Total payments	$8,000,000.00						
Net after-tax cost	$7,108,197.19						

YEAR	**8**	**9**	**10**	**11**	**12**	**13**	**14**	**15**
A/R								
Depreciation								
Inventory								
Section 197 intangibles	$0.00	$0.00	$0.00	$0.00	$0.00	$0.00	$0.00	$0.00
Consulting								
Noncompete	$20,000.00	$20,000.00	$20,000.00	$20,000.00	$20,000.00	$20,000.00	$20,000.00	$20,000.00
Goodwill	$0.00	$0.00	$0.00	$0.00	$0.00	$0.00	$0.00	$0.00
Total annual tax deductions	$20,000.00	$20,000.00	$20,000.00	$20,000.00	$20,000.00	$20,000.00	$20,000.00	$20,000.00
Tax savings	$8,000.00	$8,000.00	$8,000.00	$8,000.00	$8,000.00	$8,000.00	$8,000.00	$8,000.00
Present value of tax savings	$3,732.06	$3,392.78	$3,084.35	$2,803.95	$2,549.05	$2,317.32	$2,106.65	$1,915.14
Total PV benefit								
Total payments								
Net after-tax cost								

little or no offset for future tax benefits because the tax basis in stock is generally "dead" money. By contrast, if $100 is allocated to consulting payments, the payee will be taxed at ordinary income rates (estimated 40-percent tax rate, federal and state) plus will have SE tax liability (estimated three-percent additional tax), for an estimated tax bill of $43, but the Buyer will be able to deduct the $100 currently. Assuming a 40-percent tax rate on corporate income (federal and state), the Buyer recoups $40 in tax savings, leaving the taxing authorities ahead by $3.

Similarly, because noncompete payments will be taxed to the payee at an estimated 40-percent rate, a $100 noncompete payment would result in $40 of state and federal tax. However, the Buyer would be permitted to amortize the $100 ratably over fifteen years, resulting in $40 of tax savings spread over fifteen years. Although this is nominally an equal tax offset (the taxing authorities collect $40 of tax and "give back" $40 in tax savings), time value of money suggests that the taxing authorities come out significantly ahead in this latter arrangement. Informal calculations suggest that the present value tax savings of amounts amortized over fifteen years is approximately half of the tax savings that would be realized from deducting the entire amount in the first year. Using this informal "rule of thumb", the tax benefit to the Buyer of $40 capitalized and amortized over fifteen years would be approximately $20 in tax savings on a present-value, after-tax basis. Therefore, an allocation of purchase price to stock purchase and an allocation to noncompete payments arguably produce a comparable present-value, after-tax result, namely for every $100, the taxing authorities end up ahead by $20 in net tax revenues on an adjusted present-value, after-tax analysis.

Summary of negotiations from Example 1 through Example 4. The Seller is getting happy with the deal configuration because the selling shareholders have increased their proposed after-tax, present-value benefit from $5,495,000 in Example 1 to $6,153,000 in Example 4, an increase of approximately $650,000. The Buyer, meanwhile, is also happy because the Buyer has reduced its after-tax, present-value cost of acquisition from $7,564,539 in Example 1 to $7,108,197.19 in Example 4, a reduction of approximately $450,000.

The reduction in tax between Example 1 and Example 4 reflects the combined effects of two important elements of acquisition tax-planning. First, there is a huge difference in a Seller's tax cost between a sale of assets subject to double taxation (resulting in effective tax rates over 50 percent when the two taxes are combined through a sale-liquidation) and a stock sale (subject to an approximated 20-percent combined federal and state tax). Second, that tax differential allows a Seller to drop the price of the stock sale quite substantially and still come out ahead. In particular, Example 2 shows that, compared to a $10 million asset sale in Example 1, a $7 million stock sale gives the selling shareholders an extra $125,000 in after-tax, present-value benefit, while reducing the Buyer's after-tax, present-value cost by approximately $1.1 million. Example 3 shows that even if the Seller then pushes back and asks for an $8 million purchase price in a stock sale, the Buyer still saves $100,000, while the Seller increases its after-tax, present-value benefit to almost $1 million.

Example 5: *Sale of stock for $7.5 million.* If the Seller and Buyer were trying to structure the transaction solely as a stock sale, the results from Examples 2 and 3 might suggest to one side, or both, that the "right" purchase price for a stock acquisition would be approximately $7.5 million because that would leave both parties approximately $500,000 "better off" compared to the original $10 million asset acquisition. In fact, running the tax computations at $7.5 million of stock purchase price (and no allocations to consulting or noncompete payments) shows the results in **Figure 6.5**.

Seller-side tax consequences. The Target shareholders would, under the projections, sell their stock for $7.5 million, and, taking into account $100,000 of tax basis in the shares, report $7.4 million of LTCG. After paying tax of $1,480,000 ($7,400,000 × 20%) to federal and state taxing authorities, they would enjoy an after-tax, present-value benefit of $6,020,000, which is $525,000 better than their projected benefit in Example 1.

Buyer-side tax consequences. Meanwhile, the Buyer would enjoy the limited tax benefits from its inherited tax basis in the Target assets, and would bear an estimated after-tax, present-value cost of $6,967,468.07, which is approximately $600,000 less than the projected present-value, after-tax cost of $7,564,539.65 in Example 1.

As expected, the Target shareholders and the Buyer have identified a price at which each is approximately

Figure 6.5

Basic Tax Assumptions			
Aggregate purchase price of business			$7,500,000.00
Assumed discounting rate			10.00%
Combined corporate tax rate			40.00%
Combined individual tax rate			40.00%
Combined individual LTCG rate			20.00%
Approximated SE tax			3.00%
C Corporation Assets	***Original Purchase Price***	***Current Tax Basis***	***Current Fair Market Value***
Accounts receivable (Class III assets)	$400,000.00	$400,000.00	$400,000.00
Inventory (Class IV assets)	$600,000.00	$600,000.00	$600,000.00
Depreciable assets (Class V)	$1,250,000.00	$500,000.00	$500,000.00
Various Section 197 intangibles (excluding goodwill)	$0.00	$0.00	$2,500,000.00
Consulting ($0/yr. for 3 yrs.)			$0.00
Noncompete			$0.00
Non-goodwill total			$4,000,000.00
Goodwill	$0.00	$0.00	$3,500,000.00
Total	$2,250,000.00	$1,500,000.00	$7,500,000.00
Tax Consequences to Selling C Corporation			
Corporation			***Stock Sale***
Purchase price			$0.00
Asset tax basis			$1,500,000.00
Net income or gain			$0.00
NOL			$0.00
Net taxable gain			$0.00
Tax (40%)			$0.00
Liquidating distribution			$0.00
Tax Consequences to Shareholders on Stock Sale			
Compensation to shareholder			$0.00
Combined income and SE tax on comp (43%)			$0.00
Net compensation			$0.00
Noncompete payment			$0.00
Tax (40%)			$0.00
Net after-tax noncompete			$0.00
Stock purchase price			$7,500,000.00

Figure 6.5 (cont'd)

Aggregate tax basis in stock	$100,000.00
Taxable gain	$7,400,000.00
Tax (20%)	$1,480,000.00
After-tax proceeds of stock sale	$6,020,000.00
Total after tax benefits to shareholders	$6,020,000.00

Tax Consequences to Buyer Stock Purchase

YEAR	1	2	3	4	5	6	7
A/R	$400,000.00						
Depreciation	$200,000.00	$200,000.00	$100,000.00				
Inventory	$600,000.00						
Section 197 intangibles	$0.00	$0.00	$0.00	$0.00	$0.00	$0.00	$0.00
Consulting	$0.00	$0.00	$0.00				
Noncompete	$0.00	$0.00	$0.00	$0.00	$0.00	$0.00	$0.00
Goodwill	$0.00	$0.00	$0.00	$0.00	$0.00	$0.00	$0.00
Total annual tax deductions	$1,200,000.00	$200,000.00	$100,000.00	$0.00	$0.00	$0.00	$0.00
Tax savings	$480,000.00	$80,000.00	$40,000.00	$0.00	$0.00	$0.00	$0.00
Present value of tax savings	$436,363.64	$66,115.70	$30,052.59	$0.00	$0.00	$0.00	$0.00
Total PV benefit	$532,531.93						
Total payments	$7,500,000.00						
Net after-tax cost	$6,967,468.07						

YEAR	8	9	10	11	12	13	14	15
A/R								
Depreciation								
Inventory								
Section 197 intangibles	$0.00	$0.00	$0.00	$0.00	$0.00	$0.00	$0.00	$0.00
Consulting								
Noncompete	$0.00	$0.00	$0.00	$0.00	$0.00	$0.00	$0.00	$0.00
Goodwill	$0.00	$0.00	$0.00	$0.00	$0.00	$0.00	$0.00	$0.00
Total annual tax deductions	$0.00	$0.00	$0.00	$0.00	$0.00	$0.00	$0.00	$0.00
Tax savings	$0.00	$0.00	$0.00	$0.00	$0.00	$0.00	$0.00	$0.00
Present value of tax savings	$0.00	$0.00	$0.00	$0.00	$0.00	$0.00	$0.00	$0.00
Total PV benefit								
Total payments								
Net after-tax cost								

$500,000 better off than compared to the results in Example 1.

Comment: Why is "splitting" this tax savings the "right" result? In an abstract sense, there is no right or wrong answer in negotiating the acquisition price. In a very fundamental and practical sense, however, if the parties start their tax planning and business structuring discussions based on a "model" of the transaction as a $10 million asset acquisition, this starting point for the discussions quickly evolves into the "benchmark" against which all subsequent structuring changes are measured. If either party proposes a major restructuring of the deal, once the negotiations are relatively far along, because of a perceived tax savings, it is both incumbent and almost necessary to "share" that tax savings with the other side.

The lesson in this should be obvious: If you are the Seller, you do not want to start the negotiations using as a benchmark the structure in Example 1, but rather you want to do your tax homework before the negotiations start and begin the process by proposing the structure in Example 3! Above all else, you want to avoid establishing as the benchmark for the negotiations an unfavorable initial tax structure!

"Goosing Up" the Tax Benefits on a Stock Sale

As previously noted, moving from an asset sale to a stock sale makes tax sense because the Target shareholders are so much better off with a combined 20-percent federal and state capital gains tax rate, compared to double taxation at or near the 50-percent level, that the Seller can lower its price dramatically and both the Seller and Buyer will come out ahead. However, as Example 4 illustrates, it is possible to make the stock sale even more tax favorable to the extent that the parties can allocate part of the purchase price to consulting payments and other personal payments (or parallel payments). Basically, a stock sale produces a net 20 percent "tax toll"—the Target shareholders pay 20-percent tax while the Buyer enjoys essentially zero tax benefit.

As Examples 1, 2, and 3 demonstrate, the 20-percent tax toll on a stock sale is not as heavy as the tax toll on a corporate asset sale, where the Seller group pays roughly a 50-percent tax (the effects of double taxation) while the Buyer enjoys only a 40-percent tax benefit, which is greatly reduced on a present-value basis because of the fifteen-year amortization that applies to a significant portion of the purchase price.

Significantly, compensation payments and other personal payments or parallel payments (e.g., rent payments under a lease of real property owned by the Target shareholders and retained by them after the sale of the Target) that are paid and deducted currently reduce the "tax toll" to an amount at or near zero. Intuitively, anything that is not good for the taxing authorities is almost necessarily good for the parties to a transaction because, as demonstrated in Example 5, it is usually easy to "share" or split tax savings. Accordingly, Example 4 demonstrates how the Buyer can pay more in gross payments but pay less on an after-tax, present-value basis. The answer is to find, to the extent possible, defensible categories where the payments are ordinary income to the Seller group but immediately deductible to the Buyer.

Example 6: *Sale of stock for $4.7 million plus $3.3 million in other payments.* The Buyer and Seller like the framework for the transaction described in Example 4 and decide that the key shareholder/employee should be hired "permanently" under an employment contract. Or, the parties may find that the selling shareholders also own individually (or through an LLC) the real estate used by the Target as its principal place of business, and both the Buyer and Seller Group are interested in executing a long-term lease at favorable rates.

Example 6 assumes that the Acquirer is willing to pay $8 million in total payments related to the acquisition. The Acquirer has agreed to hire the principal Target shareholder for a salary of $500,000 per year over five years, a total payment of $2.5 million, and also agreed to lease payments of an additional $500,000, paid $100,000 per year for five years. The Acquirer is also allocating $300,000 to a noncompete payment paid in the first year. The allocation to the stock purchase component of the transaction is now $4.7 million.

Seller-side tax consequences. The Target shareholder(s) now have income streams from a variety

Figure 6.6 illustrates estimated tax consequences to the parties as follows:

Basic Tax Assumptions			
Aggregate purchase price of business			$8,000,000.00
Assumed discounting rate			10.00%
Combined corporate tax rate			40.00%
Combined individual tax rate			40.00%
Combined individual LTCG rate			20.00%
Approximated SE tax			3.00%
C Corporation Assets	***Original Purchase Price***	***Current Tax Basis***	***Current Fair Market Value***
Accounts receivable (Class III assets)	$400,000.00	$400,000.00	$400,000.00
Inventory (Class IV assets)	$600,000.00	$600,000.00	$600,000.00
Depreciable assets (Class V)	$1,250,000.00	$500,000.00	$500,000.00
Various Section 197 intangibles (excluding goodwill)	$0.00	$0.00	$2,500,000.00
Salary ($500,000/yr. for 5 yrs.)			$2,500,000.00
Noncompete			$300,000.00
Adjusted lease ($100,000/yr. for 5 yrs.)			$500,000.00
Non-goodwill total			$7,300,000.00
Goodwill	$0.00	$0.00	$700,000.00
Total	$2,250,000.00	$1,500,000.00	$8,000,000.00
Tax Consequences to Selling C Corporation			
Corporation			***Stock Sale***
Purchase price			$0.00
Asset tax basis			$1,500,000.00
Net income or gain			$0.00
NOL			$0.00
Net taxable gain			$0.00
Tax (40%)			$0.00
Liquidating distribution			$0.00
Tax Consequences to Shareholders on Stock Sale			
Compensation to shareholder			$2,500,000.00
Combined income and SE tax on comp (43%)			$1,075,000.00
Net compensation			$1,425,000.00
Noncompete payment			$300,000.00
Tax (40%)			$120,000.00
Net after-tax noncompete			$180,000.00

Figure 6.6 (cont'd)

Lease payments							$500,000.00
Tax (40%)							$200,000.00
Net after tax lease							$300,000.00
Stock purchase price							$4,700,000.00
Aggregate tax basis in stock							$100,000
Taxable gain							$4,600,000.00
Tax (20%)							$920,000.00
After-tax proceeds of stock sale							$3,780,000.00
Total after tax benefits to shareholders							$5,685,000.00
Tax Consequences to Buyer Stock Purchase							
YEAR	**1**	**2**	**3**	**4**	**5**	**6**	**7**
A/R	$400,000.00						
Depreciation	$200,000.00	$200,000.00	$100,000.00				
Inventory	$600,000.00						
Section 197 intangibles	$0.00	$0.00	$0.00	$0.00	$0.00	$0.00	$0.00
Salary	$500,000.00	$500,000.00	$500,000.00	$500,000.00	$500,00.00	$2,500,00.00	
Lease payments	$100,000.00	$100,000.00	$100,000.00	$100,000.00	$100,000.00		
Noncompete	$20,000.00	$20,000.00	$20,000.00	$20,000.00	$20,000.00	$20,000.00	$20,000.00
Goodwill	$0.00	$0.00	$0.00	$0.00	$0.00	$0.00	$0.00
Total annual tax deductions	$1,820,000.00	$820,000.00	$720,000.00	$620,000.00	$620,000.00	$20,000.00	$20,000.00
Gross tax savings (40% fed and state)	$728,000.00	$328,000.00	$288,000.00	$248,000.00	$248,000.00	$8,000.00	$8,000.00
Non-PV payments	$600,000.00	$600,000.00	$600,000.00	$600,000.00	$600,000.00	$0.00	$0.00
Tax savings on non-PV payments (40%)	$240,000.00	$240,000.00	$240,000.00	$240,000.00	$240,000.00	$0.00	$0.00
PV tax deductions	$1,220,000.00	$220,000.00	$120,000.00	$20,000.00	$20,000.00	$20,000.00	$20,000.00
PV tax savings	$728,000.00	$328,000.00	$288,000.00	$248,000.00	$248,000.00	$8,000.00	$8,000.00
Present value of PV tax savings	$661,818.18	$271,074.38	$216,378.66	$169,387.34	$153,988.49	$4,515.79	$4,105.26
Total PV benefit	$2,703,169.39						
Total payments	$8,000,000.00						
Net after-tax cost	$5,296,830.61						

Figure 6.6 (cont'd)

Tax Consequences to Buyer Stock Purchase								
YEAR	**8**	**9**	**10**	**11**	**12**	**13**	**14**	**15**
A/R								
Depreciation								
Inventory								
Section 197 intangibles	$0.00	$0.00	$0.00	$0.00	$0.00	$0.00	$0.00	$0.00
Salary								
Lease payments								
Noncompete	$20,000.00	$20,000.00	$20,000.00	$20,000.00	$20,000.00	$20,000.00	$20,000.00	$20,000.00
Goodwill	$0.00	$0.00	$0.00	$0.00	$0.00	$0.00	$0.00	$0.00
Total annual tax deductions	$20,000.00	$20,000.00	$20,000.00	$20,000.00	$20,000.00	$20,000.00	$20,000.00	$20,000.00
Gross tax savings (40% fed and state)	$8,000.00	$8,000.00	$8,000.00	$8,000.00	$8,000.00	$8,000.00	$8,000.00	$8,000.00
Non-PV payments	$0.00	$0.00	$0.00	$0.00	$0.00	$0.00	$0.00	$0.00
Tax savings on non-PV payments (40%)	$0.00	$0.00	$0.00	$0.00	$0.00	$0.00	$0.00	$0.00
PV tax deductions	$20,000.00	$20,000.00	$20,000.00	$20,000.00	$20,000.00	$20,000.00	$20,000.00	$20,000.00
PV tax savings	$8,000.00	$8,000.00	$8,000.00	$8,000.00	$8,000.00	$8,000.00	$8,000.00	$8,000.00
Present value of PV tax savings	$3,732.06	$3,392.78	$3,084.35	$2,803.95	$2,549.05	$2,317.32	$2,106.65	$1,915.14
Total PV benefit								
Total payments								
Net after-tax cost								

of sources related to the acquisition transaction. After paying estimated combined income taxes of 43 percent (federal, state, and SE tax) on the compensation, 40 percent on the lease payments and noncompete payments, and 20 percent on the stock sale, the total after-tax benefit enjoyed by the Target shareholder(s) is $5,685,000.

Buyer-side tax consequences. The Buyer, meanwhile, has increased significantly the portion of the payments that can be deducted in the first five years of the transaction. Based on total payments of $8 million, the Buyer's present-value, after-tax cost is now reduced to $5,296,803.61.

> ***Example 7:*** *Stock purchase for $5.5 million plus $3.3 million in additional payments*. Example 7 increases the aggregate payments to $8.8 million, with an additional $800,000 allocated to stock purchase price.

Seller-side tax consequences. The tax projections are essentially the same as in Example 6, except that the Target shareholders receive an additional $800,000 of purchase price allocated to the Target stock, with the result that the net present-value, after-tax benefit is increased to a projected amount of $6,325,000. This is close to the Seller's projected benefit in Example 3 ($6,420,000) and well above the Seller's projected benefit in all the other examples.

Buyer-side tax consequences. The Buyer, meanwhile, has increased its projected net present-value, after-tax cost to $6,092,830.61, which is likewise very favorable compared to the projected after-tax costs in most of the other examples.

Summary

The point is that the Buyer and Seller can push additional payments toward the items that produce the best tax results and can share the tax savings—up to the point where the allocations become unreasonable. The final but perhaps most important advice in any structuring situation involving tax-sensitive allocations is to be reasonable in a self-serving way, but above all reasonable. The simple canard, trite but true, is that "the Bulls and the Bears win, and the Pigs lose". Making intelligent, defensible tax allocations is both financially prudent and entirely legal and ethical. However, there are lines, however vague and chimerical they may be, that should not be crossed.

GAME THEORY: THE "IRRATIONAL" NEGOTIATION

Evaluating a business acquisition on a present-value, after-tax basis assumes that both parties to the transaction are acting in an economically rational, self-interested manner. Although the author generally advocates rational analysis, the author is also quick to concede that "rationality" is often the first casualty of a business negotiation. In particular, many, and perhaps most acquisition transactions are negotiated, at least initially, by business people with little training and no instinct for tax issues.

A typical negotiation can go something like this: Two individuals, Brian and Sam, are sitting in the 19th hole of the local golf course. Sam, the owner and president of a successful small business, mentions that he wishes he could pack it all in and spend the rest of his days golfing; Brian, a younger person, jokingly offers to buy Sam's company, and pretty soon the discussion is not so joking. At the end of the night, Brian and Sam agree on a sales price—$5 million—and they shake hands. The deal, in their minds, is done. They buy another round of drinks to toast the agreement.

The next day, one of them comes to someone who knows a little bit about structuring transactions. Usually, the person brings a cocktail napkin, written in a near-indecipherable code containing "all" the business terms. The business terms as defined by Brian and Sam are usually a bunch of irrelevancies ("my secretary gets to keep her green mouse pad"), plus a firm and unequivocal price: $5 million. Unfortunately, the parties to the cocktail napkin deal usually neglect to identify whether the transaction is an asset sale or a stock sale. They have made no effort to allocate price between and among assets, nor have they quantified the amount allocated to consulting payments, noncompetes, and other personal or parallel payments. Both parties will confidently state that they reached an agreement on price. However, after discussing the matter with their respective accountants or legal counsel, the Buyer will clearly remember the agreement was intended to be an asset sale, and the Seller will just as clearly remember that it was intended to be a stock sale. The discussions can easily devolve from there.

A sensible response to this type of situation might be for the parties to say: "Hey, we didn't know what we were doing. Why don't we do it again with a little less beer and a lot more tax advice?" However, that is not what happens in many real-world deals. What

Figure 6.7 shows estimated tax consequences to the parties as follows:

Basic Tax Assumptions			
Aggregate purchase price of business			$8,800,000.00
Assumed discounting rate			10.00%
Combined corporate tax rate			40.00%
Combined individual tax rate			40.00%
Combined individual LTCG rate			20.00%
Approximated SE tax			3.00%
C Corporation Assets	***Original Purchase Price***	***Current Tax Basis***	***Current Fair Market Value***
Accounts receivable (Class III assets)	$400,000.00	$400,000.00	$400,000.00
Inventory (Class IV assets)	$600,000.00	$600,000.00	$600,000.00
Depreciable assets (Class V)	$1,250,000.00	$500,000.00	$500,000.00
Various Section 197 intangibles (excluding goodwill)	$0.00	$0.00	$2,500,000.00
Salary ($500,000/yr. for 5 yrs.)			$2,500,000.00
Noncompete			$300,000.00
Adjusted lease ($100,000/yr. for 5 yrs.)			$500,000.00
Non-goodwill total			$7,300,000.00
Goodwill	$0.00	$0.00	$1,500,000.00
Total	$2,250,000.00	$1,500,000.00	$8,800,000.00
Tax Consequences to Selling C Corporation			
Corporation			***Stock Sale***
Purchase price			$0.00
Asset tax basis			$1,500,000.00
Net income or gain			$0.00
NOL			$0.00
Net taxable gain			$0.00
Tax (40%)			$0.00
Liquidating distribution			$0.00
Tax Consequences to Shareholders on Stock Sale			
Compensation to shareholder			$2,500,000.00
Combined income and SE tax on comp (43%)			$1,075,000.00
Net compensation			$1,425,000.00
Noncompete payment			$300,000.00
Tax (40%)			$120,000.00
Net after-tax noncompete			$180,000.00

Figure 6.7 (cont'd)

Lease payments							$500,000.00
Tax (40%)							$200,000.00
Net after tax lease							$300,000.00
Stock purchase price							$5,500,000.00
Aggregate tax basis in stock							$100,000
Taxable gain							$5,400,000.00
Tax (20%)							$1,080,000.00
After-tax proceeds of stock sale							$4,420,000.00
Total after tax benefits to shareholders							$6,325,000.00
Tax Consequences to Buyer Stock Purchase							
YEAR	**1**	**2**	**3**	**4**	**5**	**6**	**7**
A/R	$400,000.00						
Depreciation	$200,000.00	$200,000.00	$100,000.00				
Inventory	$600,000.00						
Section 197 intangibles	$0.00	$0.00	$0.00	$0.00	$0.00	$0.00	$0.00
Salary	$500,000.00	$500,000.00	$500,000.00	$500,000.00	$500,00.00	$2,500,00.00	
Lease payments	$100,000.00	$100,000.00	$100,000.00	$100,000.00	$100,000.00		
Noncompete	$20,000.00	$20,000.00	$20,000.00	$20,000.00	$20,000.00	$20,000.00	$20,000.00
Goodwill	$0.00	$0.00	$0.00	$0.00	$0.00	$0.00	$0.00
Total annual tax deductions	$1,820,000.00	$820,000.00	$720,000.00	$620,000.00	$620,000.00	$20,000.00	$20,000.00
Gross tax savings (40% fed and state)	$728,000.00	$328,000.00	$288,000.00	$248,000.00	$248,000.00	$8,000.00	$8,000.00
Non-PV payments	$600,000.00	$600,000.00	$600,000.00	$600,000.00	$600,000.00	$0.00	$0.00
Tax savings on non-PV payments (40%)	$240,000.00	$240,000.00	$240,000.00	$240,000.00	$240,000.00	$0.00	$0.00
PV tax deductions	$1,220,000.00	$220,000.00	$120,000.00	$20,000.00	$20,000.00	$20,000.00	$20,000.00
PV tax savings	$728,000.00	$328,000.00	$288,000.00	$248,000.00	$248,000.00	$8,000.00	$8,000.00
Present value of PV tax savings	$661,818.18	$271,074.38	$216,378.66	$169,387.34	$153,988.49	$4,515.79	$4,105.26
Total PV benefit	$2,703,169.39						
Total payments	$8,800,000.00						
Net after-tax cost	$6,096,830.61						

Figure 6.7 (cont'd)

Tax Consequences to Buyer Stock Purchase								
YEAR	**8**	**9**	**10**	**11**	**12**	**13**	**14**	**15**
A/R								
Depreciation								
Inventory								
Section 197 intangibles	$0.00	$0.00	$0.00	$0.00	$0.00	$0.00	$0.00	$0.00
Salary								
Lease payments								
Noncompete	$20,000.00	$20,000.00	$20,000.00	$20,000.00	$20,000.00	$20,000.00	$20,000.00	$20,000.00
Goodwill	$0.00	$0.00	$0.00	$0.00	$0.00	$0.00	$0.00	$0.00
Total annual tax deductions	$20,000.00	$20,000.00	$20,000.00	$20,000.00	$20,000.00	$20,000.00	$20,000.00	$20,000.00
Gross tax savings (40% fed and state)	$8,000.00	$8,000.00	$8,000.00	$8,000.00	$8,000.00	$8,000.00	$8,000.00	$8,000.00
Non-PV payments	$0.00	$0.00	$0.00	$0.00	$0.00	$0.00	$0.00	$0.00
Tax savings on non-PV payments (40%)	$0.00	$0.00	$0.00	$0.00	$0.00	$0.00	$0.00	$0.00
PV tax deductions	$20,000.00	$20,000.00	$20,000.00	$20,000.00	$20,000.00	$20,000.00	$20,000.00	$20,000.00
PV tax savings	$8,000.00	$8,000.00	$8,000.00	$8,000.00	$8,000.00	$8,000.00	$8,000.00	$8,000.00
Present value of PV tax savings	$3,732.06	$3,392.78	$3,084.35	$2,803.95	$2,549.05	$2,317.32	$2,106.65	$1,915.14
Total PV benefit								
Total payments								
Net after-tax cost								

happens is that both Brian and Sam have agreed on a price, and that remains the price—even though neither of them really knew what he was agreeing to! The typical dynamic is that the price doesn't budge—or doesn't budge much—and the parties argue about whether it will be structured as an asset sale or a stock sale. Usually the Buyer wins that discussion, if only because the golden rule prevails—whoever has the gold makes the rules.

Whether or not it starts in a "tax crazy" manner, the key for a Seller in negotiating a sale of a business is to have "sitting power"—the ability to sit in the negotiating chair and demonstrate a willingness to nix the deal unless all the terms are satisfactory. However, as the vignette above suggests, a Seller who gets well into the process of negotiating a business sale is, almost by definition, mentally ready to check out and head for the golf course. Moreover, in many cases the Buyer knows the Seller's mindset all too well. In general, once the Seller gets his or her "price"—and $5 million is probably the right number in this hypothetical napkin deal—the Seller starts to check out mentally and often gives off the body language that confirms this all too clearly. Once that happens, the Buyer has control of the negotiation, and the Seller will end up conceding almost all the business points from then on. Therefore, a Seller must try to give off "sitting power" vibes, even if the Seller is desperate to do the deal. Meanwhile, it is almost always in the Seller's interest to get the deal done as fast as possible because if a Seller really wants to get a deal completed, then time is almost always on the Buyer's side.

From the other side of the table, a Buyer should look for evidence that the Seller has taken the bait. Negotiating a purchase is a lot like fishing when you are the Buyer trying to land a deal. The Buyer's objective is to reel the deal in . . . slowly. Once the Seller has his price, a Buyer can usually get all kinds of additional concessions, benefits, adjustments, and changes. Although this book advocates an after-tax, present-value analysis of economic benefit, it is an absolute fact that most Sellers, even sophisticated business people with strong financial backgrounds, tend to be mesmerized by the top line of an offering price instead of the bottom line of present-value, after-tax benefit.

The point is that deals are done in lots of ways, with varying degrees of sense and logic. However, in all acquisition transactions one fundamental rule always prevails: Both parties are very willing to help each other reduce their respective tax bills, especially if they can figure a way to share or split the tax savings. In the end, the ability to create more after-tax benefit for both parties can be the difference between whether or not an acquisition closes.

CHAPTER ENDNOTES

1. *General Utilities v. Helvering*, 296 U.S. 200 (1935).
2. IRC Sec. 11(b)(2).
3. IRC Sec. 55(b)(1)(B).

TAX-FREE ACQUISITIONS OF CORPORATE STOCK OR ASSETS

CHAPTER 7

OVERVIEW

The principal focus of this book is taxable acquisition transactions, but any discussion of business acquisitions must necessarily examine the circumstances when a "tax-free" acquisition strategy is appropriate. In general, tax-free acquisitions or reorganizations involve an exchange by the Target shareholders of their Target stock in return for a substantial continuing stock interest in the Acquiring Corporation. A transaction can be wholly tax-free or partially tax-free. The latter is often an attractive alternative because it allows a group of selling shareholders to get some cash (called "boot") for a portion of the Target stock, while exchanging the remaining stock on a tax-free basis. However, as will be examined in significant detail below, there are often important limitations on the amount of cash or other boot that can be received in a "tax-free" transaction, depending on the form of the transaction.

Tax-free transactions are generally attractive to Sellers when one of three scenarios is present: (1) the stock of the Acquirer being received in the transaction is publicly traded, or otherwise is reasonably liquid (or the Acquirer stock can in some way can be liquidated without onerous penalties or discounts); (2) the transaction is partially tax-free, but the selling shareholders receive sufficient cash boot to make the illiquidity of the remaining stock an acceptable alternative; or (3) the transaction is really a business merger, bringing two or more businesses together to create a larger, more valuable whole, and the respective owners are not really looking at the transaction as a "sale."

Buyers, by contrast, are often interested in a tax-free acquisition because it allows the Acquirer to "purchase" valuable Target business assets using Acquirer stock instead of using the Acquirer's often-scarce cash resources. The nature of a tax-free acquisition is that the Acquirer "pays" for the acquisition of the Target by diluting the equity of the Acquirer shareholders and in effect reaching into their pockets (or, more accurately, into their investment portfolios) to fund the acquisition, instead of using Acquirer resources to fund the purchase. A "tax-free" acquisition is, in substance, a merger of two businesses, whether or not formally structured as such. In theory a merger can be priced such that the Target shareholders get the "right" amount of Acquirer stock to reflect the corresponding value of the Target assets, and then everyone (again, in theory) benefits jointly as the Acquirer enjoys post-acquisition synergies and economies of scale.

As a practical matter, most Target shareholders, if they are viewing the acquisition transaction as a "sale" of the Target rather than as a "merger" into a continuing, larger business, would prefer to get cash rather than Acquirer stock. Therefore, in order to induce a Target to agree to be acquired on a tax-free basis, the Acquirer generally must offer to pay a "premium" over the perceived current value of Target stock. Among publicly traded corporations (where the market can render an immediate verdict on the terms of an acquisition) it is relatively common for the acquisition price to be above the Target's current market value. The stock price of the Acquirer usually drops, often significantly.

Example 1: Acquirer, a closely held company, has 10 million shares of voting common stock, its only class of equity, issued and outstanding, and its stock is worth $10 million. Target's stock is worth $2 million. In theory, Acquirer could offer to issue 2 million Acquirer shares to Target shareholders in a tax-free transaction for all their Target stock (the number of Target shares, whether it is one share or one billion shares, is irrelevant). Acquirer shareholders and Target shareholders would, collectively, after the acquisition, hold 12 million shares in a combined business that is (theoretically) worth $12 million—or more than $12 million, if, as in most acquisition transactions, the parties believe there will be synergies and economies of scale.

Example 2: Same facts as in Example 1, except that Target shareholders, quite sensibly, view taking a minority interest in Acquirer corporation as an arrangement that imposes an inherent "minority discount" on the value of their equity. Suppose, for example, that the parties enter into the transaction and that the synergies and economies of scale create a post-merger Acquirer worth a theoretical $15 million instead of $12 million. The 2 million Acquirer shares held by former Target shareholders pursuant to the tax-free acquisition would be worth $2.5 million on a pro-rated basis. However, with just 16.67 percent of the total voting power, the former Target shareholders might, with significant logic, apply a 40 percent discount to the value of their Acquirer shares, meaning that the "real" value of the 2 million shares is just $1.5 million.

This is a simple but very real phenomenon in acquisition transactions, and helps explain why, in fact, Target shareholders want a premium over a "fair" exchange price (meaning an exchange price determined in a manner similar to the model illustrated in Example 1). It also helps explain why tax-free acquisition transactions can be especially interesting and complicated.

Although both the Seller and Buyer are often interested in exploring a "tax-free" acquisition, at least initially, most Target shareholders are not inclined to exchange control of a valuable and successful Target business for a minority interest in a different closely held Acquiring Corporation, absent an appropriate premium. If "tax-free" can be implemented in a way that leaves the Target shareholders with a satisfactory combination of liquidity and control, then it is always a very interesting alternative. The problem is that a tax-free acquisition usually makes sense only if the Acquirer is publicly traded or provides its own, custom-tailored mechanism for providing liquidity. By contrast, liquidity in the Acquirer stock usually reduces, often dramatically, the Target shareholders' concerns about minority discount.

On the other hand, the Acquirer may prefer not to use its stock as the currency in an acquisition because the Acquirer (especially if it is publicly traded) is looking to enhance the per share earnings potential of its stock. In such a case, the Acquirer's goal may be to acquire the assets of the Target for a fixed cash price (often, with borrowed financing secured by the Target's assets and/or funded out of the Target's projected future cash flow) and then let the synergies and economies of scale be enjoyed only by the existing shareholders of the Acquirer. If the business assumptions and the pricing expectations are correct—a huge and complicated "if"—both Target shareholders and Acquirer shareholders come out ahead.

Example 3: Same facts as in Example 1 and Example 2, above, except that Acquirer offers to buy all Target stock for $2.5 million ($500,000 above the current identified value of such Target stock). Acquirer borrows $2.5 million from the bank to fund the acquisition and secures the loan with the assets of Target and Acquirer. Target then realizes the anticipated economies of scale, and the value of the merged businesses is now $15 million, subject to a debt burden of $2.5 million, leaving net value of $12.5 million for the original Acquirer shareholders. Thus, Target shareholders are paid a premium for their shares, in cash, while Acquirer shareholders own a post-acquisition business worth $12.5 million (net of debt), which amount obviously compares favorably to the $10 million of identified value of Acquirer prior to the acquisition.

The point of this introductory discussion, more a summary of Economics and Finance 101 than a discussion of federal income tax issues, is to point out that tax-free acquisition transactions tend to be dominated by the issues of tax-deferral, liquidity, timing, and control. In Chapters 4, 5, and 6, the dominant objective was to analyze and compare a taxable asset acquisition to a taxable stock purchase on an after-tax, present-value basis, in order to reduce a complicated computational exercise into a direct apples-to-apples comparison. By contrast, in a tax-free acquisition, the nature of the transaction is more resistant to this type of direct numerical reduction. Because a tax-free transaction results in no tax to the Target or its shareholders and allows the Acquirer to pay, in effect, with someone else's money, any comparison of a taxable acquisition to a tax-free acquisition is inherently of the apples-to-oranges variety. Clients will, in the end, find ways to choose between an apple and an orange, and the goal of this chapter is to identify and articulate exactly what it means to choose and then structure an "orange" transaction—and keep an "orange" tax-free acquisition from turning into a "lemon."

FEDERAL INCOME TAX ASPECTS OF TAX-FREE ACQUISITIONS

This chapter focuses solely on tax-free acquisition strategies involving domestic corporations, as defined in Code section 7701(3) and (4) (i.e., where both the Acquirer and Target operate as domestic entities taxable for federal income tax purposes as corporations). This could include, for example, a limited liability company electing to "check the box" and be taxed as a corporation for federal tax purposes. In general, the ability to participate in tax-free reorganizations is one of the few truly important tax advantages that a corporation (whether taxable as a C corporation or an S corporation) enjoys over an LLC taxable as a partnership. As discussed in Chapter 2, in almost every other respect, from a federal income tax perspective (note carefully this qualifying language), an LLC taxable as a partnership (or as a disregarded entity) enjoys tax benefits that compare favorably to those of a corporation. In general, and as we will explore in great detail in Chapters 8 and 9, which address acquisition transactions involving S corporations and partnerships, there is usually a major federal income tax benefit to starting with and then retaining (for as long as possible) pass-through tax status.

There are three principal provisions in the Code that permit tax-free business restructurings, Code section 368 (reorganizations), Code section 351 (tax-free contributions of assets to a controlled corporation), and Code section 721 (tax-free formation of a partnership). The principal provisions addressed in this chapter are Code sections 368 and 351, since both provisions can be used to structure a corporate acquisition of business assets. We will also explore Code section 351 again in Chapter 9 when addressing how to do the equivalent of a tax-free "merger" of an LLC into a corporation. This book will not address the treatment of cross-border transactions under Code section 367. However, it is important to note that transfers of property between domestic and foreign (as defined in Code section 7701(5) and Reg. § 301.7701-2(b)(8)) corporations are subject to special tests for receiving non-recognition treatment. Generally, under Code section 367(a), with limited exceptions, a foreign corporation receiving property from a domestic corporation (an "Outbound Transaction") is NOT treated as a "corporation" for the purposes of provisions affecting reorganizations, liquidations and Code section 351 contributions, and thus such transfers are taxable. By contrast, per Code section 367(b), with respect to "nonoutbound" tax-free transfers, a foreign corporation is considered a "corporation" except to the extent provided in the regulations thereunder. The take away point is that cross-border transactions, which might otherwise be tax-free if made between domestic entities, can be subject to significant U.S. tax liability.

Both Code sections 351 and 368 contain very specific and particular technical rules that must be satisfied in order to enjoy non-recognition treatment for federal income tax purposes. In general, if an acquisition transaction involving two corporations does not qualify under one of these two provisions, then, except for some specific (and relatively narrow) non-recognition provisions described at the end of this chapter, the transaction will be a taxable acquisition that is subject to taxation under the rules described in Chapters 4 through 6.

Before moving on to a technical discussion of Code sections 351 and 368, it is useful to outline the "apples-to-oranges" comparison of a taxable stock acquisition to a tax-free stock acquisition, and a taxable asset acquisition to a tax-free asset acquisition. The principal tax characteristics of each of these four alternatives are outlined in the following examples:

Example 4: *Taxable stock acquisition.* In this transaction, assume the Acquirer purchases Target stock for $2 million in cash.

a. The Target itself does not recognize gain or loss on the transaction, unless an election is made under Code section 338. See Chapter 12.

b. The Target shareholders recognize individual gain or loss on the transaction equal to the difference between their respective proceeds from the sale minus their respective tax bases in their Target shares. Target shareholders have no continuing interest in the Acquirer.

c. The Acquirer's tax basis in the Target shares is $2 million.

d. The Acquirer can increase the Target's tax basis in its assets only by inflicting a second taxable transaction, i.e., by electing under Code section 338 (or jointly with Target shareholder(s) under Code section 338(h)(10)) to treat the Target as selling assets to itself in a hypothetical sale. See Chapter 12.

Example 5: *Tax-free stock acquisition.* Assume the Acquirer enters into a 100 percent tax-free acquisition of Target stock in exchange for $2 million of Acquirer voting stock.

a. The Target itself does not recognize gain or loss on the transaction.[1]

b. Target shareholders do not recognize gain or loss on the transaction.[2]

c. Depending on the form of the acquisition transaction (discussed more fully below), the Acquirer's tax basis in the Target shares will either be a carryover basis equal to the basis such stock had in the hands of the Target's former shareholders, or the Acquirer may take carryover basis in the Target stock equal to the Target's adjusted tax basis in its net assets. In either case, the tax basis in many or most cases will probably be significantly below the $2 million value of the Acquirer stock given to Target shareholders in the transaction.

d. The Acquirer's tax basis in the Target assets will be the carryover tax basis. No Code section 338 election is permitted. The Target's tax attributes will generally carry over as well, subject to possible limitations on the use of loss and credit carryforwards in the hands of the Acquirer.[3]

Comment: Some forms of "tax-free" acquisitions will allow the Acquirer to pay a permitted amount of "boot" in connection with the transaction. Boot does not qualify for non-recognition treatment and, subject to the form of the transaction, will generally be taxable to the Target shareholders. Target shareholders, in turn, will generally adjust their tax basis in Acquirer stock received in the "tax-free" portion of the transaction. They will increase their tax basis for the "boot" recognized as gain, and decrease their tax basis by the value of the boot received by them.[4]

Example 6: *Taxable asset acquisition.* In this transaction, assume the Acquirer purchases Target assets for $2 million.

a. The Target has a fully taxable disposition of its assets for $2 million, and recognizes gain or loss equal to the difference between the proceeds received by it and its tax basis in its various assets. A portion of any gain or loss so recognized may be characterized as ordinary income or loss. (The character of the Target's gain usually will not matter if the Target is a C corporation, because a C corporation does not have a preferential long-term capital gains tax rate; but the character of the gain will usually make a significant difference if the Target is an S corporation.)

b. Target shareholders do not have an immediate tax recognition event as a result of the asset sale (unless the Target is an S corporation, in which case the gain or loss passes through). However, in order to enjoy the proceeds paid to the Target in connection with the sale, the shareholders will need to distribute the sale proceeds (after payment of the Target's corporate-level tax liabilities, if any), and this distribution will likely be characterized either as a taxable dividend to the Target shareholders or as a taxable disposition of the Target shareholders' stock (in the Target) in exchange for the distribution.

c. The Acquirer does not hold the stock of the Target corporation following the transaction.

d. The Acquirer's tax basis in the Target assets will be the purchase price paid for such assets, which purchase price will be apportioned among the assets in accordance with Code section 1060 principles (see Chapter 3). Because the assets are acquired in connection with a business acquisition, Code section 197 will apply to intangible assets and require fifteen-year amortization of all Section 197 intangibles, including goodwill and any non-compete payments made in connection with such acquisition (see Chapter 11).

Example 7: Tax-free asset acquisition. Assume that the Acquirer acquires the assets of the Target in a tax-free transaction and that, pursuant to the acquisition transaction, the Target corporation does not continue in existence. This could be, for example, a Type "A" merger transaction, where the Target merges into the Acquirer and goes out of existence (including a "forward-triangular merger," where the Target is merged into a subsidiary of the Acquirer), or it could be a Type "C" reorganization, where the Acquirer receives Target assets in exchange for its stock, the Target is liquidated, and Acquirer stock received by the Target is distributed to the Target shareholders.

a. The Target generally recognizes no gain or loss on the transaction. The Target goes out of existence, and its existing tax attributes are generally transferred to the Acquirer as part of the transaction.

b. Target shareholders do not recognize any gain or loss on the transaction (except that Target shareholders will be taxed on any "boot" received by them in connection with and to extent permitted to an otherwise "tax-free" transaction). The Target shareholders take carryover tax basis in the Acquirer shares (i.e., the tax basis in their Target shares), adjusted upward for boot gain recognized, and adjusted downward for the amount of boot received.

c. The Acquirer does not hold stock in the Target following the transaction, and the Target generally ceases to exist.

d. The Acquirer has a tax basis in Target assets equal to the Target's tax basis in such assets before the acquisition, increased by any gain recognized by the Target.

CODE SECTION 368—OVERVIEW

Code section 368 technically does not provide "nonrecognition" treatment for tax purposes. Rather, Code section 368 merely defines (in elaborate detail) the meaning of the term "reorganization." Code section 361, in turn, provides that "no gain or loss shall be recognized to a corporation if such corporation is a party to a reorganization and exchanges property, in pursuance of the plan or reorganization, solely for stock or securities in another corporation a party to the reorganization." Code sections 354, 355, and 356 define the circumstances in which a shareholder of a corporation engaged in a reorganization transaction will (or will not) enjoy nonrecognition treatment and the tax rules governing the recognition of "boot."

Code section 368 is divided into numerous subdivisions and subparagraphs. Code section 368(a)(1)(A) through 368(a)(1)(G) are often used to provide a short-hand, alphabetic label to certain specific tax-free transactions permissible under Code section 368. These subparagraphs treat as tax-free the following transactions:

1. Statutory mergers and consolidations (an "A" reorganization).
2. Stock-for-stock exchanges (a "B" reorganization).
3. Stock-for-assets exchanges (a "C" reorganization).
4. Transfers of assets to controlled corporations, including divisive reorganizations (referred to as a "divisive D reorganization" and a "nondivisive D reorganization").
5. Recapitalizations (an "E" reorganization).
6. Mere changes in the identity, form, or place of organization of one corporation (an "F" reorganization).
7. Certain changes arising from bankruptcy or insolvency (a "G" reorganization).

The various reorganization transactions described above can be further subdivided into still more specialized versions of these transactions. Among the most popular forms for structuring an acquisition transaction are the following variations of a Type "A" merger:

1. A forward-triangular merger, under Code section 368(a)(2)(D), pursuant to which a Target corporation is merged into a subsidiary of the Acquirer, Target shareholders receive stock of the Acquirer (and possibly some boot), and the Acquirer holds the subsidiary as the surviving merger entity.

2. A reverse-triangular merger, under Code section 368(a)(2)(E), pursuant to which the Acquirer subsidiary is merged into the Target, Target shareholders receive stock of the Acquirer (and possibly some boot), and the Acquirer holds the Target as the surviving merger entity.

GENERAL REQUIREMENTS IMPOSED ON ALL TYPES OF TAX-FREE REORGANIZATIONS

Certain requirements have to be satisfied by all types of tax-free reorganizations:

1. Business purpose requirement.
2. Continuity of interest requirement.
3. Continuity of business enterprise requirement.
4. Plan of reorganization requirement.
5. Disclosure requirement.

Business Purpose Requirement

A transaction that technically complies with all the requirements of one or more categories of tax-free reorganizations will nonetheless not be recognized as tax-free unless the transaction has a bona fide business purpose. This requirement is found in Reg. § 1.368-1(b), and is derived from historic case law.[5] The case law is fuzzy on whether this "business purpose" may be a shareholder purpose rather than a corporate purpose.[6] Reg. § 1.368-2(g) requires that "the readjustments involved in the exchanges or distributions effected in the consummation thereof must be undertaken for reasons germane to the continuance of the business of a corporation a party to the reorganization."

Comment: In an acquisition transaction between unrelated parties, this requirement is easily met.

Continuity of Interest Requirement

Stockholders of a Target must receive a substantial proprietary interest in the Acquiring Corporation. The IRS takes the position for ruling purposes that stockholders of the Target must receive stock of the Acquiring Corporation having a value at least 50 percent of the value of Target stock,[7] while case law goes as low as 38 percent.[8] Sales and redemptions of stock before or after the transaction will be taken into account if they are in effect part of the overall plan of reorganization.[9] Note that the continuity of interest requirement looks at the aggregate group of shareholders. Therefore, some individual stockholders can receive little or no stock in the Acquiring Corporation so long as the existing Target shareholders in the aggregate satisfy the continuity requirements.

Comment: Until 1998, continuity of interest required that the Target shareholders receiving stock of an Acquirer needed to hold that stock for a vague and undefined period of time, so that the continuity was not temporary or illusory. However, as a practical matter, a large percentage of tax-free acquisitions involve stock of publicly traded companies being offered in exchange for Target stock, and it was, practically speaking, difficult to determine whether the exchanging shareholders were holding enough Acquirer stock for a long enough period to meet this already-vague standard. Accordingly, in 1998, the applicable regulations were substantially modified to provide that, so long as the continuity of interest requirements were met at the time of the acquisition, the test would be deemed satisfied.[10] Thus, so long as the requisite standard (e.g., the 50 percent standard of Rev. Proc. 77-37, or possibly the 38 percent standard in *J.A. Nelson Co.*[11]) is met at the time of the reorganization transaction, the requirement will be deemed met even if all the shareholders sell their Acquirer stock the next day.

Continuity of Business Enterprise Requirement

The Acquiring Corporation must maintain continuity of the business enterprise conducted by the Target corporation. Originally this was interpreted to mean that the Acquiring Corporation must conduct the same type of business activities as the Target.[12] The current definition requires that the Acquiring Corporation either continue the Target corporation's historic business or use a significant portion of the Target's historic business assets in a business.[13] The Acquiring Corporation must thereafter "continue" the enterprise, for a sufficient period of time to negate a step transaction.

Plan of Reorganization Requirement

Reg. § 1.368-1(c) provides that tax-free reorganization treatment is inapplicable unless there is a plan of reorganization. Such plan must contemplate the bona fide execution of one of the transactions specifically described as a reorganization in Code section 368(a) and must provide for the bona fide consummation of each of the requisite acts under which non-recognition of gain is claimed.[14]

> *Comment:* Case law has basically defined this requirement out of existence by holding that virtually any type of evidence, even "discussions and negotiations," can constitute the requisite "plan."[15]

Disclosure Requirement

Every corporation that is a party to a reorganization must file as part of its tax return for the year in which the reorganization occurs a complete statement of all facts pertinent to the transaction, including a copy of the plan of reorganization and various other information detailed in the regulations.[16]

REQUIREMENTS OF SPECIFIC TYPES OF TAX-FREE REORGANIZATIONS

There are seven basic types of reorganizations:

1. Type "A" reorganization.
2. Type "B" reorganization.
3. Type "C" reorganization.
4. Type "D" reorganization.
5. Type "E" reorganization.
6. Type "F" reorganization.
7. Type "G" reorganization.

Type "A" Reorganization[17]

This transaction involves a statutory merger of the Target into the Acquiring Corporation (or, far less likely, a merger of the Acquirer into the Target, or a consolidation of the two into a new third entity) pursuant to state law, and does not involve any special mechanical tests or rules beyond the general requirements set forth in the regulations and compliance with the applicable state law. Cash or other boot can be used in addition to voting or nonvoting stock, subject to the continuity of interest requirement. Realistically, a Type "A" reorganization usually has no more than 50 percent cash or other boot (there can be as much as 60 percent cash and other boot if tax counsel is willing to rely on the case law rather than the Rev. Proc. 77-37[18]), so it does allow for a considerable cash component in the transaction. However, it also involves accepting various less-than-attractive liability risks, discussed below.

In a merger, one corporation or the other is deemed to "survive," in a legal sense, although as a practical matter the survivor carries over many of the attributes, including the legal liabilities and most or all of the tax attributes, of the disappearing corporation. A consolidation, by contrast, involves a combination of two or more corporations to create what is viewed legally as a "new" entity with both of the old corporations legally going out of existence. In all of these transaction structures, the shareholders (and frequently the creditors) of the disappearing corporation(s) automatically become shareholders (and creditors) of the surviving corporation by operation of law.

The classic Type "A" merger transaction is easy to understand, relatively easy to implement, and allows for payment of a significant amount of cash boot. However, if the Acquirer is concerned about the Target's possible legal liabilities (and that will almost always be the case), an "A" reorganization may be unattractive precisely because the post-merger entity now bears all of the Target's legal liabilities. To protect against unexpected or undisclosed liabilities, the Acquirer may prefer one of the alternative reorganization structures that keeps the Target legally separate and isolated for limited liability purposes.

Type "B" Reorganization[19]

A Type "B" reorganization is "the acquisition by one corporation, in exchange solely for all or part of its voting stock (or in exchange solely for all or a part of the voting stock of a corporation which is in control of the acquiring corporation), of stock of another corporation if, immediately after the acquisition, the acquiring corporation has control of such other corporation (whether or not such acquiring corporation had control immediately before the acquisition)."

"Control" for this purpose is defined under Code section 368(c) as the ownership of 80 percent of the total combined voting power of all voting stock plus 80 percent of the total number of shares of all other classes of stock of the corporation.

A Type "B" reorganization is a relatively rigid transaction structure since the sole consideration that can be used in the acquisition is voting stock of either the Acquiring Corporation or its parent (but not a combination of stock from both corporations). Note that the voting stock can be either common or preferred, but otherwise the voting stock requirement is interpreted narrowly and does not include options or warrants to purchase voting stock.

As a practical matter, the inability to give boot to dissenting shareholders, or otherwise to give anything other than Acquirer (or Acquirer parent) voting stock to Target shareholders, is often a significant impediment to the use of a Type "B" reorganization. Realistically, a Type "B" reorganization is too easy to mishandle (even a penny of "boot" will disqualify the transaction), and so a pure "B" reorganization is relatively uncommon. There are planning and structuring mechanisms that can address some of the concerns and problems with a "B" reorganization. For example, it is possible for the Target to redeem for cash the stock of dissenting shareholders, and it is possible to have willing parties buy the shares of the dissenting shareholders before the implementation of a "B" reorganization. If the parties decide to go forward with a "B" reorganization in such circumstances, however, it is usually considered prudent to seek an IRS ruling prior to implementation of the transaction.

Type "C" Reorganization[20]

A Type "C" reorganization is "the acquisition by one corporation, in exchange solely for all or a part of its voting stock (or in exchange solely for all or part of the voting stock of a corporation which is in control of the acquiring corporation), of substantially all of the properties of another corporation, but in determining whether the exchange is solely for stock the assumption by the acquiring corporation of a liability of the other shall be disregarded." A transaction will fail to meet these requirements unless the Target corporation distributes the stock, securities, and other property it receives, as well as its other properties, in pursuance of the plan of reorganization. For purposes of the preceding sentence, if the Target corporation is liquidated pursuant to the plan of reorganization, any distribution to its creditors in connection with such liquidation shall be treated as pursuant to the plan of reorganization.[21]

Although Code section 368(a)(1)(C) by its terms imposes a stringent limit on the acquisition consideration (solely voting stock of the Acquirer or its parent), Code section 368(a)(2)(B) provides a limited amount of relief from that stringent limitation. Code section 368(a)(2)(B) provides that, if an acquisition would otherwise qualify under Code section 368(a)(1)(C) except that the consideration for the acquisition includes "money or other property in addition to voting stock," the acquisition will, nonetheless, be treated as qualifying under Code section 368(a)(1)(C) if "the acquiring corporation acquires, solely for voting stock described in [Code section 368(a)(1)(C)], property of the other corporation having a fair market value which is at least 80 percent of the fair market value of all of the property of the other corporation..."

Therefore, there are two alternative tests for whether the "solely for voting stock" requirement is met: (a) the Acquiring Corporation must transfer only voting stock, except that it may use boot to the extent that such boot plus any Target liabilities assumed by the Acquiring Corporation do not exceed 20 percent of the gross fair market value of the Target's assets; or (b) the Acquiring Corporation must transfer only voting stock, and no boot whatsoever, but then it can assume in connection with such acquisition an unlimited amount of the Target's liabilities.

Another key requirement of a "C" reorganization is that the Target must transfer "substantially all" its assets. The IRS has indicated that for ruling purposes it will rule that the "substantially all" requirement is met if the Acquirer acquires Target assets constituting 70 percent of the gross value of the Target's assets, and 90 percent of the net value of the Target's assets.[22] If an acquisition of stock in what would otherwise be a Type "B" reorganization is followed by liquidation of the Target by the Acquiring Corporation, the IRS will treat the two steps as an asset acquisition and "test" the transaction as a Type "C" reorganization.[23]

As a practical matter, the Target in a "C" reorganization is required to be liquidated.[24] After the transfer of "substantially all" Target assets in exchange for Acquirer stock, the Acquirer stock (and any remaining assets of the Target and any property received from the Acquirer) must be distributed pursuant to the plan of reorganization to the Target shareholders.[25] The benefits of including the liquidation of the Target as part of the "plan" is that distributions of property received from the Acquirer to pay off creditors will be treated as "pursuant to the plan" and will not trigger adverse consequences.[26]

A Type "C" reorganization can be characterized as a "tax-free" acquisition of Target assets in exchange for stock of the Acquiring Corporation, which stock is then transferred to the Target shareholders. Type "C" reorganizations are popular for the same reason as a purchase of assets in a taxable transaction—namely, the Acquiring Corporation wants to acquire the Target's business assets but avoid the Target's legal liabilities. The Acquiring Corporation inherits the general tax characteristics of the Target.[27]

A Type "C" reorganization can be more than a little complicated because of the mathematical and valuation tests that must be satisfied in connection with the "solely for voting stock" and "substantially all the assets" requirements. These tests are applied in a rigid, mathematical fashion to facts that may be murky, confused, contradictory, or entirely inaccurate at the time the transaction is being structured and these crucial legal calculations are being determined. Thus, concluding that the Target has transferred "substantially all" of its assets "solely" for voting stock is an exercise that requires in equal measure mathematics, valuation skills, forensic accounting, and blind faith.

Example 8: Tek Corporation has $800 worth of operating assets, liquid assets (cash and receivables) worth $200, and liabilities in the face amount of $200. If Tek Corporation transfers its $800 of operating assets to Aplex Corporation, but retains the liquid assets to pay off its liabilities, the "substantially all" requirement will be satisfied, since Tek Corporation is transferring more than 90 percent (actually 100 percent) of its net worth and more than 70 percent (actually 80 percent) of its gross assets.

Example 9: Assume the same facts as in Example 8, except that Tek Corporation's liabilities are $400, and Tek Corporation transfers $600 of operating assets to Aplex Corporation, liquidates the remaining operating assets for $200, and uses the proceeds plus the other liquid assets to pay off its liabilities. On these facts, Tek Corporation has not met the "substantially all" requirement. Tek Corporation has transferred 100 percent of its net worth, but has only transferred 60 percent of its gross assets, and therefore Tek Corporation would not meet the 70 percent prong of the test.

Another computational issue that needs to be addressed carefully in a "C" reorganization is the amount of Target liabilities that are being assumed by the Acquiring Corporation when the Acquiring Corporation transfers boot to Target shareholders. Basically, under Code section 368(a)(1)(C), an Acquiring Corporation can assume liabilities in any amount provided that it transfers *only* voting stock in the acquisition transaction. However, if the Acquiring Corporation transfers any cash or other boot, then the total value of the boot *plus* all liabilities assumed by the Acquiring Corporation cannot exceed 20 percent of the gross fair market value of the Target's assets.

Example 10: Assume Tan Corp. has assets worth $1,000 and liabilities of $150. Under a Type "C" reorganization, Amber Inc. could transfer voting stock worth $800, cash of $50 and assume all of Tan's ($150) liabilities. On these facts, the liabilities assumed plus boot equals $200 ($150 + $50), and $200 is exactly 20 percent of $1,000, which is the gross fair market value of Tan's assets. However, this would be an extremely dangerous transaction to implement, since, if there is even a slight valuation miscalculation, and the voting stock transferred in the transaction (and, thus, the value of the assets acquired in exchange for such voting stock) is later determined to have a fair market value less than $800, the transaction would fail the 20 percent test. For example, if the fair market value of the stock is $799 instead of $800, and the fair market value of Tan's assets is determined to be $999 instead of $1000, then liabilities plus boot of $200 will exceed 20 percent of $999 (the exact percentage will be 20.02 percent, which is greater than 20 percent), and the transaction will no longer be eligible for tax-free treatment under Code section 368(a)(1)(C).

Generally, a "C" reorganization is most attractive if the Acquirer is deeply concerned about the legal liability risks of the Target, and thus wants to avoid assuming any ongoing liability obligations. However, because of the complicated and often uncertain mathematical and computational requirements of a "C" reorganization, parties must either accept a very simplified transaction structure or accept risk of failing to meet these statutory requirements. As a practical matter, an Acquirer and a Target may conclude that a better way to deal with ongoing liability risks is to isolate rather than eliminate these risks (e.g., by implementing a forward-or reverse-triangular merger of a Target into an Acquirer subsidiary). The Acquirer could then at least isolate the ongoing risks from its other business assets, and could look to the indemnification provisions from the Target and its shareholders, including possibly an indemnification escrow, to address these perceived economic risks.

Type "D" Reorganization

A Type "D" reorganization is "a transfer by a corporation of all or a part of its assets to another corporation if immediately after the transfer the transferor, or one or more of its shareholders (including persons who were shareholders immediately before the transfer), or any combination thereof, is in control of the corporation to which the assets are transferred; but only if, in pursuance of a plan, stock or securities of the corporation to which the assets are transferred are distributed in a transaction that qualifies under [Code] section 354, 355 or 356." Although a "D" reorganization is not generally used for structuring a tax-free acquisition transaction by an unrelated Acquirer, it is a very common transaction structure in transactions among the existing owners of a business, and so it deserves a brief but appropriate discussion.

Type "D" reorganizations can be divided into two basic categories: "divisive 'D'" reorganizations and "nondivisive 'D'" reorganizations.

In a divisive "D" reorganization, a corporation transfers part of its assets to a controlled corporation and then distributes stock of the controlled corporation to shareholders in a transaction that effectively divides the existing corporation into two surviving or successor corporations. Depending on which shareholders of the dividing corporation receive what interest in each of the two survivors, the transaction can be termed a "spin-off," "split-off," or "split-up:"

a. *Spin-off.* In a "spin-off," the transferor corporation transfers certain business assets to a newly formed subsidiary, and the stock of the subsidiary is then distributed to the existing shareholders of the transferor corporation, pro rata. Following the spin-off, the shareholders now own, in the same proportions, the stock of two corporations, each holding a portion of the business assets formerly held by the transferor.

b. *Split-off.* In a "split-off," the transferor corporation transfers business assets to a newly formed subsidiary, but this time the stock of the subsidiary in not distributed pro rata. Instead, the stock is distributed to some of the shareholders in exchange for their shares of the transferor. It is used as a mechanism for separating the shareholders into separate ownership interests in the two respective corporations.

c. *Split-up.* In a "split-up," the assets of the transferor corporation are transferred into two new corporations, and the transferor liquidates and transfers the stock of each of the two newly formed corporations to its shareholders.

In a divisive "D" reorganization, the distribution of stock by the transferor corporation is "tax-free" to its distributee shareholders under Code section 355. To satisfy Code section 355, both the distributing corporation and the controlled corporation must, immediately after the distribution, be engaged in an "active business," as defined in Code section 355(b). See the discussion of Code section 355 below.

***Example 11:** Split-off transaction.* Arnold Black and Betty White are the 50-50 owners of the Dashing Haberdashery, Inc., a C corporation engaged in running two men's clothing stores located, respectively, in Boston and Worcester, two cities located 40 miles apart. Arnold runs the Boston store, and Betty runs the Worcester store. Arnold and Betty have decided, after twenty years of running the business together, to part ways, and they want to divide the business into two separate corporations, with Arnold and Betty each owning and operating one of the two stores. The Boston and Worcester stores each qualify as a separate line of business. Pursuant to a plan of reorganization, the Dashing Haberdashery, Inc. creates a wholly owned subsidiary, the Smashing Haberdashery, Inc., and contributes all assets of the Worcester business to the newly formed subsidiary.

Because the Boston store has somewhat greater assets and value than the Worcester store, Dashing Habadashery, Inc. contributes some extra cash to the subsidiary to equalize the net asset values of the two corporations. The stock of Smashing Haberdashery, Inc. is then distributed to Betty in exchange for all of her stock in the parent corporation. This transaction is a "split-off" that qualifies as a divisive "D" reorganization.

A nondivisive "D" reorganization, by contrast, is a transaction that results in a nondivisive restructuring of an existing corporate group.

Example 12: Pants and More, Inc., a parent corporation, has two subsidiaries, Shirts Unlimited and Socks Galore. If Pants and More decides to merge Shirts Unlimited and Socks Galore, it could do a statutory merger or consolidation. However, another possible way to accomplish the same transaction would be for Socks Galore to transfer all its assets to Shirts Unlimited in exchange for additional shares of Shirts Unlimited, and then have Socks Galore liquidate and distribute the stock in Shirts Unlimited to Pants and More. This might be a viable restructuring alternative if, for example, Shirts Unlimited and Socks Galore had been combined for operational purposes before the end of a particular tax year, but the parties had failed to file appropriate merger documents with state authorities through oversight.

A Type "D" reorganization has a technical requirement that there be a distribution of stock of the controlled corporation that qualifies under Code sections 354, 355, or 356. In a nondivisive "D" reorganization, there must be a transfer of substantially all of the assets of the transferor, and then the transferor must in turn distribute all of its assets, including all transferee stock, in pursuance of the plan of reorganization.[28] By contrast, divisive "D" transactions will normally qualify under Code section 355, or Code section 355 in conjunction with Code section 356, and therefore allow a transfer of part, but not all, of the transferor's assets.

When a transaction meets the requirements of both a Type "C" reorganization and Type "D" reorganization, it will be treated as a Type "D" reorganization. Code section 368(a)(2)(A). This rule was intended to address obscure concerns and issues, since a reorganization that meets both the Type "C" reorganization and the Type "D" reorganization test does not seem to be restricted in any meaningful way by being treated solely as a Type "D" reorganization. Note that Type "D" reorganizations are subject to Code section 357(c) and can generate a current income recognition event to the extent that liabilities assumed exceed the adjusted basis of property transferred in the transaction.

Type "E" Reorganization

An "E" reorganization is a "recapitalization" of an existing corporation. For example, a typical recapitalization involves the exchange of preferred stock in a corporation for common stock, or vice versa.[29] An "E" reorganization generally involves an agreement among the existing shareholders of a corporation to restructure and reconfigure their arrangement. It is generally not relevant to an acquisition of a Target by an unrelated Acquirer, but it is often highly relevant in a transaction that involves transfers or shifts of ownership among existing owners.

The continuity of interest requirement that normally applies to a "reorganization" is not required for a recapitalization.[30]

The "E" reorganization provisions made it possible to recapitalize closely held corporations in the 1980s in order to implement "estate freeze" transactions. (The estate freeze area has itself been largely "frozen" by various legislative initiatives of Congress, including Code section 2701 *et seq.*)

A recapitalization of a corporation that meets the requirements of Code section 2701 *et seq.* is, in essence, the economic equivalent of an "installment sale" of a family-owned corporation to the next generation of the family.

Type "F" Reorganization

A Type "F" reorganization is a "mere change in identity, form, or place of organization of one corporation, however, effected." A typical "F" reorganization would be the merger of an existing corporation formed in one state into a new corporation organized in a second state.

Type "G" Reorganization

A Type "G" reorganization involves a transfer by a corporation of all or part of its assets to another corporation in a Title 11 or similar situation, but only if, in pursuance of the plan of reorganization, stock or securities of the corporation to which the assets are transferred are distributed in a transaction that qualifies under Code sections 354, 355, or 356.

SUBSIDIARY/TRIANGULAR REORGANIZATIONS

As a practical matter, perhaps the most common acquisition structure, when the parties determine to proceed on a tax-free basis, is for the Acquirer to structure its acquisition of the Target as a so-called "triangular merger" pursuant to which the Target merges with a subsidiary of the Acquirer. In a "forward-triangular merger," the subsidiary of the Acquirer is the surviving corporation; in a "reverse-triangular merger," the Target is the surviving corporation. In both cases, the Target shareholders receive stock of the Acquirer and possibly boot (although the boot rules differ quite considerably between a forward and reverse-triangular merger, as discussed more fully below). In both transaction structures, the Acquirer successfully isolates the business risks and liabilities of the Target within the post-merger subsidiary, and thus does not contaminate or jeopardize the assets of the parent Acquirer.

The choice between doing a forward-triangular or a reverse-triangular merger typically depends on whether it is necessary to keep the Target in existence for various nontax purposes, such as covenants in existing third-party contracts or loan agreements, franchise relationships, or other contractual arrangements that may terminate or otherwise trigger adverse legal consequences if the Target is deemed to be legally liquidated or otherwise terminated. Because contractual rights and intellectual property rights play an ever-increasing role in modern commerce, a large and growing portion of acquisition transactions are structured as reverse-triangular mergers.

> ***Comment:*** Although it is usually pretty easy to understand what party is the "Acquirer" and what party is the "Target," it can become confusing in discussing triangular mergers. In a forward-triangular merger, the subsidiary of the acquiring group is technically the "acquirer," even though stock of the parent is given in exchange for the stock of the Target, and the parent is referred to as the "controlling" corporation. In a reverse-triangular merger, the subsidiary of the acquiring group is referred to as the "merged" corporation, the parent is the "controlling" corporation, and the Target is the "surviving corporation." For the sake of consistency, this chapter will continue to use the terms "Acquirer" and "Target," where appropriate, but will supplement this by identifying the Parent and the Subsidiary, where appropriate, to clarify the structure of a triangular merger.

Forward-Triangular Merger of Target into Subsidiary of Acquiring Corporation under Code Section 368(a)(2)(D)

Code section 368(a)(2)(D) provides that the "acquisition by one corporation, in exchange for stock of a corporation (referred to as 'controlling corporation') which is in control of the acquiring corporation, of substantially all of the properties of another corporation shall not disqualify a transaction under paragraph (1)(A) or (1)(G) if—(i) no stock of the acquiring corporation is used in the transaction, and (ii) in the case of a transaction under paragraph (1)(A), such transaction would have qualified under paragraph (1)(A) had the merger been into the controlling corporation."

In this transaction, the Acquiring Parent typically forms a new Subsidiary, and the Target is merged into that Subsidiary and ceases to exist. The new Subsidiary is the surviving corporation and holds the assets formerly held by the Target. What makes this a "triangular" merger is that Parent stock, rather than Subsidiary stock, is given to the Target shareholders in exchange for their Target shares. Note that if the Subsidiary's stock were used instead, the transaction would qualify as a standard "A" merger.

A forward-triangular merger requires that substantially all of the properties of the Target must be acquired by the Subsidiary. This "substantially all" test has the same meaning as for Type "C" reorganizations.[32,31] However, unlike a "C" reorganization, the forward-triangular merger does not also have a "solely for voting stock" requirement. Therefore, that second layer of computational complexity is not present. Instead, the only additional requirement is that the forward-triangular merger must satisfy the general requirements of an "A" merger, the most important of which is the continuity of interest test.

Because it is generally tested as a form of "A" reorganization (with the added requirement of meeting the "substantially all" test), a forward-triangular merger generally allows more flexible forms of consideration (including nonvoting stock of the Parent, debt securities, and significant cash) compared to a reverse-triangular merger. The most significant requirement is meeting the general continuity of interest requirement. As previously described, the IRS ruling standards permit up to 50 percent boot, and case law may permit an even higher percentage. As a practical matter, a forward-triangular merger is only slightly more onerous to satisfy than a conventional Type "A" merger, and significantly less restrictive than a Type "B," Type "C" or reverse-triangular merger.

One major business reason not to use a forward-triangular merger structure is that the Target corporation legally goes out of existence and is deemed to "transfer" its assets to the acquisition Subsidiary. Such a transfer may jeopardize various valuable contractual and other rights that are central to the acquisition from a business standpoint., Another drawback is that, in practice, the forward-triangular merger can often be surprisingly complex.[32] Experience shows that the "substantially-all" requirement might be tricky to meet. The slightest valuation miscalculation or even a previous bona fide asset distribution performed in the regular course of business can disqualify the transaction and trigger burdensome tax consequences. In that case, not only would the Target shareholders receive an unexpected tax bill, but also the Acquirer could end up having to send a check to the IRS as well. These potential tax liabilities arise from the fact that Target shareholders are deemed to make a taxable exchange of their Target stock for Acquirer stock, and Acquirer, through its ownership of the surviving subsidiary, takes on Target's tax liabilities under Code section 381, which tax liabilities immediately following the transaction are deemed to include a taxable exchange of Target's assets as part of the transaction.

If a forward-triangular merger is blown, the Target shareholders will be treated as exchanging their Target shares for Acquirer shares in a taxable transaction, what may trigger boatloads of taxable gain with no cash to pay the tax. Meanwhile, the Acquirer corporation will acquire the tax attributes of the Target, and those tax attributes will include a deemed sale of Target's assets to the newly-formed subsidiary as part of the (unsuccessful) forward triangular reorganization.

To control and mitigate the risks inherent in a forward-triangular merger reorganization, the received wisdom has been to implement the merger as a "two-step" transaction.

First, it is useful to remember that, as an alternative to a reverse triangular merger under Code section 368(a)(2)(E), a forward triangular merger under Code section 368(a)(2)(D) offers more flexible boot rules, and thus can accommodate a transaction where Target shareholders insist on cash payments in excess of the amounts of boot allowable under a reverse triangular merger (e.g., more than 20 percent). In particular, the forward triangular merger structure does not have the stringent boot restrictions of a reverse triangular merger, and therefore the only real boot limitation is the requirement that the transaction meet the judicially created continuity of interest limitation (COIL). As mentioned before, in Rev. Proc. 77-37, the IRS established a ruling guideline (often treated as a de facto "safe harbor") concluding that the shareholders of the Target corporation in a forward merger (including a forward triangular merger) will satisfy the COIL requirement if they have a continuing interest through stock ownership in Acquirer which is, in the aggregate, equal in value to at least 50 percent of the value of all of the formerly outstanding Target stock.[33] Case law has ruled favorably on transactions where the percentage of Acquirer equity received by Target shareholders was as low as 38 percent, and the boot amount was as large as 62 percent.[34] Obviously, this allows a pretty substantial amount of leeway for boot in a forward triangular merger.

However, a forward triangular merger still has the two potential drawbacks noted above, namely, (1) the transaction likely results in a legal assignment and transfer of Target assets, notably its valuable contracts, which in turn will likely trigger the "assignment" clauses in those contracts, and (2) there is a concern about a nasty tax hit to Acquirer if Target (through actions unknown to Acquirer and possibly not even necessarily known or recognized by Target) violates the "substantially-all-the-assets" test. If the contract issue is a deal killer—and it can be, especially if the Target's primary asset is one or more valuable contracts—then a forward triangular merger is a non-starter. But if contracts are not a central issue, or if, as often happens, the third parties can be convinced to approve an assignment of their contracts under appropriate terms, then the first problem can be ameliorated.

Meeting the "substantially-all-the-assets" test (which, as noted above, is generally interpreted under Revenue Procedure 77-37 to mean that the Acquirer acquires 70 percent of Target's gross assets and 90 percent of Target's net assets in the acquisition transaction) is a legitimate worry for an Acquirer, particularly if (as is increasingly common is these economically challenging times) the Target is a distressed company, as explained above.

To forestall this extremely painful tax result, the current wisdom is to implement a forward triangular merger as a two-step process, namely, (1) the first step (Step 1) is to implement a reverse triangular merger of the Target into a newly-formed transitory subsidiary of the Acquirer, and (2) immediately thereafter, as part of a single integrated plan (Step 2), merge the newly-acquired Target corporation (which the instant before has become a wholly-owned subsidiary of Acquirer) with and into a second newly- formed subsidiary of the Acquirer in a "Type A" merger, with this second newly-formed subsidiary as the surviving corporation.

To repeat in a little more detail, the Acquirer sets up two newly-formed subsidiaries, Subsidiary 1 and Subsidiary 2. Subsidiary 1 mergers with and into the Target corporation in a reverse triangular merger, and, as a result of this first transaction, the Target shareholders receive Acquirer stock and the Target is now a wholly-owned subsidiary of the Acquirer. Immediately thereafter, as part of a single integrated plan, the Acquirer merges the Target corporation (now a wholly-owned subsidiary of Acquirer) with and into the second newly-formed subsidiary, Subsidiary 2, with Subsidiary 2 as the survivor.

The IRS has indicated in authority such as Rev. Rul. 2001-2625 and Rev. Rul. 2001-4626 that certain two-step transactions can be combined or "stepped together" into a single integrated transaction that will be treated as a "reorganization" (See comments on Step Transaction Doctrine below). However, the combining of the steps assumes that the integrated transaction as a whole will meet the requirements of Code section 368(a)(2)(D). The clever element in this two-step transaction structure is that, if the transaction does not qualify as a forward triangular merger because it flunks the substantially-all-the-assets test, it will also flunk the substantially-all-the-assets requirement of a reverse triangular merger, and thus will become a taxable transaction instantly upon the implementation of Step 1.

> ***Comment:*** The authority suggesting a "disaggregation" for tax purposes upon Step 1 includes Rev. Rul. 2008-25, where Acquirer acquired Target in a "good" reverse triangular merger, for 90 percent Acquirer stock and less than 10 percent cash, but then followed the merger with a preplanned liquidation of Target into Acquirer. The IRS ruled that the integrated transaction, taken collectively, did not qualify as a reorganization (because Target liquidates and distributes its assets to Acquirer as part of the integrated transaction, it does not satisfy the "substantially all the assets" test immediately after the transaction). Instead, the IRS ruled that the first step in that two-step transaction was a failed (taxable) transaction under Code section 368(a)(2)(E), and thus the transfer of Target shares by the Target shareholders for Acquirer stock was a fully taxable transaction. The second step of the transaction under Rev. Rul. 2008- 25 was then characterized by the IRS as a Code section 332 liquidation of Target into Acquirer (i.e., a liquidation of a controlled subsidiary into its parent, resulting in non-recognition of gain on the transfer of Target assets to Acquirer and carryover tax basis in such assets in the hands of Acquirer). Significantly, as a result of the integration analysis, the first step in 2008-25 was treated as a taxable transaction (even though, if standing alone, it would have been a "good" reverse triangular merger), and the second step was nonetheless treated as eligible for the non-recognition benefits of the applicable Code provision (in that case, Code section 332).

Thus, in effect, if and when the proposed transaction "blows up," it blows up on Step 1 and hurts only the Target shareholders, causing that transaction to be fully taxable at that point in time. In particular, if Step 1 is not a successful reverse triangular merger then the Target shareholders will have a fully taxable exchange of their shares for the Acquirer shares. Immediately following this fully taxable transaction, the Type A merger of Target into Subsidiary 2 will occur and arguably will not trigger any further tax consequences to any party, because a Type A merger of Target into Subsidiary 2 will be analyzed as a Type A merger under Code section 368(a)(1)(A) and will not have a substantially- all-the-assets requirement (see note above). Instead, as long as the COIL requirements are met (e.g., no more than 50 percent boot) the Step 2 transaction should be treated as a standalone tax-free Type A reorganization.

That, at any rate, is the current thinking on how to implement a forward triangular merger.

Reverse-Triangular Merger of Subsidiary of Acquiring Corporation into Target under Code Section 368(a)(2)(E)

A reverse-triangular merger requires that the surviving Target must hold, after the merger into the

Subsidiary, substantially all of its properties and the properties of the merged corporation and that the Target's former shareholders must receive in the transaction "solely" voting stock of the merged corporation's Parent in exchange for "an amount of the stock of the surviving corporation that constitutes control."[35] "Control" for this purpose means stock possessing at least 80 percent of the total combined voting power of all classes of Target stock entitled to vote and at least 80 percent of the total number of shares of all other classes of stock of the Target.[36] The IRS interprets Code section 368(a)(2)(E) as requiring that the Subsidiary must be a first-tier subsidiary of the Parent.[37]

Creeping control, which is permitted in a Type "B" reorganization, is not permitted in a reverse-triangular merger.

The Target after the transaction must hold substantially all of its assets and substantially all of the assets of the Subsidiary. "Substantially all" is defined in the same way as for a Type "C" reorganization.[38] Likewise, the IRS has stated that for ruling purposes it will use the same tests that it applies to a "C" reorganization, i.e., "substantially all" means 70 percent of the fair market value of the gross assets and 90 percent of the fair market value of the net assets. However, whereas in a "C" reorganization the "substantially all" test applies only to Target assets, in a reverse-triangular merger it applies both to Target and Subsidiary assets. Assets contributed by the Parent to the Subsidiary to be used in the acquisition (e.g., Parent stock, and possibly cash or other boot) are not counted as part of the Subsidiary's assets for purposes of the substantially all test.

As a practical matter, a reverse-triangular merger has relatively stringent mechanical requirements that limit both the amount of boot that can be given to Target shareholders as part of the transaction, and flexibility in spinning off assets or otherwise accommodating shareholders of the Target that do not want to receive stock of the Parent. For example, the "substantially all" requirement prevents a Target from spinning off or distributing more than a relatively limited amount of its assets to its shareholders prior to the merger, and may even prevent a reverse-triangular merger entirely if the Target has made a recent distribution or spin off of assets. Basically, since the "substantially all" test requires that the Target hold at least 90 percent of its net assets (as well as 70 percent of gross assets), the Target can distribute no more than 10 percent of its net assets to shareholders in connection with the plan of reorganization. Meanwhile, the requirement that the Parent exchange "solely" its voting stock for an amount of Target stock representing "control" essentially mandates that at least 80 percent of the acquisition consideration must be Parent voting stock, with no more than 20 percent of the acquisition consideration in the form of cash or other boot.

The regulations take the position that the amount of stock constituting "control" of the Target is determined immediately before the acquisition transaction.[39] The regulation expressly states that Target stock surrendered in the transaction (by any shareholder except the controlling corporation) in exchange for consideration furnished by the Target (and not by the Subsidiary or the Parent) is considered not to be outstanding immediately before the transaction.[40] However, the amount of Target stock that can be so redeemed is effectively limited by the "substantially all" test to 10 percent of the Target's net assets, since "consideration furnished in the transaction by the surviving corporation [Target] in exchange for its stock is property of the surviving corporation which it does not hold after the transaction."[41] In turn, the requirement that the Parent exchange "solely" its voting stock for Target stock constituting "control" means that the Parent can give 20 percent cash boot to Target shareholders, in addition to the cash redemptions permitted under the authority above. This means that the maximum theoretical amount of boot in a reverse-triangular merger is 28 percent, as illustrated below.

Comment: The Parent may assume liabilities of the Target without disqualifying the transaction under Code section 368(a)(2)(E).[42] The assumption of liabilities is treated as a contribution to the Target's capital by the Parent.[43]

Example 13: Target has outstanding 100 shares of its stock. Target has $1200 of gross assets, $200 of liabilities, and $1000 of net assets, including $100 of cash. Target, using its $100 of cash, redeems 10 of the outstanding Target shares immediately before engaging in a reverse-triangular merger involving the Parent and Subsidiary. Because the redemption by Target involves consideration furnished solely by Target, the amount of Target shares counted for purposes of the "control" test does not include the 10 redeemed shares, thereby reducing the number of shares outstanding for "control" purposes to 90. Meanwhile, Target's gross assets are reduced to $1100, and net assets to $900. Since its net assets started at $1000, Target now still meets the "substantially all" test because it holds exactly 90 percent of its net assets (as determined before the redemption) and well over 70 percent of its gross assets as determined before the redemption.

Target can keep its existing liabilities, or Parent can assume these liabilities, without an adverse impact on the reverse-triangular merger. In fact, Target, if it so chose, could apply $200 of its gross assets to pay off the $200 in liabilities, and would still have $900 in gross assets as well as $900 in net assets, and would meet the 90 percent test ($900/1000 = 90%) and the 70 percent test ($900/1200 = 75%).

Next, Target merges into Subsidiary, with Target as the survivor, and Parent gives Target shareholders Parent voting stock valued at $720 in exchange for 72 Target shares, and gives the Target shareholders $180 in cash for the remaining 18 Target shares. This transaction meets the 80 percent control test (72/90 = 80%). Therefore, Target shareholders have received $100 from Target immediately before the merger, and $180 from Parent as part of the merger, for a maximum "boot" percentage of 28 percent.

Comment: Needless to say, few transactions will be structured to push the boot amount to this limit, since a minor calculation mistake in the wrong direction could cause the transaction to fail one of these precise mathematical tests.

Notwithstanding these difficulties and challenges, the reverse-triangular merger is one of the more popular forms of tax-free reorganization because it allows the Parent to gain control of the Target with all of the Target's existing contracts and other relationships intact. For example, a Target that has valuable franchise or contract rights might be acquired through a reverse-triangular merger so that the Acquirer does not need to obtain the permission or consent of the other parties to these valuable contracts.

Comment: Almost all contracts have restrictions or prohibitions against assignment of the contract without the consent of the other party, but many or most contracts do not have a provision that allows the other party to terminate the contract if there is a change of control or ownership of the first contracting party. Such a termination provision might in fact be appropriate to put into contracts if the contracting parties want the right to terminate (or more likely re-negotiate) a contract when and if there is a change of control in another party to the contract.

A reverse-triangular merger is very similar in result to a "B" reorganization, in that the Target ends up as a controlled corporation of the Acquirer. A "B" reorganization and a reverse-triangular merger are generally viewed as "stock acquisitions," while "A," "C" and forward-triangular mergers are each viewed as "asset acquisitions." Nonetheless, as discussed more thoroughly below, the "double dummy" structures might be useful to achieve the same non-recognition results under Code section 351 if a transaction fails to meet any qualifying requirements under Code section 368.

CODE SECTION 355— SPIN-OFFS, SPLIT-OFFS, AND SPLIT-UPS

When the requirements of Code section 355 are met, a corporation may distribute a controlling stock interest in an existing or newly formed Subsidiary to its shareholders tax-free, whether or not such a distribution is pro rata. There are three common variations on a divisive reorganization:

1. *Spin-off.* In a "spin-off," a corporation creates a new Subsidiary, contributes a portion of its assets constituting a separate line of business to that new Subsidiary, and then transfers the Subsidiary stock proportionately to its existing shareholders.

2. *Split-off.* In a "split-off," a corporation creates a new Subsidiary holding assets that constitute a separate line of business, and this time some of its existing shareholders get stock in the new Subsidiary corporation in exchange for their existing shares in the Parent corporation, while the remaining shareholders keep their stock in the existing Parent corporation (i.e., there is now nonproportionate share ownership between the shareholders of the existing corporation and the new Subsidiary).

3. *Split-up*. In a "split-up," a corporation creates two new Subsidiaries rather than one, and then distributes the stock of both Subsidiaries to its existing shareholders in liquidation of the existing corporation.

A divisive "D" reorganization must comply with two Code sections, Code section 368(a)(1)(D) and Code section 355. In a classic divisive "D" reorganization, a corporation drops a specific group of its assets into a controlled Subsidiary and then distributes the Subsidiary's stock, pursuant to a plan of reorganization, to one or more shareholders of the transferor-parent corporation.

For distributees of stock to enjoy tax-free treatment, the distribution must be to shareholders "with respect to their stock."[44] In addition, the following requirements must be satisfied:

- *Control immediately before the distribution*. The distributing corporation must control the corporation whose shares are being distributed.[45] Control is defined in Code section 368(c), and means the distributing corporation must own Subsidiary stock possessing at least 80 percent of the total combined voting power and at least 80 percent of the total number of shares of all of the other classes of stock issued by the Subsidiary.

- *Active conduct to two or more businesses following distribution*. Immediately after the distribution, both the distributing corporation and the controlled corporation must be engaged in the active conduct of a trade or business.[46]

- *Five-year pre-distribution business rule*. The active conduct of a trade or business requirement is satisfied only if each respective trade or business (a) was actively conducted through the five-year period ending on the date of the distribution, (b) neither business was acquired within the five-year period in a taxable transaction and (c) neither business was conducted by another corporation the control of which was acquired (directly or indirectly) during the five-year period in a taxable transaction.[47] Basically, this set of inter-related five-year rules is designed to prevent corporations from making a tax-free distribution of assets as a substitute for a current dividend. The first rule prevents shareholders from having an existing corporation build up a new business and then spin it off to them tax-free rather than paying ordinary dividends to the shareholders who would then use the money to set up the new business.[48] The other requirements are designed to prevent a corporation from purchasing a new business as a temporary investment in anticipation of a tax-free distribution.[49]

- *Distribution of all stock and securities in the controlled corporation*. The distributing corporation must distribute all of its stock and securities in the controlled corporation or an amount of stock constituting control of the controlled corporation, if it meets certain anti-abuse rules.[50]

- *Not a device for distributing earnings and profits*. The transaction must not be used principally as a device for the distribution of earnings and profits.[51] This is a general anti-abuse provision designed to target such transactions as a pre-arranged sale of stock or securities following the divisive transaction.

Special Gain Recognition Rule under Code Section 355(d)

The Revenue Reconciliation Act of 1990[52] added a parent-level gain recognition rule under Code section 355(d) if the transaction is a "disqualified distribution." A "disqualified distribution" is one where any person holds, immediately after the transaction, disqualified stock that constitutes a 50 percent or greater interest (by a vote or value) in either the Parent or the distributed Subsidiary. "Disqualified stock" means any stock acquired by "purchase" within the five-year period preceding the distribution. This anti-abuse rule is designed to prevent disguised corporate-level tax-free "sales" through the use of Code section 355 distributions. For example, this provision would tax so-called "back-in transactions" where a purchaser buys some but not all the stock of a Target corporation, the Target corporation then splits off one or more Subsidiaries to the Target's historic shareholders, and the purchaser is left with 50 percent or more of the Target's stock.

Comment: Code section 355(d) applies only if the distribution otherwise qualifies for Code section 355 treatment at the shareholder level. Note also that if a distribution fails to qualify for Code section 355 treatment, the Parent will not be eligible for non-recognition under Code section 355(c) but instead will be taxable under Code section 311 or 336.

Anti-Morris Trust Rules

The Taxpayer's Relief Act of 1997 (P.L. 105-34) introduced rules, contained in Code section 355(e), designed to prevent the perceived abuse embodied by the *Morris Trust* case. Code section 355(e) operates such that if a distributing corporation (D) distributes stock of a controlled corporation (C), and, as part of a plan, 50 percent or more of either C or D is then acquired (whether in a tax-free or taxable acquisition), the distribution of C stock is treated as a taxable sale by D[53] but is not treated as a taxable distribution to shareholders receiving the C stock.[54] A "plan" is presumed to exist if a 50-percent-or-greater acquisition occurs within the four-year period beginning two years before the distribution date.[55]

Example 14: Pursuant to a plan, Corporation T spins off its wholly owned subsidiary, S, to the T shareholders, and Corporation A then acquires T in a transaction that qualifies as a "B" reorganization under Code section 368, with the T shareholders receiving solely voting stock of A. Under these facts, T is treated as making a taxable sale of the S stock. However, T shareholders do not have a tax-recognition event and do not received a step-up in their basis in the S stock. Instead, the shareholders' original basis in their T stock is spread ratably over the T stock and S stock in proportion to their respective fair market values.[56] On the subsequent B reorganization, the T shareholders will receive A shares with the same basis and holding period as they had in the T shares immediately after the spin-off.[57] Note that T would also be deemed to have a taxable sale of S stock if, instead of acquiring T, Corporation A chose to acquire S.

Comment: Code section 355(e) is a peculiar provision and no one has ever made a particularly compelling argument about why it needed to be enacted in the first place. Among the odd and ironic aspects of this provision is that fact that, despite being widely described as the "anti-*Morris Trust*" legislation, Code section 355(e) would not be triggered by the facts in the *Morris Trust* case! Another anomaly is that Code section 355(e), when triggered, imposes tax on the distributing corporation but not the shareholders. Moreover, since the tax imposed on the distributing corporation does not result in a basis step-up to either the distributee shareholders with respect to the distributed stock or to the controlled corporation with respect to its assets, this Code section 355(e) regime arguably results a three-tier tax! The regulations under Code 355(e), which were positively draconian when first issued, are now more reasonable, but this remains a strange and potentially dangerous provision in the context of acquisition transactions.

Other Aspects of Code Section 355

Code section 355 does not restrict the type of stock that can be distributed, but if preferred stock is used it may constitute "Section 306 stock," in which case its later sale or redemption will produce dividend income rather than capital gain. Code section 355 is primarily concerned with the impact of a divisive transaction on the persons receiving the distributed stock or securities. It does not generally address the impact of the transaction on the distributing corporation (except that Code section 355(c) provides for corporate non-recognition when there is no accompanying "D" reorganization).

E&P adjustments. One potentially important issue is the impact on the distributing corporation's earnings and profits. The rule is that the distributing corporation's earnings and profits are decreased by the lesser of (a) the amount of the E&P adjustment that would have been required had the distributing corporation transferred the stock of the controlled corporation to a new Subsidiary and then distributed the new Subsidiary's stock pursuant to a Type "D" reorganization or (b) the net worth of the controlled corporation. Note also that the controlled corporation apparently retains its own earnings account in such a transaction.

A nonreorganization distribution pursuant to Code section 355(c) is similar to a divisive "D" reorganization except that the distribution does not constitute a "reorganization." Basically, Code section 355(c) provides non-recognition rules for the transferor-parent corporation that parallel those found in Code section 361(c) for reorganizations. Thus, under Code section 355(c), no gain or loss is recognized to the distributing corporation if the distribution consists of "qualified property," which is defined as consisting solely of stock or securities of the controlled Subsidiary. Likewise, Code section 355(a) makes a spin-off transaction tax-free to the shareholders and security holders who receive the distribution of stock in the Subsidiary corporation.

TAXATION OF THE VARIOUS PARTIES TO A TAX-FREE REORGANIZATION

Different tax rules apply to each party to a tax-free reorganization.

Parent/Acquiring Corporation

A Parent/Acquiring Corporation does not recognize gain or loss when it issues its stock pursuant to a reorganization in exchange for a Target corporation's stock or assets.[58] This is true, by the way, even if the transaction does not meet the technical requirements of a tax-free reorganization because Code section 1032 provides for non-recognition whenever a corporation issues its stock for other property.

Because in the case of a forward-triangular merger, a reverse-triangular merger, a triangular "C" reorganization, or a triangular "B" reorganization (each described in Reg. § 1.358-6(b)), the Subsidiary corporation transfers (or is deemed to transfer) Parent corporation stock rather than its own stock, technically Code section 1032 does not apply because the Subsidiary is not transferring its "own" stock in exchange for the Target assets or stock. However, when the transaction qualifies as a reorganization, the regulations provide that the Parent will be treated as the transferor of its own stock in exchange for the Target's assets or stock. Thus the transaction is eligible for non-recognition of gain or loss under Code section 1032.[59] This non-recognition rule only applies to stock provided to or on behalf of the Subsidiary pursuant to the reorganization transaction, not to any Parent stock already owned by the Subsidiary.[60]

Example 15: Parent Corporation ("Parent"), its wholly owned subsidiary ("Subsidiary"), and Target Corporation ("Target") agree to participate in a forward-triangular merger, pursuant to which Target is merged into Subsidiary in exchange for $100 worth of Parent stock. Subsidiary owns $30 (with a $20 tax basis) worth of Parent stock from a prior transaction. Parent agrees to provide an additional $70 of Parent stock as part of the transaction. Neither Parent nor Subsidiary has taxable gain or loss on the exchange of the $70 worth of Parent stock provided by Parent in connection with the reorganization. However, Subsidiary recognizes $10 of gain on the exchange of its "old and cold" Parent stock because it did not receive these shares pursuant to the plan or reorganization.[61]

Comment: The regulations under Code section 1032 extend non-recognition treatment to certain transactions that do not qualify as tax-free reorganizations (e.g., to a forward-triangular merger transaction that does not meet all the technical requirements of Code section 368(a)(2)(D)).[62]

The tax basis rules in a reorganization are strikingly different from the rules in a taxable acquisition. In a reorganization that involves the acquisition of assets (an "A" or "C" reorganization), the Acquiring Corporation generally takes a carryover tax basis in the Target assets, increased by any gain (generally there is none) recognized by the Target on such transfer.[63] Note that if a permitted amount of "boot" is given to Target shareholders in an "A" reorganization, neither the amount of the boot, nor even the amount of the gain recognized by the Target shareholders, will cause an increase in the Acquiring Corporation's tax basis in the Target assets, because, under Code section 362(b), only gain recognized by the "transferor" (meaning the Target corporation in this situation) is added to tax basis; tax basis is not adjusted for any gain recognized by the Target's shareholders. In determining an Acquiring Corporation's holding period in the acquired assets, there is also a tacking of the Target's holding period.[64]

In a "B" reorganization, the Acquiring Corporation takes the same tax basis in Target stock that the stock had in the hands of the transferors (i.e., the Target shareholders), increased by any gain recognized on the transaction by such transferors. Because a "B" reorganization does not permit any boot to be paid to Target shareholders, Target shareholders normally do not recognize any gain from a "B" reorganization. The exception to this general rule is if the Acquiring Corporation issues voting nonqualified preferred stock ("NQ Pfd"), as defined in

Code section 351(g)(2), in which case the NQ Pfd would be considered "boot" for purposes of Code section 356 even though it qualifies as eligible voting stock in the "B" reorganization.

Comment: It is often difficult to obtain tax basis information from existing Target shareholders, and may be essentially impossible if the Target has numerous shareholders. To address this problem the IRS has issued Rev. Proc. 2011-35,[65] which provides guidelines for estimating the tax basis of Target stock acquired in a "B" reorganization.

In the case of a forward-triangular merger, the regulations call for the Parent corporation's tax basis in the Subsidiary following the acquisition to be adjusted as if (1) the Parent acquired the Target's assets and liabilities directly from the Target in a transaction where the Parent's basis in the Target assets was determined under Code section 362, and (2) the Parent then contributed the acquired assets to the Subsidiary in a transaction governed by the basis rules of Code section 358.[66]

Example 16: Target has assets with aggregate tax basis of $60 and fair market value of $100, and no liabilities. Pursuant to a plan, Parent forms Subsidiary with $5 cash (which Subsidiary retains) and Target merges into Subsidiary. Target shareholders receive Parent stock worth $100 in exchange for their Target stock. The transaction meets the requirements of Code section 368(a)(1)(A) and (a)(2)(D).

On these facts, Parent's tax basis in Subsidiary is adjusted as if Parent acquired the Target assets directly from Target, with basis determined under Code section 362(b). Under Code section 362(b), Parent would have an aggregate tax basis of $60 in the Target assets, and on a deemed contribution of these assets to Subsidiary, Parent would increase its basis in the Subsidiary stock from $5 to $65.

In the case of a reverse-triangular merger, the Parent corporation's tax basis in the Target (technically, the "surviving corporation") is determined as if the Target had merged into the Subsidiary in a forward-triangular merger.[67] As noted above, the Parent is generally treated as (1) acquiring Target assets with carryover basis under Code section 362(b), followed by (2) a deemed contribution of the acquired assets to the Subsidiary (the surviving corporation, of course, is actually the Target) with tax basis determined under Code section 358.

Although Code section 362(b) generally provides that the Acquirer in a reorganization takes carryover tax basis in Target assets or stock, the Acquirer's expenses of the acquisition transaction should probably be capitalized in a manner similar to expense incurred in a taxable acquisition.[68] However, the regulations under Code section 263, issued in 2003, were conspicuously silent about the treatment of capitalized costs incurred in reorganization transactions.[69]

If the Acquiring Corporation (i.e., the Subsidiary in the case of a forward-triangular merger) acquires the Target's assets, Code section 381 generally provides that the Acquiring Corporation will succeed to and take into account various items from the Target. There are a total of 23 specific tax attributes identified in Code section 381(c). The list includes NOLs, earnings and profits, capital loss carryovers, accounting methods, depreciation and installment method accounting, and tax credits. The use of losses and credits is subject, of course, to limitations under Code sections 269, 382, and 383.

Target Corporation

The Target corporation generally does not recognize gain or loss in a reorganization transaction, either when it receives Acquirer stock or when it makes a liquidating distribution of such Acquirer stock to the Target shareholders.[70]

The Target's transfer of assets to the Acquirer, and receipt of property from the Acquirer, pursuant to a reorganization, is not subject to recognition of gain or loss so long as any "boot" received by the Target as part of the transaction (a) does not exceed the boot limits permitted for the particular type of reorganization and (b) the Target distributes the boot to its shareholders or creditors in pursuance of the plan of reorganization.[71]

The Target will not recognize gain or loss on the distribution to its shareholders of Acquirer stock, rights to acquire Acquirer stock, and Acquirer debt (collectively called "Qualified Property").[72] However, the Target can recognize gain (but not loss) on a distribution to its shareholders of appreciated property comprised of either (a) existing Target property retained by the Target and not transferred to the Acquirer pursuant to the reorganization, or (b) all non-Qualified Property received from the Acquirer to the extent the non-Qualified Property has appreciated in value after it is received by the Target and before it is distributed.[73] To implement this latter rule, the Target is treated as holding non-Qualified Property with a tax basis equal to the fair market value of such property on the date received by the Target from the Acquirer.[74]

The Target's tax basis in any Acquirer stock it receives will be the same as the basis in the Target property exchanged, *decreased* by any money received by the Target in the exchange, the fair market value of any other property received by the Target, and any Target liabilities assumed by the Acquirer; and *increased* by any gain recognized by the Target on the exchange and any Acquirer liabilities transferred to the Target.[75]

Target Shareholders

Target shareholders generally do not recognize gain or loss upon receipt of Acquirer stock.[76] However, a Target shareholder is taxed on any boot (money and other property) received in the reorganization transaction, up to the sum of such money and the fair market value of such other property.[77]

Target shareholders receive basis in the Acquiring Corporation's shares equal to their old basis in the Target's shares, decreased to the extent that boot is received and increased to the extent gain is recognized.[78] The Target shareholders' holding period for the Acquirer stock received in the reorganization includes the holding periods for their old shares.[79]

TAX-FREE REORGANIZATIONS INVOLVING S CORPORATIONS

The corporate organization and reorganization provisions of the Code[80] are contained in subtitle A, chapter 1, subchapter C, which applies only to corporations. However, subchapter S, governing S corporations, generally applies subchapter C to an S corporation and its shareholders "except to the extent inconsistent with this subchapter [S]."[81] Therefore, an S corporation, unlike a partnership, can be a party to a tax-free reorganization. However, tax-free reorganizations involving S corporations can have certain unique consequences, which will be reviewed briefly in this section and in greater detail in Chapter 8.

Even before the S corporation rules were substantially revamped in 1996, GCM 39768[82] concluded that an S corporation was not precluded from transferring assets in an "A," "C," "D" or "F" reorganization. Among other things that GCM rejected a technical interpretation of then-applicable Code section 1371(a)(2), which would have prevented an S corporation from qualifying for reorganization treatment. (The argument was that an S corporation, in its capacity as a shareholder, is treated as an individual and therefore cannot participate in a reorganization because it is not a "corporation" for that purpose.) Code section 1371(a)(2) was repealed in 1996.

As a practical matter, the nature and technical requirements of S status often limit the types of reorganization transactions in which an S corporation is likely to engage. An S corporation, of course, can be and often is the Target in various acquisition transactions. An S corporation can participate in an "A" merger with or into another entity, and can engage in a divisive "D" reorganization. Note that these are all transactions that generically involve a restructuring of ownership among existing shareholders. On the other hand, limitations on the number (maximum 100) and eligibility requirements for S corporation shareholders mean that, as a practical matter, an S corporation faces serious technical problems in acting as an Acquiring Corporation. For example, if a Target has 101 existing shareholders, or has corporate shareholders or foreign nonresident individuals, a tax-free acquisition would result in a termination of the S corporation's S status unless ineligible shareholders were paid in cash instead of stock and the transaction was structured within allowable boot limits.

When an S corporation is a Target and its assets are transferred in a Type "A," Type "C," or nondivisive Type "D" reorganization, the S corporation's legal existence will terminate following the transaction. In other reorganization transactions, the S corporation may continue to exist as the surviving corporation but may lose its S status. However, the S corporation election will be valid up to the date of any such termination transaction. An S corporation that is the surviving entity in a merger or other transaction, and that does not otherwise become ineligible as a result of the reorganization (e.g., the S corporation is the surviving entity in an "A" or "B" reorganization and no S corporation shares are issued to ineligible shareholders) will generally continue to be an S corporation.[83]

A potentially important aspect of a tax-free reorganization is that the transfer of S corporation assets pursuant to a reorganization solely for stock of the Acquirer does not trigger gain recognition to the "S" Target. Therefore, the built-in gains tax is not triggered.[84] If the Acquirer is also an S corporation, any

Target assets subject to Code section 1374 in the hands of the Target will have a carryover of the "built-in gain" attributes and thus will continue to be subject to Code section 1374 after the transaction for the remainder of the ten-year period.[85] If the Acquirer is an S corporation and the Target is a C corporation, the Target assets will be generally subject to a possible built-in gains tax under Code section 1374 on any subsequent disposition of the Target assets within the ten-year recognition period, which ten-year period starts on the date the assets were acquired by the S corporation rather than the beginning of the first tax year the corporation was an S corporation.[86] The S corporation will generally take carryover basis in the Target assets, and the built-in gain will be the difference between the fair market value of the Target assets on the acquisition date and the Target's tax basis (i.e., the S corporation's carryover tax basis) on such date.[87]

If an S corporation is a Target corporation in a tax-free reorganization (an "S" Target), the transaction generally causes a closing of the S Target's books, and its shareholders are allocated all of the corporation's income up to the date of the reorganization.[88] By contrast, if an S corporation is an Acquirer in a reorganization transaction (an "S Acquirer"), and the S Acquirer survives and retains its S status, the S corporation's tax year generally will not close or terminate. Moreover, absent an affirmative election, the S Acquirer's income and deductions for that tax year will be allocated among all its shareholders on a per share, per day basis.[89] This could result in shifting of income or loss in ways that the shareholders probably do not expect or intend. Normally, it is better for the participants in such an acquisition to agree that the S corporation will elect to close its books on the date of the merger, pursuant to Code section 1377(a)(2).

Example 17: S Acquirer, an S Corporation, uses a calendar tax year and is owned 50-50 by two individuals, A and B. S Acquirer earns $3 million of taxable income in the first six months of the calendar tax year. On July 1, S Acquirer merges with Target, owned by two individuals C and D, and C and D are issued enough stock such that A, B, C and D each own 25 percent of S Acquirer after the merger. Assume that, because of the business disruptions and costs of merging the two corporations, S Acquirer earns zero income over the last six months of the calendar tax year following the merger. Absent an election under Code section 1377(a)(2), the taxable income of S Acquirer will be allocated among A, B, C and D on a per share, per day basis. If A, B, C and D each own 100 shares, if the calendar year is assumed to have 365 days, and C and D owned their shares for 184 days (July 1 to December 31), C and D would each have 18,400 share-days, A and B would each have 36,500 share-days, and the total number of share-days is 109,800. C and D would therefore each be allocated $502,732.20 ($3,000,000 × 18,400/109,800) of the S Acquirer's taxable income for the taxable year, even though *all* of that income was earned during periods before they became shareholders.

By contrast, an election under Code section 1377(a)(2) would result in an interim closing of the books and an allocation of all pre-July 1 income ratably to A and B on a 50-50 basis. This is probably what all parties would expect.

An election under Code section 1377(a)(2) can be made by an acquiring S corporation on the date of a merger if the transaction qualifies, i.e., if one or more new shareholders is issued an amount of stock equal to at least 25 percent of the previously outstanding stock.

An S Target's shareholders can receive money or other property in addition to stock, pursuant to a tax-free reorganization. There is confusion as to which Code provisions should govern the taxation of this boot. Code section 1368 generally determines the tax consequences of distributions to S corporation shareholders. However, it may be that the boot distribution is governed by Code section 356 instead. If Code section 1368 governs and if the S Target has no accumulated E&P from prior C corporation years, the boot would be tax-free to the extent of the shareholders' basis in their stock; any excess would be taxed as capital gain. If Code section 1368 governs and the S Target had accumulated E&P, the boot would be tax-free to the extent of the S Target's accumulated adjustments account, then taxed as a Code section 301 dividend distribution to the extent of the S Target's E&P, then tax-free to the extent of any remaining stock basis, and finally taxed as capital gain on the excess.

On the other hand, if Code section 356 controls the boot analysis, a determination must first be made as to whether the boot is taxable as capital gain under Code section 356(a)(1) or as a boot dividend under Code section 356(a)(2). If the boot distribution is capital gain, the shareholders of the S Target will recognize capital gain equal to any gain realized (but otherwise not recognized) as a result of the reorganization, up to the full amount of the boot. By contrast, if the boot is a dividend, the transaction will be treated as a dividend up to the amount of any undistributed E&P of the S Target, and the remainder will be treated as capital gain, up to the amount of any gain realized (but otherwise not recognized) pursuant to the reorganization.

Planning Point: Because it is not clear whether Code section 1368 or 356 should apply to boot, the S Target should always, prior to the reorganization, distribute excess cash to its shareholders so that Code section 1368 clearly governs the tax consequences of such distributions.

One of the interesting tax issues that arises in tax-free reorganizations involving S corporations is the treatment of Target tax attributes under Code section 381. If an S Acquirer acquires a Target C corporation with accumulated earnings and profits (E&P), the S Acquirer succeeds to the Target's E&P.[90] This can later come back to haunt the S corporation if it subsequently has sufficient passive income to trigger the tax imposed under Code section 1375 on excess net passive investment income, and termination of S status under Code section 1362(d)(3) if it has excess passive income for three consecutive years.

CODE SECTION 351—TAX-FREE CONTRIBUTION TRANSACTIONS

Code section 351 normally provides the statutory basis for forming a new corporation without triggering tax consequences. However, there are a variety of acquisition arrangements where a transaction may fall outside of the scope of Code section 368 but comes within the scope of Code section 351.

Code section 351(a) provides that "[n]o gain or loss shall be recognized if property is transferred to a corporation by one or more persons solely in exchange for stock in such corporation and immediately after the exchange such person or persons are in control (as defined in Code section 368(c)) of the corporation." This can be broken down into the following elements:

1. There must be a *transfer* of *property* to the corporation by one or more transferors – which in turn can be further divided into the "transfer" and the "property" requirements, as discussed below.

2. The transferor must receive, in exchange, stock in the corporation. If something other than stock is received, this "boot" is subject to tax.

3. Immediately after the exchange, the transferors as a group must "control" the corporation, which means the group must possess both (i) 80 percent of the total combined voting power of all classes of stock entitled to vote and (ii) at least 80 percent of the total number of shares of all other classes of stock.

One common situation where a Code section 351 acquisition transaction makes sense is if the Acquirer is a corporation but the Target is a partnership, and thus ineligible to participate in a reorganization under Code section 368. In that case, the partners could contribute their partnership assets to the Acquirer. If enough Acquirer shareholders help out by making appropriate property contributions in exchange for additional shares of Acquirer stock, the result is a tax-free combination of a partnership and a corporation. The relevant rule is that, if there is more than one property transferor in connection with a contribution transaction, each such transferor is counted for purposes of the 80 percent control calculation only if such person receives in exchange stock (i.e., not boot) having more than a "relatively small value" in comparison to the value of the stock (i) already owned (if any) by such transferor or (ii) to be received for services rendered or to be rendered by such transferor.[91] In Rev. Proc. 77-37,[92] the IRS stated that corporate stock would not be considered to be of "relatively small value" if the fair market value of the property transferred by such person is at least 10 percent of the fair market value of the stock already owned (or to be received for services) by such person.

Example 18: Acquirer, a corporation, wants to acquire the business assets of a partnership owned by two individuals, X and Y, and wants to issue to X and Y Acquirer stock representing a 20 percent stake in Acquirer following the transaction. Acquirer has issued and outstanding a single class of voting common stock, which is currently owned by A (100 shares), by B (60 shares), and by C (40 shares). Acquirer proposes to issue 25 shares to each of X and Y, or a total of 50 additional shares, representing a 20 percent interest in Acquirer on a post-transaction basis. X and Y by themselves fail the 80 percent control requirement because they only hold 20 percent immediately after the exchange, but if A and B also contribute property to the corporation at the same time, and such contributions meet the 10 percent safe harbor and thus are deemed to be more than a "relatively small value," then A, B, X, and Y collectively would be counted toward meeting the control requirement.[93] Thus, if A contributes additional property with an appropriate value and receives 10 additional shares, and B contributes property with an appropriate value and receives 6 additional shares, all the shares owned by the contributing group immediately following the exchange would include all of A's shares (110), B's shares (66), X's shares (25), and Y's shares (25), which would total 226 out of a total issued and outstanding of 266. Therefore, the control group would hold 226/266 = 84.96% of the total number of shares issued and outstanding, which would exceed the requisite 80 percent threshold.

Comment: One of the problems with a Code section 351 "acquisition" transaction that relies on the 10 percent safe harbor under Rev. Proc. 77-37[94] is that adding an additional 10 percent stock issuance for existing shareholders changes the percentage ownership. In the above example, X and Y were earmarked to receive 50 shares representing 20 percent of the total; however, due to the issuance of 10 shares to A and 6 shares to B, X and Y end up with 50/266 = 18.8%. One can make various adjustments in valuation of contributed property to try and make it come out "right," but this can sometimes be a challenging exercise, especially where, as here, there is a party, C, who is not contributing property and who will likely have a stake in making sure any additional stock is issued for fair value.

Example 19: Acquirer is a closely held corporation owned by X, its sole shareholder. Acquirer wants to do a "B" reorganization to acquire Target and plans to give Target shareholders voting stock representing 40 percent of Acquirer. This would qualify as a "B" reorganization. However, if X decides to offer only nonvoting stock to the Target shareholders, then the transaction cannot by its terms qualify as a "B" reorganization. However, if X agrees to put in sufficient property to satisfy the 10 percent requirement under Rev. Proc. 77-37[95] so as to provide the requisite control group, then the transaction can be implemented under Code section 351 as a tax-free contribution of property (i.e., Target stock) instead of as a reorganization.

When stock is issued tax-free pursuant to Code section 351, the transferor's tax basis in the stock is the same as the transferor's tax basis in the contributed property, with the following adjustments:

1. It is *increased* by the amount any gain recognized on the exchange and any corporation liabilities transferred to the property transferor.

2. It is *decreased* by any money received in the exchange, the fair market value of any other boot received, including any debt obligations received, any liabilities transferred from the property transferor to the corporation, and any loss the transferor recognizes on the exchange.[96]

To the extent the property contributed to the corporation was, in the hands of the transferor, either a capital asset (as defined in Code section 1221) or property described in Code section 1231, the transferor's holding period in stock received includes the holding period in the property contributed to the corporation under Code section 351.[97] On the other hand, a contribution of inventory or another ordinary asset would not result in a "tacking" of the holding period.

Moreover, in order to enjoy non-recognition treatment under Code section 351, the statute further requires that the following two requirements be met:

1. The requirement that the consideration contributed or transferred in the transaction constitutes "property" (the "property requirement"); and

2. The requirement that the transaction be in the nature of a "transfer" (the "transfer requirement").

The "Property Requirement"

(a) The Meaning of "Property" under Code Section 351(a).

Neither Code section 351 nor the Regulations contain any definition of "property," although it is clear that money is considered "property" within the meaning of Code section 351. The Regulations clearly contemplate that at least some forms of intellectual property or intangible property constitute "property" for purposes of Code section 351 since Regulation section 1.351-1(a)(2), Example (1), includes a transfer of a patent to a corporation in a transaction that qualifies for non-recognition treatment under Code section 351. Instead, the definition of "property" for Code section 351 purposes has historically been derived from a combination of case law and IRS pronouncements. In general, the IRS has taken a more narrow position than the courts in defining what kinds of intellectual or intangible property constitute "property" for purposes of Code section 351, and, in particular, has taken the position in its published rulings that a transfer will constitute a transfer of property within the meaning of Code section 351 only if in a taxable transaction it would constitute a "sale or exchange" of property rather than a license for purposes of determining gain or loss.

Absent any clear and explicit statutory or regulatory guidance on the meaning of the term "property" for purposes of section 351, the authority is provided by court decisions and IRS rulings.

The courts have ruled on the scope of "property" for purposes of section 351, and also for purposes of Code section 721, a similar provision applicable under partnership tax law to a "contribution of property" to a partnership. Significantly, the courts have defined "property" very broadly both for purposes of Code sections 351 and 721.

In *E.I. DuPont de Nemours & Co. v. U.S.*, the U.S. Court of Claims addressed a situation in which a corporation created a new subsidiary and then transferred a royalty-free, non-exclusive license in a patent to the subsidiary in exchange for 100 percent of the subsidiary's stock. The IRS challenged whether the transaction qualified as a "transfer" of "property" under Code section 351. The IRS asserted its position that all substantial rights to intangible property must be transferred in order for the transaction to qualify as a "transfer" of "property" under Code section 351. The IRS further argued that the standard for a "transfer" of "property" under Code section 351 should be the same as the standard for determining whether a license of intangible property rights constituted a "sale or exchange" of a "capital asset" under Code section 1221. However, the Court of Claims rejected the IRS's position and noted that capital gains rules were not apposite to Code section 351 because Code section 351 dealt with "transfers" not "sales or exchanges" and also covered "property" rather than just "capital assets." The Court of Claims then went on to hold that although the rights transferred to the subsidiary in exchange for the stock were not all rights under the patents (and indeed were non-exclusive), they were nonetheless "perpetual, irrevocable, and quite substantial in value," and thus constituted "property" for purposes of Code section 351. The Court went on to suggest that any "positive business asset" or item "of value" constitutes property for purposes of section 351.

In *H.B. Zachry Co. v. Commissioner*, a corporation exchanged a "carved-out oil payment" in the amount of $650,000 for all ten authorized shares of the subsidiary's common stock. The taxpayers took the position that the transfer of the carved-out oil payment in exchange for stock was a transfer of property within the meaning of Code section 351, while the IRS asserted, among other arguments, that the carved-out oil payment did not constitute "property" within the meaning of Code section 351(a) because it was an assignment of a pure income right. However, the Tax Court cited authority indicating that the oil payments were considered interests in land and were severable and separable from the ownership of the surface estate, and thus were property rights. The Tax Court therefore held that a carved-out oil payment was "property" for purposes of Code section 351. The Tax Court went on to state that, "Even if the oil payment is a "pure income right," it has present value and is an interest in land. Therefore, we view it as 'property' within the common law definition and within the intendment of section 351."

In Rev. Rul. 64-56, the IRS expressly acknowledged that "know how" could constitute "property" for purposes of Code section 351, stating as follows:

> The term "property" for purposes of section 351 of the Code will be held to include anything qualifying as "secret processes and formulas" within the meaning of sections 861(a)(4) and 862(a)(4) of the Code and any other secret information as to a device, process, etc., in the general nature of a patentable invention without regard to whether a patent has been applied for,[98] and without regard to whether it is patentable in the patent law sense.[99] Other information which is secret will be given consideration as "property" on a case-by-case basis.

In that same ruling, the IRS also ruled that the fragmentation of an intangible property right into an exclusive right to use such property within the territory of a country would also constitute "property" for purposes of Code section 351.

(b) Code Section 351(d) Exception for Services.

Although Code section 351 does not define what "property" is, Code section 351(d) expressly identifies what it is not by excluding services and certain kinds of indebtedness and accrued interest from the meaning of "property" for purposes of section 351. This "services exception" was first introduced in the 1954 Internal Revenue Code as a codification of existing case law. The policy underlying the exception is that remuneration for services should be immediately taxable as ordinary income, regardless of the form of the remuneration.

The Tax Court, in *Zachry*, emphasized the existence of the services exception in Code section 351(d), and quoted the Latin phrase expressio unius est exclusio alterius to assert that such a "singular and extraordinary exception" was evidence that the definition of "property" should otherwise be construed broadly.

The IRS has provided certain limited guidance on the meaning and scope of this "services" exception. Rev. Rul. 64-56 states that the following three items will always be treated as the provision of services rather than property:

1. Training the transferee's employees in a recognized profession, craft, or trade.

2. Continuing technical assistance after the starting-up phase.

3. Assistance in the construction of a plant building to house machinery transferred, or to house machinery to be used in applying a patented or other process or formula which qualifies as property transferred ... Similarly, advice as to the lay-out of plant machinery and equipment.

On the other hand, various forms of intangible property, including a copyright, are inherently the product of the transferor-creator's personal efforts, and the issuance of corporate stock for such property could arguably be viewed as at least similar or analogous to an issuance of stock for services. However, the IRS has never asserted this position with respect to the most prominent forms of intellectual property, including patents, copyrights, trademarks and trade names. In Rev. Rul. 64-56, the IRS made the following observations and distinctions:

> Once it is established that "property" has been transferred, the transfer will be tax-free under section 351 even though services were used to produce the property. Such is generally the case where the transferor developed the property primarily for use in its own manufacturing business. However, where the information transferred has been developed specially for the transferee, the stock received in exchange for it may be treated as payment for services rendered. See Regenstein, supra, where the taxpayer developed a plan for selling insurance which he ultimately sold to certain insurance companies. The court held that the consideration received was payment for services.

The "Transfer Requirement"

Assuming that an asset or right constitutes "property," Code section 351 further requires that such property be "transferred" to the corporation in exchange for stock.

The IRS's position, asserted for many years in litigation and never subsequently modified by a public pronouncement, has been that a "transfer" occurs only if the transaction, but for Code section 351, would result in the recognition of capital gain or loss under Code section 1221 and Code section 1222 equal to the difference between the amount realized and the adjusted basis in the property. With respect to transfers of interests in copyrights, Rev. Proc. 83-59 requires, for advance ruling purposes under Code section 351, a representation that all rights, title and interests for each copyright, in each medium of exploitation, will be transferred. However, this ruling standard is arguably more stringent than, and inconsistent with, the IRS's own position in Rev. Rul. 60-226, in which the IRS ruled that the transfer of an exclusive right to exploit a copyright in a specific medium for the life of the copyright shall be treated as a sale of the right and not a license.

The courts have consistently rejected the IRS's interpretation of the "transfer" requirement. In particular, the case law clearly indicates that transactions that would not qualify as a sale or exchange of underlying property – including leases, licenses, and other partial conveyances of property interests – nonetheless satisfy the "transfer" requirement so long as the transferred right or privilege has some "value."

In *Dupont*, the U.S. Court of Claims offered a detailed analysis and rejection of the IRS's sale-or-exchange argument, and instead suggested that the transfer of property requirements could be met by a transfer of any "positive business asset" or item "of value." After finding that a non-exclusive license of patent rights constituted "property," the Court in *Dupont* also concluded that the "transfer" requirement was met, noting that the transferor "handed over something of value and received stock in return; in normal understanding there was a mutual exchange."

Significantly, following the carefully reasoned rejection of the IRS's litigation position in the *DuPont* case, the Chief Counsel of the IRS issued two General Counsel Memoranda concluding that the court in *DuPont* reached the correct result and recommended that the IRS conform its position to that taken by the court. In GCM 36922, issued in 1976 in response to a request for guidance regarding whether a transfer of less than all substantial rights held by a transferor in "know-how" or a patent constitutes a transfer for purposes of section 351, the Chief Counsel stated that, in light of the decision in *DuPont*, his office no longer believed that the IRS should maintain that all substantial rights in "know-how" or a patent must be transferred to qualify as a transfer for purposes of Code section 351. GCM 36922 advocated modification of Rev. Rul. 64-56 and 69-156 to comply with this position. Similarly, in 1977, GCM 37178 was issued in response to the inquiry as to whether the granting of a usufruct with respect to a tract of land to a corporation could constitute a transfer for purposes of Code section 351. The GCM stated that as a result of the decision in *DuPont*, it is now the IRS's position that the concept of "transfer in exchange" is not tied to and does not have the same scope as the concept "sale or exchange" under the capital gains provisions and the transaction should qualify as a transfer for purposes of Code section 351.

Despite the issuance of these GCMs in the late 1970s, the IRS has never formally modified, withdrawn or revoked its rulings that apply the "sale or exchange" standard for transfers under Code section 351. Thus, the "sale or exchange" standard appears to remain the publicly announced position of the IRS with respect to transfers of property under Code section 351.

A Transaction That Does not Qualify as "Reorganization" under Code Section 368 can Nonetheless Qualify for Non-Recognition Under Code Section 351

As mentioned before, Code section 351 and Code section 368 have significantly different qualification rules, and so a transaction that fails to qualify as a tax-free "reorganization" under Code section 368 can nonetheless qualify for non-recognition under Code section 351. In Rev. Rul. 84-71,[100] the IRS reversed and revoked its earlier position in Rev. Rul. 80-284,[101] and ruled that a transaction meeting the requirements of Code section 351 would be eligible for non-recognition treatment even though the larger transaction of which it was a part did not qualify for non-recognition treatment under Code section 368.

In Rev. Rul. 80-284 and 84-71 (generally based on the facts of *National Starch & Chemical Corp.*[102]), P, publicly held corporation, wished to purchase the stock of T, and all T stockholders except A, holding 14 percent of T, were willing to sell their T stock for cash. A wished to avoid recognition of gain. First, P and A formed a new corporation, S. P transferred cash and other property to S in exchange solely for all of S's common stock; A transferred T stock to S solely in exchange for all of S's preferred stock. These transfers were intended to be tax-free under Code section 351. Second, S organized a new corporation, D, and transferred to D the cash it had received from P in exchange for all the D common stock. Third, D was merged into T under state law. As a result of the merger, each share of T stock, except those shares held by S, were surrendered for cash equal to the stock's fair market value and each share of D stock was converted into T stock.

The formation of S met the requirements for non-recognition under Code section 351, but the larger transaction involving P's acquisition of T did not qualify for non-recognition under Code section 368. In Rev. Rul. 84-71,[103] the IRS concluded that the fact that "larger acquisitive transactions" fail to meet the requirements for tax-free treatment under the reorganization provisions of the Code does not preclude the applicability of Code section 351(a) to transfers that are part of such larger transactions. Thus, A's transfer to S was eligible for non-recognition treatment under Code section 351.

a. The "double/single dummy"

And so, tax lawyers have invented, with the connivance and blessing of the IRS, an increasingly broad use of Code section 351 as an alternative method to implement the equivalent of a "reorganization" without having to comply with the stringent particulars of Code section 368. In companion IRS private letter rulings 199911028 and 199911029 (Dec. 17, 1998), the IRS concluded that, in a "double dummy" transaction where two target corporations were each engaged in a reverse subsidiary merger in exchange for parent holding company stock, and neither of the two reverse subsidiary merger transactions qualified as a reorganization under Code section 368(a)(2)(E) because neither reverse subsidiary merger met the applicable control requirement due to the fact that a Third Party acquired and retained non-voting preferred stock issued by each of Targets, the transaction could nonetheless qualify for non-recognition treatment under Code section 351.

The result is that, by coming under Code section 351 rather than Code section 368, a transaction may qualify for tax-free treatment with respect to the exchange of stock, while allowing a greater amount of boot than would be permitted under a reverse triangular merger itself. To illustrate, assume Acquirer wants to acquire Target, but the Target shareholders want 50 percent cash and 50 percent stock of Acquirer in the transaction. That is too much boot to qualify under Code section 368(a)(2)(E) as a reverse triangular merger. However, the parties might agree to implement a so-called "double dummy" structure, pursuant to which they would form Newco as a new "parent" corporation, and in turn have Newco create two new transitory (temporary) subsidiaries. Acquirer would merge with one of the transitory subsidiaries, with Acquirer as the survivor, and Target would merge with the other transitory subsidiary, with Target as the survivor. As a result of this transaction, Newco would be the new parent, with Acquirer as a first-tier subsidiary and Target as a first-tier subsidiary. (Acquirer and Target end up as brother-sister corporations instead of being in a parent-subsidiary relationship, but often that is not a major issue or problem.) Because each of the reverse triangular merger transactions is treated as if the applicable shareholders contributed their stock to the Newco in connection with the formation of Newco, and because the former shareholders of Acquirer and Target will now (very likely) collectively meet, with respect to Newco, the 80 percent "control test" under Code section 351 immediately after completion of the integrated transaction, the result is that the Target shareholders can receive 50 percent cash and 50 percent stock of Newco and the later can be received tax-free (the cash consideration, of course, will be taxable under the boot rules). At the same time, the Acquirer shareholders will swap their Acquirer stock for stock of Newco (they can even get cash as well, if the parties want that as part of the transaction), and this transaction likewise qualifies for non-recognition under Code section 351 to the extent that any of the Acquirer shareholders are receiving stock of Newco in exchange for their Acquirer shares (again, cash consideration will be taxable under the boot rules).

This is a very good solution from the perspective of a tax lawyer. However, one obvious drawback of the "double dummy" transaction described above is that, if Acquirer is currently a publicly-traded company, the parties will likely want to create Newco as a publicly-traded company, if they want to achieve the (typical) goal of having all shareholders hold publicly-traded stock at the end of the transaction. However, creating Newco as a publicly- traded company is not easily, quickly or inexpensively accomplished.

This factor, and others, can make a double dummy unattractive for largely non-tax reasons. A vexing real-life constraint for tax professionals is that an elegant tax solution is not always a practical business answer to a particular transactional challenge. A "double dummy" transaction generally has "tax plusses and business minuses," meaning that it solves certain tax problems but introduces cost and complexity that may make it unacceptable from a business standpoint.

The Step Transaction Doctrine Applied to Code Section 351

The judicial application of the step transaction doctrine, when applied to determine if transferors have control of a transferee corporation under Code section 351, has varied and no uniform test has developed. As a result, there are no clearly defined guidelines for taxpayers. Nevertheless, the courts and the IRS have attempted to articulate doctrines that can be applied in all cases. The result has been the following three tests:

1. *End result test* – Under this test, ostensibly separate transactions are amalgamated when it appears they were really component steps of a single transaction and that each of the steps was intended for the purpose of reaching one end result.[104]

2. *Mutual interdependence test* – Under this test, the courts consider whether steps are so interdependent that the legal relationships created by one transaction would be fruitless without the completion of the entire series of transactions. Unlike the end result test, the mutual interdependence test focuses on the relationship of the steps, not merely on the end result.[105]

3. *Binding commitment test* – Under this test, a transaction is aggregated with other transactions if

> there is a binding commitment for the parties to undertake the other transactions. Generally, as long as there is a moment in which the transferors "control" the stock of the transferee corporation without being subject to a binding obligation that would cost them "control," the step transaction doctrine is not applied.[106]

Although no single set of factors determines if the step transaction doctrine should be applied, the courts generally (i) look at the intention of the parties, (ii) the time interval between the transfers, and (iii) whether the transactions are interdependent when applying the mutual interdependence test.

Perhaps the single most important factor in determining the applicability of the step transaction doctrine is whether the transactions are so interdependent that none of the transactions would have been effected without the others. The courts have held that, when two or more transactions are intended and each transaction is planned before the first is consummated, the transactions may not be integrated if each transaction has substance by itself and has its own separate business purpose.[107] If, however, the latter transactions are the *sine qua non* of the former, the courts will treat the individual transactions as one transaction.[108] Also, if there is a binding commitment to undertake the second transaction at the time of the first transaction, even if the steps are mutually independent the transactions may be stepped together under the binding commitment test.[109]

Many courts in finding that the Code section 351 control requirement has not been satisfied have pointed to a commitment binding on the parties purportedly "in control" of the transferee corporation to sell or otherwise reduce their controlling stock interests in the corporation.[110] The courts, however, have declined to apply the step transaction doctrine when there is a written agreement among the parties but: (1) the agreement is not binding: and (2) the transferor has at least momentary control of the transferee corporation.[111]

The IRS has generally attempted to apply the step transaction doctrine in order to deny the application of the Code section 351 non-recognition provisions to a transaction, and so IRS ruling authority is generally narrower and more taxpayer adverse than case law. However, it should be noted that in most IRS rulings the factual integration and interdependency of the various steps is either assumed or otherwise is in not seriously in dispute.

Summary of Requirements for Non-Recognition under Code Section 351

To summarize the discussion above, in order for a transaction to qualify under Code section 351, each of the following requirements must be met:

(1) there must be "property;"

(2) the property must be "transferred to a corporation;"

(3) such transfer must be made by "one or more persons;"

(4) the transfer must be "solely in exchange for stock in such corporation;"

(5) "immediately after the exchange" the control group must be tested on the applicable testing date to determine whether it has control, which includes an analysis of the step transaction doctrine; and

(6) on the testing date, the control group must have "control."

HYPOTHETICAL SITUATIONS ILLUSTRATING TAX-FREE ACQUISITIONS

The following are a series of hypothetical situations illustrating the tax issues and related tax consequences that can arise in a tax-free business acquisition.

Hypothetical Situation #1

P, a publicly traded corporation, plans to acquire all the shares of T, a privately owned C corporation. T has a large number of contracts with unrelated third parties. The contracts contain assignment clauses that generally require the consent of such third parties to an assignment but do not require consent in the event there is a change of control of T. P has a single class of voting common stock.

The T shareholders are willing to transfer their T shares solely in exchange for voting common stock of P, and P is willing to acquire T and accept the risks of its existing corporate liabilities. The T stock is worth

$5 million, and P is willing to deliver $5 million of its voting common stock in exchange for the T shares. The T shareholders have $100,000 of tax basis in their shares, and have held these shares for ten years.

Comment on Hypothetical Situation #1. On these facts, there are several types of a tax-free reorganization that could be implemented, but perhaps the simplest would be a Type "B" reorganization, which would involve the acquisition of all T shares solely in exchange for voting stock of P. Normally, a "B" reorganization is not a particularly favored transaction structure because no boot whatsoever is allowed in a "B" reorganization and there is always a fear that even a de minimis amount of boot, however inadvertent, could disqualify the transaction from non-recognition treatment. However, for purposes of Hypothetical Situation #1, it will be assumed that the parties are not concerned with this issue and have the capacity to monitor and control carefully the boot issue.

Upon completion of a "B" reorganization, T would be a wholly owned subsidiary of P, and the T shareholders would own $5 million worth of the voting common stock of P. P's tax basis in the T stock would be the carryover tax basis from the former T shareholders, or $100,000, pursuant to Code section 362(b), and P would have a holding period determined by reference to the holding period of the former T shareholders (i.e., ten years).

Meanwhile, the T shareholders would have carryover basis[112] and carryover holding periods[113] from their old T shares to their newly issued voting common shares and thus would have $100,000 of tax basis in the P shares and would have a ten-year holding period, more than long enough to claim long-term capital gains treatment on a subsequent sale.

Hypothetical Situation #2

The same facts as in Hypothetical Situation #1, except that P wants to structure the transaction as a Type "A" merger so that the T assets will be held directly by P immediately following the transaction. P's business-driven reason for structuring the transaction in this manner is that P has a patent license that allows P and only P to manufacture and sell products governed by the patent; therefore P needs to acquire the T assets and own them directly, rather than through a subsidiary.

Because it is no longer subject to the prohibition against any boot that would apply to a "B" reorganization, P is proposing to deliver $4 million of P common stock and $1 million of cash to the T shareholders in exchange for their shares. T has held its assets for various holding periods and has $2.5 million of tax basis in its assets.

Comment on Hypothetical Situation #2. A Type "A" reorganization is a statutory merger pursuant to which T would be merged into P, with P as the surviving corporation, and the former T shareholders would surrender their T shares in exchange for the proposed consideration (i.e., an appropriate number of P shares plus a share of the proposed cash payment). Unlike a "B" reorganization, an "A" does not mandate that the P shares received by the former T shareholders must be voting shares; however, since P only has a single class of voting common, it is a moot point.

As previously noted, an "A" reorganization allows for payment of a significant amount of boot to the T shareholders, subject only to the continuity of interest limitations. Also as previously noted, Rev. Proc. 77-37[114] permits boot to constitute up to 50 percent of the total consideration in an "A" reorganization, and case law has permitted an "A" to have as much as 62 percent cash boot and still meet the continuity of interest requirement. The facts as presented in this Hypothetical Situation #2 anticipate payment of $1 million of boot, which is just 20 percent of the total consideration and thus will not jeopardize the tax-free portion of the transaction. The T shareholders will recognize boot gain equal to the lesser of the gain realized or the amount of boot received.[115] The gain so recognized will likely be treated as capital gain with respect to the surrendered stock, unless it somehow "has the effect of the distribution of a dividend."[116] The dividend issue is significantly less important than before because today the dividend tax rate and long-term capital gain tax rate for federal income tax purposes are both 15 percent.

Pursuant to an "A" reorganization, T would be merged directly into P, and the T shareholders would receive P common stock. P would take carryover tax basis in these T assets, determined by the tax basis of the assets in the hands of T immediately prior to the merger, and increased by gain recognized by T on the exchange.[117] Note that P does not enjoy any increase in its tax basis in the T stock as a result of the $1 million gain recognized by the former T shareholders.[118] Therefore P would acquire the T assets with a carryover of T's existing tax basis in the assets or $2.5 million. P would succeed to all of T's tax attributes, pursuant to Code section 381, subject to limitations on the use of

NOLs, capital loss carryforwards, and credits imposed by Code sections 269, 382, and 383.

The former T shareholders would have the same tax basis in their newly acquired P stock that they had in the exchanged T shares, or $100,000, increased by the amount of gain recognized in the exchange, and decreased by the amount of money received.[119] Because the gain amount recognized by the T shareholders under Code section 356(a)(1) as a result of receiving boot in the transaction exactly equals the amount of money received (i.e., $1 million), the net tax basis of the former T shareholders in their newly acquired P shares will remain $100,000. If the T shareholders held the T stock as capital assets (very likely), then the P shares received in the transaction would have carryover holding periods from the T shares surrendered in connection with the merger.[120]

Hypothetical Situation #3

Hypothetical Situation #3 is based on the same facts as Hypothetical Situation #2, except P has become very concerned about possible liabilities that may arise as a result of lawsuits threatened against T. Therefore, P has decided that it wants to acquire only the T assets, not the legal operating history of T. Accordingly, the parties decide to structure the transaction as a Type "C" reorganization.

T has assets and liabilities comprised of the following:

T has operating assets worth $5 million, liquid assets (comprised of cash and receivables) worth $700,000, and accounts payable in the face amount of $200,000. T also has a $500,000 liability owed to a bank under a line of credit. T proposes to transfer the $5 million worth of operating assets to Corporation P in exchange for $4 million of voting stock and $1 million of cash, but T proposed to retain the $700,000 of liquid assets to pay off its $200,000 worth of accounts payable and $500,000 bank liability.

Comment on Hypothetical Situation #3. For a transaction to qualify as a "C" reorganization, the transaction must satisfy the "solely" for voting stock requirement and the "substantially all" the Target assets requirement. With respect to the former, Code section 368(a)(2)(B) provides that, if an acquisition of assets would qualify under Code section 368(a)(1)(C) but for the fact that the Acquiring Corporation exchanges money or other property in addition to its voting stock and if the Acquiring Corporation acquires solely for its voting stock property of the Target corporation having a fair market value that is at least 80 percent of the fair market value of all of the property of the Target corporation, then the acquisition will be treated as qualifying under Code section 368(a)(1)(C). Solely for the purpose of applying the preceding rule, the amount of any liability assumed by the Acquiring Corporation will be treated as money paid for the property.[121] In substance, these rules state that an Acquirer is permitted to pay boot in a "C" reorganization, but only if voting stock represents 80 percent of the gross fair market value of all Target assets.

Based on the foregoing, the proposed structure would not satisfy the requirements of a C reorganization. The amount of cash "boot" being offered, $1 million, is exactly 20 percent of the total proposed consideration from P. However, the 80 percent voting stock test in Code section 368(a)(2)(B) is based on the gross assets of T and not the "net" amount. Therefore, since T has gross assets of $5.7 million, 80 percent of this amount would be $4,560,000, and $4 million of P stock is not sufficient to meet the requirements of Code section 368(a)(2)(B). Note that the proposed transaction would meet the "substantially all" test because the assets being transferred are more than 90 percent of the net value (actually, 100 percent) and more than 70 percent of the gross value (the percentage is $5 million/$5.7 million, or approximately 87.72 percent). However, because T's liabilities total $700,000, this amount, plus the cash payment of $1 million, will constitute more than 20 percent of the gross value of all T assets.

Comment: Under the language of Code section 368(a)(2)(B), because the 80 percent test is based on the gross assets of T, it does not matter whether T transfers its net assets of $5 million, and keeps $700,000 to pay its outstanding liabilities, or whether T transfers all its assets, worth $5.7 million, and P assumes the $700,000 of liabilities. In the latter case, the assumed liabilities are added to the amount of boot deemed paid. This treatment of assumed liabilities as money paid for the property is a rule applied exclusively to determine whether the 80 percent test is met under Code section 368(a)(2)(B).

Since the proposed transaction fails the "solely" for voting stock requirement, the acquisition would need to be restructured. A possible alternative structure would be to reduce the amount of boot and increase the amount of voting stock to meet the 80 percent requirement. Thus, if the amount of voting stock is increased in value to $4.6 million and the cash payment is reduced to $400,000, the transaction would now meet the 80 percent boot relaxation rule ($4.6 million/$5.7 million = 80.7%). Note that because no liabilities of T are being assumed by P, the assumption of liabilities is not being added into the calculation of the amount of money paid for the property. Again, however, in computing the 80 percent threshold when cash has been transferred, P must include in the "bad" 20 percent (1) the amount of any boot, plus (2) T's liabilities transferred to P, plus (3) the fair market value of any of T's assets not transferred to P. In effect, when T tries to hold back enough assets to pay its outstanding liabilities, it does not reduce the computation of the 80 percent threshold amount. In particular, the 80 percent formula operates such that either the T liabilities are assumed by P and thus are treated as additional cash paid for the T property, pursuant to Code section 368(a)(2)(B), final sentence, or, if T retains the liabilities and sufficient assets to pay them, T's retained assets are added to the gross asset value against which the 80 percent is measured (and in effect is added in computing the "bad" 20 percent).

Assuming both parties are satisfied with the proposed restructuring of the transaction, the transaction would include $4.6 million of P stock, and T would have $5.7 million in gross assets. Thus, the transaction would meet the 80 percent boot relaxation rule of Code section 368(a)(2)(B) (4.6/5.7 = 80.7%). In addition, since T is transferring its $5 million of operating assets and keeping $700,000 in cash to liquidate its $700,000 in outstanding liabilities, the transaction would also meet the "substantially all" test standards of Rev. Proc. 77-37 (i.e., 90 percent net asset test and 70 percent gross asset test), and the transaction would therefore qualify as a C reorganization.

Based on the revised transaction described above, P would have the same tax basis in the acquired T assets that T had in such assets before the exchange, increased by any gain recognized by T (which is zero; gain recognized by the T shareholders does not result in increased tax basis in the hands of T).[122] P would also succeed to the tax attributes of T pursuant to Code section 381(a)(2), subject to limitations under Code sections 269, 382, and 383.

T shareholders, meanwhile, would recognize boot gain of $400,000 under Code section 356(a)(1). The T shareholders' tax basis in the P voting stock would be their carryover tax basis from the T shares exchanged, or $100,000, increased by the boot gain recognized and decreased by the boot received. Therefore, the tax basis nets down to $100,000. The holding period of the P shares in the hands of the former T shareholders will include their holding periods with respect to the T shares.

Hypothetical Situation #4

Assume the same facts as Hypothetical Situation #3, except that P has become comfortable that it can obtain the necessary license rights for its wholly owned subsidiaries without undue complication and has carefully investigated in the due diligence process T's exposure to future law suits and feels that it is at least manageable, although P believes it would be wise to keep those liability risks isolated from P's other assets and activities. P continues to believe that seeking permission to assign T's third-party contracts will be protracted and difficult, and now believes that the best alternative is to acquire T as a first-tier subsidiary, and keep T in existence after the acquisition.

Comment on Hypothetical Situation #4. On these facts, the transaction requirements are clearly pointing toward a reverse-triangular merger. P would form a new wholly owned subsidiary ("S"), and then merge S into T, with T as the surviving corporation. This transaction would keep T intact as a wholly owned subsidiary of P. P would transfer to T shareholders, in exchange for their shares, P shares (and no S shares) together with a small amount of boot. Since the parties were looking at $400,000 of boot in Hypothetical Situation #3, this is the initial proposal by the T shareholders.

A reverse-triangular merger imposes two transactional tests: First, the "substantially all" assets test, which requires that, following the merger of S into T, T must hold substantially all of its properties and substantially all of S's properties (other than stock of P distributed in the transaction). Second, T's shareholders must exchange, for an amount of voting stock of P, an amount of T stock that constitutes "control" of T.

With respect to the first test, the "substantially all" requirement, the term "substantially all" is defined in the same way as for a "C" reorganization (i.e., T must hold 70 percent of the gross assets and 90 percent of the net assets of each of T and S, as determined immediately before the merger).[123] Because the proposed transaction in Hypothetical Situation #3 meets the requirements of a C reorganization, it will likewise meet the "substantially all" test under Code section 368(a)(2)(E).

With respect to the "control" test, a reverse-triangular merger permits P to offer a limited amount of boot to the T shareholders, so long as at least 80 percent of the stock of T outstanding immediately before the transaction is acquired in exchange for P voting stock. Technically, T could use up to 10 percent of its net assets to redeem shares of T shareholders immediately before the merger transaction,[124] and then would need to meet the 80 percent control test with respect to the remaining (post-redemption) outstanding T shares.

The proposed transaction calls on T to merge with S, and for T shareholders to receive $4.6 million of P voting stock and $400,000 of cash boot. T can retain all of its gross and net assets in the transaction, or it could decide to use its $700,000 in liquid assets to pay off its $700,000 in liabilities, and it would still meet the 90/70 tests. (The net assets test would be $5 million/$5 million = 100%, and the gross assets test would be $5 million/$5.7 million = 87.7%). The transaction will also meet the 80 percent test because the stock of T is being exchanged for $4.6 million of P stock, which represents 92 percent of the consideration, well above the 80 percent threshold.

Note that if the parties wanted to push the envelope, they could use $500,000 of T's liquid assets to redeem 10 percent of the outstanding T shares. So long as only T assets are being used in the redemption (and the property used in the redemption is not supplied by P or S), those redeemed T shares will not be taken into account for purposes of the 80 percent control test. T would then merge with S and would hold $5.2 million of former T assets, and $700,000 of former T liabilities, and $4.5 million of net assets. The transaction therefore meets (exactly) the 90 percent net assets test (4.5/5.0 = 90%) and more easily meets the 70 percent gross assets test (5.2/5.7 = 91.2%). As consideration for the acquisition of the T shares, P could give $3.6 million of its stock, and $900,000 in cash, in exchange for the 90 percent of the T shares still issued and outstanding, and this would meet (again, exactly) the 80 percent control test (P gives $3.6 million of P voting shares for 80 percent of the T stock still issued and outstanding, and $900,000 in cash for the remaining 20 percent of the T stock).

This Hypothetical Situation shows that T shareholders could potentially receive as much as $1.4 million in cash, $500,000 from T assets in a redemption immediately before the merger, and $900,000 from P in connection with the merger, and still technically meet the "substantially all" and the "control" tests under Code section 368(a)(2)(E). Hopefully, no one would attempt to cut the transaction qualifications that closely.

Following the merger transaction, P's tax basis in the T stock would be determined in the same manner as if T had merged into S in a forward-triangular merger.[125] P is generally treated as (1) acquiring T assets with a carryover tax basis under Code section 362(b), followed by (2) a deemed contribution of the acquired assets to S (the surviving corporation is, of course, actually T) with tax basis determined under Code section 358.

In the present case, T is assumed to have $2.5 million of tax basis in its assets. Assume P capitalized S with assets having $100,000 of tax basis prior to the merger, and that P's tax basis in its S stock was therefore $100,000. The tax basis of P in the T stock following the merger is $100,000 (initial basis in S stock), plus $2,500,000 (basis in T assets), minus $700,000 (assumed liabilities) = $1,900,000. T will continue to have a continuation of its existing tax attributes, including tax basis and holding periods with respect to its assets. (Code section 381 does not technically apply since T's corporate existence is preserved.)

The former T shareholders will have carryover tax basis from their T shares to the P shares received in the exchange.[126] Assuming that the former T shareholders held the T stock as a capital asset, they will have a tacking of the holding period.[127]

Hypothetical Situation #5

Same facts as in Hypothetical Situation #4, except that the T shareholders now insist on receiving 50 percent cash "boot" and 50 percent P stock in connection with the transaction, and refuse to go forward otherwise. P, after evaluating the challenges of obtaining contract assignments, decides it will acquire the T stock on those terms. However, P wants to structure the transaction as a forward-triangular merger so that the liability risks of T are separated from P.

Following the merger, P will hold the stock of S, the survivor of the merger with T.

Comment on Hypothetical Situation #5. A forward-triangular merger must meet the same continuity of interest requirements as a regular "A" reorganization. Therefore, under the applicable ruling standards of

Rev. Proc. 77-37,[128] a combination of 50 percent cash "boot" and 50 percent P stock would meet the applicable standards.

In a forward-triangular merger, P is treated as the transferor of its own stock in exchange for T shares. Thus, the transaction is eligible for non-recognition treatment.[129] S continues to have T's existing tax basis in its assets, and P's tax basis in the S stock is adjusted as if (1) P acquired T's assets and liabilities directly from T in a transaction where P's tax basis in the T assets was determined under Code section 362(b), and (2) P then contributed the acquired assets to S in a transaction governed by the basis rules of Code section 358.[130] Therefore, P would start with whatever tax basis it has in its S shares immediately before the transaction. P would then be deemed to receive, in exchange for P stock, T's assets and liabilities with a carryover of T's tax basis in such assets, adjusted by any T gain recognized in the transaction (there should be zero adjustment). P would then be deemed to contribute such assets and liabilities to S and to take additional basis in its S shares determined under Code section 358. Practically speaking, this means that P's tax basis in S is generally going to equal the sum of (1) P's starting tax basis in S, increased by (2) the tax basis of T in its assets, and reduced by (3) T's liabilities.

In the present case, assume P had $100,000 of tax basis in S, representing assets contributed to S under Code section 351 prior to the merger. T's assets have a tax basis of $2.5 million, and are subject to liabilities of $700,000. Therefore, P's tax basis in S is adjusted by increasing it for the tax basis of T's assets ($2.5 million) and reduced by T's liabilities ($700,000), resulting in post-merger basis in the S shares of $1.9 million.

S will hold T's assets with a carryover of the tax basis T had in such assets.[131] S will likewise succeed to all of T's tax attributes pursuant to Code section 381, including the holding period.

T's former shareholders, meanwhile, will recognize gain equal to the $2.5 million of cash boot received in the transaction, and will take carryover tax basis of $100,000 from their old T shares to the new P shares received in the exchange[132] and will have a tacking of the holding period.[133]

Hypothetical Situation #6

Assume the general facts in each of the Hypothetical Situations #1–5, except that T, instead of being a C corporation, is an S corporation.

The reason to raise this factual variation is to point out that there could likewise be five different structures for acquisition transactions when the S corporation is the Target. There are no significant tax differences if Target shareholders are receiving primarily stock in the transaction. Even if they also receive "boot" in the transaction, it will not have adverse tax consequences at the S corporation level (e.g., such as a disposition of assets that are treated as Code section 1374 built-in gain or subject to the "sting" tax, discussed more fully in Chapter 8). In particular, in a "B" reorganization, as in Hypothetical Situation #1, because there is an exchange of Target stock solely for voting stock of the Acquirer, there is no tax recognition event whatsoever. In Hypothetical Situation #2, a type "A" merger, there is no tax recognition event unless "boot" is provided, but even if the merger involves a permitted amount of cash "boot" (e.g., up to 50 percent), the "boot" is recognized only at the shareholder level, not at the S corporation level.

In Hypothetical Situation #3, a "C" reorganization, the rules under Code section 362(b) expressly indicate that, so long as any "boot" received in the transaction is distributed out to the shareholders in liquidation of the Target corporation, the Target will not recognize taxable gain at or on the disposition of its assets or on the distribution of the property to its shareholders. Instead, the shareholders again will recognize gain upon receiving "boot."

Comment: As previously discussed, to the extent that the S corporation has its own cash, it is usually prudent for an S corporation that is a Target in an acquisition to distribute all of its cash immediately before the acquisition so that it is governed by Code section 1368, and not subject to potential "boot" characterization under Code section 356.

CHAPTER ENDNOTES

1. IRC Sec. 361.
2. IRC Sec. 354.
3. See IRC Secs. 269, 382 and 383.
4. See, *e.g.*, IRC Sec. 356.
5. *E.F. Gregory*, S.Ct., 293 US 465 (1935).
6. Compare *J.R. Bazley*, S.Ct., 332 US 67 S.Ct. 1489 (1947), with J.B. Lewis Estate, 176 F2d 646.
7. See Rev. Proc. 77-37, 1977-2 CB 568.

8. *J.A. Nelson Co.*, 296 U.S. 374, 56 S.Ct. 273 (1935).
9. See *Yoc Heating Corp.*, 61 TC 168 (1973).
10. Reg. § 1.368-1(e).
11. *J.A Nelson*, supra.
12. See Rev. Rul. 56-330, 1956-2 CB 204, subsequently revoked by Rev. Rul. 63-29, 1963-1 CB 77.
13. See Reg. § 1.368-1(d).
14. Reg. § 1.368-1(c).
15. *Transport Products Corp.*, 25 TC 853, Dec. 21,535, aff'd, CA-6, 57-1 USTC ¶ 9279, 239 F2d 859.
16. Reg. § 1.368-3.
17. IRC Sec. 368(a)(1)(A).
18. 1977-2 CB 568.
19. IRC Sec. 368(a)(1)(B).
20. IRC Sec. 368(a)(1)(C).
21. IRC Sec. 368(a)(2)(G).
22. Rev. Proc. 77-37, 1977-2 CB 568.
23. Rev. Rul. 67-274, 1967-2 CB 141.
24. IRC Sec. 362(a)(2)(G).
25. IRC Sec. 368(a)(2)(G).
26. IRC Sec. 361(b)(3).
27. See the discussion of IRC Sec. 381 *et seq.* in Chapter 13.
28. IRC Sec. 354(b)(1)(B).
29. See Reg. § 1.368-2(e).
30. Reg. § 1.368-1(b).
31. Reg. § 1.368-2(b)(2).
32. See "The Forward Triangular Merger: A Not-So-Straight-Forward Transaction," by Joseph B. Darby III, Practical US/Domestic Tax Strategies, Thomson Reuters, August 2009, Vol. 9, No. 8.
33. Rev. Proc. 77-37, § 3.02.
34. *J.A. Nelson Co.*, 296 U.S. 374, 56 S.Ct. 273 (1936).
35. IRC Sec. 368(a)(2)(E).
36. IRC Sec. 368(c).
37. Rev. Rul. 74-564, 1974-2 CB 124; Rev. Rul. 74-565, 1974-2 CB 125.
38. Reg. § 1.368-2(j)(3)(iii).
39. Reg. § 1.368-2(j)(3)(i).
40. Reg. § 1.368-2(j)(3)(i).
41. Reg. § 1.368-2(j)(3)(iii).
42. Reg. § 1.368-2(j)(4).
43. *Id.*
44. IRC Sec. 355(a)(1)(A)(i). See *O.E. Bann*, 382 F2d 485 (1967).
45. IRC Sec. 355(a)(1)(A).
46. IRC Sec. 355(a)(1)(C), (b).
47. IRC Sec. 355(b)(2)(B), (C) and (D).
48. IRC Sec. 355(b)(2)(B).
49. IRC Sec. 355(b)(2)(C) and (D).
50. IRC Sec. 355(a)(1)(D).
51. IRC Sec. 355(a)(1)(B).
52. P.L. 101-508.
53. IRC Secs. 355(e), 355(c)(2), and 361(c)(2).
54. IRC Sec. 355(e) does not modify or over-ride the non-recognition provisions of IRC Sec. 355(a), applicable to distributees of stock in a controlled corporation.
55. IRC Sec. 355(e)(2)(B).
56. See IRC Sec. 358(c).
57. IRC Secs. 358(a)(1) and 1223(1).
58. IRC Sec. 1032.
59. Reg. § 1.1032-2(b).
60. Reg. § 1.1032-2(c).
61. See Reg. § 1.1032-2(d).
62. Reg. § 1.1032-3.
63. IRC Sec. 362(b).
64. IRC Sec. 1223(2).
65. 2011-25 IRB 890.
66. Reg. § 1.358-6(c).
67. Reg. § 1.358-6(c)(2).
68. See *McCrory Corp.*, 651 F2d 828 (1981).
69. See Reg. § 1.263(a)-5(g)(1), "reserving" comment on transaction costs incurred in a transaction described under IRC Sec. 368.
70. IRC Sec. 361.
71. IRC Sec. 361.
72. IRC Sec. 361(c)(1) and (c)(2)(B).
73. IRC Sec. 361(c)(2).
74. IRC Sec. 358(a)(2).
75. IRC Sec. 358(a)(1)(d).
76. IRC Sec. 354(a)(1).
77. IRC Sec. 356(a)(1).
78. See IRC Sec. 358(a)(1).
79. See IRC Sec. 1223(1).
80. IRC Secs. 351-368.
81. IRC Sec. 1371(a).
82. February 12, 1985.
83. See Rev. Rul. 69-566, 1969-2 CB 165.
84. See IRC Sec. 1374(d)(3).
85. IRS Ann. 86-128, IRB 1986-51, 128.
86. IRC Sec. 1374(d)(8).
87. *Id.*
88. See IRC Sec. 1362(e).
89. IRC Sec. 1377(a)(1).
90. IRC Sec. 381(c)(2).
91. Reg. § 1.351-1(a)(ii).
92. 1977-2 CB 568.
93. Reg. § 1.351-1(a)(1)(ii).
94. 1977-2 CB 568.
95. 1977-2 CB 568.
96. IRC Sec. 358(a)(1) and (d).
97. IRC Sec. 1223(1).
98. See G.C.M. 21507, CB 1939-2, 189; *Wall Products Inc. v. Comm.*, 11 T.C. 51, at 57 (1948), acquiescence, CB 1949-1, 4; *Ralph L. Evans v. Comm.*, 8 B.T.A. 543 (1927).

99. See *Marvin R. Thompson v. Johnson*, United States District Court for the Southern District of New York, entered July 26, 1950, 50-2, U.S. Tax Cases, paragraph 9428, 42 American Federal Tax Reports 1284.
100. 1984-1 CB 106.
101. 1980-2 CB 117.
102. 93 TC 67 (1989), *aff'd*, 918 F.2d 426 (3d Cir. 1990).
103. 1984-1 CB 106.
104. See *Kuper v. Comm.*, 533 F.2d 152 (5th Cir. 1976); *Culligan Water Conditioning of Tri-Cities, Inc. v. U.S.*, 567 F.2d 867 (9th Cir. 1978) (the step transaction doctrine was inapplicable because there was no obligation or plan to dispose of the transferee corporation's stock at the time of incorporation); *King Enterprises, Inc. v. U.S.*, 418 F.2d 511 (Ct. Cl. 1969); TAM 200036002 (end result test may be used to determine if distributions from wholly owned subsidiary to its parent may be treated as boot in a § 351 transaction).
105. See *Redding v. Comm.*, 630 F.2d 1169 (7th Cir. 1980), *cert. denied*, 450 U.S. 913 (1981) (step transaction doctrine in the context of a § 355 spinoff); *Manhattan Bldg. Co. v. Comm.*, 27 T.C. 1032 (1957), *acq.*, 1957-2 CB 5; *American Bantam Car Co. v. Comm.*, 11 T.C. 397 (1948), *aff'd per curiam*, 177 F.2d 513 (3d Cir. 1949), *cert. denied*, 339 U.S. 920 (1950); Rev. Rul. 78-130, 1978-1 CB 114; Rev. Rul. 70-225, 1970-1 CB 180, *obsoleted by* Rev. Rul. 98-44, 1998-37 I.R.B. 4; Rev. Rul. 61-156, 1961-2 CB 62; Rev. Rul. 54-96, 1954-1 CB 111; Rev. Rul. 56-100, 1956-1 CB 624.
106. See *Comm. v. Gordon*, 391 U.S. 83 (1968); *J.E. Seagram Corp. v. Comm.*, 104 T.C. 75 (1995); *Intermountain Lumber Co. v. Comm.*, 65 T.C. 1025 (1976); *Hazeltine Corp. v. Comm.*, 89 F.2d 513 (3d Cir. 1937); Rev. Rul. 79-194, 1979-1 CB 145; Rev. Rul. 79-70, 1979-1 CB 144; Rev. Rul. 70-522, 1970-2 CB 81; CCA 200350016; TAM 8735009.
107. See, e.g., *Stephens, Inc. v. U.S.*, 464 F.2d 53 (8th Cir. 1972), *cert. denied*, 409 U.S. 1118 (1973); *Weikel v. Comm.*, T.C. Memo 1986-58; *Zachry Co. v. Comm.*, 49 T.C. 73 (1967); *Nat'l Bellas Hess, Inc. v. Comm.*, 20 T.C. 636 (1953), *acq.* in part, 1953-2 CB 5, aff'd, 220 F.2d 415 (8th Cir. 1955); *Scientific Instrument Co. v. Comm.*, 17 T.C. 1253 (1952), *aff'd per curiam*, 202 F.2d 155 (6th Cir. 1953). *See also* Rev. Rul. 79-250, 1979-2 CB 156. *Cf.*, Rev. Rul. 96-29, 1996-1 CB 50.
108. *South Bay Corp. v. Comm.*, 345 F.2d 698 (2d Cir. 1965); *American Wire Fabrics Corp. v. Comm.*, 16 T.C. 607 (1951), *acq.*, 1951-2 CB 1; *American Bantam Car Co. v. Comm.*, 11 T.C. 397 (1948), *aff'd per curiam*, 177 F.2d 513 (3d Cir. 1949), *cert. denied*, 399 U.S. 920 (1950). *See also* TAM 9304002 (the exchange of property by some shareholders of a corporation for notes issued by the corporation was not a sale of assets to the corporation because the exchange was part of a larger transaction in which other shareholders exchanged property for stock, with the result that the transaction as a whole was governed by pre-1989 RRA § 351.
109. See *J.E. Seagram Corp. v. Comm.*, 104 T.C. 75 (1995).
110. See, e.g., *S. Klein on the Square, Inc. v. Comm.*, 188 F.2d 127 (2d Cir. 1951), *cert. denied*, 342 U.S. 824 (1951); *Hazeltine Corp. v. Comm.*, 89 F.2d 513 (3d Cir. 1937); *Bassick v. Comm.*, 85 F.2d 8 (2d Cir. 1936), *cert. denied*, 299 U.S. 592 (1936); *Manhattan Bldg. Co. v. Comm.*, 27 T.C. 1032 (1957), *acq.*, 1957-2 CB 5; *American Bantam Car Co. v. Comm.*, 11 T.C. 397 (1948), *aff'd per curiam*, 177 F.2d 513 (3d Cir. 1949), *cert. denied*, 339 U.S. 920 (1950).
111. See *Intermountain Lumber Co. v. Comm.*, 65 T.C. 1025 (1976); *Stanton v. U.S.*, 512 F.2d 13 (3d Cir. 1975); *Stephens, Inc. v. U.S.*, 464 F.2d 53 (8th Cir. 1972), *cert. denied*, 409 U.S. 1118 (1973); *American Bantam Car Co. v. Comm.*, 11 T.C. 397 (1948), *aff'd per curiam*, 177 F.2d 513 (3d Cir. 1949), *cert. denied*, 339 U.S. 920 (1950); *D'Angelo Assocs., Inc. v. Comm.*, 70 T.C. 121 (1978); TAM 8220002; PLR 200017002 (a governmental entity "controlled" the corporation to which it contributed an insurance business because it retained the power to decide whether to keep the interests it received or transfer them to private owners).
112. IRC Sec. 358.
113. IRC Sec. 1223(1).
114. 1977-2 CB 568.
115. IRC Sec. 356(a)(1).
116. IRC Sec. 356(a)(2).
117. IRC Sec. 362(b).
118. See Rev. Rul. 72-327, 1972-2 CB 197.
119. IRC Sec. 358(a)(1).
120. IRC Sec. 1223(1).
121. IRC Sec. 368(a)(2)(B).
122. IRC Sec. 362(b).
123. Reg. § 1.368-2(j)(3)(iii); Rev. Proc. 77-37, 1977-2 CB 568.
124. See Reg. § 1.368-2(j)(3)(iii).
125. Reg. § 1.358-6(c)(2).
126. IRC Sec. 358.
127. IRC Sec. 1223(1).
128. 1977-2 CB 568.
129. Reg. § 1.1032-2(b).
130. Reg. § 1.358-6(c).
131. IRC Sec. 362(b).
132. IRC Sec. 358.
133. IRC Sec. 1223(1).

ACQUISITION AND SALE OF AN S CORPORATION BUSINESS

CHAPTER 8

OVERVIEW

An S corporation is a corporation for all nontax purposes. It is differentiated from a C corporation only for purposes of federal and (usually) state income taxation. In general, under subchapter S of chapter 1 of the Code, an S corporation is treated for most federal income tax purposes as a pass-through entity, which means that the S corporation's items of income, gain, loss, deduction, and credit are allocated and distributed proportionately to the S corporation's shareholders and are reported by the shareholders on their respective individual federal and state income tax returns. There are certain circumstances in which the S corporation itself can be subject to an entity-level federal or state tax, notably under Code sections 1374 and 1375, discussed below. However, as a general matter, the income, gain, and loss of an S corporation—including income, gain, or loss recognized by the S corporation on the sale of its assets—are taxed at the shareholder level and are not taxed at the corporate level.

As with a C corporation, the sale and acquisition of a business operated through an S corporation raises the three basic transaction structuring decisions: (a) will the transaction be taxable or tax-free? (b) if it is taxable, will the transaction be an asset sale or a stock sale? and (c) will the consideration for the acquisition be paid or delivered at closing or will some or all of it be paid on a deferred or contingent basis?

An S corporation, being a corporation, can be a participant in any "reorganization" under Code section 368, and is also governed by the provisions of Code section 351 with respect to contributions of appreciated property in exchange for stock. By contrast, an LLC taxable as a partnership cannot participate in a reorganization transaction because it is not a corporation. The inability to structure an LLC acquisition as a reorganization under Code section 368 is often considered one of the biggest disadvantages of an LLC as a business entity, particularly if the business is likely to be the subject of an acquisition by a publicly traded corporation. On the other hand, an LLC is governed by Code section 721 rather than Code section 351 on contributions of property in exchange for equity interests, and Code section 721 is generally far less onerous, particularly because it does not have the 80 percent control test imposed under Code section 351.

If an acquisition is intended to be a taxable transaction, and not a reorganization, an S corporation business can be acquired either through an asset acquisition or a stock acquisition. As this chapter will explore in great detail, *from a tax perspective, an S corporation is generally far superior to a C corporation as a target in an acquisition, regardless of whether the transaction is structured as an asset sale or a stock sale*. This is because, if the transaction is an asset sale, the pass-through taxation under subchapter S avoids the onerous double taxation imposed on a C corporation. On the other hand, if the transaction is structured as a stock sale, the availability of a Code section 338(h)(10) election means that the Acquirer can acquire stock rather than assets (usually desirable for a nontax reason) but then can step-up the tax basis of the assets by electing, with the Target shareholders, to treat the acquisition transaction as an asset acquisition rather than as a stock acquisition.[1] Similarly, if the Acquirer prefers stock sale tax treatment, the availability of a Code section 336(e) election allows a seller to unilaterally treat a stock sale as an asset sale for tax purposes.[2] As a result, the Acquirer can choose which form of acquisition transaction it prefers (i.e., stock or assets), and either choice will (usually) produce entirely or predominantly capital gain to the Seller, while allowing the Acquirer to enjoy a stepped-up basis in the acquired assets immediately after the transaction.

There are special rules, issues, and considerations that can arise if the acquisition of an S corporation is structured as an installment sale.[3] These issues are addressed in detail in Chapter 10.

TAX ISSUES INVOLVED IN AN ACQUISITION OF S CORPORATION ASSETS

A sale of assets by an S corporation, especially when followed by the liquidation of the corporation, generates significantly different tax consequences than a comparable sale of assets by a C corporation. First, on the sale of the S corporation assets, the items of income, gain, loss, deduction, and credit pass through to the S corporation shareholders (who, by definition, must be individuals or certain types of trusts) and therefore are generally taxed according to the tax rates and tax rules for individuals rather than corporations.[4] This means that, to the extent the S corporation recognizes substantial long-term capital gain on the sale of its assets (a very common occurrence), this gain is taxed for federal income tax purposes at the shareholder level at the currently favorable long-term capital gain tax rate. Note, however, that an S corporation may have corporate-level tax liabilities under Code section 1374 (built-in gains tax), or Code section 1375 (retained E&P from prior C corporation years and excess passive income), and can be subject to other corporate-level taxes in certain other limited contexts.

On the second step of the asset-sale transaction, the corporate liquidation, the S corporation is subject to gain or loss recognition under Code section 336(a) and therefore will recognize gain or loss on the distribution of any appreciated assets (or any other assets whose fair market value exceeds the corporation's tax basis in the asset). However, because it is an S corporation, this gain or loss will again pass through to the shareholder.[5] In turn, the shareholder will get a step-up in his or her "outside" tax basis in the S corporation stock, pursuant to Code section 1367, and thus will generally recognize capital gain or loss on a liquidating S corporation distribution equal to the difference between the fair market value of the distributed assets and the shareholder's basis in the S corporation stock.[6]

It is often stated, simplistically, that a liquidation of an S corporation is subject to a "single level" of tax. As the preceding discussion illustrates, the liquidation of an S corporation technically triggers the same number of tax recognition events as the liquidation of a C corporation, namely, (a) recognition at the corporation level of gain or loss based on the fair market value of each distributed asset compared to the corporation's tax basis in that asset, and then (b) recognition at the shareholder level of gain or loss based on the fair market value of the distributed assets compared to each shareholder's tax basis in his or her stock. However, the crucial difference is that when gain is recognized by the S corporation at the corporate level, both under Code section 1001 pursuant to its sale of assets and under Code section 336(a) pursuant to the liquidating distribution, such gain recognition results in a step-up in each shareholder's "outside" tax basis in the S corporation stock under Code section 1367, and such basis step-up, in turn, will reduce the gain recognized by the shareholder upon the liquidating redemption of S corporation shares; the net effect is often the equivalent of a single level of tax.

Example 1: Assume an S corporation has held for more than one year a single capital asset with a fair market value of $1 million and a tax basis in the hands of the S corporation of $100,000. Assume further that the sole shareholder in the S corporation has $100,000 of "outside" basis in the shareholder's S corporation shares. On the taxable sale of the asset to a third party for $1 million, the S corporation will recognize $900,000 of capital gain, which gain, in turn, will pass through and be taxed to the shareholder under Code section 1366. There will be a corresponding step-up or increase in the shareholder's "outside" tax basis of $900,000 under Code section 1367. If the S corporation liquidates and distributes the $1 million in cash to the shareholder, the shareholder at that moment will have $1 million of outside tax basis ($100,000 initial tax basis + $900,000 recognized on the asset sale and passed through to the shareholder under Code section 1367). Therefore, this liquidating distribution will generate no additional gain (shareholder receives $1 million in cash in exchange for stock with a tax basis at that moment of $1 million).[7]

Example 2: Same as in Example 1, except that the shareholder starts with an outside basis equal to zero. Upon the sale of the asset, the S corporation again recognizes $900,000 of gain, which passes through to the shareholder under Code section 1366 and causes, in turn, the shareholder's outside basis to be increased from zero to $900,000 under Code section 1367. Upon the subsequent liquidating distribution of $1 million, the transaction will generate gain from the sale or exchange of property (i.e., the stock) and will result in recognition by the shareholder of additional capital gain in the amount of $100,000 ($1 million of distributed cash in exchange for stock with a tax basis at that moment of $900,000).[8]

Example 3: Same as in Example 1, except that the shareholder starts with an outside basis equal to $300,000. Upon the sale of the asset, the S corporation once again recognizes $900,000 of gain, which passes through to the shareholder under Code section 1366 and causes, in turn, the outside tax basis to be increased from $300,000 to $1.2 million under Code section 1367. Upon the subsequent liquidating distribution of $1 million, the transaction will be treated as a sale or exchange of property (i.e., the stock) and will result in recognition by the shareholder of capital loss in the amount of ($200,000) ($1 million of distributed cash in exchange for stock with a tax basis at that moment of $1.2 million).[9] On this transaction, the shareholder recognizes $900,000 of capital gain on the sale of the asset by the corporation and a ($200,000) loss on the liquidation of the S corporation, which, if it all occurs in the same tax year, can partially offset and produce a net capital gain of $700,000 ($900,000 – $200,000).

Comment: If, in Example 3, the S corporation is not liquidated in year 1 (the year of the asset sale) and instead is liquidated in the following year (year 2), the shareholder may have the worst of both worlds: $900,000 of capital gain in year 1 and a $200,000 long-term capital loss in year 2. The capital loss may be almost entirely unusable because capital losses of an individual taxpayer are not eligible for a carryback[10] and can only be used to offset capital gains in the current year plus $3,000 of other income.[11] Thus, the shareholder will overpay long-term capital gain up front and may wait indefinitely to use the related capital loss carryover.[12] Even worse, if the shareholder dies before the capital loss is used up, the capital loss will disappear.[13]

CODE SECTIN 1374 ISSUES INVOLVED IN A SALE OF ASSETS BY AN S CORPORATION THAT IS A FORMER C CORPORATION

Although S corporations are generally not subject to taxation at the entity level, special rules apply if the S corporation was formerly a C corporation. Code section 1374, sometimes called the "sting tax", subjects an S corporation to an entity-level tax at the maximum corporate tax rate (currently 35 percent), in any tax year in the first five years (and sometimes even after five years) after a corporation that was formerly a C corporation elects S status if the S corporation has "net recognized built-in gain" in that tax year. The "net realized built-in gain" is an annual calculation performed under the unique accounting rules of Code section 1374, which, in the author's experience, is in many respects as distinctive and complicated as the calculation of taxable income for regular tax purposes or the calculation of alternative minimum taxable income for purposes of the alternative minimum tax.

The policy underlying Code section 1374 is that a C corporation should not be able to avoid the double taxation imposed by subchapter C by electing S status shortly before selling all or a significant portion of its business assets. Historically, the so-called "waiting period" (the period after S conversion during which the corporation is subject to Code section 1374) has changed from three years, to ten years, to now five years.

Several tax planning issues should be addressed at the outset: (a) the tax costs of selling a business are much lower if the Target is an S corporation and is not subject to Code section 1374; (b) the five-year period means that the sale or disposition of a business must be anticipated and the S election filed significantly before the anticipated sale; and (c) if an entity is a C corporation today and the shareholders want to sell the business in the near future, it may be too late to avoid Code section 1374. Instead, one must manage the calculation of the amount of built-in gain, and the related timing of recognition of built-in gain and loss, so as to minimize the Code section 1374 tax.

The rules under Code section 1374 are complex. Code section 1374 applies the highest rate of tax imposed under the corporate tax[14] to the S corporation's "net recognized built-in gain". The term "net recognized built-in gain" is defined in Reg. § 1.1374-2(a) as being the *least* of the following:

1. Its taxable income determined by using all rules applying to C corporations and considering only its recognized built-in gain, recognized built-in loss, and recognized built-in gain carryover (this is referred to as the "pre-limitation amount").

2. Its taxable income determined by using all rules applying to C corporations as modified by Code section 1375(b)(1)(B) (this is referred to as the "taxable income limitation").

3. The amount by which its net unrealized built-in gain exceeds its net recognized built-in gain for all prior tax years (this is referred to as the "net unrealized built-in gain limitation").

Code section 1374 has spawned its own unique set of concepts and, in turn, acronyms. At the time of conversion from C to S corporation status, the corporation needs to take a snapshot and identify its net unrealized built-in gain (NUBIG), which is the amount by which the fair market value of the S corporation's assets, as of the beginning of its first tax year for which an S election is in effect, exceeds the aggregate adjusted bases of its assets at such time.[15] Stated another and perhaps easier way to understand, NUBIG is the amount by which the corporation's built-in gains (corporate assets with a fair market value in excess of the corporation's tax basis in those assets) exceeds its built-in losses (corporate assets with a fair market value below the corporation's tax basis in those assets) as of the first day of S corporation status.

Example 4: An S corporation has two assets. Asset 1 has a fair market value of $7 million and tax basis of $1 million, which means that the fair market value of Asset 1 exceeds the corporation's tax basis in the asset by $6 million. Asset 2 has a fair market value of $3 million and a tax basis of $5 million, which means that the fair market value of Asset 2 is $2 million less than the corporation's tax basis in the asset. Because NUBIG puts an overall cap equal to the net unrealized built-in gains of all corporate assets on the conversion date, the NUBIG is $4 million ($10 million of aggregate fair market value, minus $6 million of aggregate adjusted tax bases).

For each of the next five years following its conversion to S status, the corporation will need to track its recognized built-in gain (RBIG) and recognized built-in loss (RBIL). These terms represent the gain or loss, respectively, recognized by the corporation on the disposition of an asset that was held by the corporation on the conversion date. Technically, RBIG means any gain recognized during the five-year recognition period, beginning on the effective date of the corporation's S election, from the disposition of any asset except to the extent that (1) the S corporation can establish that the asset disposed of was not held by it as of the effective date of its S election or (2) such asset's built-in gain (the excess of the fair market value of the asset over the corporation's adjusted tax basis in the asset) as of the effective date of the S election was less than the gain recognized by the corporation on the disposition. This means that appreciation (on an asset-by-asset basis) after conversion to an S corporation escapes the Section 1374 "sting tax".

Similarly, RBIL means any loss recognized during the five-year recognition period on the disposition of any asset to the extent that the S corporation can show that (1) such asset was held by it as of the effective date of its conversion to S status, and (2) the loss recognized does not exceed the amount of such asset's built-in loss (the excess of the corporation's adjusted tax basis in the asset over the asset's fair market value) as of the effective date of the corporation's S election.[16]

The net recognized built-in gain potentially subject to tax in any year is the sum of the RBIG, the RBIL, and any net realized built-in gain carryover from a prior tax year in which the corporation had net RBIG but was not subject to the full 1374 "sting tax" due to one of the limitations. Once the net RBIG is computed, it is then reduced by any NOL carryforwards and any capital loss carryforwards arising in a tax year during which the corporation was a C corporation.[17] In addition, any tax computed under Code section 1374 may be reduced by business and minimum tax credit carryforwards arising from years in which the corporation was a C corporation.[18] Reg. § 1.1374-6(a) provides that the credits and credit carryforwards allowed as credits against the built-in gains tax under Code section 1374(b)(3) are allowed only to the extent their use is allowed under the rules applicable to C corporations; any other credits or credit carryforwards (such as the foreign tax credit under Code section 901) are not allowed as credits against the built-in gains tax. Additionally, Reg. § 1.1374-6(b) provides that the amount of business credit carryforwards and minimum tax credit allowed against the built-in gains tax are subject to the limitations described in Code section 38(c) and Code section 53(c), respectively.

Once the net RBIG for a tax year is computed, and before applying possible tax credits from prior C corporation years, one must examine certain limitations rules to see if the net RBIG will in fact be subject to the 1374 "sting tax". The first limitation, the taxable income limitation, requires a computation of the corporation's taxable income in the manner provided by Code section 1375(b)(1)(B), which generally means a computation as if the corporation were still a C corporation. The theory underlying this limitation is that the 1374 "sting tax" is intended to prevent avoidance of the corporate level tax applied to C corporations. Therefore, it should not apply unless the corporation would have taxable income for the tax year if it had remained a C corporation. Any gain not included in RBIG because of the taxable income limitation is carried over to the next tax year.[19]

Code section 1374(c)(2) provides the NUBIG limitation, which is that the net RBIG taken into account under Code section 1374 for any tax year may not exceed the excess, if any, of (a) the corporation's NUBIG over (b) the corporation's net RBIG for all prior years during the recognition period. This simply means that the maximum amount of built-in gain subject to tax over the entire ten-year period cannot exceed the NUBIG determined as of the date of conversion to S status. The policy underlying the NUBIG limitation is that the maximum amount of built-in gain subject to tax under Code section 1374 should be capped at the amount of appreciation in the corporation's assets that occurred during its C corporation period, and excludes any post-S conversion appreciation in such assets (on a total assets level).

Code section 1374(d)(1) provides that NUBIG is the amount by which the fair market value of the corporation's assets as of the beginning of its first tax year as an S corporation exceeds the corporation's aggregate adjusted tax bases in such assets at such time. Reg. § 1.1374-3(a) provides a more detailed definition of NUBIG. It states that NUBIG is the total of:

1. the amount that would be realized if, on the first day of the recognition period, the corporation had remained a C corporation and had sold all of its assets at fair market value to an unrelated party that assumed all of its liabilities; decreased by
2. any liability of the corporation that would be included in the amount realized on this hypothetical sale, but only if the corporation would be allowed a deduction on payment of such liability; decreased by
3. the aggregate adjusted bases of the corporation's assets on the first day of the recognition period; increased or decreased by
4. The corporation's Section 481 adjustments that would be taken into account following the hypothetical sale; and increased by
5. Any recognized built-in loss that would not be allowed as a deduction under Code section 382, 383, or 384 following the hypothetical sale.

Example 5: Assume that a building has a fair market value of $1.2 million and a tax basis of $1 million at the time the corporation converts from C to S status. Four years later, the value of the property is $2 million but, because of depreciation, its tax basis is now $500,000. A sale of the building at that point in time (i.e., four years later) will result in a gain of $1.5 million. However, at the time of conversion, the net unrealized built-in gain is only $200,000 (the difference between $1.2 million and $1 million). Therefore, the NUBIG limitation will cause $200,000 of the realized gain on the sale of the asset to be characterized as RBIG for 1374 "sting tax" purposes. Note that the taxpayer will need to maintain records for up to five years, and possibly longer, to document and support these amounts.

Code section 1374(d)(5)(C) provides that a corporation's NUBIG is adjusted for built-in income and built-in deduction items, which are treated as recognized built-in gains or recognized built-in losses under Code section 1374(d)(5). These built-in income and loss items are often included in the computation of NUBIG based on accrual accounting concepts, and thus can affect NUBIG even if such items are not actually recognized during the recognition period.

Because built-in income and built-in deduction items are particularly complex, additional discussion of these items is in order. Code section 1374(d)(3) provides that RBIG means any gain recognized during the recognition period on the "disposition of any asset". This definition works well for most "assets", but not when an asset is actually an accounting item. Accordingly, the Technical and Miscellaneous Revenue Act of 1988[20] clarified that recognized built-in gain and recognized built-in loss include not only gains and losses recognized on a disposition of an asset but also certain items of income properly taken into account during the recognition period and certain amounts allowable as a deduction during the recognition period. Code section 1374(d)(5)(A) provides that any item of income that is properly taken into account during the recognition period but which is attributable to periods prior to the date of the corporation's conversion to S status will be treated as a recognized built-in gain for the tax year in which it is properly taken into account. This type of item is generally referred to as a "built-in income item", although that technical term does not expressly appear in the Code. Code section 1374(d)(5)(B) provides that any amount that is allowable as a deduction during the recognition period (determined without regard to any carryover) but is "attributable" to a period prior to the date of the corporation's conversion to S status will be treated as a recognized built-in loss for the tax year for which it is allowable. This type of item is generally referred to as a "built-in deduction item".

To determine whether an item constitutes a built-in income or built-in deduction item under Code section 1374(d)(5), the focus is on whether such item is "attributable" to a period prior to the date of the corporation's conversion to S status. To facilitate this analysis, the IRS adopted an "accrual method rule" to determine whether an income or a deduction item is attributable to a period prior to the date of the corporation's conversion to S status. Reg. § 1.1374-4(b)(1) provides that any item of income properly taken into account during the recognition period is recognized built-in gain if the item would have been properly included in gross income before the beginning of the recognition period by an accrual method taxpayer (disregarding any method of accounting for which an election by the taxpayer must be made unless the taxpayer actually used the method when it was a C corporation).

The most common example of a built-in income item subject to the built-in gains tax is an accounts receivable generated by a cash basis taxpayer in a C corporation tax year but not collected until after conversion to S status. Because accounts receivable would have been income to a C corporation year using the accrual method, collection of this income is treated as "built-in gain".

Regulation § 1.1374-4(b)(2) provides that any item of deduction properly taken into account during the recognition period is recognized built-in loss if the item would have been properly allowed as a deduction against gross income before the beginning of the recognition period by a taxpayer using the accrual method (disregarding any method of accounting for which an election by the taxpayer must be made unless the taxpayer actually used the method when it was a C corporation). A common example of a built-in deduction item is the payment of accounts payable by a cash-basis taxpayer.

Even if an item does not constitute a built-in loss item within the meaning of Code section 1374(d)(5)(B), it still may potentially affect a corporation's NUBIG. For example, an accrued bonus payable to a C corporation employee that is not paid by the corporation within the first two and one-half months following the date of the corporation's conversion to S status would not constitute a built-in deduction item under Code section 1374(d)(5)(B) because under both Code sections 267(a)(2) and 404(a)(5), such amount would not have been deductible by the corporation prior to the date of its conversion if it were an accrual-basis taxpayer. However, the accrued bonus would reduce the corporation's NUBIG limitation because Reg. § 1.1374-3(a)(2) provides that NUBIG is decreased by the amount of any liability of the corporation to the extent the corporation would be allowed a deduction on payment of such liability. In other words, the accrual method of accounting does not strictly apply in determining whether a liability decreases a corporation's NUBIG, to the extent that the "assumed payment" rule described above changes the accounting result.

Practice Pointer: See Reg. § 1.1374-4(c) for special rules regarding payments to related parties that are properly deducted under Code section 267(a)(2) during the recognition period. Such amounts constitute recognized built-in loss to the extent that all events have occurred that establish the fact of the liability to pay the amount, and the exact amount of the liability can be determined, as of the beginning of the recognition period and either the amount is paid during the first two and one-half months of the recognition period or to a related party who directly or indirectly owns less than five percent (by voting power and value) of the corporation's stock, both as of the beginning of the recognition period and when the amount is paid.

One of the notably harsh results of these rules is that an S corporation that expects to dispose of assets from its prior C corporation era needs to do some careful analysis and planning. For example, if an asset with significant built-in gain is to be sold, it may be an opportune time to also dispose of an asset with significant built-in loss. Likewise, if a built-in loss asset is being sold, triggering RBIL, it may be a good time to trigger offsetting RBIG.

Example 6: An S corporation has four assets that, at the time of conversion, had the following respective amounts of built-in gain or loss:

Asset 1 had built-in gain of $4 million. Asset 2 had built-in gain of $2 million. Asset 3 had built-in loss of $1 million. Asset 4 had built-in loss of $1 million.

The NUBIG limitation of the S corporation under Code section 1374(c)(2) is $4 million. In the first post-conversion year, the S corporation sells Asset 3, recognizing a $1 million RBIL. Since there is no RBIG in that year, the RBIL is wasted. In year 2, Asset 1 is sold, recognizing $4 million of RBIG. There is no mechanism to use the prior RBIL to reduce this RBIG. Moreover, since the NUBIG limitation is $4 million, the entire net RBIG is subject to tax at that time. By contrast, if Asset 4 were sold in year 2, the RBIL and RBIG would offset in that year, and produce a net RBIG of $3 million subject to the 1374 "sting tax".

The rules previously described are both mechanical and severe, yet there remain both tax planning opportunities and issues with controversy. First, taking an accurate "snap shot" of the fair market value of a corporation's assets at the date of conversion is critical. Second, the S corporation has control over the timing for selling its assets, and should take care not to inflict a 1374 "sting tax" foolishly or unknowingly (e.g., by failing to trigger RBIL in the same year as RBIG). Third, one can to some degree create or structure built-in loss prior to a conversion to S status by creating a bonus or compensation obligation payable to a shareholder-employee, which obligation (probably evidenced by a promissory note) would not be deductible under accrual accounting rules until paid, but, because of the assumed payment rule in Reg. § 1.1374-3(a)(2), the corporation can claim a built-in deduction and reduce its NUBIG. Fourth, a fascinating question remains about how to apply the RBIG analysis to an asset that has been subject to repair, upgrade, or other improvement after the S conversion, and the fair market value of which was arguably created or augmented after the conversion date.

Example 7: A company converts to S status after operating for many years as a C corporation. The company has a fleet of trucks. On the conversion date the fair market value of the fleet of trucks exceeded the company's tax basis in the trucks by $1 million. Over the next three years, most or all of the trucks were consumed economically by usage, and new trucks were added to the fleet. In year 4, a buyer purchases the assets of the company, including the fleet of trucks. The fleet had a built-in gain on the S conversion date of $1 million. On the date of sale, the fleet had fair market value in excess of tax basis of $1.5 million. However, virtually all of the old trucks are gone, and were disposed of at $0 as valueless scrap, or else are parked and abandoned in the parking lot behind the company's headquarters.

Code section 1374(d)(3) defines "recognized built-in gain" to mean "any gain recognized during the recognition period [i.e., five-year period beginning on the effective date of the corporation's S election] on the disposition of any asset except to the extent that the S corporation establishes that (A) *such asset was not held by the S corporation as of the beginning of the first taxable year for which it was an S corporation. . .* " [Emphasis supplied.] There does not appear to be any significant authority interpreting the phrase "*such asset was not held by the S corporation as of the beginning of the first taxable year for which it was an S corporation. . .* " However, logic and common usage of the language would appear to support the conclusion that all the trucks in the fleet acquired after the conversion date, which represent all of the current value of the fleet, were acquired after the beginning of the first tax year that the corporation was an S corporation. Thus, all gain attributable to the sale of the fleet is excluded from RBIG.

Example 8: Assume the company in question is a creator and vendor of software. Assume it operated as a C corporation for a number of years and created Super Software, a software product it licensed to customers. Assume it converted to S status, at which time the Super Software product was believed to have built-in gain of $5 million. For the next three years, the company created a variety of new software products and also modified, restructured, enhanced, and rewrote almost all of Super Software. It expensed its costs to modify, restructure, enhance, and rewrite Super Software in conformity with standard accounting practices. In year 4, a purchaser buys all the assets of the company, including Super Software, and pays $20 million for the much-improved Super Software.

This is a harder question than Example 7 only because the Super Software has been substantially refurbished and updated, rather than replaced. The author believes that because virtually all the value of the Super Software at the time of the sale related to upgrades, enhancements, and improvements from money invested over the prior three years, little or no RBIG should be attributed to the Super Software. This example underscores one of the fundamental economic flaws of Code section 1374, which is that it assumes "assets" are somehow static in nature, and that any "built-in gain" remains economically fixed and locked into the asset for a period of up to five years. This assumption might (or might not) be accurate with respect to raw land, assuming the land was not materially altered after the S conversion, but it is clearly *not* an accurate assumption regarding an asset such as software, or a fleet of trucks. One can even argue that a commercial building that is maintained through continuous expenditures and repairs has at least in part been "acquired" after the date of conversion.

All assets held by a corporation as of the effective date of its S election are subject to the Code section 1374 tax for five years. If such assets are sold during that five-year period, Code section 1374 will apply, subject to the annual income limitation and the various other limitations (e.g., the overall cap on built-in gain). However, some interesting issues can arise with respect to when and whether gain has been recognized on the sale of an asset that was held by the corporation prior to its S election. For example, inventory is generally subject to the built-in gain recognition provisions of Code section 1374. Hence, to the extent that the tax basis of such inventory is less than its fair market value on the date of the conversion, its disposition will result in RBIG. The key issue is how one values the built-in gain of such inventory on the date of conversion.

As previously discussed, a corporation's net recognized built-in gain subject to tax in any year is not greater than the corporation's taxable income, calculated as provided by Code section 1375(b)(1)(B). Basically, this calculation attempts to determine what the taxable income of the corporation would have been if the corporation were a C corporation instead of an S corporation in the applicable year. This can be a very interesting issue to address and try to control when an S corporation sells assets. For example, if, in the same year that an S corporation sells assets and recognizes built-in gain, it pays reasonable compensation bonuses to shareholder employees, the corporation may be able to legitimately reduce its taxable income under this "faux C corporation" computation to zero (or near zero) and thereby avoid all or substantially all of the "sting tax". Moreover, since the built-in gain then carries forward to the next year, the same strategy can potentially be repeated, until after the fifth year, when the exposure for carryover built-in gain disappears.

As will be discussed more fully in Chapter 10, an S corporation cannot avoid the impact of Code section 1374 by selling its assets for an installment note that provides for payment of principal after the five-year recognition period has terminated.[21]

If an S corporation can do a like-kind exchange, or other nontaxable transaction, with assets, that transaction will not trigger tax under Code section 1374 or any other provision of the regular tax (and, because it is an S corporation, it will not be subject to the alternative minimum tax applicable to C corporations under Code section 55). However, assets acquired in exchange for an asset that is subject to Code section 1374 will likewise become subject to Code section 1374.

The greatest and most obvious benefit of electing S status is that, after the five-year waiting period under Code section 1374, the corporation is "cleansed" of its former C corporation attributes and thus can sell off its assets subject to a single level tax, generally at capital gains tax rates.

Another interesting observation to make is that, in some cases, it may make sense to elect S corporation status, notwithstanding the Code section 1374 "sting tax", immediately before a sale of business assets. This is illustrated by the following example.

Example 9: Assume a corporation is currently a C corporation and has been offered $1 million for its assets, all or substantially all of which are capital assets or Code section 1231 property with little or no Code section 1245 recapture. Assume that this purchase price has been allocated 25 percent to consulting payments ($250,000), 25 percent to noncompete payments ($250,000), and the remaining balance ($500,000) to the corporate assets. The $500,000 will be subject to tax at ordinary corporate tax rates (because there is no preferential capital gains tax rate for corporations), and the liquidation of the corporation will produce a second level of tax, at capital gains rates, at the shareholder level.

Assume that the corporation can justify paying severance and/or termination bonuses to its key employees, most of whom are its principal shareholders, in an amount approximately equal to $500,000 dollars (i.e., an amount that essentially zeros out the corporate level gain). This strategy avoids the double taxation at the corporate level, but still taxes the income at ordinary income rates to the individual shareholders, which is clearly not as good as if the corporation were an S corporation and the shareholders were taxed at a single level of tax at capital gains tax rates.

Assume instead that this transaction occurs at the end of a tax year and the C corporation can elect S status and immediately thereafter sell the assets. The $500,000 of gain will be "built-in gain" for purposes of Code section 1374, subject to the "sting tax". However, the amount of "sting tax" actually imposed by Code section 1374 is limited to the lesser of the recognized built-in gain, or, if less, the amount of taxable income the S corporation would have reported if it were a C corporation.[22] A net recognized built-in gain that is not subject to Code section 1374 because of the taxable income limitation carries forward to subsequent tax years (subject to the same taxable income limitation) but not past the five-year recognition period.[23]

In this example, assuming the corporation can justify paying $500,000 of compensation to its key employees (its principal shareholders), the net recognized built-in gain for "sting tax" purposes would be zero because of the taxable income limitation. However, on the Form K-1 issued to shareholders, the corporation would separately state the $500,000 long-term capital gain and $500,000 operating loss. Assuming that the same shareholders received all or substantially all of the $500,000 in compensation income for the year, the effect would be $500,000 of W-2 income, a $500,000 operating loss on the K-1, which offsets the W-2 income, and $500,000 of capital gain. This strategy converts compensation income into capital gains through an expedient use of the taxable income limitation under Code section 1374(d)(2)(A).

TAX ISSUES UNDER CODE SECTION 1362 AND 1375

In addition to Code section 1374, there is also a "sting tax" imposed at the corporate level under Code section 1375 when an S corporation (1) has subchapter "C" earnings and profits at the close of the tax year, and (2) more than 25 percent of the corporation's gross receipts are passive investment income. Passive investment income means gross receipts derived from royalties, rents, dividends, interest, annuities, and sales or exchanges of stock or securities. If passive income exceeds this 25-percent level for three consecutive years, the S election is automatically terminated.[24] The Code section 1375 tax equals the "excess net passive income" multiplied by the highest rate of tax specified in Code section 11 (i.e., 35 percent). Code sections 1374 and 1375 are designed to be complementary (i.e., one section or the other may apply, but not both at the same time to the same income).

The Code section 1375 tax applies only to "excess net passive investment income", which is the portion of a corporation's net passive income calculated by multiplying the net passive income by a fraction, the numerator of which is the corporation's passive investment income less 25 percent of its gross receipts and the denominator of which is the corporation's passive investment income. Although this formula is complicated to apply, the basic thrust of the rule is to apply a double tax only to the extent that the passive income exceeds this 25-percent-of-gross-receipts level.

"Passive investment income" for Code section 1362 and 1375 purposes is not necessarily the same as the definition of passive income in other contexts (e.g., it is not, for example, the same as passive income under Code section 469, the so-called "passive activity loss" rules). For Code section 1375 purposes, "passive investment income" includes only gross receipts derived from royalties, rents, dividends, interest, annuities, and sales or exchanges of stock or securities. A common question is whether "rent", coupled with various other kinds of activities, is passive for the purposes of Code section 1375 or "active" income. This is a facts-and-circumstances issue, but generally, when the taxpayer provides significant additional services in addition to the rental of property, the income will not be considered "passive income" for Code section 1375 purposes.[25]

For example, if an S corporation owns and rents a yacht on a "bare boat charter" basis, whereby it provides simply the use of the boat for periods of time, such income will be passive income. However, if the S corporation provides a charter captain and significant other services to passengers, this income would not be considered passive income for these purposes.[26]

QUALIFIED SUBCHAPTER S SUBSIDIARIES

A qualified subchapter S subsidiary (QSub), is defined in Code section 1361(b)(3)(B) as any domestic corporation other than an ineligible corporation (as defined in Code section 1361(b)(2)) that meets the following requirements: (1) 100 percent of the stock of such corporation is held by the S corporation, and (2) the S corporation elects to treat such corporation as a QSub. An "ineligible corporation" as defined in Code section 1361(b)(2) means any corporation that is (a) a financial institution (such as a bank or thrift institution) that uses the reserve method of accounting for bad debts described in Code section 585, (b) an insurance company subject to tax under the rules of subchapter L of the Code, (c) a corporation that has elected to be treated as a possessions corporation under Code section 936, or (d) a Domestic International Sales Corporation (DISC) or former DISC.

Tax Consequences of a QSub Election

A qualified subchapter S subsidiary election (a "QSub election") is made by the parent S corporation, which must file timely a Form 8869. The federal income tax effect of a QSub election is that there is a deemed liquidation of the subsidiary into the parent corporation immediately before the election is effective under Code sections 332 and 337.[27] The deemed liquidation of the subsidiary under Code section 332 is a tax-free event. However, if at the time of the deemed liquidation the S subsidiary is insolvent, it will be treated as liquidating under Code section 331, not Code section 332 and/or Code section 337, which results in a recognition of asset gain to the S subsidiary.[28] According to Code section 1361(b)(3)(A), the QSub is not treated as a separate corporation following the deemed liquidation. Thus, all of the subsidiary's assets, liabilities, and items of income, deduction, and credit are treated as assets, liabilities, and such items (as the case may be) of the parent S corporation. *Note:* A final federal income tax return for the subsidiary may need to be filed it if was a separate corporation prior to the date of the deemed liquidation.

When to Make the QSub Election and the Effective Date of Such Election

The parent S corporation may make the QSub election at any time during the tax year. However, it is important to note that the effective date of the election depends upon when the election is filed with the IRS. The effective date of the QSub election cannot be more than (1) two months and fifteen days prior to the date of the filing of the election, or (2) twelve months after the date of the filing of the election.[27.5] If no date is specified on the Form 8869, the effective date of the election is as of the date the form is filed. Specific instructions regarding late filing of a QSub election are detailed on the Instructions to the Form 8869.

Termination of the Election

Once the QSub election is filed, it remains in effect until terminated. Under Code section 1361(b)(3)(C), if a QSub ceases to meet the requirements of Code section 1361(b)(3)(B), it will be treated as a new corporation acquiring all of its assets (and assuming all of its liabilities) immediately before such cessation from the S corporation in exchange for its stock. According to Code section 1361(b)(3)(D), if a corporation's status as a QSub terminates, such corporation (and any successor) shall not be eligible to make a QSub election, or an election under Code section 1362(a) to be treated as an S corporation, before its fifth tax year which begins after the first tax year for which such termination was effective, unless the IRS consents to such an election. The tax treatment of such a transaction will be determined under the Code and general principles of tax law, including the "step transaction doctrine".[29]

Employment and Excise Tax Reporting of QSubs

As a general rule, a QSub is a disregarded entity and will use the parent S corporation's employer identification number (EIN) for federal tax purposes. After the QSub election terminates, the former QSub must use the EIN it had before the election was made (or, if it had none, obtain one).[30]

However, for employment tax and certain excise taxes, this disregarded entity status is ignored and QSubs are treated as separate entities.[31] Here, the QSub itself (and not the parent S corporation) is the "employer" for purposes of withholding, reporting, and paying employment taxes.[32] In these circumstances, a QSub must have and use its own EIN.[33]

SALE OF S CORPORATION STOCK AND CODE SECTION 336(e) AND 338(h)(10) ELECTIONS

When stockholders of an S corporation sell their stock, the stockholders ordinarily are subject to federal income tax on any gain from the sale. The gain is equal to the difference between the sale proceeds received by the stockholders and the adjusted tax basis of their S corporation stock.

However, if a Code section 336(e) or 338(h)(10) election is made, the sale of the S corporation stock is ignored for federal income tax purposes. As a result of a Code section 336(e) or 338(h)(10) election, the S corporation is deemed to have sold all of its assets and distributed the sales proceeds to its stockholders in a liquidation transaction.[34]

As a prerequisite, both 336(e) and 338(h)(10) elections are only available if the stock of an S corporation is acquired in a "qualified stock purchase". Further, for a Code section 338(h)(10) election, the acquirer must be a corporation.[35] A "qualified stock purchase" is defined as the purchase during a twelve-month period of an S corporation's stock possessing at least 80 percent of the S corporation's total voting power and 80 percent of the S corporation's value.[36]

Procedurally, these elections differ. The election under Code section 338(h)(10) is made jointly by the S corporation shareholders and the purchaser.[37] Both the acquirer and the shareholders of the selling corporation must agree to make an election under Code section 338(h)(10). The election must be filed with the IRS no later than the fifteenth day of the ninth month beginning after the month in which the acquisition occurs.[38] Alternatively, a Code section 336(e) election may be made alone by the shareholders of a selling corporation, but the decision must be unanimous.[39] Here, the selling shareholders and the to-be-acquired company enter into a binding agreement, where the 336(e) election will be filed with the corporation's next timely filed tax return.[40]

As a result of a Code section 336(e) or 338(h)(10) election, the target S corporation is treated as having sold all of its assets at the close of the acquisition date in a single transaction.[41] The S corporation realizes the gain from the deemed asset sale before the close of its business activities on the acquisition date.[42] Thus, the S corporation will file a final return reporting both its operating results through the acquisition date and the gain recognized from the deemed asset sale.

An S corporation's taxable gain realized on a deemed asset sale begins with a determination of the "aggregate deemed sale price" (ADSP) for the target company's assets.[43] The ADSP is equal to the grossed-up amount realized on the sale to the purchasing corporation of the purchasing corporation's recently purchased target stock plus the liabilities of the S corporation as of the beginning of the day after the acquisition date.[44] A liability must be properly taken into account in the amount realized under general principles of tax law.[45] Liabilities may include liabilities for the tax consequences resulting from the deemed sale.[46] After determining the ADSP, it is necessary to compute the amount of the S corporation's gain from the deemed sale of assets, which is equal to the difference between the ADSP and the tax basis of the S corporation in its assets at the end of the acquisition date.[47] Here, the ADSP is allocated to assets according to the residual method in Reg. § 1.338-6. Then, the gain or loss realized on the deemed sale of assets is calculated on an asset-by-asset basis.[48]

A sale transaction where the seller receives part or all of the purchase price in notes or other deferred payment obligations may be taxed under the installment method of accounting.[49] An installment sale is defined as a disposition of property where at least one payment is to be received after the close of the taxable year in which the disposition occurs.[50]

As a result of making a Code section 336(e) or 338(h)(10) election, a company is deemed to have sold its assets for an amount that includes all consideration paid to the shareholders for their shares. If part of this consideration is payable after the close of the tax year in which the sale occurred, the transaction will meet the definition of an "installment sale", and the S corporation generally may compute its gain from the deemed asset sale under the installment sale method.[51]

The S corporation will report gain from the deemed asset sale on its final S corporation return only to the extent required under the installment sale method of accounting. Under the installment method, a seller reports gain in each year based on the installment payments received. The amount of gain to be reported each year is an amount equal to the "gross profit percentage" multiplied by the total payments received.[52] Thus, in order to compute a company's installment gain to be reported on its final S corporation return, it is necessary for the company to determine (1) the "gross profit percentage" from the sale, and (2) the amount of payments deemed to be received by the company during the tax year.

As an additional consequence of a Code section 336(e) or 338(h)(10) election, the S corporation is deemed to have liquidated immediately after the "deemed sale" of its assets.[53] The company is treated as distributing to the shareholders (pursuant to the "deemed liquidation" of the company) installment obligations (on exactly the same terms as the installment obligations received by each stockholder in the "actual" sale) and cash in an amount equal to the fair market value of all other consideration received by the stockholders in the "deemed sale".[54]

Ordinarily, a corporation's transfer or distribution of an installment obligation to its shareholders causes the corporation to recognize any gain deferred under the installment sale rules.[55] However, an S corporation does not recognize gain on the distribution of an installment obligation received as part of a liquidating sale of the corporation's assets.[56] This nonrecognition exception under Code section 453B(h) applies to a deemed liquidation of an S corporation pursuant to Code section 336(e) and 338(h)(10).[57] Accordingly, the S corporation should not recognize any gain on the deemed distribution of installment obligations to the shareholders.

For shareholders, the Code section 336(e) and 338(h)(10) elections cause the sale of stock to be ignored for federal income tax purposes. Instead, the shareholders report and pay tax on their allocable share of the S corporation's deemed gain from the deemed asset sale, which is reported on the final S corporation return. In addition, the shareholders report gain or loss (if any) on the deemed liquidation of the company.

All of the income, deductions, and items of gain or loss of the S corporation "pass through" to and are reported on the shareholders' individual returns. The gain recognized on the "deemed sale" of the assets will be reported on the final S corporation tax return for the short tax year ending on the acquisition date. The company will first compute its gain on the "deemed sale" (after application of the installment sale rules described above), and then separate the gain into components: long-term capital gain, short-term capital gain, and ordinary income.[58] Each shareholder will then include her or his pro rata share of each separate item of income or gain on the stockholder's individual income tax return.[59] The shareholders will also report on their individual returns their pro rata taxable income or loss from operations through the acquisition date.

The Code section 336(e) and 338(h)(10) elections also cause shareholders to report gain or loss on the deemed liquidation of the S corporation. This gain or loss will be equal to the amounts deemed received by each shareholder on liquidation of the corporation *less* the tax basis of the shareholder in his or her shares.[60]

As will be discussed more fully in Chapter 14, relating to installment sales by an S corporation followed by a liquidation, a liquidating distribution of substantial cash together with installment sale obligations can trigger an acceleration of gain recognition. See Chapter 14.

CHAPTER ENDNOTES

1. IRC Sec. 338(h)(10).
2. IRC Sec. 336(e); Reg. § 1.336-2(c).
3. See IRC Secs. 453(h) and 453B(h).
4. See IRC Sec. 1366.
5. IRC Sec. 1366.
6. IRC Secs. 331 and 1001.
7. IRC Secs. 331 and 1001.
8. IRC Secs. 331 and 1001.
9. IRC Secs. 331 and 1001.
10. IRC Sec. 1212(b).
11. IRC Sec. 1211(b)(1).
12. IRC Sec. 1212(b).
13. Rev. Rul. 74-175.
14. IRC Sec. 11(b).
15. IRC Sec. 1374(d)(1).
16. See IRC Sec. 1374(d)(4).

17. IRC Sec. 1374(b)(2).
18. IRC Sec. 1374(b)(3)(B).
19. IRC Sec. 1374(d)(2)(B).
20. P.L. 100-647.
21. Reg. § 1.1374-4(h)(1).
22. See IRC Sec. 1374(d)(2)(A).
23. See IRC Sec. 1374(d)(2)(B).
24. See IRC Sec. 1362(d)(3).
25. Reg. § 1.1362-2(c)(5)(ii)(B)(2).
26. IRS Letter Ruling 8916057 (January 15, 1989).
27. Reg. § 1.1361-4.
28. Reg. § 1.1361-4(d) example (5).
29. Reg. § 1.1361-3(a)(4).
30. Reg. § 1.1361-5(b)(1).
31. Reg. § 301.6109-1(i).
32. See T.D. 9356, 2007-39 I.R.B. 675
33. Rev. Rul. 2008-18, 2008-1 C.B. 674; See also General Instructions for Forms W-2 and W-3.
34. IRC Sec. 338(h)(10).
35. IRC Sec. 338(d)(3).
36. Id.
37. Reg. § 1.338(h)(10)-1(c)(3).
38. IRC Sec. 338(g).
39. Reg. § 1.336-2(h).
40. Id.
41. IRC Sec. 338(a)(1); Reg. 1.338(h)(10)-1(d)(3). When a IRC Sec. 338(h)(10) election is made, there is no actual transfer of assets. Rather, an IRC Sec. 338(h)(10) election creates a "deemed" asset sale from the existing corporation to a hypothetical "new" corporation, which obtains a tax basis in the S corporation's assets equal to the deemed purchase price. IRC Sec. 338(a)(2).
42. Reg. § 1.338(h)(10)-1(d)(3)(i).
43. Reg. § 1.338-4.
44. Reg. § 1.338-4(b). The liabilities generally are measured as of the beginning of the day after the acquisition date. Reg. §§ 1.338-4(d) and 1.338-1(a).
45. Reg. § 1.338-4(d)(1).
46. Reg. § 1.338-4(d)(1).
47. IRC Sec. 338(a)(1).
48. Reg. § 1.338-4(a).
49. IRC Sec. 453(a).
50. IRC Sec. 453(b)(1). A taxpayer can elect to *not* have the installment sale rules apply. IRC Sec. 453(d).
51. See Reg. § 1.338(h)(10)-(1)(d)(8) and Reg. § 1.336-1(a)
52. IRC Sec. 453(c).
53. Reg. § 1.338(h)(10)-1(d)(4).
54. Reg. § 1.338(h)(10)-1(d)(8)(ii).
55. IRC Sec. 453B(a).
56. IRC Sec. 453B(h).
57. See Reg. § 1.338(h)(10)-1(d)(8)(ii), (e), Example 10(iv).
58. IRC Sec. 1366(a)(1).
59. IRC Sec. 1366(a)(1). For this purpose, each stockholder's "pro rata share" will be equal to the stockholder's percentage ownership of the company's stock. IRC Sec. 1377(a)(1).
60. Reg. § 1.338(h)(10)-1(d)(5).

TAX ASPECTS OF BUYING AND SELLING A PARTNERSHIP BUSINESS

CHAPTER 9

OVERVIEW

Partnership income taxation, governed by subchapter K of chapter 1 of the Code, is arguably the most sophisticated and technically complex area of federal income tax practice. However, with the complexity comes opportunity, because the Code provisions governing partnership taxation are generally much more flexible, and allow much greater creativity, than the corresponding Code provisions governing corporate taxation.

Partnership taxation is simultaneously flexible and complicated because it attempts to combine two very different theories of taxation—often somewhat uncomfortably—into a single tax philosophy. Subchapter K sometimes treats a partnership as a group of individuals (called "aggregate theory") and sometimes treats a partnership as a single business entity (called "entity theory"). Aggregate theory is most pronounced in the provisions of subchapter K where the income of the partnership is taxed not to the partnership but to its partners.[1] In most other respects, a partnership is treated as a separate entity. For example, the assets of a partnership are treated as owned by the partnership rather than by the partners[2] and a partnership interest is treated as an asset directly owned by the partner.[3]

A partnership does not pay federal income taxes.[4] Instead, items of partnership income, gain, loss, deduction and credit pass through to the partners and are reported on the partners' individual tax returns in accordance with the sharing of such items as determined by the partnership agreement, subject to the rules and regulations of the Internal Revenue Code, particularly the regulations under Code section 704. Each partner is then personally liable for any income tax imposed as a result of such partner's allocable share of partnership income.

A partnership can be subject to certain federal taxes, including FICA,[5] FUTA and certain excise taxes, and can be subject to state income taxation in some state jurisdictions as well. In addition, a partnership must file a federal information return, Form 1065, reporting tax items even though it is not taxed on the reported income.

OVERVIEW OF SELLING A PARTNERSHIP BUSINESS

As discussed extensively in Chapters 4, 5, and 6, when the Target is operated as a corporation, there are two basic ways to structure a business acquisition: (1) as a sale of assets or (2) as a sale of stock. However, when the Target is operated as a partnership, one can easily add a third alternative transaction structure, which is a liquidation of the partnership followed by a sale of its assets.[6] The reason this third transaction path is more readily available to a partnership than a corporation has to do with the tax treatment of asset distributions. For a corporation, a distribution of appreciated corporate assets is treated as a taxable sale or exchange, whether the distribution is a liquidating distribution[7] or simply a distribution of appreciated assets.[8] By contrast, the distribution rules that apply to a partnership, under Code section 731, are what amounts to tax-free liquidation of the entity by causing gain to be recognized only by the partner[9] and only to the extent that the amount of money distributed exceeds the adjusted basis of such partner's interest in the partnership immediately before the distribution.[10] Thus, so long as the cash distributions do not exceed outside tax basis in the partnership interest, no gain will be recognized. Moreover, in the case of a liquidating distribution, the tax basis of a partner in the distributed assets will be the adjusted basis of such partner's interest in the partnership reduced by any money distributed in the same transaction.[11]

Although partnership acquisitions offer three distinctive structuring alternatives rather than two, the irony is that whereas the two alternative structures for a corporate acquisition produce markedly different tax results to both the Buyer and Seller,[12] a partnership acquisition will generally produce tax results that are usually, in the end, quite similar if not identical, regardless of which path is chosen. However, the mechanics of computing the tax consequences of the three partnership transaction paths are each quite distinctive, even if the paths, in the end, largely or entirely converge. Although these tax consequences will be explored in greater detail below, a brief overview is appropriate at this point:

- *Transaction Path 1*: A sale of assets by a partnership Seller directly to the Buyer produces initial tax results identical to the sale of assets by a sole proprietorship, i.e., purchase price is allocated to each asset pursuant to Code section 1060, and gain or loss (and the character of each tax even, e.g., long-term capital gain or loss, short-term gain or loss, or ordinary gain or loss will be determined on an asset-by-asset basis). Once computed, these tax items will then be distributed to and among the partners as provided in Code sections 702-704. A subsequent liquidating distribution of partnership assets after the sale will have the tax consequences specified in Code section 732(b). The Buyer, meanwhile, gets the conventional stepped up basis that occurs in any asset acquisition.

- *Transaction Path 2:* A sale of the partnership interests by the partners to the Buyer is taxed nominally as a sale of a capital asset under Code section 741, and initially appears to mimic a stock sale. However, Code section 751, the "hot asset" provision, basically produces the equivalent of a "look through" on the sale of the partnership interest and causes the partner to recognize ordinary income in the amount that would be realized if the assets were sold directly. This provision largely eliminates any tax differences between an asset sale and a partnership interest sale. The Buyer, meanwhile, assuming it acquires all interests in the partnership, will have an automatic liquidation of the partnership and will have the purchase price allocated to the partnership assets pursuant to Code section 732(b).

- *Transaction Path 3:* A liquidation of the partnership followed by a sale of its assets by the partners will, in form and content, again trigger the same tax consequences as a sale of assets by a sole proprietorship (i.e., allocation of purchase price among the assets under Code section 1060, with resulting tax consequences). The only variation between Path 1 and Path 3 will be if there is a difference between inside and outside tax basis that, as a result of the basis-adjustment rules under Code section 732, can benefit the selling partners in a material way. Note that the Buyer will experience no tax difference whatsoever between Path 1 and Path 3. Meanwhile, the Buyer always has the same tax consequences under Code section 1060 regardless of whether the Seller is a corporation, a partnership, or one or more individuals; for the Buyer, an asset acquisition is an asset acquisition.

An often valuable attribute of partnership taxation is that partnership assets can be divided and reorganized in a flexible manner so that some, but not all, of the business assets can be sold to an acquirer. This is in marked contrast to corporations, which often are subjected to undesirable tax costs if a Buyer wants to buy some, but not all, of the lines of business of a Target company.[13] Basically, Code section 355(e) makes it difficult to sell part, but not all, of an existing corporate entity, and much time, effort, and ultimately angst goes into structuring a partial sale of a corporate business. By way of comparison, if the same business is instead operated through a partnership, it is extremely easy to sell off certain assets and to retain or "spin off" other assets into a separate partnership or limited liability company, and thus to accomplish the desired business division easily and seamlessly.

How Contributions to a Partnership are Taxed. When a partner contributes money or other property to a partnership in exchange for an interest in the partnership, there is generally no gain or loss recognized at that time.[14] A relatively narrow exception to this nonrecognition rule arises when property is transferred to a partnership that would be treated as an "investment company" (as defined in Code section 351(e)) if the partnership were a corporation.[15] Also, a contribution of property subject to liabilities in excess of the contributor's tax basis in such property can trigger income or gain in some circumstances, as discussed

There is also an exception to nonrecognition for services contributed for certain types of partnership interests, as discussed in below.

The partnership nonrecognition provisions under Code section 721(a) are much broader than the corresponding provisions that apply to a corporation under Code section 351. These favorable partnership tax rules make it possible for one or more persons to contribute assets tax-free to a partnership in situations that would be taxable if the business entity were a corporation. A tax-free incorporation transaction requires that, among other things, (a) the property be transferred to a corporation solely in exchange for stock in the corporation, and (b) immediately after the exchange, those persons receiving such stock must be in "control" of the corporation.[16]

Example 1: An individual, Alan Phillips, owns 100 percent of an S corporation, Phillips Accounting, Inc., which is engaged in the accounting business. Bob Riley, also an individual, operates a sole proprietorship engaged in the accounting business. Alan and Bob value each of their businesses at $1 million, based on annual revenues, although each business has relatively little in the way of tangible assets (or tax basis in those assets).

If Bob were to contribute his operating assets to Phillips Accounting, Inc. in exchange for a 50 percent interest in the corporation, Bob would be taxed on the transfer because he would not satisfy the 80 percent "control" test under Code section 351 immediately after the contribution.

Example 2: Assume the same facts as in Example 1, except that Phillips Accounting is a single-member LLC rather than a corporation. Upon the contribution of assets by Bob, both Alan and Bob would be treated as if they were jointly contributing their respective business assets to a new partnership in exchange for 50-percent interests.[17] Under Code section 721(a), no gain or loss is recognized by Alan or Bob on the deemed contribution to a partnership. Under Code section 722, their tax basis in their respective partnership interests is equal to their tax basis in their respective assets treated as contributing to the newly-created partnership.

Under Code section 723, the basis of the contributed property in the hands of the partnership is the adjusted basis of that property in the hands of the contributing partner, i.e., in the hands of Alan or Bob immediately before the transaction. Under Code section 1223(1), the holding period for the partnership interests received by Alan and Bob includes their holding period in the capital and Section 1231 assets deemed contributed when the disregarded entity converted to a partnership. Under Code section 1223(2), the partnership's holding period for the capital and Section 1231 assets transferred to it includes the holding period in the hands of Alan and Bob. There is no tacking of the holding period (either at the partner level under Code section 1223(1) or at the partnership level under Code section 1223(2)) for any ordinary assets contributed to the LLC by either Alan or Bob.

Example 3: Assume the same facts as in Example 1, except that Alan and Bob decide to form a new LLC taxable as a partnership, called AlanBob Accounting, LLC, and Alan will cause Philips Accounting, Inc. to contribute its assets to the LLC, while Bob will contribute his assets to the LLC. (This structure may be viable as an alternative because Alan's S corporation can be used as a conduit to pass-through both income and cash distributions without triggering any S corporation-level income tax.) The S corporation and Bob should each be able to contribute to the LLC (taxable as a partnership) without recognition of gain under Code section 721, and with the corresponding tax basis and holding-period consequences. Note that while Alan's S corporation is now a vestigial entity, Alan will not want to liquidate it, since this would be a fully taxable transaction to the S corporation (under Code section 336(a)) and to Alan (under Code section 331, although the basis adjustment rules under Code section 1367 should limit Alan's total tax exposure to the equivalent of a "single" level of tax.

Comment: It is both possible and relatively common for the existing shareholders of a small, closely held corporation to "help" a person meet the 80 percent control test by also contributing property to the corporation. A person is treated as a property transferor for purposes of the 80 percent control calculation if such person receives stock having more than a "relatively small value" in comparison to the value of the stock already owned by such transferor.[18] Under Rev. Proc. 77-37,[19] ruling standards, if Alan were to contribute property at the same time as Bob worth 10 percent or more of the fair market value of the Phillips Accounting, Inc. stock owned by Alan immediately before such contribution, this would be treated by the IRS as having more than a "relatively small value." However, while such a transaction is feasible in a small, closely held corporation, it is usually not practical for larger businesses.

Contribution of Services. One of the many attractive aspects of partnership taxation is that equity in a partnership, under appropriate circumstances, can be issued to a partner for present and/or future services without triggering any immediate taxable event. In particular, although a partnership interest has demonstrable value at the time it is transferred to a service provider, case law and IRS pronouncements make it clear that a service partner who receives only a "profits interest" in a partnership (but no capital interest at the time the partnership interest is transferred) will not have to recognize any income or gain on receipt of that interest, unless the interest can be accurately valued.[20] By contrast, in an equivalent transaction with a corporation, it is clear under Code section 351(d)(1) that a contribution of "services" does not constitute "property" and thus does not qualify for non-recognition status.[21] Therefore, a shareholder cannot contribute services to a corporation and receive stock in a nonrecognition transaction.

Although receipt of property in exchange for services is a taxable event under Code section 83, there was always a conceptual uncertainty (rooted, at core, in the tensions between aggregate theory and entity theory in partnership taxation) about whether this rule should apply to a partnership interest in exchange for services. The IRS took the pro-tax position (big surprise) but in two famous cases, *S. Diamond*[22] and *W.G. Campbell*,[23] the courts held that receipt of a future profits interest was not currently taxable. In Rev. Proc. 93-27, the IRS announced that it would not try to tax transfers of "profits interests" in exchange for services, with a limited number of exceptions. Rev. Proc. 93-27 defines a "profits interest" being a partnership interest that would not give the holder a share of the proceeds if the partnership's assets were sold at fair market value and then the proceeds were distributed in a complete liquidation of the partnership. This determination is made at the time of receipt of the partnership interest. Rev. Proc. 93-27 contains three exceptions and does not apply:

(1) If the profits interest relates to a substantially certain and predictable stream of income from partnership assets, such as income from high-quality debt securities or a high-quality net lease;

(2) If within two years of receipt, the partner disposes of the profits interest; or

(3) If the profits interest is a limited partnership interest in a "publicly traded partnership" within the meaning of section 7704(b) of the Internal Revenue Code.

When services are contributed to a partnership in exchange for an interest, the taxability (or nontaxability) of that transaction depends entirely on the nature and form of the partnership interest received. If the service provider receives a capital interest (i.e., an immediately vested right to receive on liquidation a portion of the partnership capital) the transaction generates taxable income in the nature of a Code section 707(c) "guaranteed" payment.[24] On the other hand, if the service provider receives only a profits interest (i.e., a right to share in future partnership profits), the receipt of such interest is in most cases not taxable; and instead the service provider will recognize income as it is allocated to such interest in the future.[25] (Tax-free receipt of a future profits interest in exchange for services is a major factor in tax planning for many technology-oriented startup LLCs, and can become a major issue when and if such LLCs are "sold" shortly after startup, i.e. before expiration of the two-year holding period required as a condition to the application of the Rev. Proc. 93-27 safe harbor.

Note: On May 20, 2005, the IRS issued proposed regulations[26] that generally backtrack substantially from the broad safe harbor contained in Rev. Proc. 93-27. Instead, these proposed regulations take the general position that receipt of a partnership interest for services can and should be a taxable event, but then provide a "safe harbor" election that can be made by the partnership and all its partners to treat the fair market value of the transferred interest as being equal to the liquidation value of that interest (i.e., generally zero for a "true" profits interest). In addition, the regulations indicate that profits interests received subject to a vesting schedule (a common scheme) require the filing of a Section 83(b) election to avoid being taxed at the time the interest vests. As a practical matter, it is not clear that the proposed regulations, when and if issued (as of early 2017, the proposed regulations have not been finalized), would dramatically alter the tax treatment of most partnership profits interests, but they would require many more partnerships and partners to make timely elections—a situation that is all-but-certain to lead to errors, oversights, and mistakes on the part of taxpayers and their advisors. In short, the proposed regulations would make this area substantially more administration intensive, and would lead, inevitably, to a corresponding increase in administrative mistakes.

CONTRIBUTING PARTNER'S BASIS AND HOLDING PERIOD IN A PARTNERSHIP INTEREST

When property is contributed to a partnership, it results both in "outside" basis (the tax basis the partner has in the partnership interest) and "inside" basis (the basis that the partnership has in the contributed property). In addition, there are rules that govern the "holding period" of both the partnership interest and the property held by the partnership that are very important for purposes of the provisions of the Code that distinguish between short-term and long-term capital gain.

Under Code section 722, the "outside" tax basis of a partner in a partnership interest acquired upon a contribution of property, including money, is equal to the amount of such money and the adjusted basis of such property in the hands of the contributing partner at the time of the contribution, increased by the amount (if any) of gain recognized under Code section 721(b) to the contributing partner at such time.

Treatment of Liabilities—Code section 752. Any increase in a partner's share of the liabilities of a partnership, or any increase in a partner's individual liabilities by reason of the assumption by such partner of partnership liabilities, is treated as a contribution of money by such partner to the partnership.[27] Any decrease in a partner's share of the liabilities of a partnership, or any decrease in a partner's individual liabilities by reason of the assumption by the partnership of such individual liabilities, shall be considered as a distribution of money to the partner by the partnership.[28] For purposes of these rules, a liability to which property is subject, to the extent of the fair market value of such property, is considered a liability of the owner of the property.[29] These Code section 752 rules affect the computation of a partner's outside basis, both at the time when the partner receives his partnership interest and any time afterwards when the liability structure of the partnership is altered. Regulations under Code section 752 determine how recourse and nonrecourse liabilities of a partnership are shared by and among the partners.[30] These regulations are integrated with the regulations under Code section 704(b) to provide a comprehensive scheme governing partnership allocations and distributions.

Basis of Partnership Interests Acquired Other than by Contribution. The basis of a partnership interest acquired other than by contribution is determined under the rules set forth in part II of subchapter O of the Code (Code section 1011 *et seq.*).[31] Generally, the basis in an interest purchased for another person is equal to the purchase price.[32] The basis of an interest transferred by gift is the lesser of the donor's basis or the fair market value of the interest at the time of the gift.[33]

Basis Adjustments. After the partner's original outside basis in the partnership interest is determined under Code section 722 (relating to contributions to the partnership) or Code section 742 (relating to transfers of partnership interests), the outside basis is adjusted, pursuant to Code section 705(a), as follows:

1. It is increased by the sum of the partner's distributive share for the tax year and prior tax years of—

   a. Taxable income of the partnership (as determined under Code section 703).

   b. Income of the partnership exempt from tax under the Code.

   c. The excess of the deductions for depletion over the basis of the property subject to depletion.

2. It is decreased (but not below zero) by distributions by the partnership as provided in Code section 733 and by the sum of the partner's distributive share for the tax year and prior tax years of—

   a. Losses of the partnership.

   b. Expenditures of the partnership not deductible in computing its taxable income and not properly chargeable to capital account.

3. It is decreased (but not below zero) by the amount of the partner's deduction of depletion for any partnership oil and gas property to the extent such deduction does not exceed the proportionate share of the adjusted basis of such property allocated to such partner under Code section 613A(c)(7)(D).

Holding Period for a Partnership Interest. If a partnership interest is acquired in exchange for a contribution of property that is a capital asset or property described in Code section 1231, Code section 1223(1) provides that the holding period for the partnership interest includes the contributor's holding period for the contributed property. If the contributing partner contributes cash or any other type of asset in exchange for the partnership interest (notably a contribution of inventory assets), the holding period of the interest begins on the date the interest in acquired.

PARTNERSHIP'S "INSIDE" BASIS AND HOLDING PERIOD IN CONTRIBUTED PROPERTY

This section discusses a partnership's "inside" basis in partnership assets and its holding period in contributed property.

Basis. The partnership's basis in property contributed to the partnership by a partner is the adjusted basis of such property at the time contributed, increased by the amount (if any) of gain recognized by the contributing partner under Code section 721(b) at the time of contribution.[34]

Holding Period. A partnership's holding period for a contributed asset includes, if the asset is a capital asset or property described in Code section 1231, the holding period of the asset in the hands of the contributing partner.[35] There is no "tacking" of the holding period under Code section 1223(2) for ordinary assets.

Partnership Liabilities and Contributions of Property Subject to Liability. The "inside" basis rules become much more complicated when liabilities are involved. Code section 752, and the accompanying regulations, define a complicated interaction between the allocation rules under Code section 704, the basis rules under Code section 705 and the distribution rules under Code section 731. Code section 752 provides that an increase in a partner's share of the partnership's liabilities is treated as a contribution of money to the partnership, and a decrease in a partner's share of partnership liabilities or a decrease in a partner's individual liabilities by reason of the partnership's assumption of such liabilities is treated as a distribution of money to the partner.

The contribution of property to a partnership subject to a liability is treated as if the partnership has assumed the liability to the extent that the amount of liabilities do not exceed the fair market value of the property at the time of the contribution. A contribution of property subject to a liability or the assumption of a liability by a partnership can often result in a partner incurring both an increase and a decrease in the partner's share of partnership liabilities. The regulations state that only the net increase or decrease is taken into account.[36] This "netting" rule means that all the basis and other adjustments under Code section 752 must be taken into account simultaneously in order to determine the net effect of a transaction.

If the partnership assumes a liability of the contributor, or takes contributed property subject to a liability, the portion of the liability allocated to other partners under Code section 752 is treated as a cash distribution from the partnership to the contributing partner under Code section 752(b). This deemed distribution decreases the contributing partner's outside basis in his or her partnership interest by the amount of the deemed cash distribution, but not below zero.[37] Any deemed distributions in excess of the partner's outside basis in his or her partnership interest generate taxable capital gain under Code sections 731(a)(1) and 741. On the other hand, if a portion of the liability assumed or treated as assumed by the partnership is allocated back to the contributing partner, this can result in a deemed cash contribution to the partnership that increases the contributing partner's outside basis. These deemed decreases and increases will be netted in order to determine the tax consequence of the transaction.

Example 4: Assume that Nancy Munroe acquires a 20 percent interest in a general partnership by contributing land with the fair market value of $10,000, an adjusted basis to Nancy of $4,000, and subject to a mortgage of $2,000, which mortgage is assumed by the partnership. Assuming the partnership has no other liabilities, the basis of Nancy's interest in the partnership is $2,400, computed as follows:

Adjusted basis to Nancy of property contributed	$4,000
Relief of mortgage liability	($2,000)
Portion of mortgage allocable to Nancy following contribution (20% of $2,000)	$400
Nancy's basis in partnership interest	$2,400

Example 5: Assume the same facts as in Example 4 except that the land contributed by Nancy is subject to a mortgage of $6,000 instead of $2,000, which mortgage is assumed by the partnership. Under these facts, the basis of Nancy's interest is computed as follows:

Adjusted basis to Nancy of property contributed	$4,000
Relief of mortgage liability	($6,000)
Portion of mortgage allocable to Nancy following contribution (20% of $6,000)	$1,200
Tentative basis in partnership interest	($800)

Since, under Code section 733, a partner's basis can never be less than zero, Nancy's initial basis is zero, and she recognizes $800 of capital gain.

Example 6: Assume the same facts as in Example 4 except that Nancy remains personally liable to the creditor and none of the other partners bear any of the economic risk of loss for the liability under state law or otherwise. Nancy's basis in her partnership interest is computed as follows:[38]

Adjusted basis to Nancy of property contributed	$4,000
Relief of mortgage liability	($2,000)
Portion of mortgage allocable to Nancy following contribution	$2,000
Nancy's basis in partnership interest	$4,000

TAX ALLOCATIONS IN CONNECTION WITH CONTRIBUTIONS OF PROPERTY—CODE SECTION 704(C)

Code section 704(c) requires that, pursuant to regulations, items of income, gain, loss, deduction, and credit with respect to property contributed to a partnership by a partner must be shared among the partners so as to take account of the variation between the basis of the property to the partnership and its fair market value at the time of contribution.[39] In addition, if any property contributed to a partnership after October 3, 1989 is subsequently distributed within seven years of the contribution date, to anyone other than the contributing partner then the contributing partner (or the partner's successor) recognizes gain or loss in an amount equal to the gain or loss that would have been allocated to such partner by reason of the variation described in the preceding sentence as if the property had been sold at its fair market value at the time of the distribution.[40] The character of such gain or loss is determined by reference to the character of the gain or loss that would have resulted if such property had been sold by the partnership to the distributee, and appropriate adjustment must be made to the adjusted basis of the contributing partner's interest in the partnership and to the adjusted basis of the property distributed to reflect any gain or loss so recognized.[41]

A basic purpose of Code section 704(c) is to keep track of, and make subsequent adjustments for, the built-in tax attributes of property that exist at the time a partner contributes such property to a partnership. The general thrust of Code section 704(c) is that the contributing partner will be allocated the tax attributes arising from a variation (at the time of contribution) between the tax basis of contributed property and the fair market value of such property. This adjustment rule is "fair" because it allows a partner to contribute appreciated (or depreciated) property to a partnership without a recognition event under Code section 721, but prevents abuse of Code section 721 by essentially prohibiting a "transfer" to other partners of the built-in tax attributes of such property.

Example 7: Joe Martinez contributes $500 of cash to a partnership and Susan Perry contributes unimproved real property with a basis of $100 and a fair market value of $500. Both Joe and Susan have contributed property of equal value (i.e., $500); however, Joe has an outside tax basis of $500, and Susan has an outside basis of $100.[42] Meanwhile, the partnership has an inside tax basis of $600—$500 of basis in the cash and $100 of basis in the real property.[43] If the partnership immediately turns around and sells the real property contributed by Susan to an unrelated party for $500, the partnership will recognize gain of $400. Absent Code section 704(c), the partners might split this gain 50-50, thus effectively "transferring" a portion of the taxable gain from Susan to Joe. However, under Code section 704(c), this gain will be allocated solely to Susan, causing her to recognize $400 of gain and resulting in a corresponding increase in Susan's outside basis from $100 to $500.[44]

Comment: This example does not address the capital accounting rules under Code section 704(b), which rules have a symbiotic relationship with the tax allocation rules under Code section 704(c). In general, Code section 704 and the regulations thereunder try to assure that the economic consequences to partners are not affected by whether the tax basis of contributed property differs from its fair market value at the time of its contribution.

PARTNERSHIP ALLOCATIONS

A partner's share of the partnership items of income, gain, loss, deduction, and credit pass through to the partner and are included in the partner's taxable income for the tax year within or with which the partnership's tax year ends.[45] The partnership's taxable income is computed in the same manner as individual taxable income except that certain items that can have an impact on an individual's tax liability (e.g., capital gains and capital losses) are required to be separately stated.

Partnership items are allocated pursuant to the partnership agreement but subject to the very complicated rules set forth in the regulations under Code section 704. These regulations require that in order to be respected for federal income tax purposes an allocation must satisfy one of three alternative tests: (a) it must have "substantial economic effect"; (b) it must be in accordance with the "partner's interest in the partnership"; or (c) it must be "deemed" to be in accordance with the partner's interest in the partnership.[46]

As a practical matter, taxpayers usually attempt to comply with the first of the three tests because this is set forth in detail in the Treasury regulations. By contrast, because the second test has never been defined or implemented by regulations, its application remains uncertain. The third test is specific to certain tax attributes that have no economic corollary and thus cannot be allocated in a manner that would have substantial economic effect.

In order to meet the "substantial economic effect" test, allocations must meet two requirements: (a) the allocation must have economic effect; and (b) the economic effect must be substantial.[47]

In order for an allocation to have "economic effect," it must satisfy three requirements: (a) the partnership agreement must require the partnership to maintain capital accounts in accordance with the Treasury regulations; (b) upon liquidation of the partnership (or any partner's interest in the partnership), liquidating distributions are required to be made to partners in accordance with their positive capital account balances; and (c) on liquidation, any partner with a negative capital account is unconditionally obligated to make a contribution to the partnership in the amount of the partner's negative capital account (this contribution obligation is called a "deficit restoration obligation").[48] As a practical matter, most partners will happily comply with the first two requirements but do not want to comply with the third requirement, a deficit restoration obligation.

Therefore, partnerships generally comply with the so-called "alternate test of economic effect" set forth in the Treasury regulations, which allows partnerships to replace the third requirement (the deficit restoration obligation) with a so-called "qualified income offset" provision.[49] The qualified income offset provision provides that when a partner unexpectedly has a negative capital account, then the partnership will be required to allocate a sufficient amount of income to bring the partner's capital account back up to at least zero as quickly as possible. Although a qualified income offset provision does not guarantee that a partner will never have a negative capital account, it realistically reduces the likelihood of such an occurrence.

Comment: Although the Treasury regulations technically require a qualified income offset provision, many partnership agreements often contain other provisions that either prohibit loss allocations that will make a capital account go "negative," or a gross income allocation provision, which is actually broader and more comprehensive in its operation than a qualified income offset provision. Interestingly, although these provisions often make the qualified income offset provision redundant, the regulations expressly require a qualified income offset provision and have not been updated to permit its replacement.

Capital accounts must be maintained according to a specific accounting mechanism defined in the regulations under Code section 704. It is important to recognize that this capital accounting system is different than both tax accounting and financial accounting methods, such as GAAP. Capital accounts are maintained according to a system that measures the fair market value of assets (and ignores tax attributes such as tax basis) but differs from GAAP accounting and similar accounting methods in that it adjusts the fair market value of assets only on certain events, referred to colloquially as "book up" or "book down" events.

A partner's capital account is determined as follows:

1. The account is increased by the following:
    a. The amount of money contributed by the partner to the partnership.
    b. The fair market value of property contributed by the partner to the partnership (net of liabilities).
    c. The partner's share of partnership's income and gain.
2. The account is decreased by the following:
    a. The amount of money distributed to the partner by the partnership.
    b. The fair market value of property distributed to the partner by the partnership (net of liabilities).
    c. The partner's share of partnership expenses, losses, and deductions.

Complex rules govern the tax consequences of partnership debt, and the allocation of losses and deductions attributable to such debt. The following is a very simple summary of a very intricate and complicated area of law. Debt is divided for tax allocation purposes into two categories:

1. Recourse debt, for which a partner bears the economic risk of loss.
2. Nonrecourse debt, for which no partner bears the economic risk of loss.

The rules for debt allocation under Code section 752 and the related impact on capital accounting and other issues under Code section 704 is beyond the scope of this book. However, as a basic observation, losses, expenses, and deductions funded from partnership capital can be allocated as the partners agree, subject to the Code section 704 rules, described briefly above. Losses, expenses, and deductions that are funded from recourse debt must be allocated to the partner who bears the economic risk of loss with respect to that debt. By contrast, losses, expenses, and deductions that are funded from nonrecourse debt cannot be so allocated because no partner bears the economic risk of loss. Therefore, such losses, expenses, and deductions can be allocated among partners in accordance with complex rules specified in the Code section 752 regulations.

PARTNERSHIP DISTRIBUTIONS

One of the great tax advantages of a partnership over a corporation is that distribution of partnership property, with a few specific exceptions, does not ordinarily trigger an income or gain recognition event to partners. As previously noted, each partner has outside basis in the partner's partnership interest, which basis is initially determined at the time property is contributed to the partnership, and thereafter is increased by the partner's share of partnership income, decreased by the partner's share of partnership loss, increased by subsequent contributions of property, and decreased by subsequent distributions of property.

When a partnership distributes property to a partner, money and marketable securities are given special treatment. The partner will not recognize gain on the receipt of such assets, except to the extent that the sum of money plus the fair market value of marketable securities exceeds the partner's adjusted basis in his or her partnership interest.[50] If a distribution of money exceeds a partner's outside basis, the excess cash distribution will generate recognition of capital gain.[51]

Example 8: Chris Wong has a partnership interest in Partnership CDE, with an adjusted basis to Chris of $10,000. Chris retires from the partnership, and receives a distribution in liquidation of his entire interest equal to $13,000 in cash. This will be treated as, first, a return of Chris's $10,000 of outside basis, and will then generate $3,000 of capital gain to the extent that the distribution causes Chris's outside basis to go below zero.

Loss is recognized to a partner only upon liquidation of the partner's entire interest in the partnership, and only if the property distributed to the partner consists solely of money, unrealized receivables (as defined in Code section 751(c)), and inventory items (as defined in Code section 751(d)(2)).

Example 9: Amanda Pratt has a partnership interest in Partnership ABC with an adjusted outside basis of $10,000. Amanda retires from the partnership and receives, as a distribution in liquidation of Amanda's entire interest, her share of partnership property. This share is $5,000 in cash plus inventory with a basis to Amanda (under Code section 732) of $3,000. Amanda realizes a capital loss of $2,000, which is recognized under Code section 731(a)(2).

Example 10: Burt Wommick has a partnership interest in Partnership BCD with an adjusted outside basis of $10,000. Burt retires from the partnership and receives, as a distribution and liquidation of Burt's entire interest, his share of partnership property. This share is $4,000 in cash, real property (used in the trade or business) with an adjusted basis to the partnership of $2,000, and unrealized receivables having a basis to him (under Code section 732) of $3,000. No loss will be recognized to Burt on the transaction because he received property other than money, unrealized receivables, and inventory items. As determined in Code section 732, Burt's tax basis in the real property received is $3,000.

Under Code section 737, if a partner contributes appreciated property to a partnership and within seven years receives a distribution of other property, the partner must recognize gain in an amount generally limited by the "net pre-contribution gain" (basically, the built-in gain) attributable to the original property contributed by such partner. There is also a rule under Code section 704(c)(1)(B) that can cause a contributing partner to be taxed on the built-in gain inherent in contributed property if that property is then distributed by the partnership other than to the contributing partner within seven years of the original contribution to the partnership.[52] These rules are generally designed to prevent partners from using the nonrecognition provisions of Code sections 721 and 731 to avoid recognition of gain on transactions that are similar to, or in substance equivalent to, a sale of the appreciated property contributed to the partnership.

A partner will generally have carryover basis from property distributed from a partnership, meaning that the partner will have the same basis that the partnership had in the property immediately before the distribution. However, if the partner's outside basis at the time of the distribution is less than the carryover basis of the distributed property, the partner will only receive the lesser amount (i.e., the outside basis).[53]

A partner's outside basis in the partnership interest is reduced by the amount of the basis the partner takes in distributed property.[54]

SALE OF ASSETS BY A PARTNERSHIP

From a federal income tax perspective, the sale of business assets by a partnership is virtually identical to a sale of assets by an individual proprietorship.[55] Gain recognized by the partnership is not subject to tax at the entity level. Instead, the partnership's income is passed through and taxed to its partners. As with a sale of assets by a sole proprietorship, a sale of partnership assets raises the usual tax issues related to the allocation of purchase price among the assets under Code section 1060, the character of the assets (capital assets, as defined in Code section 1221, generate capital gain or loss; Code section 1231 assets generate ordinary income recapture, capital gain, and ordinary loss; and "ordinary assets" (neither of the first two) generate ordinary income and loss), and the holding period.[56]

The taxable income of a partnership is computed in the same manner as for an individual except for the following specific rules and variations:

1. The various items described in Code section 702(a) are separately stated.
2. The following deductions are not allowed to a partnership:[57]
    a. Deductions for personal exemptions provided in Code section 151.
    b. Deductions for taxes provided in Code section 164(a) with respect to taxes described in Code section 901, paid or accrued to foreign countries and possessions of the United States.
    c. The deduction for charitable contributions provided in Code section 170.
    d. The net operating loss deduction provided in Code section 172.
    e. The additional itemized deductions for individuals provided in Code section 211 *et seq.*
    f. The deduction for depletion under Code section 611 with respect to oil and gas wells.

The income of a partnership is then allocated to the partners in the manner determined by the partnership agreement, unless the partnership agreement does not provide for such an allocation or the allocation provided by the agreement does not have substantial economic effect.[58] Each partner takes into account separately the partner's distributive share of the following partnership items:[59]

1. Gains and losses from sales or exchanges of capital assets held for not more than one year.
2. Gains and losses from sales or exchanges of capital assets held for more than one year.
3. Gains and losses from sales or exchanges of property described in Code section 1231.
4. Charitable contributions.
5. Dividends with respect to which Code section 1(h)(11) or part VIII of chapter B applies.
6. Taxes described in Code section 901, paid or accrued to foreign countries and to possessions of the United States.
7. Other items of income, gain, loss, deduction, or credit, to the extent provided by regulations.
8. Taxable income or loss, exclusive of items requiring separate computation under the seven categories previously described.

A sale of partnership assets would typically require an allocation by the Buyer of the purchase price among the various assets, pursuant to Code section 1060.[60] Such an asset sale may be accompanied by consulting payments, and/or noncompete payments, from the Buyer to one or more partners. In this regard, the allocation between business assets and payments to the individuals who operate the business can raise the same "reasonable compensation" issues that arise on the sale of a corporate business and related payments to individual shareholders/employees of that corporate business.[61]

A substantial portion of the purchase price would presumably be allocated either to capital assets or to Code section 1231 assets, and thus may produce, among the tax items distributed to the respective partners on a Schedule K-1, capital gain or loss and/or ordinary loss. Some portion of the purchase price may be allocated to inventory, accounts receivable, recapture under Code section 1245 or 1250, unrecaptured Section 1250 gain, and other similar items that generate ordinary income or gain, rather than capital gain.

One very important distinction between the sale of assets by an S corporation and the sale of assets by a partnership is that, to the extent the partnership retains any appreciated assets that the Buyer does not want to acquire, the partnership can liquidate and distribute these appreciated assets without triggering taxable gain. By contrast, an S corporation that retains any assets and then distributes them, will trigger a gain, either under Code section 311(b) or Code section 336(a), depending on whether it is a nonliquidating distribution or liquidating distribution. In a similar vein, a partnership that sells assets on an installment basis, including a contingent sale or earn-out transaction, can distribute the installment obligation to its partners without triggering either gain recognition or the tax basis allocation problems that plague an S corporation in this type of transaction.[62]

Another very substantial benefit of partnership taxation is that subchapter K has no analogy to the corporate level taxes that apply to any C corporation, nor any analogy to the Code section 1374 taxes that apply to an S corporation. As we examined in Chapters 4, 5, and 6, a large amount of thought and effort goes into structuring corporate transactions to avoid or minimize the double taxation of C corporations. Likewise, a significant amount of planning must accompany a sale of assets by an S corporation, including consideration of Code section 338(h)(10) elections, evaluation of sting tax exposure under Code section 1374, and other issues discussed in Chapter 8.

As discussed in Chapter 7, it is not unusual for an Acquirer to request a spin-off of assets from a Target corporation, triggering the application of Code section 355(e). An LLC/partnership, by contrast, can spin off, split off and split up assets without any tax consequences, and thus can minimize the tax costs of a divisive restructuring in anticipation of a sale.

SALE OF A PARTNERSHIP INTEREST—CONSEQUENCES TO SELLER

When a partner sells all or part of his or her interest in the partnership, it is treated as a sale of a capital asset.[63] This is true regardless of whether the sale is to an unrelated third party or to another partner. Special rules apply under Code section 742 when the partnership redeems the interest of a partner.

On the surface, Code section 741 would appear to make a sale of a partnership interest similar to a sale of corporate stock. However, this general rule of capital gains treatment is modified by Code section 751, which indicates that a sale of an interest in a partnership holding "Code section 751 assets," otherwise known as "hot assets," can trigger ordinary gain. Hot assets include the following:[64]

1. "Unrealized receivables" of the partnership.

2. Inventory items.

In effect, Code section 751 applies the equivalent of "look-through" taxation to those partnership assets that, if sold separately, would be considered ordinary assets, generating ordinary income or gain. See the discussion in Chapter 3, which notes that the sale of inventory, accounts receivable, and similar assets results in ordinary income when sold by a sole proprietorship.

For purposes of Code section 751, the term "unrealized receivables" is very broadly defined to cover virtually all assets that, if sold directly by the partnership, would generate ordinary income or gain. "Unrealized receivables" include any rights (contractual or otherwise) to payment for:[65]

1. Goods delivered, or to be delivered, to the extent that proceeds therefrom would be treated as amounts received from the sale or exchange of property other than a capital asset.

2. Services rendered, or to be rendered.

The same subsection goes on to state that items that generate ordinary income due to "recapturing," under Code sections 1245 and 1250, and certain other types of recaptured property, are considered hot assets to the extent of the recapture required by those sections.[66] The term "unrealized receivables" also includes any market discount bond,[67] or any short-term obligations[68] to the extent of the amount that would be treated as ordinary income if the market discount bond or short-term obligation had been sold by the partnership.

When a partner sells the partner's entire partnership interest, but other partners continue the partnership, the partnership tax year closes for the selling partner on the date of the sale.[69] This means that the partner is not liable for any tax liabilities or income or gain generated by the partnership after the sale date. This rule is different than the "interim" closing rule for S corporations, which imposes a default rule of "per share per day," and requires a special election to create an interim cut-off date.[70]

If all the interests in an LLC taxable as a partnership are sold to a single purchaser, the transaction is treated for tax purposes as a liquidation of the LLC, followed by a purchase of assets, and the LLC will continue as a "disregarded entity."[71]

> *Example 11:* C and D, equal partners in an LLC, sell their entire LLC interests to E, an unrelated person, for $10,000 each. The LLC is deemed to make a liquidating distribution of assets to C and D, who are deemed immediately to sell the assets to E. E's basis in the assets is $20,000 under Code section 1012, and his holding period begins the day after the date of sale. The LLC going forward will be treated as a "tax-nothing" for federal income tax purposes.[72]

The general effect of Code section 741, as modified by Code section 751, is to equal, or very closely approximate, the same tax consequences that would adhere if the partnership itself sold its assets to a purchaser.

SALE OF A PARTNERSHIP INTEREST—TAX ATTRIBUTES TO BUYER

The buyer of a partnership interest has a tax basis in such interest equal to cost.[73] At that moment, there is likely to be a disparity between the outside basis held by the (new) partner in his or her interest, and the tax basis of the partnership in the new partner's proportional share of partnership assets, on a look-through basis. However, subchapter K contains extremely taxpayer-favorable provisions that alleviate this problem by allowing a purchaser, with the consent of the partnership, to elect to "step-up" the inside basis of the partnership assets to equal the outside tax basis of the purchaser in his or her partnership interest.[74] There are specific and relatively detailed rules about how to allocate this basis adjustment.[75]

When a partnership has a Code section 754 election in effect, upon the transfer of an interest in the partnership, whether by sale or exchange or as a result of the death of a partner, Code section 743(b) provides that the following adjustments occur:

1. The partnership increases the adjusted basis of partnership property by the excess of the transferee's basis for the transferred partnership interest over the transferee's share of the adjusted basis to the partnership of the partnership's property; or
2. The partnership decreases the adjusted basis of partnership property by the excess of the transferee's share of the adjusted basis to the partnership of the partnership's property over the transferee's basis for the transferee's partnership interest.

The following examples illustrate these adjustments.

Example 12: A is a member of a partnership in which the partners have equal interests in capital and profits. The partnership has made an election under section 754, relating to the optional adjustment to the basis of partnership property. A sells its interest to T for $22,000. The balance sheet of the partnership at the date of sale shows the following:

Asset	Adjusted Basis	Fair Market Value
Cash	5,000	5,000
Accounts Receivable	10,000	10,000
Inventory	20,000	21,000
Depreciable Assets	20,000	40,000
Total	**55,000**	**76,000**
Liabilities and Capital	**Adjusted Basis**	**Fair Market Value**
Liabilities	10,000	10,000
Capital:		
A	15,000	22,000
B	15,000	22,000
C	15,000	22,000
Total	**55,000**	**76,000**

The amount of the basis adjustment under section 743(b) is the difference between the basis of T's interest in the partnership and T's share of the adjusted basis to the partnership of the partnership's property. Under section 742, the basis of T's interest is $25,333 (the cash paid for A's interest, $22,000, plus $3,333, T's share of partnership liabilities). T's interest in the partnership's previously taxed capital is $15,000 ($22,000, the amount of cash T would receive if PRS liquidated immediately after the hypothetical transaction, decreased by $7,000, the amount of tax gain allocated to T from the hypothetical transaction). T's share of the adjusted basis to the partnership of the partnership's property is $18,333 ($15,000 share of previously taxed capital, plus $3,333 share of the partnership's liabilities). The amount of the basis adjustment under section 743(b) to partnership property therefore, is $7,000, the difference between $25,333 and $18,333. This adjustment will be allocated as provided in Code section 755.

Example 13: A, B and C form partnership TRS to which A contributes land (Asset 1) with a fair market value of $1 million and an adjusted basis to A of $400,000. B and C each contribute $1 million in cash. Each partner has $1 million credited to the partner's capital account. The partners share profits equally. During the first partnership tax year, Asset 1 appreciates in value to $1.3 million. At the end of that year, A sells A's one-third interest in the partnership to T for $1.1 million, at a time when the partnership has a Section 754 election in effect. On this sale, A would be allocated $700,000 of gain, comprised of $600,000 of Code section 704(c) built-in gain, plus A's one-third share of the additional appreciation in Asset 1. T, in turn, would acquire A's partnership interest and would take A's inside basis of $400,000, increased by $700,000 pursuant to a basis adjustment of Code section 743(b), and would end up with an inside basis of $1.1 million, allocated among partnership assets as provided in Code section 755.

The subchapter K tax basis step-up provisions have no equivalent or corollary in the subchapter C corporate rules, nor in the subchapter S rules. The consequence is that there is little or no tax difference to the Buyer between purchasing the partnership interest (when followed by a Code section 743/754 election) and purchasing the partnership assets directly.

Liquidation of Partnership Interests. In general, Code section 731 governs distributions of money or other property by a partnership to a partner. The rules are relatively simple and very favorable to taxpayers. Even appreciated assets can be distributed to a partner (whether or not in liquidation of the partnership) without tax consequence, unless money is distributed to a partner in excess of the partner's outside tax basis in the partner's partnership interest. Under Code section 731(a)(2), no loss is recognized unless: (a) the distribution is in liquidation of the partner's interest in the partnership, and (b) no property other than money or Section 751 assets are distributed. For purposes of Code section 731, marketable securities are treated as "money."[76] In general, no gain or loss is recognized by the partnership on these distributions.[77] Any gain recognized by a distributee partner is treated as capital gain under Code section 741, except to the extent that the money or property distributed is in exchange for the partner's interest in Code section 751 assets.[78]

The basis of the distributee-partner in the partnership assets upon a liquidation is governed by Code section 732(b), which provides that "the basis of property (other than money) distributed by a partnership to a partner in liquidation of the partner's interest shall be an amount equal to the adjusted basis of such partner's interest in the partnership reduced by any money distributed in the same transaction." Thus, upon a liquidating distribution, the basis in the applicable assets is adjusted (upward or downward) based on the outside basis of the taxpayer in the partnership interest. Presumably, a liquidation/asset sale transaction path is likely to be followed where the outside basis in the partnership interest is greater than the partnership's basis in the assets. Note that under Code section 1223(1) there is a tacking of the holding period for all assets that could generate capital gain (either capital assets or Section 1231 assets), and so a liquidation followed by an asset sale is likely to make sense (if at all) in situations where the outside basis is in excess of the inside basis. There is no detriment to the holding period for those assets (either capital assets or Section 1231 assets) where the holding period makes a difference in the tax rate.

Redemption of Retiring or Deceased Partner's Interest. Code section 731 is subject to Code section 736, when the distribution is in liquidation of a retiring partner or deceased partner's success or in interest.[79] Code section 736 is an awkwardly worded provision that generally gets where one expects to go, but sometimes in a curious manner. Code section 736(a) states that, except as otherwise provided in Code section 736(b), distributions in liquidation of a retiring or deceased partner's interest will be treated, either as guaranteed payments or as a distributive share of partnership income. However, Code section 736(b) then states that except in relatively specific circumstances, such payments will be considered as a "distribution by the partnership and not as a distributive share or guaranteed payment." In effect, the rule is the exception, and the exception is the rule.

Under Code section 736(b)(1), a payment for a retiring or deceased partner's interest in partnership property is treated as a distribution under the general rules of Code section 731. As noted above, these rules are very favorable to a taxpayer. However, under Code section 736(b)(2) and (3), for a general partner of a partnership in which capital is not a material income-producing factor, payments that are in exchange for the partner's interest in a Code section 751 "hot asset," or for the goodwill of the partnership, are treated as distributions under Code section 736(a). In other words, such distributions are treated as ordinary income, except to the extent that the partnership agreement provides for payments for a partner's interest in goodwill. This somewhat awkward statutory structure allows a service partnership to decide whether the purchase of goodwill from a retiring/deceased partner should be ordinary income to the recipient (and effectively deductible by the partnership) or capital gain to the recipient and nondeductible (but capitalizable) to the partnership.

The rules are as follows:

1. Liquidating payments to a limited partner, or to a general partner in a partnership where capital is a material income-producing factor (generally everything except for a service business). All liquidating distributions are taxed under Code section 731, except to the extent that the amount of the distribution is not for the distributee partner's interest in partnership property.

2. Liquidating payments to a general partner in a service partnership are taxed under Code section 736(b)(2) and (3). Payments in exchange for "hot assets" or goodwill are treated as ordinary income, except to the extent that the partnership agreement provides for payments for goodwill, in which case they can be treated as Code section 731 distributions.

Example 14: Assume that Partnership XYZ, a service partnership, has decided to buy out retiring general partner X for a lump-sum cash payment of $100,000. Assume that X's outside basis in X's partnership interest is $30,000. The partnership agreement provides for payments with respect to goodwill. There are $10,000 of unrealized receivables allocable to X's interest, and $40,000 of goodwill. Since there is a cash distribution in excess of the partner's tax basis in this interest, there will be a gain in this transaction of $70,000, which will be capital gain, except that the $10,000 allocable to unrealized receivables will be ordinary income to the recipient.[80]

Example 15: Assume the same facts as Example 12, but the partnership agreement does not provide for payments with respect to goodwill. The principal impact would be to convert the capital gain otherwise allowed by Code section 731(a) into ordinary income under Code section 736(a) to the extent of the amounts received by the partner for goodwill ($40,000) and unrealized receivables ($10,000).

No gain or loss is recognized by the partnership in any redemption transaction with the partner.[81]

In the case of an ongoing partnership, the liquidating redemption transaction does not affect the basis of the partnership property, despite the fact that the partnership has purchased the withdrawing partner's proportionate share of the assets.[82] However, in such a case, the partnership may elect to adjust the basis of the partnership property to reflect its payment.[83] If an election is made, or is in existence, the basis of the partnership assets would be increased (or decreased) by the amount of gain or loss recognized by the distributee.[84]

PURCHASE PRICE ALLOCATION ISSUES

Because a Code section 743/754 election creates very little difference between a sale of a partnership interest and the sale of underlying assets to either the Buyer or Seller, there are generally few allocation issues driven by the form of the partnership sale transactions. Instead, the central allocation issues are likely to turn on how to allocate purchase price among the assets of the partnership.

The most significant allocation issue is between hot assets, taxable as ordinary income under Code section 751, and the other partnership assets that will generally be taxed at capital gain tax rates. An individual partner would naturally like to reduce the amount allocated to Section 751 assets (thereby moving money from the ordinary income category to the capital gains category), while a buyer may (depending upon a variety of factors) generally prefer allocating the purchase price to hot assets.

Although an election to adjust the inside tax basis of the partnership assets, based on the purchase price paid by the Buyer of a partnership interest, is for the benefit of the Buyer, the election is actually made by the partnership. The election, when and if it is made, thereafter continues and applies to all subsequent transfers of interest.[85] A Section 754 election can be revoked only with the approval of the IRS.[86] Obviously a Section 754 election is greatly advantageous to a Buyer if and to the extent that the purchased partnership interest has a greater value than the inside tax basis (i.e., the business is generally successful!). However, a Section 754 election will have adverse effect if the inside tax basis is in excess of the amount paid by the Buyer to acquire the partnership interest. Code section 743 now requires a basis adjustment automatically if a partnership interest is transferred and the partnership has a substantial built-in loss (basis exceeds fair market value of partnership property by over $250,000).

Tax Termination of Partnership. A partnership is legally terminated for *tax purposes only* if, within a twelve-month period, 50 percent or more of the total interest in the partnership capital and profits is sold or exchanged.[87] Such a transfer of 50 percent or more of capital and profits interests is treated as a deemed liquidation of the partnership and a recontribution of the assets to a new partnership.

RECEIPT OF A PARTNERSHIP INTEREST IN EXCHANGE FOR SERVICES

Code section 721(a) by its terms applies to contributions of property to a partnership. It does not explicitly cover contributions of services to a partnership in exchange for a partnership interest.

However, Reg. § 1.721-1(b) does address contributions of "services" to some extent by indicating that, to the extent that partners transfer a capital interest in a partnership to another partner in exchange for services, the value of the capital interest so transferred is income to the recipient under Code section 61. The amount of such income is the fair market value of the capital interest so transferred, either at the time the transfer is made (in the case of past services) or at the time the services are completed (if the transfer is conditioned on the performance of future services).[88] The time when the income is realized depends on the facts and circumstances, including whether there are any substantial restrictions or conditions on the compensated partner's right to withdraw or otherwise dispose of such interest.[89]

Neither Code section 721 nor the regulations thereunder clearly addresses the tax consequences that should occur when services are contributed to a partnership in exchange for a profits interest. This lack of guidance has generated substantial uncertainty and significant litigation over the years, culminating in a decision by the U.S. Court of Appeals for the Eighth Circuit in *W.G. Campbell*.[90] Unfortunately, the *Campbell* case does not provide a clear and definitive answer to the question of whether a profits interest is or is not taxable. Instead, the Court found on the specific facts in *Campbell* that the partnership profits interest had "speculative, if any, value" and thus concluded that the receipt of that specific interest was not currently taxable. The decision suggested, however, that a receipt of future profits interest that could be valued with reasonable precision might trigger current income to a service provider.

As a follow-up to the *Campbell* decision, the IRS issued Rev. Proc. 93-27,[91] which provides that the receipt of a profits interest for the provision of services to or for the benefit of a partnership in a partner capacity (or in anticipation of becoming a partner) is not a taxable event for the partner or the partnership. Instead, the partner will recognize and report profit (and taxable income) as it is earned by the partnership and distributed to such partner. Rev. Proc. 93-27 does not apply, however, in the following situations:

1. The profits interest relates to a substantially certain and predictable stream of income from partnership assets, such as income from high quality debt securities or a high quality net lease.

2. The partner disposes of the profits interest within two years of receipt.

3. The profits interest is a limited partnership interest in a "publicly traded partnership" within the meaning of Code section 7704(b).

An interesting question is whether a profits interest that is not currently taxable, under the criteria described in Rev. Proc. 93-27, is a capital asset in the hands of the recipient partner (i.e., whether the partner will recognize capital gain or ordinary income on a sale of that partnership interest). Assuming the partner holds the profits interest for at least two years (thus satisfying the criteria in Rev. Proc. 93-27), the author believes that this should be classified as a capital asset, based on the language of Code section 741, together with the "two-year" rule embedded in Rev. Proc. 93-27. However, there is no certainty on this issue at this time.

HYPOTHETICAL SITUATIONS ILLUSTRATING TAX ISSUES IN THE SALE OF A PARTNERSHIP INTEREST

The following are a series of hypothetical situations illustrating basic tax issues in the sale of a partnership interest.

Hypothetical Situation #1. Peter, Paul, and Terry are equal partners in a partnership formed three years before to record, distribute and perform folk music. The partnership owns, among other things, cash, receivables, and a large collection of old and out-of-tune instruments, including guitars originally purchased for $10,000. Terry has a falling out with Peter and Paul and decides to sell his interest in the partnership to Barry. On the date of the sale, the partnership owns the following assets:

Asset	Adjusted Basis	Fair Market Value
Cash	$ 3,000	$ 3,000
Accounts receivable	0	3,000
Depreciable assets (guitars)	0	3,000
Goodwill of band	0	6,000
Total	**3,000**	**15,000**

Capital Accounts	Adjusted per Books	Fair Market Value
Capital:		
Peter	$1,000	$5,000
Paul	1,000	5,000
Terry	1,000	5,000
Total	**3,000**	**15,000**

Assume Terry's tax basis in his partnership interest is $1,000, and that the partnership has a Code section 754 election in effect.

If Barry pays Terry $5,000 to purchase Terry's partnership interest, and assuming Terry has $1,000 of tax basis in the partnership interest being sold, the tax consequences are as follows:

Terry: Terry has sold a partnership interest, and under Code section 741 the gain or loss on such sale is considered gain or loss from a sale of a capital asset. However, such gain, in turn, is subject to recharacterization under Code section 751. Terry's tax basis in his partnership interest is $1,000, and so Terry has a $4,000 gain recognition on the transaction. However, Terry's partnership interest includes a one-third interest in the accounts receivable, which is a hot asset under Code section 751, and also includes a one-third interest in depreciation recapture (on the guitars) under Code section 1245, which is classified as an unrealized receivable under Code section 751(c). Therefore, $2,000 of Terry's $4,000 of gain will be characterized as ordinary income. The other assets of the partnership are depreciable (Section 1231) assets and goodwill (another Section 1231 asset), and do not trigger a recharacterization of capital gain to ordinary income under Code section 751. Therefore, Terry will realize $2,000 of long-term capital gain (LTCG) and $2,000 of ordinary income (under Code section 751(a)) as a result of the sale.

Barry: Barry will have $5,000 of tax basis in his partnership interest (pursuant to Code section 1012) immediately after the acquisition. In turn, because there is a Section 754 election in effect, the tax basis will be allocated among the assets of the partnership based on Code section 755. Code section 755 and the applicable regulations provide that if the assets of the partnership constitute a trade or business, as defined in the Code section 1060 regulations, then the partnership is required to use the residual method to assign values to the partnership's Code section 197 intangibles.[92] In the present case, a reasonable allocation of purchase price based on fair market value is as follows:

Asset	Fair Market Value	Allocable Basis for Barry (1/3 interest in assets)
Cash	$3,000	$1,000
Accounts receivable	$3,000	$1,000
Depreciable assets (guitars)	$3,000	$1,000
Goodwill of band	$6,000	$2,000

Barry will be able to claim depreciation of his $1,000 of tax basis in the guitars over a five-year life under Code section 168. He will be able to amortize the goodwill over fifteen years under Code section 197. The cash and accounts receivable (A/R) are not depreciable or amortizable, but Barry has $1,000 of tax basis in the accounts receivable and will not recognize ordinary income when his share of the A/R is collected (the ordinary income recognition event on that portion of the A/R has already been recognized by Terry, thanks to the provisions of Code section 751(a)). Likewise, $1,000 of the $3,000 of cash held in the partnership is allocable to Barry, and can be distributed to Barry without generating taxable income, pursuant to Code section 731.

Hypothetical Situation #2. Hillary and Bill form an equal partnership, Hillbilly, LLC. Hillbilly will make allocations under Code section 704(c) using the remedial allocation method that is described in Reg. § 1.704-3(d). Hillary contributes nondepreciable real property with a fair market value of $100,000 and an adjusted tax basis of $150,000. Bill contributes $100,000 of cash. Hillary subsequently sells her partnership interests to Monica for $100,000. Hillbilly has a Section 754 election in effect to adjust the basis of a partnership property. Monica receives a negative $50,000 basis adjustment under Code section 743(b), which, under Code section 755, is allocated to the real property. The partnership subsequently sells the real property for $120,000. The partnership recognizes a $20,000 book gain, but a $30,000 tax loss. The book gain is allocated equally between the partners. The entire $30,000 book tax loss will be allocated to Monica under the principles of Code section 704(c). To match his $10,000 allocation of book gain, Bill will be allocated $10,000 of remedial gain, and Monica will be allocated an offsetting $10,000 of remedial loss. Monica was thus allocated a total of $40,000 of tax loss with respect to the property. However, because Monica had a negative $50,000 basis adjustment to the property, Monica actually recognized a $10,000 gain from the partnership's sale of the property.

Comment: This example shows that the Code section 704 rules in fact produce the correct result. Hillary should recognize a $50,000 loss in the sale of her interests in the partnership, and Monica should have essentially $100,000 of tax basis in her interest and in the underlying nondepreciable property. When this property is essentially sold for $120,000, there has been in effect a $20,000 gain. The partnership agrees that this gain will be split equally between Monica and Bill. Any remedial adjustments merely cause the book and tax consequences to reflect this economic reality. This hypothetical situation is based on Example 3 in Reg. § 1.743-1(j)(3)(ii).

Hypothetical Situation #3. Assume Luke, Leah, and Hank are equal one-third partners in a bookstore. Hank agrees to sell his interest to Ben for $90,000 in cash, plus the assumption by Ben of Hank's share of partnership liabilities. The partnership has inventory and, therefore, is an accrual basis taxpayer. The balance sheet of partnership is as follows:

	Fair Market Value	Tax Basis
Cash	$ 10,000	$ 10,000
Accounts Receivable	3,000	3,000
Inventory	150,000	102,000
Book Shelves and Other	31,000	10,000
Leasehold improvements	10,000	10,000
Sum of Class I–VI	$204,000	$135,000
Class VII Assets (goodwill)	96,000	0

Liabilities of the partnership are $30,000, payable to various parties. Hank's outside tax basis is $45,000.

The purchase price paid by Ben to Hank is allocated according to the asset values. Any excess of selling price over asset values would be presumed to be allocated to goodwill. The gain recognized by Hank would be computed as follows:

Cash Realized	$90,000
Liabilities assumed ($30,000 × 1/3)	$10,000
Total Purchase Price	$100,000
Minus Tax Basis	$45,000
Net Gain	$55,000

Note that the accounts receivable have already been included in income under the partnership's accrual method of accounting and, since tax basis equals fair market value, they are not "hot assets" as defined in Code section 751. The depreciation recapture on the bookshelves, representing the difference between the fair market value and the inside tax basis, is to be recaptured under Code section 1245 and, in turn, is considered an unrealized receivable and therefore subject to ordinary income treatment under Code section 751(c). The inventory is a Code section 751(a) asset. The leasehold improvements are assumed to have tax basis equal to fair market value so there is no recapture income under Code section 1245 and/or no uncaptured 1250 gain under Code section 1250(a) (either of which would have been characterized as unrealized receivables under Code section 751(c)).

Hank's gain is in proportion to Hank's one-third partnership interest. Therefore, Hank would recognize one-third of the differential in each of these items. Hank will recognize $16,000 of ordinary income under Code section 751(b) with respect to his share of the substantially appreciated inventory, $7,000 for "unrealized receivables" (the "recapture" income under Code section 1245) with respect to the bookshelves and furniture, and $32,000 of capital gain (gain of $55,000 minus $16,000 minus $7,000) with respect to his partnership interest under Code section 741.

Ben, meanwhile, will have $100,000 of outside tax basis in his partnership interest. Assuming a Code section 754 election is made, his tax basis in the allocable portion of partnership assets will be increased to the fair market value of his one-third interest in each asset, pursuant to Code section 755.

CHAPTER ENDNOTES

1. See, e.g., IRC Secs. 701, 702, 704, and 751.
2. See, e.g., IRC Secs. 723, 734, and 743.
3. See, e.g., IRC Secs. 705, 722, and 741.
4. IRC Sec. 701.
5. Reg. § 31.3401(d)-1(c), for example, defines "employer" to include a "partnership."
6. These three alternative transaction paths mimic the three alternative methods of incorporating a partnership. See Rev. Rul. 84-111.
7. IRC Sec. 336.
8. IRC Sec. 311(b); note, however, that IRC Sec. 311(b) does not apply unless the distribution trigger gain—it will not trigger loss.
9. IRC Sec. 731(b) exempts the partnership from any gain recognition whatsoever.
10. IRC Sec. 731(a)(1).
11. IRC Sec. 732(b).
12. See Chapters 4, 5, and 6.
13. See IRC Sec. 355(e); see the discussion in Chapter 7.
14. IRC Sec. 721(a).
15. IRC Sec. 721(b).
16. IRC Sec. 351.
17. See Rev. Rul. 99-5, 1999-1 CB 434.
18. Reg. § 1.351-1(a)(1)(ii).
19. 1977-2 CB 568.
20. *W.G. Campbell, 953 F2d 815 (1991)*; Rev. Proc. 93-27, 1993-2 CB 343.
21. IRC Sec. 351(a).
22. 56 TC 530, Dec. 30,838 (1971), aff'd, 492 F2d 286(1971) 1993-2 CB 343.
23. 59 TCM 236, Dec. 46,493(M), TC Memo. 1990-162.
24. Reg. § 1.721-1(b
25. See Rev. Proc. 93-27, rev'd on this issue, 943 F.2d 815(1991).
26. IRS Notice 2005-43, iss'd May 20, 2005, pub June 13, 2005.
27. IRC Sec. 752(a).
28. IRC Sec. 752(b).
29. IRC Sec. 752(c).
30. Reg. §§ 1.752-1 to 1.752-5.
31. IRC Sec.742.
32. IRC Sec. 1012.
33. IRC Sec. 1015.
34. IRC Sec. 723.
35. IRC Sec. 1223(2).
36. Reg. § 1.752-1(f).
37. IRC Sec. 733.
38. See Reg. § 1.752-1(g).
39. IRC Sec. 704(c)(1)(A); Reg. 1.704-3
40. IRC Sec. 704(c)(1)(B)(i).
41. IRC Sec. 704(c)(1)(B)(ii) and (iii).
42. IRC Sec. 722.
43. IRC Sec. 723.
44. IRC Sec. 705(a).
45. IRC Sec. 706(a).
46. Reg. § 1.704-1(b)(1)(i).
47. Reg. § 1.704-1(b)(2)(ii).
48. Reg. § 1.704-1(b)(2)(ii)(b).
49. Reg. § 1.704-1(b)(2)(ii)(d).
50. IRC Sec. 731.
51. IRC Sec. 731, treating such distributions as gain from the sale of a partnership interest.
52. A third, similar anti-abuse provision is found in IRC Sec. 707(a)(2), applicable to "disguised sales" of services or property.
53. IRC Sec. 732(a).
54. IRC Sec. 733.
55. See Chapter 3.
56. See IRC Sec. 703.
57. IRC Sec. 703(a).
58. See IRC Sec. 704(a), (b).
59. See IRC Sec. 702(a).
60. See Chapter 3.
61. See Chapter 17.
62. See Chapter 14.
63. IRC Sec. 741.

64. IRC Sec. 751(a).
65. See IRC Sec. 751(c).
66. *Id.*
67. IRC Sec. 1378.
68. IRC Sec. 1383.
69. IRC Sec. 706(c)(2)(A).
70. See IRC Sec. 1377(a)(2).
71. Rev. Rul. 99-6, 1999-1 CB 432.
72. Reg. § 301.7701-3(f)(2).
73. See IRC Secs. 741 and 1012.
74. See IRC Secs. 743(b) and 754.
75. See IRC Secs. 743(c) and 755.
76. See IRC Sec. 731(c).
77. IRC Sec. 731(b).
78. See IRC Secs. 731(a) and 731(d).
79. See IRC Sec. 731(d).
80. IRC Secs. 736(a) and 736(b)(2)(A).
81. IRC Sec. 731(b).
82. IRC Sec. 734(a).
83. See IRC Sec. 754.
84. See IRC Sec. 734(b).
85. See IRC Sec. 754.
86. See Reg. § 1.754-1(c).
87. See IRC Sec. 708(b).
88. Reg. § 1.721-1(b)(1).
89. *Id.*
90. 59 TCM 236, Dec. 46,493(M), TC Memo. 1990-162, rev'd in part, 943 F2d 815(1991).
91. 1993-2 CB 343.
92. Reg. § 1.755-1(a)(2).

INSTALLMENT SALES, CONTINGENT PAYMENTS, AND ESCROW ARRANGEMENTS

CHAPTER 10

OVERVIEW

It is very common, when a business is sold, for some or even all of the consideration to be paid to the Seller on a *deferred* basis. Naturally, the Seller wants to get as much consideration as possible, as quickly as possible, but those two objectives are not always synonymous. Meanwhile, a rational Buyer has an equally natural desire to "hold back" some portion of the purchase price to make sure the business, following the acquisition, is as successful as the parties intended.

Beyond the pure negotiating instincts of the respective parties, there are a variety of other practical factors that can come into play. For example, because a Buyer may need to use scarce capital to run the business for a period of time, the Buyer may need to use part of the "purchase price" to capitalize the business in the short term, and then pay out the balance of the purchase price over time. In substance, the business is often expected to help "pay for itself" through deferred payment of the purchase price. Another excellent reason for deferring the purchase price is so that the Buyer and Seller can more accurately decide what the final price should be. An operating business has no intrinsic or fixed-value—it is only as valuable as its post-sale performance in the hands of the Buyer. A Buyer is willing to pay more if the Buyer knows, with the absolute certainty of hindsight, that the business will perform at the expected or desired levels. Accordingly, it is very common not only to defer payment, but also to have some portion of the purchase price be *contingent* upon future events, including performance of the business over a period of months or years.

Another common acquisition arrangement is an "escrow", where a portion of the purchase price is held back to fund both anticipated and unanticipated liabilities of the Seller.

For all these reasons, and others, deferred payment arrangements can be an appropriate "business solution" to bridge the differences between the Buyer and the Seller. However, the IRS also has a stake in these arrangements. The federal income tax law generally requires that deferred payments be characterized in an economically rational and consistent manner. In particular, there are original issue discount (OID), imputed interest, and other deferred-payment rules, discussed below, which generally require that the parties to an installment sale both (a) charge a minimum rate of interest, and (b) pay or otherwise take into account each year these required interest amounts. Under these rules, if the actual or implied interest rate negotiated between the parties in a deferred payment transaction is "too low", these rules will impute interest at a specified minimum rate and will re-characterize a portion of deferred payments to include "interest", or the equivalent of interest, as part of each deferred payment transaction.

This chapter examines the key issues that need to be addressed when payment of all or some portion of the purchase price is deferred. The discussion will cover not only deferred payments of cash and/or property, but also deferred "payments" of stock in what purports to be a tax-free transaction. As we will see, deferred payment transactions often make a lot of sense, but they also can be very idiosyncratic and unique to the negotiations in a specific transaction. Because of that, their variety is exceptionally broad. At the same time, the tax rules that apply to installment sales, and especially to contingent payment transactions, are oftentimes onerous, and in all events complex.

INSTALLMENT SALES

Under Code section 453, income from an "installment sale" is required to be reported on the so-called "installment method". An "installment sale" is defined as any disposition of (eligible) property where at least one payment is received after the close of the tax year in which the sale occurs.[1] Significantly, the installment method can be used by all taxpayers, whether on the cash or accrual method of accounting, so long as the property sold is not otherwise ineligible for installment reporting. (*Note*: Publicly traded stock is generally not eligible for installment sale treatment,[2] but stock of a closely held corporation can be sold on the installment method.) Installment reporting does not apply to any sale at a loss. The installment method is mandatory, but subject to an election out: a taxpayer who sells property where at least one payment is received after the close of the tax year is *required* to recognize gain from the sale using the installment method unless the taxpayer expressly elects out of installment sale treatment.[3]

When property is sold in an installment sale, the selling taxpayer is not required to report the full gain on the date of the sale, but rather is permitted to report gain on a deferred basis. As previously noted, this is true even if the seller uses the accrual method of accounting. In effect, the installment method places a seller on the equivalent of the cash method of accounting with respect to installment payments, and allows the total gain on the transaction to be reported ratably (with some special rules and modifications) as payments are received.

Pursuant to Code section 453(c) and Temp. Reg. § 15.453-1(b)(2), each installment payment received is multiplied by the "gross profit ratio" to determine the amount of gain to be reported with respect to that payment. The balance of each payment is treated as a nontaxable recovery of basis.

The "gross profit ratio" is the fraction the numerator of which is the gross profit realized or to be realized and the denominator of which is the total contract price.[4] The concept of the "gross profit ratio" is simple, but the calculation of the ratio is actually significantly more complicated than one might initially expect.

1. The "gross profit ratio" (GPR) is a fraction or a percentage equal to the "gross profit" (GP) divided by the "contract price" (CP).

   GPR = GP/CP

2. The "gross profit" (GP) is the "selling price" (SP) minus the Seller's adjusted tax basis (ATB) in the property, which adjusted tax basis includes the selling expenses paid by the Seller.[5]

   GP = SP – ATB

3. The "selling price" (SP) is the gross selling price, including any mortgage or other encumbrance on the property and without reduction for any selling expenses paid by the Seller, but excluding any interest or original issue discount (OID) payable by the Seller.[6]

4. The "contract price" (CP) is the selling price (SP) reduced by any qualifying indebtedness (QI) (generally a mortgage or other indebtedness encumbering the transferred property, or unsecured debt incurred or assumed by the purchaser incident to the acquisition of the property) to the extent such qualifying indebtedness is not in excess of the adjusted tax basis in the property.[7]

   CP = SP – QI (but only to the extent QI is not in excess of ATB (which, in turn, includes selling expenses)).

Example 1: (a) *Facts.* Seller, the owner of a business operated as a sole proprietorship, sells all of Seller's business assets to Purchaser in exchange for $1 million. Assume (i) that Seller has $180,000 of tax basis in Seller's business assets, (ii) that none of the assets are ordinary assets that will generate either ordinary income or recapture income, (iii) that there are $20,000 of selling expenses, (iv) that there is no qualified indebtedness, and (v) that no special allocations of cash versus installment notes is made among the assets being sold. Further assume Purchaser will pay $400,000 in cash at the closing in Year 1 and will deliver a promissory note for the remaining $600,000, with $200,000 of principal due at the end of Year 2 and the remaining $400,000 due and payable at the end of Year 3, and that such promissory note will bear adequate stated interest that is due and payable at least annually or more frequently (i.e., a high enough interest rate and frequent enough payment schedule so as not to trigger the application of the OID rules).

(b) Determine GPR. In this circumstance, Seller's "gross profit" is $800,000 (selling price of $1 million – adjusted tax basis (including $20,000 of selling expenses) of $200,000), and the "contract price" is $1 million (selling price of $1 million minus zero qualifying indebtedness). Therefore the gross profit ratio (gross profit divided by contract price) is 80 percent ($800,000/$1,000,000).

(c) Identify Payments. Because, for Code section 453 purposes, payments do not include interest on the promissory note, the installment payments are the $400,000 paid at closing, the $200,000 paid in Year 2, and the $400,000 paid in Year 3.

(d) Multiply Payment × GPR to Determine Gain Recognition. On receipt of the $400,000 payment in Year 1, Seller will recognize gain of $320,000 ($400,000 × 80%). Seller will subsequently recognize gain of $160,000 ($200,000 × 80%) in Year 2, and gain of $320,000 ($400,000 × 80%) in Year 3. (*Note:* Seller will also recognize interest income in each tax year as such interest is paid on the promissory note.)

(e) Tax Consequences to Purchaser. Purchaser will capitalize and depreciate the full purchase price of $1 million, starting with the closing date, even though a significant portion of the purchase price is payable more than two years later. Purchaser will also be able to deduct the interest payments on the promissory note in each tax year as such payments are made.

Be aware that for the interest payments to be "interest", and not OID, the interest rate must be at or above the applicable federal rate for the term of the note and the interest payments must be due and payable at least annually or more frequently.[8]

Example 2: (a) *Facts.* Same facts as Example 1, including a $1 million purchase price, except that as part of the purchase that Seller transfers, and Purchaser assumes, qualifying indebtedness of $100,000, and the cash payment at closing is reduced to $300,000. Purchaser still delivers at closing a promissory note of $600,000.

(b) Determine GPR.

GP = SP ($1,000,000) – ATB ($200,000) = $800,000 CP = SP ($1,000,000) – QI ($100,000) = $900,000 GPR = GP/CP = $800,000/$900,000 = 88.89%

(c) Identify Payments. Payments do not include interest paid on the promissory note, nor the assumption of QI to the extent it is not in excess of ATB. Therefore, the payments are $300,000 at closing, $200,000 in Year 2, and $400,000 in Year 3.

(d) Compute Gain (Payment × GPR).

Seller recognizes $266,670 at closing ($300,000 × 88.89%), $177,780 in Year 2 ($200,000 × 88.89%), and $355,560 in Year 3 ($400,000 × 88.89%).

(e) Tax Consequences to Purchaser. Same as in Example 1.

Example 3: (a) *Facts.* Assume the same facts as in Example 2, except that the qualifying indebtedness is $250,000, and thus is greater than the adjusted tax basis (ATB). Purchaser delivers $150,000 in cash at closing and a $600,000 promissory note payable under the same terms as in Examples 1 and 2.

(b) Determine GPR

SP = $1,000,000

ATB (including selling expenses) = $200,000

QI = $250,000

GP = SP ($1,000,000) – ATB ($200,000) = $800,000.

CP = SP ($1,000,000) – QI not in excess of ATB ($200,000) = $800,000

GPR = GP/CP = 100%

(c) Identify Payments. Under Code section 453, payments do not include interest paid on the promissory note, nor the assumption of QI to

the extent not in excess of ATB, but do include assumptions of QI in excess of ATB. In this case, because the assumption of QI of $250,000 exceeds ATB by $50,000, this is a "payment" at closing, as is the $150,000 cash payment delivered at closing. The additional payments are $200,000 in Year 2 and $400,000 in Year 3.

(d) Compute Gain (Payment × GPR).

Seller recognizes $200,000 at closing [$50,000 (QI in excess of ATB) × 100%, plus $150,000 × 100%], $200,000 in Year 2 ($200,000 × 100%), and $400,000 in Year 3 ($400,000 × 100%).

(e) Tax Consequences to Purchaser. Same as in Example 1.

The benefit of the installment method is that the Seller does not have to pay taxes on gain realized until payment is received. This makes the Seller far more likely to enter into an installment sale transaction than if all the taxes were due up front! Meanwhile, the Buyer is allowed to borrow acquisition capital from the Seller, and in effect fund the acquisition from the future earnings power of the acquired business.

There are a variety of technical requirements that are designed to make sure that the installment method is being used properly by the parties concerned. One important issue is that the Purchaser is not supposed to receive anything that is the equivalent of cash. For example, Code section 453(f)(3) indicates that the installment method is not available with respect to a debt instrument if issued by anyone other than the Purchaser of the property. Likewise, an installment note will be considered taxable immediately, even if issued by the Purchaser of the property, if it is either payable on demand or is readily tradable.[9]

On the other hand, it is permissible and appropriate to have reasonable protection and assurance that a promissory note will ultimately be paid. Accordingly, a Purchaser obligation that is otherwise a qualified installment obligation is not made taxable solely if it is guaranteed by a third party.[10] Likewise, the regulations permit an installment note to be secured by a standby letter of credit. To qualify as a "standby" letter of credit, the letter of credit must be a nonnegotiable, nontransferable (except with the debt it secures) letter of credit issued by a bank or other financial institution serving as a guarantee of the debt it secures. A letter of credit is *not* a standby letter of credit if it may be drawn upon in the absence of a default.[11]

Other forms of payment assurances or security arrangements are also frequently used, especially in cases where a letter of credit or third-party guarantee is expensive to obtain. However, if the security provided to the Seller is cash, or its equivalent, the pledge of security may cause the installment note to be treated as a payment.[12] A common security arrangement in connection with an installment sale is for the Seller to take a security interest in the assets sold to the Buyer. This type of security arrangement is permitted under an installment sale. The issues relating to the use of escrow accounts as security devices are discussed more fully later in this chapter.

Code section 453 requires a Seller to strike a sometimes delicate balance between the Seller's security objectives and the Seller's desired federal income tax consequences. Obviously, from a purely economic standpoint, a Seller would prefer to take no risk with respect to collection of the future payments due under an installment sale. However, under Code section 453, the Seller risks accelerated gain recognition if the Seller receives too much security or too much liquidity in the debt instrument.

Immediate gain recognition can be triggered under Code section 453(e) by subsequent actions of the Buyer if the Buyer is related to the Seller and makes a second disposition of property within two years after its acquisition. This specific anti-abuse rule is designed to prevent related parties from engaging in an installment sale, deferring gain to the Seller, and then allowing the related Buyer to "flip" the property immediately in exchange for cash or other consideration. "Related person" means a person whose stock would be attributed under Code section 318(a) (other than Code section 318(a)(4)) to the person first disposing of the property or a person who bears a relationship described in Code section 267(b) to the person first disposing of the property.[13]

Example 4: Assume Father owns stock in a C corporation (stock is nondepreciable property) worth $1 million and with tax basis in his hands of $100,000. Father sells the stock to Daughter for a $1 million promissory note, bearing adequate stated interest, with interest due and payable annually or more frequently, and with the principal amount of the note due and payable as a balloon payment in ten years. Within two years, Daughter resells the stock to an unrelated

Buyer for $1 million. Daughter has purchased the stock and sold it for the same price, and therefore recognizes no gain on the transaction (her tax basis in the stock is $1 million, and she sells it for $1 million). Father, meanwhile, would (but for the application of Code section 453(e)) be eligible to report his sale to Daughter on the installment method and defer recognition of the gain for ten years, and Daughter would be able to enjoy the use of the $1 million, subject to the obligation to make annual interest payments.

Example 5: Same as Example 4, except Daughter sells the property two years and one day after the installment purchase from Father. On those facts, and assuming the transaction cannot be attacked under a step transaction or other analysis, the subsequent sale does not trigger the application of Code section 453(e) because it occurs beyond the two-year statutory period. Daughter would have the current use of the money, would have to pay current interest under the terms of the note, and would owe a balloon payment of $1 million to Father in Year 10, at which time Father would recognize gain. Father's gross profit would be $900,000 ($1 million – $100,000), and he would recognize that amount of gain at the time he received the balloon payment. Father would also report interest income as paid throughout the term of the note, and Daughter would have a corresponding interest payment in each year.

Another special acceleration rule is found in Code section 453(i), related to the recognition of Code sections 1245 and 1250 recapture. Basically, if the property in question is subject to the allowance for depreciation under Code section 167 and has a built-in recapture amount that will be recognized as recapture income on sale under Code sections 1245 or 1250 (or, if the Seller is a partnership, under Code section 751 as it relates to Code sections 1245 or 1250), this built-in recapture income is recognized as ordinary income in the year of the sale, whether or not there is a cash payment in such year. Thus, if depreciable property is sold on the installment method, recapture income must be recognized and reported by the Seller in the year of disposition. This is true even if the Seller does not receive any cash in the year. Any recapture income recognized in the year of sale under this rule is treated as additional tax basis for purposes of computing the gross profits ratio on payments, whether such payments are received in that year or any future year.[14]

Example 6: Seller, who operates a business as a single member LLC (taxable as a sole proprietorship), agrees to sell the business's assets for $1 million. The assets are comprised of depreciable equipment, purchased for $400,000 with tax basis in the hands of Seller of $100,000, and the goodwill of the business, which has zero tax basis in the hands of Seller. Buyer and Seller reasonably agree, pursuant to Code section 1060, to allocate $200,000 to the equipment and $800,000 to the goodwill. There is no qualifying indebtedness. Buyer agrees to pay $400,000 at closing and delivers a promissory note in the face amount of $600,000, secured by a stand-by letter of credit, and bearing adequate stated interest due and payable annually or more frequently. The principal balance of the promissory note is due on the last day of Year 2. The parties do not make any agreement to allocate the cash portion or the note portion of the purchase price between the assets.

On these facts, Seller will recognize $100,000 of recapture income in the year of disposition. This recognition amount will be added to the tax basis of Seller in determining the gross profits ratio, which is 80 percent, determined as follows: Gross Profit (Selling Price of $1 million minus adjusted tax basis (including recapture income recognized) of $200,000 = $800,000) divided by Contract Price (Selling Price of $1 million minus zero qualifying indebtedness). This 80 percent ratio is multiplied by the $400,000 payment received in Year 1, which means that Seller recognizes $320,000 of gain in Year 1. Note that this $320,000 of gain is in addition to the $100,000 of recapture income recognized in Year 1, which means that Seller recognizes a total of $420,000 of taxable income or gain in Year 1, even though Seller only receives $400,000 in actual payments. In Year 2, Seller will be paid $600,000 and will recognize gain of $480,000 (payment amount ($600,000) × GPR (80%)). Seller also is paid and recognizes in each year the interest income paid pursuant to the terms of the promissory note.

Buyer, meanwhile, capitalizes its entire $1 million purchase price in the applicable assets, even though payment of $600,000 of the purchase price is deferred until Year 2. Buyer deducts interest on the promissory note as it is accrued and paid.

Another anti-abuse provision is Code section 453(g), which basically acts as a complement to the rules in Code section 1239 related to sales of depreciable property to related persons. Basically, Code section 453(g) bars installment sale treatment in sales of depreciable property between related persons. Instead, all payments are treated as received in the year of the disposition. This rule can be overridden if it can be established to the satisfaction of the IRS that the disposition did not have as one of its principal purposes the avoidance of federal income tax. For purposes of Code section 453(g), the term "related persons" has the meaning given as such term in Code section 1239(b), except that such term also includes two or more partnerships having a relationship described in Code section 707(b)(1)(B)(i.e., the same persons directly or indirectly own more than 50 percent of the capital or profits interests).

Although the installment method is generally an attractive way to defer tax liabilities until cash is readily available, there may be circumstances where it actually makes sense to accelerate the gain recognition, even if the payment is deferred. Accordingly, the installment sale rules allow a taxpayer to elect out of the installment sale method. Such an election might make sense, for example, if a corporation has large capital losses that it otherwise cannot use during the five-year capital loss carry-forward limitation under Code section 1212. By electing to recognize immediately all of the gain from the sale, the corporation can avoid wasting those capital losses. An election to forego installment sale treatment is made on or before the due date (including extensions) of the Seller's tax return for the year of the sale. After the election is made, it is irrevocable without the consent of the IRS.[15]

Code section 453 does not apply to any sale at a loss. Such a loss is recognized on the date that the property is sold. This is true even if the Seller would prefer to defer recognition of the loss (e.g., to defer the running of the five-year capital loss carry-forward limitation applicable to a C corporation under Code section 1212).

The installment method is not available to any "dealer disposition" of property.[16] A "dealer disposition" is defined as (a) any disposition of personal property by a person who regularly sells or otherwise disposes of personal property of the same type on an installment plan and (b) any disposition of real property held for sale to customers in the ordinary course of the taxpayer's trade or business.[17]

One important provision that can significantly reduce the benefits of the installment method in large transactions is Code section 453A, which generally requires the Seller to pay the equivalent of an "interest charge" on the amount of tax deferred under the installment method. The provision is aimed at "large" installment sale transactions. It applies only if the obligation is incurred in an installment sale of property whose sale price exceeds $150,000, such installment obligation is outstanding at the close of the tax year, and the face amount of all such obligations held by the taxpayer that arose during, and are outstanding as of the close of, such tax year exceeds $5 million. Code section 453A imposes an annual interest charge on the Seller's deferred tax liability based on the underpayment rate in effect under Code section 6621(a)(2).[18] In substance, Code section 453A allows the federal government to charge interest (at a relatively reasonable rate) on unpaid federal taxes deferred pursuant to large installment sales.

If an installment obligation is subject to Code section 453A, the following rules apply in determining the interest charge:

1. If the installment obligations meet the $150,000/$5 million thresholds, the interest charge must be paid annually thereafter, even if the Seller receives no cash payments on the installment note before its maturity.

2. Once it applies to an installment obligation, the Code section 453A interest charge is imposed annually until the obligation is fully paid or disposed of.

3. The deferred tax liability on which interest is charged is reduced as gain is recognized.[19]

If an installment note is subsequently sold or otherwise liquidated by the Seller, the Seller recognizes gain or loss equal to the difference between the amount realized on the sale of the note and the Seller's tax basis in the note. Code section 453B(a) gain is recognized on the disposition of an installment note even though the Seller received no consideration (e.g., a gift of an installment note, including a charitable donation, causes the donor to recognize gain).[20] Likewise, an installment note issued by an Acquirer corporation in connection with an acquisition that is subsequently converted by the Seller into stock of the Acquirer will cause gain recognition upon the conversion into stock, even if the note is issued with a built-in conversion feature.[21]

Post-sale modifications to the terms of an installment note can be treated as a sale or exchange of the note under the principles of *Cottage Savings Association*[22] and Code section 1001 if the modifications are substantial. The IRS has issued regulations which indicate that relatively minor changes will not be considered a modification triggering exchange treatment of the note.[23] However, the *Cottage Savings* case and the subsequent regulations under Code section 1001 are often viewed as a "hair trigger" modification test, meaning that even a relatively inconsequential modification of the promissory note may be deemed a "modification" triggering extremely adverse tax consequences. A provision of Code section 453A triggers gain when a Seller uses an installment note received in connection with a sale of property as collateral for subsequent financing. If an installment obligation is used to secure an indebtedness, the net proceeds from the indebtedness will be treated as a payment received on such installment obligation.[24]

Although a gift made during a transferor's lifetime is considered a taxable disposition of an installment note, a transfer by will or intestacy does not cause the decedent or the decedent's estate to recognize gain.[25] However, the remaining installment payments are treated as income in respect of the decedent under Code section 691 and are taxable to the beneficiary upon receipt.[26] The beneficiary reports gain in the same manner as the decedent would have reported it if the decedent had lived, and the gain will be treated as long-term capital gain if it was so treated in the hands of the decedent.[27] However, if a note is bequeathed to the obligor, the note is regarded as cancelled, and the bequest is treated as a taxable disposition by the decedent's estate.[28]

Under Code section 453(f)(3), the term "payment" does not include "the receipt of evidence of indebtedness of the person acquiring the property". On the other hand, a note that is not indebtedness of the Purchaser, but rather indebtedness of some other party, is considered a "payment" and is included in the amount realized by the Seller when received.[29] Care should be taken to make sure that the promissory note is issued by the true "Purchaser", and not by a subsidiary or parent corporation, in connection with the corporate acquisition transaction.

An installment note is treated as an immediate "payment" if it is either: (1) payable on demand or (2) is readily tradable.[30] Whether a note is treated as payable on demand is determined under applicable state or local law.[31] A note is considered readily tradable if it is issued: (1) with interest coupons attached (whether or not the obligation is readily tradable on an established securities market); (2) in registered form (other than an obligation issued in registered form that the taxpayer establishes will not be readily tradable in an established securities market); or (3) in any other form designed to render such obligation readily tradable in an established securities market.[32]

Any installment obligation that is convertible into readily tradable stock or debt is treated as readily tradable and therefore is treated as an immediate payment. The exception to this rule is if the obligation is convertible only at a "substantial discount". Whether an obligation is convertible at a substantial discount depends upon the particular facts and circumstances. A substantial discount will be considered to exist if at the time of issue the fair market value of the securities into which the note is convertible is less than 80 percent of the fair market value of the note. A substantial discount also will be considered to exist if the conversion privilege cannot be exercised within a period of one year from the date of issue.[33]

EARN-OUTS AND OTHER CONTINGENT PAYMENT TRANSACTIONS

An "earn-out" is an installment sale in which the purchase price is contingent on the future earnings of the Target in the hands of the Buyer. A tax-free reorganization transaction can also call for a contingent future payment in the form of additional stock, additional cash, or both. A so-called "contingent payment" transaction is actually a very specific form of installment sale. Technically, a "contingent payment sale" is defined as a sale or other disposition of property in which the selling price cannot be determined as of the close of the tax year in which the sale of the disposition occurs.[34] A contingent payment sale can be entirely contingent, or, more commonly, it can have both a fixed amount component and a contingent payment component. In the latter case, the contingent payment component is often referred to as an "earn-out".

Comment: Sometimes it can be difficult to determine whether a contingent payment arrangement is merely a sale in which the final selling price is not determined at the end of the year or a retention of an interest in the property that has been sold. Realistically, even in a contingent payment sale that qualifies as a true sale for tax purposes, the Seller often has an ongoing, quasi-equity stake in the success of the transferred asset, especially when the asset in question is a functioning business and the contingent payment amount will be determined by the profitability or success of that business.

Contingent payment arrangements are especially popular when the value of a business is difficult to determine at the date of sale and both the Buyer and Seller would like to see how the business performs in the hands of the Buyer before setting a final purchase price. It is very common for the parties to agree that the sale price will be modified in the future, usually upward but sometimes downward, to take into account future gross sales, future earnings, or other factors based on the performance of the business in the hands of the Buyer.

The difficulty with contingent payment arrangements is that they call for the simultaneous application of two distinct and not-very-well-integrated provisions of the Code: (1) the installment sale rules under Code section 453 and (2) the original issue discount (OID) rules and imputed interest rules under Code sections 1274 and 483. As a starting point, a contingent payment sale of nonpublicly traded property is treated as an installment sale governed by Code section 453. For these purposes, a contingent payment sale is defined as a sale or other disposition of property in which the aggregate selling price cannot be determined by the close of the taxable year in which the sale or disposition occurs.[35]

In general, all installment sales must divide the deferred payments into three specific portions for tax purposes: (1) the portion of each payment representing "interest" (or OID) to compensate the Seller for the time value of money, (2) the portion of each payment representing income or gain recognized by the Seller, and (3) the portion of each payment representing a tax-free return of basis. So long as the timing and amount of all payments is known, the rules are mathematically precise and, if not exactly easy to apply, at least can be applied with certainty. However, when the payment amounts are contingent as to time, or amount, or both, a different set of rules are required to be applied.

First, under the time-value-of-money rules, where a Purchaser issues a nonpublicly traded contingent debt instrument to acquire nonpublicly traded property (the standard situation in any business acquisition), the instrument is bifurcated into contingent and noncontingent parts.[36] The noncontingent part is characterized for tax purposes under the usual rules of Code section 1274, i.e., the noncontingent portion is treated as a debt instrument with an issue price equal to the lesser of (1) the sum of all noncontingent principal payments or (2) the sum of the present values of all noncontingent payments discounted using the applicable federal rate (AFR).[37] Although the terminology is complex, the consequence of this rule is relatively easy to describe: the noncontingent portion will be recharacterized if and only if it does not bear adequate stated interest.

The contingent payments, by contrast, are taken into account in the tax year that each such payment is made.[38] At that point in time, assuming the contingent payment obligation does not provide for adequate stated interest to be added to the contingent payment amount (which is a very safe assumption in most transactions), the contingent payment amount is discounted using the applicable AFR from the original issue date to the payment date, thereby determining the portion of such payment to be treated as principal, and the balance as interest.[39] Special rules apply if the contingency becomes fixed more than six months before payment is due (not usually the case, but possible). Curiously, the apportionment between principal and interest under these rules is mandatory, and applies even if the parties agreed to treat the entire contingent payment as interest.[40]

After determining the portion of each contingent payment that is considered "principal" versus interest (or OID), the principal amount must then be allocated a portion of the tax basis to determine the amount of gain recognized at the time of payment. The regulations provide interesting, complicated, and sometimes troublesome rules for apportioning tax basis in contingent payment sales.[41] Basically, the regulations address three specific contingency scenarios: (a) contingent sales where there is a stated maximum selling price, (b) contingent sales where there is no stated maximum selling price, but there is a fixed period of time over which payments may be received, and (c) contingent sales where there is neither a specified maximum selling price or fixed payment period. Each of these three scenarios is discussed more fully below. Be aware, however, that these contingent-payment rules are generally adverse to both the Buyer and Seller and may profoundly alter what the parties will accept in terms of contingent payment arrangements. These rules are especially important to study when an installment sale includes a specified "upside" to the Seller based on future performance of the business in the hands of the Buyer because in many cases the contingent payment rules are very onerous and produce nasty and unexpected tax results.

When there is a *stated maximum selling price* (which means that the maximum amount that the Seller can receive can be determined as of the end of the tax year in which the sale occurred), the Seller reports the gain with respect to each payment received under the installment obligation by treating the stated maximum selling price as the selling price. The stated maximum selling price is determined by assuming that all of the contingencies contemplated by the agreement are met or otherwise resolved in a manner that will maximize the selling price and accelerate payments to the earliest date or dates permitted under the agreement.[42]

Example 7: Seller, an S corporation, sells all of its assets to Buyer in exchange for $20 million in cash, plus an earn-out equal to five percent of Target's profits over the next three years, up to a maximum additional "earn-out" amount of $5 million. Assume (somewhat artificially in order to simplify this example) that the contingent payments are made with an additional payment each time representing adequate stated interest. Assume there is $10 million of tax basis in the business assets, that there are no ordinary income assets and no recapture income on the sale, and no assumption of qualifying indebtedness.

In computing the gross profit ratio, Seller must assume that Seller will receive the maximum possible amount at the earliest possible time. Therefore, the GPR is computed assuming a total selling price of $25 million. Therefore, the gross profit ratio will be 60 percent (selling price ($25 million) minus adjusted tax basis ($10 million) = $15 million, divided by the contract price of $25 million). This means that with respect to the $20 million payment received in the first year, 60 percent, or $12 million, will be recognized as gain for the first tax year. Note that, as a result of the contingent payment rules applied to these simplified facts, $2 million of adjusted tax basis is not recovered in the first year but instead will be apportioned to the theoretical maximum of $5 million of "contingent" payments, and thus will be recovered as these payments are received over the next three years.

Assume that, at the end of Year 2, an additional $2 million of contingent purchase price is payable under the earn-out formula, together with adequate stated interest. Applying the gross profit ratio of 60 percent, this means that an addition of $1.2 million of gain will be recognized in Year 2 (payment amount ($2,000,000) × GPR (60%) = $1,200,000).

Assume that, at the end of Year 3, the remaining contingencies are not met and that the contingent obligation expires without triggering further payment obligations by Buyer. At that point in time, Seller will recognize a $1.2 million capital loss (representing the amount of tax basis not previously recovered under the installment sale reporting rules). Bear in mind that, because capital losses cannot be carried backward by individuals, this will result in a serious mismatching of gain and loss for Seller's individual shareholders. Although Seller actually realizes $22 million of proceeds on the sale transaction and reports a gain of $12 million ($22 million of total sales proceeds (exclusive of interest) minus $10 million of tax basis), because of how the rules apply to a contingent installment sale transaction, Seller will report $12 million of gain in the year of the sale and $1.2 million of gain in Year 2 of the installment sale period, or a total of $13.2 million of capital gain. In Year 3, when all contingent payment rights terminate, Seller will report a $1.2 million long-term capital loss.

Although in the broad sense there is a "netting" of capital gain and capital loss, resulting in a $12 million net gain, the tax accounting rules do not permit the $1.2 million capital loss in Year 3 to be carried back and applied against the $13.2 million of gain recognized in the prior years. Therefore, the taxpayer not only will pay gain on an "extra" $1.2 million initially, but also may have very limited ability to utilize this $1.2 million capital loss going forward. This is especially true in transactions where an individual is selling all of his or her interest in an ongoing business and does not have any ready source of additional capital gains (a very common situation for parties whose principal investment and source of wealth is their business).

The problem described in Example 7 is created because the rules applicable to a contingent payment sale with a stated maximum selling price tend to back-load the benefits of tax basis and can produce losses if the earn-out projections are inflated or overly optimistic. (In fact, earn-out structures often call for exaggerated "maximum" payouts based on fanciful projections of future income and growth. This is a "natural" agreement for both the Buyer and Seller to negotiate because the Seller would like to receive additional money if the business is wildly successful in the hands of the Buyer, and the Buyer is usually quite amenable to making additional payments if the business in fact succeeds beyond the Buyer's wildest expectations. The problem is that this kind of logical "win-win" arrangement between the Buyer and the Seller turns out to be strictly a "lose-lose" proposition under the Code if the Seller ends up with unusable capital losses because of a too-optimistic earn-out structure.)

A possible "solution" to this earn-out problem is to keep the earn-out figures as realistic as possible. Another possible strategy is to "allocate" purchase price and forms of payment among the assets in the sale (e.g., allocate the cash portion of the purchase price to those assets that have significant tax basis and allocate the "earn-out" installment to the assets that typically have a very low tax basis, such as the goodwill of the company, which will almost always be low or zero unless it has been recently purchased from another business as part of the acquisition of that business).[43] Another possible solution is to separate the sale transaction into two discrete components.

As if these types of transactions were not already complex, additional computational adjustments must be made in cases where the "earn-out" formula calls for payments and (as is far more likely the case) does not provide for additional adequate stated interest.

> ***Example 8:*** Same facts as Example 7, except there is not adequate stated interest added to contingent deferred payments. In Year 2, the $2 million contingent payment received by Seller will first be divided into an interest component and a principal component by applying Code section 1274 and Reg. § 1.1275-4(a) and other computational assumptions (including assuming that all remaining contingent payments will be due and payable at the earliest possible time). Assume, based on the application of the regulations, that the principal component of the payment is .80. This means that $1.6 million of the $2 million payment is principal, $400,000 is interest, and unapplied the tax basis of $2 million will be prorated between the deemed principal payment of $1.6 received in Year 2, and the deemed principal payment attributable to the remaining maximum contingency of $3 million. If the $3 million is deemed payable in full at the earliest possible time (in this case, Year 3 of the earn-out period) and if under the regulations the $3 million is treated in Year 3 as having a principal component of .70 (these numbers are being intentionally rounded for illustrative purposes), this means that the maximum imputed principal is $1.6 million plus $2.1 million (the $3 million payment in Year 3 multiplied by .70), or a total imputed principal balance of $3.7 million. Therefore, the portion of the tax basis allocated to the $1.6 million of deemed principal payment in Year 2 of the earn-out is $2 million of deferred tax basis multiplied by the fraction 1.6/3.7 (i.e., the principal payment in Year 2 divided by the total imputed maximum principal payment under the contingent payment arrangement), which equals $864,865. This means that in Year 2, Seller recovers this amount of tax basis, recognizes $400,000 of interest income and $735,135 of gain ($1.6 million of principal payment minus $864,865 of recovered tax basis).

When there is *no maximum stated selling price*, but the arrangement involves *a maximum or fixed period of payment* (i.e., there is an outside time limit on when contingent payments will be received), the Seller's basis is allocated over such period in equal annual increments, and the gain with respect to payments in each year is reported accordingly. If the payments during a year are less than the portion of the Seller's basis allocated to that year, the unrecovered basis is carried forward to the next year, and the taxpayer is not allowed to report a loss unless and until the last year of the installment period, at which time any remaining unrecovered basis is deducted as a loss.[44] Once again, because such loss is almost always a capital loss, it will be subject to the limitations on utilization of capital losses.

> ***Example 9:*** Assume that Seller, an S corporation, sells its business assets, in which it has a tax basis of $5 million, and Buyer is contractually obligated to make purchase payments, based on productivity, over a five-year period. Assume there is no recapture income or other ordinary income, nor any assumption of qualifying indebtedness. Assume the principal payment the first year is $4 million, together with adequate stated interest (again, it is relatively unusual to include an interest component, but for

illustrative purposes it eliminates the complexities of the OID rules). Seller would allocate its $5 million of tax basis ratably over five years, and thus would apply $1 million of basis to the first year, and would recognize $3 million of capital gain in the first year.

Assume in Year 2 that there is only a payment of $200,000, plus adequate interest, made to Seller under the productivity formula. Seller would be allowed to allocate up to $1 million of tax basis to Year 2, but because the installment payment for Year 2 (exclusive of interest) is only $200,000, Seller is limited under the regulations to claiming only $200,000 of tax basis in Year 2 and must carry the remaining $800,000 of tax basis initially allocated to Year 2 over to Year 3.

Where there is *neither a stated maximum selling price nor a maximum or fixed payment period*, the transaction is supposed to be scrutinized to determine whether in substance it is a rent or royalty agreement rather than a sale. If sales treatment is determined to be appropriate, the Seller is permitted to recover his or her tax basis in equal annual increments over fifteen years.

All three of these contingent payment rules allocating tax basis are disadvantageous to taxpayers. Note that the second rule, which applies to a contingent payment sale with no maximum stated selling price but a fixed period over which payments can be made, is particularly onerous because the tax basis is recovered ratably over the maximum fixed period of payment, whereas in many cases the largest economic value in a contingent payment arrangement will be expected by both parties to be earned in the early years of the contingency period. For example, assume the Seller sells a patent for a contingent purchase price payable over the twenty-year life of the patent based on the gross revenue earned from the patent by the Buyer. Assume, as is often the case, that the patent value is expected to peak in the early years and then decline. The second rule would allocate tax basis ratably over the twenty-year period even though most or all of the income under the contingent payment formula may be recognized by the Seller in the early years.

The fundamental problem with each of these three contingent payment alternatives is that federal income tax law (and most if not all state tax laws) place limits on carrying capital losses backwards and forwards. Historically, the Code has never allowed individuals to carry back their capital losses; instead, capital losses are carried forward indefinitely, subject to termination on the death of the individual taxpayer.[45] Corporations can carry back capital losses three years and carryforward capital losses to only five years.[46]

INDEMNIFICATION ESCROWS

Sometimes the Seller and Buyer agree to place a portion of the purchase price into escrow as a "hold back" so that the Buyer can easily recover money if there is a breach of the representations and warranties made by the Seller in the purchase and sale agreement. A typical escrow arrangement on a $10 million acquisition transaction might call for $7-9 million of the acquisition price to be paid to Seller at closing but for $1-3 million (and sometimes more) to be placed in escrow, and then released at the end of a specified period (usually twelve to thirty-six months) if the Buyer does not raise indemnification claims or disputes within that period.

While the reasons for creating an indemnification escrow are simple and obvious, the tax consequences are not. In a taxable transaction, an escrow account usually contains cash, but may also contain stock of the Buyer. In a tax-free transaction, by contrast, an escrow usually contains stock of an Acquirer, but may also contain cash. In all escrows, the cash is almost always invested so that it earns interest income while sitting in the escrow account. Stock held in the escrow sometimes earns dividends while in escrow and almost always has voting rights. The question of who or what person, if any, is supposed to pay tax on this income is a surprisingly nuanced and complicated issue.

In some early cases, the courts concluded that income earned in escrow was not required to be reported by anyone until the identity of the payee was established.[47] However, the Technical and Miscellaneous Revenue Act of 1998[48] provided considerable clarity to this area by enacting Code section 468B(g), which reads as follows:

> Nothing in any provision of law shall be construed as providing that an escrow account, settlement fund, or similar fund is not subject to current income tax. The Secretary shall prescribe regulations providing for the taxation of any such account or fund whether as a grantor trust or otherwise.

In January 1999, the IRS issued proposed regulations under Code section 468B, Prop. Reg. § 1.468B-8, covering "contingent at closing escrow". A "contingent at closing escrow" is defined as any escrow account satisfying the following three requirements:[49]

1. The escrow is established in connection with the sale or exchange (other than an exchange to which Code section 354, 355, or 356 applies) of real or personal property used in a trade or business or held for investment (including stock in a corporation or an interest in a partnership).

2. Depending on whether events specified in the purchase agreement that are subject to bona fide contingencies occur or fail to occur, the escrow's assets (except for assets set aside for taxes or expense) are distributable entirely to the Buyer, entirely to the Seller, or in part to the Buyer with the remainder to the Seller. Bona fide contingencies do not include events that are certain, or reasonably certain, to occur, such as the passage of time, or that are certain, or reasonably certain, not to occur.

3. The escrow is not a qualified escrow account or a qualified trust established in connection with a deferred exchange under Code section 1031(a)(3).

Under the proposed regulations, the Buyer is treated as owning the assets of the "contingent at closing escrow" for the period prior to the date on which the last of the events subject to a bona fide contingency either has or has not occurred. (This is referred to as the "determination date".)[50] Therefore, all the escrow's items of income, deduction, and credit are included in the Buyer's income for this period. The proposed regulations address only the issue of who is taxed under Code section 468B on income earned by the escrow account. The proposed regulations specifically state that no inference should be drawn concerning the tax treatment of a "contingent at closing escrow", or of parties to the escrow, under Code sections other than Code section 468B.

There are a number of important issues on which the proposed regulations are silent. For example, if the Seller is reporting the escrow sale proceeds on the installment method and later receives both the escrow amount and the interest that has been previously taxed to the Buyer, there is no explanation of how the Seller should properly report this transaction. Arguably the aggregate amount received by the Seller should be treated as a deferred payment of the purchase price so that a portion of the payment would be characterized as imputed interest (or OID) under Code section 1274, and the remainder would be characterized as proceeds from a stock sale. This means that the Seller would have an appropriate amount of interest income (or OID), and the Buyer would be allowed a deduction for the amount of payment recharacterized as interest (or OID). From a practical standpoint, this would have the effect of giving the Buyer an interest deduction that should offset, or substantially offset, the interest taxed to the Buyer under Proposed Reg. § 1.468B-8.

Under the present rules, including the proposed regulations under Code section 468B (which are not formally binding on taxpayers until adopted by the IRS), the Seller and Buyer can generally agree on the structure of the escrow such that the escrow funds can be treated as sale proceeds triggering gain or loss recognized immediately by the Seller or, if preferable, as money that belongs to the Buyer until all the contingencies are resolved and the escrow funds are released to the Seller. To defer tax recognition to the Seller while protecting the funds from access by the Buyer, the parties could use a so-called "Rabbi trust". To produce immediate tax recognition by the Seller, the parties could use a so-called "secular trust". In the case of a "Rabbi trust", the escrowed funds are reachable by creditors of the Buyer during the escrow period. In the case of a "secular trust", the gain to the Seller is recognized immediately, the escrowed funds are not reachable by creditors of the Buyer, and the economic benefits of the escrowed funds (including any interest that accrues on the funds) inure to the benefit of the Seller.

IMPUTED INTEREST AND OID RULES (CODE SECTIONS 483 AND 1274)

When there is a deferred payment in a sale or exchange of nonpublicly traded property and adequate stated interest is not provided on the deferred payment, a portion of the payment will be recharacterized as interest for federal income tax purposes under Code section 483 or 1274. The main set of rules governing such deferred payments is set forth in Code section 1274. Code section 483 covers certain sales and exchanges not covered by Code section 1274. A significant difference between the two provisions is that interest imputed under Code section 1274 is subject to the OID rules of Code sections 1272 and 1273 and must be reported by the Buyer and Seller each year whether or not any payment is made during the year. Under Code section 483, imputed interest is taken into account in accordance with the taxpayer's method of accounting.

The OID rules are very complicated, but their intention is quite simple: all debt instruments, including those given for property in an installment sale, are required to charge a minimum rate of interest (referred to as "adequate stated interest"). Interest is adequate stated interest if it equals the applicable federal rate (which is redetermined each month and varies depending on the term of the debt instrument), compounded semiannually. If this minimum rate of interest is not charged, interest is imputed to the debt instruments at the applicable federal rate. The amount of imputed interest (OID) determined under these rules is then taken into account by both the holder of the debt and the issuer (i.e., the Seller and the Buyer in a sale of property) using the accrual method of accounting, without regard to when the actual payments are made. The applicable federal rate is actually three rates: (i) the federal short-term rate applies to debt instruments with a term (maturity date) of not over three years; (ii) the federal mid-term rate applies to debt instruments with a term of over three years but not over nine years; and (iii) the federal long-term rate applies to debt instruments with a term of over nine years. These rates are published monthly by the IRS in the IRS Bulletin.

A substantial portion of the OID rules deal with debt instruments that do not require adequate stated interest on deferred payments. Although most of these rules are not relevant to the rules under Code section 1274, which deals with nonpublicly traded debt instruments that are issued in consideration for the sale or exchange of nonpublicly traded property, a brief summary of important terminology is required. OID is defined as the difference between a debt instrument's "stated redemption price at maturity" and its "issue price".[51] The concept is that if a bond is sold at a discount (i.e., below its redemption price at maturity), the difference between the issue price and the redemption price reflects built-in interest. For example, if a bond is issued for $7,000 and is redeemable in five years at $10,000, the $3,000 "discount" on original issue is OID and will be accrued as the equivalent of interest ratably over the applicable period.

A debt instrument with an issue price of $10,000 and a stated redemption price at maturity of $10,000 can have OID under Code section 1274 if it does not pay "adequate stated interest" (i.e., interest at a rate equal to or in excess of the applicable federal rate (AFR)) unconditionally at fixed periodic intervals of one year or less during the entire term of the debt instrument. If the stated interest is payable at fixed periodic intervals of one year or less during the entire term of the debt instrument, but the rate of interest is below the AFR, OID will be imputed to bring the total interest rate (stated and imputed) up to the AFR.

Example 10: Assume Buyer gives Seller an installment note on January 1 of Year 1 to purchase unimproved land held for more than one year with tax basis in the hands of Seller of $100,000. Assume Buyer delivers to Seller, as full payment for such purchase, a promissory note in the original face amount of $1 million, bearing no stated interest, and payable as a single balloon payment on January 1 of Year 3. Assume the applicable federal short-term rate at the time of the purchase is five percent per annum. Seller is treated as receiving an installment note with an imputed principal amount of $907,029.48 and OID of $92,970.52 ($1 million – $907,029.48). Seller is deemed to have sold the land for $907,029.48, plus interest accruing at a rate of five percent per annum over the next two years. Assume no election is made under Code section 1274A. Buyer will be deemed to pay, and Seller to receive, $45,351.48 of OID in Year 1, and $47,619.04 of OID in Year 2. In Year 3, Seller will be deemed to receive a payment of $907,029.48 for the land, in which Seller has a tax basis of $100,000, so Seller will report long-term capital gain of $807,029.48 in Year 3.

The Seller must report as income any OID accrued with respect to the debt instrument in the year of such accrual, whether or not any payment is made to the Seller in that year. In addition, as noted above, all OID payments accruing under a debt instrument are subtracted in determining the Seller's sales proceeds in applying the installment sale rules for purposes of Code section 453. Thus, it is often practical to state adequate interest (usually at the lowest AFR applicable to the transaction) so that the parties to the transaction clearly understand the respective amounts of principal and interest in a deferred payment transaction.

The Buyer deducts OID under Code section 163(e), as the OID accrues, not when the interest is actually paid. The Buyer subtracts the OID from the amounts paid to the Seller in determining the Buyer's tax basis in the acquired assets.

Code section 1274 applies to any debt instrument issued in exchange for property if: (1) the stated redemption price at maturity exceeds the stated principal amount, if there is adequate stated interest, or the imputed principal amount of the debt instrument, in any other case, and (2) some or all of the payments due under such debt instrument are due more than six months after the date of such sale or exchange.[52] However, Code section 1274 does not apply to the following:[53]

- A debt instrument that is publicly traded or issued for publicly traded property.
- A debt instrument arising from the sale or exchange of a farm for $1 million or less by an individual, estate, or testamentary trust, small business corporation, or a partnership that meets requirements similar to those that must be met by a corporation to qualify as a small business corporation.
- A debt instrument arising from the sale or exchange by an individual of the individual's principal residence.
- A debt instrument arising from the sale or exchange of property for $250,000 or less.
- In the case of a sale or transfer of substantial rights to a patent, any amount contingent on the productivity, use or disposition of the property transferred.
- A debt instrument to the extent it is governed by Code section 483(e) (involving certain land transfers between related parties).

A detailed discussion of the scope and nuances of the OID rules is beyond the scope of this book. However, some examples will help illustrate and hopefully illuminate this very important aspect of sale transactions. As noted above, the "simple" way to avoid having to deal with OID on an installment sale is to provide for adequate stated interest in the debt instrument and by making such stated interest payable at least annually or more frequently over the entire term of the debt instrument.

Examples from § 1.1274-1 Regulations. The following examples illustrate the rules of this section.

Example (1): *Single stated rate paid semiannually.* A debt instrument issued in consideration for the sale of nonpublicly traded property in a transaction that is not a potentially abusive situation calls for the payment of a principal amount of $1,000,000 at the end of a ten-year term and twenty semiannual interest payments of $60,000. Assume that the test rate of interest is 12 percent, compounded semiannually. The debt instrument is not subject to section 1274 because it provides for interest equal to the test rate and all interest payable on the instrument is qualified stated interest.

Example (2): A purchases an office building from B on December 31, 2003, for a purchase price of $10,000,000. However, payments are not due until December 31, 2005. If we assume that the short-term accrual of federal rate is 5 percent, compounded annually, then the present value of $10 million due two years from now, and discounted at a 5 percent rate, produces an imputed principal amount of $9,070,294.78. In this example, the stated principal amount of maturity is $10,000,000 and the imputed issue price is $9,070,294.78, so the difference is OID in the amount of $929,705.22. This OID will be accrued ratably under economic accrual principals, for the tax years 2003 and 2004. The exact payment amounts of OID attributes each year are $453,514.74 for the first year and $476,190.48 for the second year.

Comment: This all makes basic mathematical sense, because if the sale price was $9,070,294.78, and the interest rate was 5 percent, the amount of interest that would accrue on $9,070,294.78 over the first year would be $453,514.74. In turn, if this $453,514.74 amount is treated as added to principal, including the amount loaned to the Borrower, so that the principal amount for year two is now $9,523,809.52, then the 5 percent interest charged on this new amount would be $476,190.48.

Examples from Regulation § 1.1274-2(h). Each example assumes a 30-day month, 360-day year. In addition, each example assumes that the debt instrument is not a qualified debt instrument (as defined in Code section 1274A(b)) and is not issued in a potentially abusive situation.

Example (1): *Debt instrument without a fixed rate over its entire term.* (i) *Facts.* On January 1, 1995,

A sells nonpublicly traded property to B for a stated purchase price of \$3,500,000. In consideration for the sale, B makes a down payment of \$500,000 and issues a ten-year debt instrument with a stated principal amount of \$3,000,000, payable at maturity. The debt instrument calls for no interest in the first 2 years and interest at a rate of 15 percent payable annually over the remaining 8 years of the debt instrument. The first interest payment of \$450,000 is due on December 31, 1997, and the last interest payment is due on December 31, 2004, together with the \$3,000,000 payment of principal. Assume that the test rate of interest applicable to the debt instrument is 10.5 percent, compounded annually.

(ii) *Applicability of section 1274.* Because the debt instrument does not provide for any interest during the first 2 years, none of the interest on the debt instrument is qualified stated interest. Therefore, the issue price of the debt instrument is determined under section 1274. See Reg. § 1.1274-1(b)(1). If the debt instrument has adequate stated interest, the issue price of the instrument is its stated principal amount. Otherwise, the issue price of the debt instrument is its imputed principal amount. The debt instrument has adequate stated interest only if the stated principal amount is less than or equal to the imputed principal amount.

(iii) *Determination of imputed principal amount.* To compute the imputed principal amount of the debt instrument, all payments due under the debt instrument are discounted back to the issue date at 10.5 percent, compounded annually, as follows:

(A) The present value of the \$3,000,000 principal payment payable on December 31, 2004, is \$1,105,346.59, determined as follows:

$$\$1,105,347.59 = \frac{\$3,000,000}{(1+.105/1)^{10}}$$

(B) The present value of the eight interest payments of \$450,000 as of January 1, 1997, is \$2,357,634.55, determined as follows:

$$\$2,357,634.55 = \frac{\$450,000 \times 1-(1+.105/1)^{-8}}{(.105/1)}$$

(C) The present value of this interim amount as of January 1, 1995, is \$1,930,865.09, determined as follows:

$$\$1,930,865.09 = \frac{\$2,357,634.55}{(1+.105/1)^{2}}$$

(iv) *Determination of issue price.* The debt instrument's imputed principal amount (that is, the present value of all payments due under the debt instrument) is \$3,036,211.68 (\$1,105,346.59 + \$1,930,865.09). Because the stated principal amount (\$3,000,000) is less than the imputed principal amount, the debt instrument provides for adequate stated interest. Therefore, the issue price of the debt instrument is its stated principal amount (\$3,000,000).

Example (2): *Debt instrument subject to issuer call option.* (i) *Facts.* On January 1, 1995, in partial consideration for the sale of nonpublicly traded property, H Corporation issues to G a ten-year debt instrument, maturing on January 1, 2005, with a stated principal amount of \$10,000,000, payable on that date. The debt instrument provides for annual payments of interest of 8 percent for the first five years and 14 percent for the final five years, payable on January 1 of each year, beginning on January 1, 1996. In addition, the debt instrument provides H with the unconditional option to call (prepay) the debt instrument at the end of five years for its stated principal amount of \$10,000,000. Assume that the Federal mid-term and long-term rates applicable to the sale based on annual compounding are 9 percent and 10 percent, respectively.

(ii) *Option presumed exercised.* Assuming exercise of the call option, the imputed principal amount as determined under paragraph (d) of this section is \$9,611,034.87 (the present value of all of the payments due within a five-year term discounted at a test rate of 9 percent, compounded annually). Assuming nonexercise of the call option, the imputed principal amount is \$10,183,354.78 (the present value of all of the payments due within a ten-year term discounted at a test rate of 10 percent, compounded annually). For purposes of determining the imputed principal amount, the option is presumed exercised because the imputed principal amount, assuming exercise of the option, is less than the imputed principal amount, assuming the option is not exercised. Because the option is presumed exercised, the debt instrument fails to provide for adequate stated interest because the imputed principal amount ($9,611,034.87) is less than the stated principal amount ($10,000,000). Thus, the issue price of the debt instrument is $9,611,034.87.

Example (3): *Variable rate debt instrument with a single rate over its entire term.*

Facts. On January 1, 1995, A sells B nonpublicly traded property. In partial consideration for the sale, B issues a debt instrument in the principal amount of $1,000,000, payable in five years. The debt instrument calls for interest payable monthly at a rate of 1 percentage point above the average prime lending rate of a major bank for the month preceding the month of the interest payment. Assume that the test rate of interest applicable to the debt instrument is 10.5 percent, compounded monthly. Assume also that 1 percentage point above the prime lending rate of the designated bank on the date of the sale is 12.5 percent, compounded monthly, which is greater than 1 percentage point above the prime lending rate of the designated bank on the first date on which there is a binding written contract that substantially sets forth the terms under which the sale is consummated.

Debt instrument has adequate stated interest. The debt instrument is a variable rate debt instrument (within the meaning of Reg. § 1.1275-5) that provides for stated interest at a qualified floating rate. Under paragraph [Reg. § 1.1274-2](f)(1)(i) of this section, the debt instrument is treated as if it provided for a fixed rate of interest equal to 12.5 percent, compounded monthly. Because the test rate of interest is 10.5 percent, compounded monthly, the debt instrument provides for adequate stated interest.

Example (4): *Debt instrument with a capped variable rate.* On July 1, 1995, A sells nonpublicly traded property to B in return for a debt instrument with a stated principal amount of $10,000,000, payable on July 1, 2005. Interest is payable on July 1 of each year, beginning on July 1, 1996, at the Federal short-term rate for June of the same year. The debt instrument provides, however, that the interest rate cannot rise above 8.5 percent, compounded annually. Assume that, as of the date the test rate of interest for the debt instrument is determined, the Federal short-term rate is 8 percent, compounded annually. Assume further that, as a result of the interest rate cap of 8.5 percent, compounded annually, the expected yield of the debt instrument is significantly less than the expected yield of the debt instrument if it did not include the interest rate cap. Under paragraph [Reg. § 1.1274-2(f)(1)(ii)] of this section, the variable payments are treated as contingent payments for purposes of this section.

CHAPTER ENDNOTES

1. IRC Sec. 453(b)(1).
2. IRC Sec. 453(k)(2)(A).
3. IRC Sec. 453(d).
4. Temp. Reg. § 15A.453-1(b)(2).
5. Temp. Reg. § 15A.453-1(b)(2)(v).
6. Temp. Reg. § 15A.453-1(b)(2)(ii).
7. Temp. Reg. § 15A.453-1(b)(2)(iii).
8. See IRC Sec. 1274.
9. IRC Sec. 453(f)(4).
10. IRC Sec. 453(f)(3).
11. See Temp. Reg. § 15A.453-1(b)(3)(iii).
12. See Temp. Reg. § 15A.453-1(b)(3)(i).
13. IRC Sec. 453(f)(1).
14. IRC Sec. 453(i).
15. IRC Sec. 453(d)(3).
16. IRC Sec. 453(b)(2)(A).
17. IRC Sec. 453(l).
18. IRC Sec. 453A(c)(2).
19. IRC Sec. 453A(c)(3).
20. Rev. Rul. 79-371, 1979-2 CB 294.
21. Rev. Rul. 72-264, 1972-1 CB 131.
22. 499 U.S. 554 (1991).
23. Reg. § 1.1001-3.
24. IRC Sec. 453A(d)(1).
25. IRC Sec. 453B(c).
26. IRC Sec. 691(a)(4).
27. IRC Sec. 691(a)(3).
28. IRC Sec. 691(a)(5).
29. See, e.g., IRS Letter Ruling 8622002, February 20, 1986 (installment method not applicable where payment was made in certificates of deposit).

30. IRC Sec. 453(f)(4).
31. Temp. Reg. § 15A.453-1(e)(3).
32. IRC Sec. 453(f)(5).
33. Temp. Reg. § 15A.453-1(e)(5).
34. Reg. §15A.453-1(c)(1).
35. Temp. Reg. § 15A.453-1(c)(1).
36. Reg. § 1.1275-4(c).
37. See generally IRC Sec. 1274.
38. Reg. § 1.1275-4(c)(4).
39. Reg. § 1.1275-5(c)(4)(ii).
40. Reg. § 1.1275-4(c)(7).
41. Temp. Reg. § 15A.453-1(c).
42. Temp. Reg. § 15A.453-1(c)(2)(i)(A).
43. See Rev. Rul. 68-13, 1968-1 CB 195.
44. Temp. Reg. § 15A.453-1(c)(3).
45. Rev. Rul. 74-175, 1974-1 CB 52.
46. See IRC Sec. 1212.
47. See, e.g., *C. Chaplin*, 136 F2d 298 (9th Circuit 1943) (dividends paid on escrow stock were not taxable until distributed out of escrow).
48. P.L. 100-647.
49. Prop. Reg. § 1.468B-8(b).
50. Prop. Reg. § 1.468B-8(c).
51. IRC Sec. 1273(a)(1)
52. IRC Sec. 1274(c)(1).
53. IRC Sec. 1274(c)(3).

AMORTIZATION OF INTANGIBLES—CODE SECTION 197

CHAPTER 11

OVERVIEW

Intangible property is the driving engine of the U.S. economy and much of the international economy. Studies have shown that whereas thirty or forty years ago, intangible property represented approximately 30 percent of the total value on the balance sheet of a typical corporation, today it represents on average an estimated 70 percent of the total value. This reflects the fact that the modern economy no longer creates wealth with large amounts of expensive tangible property, but rather relies on intangible assets. In effect, steel mills and shoe factories have been replaced with patents, trademarks, know-how, goodwill, and other similar "assets." Given recent trends in history, it seems likely that this evolution and direction will continue well into the future.

The tax treatment of intangibles has developed, rather belatedly, as intangibles have surged in importance. Before the Revenue Reconciliation Act of 1993 (P.L. 103-66), amortization of intangibles was a major source of litigation between taxpayers and the IRS. Under prior law, "goodwill" was not considered amortizable for income tax purposes based on the IRS's position, asserted in regulations, that goodwill does not have a useful life that can be estimated with reasonable certainty. Therefore, the regulations mandated that no deduction was allowable with respect to goodwill.[1] However, because taxpayers are loath to pay good money for a non-amortizable or non-depreciable asset, various efforts—often highly creative—were made to identify specific assets, within the category of goodwill, which had a reasonably determinable useful life. See, e.g., the Supreme Court case of *Newark Morning Ledger Co.*,[2] in which the Supreme Court held that "a taxpayer able to prove that a particular asset can be valued and that it has a limited useful life may depreciate its value over its useful life regardless of how much the asset appears to reflect the expectancy of continued patronage . . . " In that case, the taxpayer, which acquired the publishers of daily and Sunday newspapers in eight communities, allocated a substantial portion of the purchase price to an asset that it identified as "paid subscribers," and then amortized these assets on a straight-line basis over their estimated useful lives, which it estimated ranged from 14.7 to 23.4 years.

Contemporaneous with the *Newark Morning Ledger Co.* case, taxpayers developed new kinds of assets (e.g., "workforce in place") which were intended to have a value and an amortizable life over which their cost would be recovered. Endless rounds of litigation ensued over (1) whether the identified asset actually existed at all, (2) what part of the purchase price should be allocated to this asset, and (3) the proper period of time for recovering this cost.

In response to the endless legal disputes over the amortization of goodwill, Congress enacted Code section 197, which provided for the first time a comprehensive set of rules not only for goodwill and noncompete payments, but also for all kinds of intangible assets acquired in connection with the sale of a business. As will be discussed more fully below, Code section 197 allows any "Section 197 intangible" to be amortized on a straight-line basis over a fifteen-year period.

Code section 197 is an important provision in the Code and grows more so every year as intangible assets become increasingly dominant in the U.S. and international economy. Part of Code section 197's importance is probably unintentional: It is the one section of the Code that makes a relatively detailed effort to address the definition of a variety of categories of intangible assets. Basically, because the nature of intangible assets is inherently abstract (hence the term intangible) the very amorphousness of the asset category almost necessarily cries out for a concrete definition. Code section 197 does that by providing a detailed description of a wide variety of common intangible assets.

In contrast to the rules of Code section 197, which generally apply when intangible assets are acquired in connection with a business or a substantial interest in a business, it is useful to briefly discuss the treatment of self-created intangible assets. In general, the costs associated with creating most intangible assets are deductible as research expenses under Code section 174 or as ordinary and necessary business expenses under Code section 162. Indeed, it is not unusual for a self-created intangible asset to have little or no tax basis, given the deductibility of most of the expenses incurred to create it.

When the costs incurred to create an intangible asset are required to be capitalized as basis in the asset, the regulations under Code section 167 permit the depreciation of such costs if the useful life of the asset can be reasonably estimated. If an intangible asset is known from experience or other factors to be of use in a business only for a limited period of time, the length of which can be estimated with reasonable accuracy, the asset may be subject to the depreciation allowance.[3] Examples used in the regulations are patents and copyrights. Conversely, an intangible asset whose useful life is not limited is not subject to the allowance for depreciation. No allowance is permitted merely because, in the unsupported opinion of the taxpayer, the intangible asset has a limited useful life.[4]

With respect to intangible assets created on or after December 31, 2003 (other than intangible assets that have a useful life that can be estimated with reasonable accuracy and intangible assets purchased from another person), a safe harbor permits taxpayers to treat the intangible asset as having a useful life equal to fifteen years solely for the purpose of determining the depreciation allowance.[5]

OVERVIEW OF CODE SECTION 197

General Rule

Code section 197 provides that a taxpayer is entitled to an amortization deduction with respect to any "amortizable Section 197 intangible."[6] The amount of such deduction is determined by amortizing the adjusted basis of such intangible ratably over the fifteen-year period beginning with the month in which such intangible was acquired.[7]

The deduction allowed under Code section 197(a) is the exclusive mechanism for amortizing or depreciating any amortizable Section 197 intangible. No other depreciation or amortization deduction is allowable.[8]

The term "amortizable Section 197 intangible" means any Section 197 intangible that (1) is acquired by the taxpayer after the date of the enactment of Code section 197 (August 10, 1993) and (2) that is held in connection with the conduct of a trade or business or an activity described in Code section 212. However, the term "amortizable Section 197 intangible" does not include so-called "self-created intangibles," meaning intangibles created by the taxpayer, unless the intangible involves (1) rights granted by a government, (2) a covenant not to compete entered into in connection with an acquisition of an interest in a trade or business, or (3) any franchise, trademark, or trade name[9] Note that even the relatively rare categories of "self-created intangibles" that fall within Code Section 197 are not subject to Section 197 if such intangibles are created in connection with a transaction or series of related transactions involving the acquisition of assets constituting a trade or business or substantial portion of a trade or business.[10]

Effective Date

In general, Code section 197 applies to property acquired after August 10, 1993. However, taxpayers could elect for Code section 197 to have an effective date of July 25, 1991. In addition, taxpayers could have elected not to apply Code section 197 to any binding contract that was in effect on August 10, 1993, provided that the taxpayer did not also elect to treat July 25, 1991, as the effective date.

"SECTION 197 INTANGIBLE" DEFINED

Code section 197(d) defines "Section 197 intangible" to mean:

1. Goodwill.

2. Going concern value.

3. Any of the following intangibles:

   a. Workforce in place, including its composition and terms and conditions (contractual or otherwise) of its employment,

   b. Business books and records, operating systems, or any other information base (including lists or other information with respect to current or prospective customers).

   c. Any patent, copyright, formula, process, design, pattern, know-how, format, or other similar item.

   d. Any customer-based intangible.

   e. Any supplier-based intangible.

   f. Any other similar item.

4. Any license, permit, or other right granted by a governmental unit or an agency or instrumentality thereof.

5. Any covenant not to compete (or other arrangement to the extent such arrangement has substantially the same effect as a covenant not to compete) entered into in connection with an acquisition (directly or indirectly) of an interest in a trade or business or a substantial portion thereof.

6. Any franchise, trademark, or trade name.

Comment: Under the list of items in 3 (corresponding to Code section 197(d)(1)(C)(i through vi)), Code section 197 applies to "any other similar item" to those found in that list. However, the legislative history provides no indication as to the scope of this provision and really gives the IRS legislative flexibility to identify additional items and address them with the regulations.

Another significant expansion of the list of Section 197 intangibles is a provision in the regulations providing that any right under a license, contract, or other arrangement for the use of a Section 197 intangible is itself a Section 197 intangible.[11] In addition, a term interest, whether outright or in trust, in any Section 197 intangible is itself a Section 197 intangible.[12] Conversely, it stands to reason that if one of the exclusions from the definition of Section 197 intangible applies to a particular asset, then any right under a license, contract, or other arrangement for the use of that asset should not constitute a Section 197 intangible.

Exclusions from Definition of Section 197 Intangible

Code section 197(e) excludes the following assets from the definition of a Section 197 intangible:

1. Any interest in a corporation, partnership, trust, or estate, or any interest under an existing futures contract, foreign currency contract, notional principal contract, or other similar financial contract.

2. Any interest in land.

3. Computer software that is readily available for purchase by the general public if it is subject to a nonexclusive license and has not been substantially modified and other computer software not acquired as part of the acquisition of a trade or business.

4. Any of the following if not acquired in a transaction involving the acquisition of assets constituting a trade or business:

   a. Any interest in a film, sound recording, videotape, book, or similar property.

   b. Any right to receive tangible property or services under a contract or granted by a governmental unit or agency or instrumentality thereof.

   c. Any interest in a patent or copyright.

   d. Any right to receive tangible property or services under a contract or from a governmental unit.[13]

5. Any interest under an existing lease of tangible property (thus, that portion of a leasehold that is attributable to a favorable location, for example, is not a separate Section 197 intangible) and any interest in existing indebtedness.

6. A franchise to engage in a professional sport, and any item acquired in connection with such a franchise, if acquired on or before October 22, 2004.

7. Any right to service indebtedness that is secured by residential real property unless the right is acquired in a transaction (or series of related transactions) involving the acquisition of assets constituting a trade or business. Such rights are amortizable over nine years.[14]

8. Fees for professional services, and any transaction costs, incurred by parties to a tax-free reorganization. Such amounts are not deductible under the U.S. Supreme Court's decision in *INDOPCO, Inc.*[15]

In general, the excluded assets fall into two basic categories: (1) those that are excluded from the definition of Section 197 intangible regardless of how the assets are acquired and (2) assets that are potentially Section 197 intangibles, but are not acquired in connection with the acquisition of trade or business or a substantial portion of a trade or business. This latter category of assets is sometimes referred to as "separately acquired" assets. Excluded assets in the first category are amortizable or depreciable, if at all, under other sections of the Code. The assets in the second category -- separately acquired assets -- are typically used in the trade or business of the acquirer and are depreciated under Code section 167.[16]

Although it often seems relatively clear which assets are included or excluded from the definition of a Code section 197 intangible, it is in the nature of intangible assets to be subject to sophisticated evolution and permutation at the hands of savvy, tax-motivated professionals. Although Code section 197 covers many categories of intangible assets, there remains a sophisticated effort to convert some excluded assets into Section 197 intangibles, particularly if the otherwise excluded asset would not be amortizable or deductible under other code sections.

The assets excluded from Code section 197 have been excluded for reasons inherent in each of the types of assets. For example, the various financial interests excluded by Code section 197(e) (1) (e.g., an interest in a corporation, partnership, trust, or estate) must be excluded from any type of amortization, to be consistent with the history of the Code.

Code section 197(e)(2) excludes any interest in land, because land has never been depreciable under any provision of the Code.

Certain kinds of computer software, notably so-called "off the shelf" software, are excluded as Section 197 intangibles and are amortizable over three years.[17] Such software generally has a very short useful life, and a fifteen-year amortization period would be inappropriate. Interests in leases of tangible property present a very interesting situation. Code section 197(e)(5) excludes any interest, either as a lessor or as a lessee, in an existing lease of tangible property. In general, with respect to an acquisition of an interest in property in which there is an underlying lease, and where the acquirer becomes a lessor, Code section 167(c)(2) provides that no portion of the adjusted basis of the property is allocated to the leasehold interest. Instead, the entire adjusted basis is to be taken into account in determining depreciation deductions with respect to the property subject to the lease. Code section 167(c)(2) was enacted in 1993 at the same time as Code section 197. Legislative history to Code section 197 provides, as an illustration, that if a taxpayer acquires a shopping center leased to tenants operating retail stores, the portion of the purchase price of the shopping center attributable to favorable characteristics of the leases will be added to the basis of the shopping center.

By contrast, the cost of acquiring an interest as a lessee in an existing lease arrangement, which is excluded from Code section 197, is amortizable in accordance with Code section 178 and the regulations under Code section 162. In particular, to the extent any premium is paid to acquire an interest as a lessee in a lease (because the lease rent is below market), the premium is deductible ratably over the remaining term of the lease.[18] Code section 178 provides that the term of the lease includes all renewal option periods, as well as other periods for which the parties reasonably expect the lease to be renewed, if less than 75 percent of the cost of the lease is attributable to the remaining term of the lease.[19]

Example 1: On January 1, 1959, Lessee A pays $10,000 to acquire a lease of twenty years with two options exercisable by A to renew for periods of five years each. Of the total $10,000 cost to acquire the lease, $7,000 was paid for the original twenty-year lease period, and the balance of $3,000 was paid for the renewal options. Since the $7,000 cost of acquiring the initial lease is less than 75 percent of the $10,000 cost of the lease ($7,500), the term of the lease should be treated as including the original lease period and the two renewal periods, or thirty years.[20]

When intangible assets acquired in a business acquisition transaction are amortizable over fifteen years, and at the same time there is an acquisition of a lessee's interest in a lease of tangible property with a considerably shorter term remaining, purchasers might be tempted to assign as much of the purchase price as possible to the leasehold interest to accelerate the enjoyment of tax benefits. Code section 197 legislative history anticipates this situation and requires that the portion of the total purchase price that is allocable to the interest as a lessee is not to exceed the excess of (1) the present value of the fair market value rent for the use of the tangible property for the term of the lease, over (2) the present value of the rent reasonably expected to be paid for the use of the tangible property for the term of the lease.[21]

Code section 197(e)(7) excludes transaction costs, which are "any fees for professional services, and any transaction costs, incurred by parties to a transaction with respect to which any portion of the gain or loss is not recognized under Part III of subchapter C." This exclusion is viewed as the embodiment of the Supreme Court decision in *INDOPCO*.[22] By virtue of being excluded from Code section 197, transaction costs are not automatically amortizable over fifteen years. Rather, under the *INDOPCO* authority the cost must be capitalized under Code section 263, but may be amortizable or deductible, depending on whether such costs are allocable to any specific amortizable or depreciable assets.

Various assets that would otherwise be subject to Code section 197 if acquired as part of the acquisition of a business are not governed by this provision if acquired separately. Such assets are listed in Code section 197(e)(4) and also include computer software under Code section 197(e)(3)(A)(ii). Rules for determining when an asset or group of assets constitutes a trade or business or a substantial portion of a trade or business are set forth in Reg. § 1.197-2(e). For example, an asset or group of assets constitutes a trade or business or a substantial portion of a trade or business if goodwill or going concern value under any circumstances can attach to the assets.[23] The acquisition of a franchise, trademark, or trade name automatically constitutes the acquisition of a trade or business or substantial portion of a trade or business.[24]

RULES APPLICABLE TO COMPUTER SOFTWARE

Computer software that is excluded from the definition of a "Section 197 intangible" is generally eligible for depreciation or amortization using one of the following three methods: (1) inclusion in the cost of the accompanying computer hardware and recovered over the period applicable to the hardware, (2) recovered ratably over thirty-six months beginning with the month the software is placed in service, or (3) expensed pursuant to Code section 179.

So-called "off the shelf" software is expressly excluded from the definition of Section 197 intangibles. This benefits taxpayers because such software is typically amortized on a straight-line basis over thirty-six months.[25] Off-the-shelf software is defined in Code section 197(e)(3)(A)(i) as software that (1) is readily available for purchase by the general public, (2) is subject to a non-exclusive license, and (3) has not been substantially modified.

Comment: The exception is broad and not limited to so-called "shrink wrap" software that is typically sold in retail stores. The definition of off-the-shelf software describes software that has "not been substantially modified," suggesting that it can be modified a little bit, just not too much. The "not substantially modified" requirement is satisfied if the cost of all modifications to the version of the software that is readily available to the general public does not exceed the greater of 25 percent of the price at which the unmodified version of the software is readily available to the general public or $2,000. The requirement that the software be readily available to the general public can be met even though the software is not available through a system of retail distribution.[26]

Code section 197 also excludes "separately acquired" software, which means software not acquired in a transaction (or series of related transactions) involving the acquisition of assets constituting a trade or business or a substantial portion of a trade or business. Such software is amortized over thirty-six months.[27]

SELF-CREATED INTANGIBLES

In General

"Self-created intangibles" are generally not "amortizable Section 197 in-tangibles."[28] Self-created intangibles are intangibles that are created by the taxpayer but are not created in connection with a transaction (or series of transactions) that involves the acquisition of assets that constitute a substantial portion or all of a trade or business. These intangibles are expensed or deducted in the usual manner. For example, a company's costs of developing a "workforce in place" (e.g., by sponsoring a training program) would generally be deductible as an ordinary and necessary business expense. Similarly, general advertising costs should be currently deductible even though advertising serves to increase the company's goodwill.

Exception

Certain Section 197 intangibles are subject to fifteen-year amortization even if self-created. These are (1) governmental licenses and permits (e.g., liquor licenses and broadcast rights), (2) covenants not to compete entered into in connection with the acquisition of a trade or business (which should be excluded from the definition of self-created anyway), and (3) franchises, trademarks, and trade names.[29] For example, the capitalized costs incurred in connection with the development and registration of a trademark or trade name are amortized over fifteen years.

ANTI-CHURNING RULES

Overview of the Rules

Special anti-churning rules are provided in Code section 197(f)(9) to prevent taxpayers from converting goodwill or going concern value, or any other Section 197 intangible for which a depreciation or amortization deduction would not be allowable but for Code section 197 into amortizable Section 197 intangibles. These rules apply if:

1. the intangible is acquired by the taxpayer after August 10, 1993; and
2. either:
    a. the taxpayer or a "related person" held or used the property at any time on or after July 25, 1991, and on or before August 10, 1993;
    b. the taxpayer acquires the property from a person who held the intangible at any time on or after July 25, 1991, and on or before August 10, 1993, and the user of the intangible does not change; or
    c. the taxpayer grants the right to use the intangible to a person (or a person related to that person) who held or used the intangible at any time on or after July 25, 1991, and on or before August 10, 1993.

Election Out

A taxpayer is not subject to the anti-churning rules if the person from whom the taxpayer acquired the intangible elects to recognize gain on the disposition of the intangible and pay a tax on that gain equal to the amount of the gain multiplied by the highest rate of income tax applicable to that person under the Code.[30]

Definition of Related Persons

For purposes of the anti-churning rules, Code section 197 applies the commonly used Section 267(b) and Section 707(b)(1) tests, as well as the common control test of Section 41(f)(1) to define when persons are related.[31] However, in applying the tests of Code sections 267(b) and 707(b)(1), a much lower 20-percent ownership standard is substituted for the 50-percent standard that would normally apply in those sections.[32] This makes it correspondingly more difficult to avoid these anti-churning restrictions.

Special Rule for Partnerships

With respect to any increase in the basis of partnership property under Code sections 732, 734, or 743, determinations are made at the partner level, with each partner treated as having owned and used the partner's proportionate share of partnership assets.[33]

Death

The anti-churning rules do not apply to acquisitions by reason of death.[34]

SPECIAL RULES

Contingent Purchase Price Adjustments

If a portion of the cost of acquiring an amortizable Section 197 asset is contingent (e.g., additional future payments may be made depending on specified factors or conditions), the adjusted basis of such asset is increased as of the beginning of the month that the additional amount is paid or incurred. This additional adjusted basis will then be amortized ratably over the remaining months in the fifteen-year amortization period.[35] The amount added to amortizable tax basis is determined in the same manner that the principal payment amount is determined on contingent amounts payable under a debt instrument given in consideration for the Section 197 intangible.[36]

Dispositions of Section 197 Intangibles

No loss is recognized on the disposition of Section 197 intangibles if the taxpayer retains other Section 197 intangibles acquired in the same or a series of related transactions.[37] Instead, the basis in the retained assets is increased.[38] For example, if a taxpayer acquires two trademarks in the same transaction for $100,000 each and one is abandoned as worthless after five years, then the $66,667 (i.e., $100,000 reduced by five years of amortization) of remaining amortization for that trademark is added to the basis of the other trademark and recovered over the remaining ten years.

Nonrecognition Events

In general, the transferee is treated as the transferor (and continues on the same fifteen-year amortization schedule started by the transferor) in transactions described in Code sections 332 (liquidations subsidiaries), 351 (incorporation transfers), 361 (mergers, etc.), 721 (contributions to partnerships), 731 (distributions by partnerships), 1031 (like-kind exchanges), and 1033 (involuntary conversions).[39]

FINAL THOUGHTS ON SECTION 197 INTANGIBLES

Realistically, fifteen-year amortization is acceptable but not great from the perspective of the Buyer. After all, consulting or compensation payments can be deducted immediately when paid, and tangible assets can generally be amortized over a five-year period. On the other hand, nonresidential real estate is egregiously unattractive, depreciable over thirty-nine years on a straight-line basis, and there are many types of tangible assets, such as depreciable machinery or other assets used in a trade or business, that are subject to recapture income in the hands of the Seller (see Chapter 3).

Another attribute of Section 197 intangibles is that it is often hard to put an intrinsic value on these assets. Unlike a truck or an automobile, which often has a relatively specific "blue book" value that can be readily accessed by many people (including IRS audit agents), there isn't always a readily available or widely accepted method for determining the value for intangibles.

Some assets have a statutory period of legal protection that may in fact be shorter, sometimes substantially shorter, than the fifteen-year amortization period provided by Code section 197. On the other hand, a patent may be an excludable asset under Code section 197(e)(4). Accordingly, buying patent rights that will enjoy legal protection for three years, when the patent expires, but have to be amortized over fifteen years is an unpalatable deal for the Buyer. The determination of whether a patent is an excludable asset depends on whether it was acquired in a transaction (or series of related transactions) involving the acquisition of assets constituting all or a substantial portion of a trade or business.

The regulations under Code section 197 attempt to address the almost metaphysical aspects of whether an acquisition of assets constitutes the acquisition of a trade or business. This all underscores essentially the unpalatable aspect of Code section 197, which stretches out the purchase price over a fifteen-year period, under the general notion that this is an appropriate legislative approximation of the value of an aggregated business, which is the core concept underlining Code section 197.

An interesting concept to bear in mind in the course of a negotiation, especially when it comes time to allocate purchase price among assets, is that straight-line fifteen-year amortization is "roughly" equivalent, on a present value basis, to deducting the entire intangible purchase price amount seven or eight years in the future. (This is not exactly right, because present value discounting is a geometric rather than arithmetic process, but for approximation purposes it is a useful estimate). In all events, if an amount were paid today and deducted seven years in the future, with an aggregate federal and state tax savings of 40 percent (representing an estimate of the combined federal and state tax on corporations at the maximum tax bracket), the present value benefit of such payments amortized over fifteen years is roughly 20 percent of the payment price. In other words, amortizing $1.00 over fifteen years is worth about half the tax savings (a 20-percent effective present value savings) that would be enjoyed if the payment were currently deductible (assuming $1.00 has a 40-percent present value benefit to the Buyer).

This very rough "rule of thumb" is useful in deciding, in a real-time negotiation, the approximate tax benefits of various allocations.

Note that the apportionment of the purchase price among assets is the central issue in a rational after-tax present value analysis, yet it is often done "on the fly" in the midst of the negotiation (and often after the purchase price has been set). As it should by now be clear, this process is entirely backwards, but it also rather accurately describes how the large majority of negotiations are conducted. Be prepared to fix the price first, then do tax allocations to determine the "real" price to each party. Realistically, armed with the simple rule of thumb described in this section, you will be ahead of other parties in understanding the real cost and benefit of an allocation strategy. Note also that if an allocation strategy has been agreed to (often at the end of a marathon negotiating session) and you shake hands on it, the chances are you can make it stick, especially if you write it down immediately and everyone signs off on it. In general, business negotiations are far closer to a marathon than to a sprint, and this is an important aspect of being ready to run the last mile of the negotiations.

CHAPTER ENDNOTES

1. See Reg. § 1.167(a)-3.
2. 507 U.S. 546, 113 S.Ct. 1670 (1930).
3. Treas. Reg. § 1.167(a)-3(a).
4. *Id.*
5. Treas. Reg. § 1.167(a)-3(b).
6. IRC Sec. 197(a).
7. *Id.*
8. IRC Sec. 197(b).
9. IRC Sec. 197(c)(2). Trademarks, trade names and franchise rights, as a practical matter, are the most important "self-created intangibles" that are subject to amortization over fifteen years under Section 197.
10. IRC Sec. 197(c)(2), last sentence.
11. Treas. Reg. § 1.197-2(b)(11).
12. Treas. Reg. § 1.197-2(b)(11).
13. Treas. Reg. § 1.197-2(c)(6).
14. IRC Sec. 167(f)(3).
15. 503 U.S. 79, 112 S.Ct. 1039 (1992)
16. For example, separately acquired patents and copyrights are typically depreciated under the income forecast method described in Code Sec. 167(g), while software is typically depreciated on a straight line basis over thirty-six months under Code Sec. 167(f).
17. IRC Sec. 167(f).
18. Treas. Reg. § 1.162-11(a).
19. IRC Sec. 178(a).
20. Treas. Reg. § 1.178-1(b)(6), Example 4.
21. House Ways and Means Committee Report No. 103-11, H.R. 2141, p. 331.
22. 503 U.S. 79, 112 S.Ct. 1039 (1992)
23. Treas. Reg. § 1.197-2(e)(1).
24. Treas. Reg. § 1.197-2(e)(2).
25. IRC Sec. 167(f)(1).
26. See Treas. Reg. § 1.197-2(c)(4)(i).
27. IRC Sec. 167(f).
28. IRC Sec. 197(c)(2).
29. IRC Sec. 197(c)(2)(A).
30. IRC Sec. 197(f)(9)(B).
31. IRC Sec. 197(f)(9)(C).
32. *Id.*
33. IRC Sec. 197(f)(9)(E).
34. IRC Sec. 197(f)(9)(D).
35. Treas. Reg. § 1.197-2(f)(2); see Chapter 5.
36. Treas. Reg. § 1.197-2(f)(2)(iii); see Chapter 10.
37. IRC Sec. 197(f)(1)(A).
38. *Id.*
39. IRC Sec. 197(f)(2).

SECTION 338 AND 336(e) ELECTIONS

CHAPTER 12

OVERVIEW

People often want to have things "both ways," and this same impulse extends to the world of business acquisitions. In particular, an Acquirer may want to structure an acquisition of a Target as a stock purchase for business reasons, but may also want to treat it as an asset acquisition for tax reasons. Similarly, a Target (or its shareholders) may prefer asset disposition tax treatment for a transaction that is structured as a stock sale (or series of stock sales). To address these conundrums, Code Sections 338 and 336(e) are what might be described as "eat your cake and have it, too" provisions because they allow the parties to implement a transaction in the form of a stock sale but produce the tax consequences of an asset sale, thereby producing a win-win situation for tax purposes.

Section 338 Elections. An Acquirer of Target stock under certain circumstances has the opportunity to make either of two elections available under Code section 338. The first is under Code section 338(g), and the second is under Code section 338(h)(10). Both elections have the effect for federal income tax purposes of triggering a "hypothetical" sale of assets, with the result that taxable gain from the deemed sale of assets is recognized and tax basis in the assets is correspondingly increased, even though the transaction is, in form, a stock sale.

To be eligible to make a Section 338 election, a single corporate Acquirer must make a "qualified stock purchase" by purchasing stock possessing at least 80 percent of the voting power, and having a value equal to at least 80 percent of the total value, of the stock of the Target corporation within a twelve-month period.[1] The Acquirer can then irrevocably elect to treat the stock purchase as an asset acquisition.[2] Pursuant to such an election, the Target ("Old Target") is treated as if it sold all of its assets to a newly formed corporation ("New Target") at the close of the first day that the Acquirer completed a qualified stock purchase (the "Acquisition Date").[3] New Target is then treated as if it purchased, as of the beginning of the day after the Acquisition Date, all of the Old Target's assets for a price determined by the price paid by the Acquirer for the Old Target stock, adjusted for the Old Target's liabilities and certain other adjustments.[4] The New Target then allocates this deemed purchase price among its assets using the residual method prescribed in the Code section 338 regulations.

Comment: The residual method is familiar territory because it is also applied under Code section 1060. See the discussion in Chapter 3.

A Code section 338(g) election triggers double taxation: The Seller is liable for the tax consequences of a stock sale, and the Acquirer (now the owner of the Target) must bear the tax consequences of the hypothetical asset sale by the Old Target, which is deemed to occur on the first day that the Acquirer acquires sufficient stock to satisfy the 80-percent threshold. Thus (absent a contractual agreement otherwise), the tax consequences of the deemed asset sale are borne by the Acquirer as the owner of the Target. However, the Acquirer (i.e., through its ownership of the New Target) enjoys a corresponding step-up in tax basis in the Target assets, and will therefore benefit prospectively from increased amortization and depreciation deductions.

A Code section 338(h)(10) election, by contrast, produces significantly different tax consequences. Such an election must be jointly made by the Acquirer and Seller.[5] Under a Code section 338(h)(10) election, the

Figure 12.1

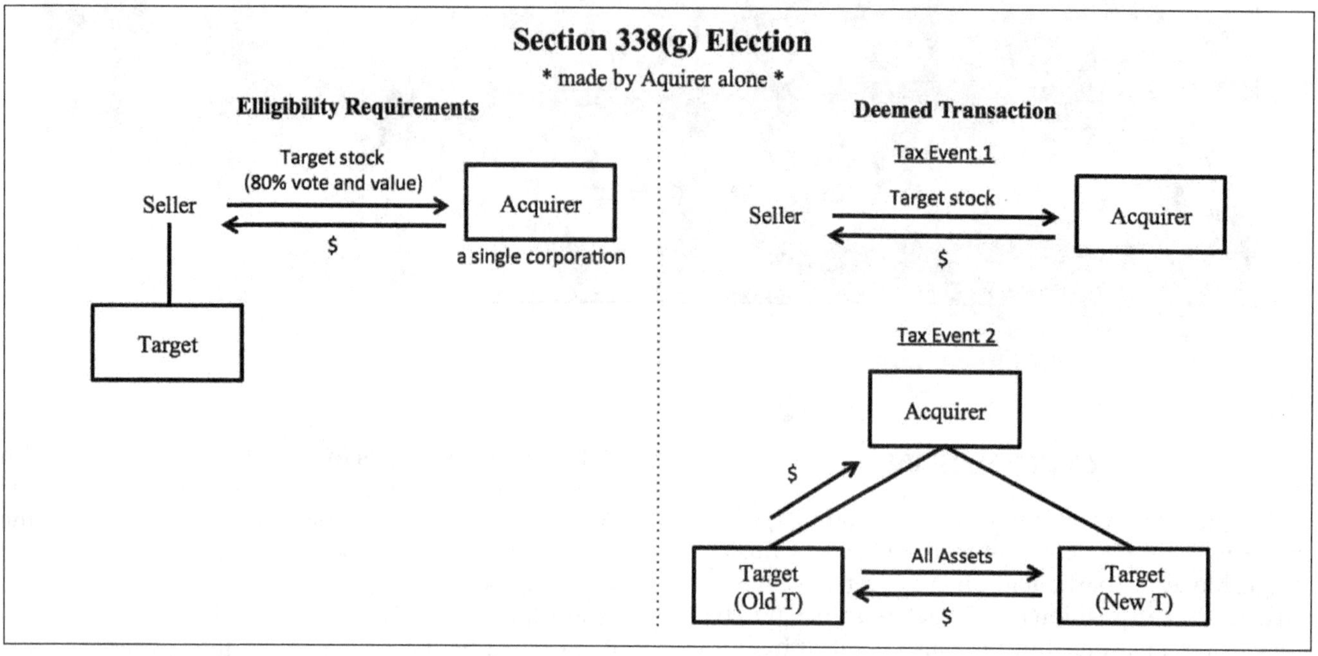

Figure 12.2

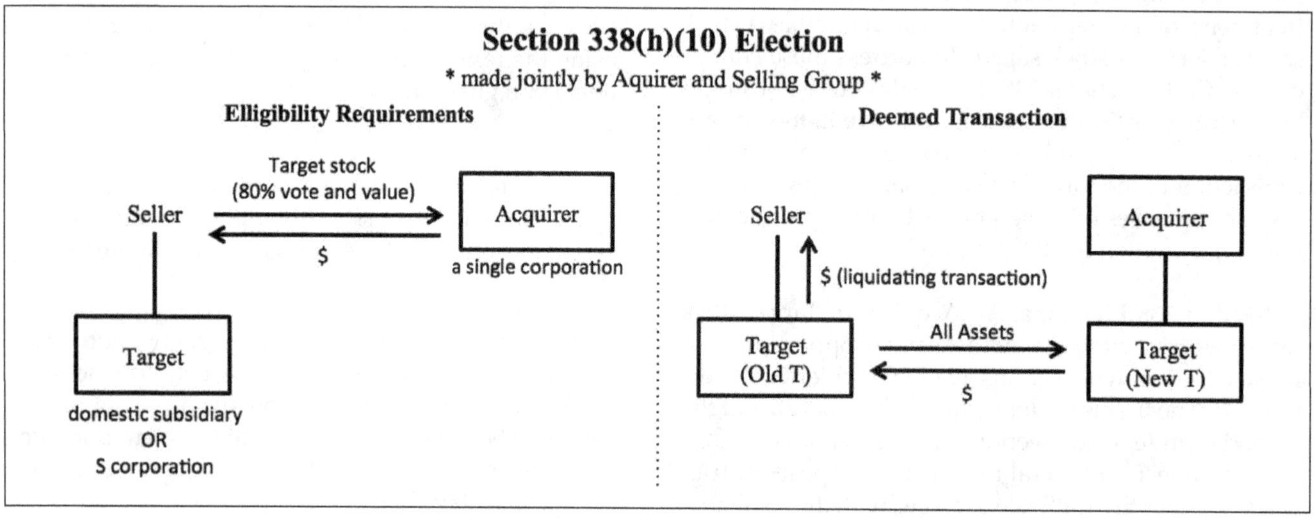

acquisition transaction is characterized as a sale of assets by the Old Target (owned by the Seller) to the New Target (owned by the Acquirer) followed by a liquidation of the Old Target (still owned by the Seller).[6] This "transaction path" means that the tax liabilities that result from the deemed asset sale are borne by the Seller rather than the Acquirer. Because of the limited circumstances in which a Code section 338(h)(10) election can be made, the deemed liquidation of the Old Target by the Seller generally does not produce a second level of tax. (By contrast, a Code section 338(g) election always triggers two tax events, the first borne by the Seller on the sale of Target stock and the second borne by the Acquirer on the deemed asset sale from the Old Target to the New Target). The circumstances in which a Code section 338(h)(10) election can be made are limited to situations where the Target is (1) a domestic corporation that is a member of a consolidated group, (2) a domestic corporation that is a subsidiary of an affiliated group not filing a consolidated return, or (3) an S corporation.[7]

In both types of elections, either the Acquirer (in a Code section 338(g) election) or the Acquirer and the

Seller electing jointly (in a Code section 338(h)(10) election) is making the decision to intentionally trigger a taxable disposition of assets—presumably because in the specific circumstances of that transaction, the resulting voluntary recognition of income and gain, and corresponding step-up in tax basis in the assets, produces a more advantageous result than not making the election.

The Code section 338(g) election is almost never a tax-efficient structure because taxpayers (especially C corporations, which do not enjoy an advantageous LTCG tax rate) rarely want to trigger gain recognition today in exchange for depreciation deductions tomorrow. Therefore, Code section 338(g) elections are relatively unusual and are generally limited to very specific factual circumstances, notably when the Target corporation has substantial net operating losses or other carryover items that would otherwise expire or be substantially limited (e.g., under Code section 382) and which can, in substance, be converted into recoverable tax basis by virtue of a deemed asset sale.

By contrast, a Code section 338(h)(10) election has proven to be significantly more popular in recent years, particularly when the Target is an S corporation. The effect of a stock purchase coupled with a Code section 338(h)(10) election is that the Acquirer acquires the stock of the Target, but both the Buyer and Seller treat the transaction for federal income tax purposes as if the Buyer has purchased the Seller's assets, followed by a liquidation of the Old Target (deemed still to be owned by the Seller). As will be discussed in greater detail below, this is often a good tax strategy for federal income tax purposes because the Seller generally recognizes approximately the same amount of capital gain on the sale, whether it sells assets or stock, and the Acquirer dramatically improves its tax results by increasing its tax basis in the Target assets (which basis is recoverable through amortization and depreciation) rather than having the tax basis allocated merely to the Target stock (classic "dead" money, as discussed in Chapter 5). Typically, a Seller making a Code section 338(h)(10) election generally avoids a second level of tax on the deemed liquidation transaction (e.g., because of the application of the consolidated return rules, or because, under the S corporation rules, the asset disposition creates outside tax basis that eliminates most or all gain on the deemed liquidation). Therefore, a Code section 338(h)(10) election often makes it possible for the parties to "share" economically the enhanced tax benefits enjoyed by the Acquirer as a result of the election.

The Section 336(e) Election. In general, a Code section 336(e) election allows the parties involved in a corporate stock sale to enjoy the tax benefits of a Code section 338(h)(10) election in circumstances that would not otherwise qualify under section 338(h)(10). A Code section 336(e) election is available if a Seller (who can

Figure 12.3

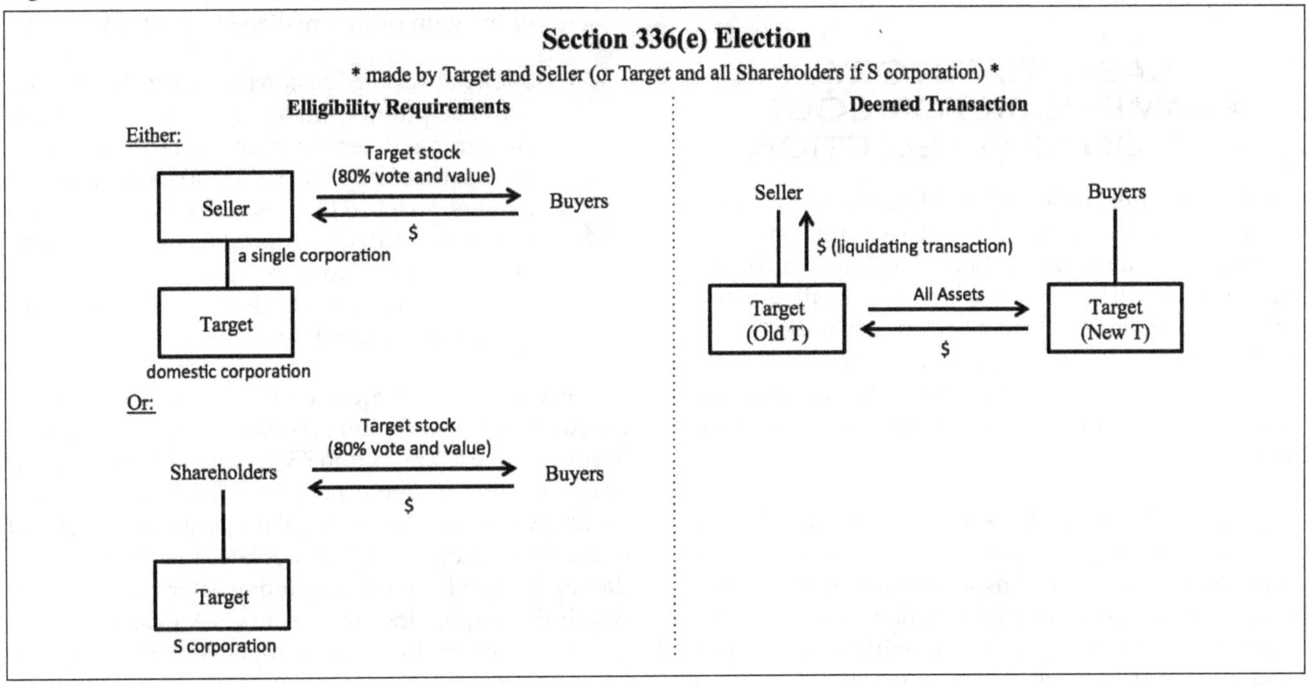

be either a domestic C corporation or the shareholders of an S corporation) sells the Target (which can be, respectively, any domestic C corporation or an S corporation) in a "qualified stock disposition," namely, by selling stock possessing at least 80 percent of the voting power and having a value equal to at least 80 percent of the total value of the stock of the Target corporation within a twelve-month period.[8]

Because a Code section 336(e) election is generally designed to mirror or mimic the tax effects of a Code section 338(h)(10) election, there is a potential for overlap between events qualifying as a "qualified stock purchase" under Section 338(h)(10) and as a "qualified stock disposition" under Section 336(e). In general, the latter election accommodates a broader set of transactional and factual circumstances because the buyer does not need to be a single corporation. Instead, a qualified stock disposition may arise even if there are multiple unrelated buyers of the stock, or an individual (non-corporate) purchaser of the stock, so long as the aggregate dispositions exceed the 80 percent threshold during the applicable twelve-month period. If the qualifying dispositions occur over a period of time rather than in a single transaction it is sometimes referred to as a "creeping QSD."

Mechanically, a Code section 336(e) election achieves the same tax results as a Code section 338(h)(10) election, but uses different terms and definitions to accomplish this result. See discussion below, for further details.

BASIC STATUTORY FRAMEWORK FOR CODE SECTION 338(g) ELECTION

If the Acquirer makes a "qualified stock purchase" with respect to the Target, then the Acquirer can make an election under Code section 338(g), in which case the Target (1) will be treated as having sold all its assets at the close of the acquisition date at fair market value in a single transaction and (2) will be treated as a new corporation that purchased all the assets referred to in (1) as of the beginning of the day after the acquisition date.[9]

Qualified Stock Purchase. The term "qualified stock purchase" means any transaction or series of transactions in which stock (meeting the requirements of Code section 1504(a)(2)) of one corporation is acquired by another corporation by purchase within the twelve-month acquisition period.[10] As a practical matter, a qualified stock purchase means that the Acquirer purchases within a twelve-month period (1) at least 80 percent of the total combined voting power of all classes of target stock entitled to vote, and (2) at least 80 percent of the total value of the stock of the Target (except nonvoting stock that is limited and preferred as to dividends and does not participate in corporate growth to any significant extent, that has redemption and liquidation rights that do not exceed its issue price (except for a reasonable redemption or liquidation premium), and that is not convertible into another class of stock).[11]

"Purchase" Defined Generally to Mean "Taxable Acquisition". Code section 338(h)(3)(A) defines a "purchase" as "any acquisition of stock," but only if the following conditions are satisfied:

1. *Stock not acquired with carryover basis.* The basis of such stock in the hands of the Acquirer is not determined (a) in whole or in part by reference to its adjusted basis in the hands of the transferor (i.e., no carryover basis transactions, such as in tax-free mergers), or (b) under Code section 1014(a) (i.e., because it was acquired from a decedent).

2. *Stock not acquired in tax-free reorganization.* Such stock is not acquired in an exchange to which Code sections 351, 354, 355, or 356 applies or in any other transaction described in regulations in which the transferor recognizes less than all of the gain or loss realized in the transactions.

3. *Stock not acquired from related party.* Such stock is not acquired from a person "related" to the Acquirer as determined under the related party rules under Code section 318(a) (and excluding for this purpose Code section 318(a)(4)). This requirement does not apply to an acquisition of stock from a related corporation if at least 50 percent in value of the related corporation's stock was acquired by purchase.

Election. If an Acquirer makes a qualified stock purchase, the corporation may elect under Code section 338(g) to have Code section 338(a) applied. (Permission or cooperation from the Target is not required.) Except as otherwise provided in regulations, an election must be made by filing Form 8023 not later than the fifteenth day of the ninth month beginning after the month in which the acquisition date occurs.[12] An election, once made, is irrevocable.[13] Note that, depending on the "Acquisition Date," the election may be required to be filed *before* the due date of the Acquirer's tax return for the tax year in which the acquisition occurs.

CONSEQUENCES OF CODE SECTION 338(g) ELECTION

Tax Consequences of Election. When a stock acquisition is accompanied by a Code section 338(g) election, there are two distinct tax recognition events: (1) a stock sale by the Seller and (2) a deemed hypothetical sale by the Old Target to the New Target.

The first tax recognition event is determined under the normal rules governing a sale of stock. The Seller will recognize gain or loss equal to the difference between the amount realized and the Seller's tax basis in the shares.[14] If the Target is a domestic corporation, the subsequent deemed sale of assets will not affect the Seller's calculation of gain. However, if the Target is a foreign corporation, the deemed sale of assets can affect the character of the Seller's gain on the stock sale and trigger other consequences.[15]

The second level of tax occurs when the Old Target is treated as selling its assets to the New Target at fair market value in a single taxable transaction as of the beginning of the day after the Acquisition Date. The regulations provide formulas for converting the price paid for the Target stock into the price paid for each of its assets.[16] The aggregate deemed sale price (ADSP) is determined for the Old Target, and that ADSP is allocated among the Old Target's assets to determine the amount for which each asset is deemed to have been sold. ADSP is the sum of (1) the grossed-up amount realized on the sale to the Acquirer of the Acquirer's recently purchased Target stock plus (2) the liabilities of the Old Target.[17]

Comment: The ADSP calculation does not affect either the amount of gain or loss recognized by the Seller, or the Acquirer's tax basis in the Target stock, both of which are determined under the usual rules applicable to a stock purchase.

Upon making a Code section 338 election, the Old Target must recognize taxable gain on the deemed disposition of its assets for the ADSP. The ADSP is allocated among the Target's assets, and gain or loss is computed by reference to the ADSP allocated to each asset.[18] The Old Target may offset against the gain recognized any net operating losses (NOLs). Note that as a result of the Code section 338 election, the Target loses all its former tax attributes, including any unused NOLs, and the New Target starts as a fresh corporation without inheriting the tax history of the Old Target under Code section 381.

Example 1: ADSP is a unique and highly complex calculation used solely for purposes of determining the gain recognized pursuant to a Code section 338(g) election. The full flavor and nuance of the ADSP is beyond the scope of this book, but the following example from Reg. § 1.338-4(g), Example 1 provides some flavor of the complexity of this calculation:

For purposes of [this example...], T is a calendar year taxpayer that files separate returns and that has no loss, tax credit, or other carryovers to Year 1. Depreciation for Year 1 is not taken into account. T has no liabilities other than the Federal income tax liability resulting from the deemed asset sale, and the T shareholders have no selling costs. Assume that T's tax rate for any ordinary income or net capital gain resulting from the deemed sale of assets is 34 percent and that any capital loss is offset by capital gain. On July 1 of Year 1, P purchases all of the stock of T and makes a section 338 election for T.[...]

(i) On July 1 of Year 1, T's only asset is an item of section 1245 property with an adjusted basis to T of $50,400, a recomputed basis of $80,000, and a fair market value of $100,000. P purchases all of the T stock [(T has one class of stock)] for $75,000, which also equals the amount realized for the stock determined as if the selling shareholder(s) were required to use old target's accounting methods and characteristics.

(ii) ADSP is determined as follows (for purposes of [this example], G is the grossed-up amount realized on the sale to P of P's recently purchased T stock, L is T's liabilities other than T's tax liability for the deemed sale tax consequences, TR is the applicable tax rate, and B is the adjusted basis of the asset deemed sold):

ADSP = G + L + TR (ADSP-B)

ADSP = ($75,000/1) + $0 + .34 ×
(ADSP – $50,400)

ADSP = $75,000 + .34ADSP – $17,136

.66ADSP = $57,864 ADSP = $87,672.72

(iii) Because ADSP for T ($87,672.72) does not exceed the fair market value of T's asset ($100,000), a Class V asset, T's entire ADSP is allocated to that asset. Thus, T's deemed sale results in $37,272.72 of taxable income (consisting of $29,600 of ordinary income and $7,672.72 of capital gain).

(iv) The facts are the same as in paragraph (i) of this *Example 1*, except that on July 1 of Year 1, P purchases only 80 of the 100 shares of T stock for $60,000. The grossed-up amount realized on the sale to P of P's recently purchased T stock (G) is $75,000 ($60,000/.8). Consequently, ADSP and the deemed sale tax consequences are the same as in paragraphs (ii) and (iii) of this *Example 1*.

(v) The facts are the same as in paragraph (i) of this *Example 1*, except that T also has goodwill (a Class VII asset) with an appraised value of $10,000. The results are the same as in paragraphs (ii) and (iii) of this *Example 1*. Because ADSP does not exceed the fair market value of the Class V asset, no amount is allocated to the Class VII asset (goodwill).

Determination of Tax Basis in Target Assets after Deemed Purchase. The New Target is deemed to have purchased all of its assets for the adjusted grossed-up basis (AGUB).[19] AGUB is the sum of the grossed-up basis in the Acquirer's recently purchased Target stock (i.e., Target stock purchased by the Acquirer during the twelve-month acquisition period), the Acquirer's basis in nonrecently purchased Target stock, plus the liabilities of the New Target.[20] AGUB is allocated among the New Target's assets in accordance with Reg. § 1.338-6 to determine the price at which the assets are deemed to have been purchased.[21]

Grossed Up Basis. The "grossed up basis" of recently purchased stock is an amount equal to (1) the Acquirer's basis in recently purchased stock at the beginning of the day after the acquisition date; (2) multiplied by a fraction the numerator of which is 100 percent, minus the percentage of stock (by value) in the Target attributable to the Acquirer's not recently purchased stock, and the denominator of which is the percentage of stock (by value) in the Target attributable to the Acquirer's recently purchased Target stock; and (3) plus acquisition costs the Acquirer incurred in connection with its purchase of the recently purchased stock that are capitalized in the basis of such stock (e.g., brokerage commissions and any similar costs incurred by the Acquirer to acquire the stock).[22] The term "recently purchased stock" means any stock in the Target that is held by the Acquirer on the acquisition date and that was purchased by such corporation during the twelve-month acquisition period.[23] The term "nonrecently purchased stock" means any stock in the Target held by the Acquirer on the acquisition date that is not recently purchased stock.[24]

Grossed Up Basis Explained. Although the term is somewhat arcane, the "grossed up basis" in recently purchased stock, assuming the Target has a single class of outstanding stock, is equal to the total price that the Acquirer would have paid for all the outstanding stock of the Target (other than nonrecently purchased stock) had such stock been purchased for a price per share equal to the average price per share paid for the recently purchased stock.

Example 2: If the Acquirer purchases 100 percent of the Old Target's stock within the applicable twelve-month acquisition period, the grossed up basis will equal the Acquirer's actual basis in the Target stock. If less than 100 percent of the Old Target stock is acquired by a purchase during the 1 twelve-month acquisition period and there is no nonrecently purchased stock, the definition of "grossed up basis" treats the transaction for basis purposes as if 100 percent of the stock had been acquired at a proportionate price, Thus, if the Acquirer purchases 90 percent of the Target's stock for $900,000 and elects Code section 338(a) treatment, the grossed up basis of the Target stock is $1 million ($900,000 × 100% ÷ by 90%).

Example 3: If the Acquirer purchases 90 percent of the Target's stock for $900,000 and previously purchased 10 percent of the stock five years earlier for $10,000, the sum of the grossed-up basis and the basis in nonrecently purchased stock would be $910,000 rather than $1 million. This situation is very different than if 10 percent of the Target's shares are held by an unrelated party, in which case the Target's assets would have a grossed up basis of $1 million ($900,000 × (100% ÷ 90%)).

Code section 338(b)(3) provides for an election to step up the basis of an Acquirer's not recently purchased stock to an amount that equals the "grossed up basis" that would apply if the stock were held by an unrelated party. In return for this step up in the basis of the New Target's assets, the Acquirer is required to recognize gain as if the not recently purchased stock had been sold on the acquisition date for an amount equal to its grossed-up basis.

> *Example 4:* If the grossed-up basis of recently purchased stock (representing 90 percent of the Target's stock) is $900,000, and if the Acquirer has 10-percent not recently purchased stock, a Code section 338(b)(3) election means the not recently purchased stock will be treated as if it had been sold on the acquisition date for an amount equal to $900,000 multiplied by a fraction, the numerator of which is the percentage of stock (by value) in the Target attributable to the Acquirer's not recently purchased stock (in this case 10 percent) and the denominator of which is 100 percent minus the percentage referred to in the numerator (100% – 10% = 90%). This equals a fraction of one-ninth, which when multiplied by the grossed-up basis of $900,000 results in $100,000. Thus, the Acquirer's basis in the Target stock is $1 million, and the Acquirer is deemed to have sold its 10-percent not recently purchased stock for $100,000 on the acquisition date.

> *Example 5:* Like ADSP, AGUB is a unique and highly complex calculation made under Code section 338 and the applicable regulations. Although a full explanation of AGUB is beyond the scope of this book, the following example from Reg. § 1.338-5(g), Example 1 illustrates the nature of the AGUB calculation:
>
> For purposes of [this example…], T has no liabilities other than the tax liability for the deemed sale tax consequences, T shareholders incur no costs in selling the T stock, and P incurs no costs in acquiring the T stock. The examples are as follows:[…]
>
> (i) Before July 1 of Year 1, P purchases 10 of the 100 shares of T stock for $5,000. On July 1 of Year 2, P purchases 80 shares of T stock for $60,000 and makes a section 338 election for T. As of July 1 of Year 2, T's only asset is raw land with an adjusted basis to T of $50,400 and a fair market value of $100,000. T has no loss or tax credit carryovers to Year 2. T's marginal tax rate for any ordinary income or net capital gain resulting from the deemed asset sale is 34 percent. The 10 shares purchased before July 1 of Year 1 constitute nonrecently purchased T stock with respect to P's qualified stock purchase of T stock on July 1 of Year 2.
>
> (ii) The ADSP formula as applied to these facts is the same as in § 1.338-4(g) *Example 1.* Accordingly, the ADSP for T is $87,672.72. The existence of nonrecently purchased T stock is irrelevant for purposes of the ADSP formula, because that formula treats P's nonrecently purchased T stock in the same manner as T stock not held by P.
>
> (iii) The total tax liability resulting from T's deemed asset sale, as calculated under the ADSP formula, is $12,672.72.
>
> (iv) If P does not make a gain recognition election, the AGUB of new T's assets is $85,172.72, determined as follows (in the following formula below, GRP is the grossed-up basis in P's recently purchased T stock, BNP is P's basis in nonrecently purchased T stock, L is T's liabilities, and X is P's acquisition costs for the recently purchased T stock):

$$AGUB = GRP + BNP + L + X$$

$$AGUB = \$60,000 \times [(1 - .1)/.8] + \$5,000 + \$12,672.72 + 0 \quad AGUB = \$85,172.72$$

> (v) If P makes a gain recognition election, the AGUB of new T's assets is $87,672.72, determined as follows:

$$AGUB = \$60,000 \times [(1 - .1)/.8] + \$60,000 \times [(1 - .1)/.8] \times [.1/(1 - .1)] + \$12,672.72$$

$$AGUB = \$87,672.72$$

> (vi) The calculation of AGUB if P makes a gain recognition election may be simplified as follows:

$$AGUB = \$60,000/.8 + \$12,672.72$$
$$AGUB = \$87,672.72$$

(vii) As a result of the gain recognition election, P's basis in its nonrecently purchased T stock is increased from $5,000 to $7,500 (i.e., $60,000 × [(1 − .1)/.8] × [.1/(1 − .1)]). Thus, P recognizes a gain in Year 2 with respect to its nonrecently purchased T stock of $2,500 (i.e., $7,500 – $5,000).

Comparison of AGUB with ADSP. AGUB, used to determine the Acquiring Corporation's tax basis in the New Target assets after a Code section 338(g) election, will differ from ADSP, used to determine the price at which the Target is deemed to have sold all of its assets in the hypothetical sale under Code section 338(a)(1), whenever the Acquirer holds not recently purchased Target stock with a tax basis that differs from the Acquirer's tax basis in recently purchased Target stock. This difference reflects the fact that the ADSP formula treats an Acquirer's not recently purchased Target stock in the same manner as the Target stock not held by the Acquirer. If an election is made under Code section 338(b)(3) to treat the not recently purchased stock as if it is sold on the acquisition date, the difference between the AGUB formula and the ADSP formula is eliminated.

Code Section 338 Election for Target Subsidiaries. If stock in a Target affiliate (i.e., subsidiary) is deemed acquired by the New Target pursuant to a Code section 338 election, and this deemed stock acquisition is itself a qualified stock purchase (i.e., meets the 80-percent tests), then the Target affiliate is also a target eligible for a Section 338 election.[25] To avoid double counting of gains, the regulations provide no gain or loss is recognized by the Old Target on the deemed sale of subsidiary stock to the New Target when a Section 338 election is made for a subsidiary and certain other conditions are met.[26]

CONSISTENCY AND OTHER RULES

Code section 338 and the accompanying regulations contain certain rules (the so-called "Consistency Rules") that try to prevent the Acquirer from "picking and choosing" among the Old Target assets to obtain a step-up in tax basis (at the cost of tax liability) with respect to some assets but a carryover basis (and no tax liability) for others. The Consistency Rules generally require that the Acquirer (and its affiliates) treat all acquisitions from the Target (or the Target's affiliates) consistently as either stock purchases or asset purchases.

Code section 338(e)(1) (the "Asset Consistency Rule") states that an Acquirer shall be treated as having made an election under Code section 338 with respect to any Target if, at any time during the consistency period, it acquires any asset of the Target (or a target affiliate). A "Target" means any corporation whose stock has been acquired by another corporation in a qualified stock purchase (i.e., 80 percent acquired).[27]

Code section 338(f) (the "Stock Consistency Rules") states that if an Acquirer makes a qualified stock purchase with respect to the Target and one or more of the Target's affiliates during any Consistency Period then, subject to certain statutory exceptions, any election under Code section 338 with respect to the first purchase shall apply to each other purchase, and no election may be made under Code section338 with respect to the second or subsequent purchase if such election was not made with respect to the first such purchase.

The term "Consistency Period" means the period consisting of (1) the one-year period before the beginning of the twelve-month acquisition period for the Target, (2) such acquisition period (up to and including the acquisition date) and (3) the one-year period beginning on the day after the acquisition date. Thus, the Consistency Period is a three-year period including the year before and after the twelve-month acquisition period.[28]

Regulatory Modifications to Asset and Stock Consistency Rules. The Treasury Department concluded, after the *General Utilities* repeal in 1986, that the Consistency Rules should be largely abandoned. Today, the Asset Consistency Rules address relatively limited schemes under the consolidated return rules, e.g., where the Acquirer purchases an asset from the Target (part of a consolidated group), basis is adjusted in Target stock, and then the Target stock is sold to the Acquirer within the consistency period.[29] The only consequence of a violation is that the Acquirer must take carryover basis in the asset unless a Section 338 election is made for the Target.[30] The Stock Consistency Rules exist only to support the Asset Consistency Rules.[31]

Target Alone is Subject to Tax upon Section 338 Election. If the Old Target recognizes income and gain as a result of a Section 338 election, such income and gain are taxed to the Old Target; they are not reported on any consolidated return filed by the Acquirer.[32] Congress sought to prevent the offset of the Old Target's income and gain with losses of the Acquirer's consolidated group.

Purchases of Stock of the Target which Was Member of Affiliated Group Filing Consolidated Return. The Old Target is treated as having a one-day tax year (including only day of sale) so that the selling group is not liable for the Old Target's taxes attributable to the election.[33]

Grant of Regulatory Authority. Code section 338 bestows unusual authority on the Treasury Department to deal with "tax avoidance" and certain plans through substantive rules in regulations.[34] The Treasury Department initially issued absurdly complex regulations, but has since rewritten (and simplified significantly) this still-daunting body of rules.

CODE SECTION 338(h)(10) ELECTIONS

A Code section 338(h)(10) election may be made for the Target if the Acquirer purchases sufficient Target stock to meet the applicable requirements for a "qualified stock purchase" and the Target is (1) a domestic corporation that is a member of a consolidated group, (2) a domestic corporation that is a subsidiary of an affiliated group not filing a consolidated return, or (3) an S corporation.[35]

Technically, when an acquiring corporation "A" acquires the stock of target corporation "T" and A and the selling consolidated group (or the selling affiliate or the S corporation shareholders) jointly make a Code section 338(h)(10) election, the following results occur:

1. "Old T" is treated as selling its assets in a single transaction to a new corporation, "New T," owned by A. The price at which each asset of Old T is deemed to have been sold is calculated by (a) determining the ADSP and (b) then allocating ADSP among the assets of Old T in accordance with the general allocation rules (with certain modifications).

2. Old T is treated as then having liquidated.

3. New T is treated as purchasing Old T's assets as of the beginning of the day after the acquisition date. New T's tax basis in its assets is determined under the same rules that apply to a Code section 338(g) election.

4. New T takes on basis for Old T's assets equal to the aggregate purchase price A pays for Old T's stock plus Old T's liabilities inherited by New T plus certain other items.[36]

The result of a Code section 338(h)(10) election is that (1) the ADSP is treated as if paid for the Target's assets, (2) the losses of other members of the selling group may be used to offset the gain recognized by the Target in the hypothetical sale transaction, (3) the Target is deemed to have sold all its assets and distributed the proceeds in complete liquidation (generally a tax-free liquidation, either because of the application of Code section 332 in the case of a corporate group, or because of the basis step-up rules under Code section 1367 in the case of an S corporation), and (4) the Acquirer obtains a step up in basis of assets while the transaction in the aggregate triggers only a single level of tax (i.e., the sale of assets by the Target that is reported by the seller). No gain or loss is recognized on the sale of stock by the selling consolidated group (or the selling affiliate or an S corporation shareholder). Instead, the Target is taxed on the deemed sale of assets followed by a deemed liquidation, and its shareholder(s) are then taxed under the applicable rules (consolidated return, S corporation, etc.).

The tax treatment of an S corporation is very different from a C corporation because of the pass-through tax treatment. In particular, the transaction is treated as a sale of assets by "Old T" to "New T" for an amount equal to the ADSP—roughly the gross amount realized on the sale of stock plus "New T's" liabilities acquired from "Old T." Significantly, Old T is treated as making this asset sale while still owned by the existing S corporation shareholders. Thus, the S corporation shareholders recognize the gain on a pass-through basis. Under normal S corporation rules, the gain on the deemed asset sale flows through to the pre-acquisition shareholders and is reported on their tax returns.[37] The S corporation will be subject to the Code section 1374 "sting tax," if it has "built-in" gain.

The gain recognized by selling shareholders is computed as if it were an asset sale, and no gain or loss is computed based on the sale of the stock. Old T is treated as receiving the stock sale proceeds and distributing such proceeds to its pre-acquisition shareholders in a complete liquidation under Code section 331. Therefore, the existing shareholders are treated as receiving the deemed liquidation of proceeds as full payment in exchange for their stock, and each shareholder recognizes corresponding capital gain or capital loss to the extent the shareholder's deemed liquidation proceeds exceed or are less than the shareholder's basis in the S corporation stock. Because there is an adjustment in outside basis as a result of any gain recognized by the corporation, the shareholders' tax basis for purposes of the deemed liquidation will be the (1) existing tax basis on the date of the sale transactions increased by (2) the amount of gain that flows through to each respective shareholder as a result of the deemed sale of assets. That shareholders of a Target S corporation can make a Code section 338(h)(10) election has made this type of election far more common than it would otherwise be. In general, there are a number of situations where the Acquiring Corporation would like to acquire assets rather than stock of the Target but cannot do so (e.g., because the Target has valuable contract rights or other relationships that would be potentially voidable if such contracts were transferred from the Target to the Acquiring Corporation). Thanks to the Code section 338(h)(10) election, an Acquiring Corporation can purchase the stock of an S corporation but elect (if joined by the Target shareholders) to have the transaction taxed as a purchase of assets, which generally produces substantially more favorable tax consequences.

It is interesting to make a brief comparison between a Code section 338(g) election and a Code section 338(h)(10) election. In the former case, the Acquirer alone makes the election, and the election does not affect the seller since the hypothetical sale of the Target's assets is deemed to occur at the close of the acquisition date. Although the deemed sale is not included in any consolidated return of a corporate purchaser, the tax impact of the transaction is effectively borne by the purchaser because the purchaser now owns the Target that owes the tax.

By contrast, a Code section 338(h)(10) election requires a joint election by the Acquirer and Selling Group, and the tax consequences are borne by the Selling Group. Depending on the tax circumstances of the Selling Group (e.g., such as whether the Selling Group has net operating losses as part of a consolidated return, or whether the Selling Group are the shareholders of an S corporation), there may be no significant tax difference to the Selling Group between a stock sale and a deemed asset sale. Therefore, the Selling Group may have little or no objection to bearing the tax costs, provided that it can negotiate a suitable increase in price.

Comment: A savvy Seller is likely to extract a premium for agreeing to a Code section 338(h)(10) election even if it is an S corporation and even if there is no tax detriment between a deemed sale of stock and a deemed sale of (capital) assets. For the Acquirer, the tax benefits of a Code section 338(h)(10) election can be significant because tax basis in the Target's stock is likely to be far less beneficial than if the same purchase price is deemed paid for the Target's assets, which assets are likely to be largely depreciable, amortizable, or even deductible or the equivalent of deductible (e.g., a purchase of receivables will result in the allocable tax basis being liquidated into cash almost immediately by the Target after the acquisition date).

A Code section 338(h)(10) election is made by filing Form 8023 not later than the fifteenth day of the ninth month beginning after the month in which the acquisition date occurs.[38] A Code section 338(h)(10) election must be made *jointly* by the Acquiring Corporation and the selling consolidated group, the selling affiliate, or the S corporation shareholders. Obviously, such an election decision is negotiated as part of the purchase and sale agreement in such transactions.

A Code section 338(h)(10) election is irrevocable.[39] Although for non-tax purposes there is only one Target corporation, for tax purposes the deemed asset sale and liquidation is treated as if it actually occurred and as if there are two corporations: Old T and New T. If a Section 338(h)(10) election is made for the Target (which becomes Old T), a Section 338 election is deemed made for the Target (as New T) as well, so Target must re-determine its basis in assets to be consistent with a Code section 338 election.[40]

No gain or loss is recognized on the stock sale by the selling consolidated group (or the selling affiliate or an S corporation shareholder) if the Target's stock is part of a qualified stock purchase under Code section 338(h)(10). Instead, the Target is taxed on the deemed sale of assets, followed by deemed liquidation. The Target's selling shareholders are taxed on any gain or loss under the applicable rules (e.g., consolidated return, S corporation, etc.).

The price at which each asset of the Old Target is deemed to have been sold is calculated by (1) determining the ADSP and (2) then allocating ADSP among the assets of the Old Target in accordance with the general allocation rules (with certain modifications).

Making this election permits the Seller to avoid recognizing income or gain on its disposition of Old Target stock at the cost of the deemed asset sale (i.e., a sale of assets by the Target followed by liquidation of the Target) described above. As a result, the Acquirer can obtain a step-up in asset basis at the cost of what is generally a single level of tax to the Seller. Practical experience shows that the Acquirer will pay more to the Seller if a Code section 338(h)(10) election is made.

A Code section 338(h)(10) election may also be advantageous if the consolidated selling group has a lower "outside" basis in the stock of the Target than the Target's "inside" basis in its assets. In such a situation, the consolidated selling group may even accept a lower price for the sale of the Target stock with the Code section 338(h)(10) election than for a sale without such an election.

The following example from Reg. § 1.338(h)(10)-1(e), Example 5 illustrates the consequences of a Code section 338(h)(10) election:

Example 5. (i) T, a member of a selling consolidated group, has only one class of stock, all of which is owned by S1. On March 1 of Year 2, S1 sells its T stock to P for $80,000, and joins with P in making a section 338(h)(10) election for T. There are no selling costs or acquisition costs. On March 1 of Year 2, T owns land with a $50,000 basis and $75,000 fair market value and equipment with a $30,000 adjusted basis, $70,000 recomputed basis, and $60,000 fair market value. T also has a $40,000 liability. S1 pays old T's allocable share of the selling group's consolidated tax liability for Year 2 including the tax liability for the deemed sale tax consequences (a total of $13,600).

(ii) ADSP of $120,000 ($80,000 + $40,000 + 0) is allocated to each asset as follows:

Assets	*Basis*	*FMV*	*Fraction*	*Allocable ADSP*
Land	$50,000	$75,000	5/9	$66,667
Equipment	$30,000	$60,000	4/9	$53,333
Total	$80,000	$135,000	1	$120,000

(iii) Under Reg. § 1.338(h)(10)-1(d)(3), old T has gain on the deemed sale of $40,000 (consisting of $16,667 of capital gain and $23,333 of ordinary income).

(iv) Under Reg. § 1.338(h)(10)-1(d)(5)(iii), S1 recognizes no gain or loss upon its sale of the old T stock to P. S1 also recognizes no gain or loss upon the deemed liquidation of T. (See Reg. § 1.338(h)(10)-1(d)(4) and Code section 332.)

(v) P's basis in new T stock is P's cost for the stock, $80,000. (See Code section 1012.)

(vi) Under § 1.338-5, the AGUB for new T is $120,000, i.e., P's cost for the old T stock ($80,000) plus T's liability ($40,000). This AGUB is allocated as basis among the new T assets under §§ 1.338-6 and 1.338-7.

INTERACTION OF CODE SECTION 338(h)(10) AND CODE SECTION 453 INSTALLMENT SALES

In general, regulations under Code section 338(h)(10) recognize that there are technical problems with the interaction of a Code section 338(h)(10) election and the installment sale rules of Code sections 453, 453A, and 453B. The technical glitch is that, under Code sections 453(f)(3), (h), and 453B(h), a seller generally is not considered to receive payment with respect to an installment sale upon receipt of indebtedness if the issuer of the debt instrument is the person acquiring the property. However, the seller generally would be considered to have received payment with respect to an installment sale on the receipt of evidence of indebtedness issued by a person other than the person acquiring the property.[41] In the latter case, the seller will recognize income immediately upon receipt of such indebtedness.

The concern was raised early on that because under a Code section 338(h)(10) election, there is a deemed sale of assets by the Old Target to the New Target, technically the New Target may be delivering to the Old Target a promissory note issued by someone other than the New Target (i.e., the promissory note of the Acquirer, which is distinct from the New Target).

To address this issue, the regulations under Code section 338(h)(10) modify the tax consequences of a deemed asset sale solely for determining eligibility under the installment sale provisions of Code sections 453, 453A, and 453B.[42] The adjustments include the following:

In the deemed asset sale:

1. The Old Target is treated as receiving in the deemed asset sale new Target installment obligations, the terms of which are identical (except as to the obligor) to Acquirer installment

obligations issued in exchange for recently purchased stock of the Target.

2. The Old Target is treated as receiving in cash all other consideration in the deemed asset sale other than the assumption of, or taking subject to, old Target liabilities.

3. The amount realized for recently purchased stock taken into account in determining ADSP is adjusted (and thus ADSP is redetermined) to reflect the amounts paid under an installment obligation for the stock when the total payments under the installment obligation are greater or less than the amount realized.

In the deemed liquidation:

1. The Old Target is treated as distributing in the deemed liquidation the new Target installment obligations that it is treated as receiving in the deemed asset sale.

2. Members of the selling consolidated group, the selling affiliate, or the S corporation shareholders are treated as receiving in the deemed liquidation the new Target installment obligations that correspond to the Acquirer installment obligations that they actually received in exchange for their recently purchased stock.

3. Members of the selling consolidated group, the selling affiliate, or the S corporation shareholders are treated as receiving all other consideration in the deemed liquidation in cash.

The following example is taken from Reg. § 1.338(h)(10)-1(e), Example 10:

Example 10. (i) T is an S corporation whose sole class of stock is owned 40 percent each by A and B and 20 percent by C. T, A, B, and C all use the cash method of accounting. A and B each has an adjusted basis of $10,000 in the stock. C has an adjusted basis of $5,000 in the stock. A, B, and C hold no installment obligations to which section 453A applies. On March 1 of Year 1, A sells its stock to P for $40,000 in cash and B sells its stock to P for a $25,000 note issued by P and real estate having a fair market value of $15,000. The $25,000 note, due in full in Year 7, is not publicly traded and bears adequate stated interest. A and B have no selling expenses. T's sole asset is real estate, which has a value of $110,000 and an adjusted basis of $35,000. Also, T's real estate is encumbered by long-outstanding purchase-money indebtedness of $10,000. The real estate does not have built-in gain subject to section 1374. A, B, and C join with P in making a section 338(h)(10) election for T.

(ii) Solely for purposes of application of sections 453, 453A, and 453B, old T is considered in its deemed asset sale to receive back from new T the $25,000 note (considered issued by new T) and $75,000 of cash (total consideration of $80,000 paid for all the stock sold, which is then divided by .80 in the grossing-up, with the resulting figure of $100,000 then reduced by the amount of the installment note). Absent an election under section 453(d), gain is reported by old T under the installment method.

(iii) In applying the installment method to old T's deemed asset sale, the contract price for old T's assets deemed sold is $100,000, the $110,000 selling price reduced by the indebtedness of $10,000 to which the assets are subject. (The $110,000 selling price is itself the sum of the $80,000 grossed-up in paragraph (ii) above to $100,000 and the $10,000 liability.) Gross profit is $75,000 ($110,000 selling price - old T's basis of $35,000). Old T's gross profit ratio is 0.75 (gross profit of $75,000 ÷ $100,000 contract price). Thus, $56,250 (0.75 × the $75,000 cash old T is deemed to receive in Year 1) is Year 1 gain attributable to the sale, and $18,750 ($75,000 – $56,250) is recovery of basis.

(iv) In its liquidation, old T is deemed to distribute the $25,000 note to B, since B actually sold the stock partly for that consideration. To the extent of the remaining liquidating distribution to B, it is deemed to receive, along with A and C, the balance of old T's liquidating assets in the form of cash. Under section 453(h), B, unless it makes an election under section 453(d), is not required to treat the receipt of the note as a payment for the T stock; P's payment of the $25,000 note in Year 7 to B is a payment for the T stock. Because section 453(h) applies to B, old T's deemed liquidating distribution of the note is, under section 453B(h), not treated as a taxable disposition by old T.

(v) Under section .1366, A reports 40 percent, or $22,500, of old T's $56,250 gain recognized in Year 1. Under section 1367, this increases A's $10,000 adjusted basis in the T stock to $32,500. Next, in old T's deemed liquidation, A is considered to receive $40,000 for its old T shares, causing it to recognize an additional $7,500 gain in Year 1.

(vi) Under section 1366, B reports 40 percent, or $22,500, of old T's $56,250 gain recognized in Year 1. Under section 1367, this increases B's $10,000 adjusted basis in its T stock to $32,500. Next, in old T's deemed liquidation, B is considered to receive the $25,000 note and $15,000 of other consideration. Applying section 453, including section 453(h), to the deemed liquidation, B's selling price and contract price are both $40,000. Gross profit is $7,500 ($40,000 selling price - B's basis of $32,500). B's gross profit ratio is 0.1875 (gross profit of $7,500 ÷ $40,000 contract price). Thus, $2,812.50 (0.1875 × $15,000) is Year 1 gain attributable to the deemed liquidation. In Year 7, when the $25,000 note is paid, B has $4,687.50 (0.1875 × $25,000) of additional gain.

(vii) Under section 1366, C reports 20 percent, or $11,250, of old T's $56,250 gain recognized in Year 1. Under section 1367, this increases C's $5,000 adjusted basis in its T stock to $16,250. Next, in old T's deemed liquidation, C is considered to receive $20,000 for its old T shares, causing it to recognize an additional $3,750 gain in Year 1. Finally, under paragraph (d)(5)(ii) of this section, C is considered to acquire its stock in T on the day after the acquisition date for $20,000 (fair market value = grossed-up amount realized of $100,000 × 20%). C's holding period in the stock deemed received in new T begins at that time.

STATUTORY FRAMEWORK AND MECHANICS OF CODE SECTION 336(e)

The applicable regulations state that the federal income tax consequences of an election under Code section 336(e) should "coincide" with those of Code section 338(h)(10).[43] Therefore, like a Code section 338(h)(10) election, under a Code section 336(e) election:

1. Seller recognizes no gain or loss on the actual sale of stock.[44]
2. There is a deemed sale of assets before the close of the disposition, while the Target is owned by the Seller. The deemed sale price, here called the aggregate deemed asset disposition price (ADADP), is determined in the same manner as the ADSP in a deemed sale under Code section 338(h)(10).[45]
3. Old Target's gain or loss from the deemed sale is determined by allocating the ADADP (the amount realized from the deemed sale) to assets under Reg. §§ 1.338-6 and -7.[46] If the Target was an S corporation, this gain or loss flows through to the Seller and increases Seller's basis in Target stock under Code Sections 1366 and 1367 since Target's S election status persists through the close of the disposition date.[47]
4. Seller recognizes gain or loss in a deemed liquidation, where old Target transfers all consideration received in the deemed sale (the ADADP) to Seller in exchange for Seller's Target stock. Like in a 338(h)(10) election, this deemed exchange is taxed as a complete liquidation transaction, as if it actually occurred.[48]
5. New Target increases basis in assets by allocating the adjusted grossed-up basis (the AGUB) to assets under Reg. §§ 1.338-6 and -7. Here, the AGUB is determined for a Code section 336(e) election in the same manner as for a Code section 338(h)(10) election.[49]

Making the Election. Interestingly, although the Buyer(s) are likely the biggest and most obvious tax beneficiaries of a Code section 336(e) election, the election itself does not require the Buyers' consent or even participation. Unlike a Code section 338(h)(10) election (which must be filed jointly by the Buyer and the Seller), a Code section 336(e) election is made by Seller and Target entering into a binding agreement and Target (or Seller if the Target was a consolidated subsidiary) attaching the applicable election statement to its next timely filed tax return.[50]

Comment: Code section 336(e) elections operate as a supplement, and not an override, to Code section 338(h)(10) elections. If a transaction qualifies as both a qualified stock purchase and a qualified stock disposition, only Code section 338(h)(10) may be used.[51] This prevents Sellers from circumventing a Buyer's joint participation in the election in these situations.

Dealing with Retained Stock. Similar to a Code section 338(h)(10) election, minority shareholders who retain their stock will not be subject to tax under the deemed liquidation portion a Code section 336(e) election, but may still incur additional tax from the transaction if the Target was an S corporation; there is no provision to divert Old Target's gain to only participating shareholders and shield non-participating shareholders.[52]

If the Seller retains a portion of their stock (while still disposing of enough to meet the qualifying stock disposition requirements), Code section 336(e) provides that the Seller will still be treated as if it liquidated all of its Target stock, and then bought back the retained stock the day after the disposition.[53]

Example 6: Assume the same facts as Reg. § 1.338(h)(10)-1(e), Example 10, except now P is an individual, not a corporation. Now this transaction no longer constitutes a qualified stock purchase and Code section 338(h)(10) is inapplicable. However, this meets the requirements of a qualified stock disposition since (1) the target is an S corporation, and (2) sellers sold stock in the target representing 80 percent or more of the vote and value. Here, the S corporation may make a Code section 336(e) election to create identical tax results as Reg. § 1.338(h)(10)-1(e), Example 10.

Example 7: Assume the same facts as Reg. § 1.338(h)(10)-1(e), Example 10, except now there are two buyers, P and Q. Assume P buys all of A's shares (representing 40 percent interest in the S corporation) for $40,000 cash, and Q buys all of B's shares (representing 40 percent interest in the S corporation) by issuing a $25,000 note and giving property with a fair market value of $15,000. This transaction no longer constitutes a qualified stock purchase since 80 percent of target stock was not purchased by "a corporation." However, like ***Example 6***, this meets the requirements of a qualified stock disposition and the S corporation may make a Code section 336(e) election to create identical tax results as Reg. § 1.338(h)(10)-1(e), Example 10. Note the irrelevancies here:

- It doesn't matter whether P and Q are individuals or corporations.

- P and Q may be buyers working together to acquire the S corporation, or unrelated parties who don't know each other (as long as they both buy stock representing 80 vote and value within twelve months of each other).

However, note how this transaction could also be done differently to still utilize Code section 338(h)(10): P and Q could form a new S corporation "Newco" that would buy the target S corporation stock from A and B, Newco and the target S corporation could make a Code section 338(h)(10) election, and then the target S corporation could make a Qualified Subchapter S Subsidiary (QSSS) election. This achieves identical tax results as above, but with a different corporate structure (which may or may not have significance to the parties).

PROTECTIVE SECTION 336(e) ELECTIONS FOR BAD DISTRIBUTIONS OF SUBSIDIARY STOCK UNDER SECTION 355

In addition to converting an actual stock sale into a deemed asset sale, a protective Code section 336(e) election may be used to convert a deemed stock sale under Code Sections 355(d) or (e) into a deemed asset sale.

Summary of Code Section 355 Stock Distributions. Generally, Code section 355 provides tax-free status for distributions of subsidiary stock to a parent's shareholders. Further, Code section 355 distributions can be part of a tax-free reorganization if preceded by a contribution of assets to a subsidiary (called a "divisive D reorganization"). However, in both situations, there are two ways that this tax-free distribution can go wrong:

1. *The transaction fails a basic requirement of Code Section 355* – To obtain tax-free status, some core requirements must be met:

    - Parent must control the subsidiary;

    - Parent must distribute stock, and this must be enough for control of the subsidiary;

- The transfer must not be a device for distributing earnings and profits;
- Both corporations must conduct an active trade or business after the transfer;
- There must be a business purpose for the distribution (as opposed to solely tax purpose); and
- There must be some continuity of interest between the shareholders owning the parent before the transaction and the shareholders owning the subsidiary after the transaction.

Here, a transfer will fail the active trade or business requirement if either 80 percent of the parent or the subsidiary was purchased within the past five years.[54]

If all of these requirements aren't met, then the distribution of subsidiary stock will be taxed as any other distribution of corporate property; the parent corporation recognizes gain as if the subsidiary stock was sold at fair market value, and shareholders treat the distribution as either a dividend or return of capital. See Chapter 15.

2. *The transaction passes the basic requirements, but implicates Code Section 355(d) or (e)* – Code section 355(d) and (e) are best rationalized as an intermediate punishment for the purchase of between 50 and 80 percent control of either the parent or subsidiary within the past five years or as part of a disguised sale plan.[55] Here, the parent corporation still recognizes gain as if the subsidiary stock was sold at the fair market value, but the recipient shareholders do not treat this as a taxable corporate distribution.[56] Instead, shareholders treat still treat this as a good Code section 355 transaction and allocate their pre-transaction basis in parent stock to their post-transaction stock in the parent and subsidiary.

Protective Code Section 336(e) elections. In life it is generally a good strategy to hope for the best but plan for the worst, and Code section 355 distributions are no exception. Although it's easy to tell when five years have passed, transactions involving the purchase of 50 percent or more of a parent or subsidiary are never fully safe from the subjective "part of a plan" application of Code section 355(d) and (e). However, if the assets in the subsidiary have considerable basis, making a protective Code section 336(e) election may mitigate the effect of a Code section 355(d) or (e) violation.

Here, the 336(e) election operates in a modified manner. Similar to a normal 336(e) election,

1. Seller (the parent corporation) recognizes no gain or loss on the deemed sale of subsidiary stock (triggered by Code section 355(d) and (e));[57] and

Figure 12.4

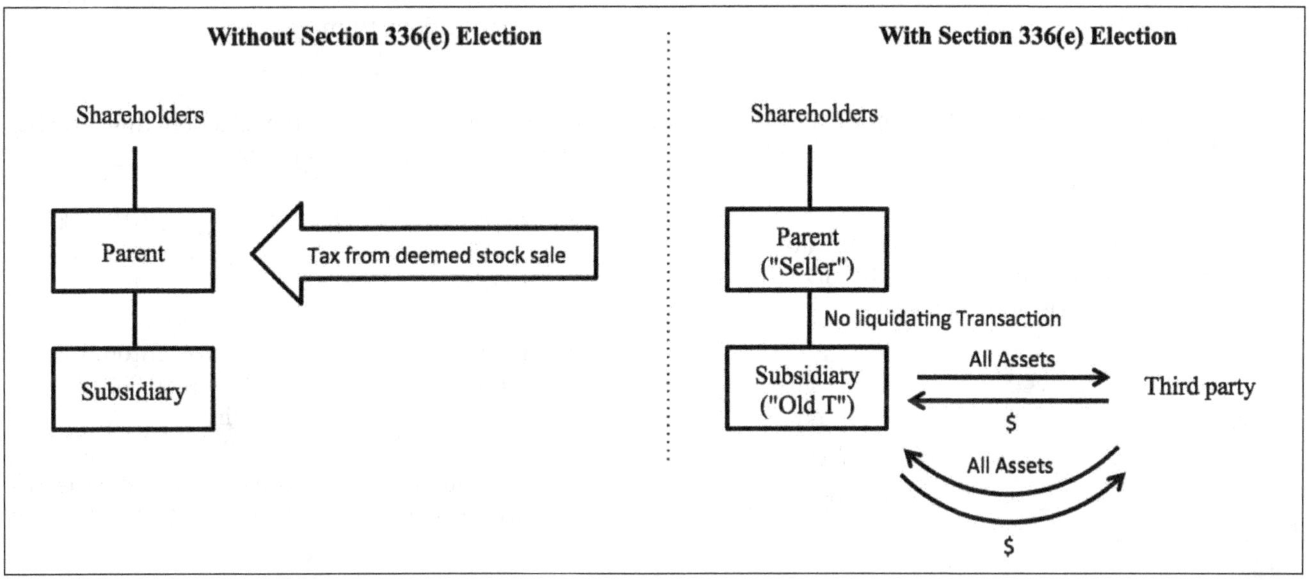

2. There is still a deemed sale of assets where Controlled (the subsidiary) recognizes gain or loss as if assets are sold to an unrelated third party and steps up basis in its assets as if it bought the assets back after.[58]

However, unlike a normal 336(e) election, there is no deemed liquidation to create tax to Seller (the parent corporation).[59]

INTERACTION OF CODE SECTION 336(e) AND CODE SECTION 453 INSTALLMENT SALES

Similar to Code section 338, the regulations of Code section 336(e) recognize the technical difficulties of applying Code section 453 installment sale treatment to a deemed asset sale. Accordingly, the Code section 336(e) regulations piggyback on the Code section 338(h)(10) solution by cross-referencing Reg. § 1.338(h)(10)-1(d)(8) in the discussion of Old Target's gain or loss recognition,[60] and stating generally:

> "§ 1.338(h)(10)-1(d)(8), concerning the availability of the section 453 installment method, may apply with respect to Section 336(e)."[61]

This solution derives from a larger willingness to apply Section 338 principles to Section 336(e). The regulations under Code section 336(e) expressly provide that, to the extent not inconsistent with Section 336(e) (and the regulations thereunder) the principles of Section 338 (and the regulations thereunder) apply for purposes of the 336(e) regulations.[62]

Example 8: Assume the following facts, which modify Reg. § 1.338(h)(10)-1(e), Example 10 to illustrate these concepts:

X, an S corporation, has a single class of stock and three shareholders with the following ownership interests and tax basis:

	Ownership	Basis
A	40%	10,000
B	40%	10,000
C	20%	5,000

Deciding to bring in a new partner D, each shareholder agrees to sell half of his or her stock to D. However, D is short on cash and has a great idea: D will have Y, a wholly owned S corporation of his, buy the S corporation stock for him. A, B, and C agree, so bought Y buys X stock as follows: 20 percent from A for $20,000 cash, 20 percent from B for $20,000, and 10 percent from C for $10,000. After this transaction, X shareholders have the following ownership interests and tax basis:

	Ownership	Basis
A	20%	5,000
B	20%	5,000
C	10%	2,500
Y	50%	50,000

With D's help, X is wildly successful and quickly triples in value.

A year later, D decides to distribute the X stock to himself since it was really annoying having to wait for the Form K-1 from X's taxes to do his Y taxes. Here, this distribution of X stock squarely implicates Code section 355(d) as a distribution of stock in a controlled subsidiary where 50 to 80 percent of the controlled company (X) was purchased within the past five years. At the time of distribution, D's interest in Y has a fair market value of $1,500,000 (including Y's interest in X) and a basis of $300,000; and Y's interest in X has a fair market value of $150,000 but coincidentally still a $50,000 basis after pass-through income and distributions from the year.

Without a Code section 336(e) election, this distribution would create the following tax:

- Y would recognize $100,000 gain ($150,000 fair market value – $50,000 basis) on the sale of X stock.
- Y's $100,000 gain would pass through to D and increase his basis in Y to $400,000 (300,000 starting basis + 100,000 gain).
- D would allocate his pre-transaction basis in Y stock (increased by the $100,000 above) to his

Figure 12.5

	Before Distribution	After Distribution	
Y stock	400,000 basis	360,000 basis	$400{,}000 \times \left(\frac{(1{,}500{,}000 - 150{,}000)}{1{,}500{,}000}\right)$
X stock		40,000 basis	$400{,}000 \times \left(\frac{150{,}000}{1{,}500{,}000}\right)$

post-transaction interest in Y and X stock by the respective fair market value:

With a Code section 336(e) election, this distribution would instead create very different tax consequences:

- X would be deemed to sell all of its assets to an unrelated third party for $100,000 (50,000 / 0.5). Depending on X's basis in its assets, this may produce either a large or small gain.
- X's gain would pass through to A, B, C, and D, and increase their basis in X stock accordingly.
- X would be deemed to buy all of its assets back from the third party for $100,000 (50,000 / 0.5) and increase its basis in assets.

Note that although a Code section 336(e) election for Code section 355(d) and (e) transactions may reduce the overall tax, it may also shift the tax burden amongst the involved parties as it did here.

CHAPTER ENDNOTES

1. IRC Sec. 338(d)(3).
2. IRC Sec. 338(g).
3. IRC Sec. 338(a)(1).
4. IRC Sec. 338 (a)(1) and (b).
5. Reg. § 1.338(h)(10)-1(c)(3).
6. See Reg. § 1.338(h)(10)-1(d).
7. Reg. § 1.338(h)(10)-1(c)(1).
8. Reg. § 1.336-1(b)(6).
9. IRC Sec. 338(a).
10. IRC Sec. 338(d)(3).
11. IRC Sec. 1504(a)(2), (4).
12. IRC Sec. 338(g)(1).
13. IRC Sec. 338(g)(3).
14. IRC Sec. 1001.
15. Reg. § 1.338-4(h).
16. Reg. § 1.338-4.
17. Reg. § 1.338-4(b)(1).
18. Reg. § 1.338-4(e).
19. Reg. § 1.338-5(a).
20. Reg. § 1.338-5(b)(1).
21. Reg. § 1.338-5(a).
22. IRC Sec. 338(b)(4); Reg. § 1.338-5(c).
23. IRC Sec. 338(b)(6)(A).
24. IRC Sec. 338(b)(6)(B).
25. Reg. § 1.338-2(c)(18); Reg. § 1.338-3(b)(4)(i).
26. Reg. § 1.338-4(h)(2).
27. IRC Sec. 338(d).
28. IRC Sec. 338(h)(4).
29. Reg. § 1.338-8(b), (c), and (d).
30. Reg. § 1.338-8(a), (d).
31. *Id.*
32. Reg. § 1.338-10(a)(1).
33. Reg. § 1.338-10(a)(1).
34. See IRC Sec. 338(e)(3), (i).
35. Reg. § 1.338(h)(10)-1(c).
36. Reg. § 1.338(h)(10)-1(d).
37. See IRC Sec. 1366.
38. Reg. § 1.338(h)(10)-1(c).
39. Reg. §1.338(h)(10)-1(c)(4).
40. Reg. § 1.338(h)(10)-1(c)(4).
41. See Reg. § 15A.453-1(b)(3)(i).
42. Reg. § 1.338(h)(10)-1(d)(8).
43. Reg. § 1.336-1(a)(1)
44. Reg. § 1.336-2(b)(1)(i)(A).
45. *Compare* Reg. § 1.336-3(b) *with* Reg. § 1.338-4(b).
46. Reg. § 1.336-2(b)(1)(i)(A).
47. Reg. § 1.336-2(b)(1)(i)(A).
48. Reg. § 1.336-2(b)(1)(iii)(A).
49. See Reg. § 1.336-4 (referencing Reg. § 1.338-5 and merely modifying terms to reflect that a § 336(e) election relates to a disposition rather than an acquisition).
50. Reg. § 1.336-2(h).
51. Reg. § 1.336-1(b)(6)(ii)(A).
52. *See* Reg. § 1.336-3(d).

53. Reg. § 1.336-2(b)(1)(v).
54. IRC Sec. 355(b)(2)(D).
55. *Compare* IRC Sec. 355(b)(2)(B) *with* IRC Sec. 355(d)(2) and (e)(2).
56. *South Tulsa Pathology Lab v. Comm'r.*, 118 T.C. 84 (2002).
57. Reg. § 1.336-2(b)(2)(iii).
58. Reg. § 1.336-2(b)(2)(i) and (ii).
59. Reg. § 1.336-2(b)(2)(i)(A)(1).
60. Reg. § 1.336-2(b)(1)(i)(B)(1) and -2(b)(2)(i)(B)(1).
61. *Id.*
62. Reg. § 1.336-1(a)(1)(i).

POST-ACQUISITION LIMITATIONS ON NOLs

CHAPTER 13

OVERVIEW

Unlike a taxable sale of assets, which transfers the business but generally leaves behind both the legal and financial history of the Target, a purchase of stock allows the Buyer to acquire the tax history of the Target as well as its assets and business. Over the years, Congress became concerned about the trafficking in corporations that had built-in net operating losses (NOLs). Code section 382 was introduced and amended several times in an effort to restrict the trafficking in so-called "loss corporations."

The early versions of Code section 382 attempted to prevent the purchase of loss corporations for the purpose of using net operating losses to offset income from entirely unrelated businesses. However, the early versions of Code section 382 did not limit the use of NOLs so long as the buyers continued to carry on the loss corporation's existing trade or business. Also, tax-free reorganizations generally did not limit the use of NOLs so long as the loss corporation's shareholders retained a continuing stock interest representing 20 percent or more of the value of the successor corporation.

The Tax Reform Act of 1986 (TRA-86) (P.L. 99-514) substantially expanded the scope and application of Code section 382 to purchases of corporate stock. Today, a change in ownership of more than 50 percentage points of a loss corporation's stock over the lowest percentage of stock of the loss corporation (or any predecessor corporation) owned by such shareholders at any time during the testing period[1] triggers the application of Code section 382. When an "ownership change" occurs, Code section 382 limits the amount of net operating losses that can be used in each year to an amount equal to a statutory rate of return multiplied by the fair market value of the loss corporation's stock immediately before the ownership change. The concept underlying current Code section 382 is that purchasing net operating losses to offset income is the equivalent of investing for a tax-exempt return. Therefore, Congress sought to make the value of the net operating losses in a loss corporation roughly equal to the value of investing the same proceeds in a tax-exempt bond or comparable tax-exempt investment.

Although purchasing the stock of the Target is probably the most common way to acquire both the business and the tax history of an incorporated business (and trigger the application of Code section 382), Code section 381 defines certain transactions where an acquisition of business assets can lead to a carryover of tax attributes. Generally, Code section 381 applies when the Acquiring Corporation acquires assets (1) in a distribution to which Code section 332 applies or (2) in a transfer to which Code section 361 (relating to non-recognition of gain or loss to corporations) applies, but only if such transfer is pursuant to a tax-free reorganization described in subparagraph (A), (C), (D), (F), or (G) of Code section 368(a)(1).[2] In the case of a Type "D" and Type "G" reorganization, the transfer must also meet certain requirements under Code section 354(b)(1).[3] A corporation that succeeds to the tax attributes of another corporation pursuant to Code section 381(a) is subject to limitations imposed by Code sections 381(b) and (c), 382, 383, and 384.

The consolidated return regulations also place limitations on the use of acquired net operating losses. However, consolidated return issues are beyond the scope of this chapter.

CODE SECTION 382—LIMITATION ON NET OPERATING LOSS CARRYFORWARDS

Code section 382 limits (the "Section 382 limitation") the amount of taxable income of any "new loss corporation" for any "post-change year" that may be offset by "pre-change" losses.[4] The Section 382 limitation for any post-change year is an amount equal to the value of the old loss corporation, multiplied by the long-term tax-exempt rate.[5] The Section 382 limitation will be zero if the new loss corporation does not continue the business enterprise of the old loss corporation at all times during the two-year period beginning on the change date.[6] The continuity of business enterprise requirement is defined in Reg. § 1.368-1(d).

Example 1: X corporation has a $10 million net operating loss carryforward. On January 1, 1994, Y corporation acquires all the stock of X corporation for $5 million in cash in a transaction that constitutes an ownership change under Code section 382. The long-term tax-exempt rate in effect at the time of the transaction is seven percent. Based on these facts, X may use its NOL carryforward. In 1994 and later years, only an amount of income equal to seven percent of $5 million, or $350,000, can be offset by the NOL. The unused NOLs will eventually expire since the maximum period that NOLs can be carried forward is twenty years.[7]

Pre-Change Loss and Post-Change Year. Code section 382(d)(1) defines a "pre-change loss" as "any net operating loss carryforward of the old loss corporation to the taxable year ending with an ownership change or in which the change date occurs," plus "the net operating loss of the old loss corporation for the taxable year in which the ownership change occurs to the extent such loss is allocable to the period in such year on or before the change date." Basically, the term "pre-change loss" means all of the NOLs of a corporation that are attributable to the period prior to an "ownership change." The term "post-change year" means "any taxable year ending after the change date."[8] The term "change date" means (1) in the case where the last component of an ownership change is an owner shift involving a 5-percent shareholder, the date on which such shift occurs, and (2) in the case which the last component of an ownership change is an equity structure shift, the date of the reorganization.[9]

Value of Old Loss Corporation. The value of the old loss corporation is generally the value of the stock of such corporation (including any stock described in Code section 1504(a)(4)) immediately before the ownership change.[10] The term "value" means fair market value.[11]

Long-Term Tax-Exempt Rate. The "long-term tax-exempt rate" is the highest of the adjusted federal long-term rates in effect for the three-calendar-month period ending with the calendar month in which the change date occurs.[12] The adjusted federal long-term rate is the applicable federal rate determined under Code section 1274(d) (1) properly adjusted for differences between rates on long-term taxable and tax-exempt obligations.[13]

Ownership Change. There is an "ownership change" if, "immediately after any 'owner shift involving a 5-percent shareholder' or any 'equity structure shift' the percentage of the stock of the loss corporation owned by one or more 5-percent shareholders has increased by more than 50 percentage points over the lowest percentage of stock of the loss corporation (or any predecessor corporation) owned by such shareholders at any time during the testing period."[14]

Owner Shift and Equity Structure Shift. Code section 382(g)(2) defines an "owner shift involving a 5 percent shareholder" to exist if "(A) there is any change in the respective ownership of stock of a corporation, and (B) such change affects the percentage of stock of such corporation owned by any person who is a 5- percent shareholder before or after such change." The term "equity structure shift" means any reorganization within the meaning of Code section 368. However, that term does not include any Type "D" or Type "G" reorganization unless the requirements of Code section 354(b)(1) are met or any Type "F" reorganization.[15] The term "equity structure shift" also includes taxable reorganization-type transactions, public offerings, and similar transactions, to the extent provided in regulations.[16] However, special rules exempt from the definition of an owner shift a transfer of stock by reason of death, gift, divorce, separation, or similar transaction.[17] In particular, this rule states that if the basis of any stock in the hands of any person is determined under (1) Code section 1014 (relating to property acquired from a decedent), (2) Code section 1015 (relating to property acquired by a gift or transfer in trust), or (3) Code section 1041(b)(2) (relating to transfers of property between spouses or incident to divorce), such person is treated as owning the stock during the period such stock was owned by the person from whom it was acquired.[18] Likewise, stock received by any person in satisfaction of a right to receive a pecuniary bequest or stock acquired by a person pursuant to any divorce or separation instrument (within the meaning of Code section 71(b)(2)) is treated as owned by such person during the period such stock was owned by the person from whom it was acquired.[19]

5-Percent Shareholder. The term "5-percent shareholder" means "any person holding 5 percent or more of the stock of the corporation at any time during the testing period."[20] Generally, all stock owned by shareholders who are not 5-percent shareholders is aggregated and treated as stock owned by one 5-percent shareholder.[21] Stock owned by a group of persons who, pursuant to a formal or informal understanding among themselves, acquire five percent or more of the stock of a loss corporation, is aggregated and treated as stock owned by a separate 5-percent shareholder, even though each member of the group individually owns less than five percent of the stock.[22] Except as provided in regulations and in Code section 382(e) (relating to the determination of value of a corporation), the term "stock" means stock other than stock described in Code section 1504(a)(4).[23]

Comment: In effect, the stock used to measure changes in ownership interests for purposes of Code section 382 excludes non-voting, non-convertible preferred stock, which is sometimes called "straight preferred."

The determination of the percentage of stock of any corporation held by any person is made on the basis of value.[24] Except as provided in regulations, changes in proportionate ownership attributable solely to fluctuations in the relative fair-market values of different classes of stock are disregarded.[25]

Testing Period. The term "testing period" means "the three-year period ending on the day of any owner shift involving a 5 percent owner or equity structure shift."[26] If there has been a prior ownership change, the testing period for determining whether a subsequent ownership change has occurred does not begin until the first day following the change date for the earlier change.[27] The testing period does not begin before the earlier of the first day of the first tax year from which there is a carryforward of a loss or of an excess credit to the first post-change year or the tax year in which the transaction being tested occurs.[28]

Testing Date. To implement the ownership change test, the regulations introduce the concept of "testing date."[29] The computation of the percentage increase in ownership is made as of the close of each testing date.[30]

Only Increases Considered. In order to determine whether an ownership change has occurred on a testing date, the loss corporation must identify each 5-percent shareholder whose percentage of stock ownership in the loss corporation immediately after the close of the testing date has increased, compared to such shareholder's lowest percentage of stock ownership in such corporation at any time during the testing period.[31] The amount of the increase in the percentage of stock ownership in the loss corporation of each 5-percent shareholder must be computed separately by comparing the percentage ownership of each such 5-percent shareholder immediately after the close of the testing date to such shareholder's lowest percentage ownership at any time during the testing period.[32] Each such increase in the percentage ownership of each 5-percent shareholder is then added together with all other such increases of other 5-percent shareholders to determine whether an ownership change has occurred.[33] Because only those 5-percent shareholders whose percentages of stock ownership have increased are taken into account, a 5-percent shareholder is disregarded if that shareholder's percentage of stock ownership, immediately after the close of the testing date, has decreased (or has remained the same), compared to his lowest percentage ownership interest on any previous date during the testing period.[34]

Old Loss Corporation and New Loss Corporation. The term "loss corporation" means "a corporation entitled to use a net operating loss carryover or having a net operating loss for the taxable year in which the ownership change occurs."[35] Except to the extent provided in regulations, such term includes any corporation with a net unrealized built-in loss.[34] The term "old loss corporation" means "any corporation – (A) with respect to which there is an ownership change, and (B) which (before the ownership change) was a loss corporation."[36] The term "new loss corporation" means "a corporation which (after an ownership change) is a loss corporation."[37] The same corporation may be both an old loss corporation and a new loss corporation.[38]

To illustrate the computation of increases in percentage ownership, Temp. Reg. § 1.382-2T(c)(2) gives the following example:

(i) A and B each own 40 percent of the outstanding L stock. The remaining 20 percent of L stock is owned by 100 unrelated individuals, none of whom own as much as five percent of the L stock ("Public L"). C negotiates with A and B to purchase all their stock in L.

(ii) The acquisitions from both A and B are completed on September 30, 1990. C's acquisition of 80 percent of L stock results in an ownership change because C's percentage ownership has increased by 80 percentage points as of the testing date, compared to C's lowest percentage ownership in L at any time during the testing period (0 percent).

The determination whether an ownership change has occurred is made without regard to whether the changes in stock ownership of the loss corporation (by one or more 5-percent shareholders) result from related or unrelated events.[39]

Temp. Reg. § 1.382-2T(c)(4), gives the following example:

(i) L has outstanding 200 shares of common stock. A, B and C respectively own 100, 50 and 50 shares of the L stock. On January 2, 1988, A sells 60 shares of L stock to B. Thus, B's percentage ownership interest in L increases by 30 percentage points, from 50 shares to 110 shares. On January 1, 1989, A purchases C's entire interest in L. Thus, A's percentage ownership interest in L increases by 25 percentage points, compared to his lowest percentage ownership interest in L, from 40 shares immediately following the January 2, 1988 sale to B to 90 shares. Even though A's ownership interest in L as of January 1, 1989 has decreased, compared to A's 50 percent ownership interest at the beginning of the testing period, A is a 5-percent shareholder who must be taken into account for purposes of the computation required under [Temp. Reg. § 1.382-2T(c)(1)] because his interest in L on that testing date (45 percent) has increased, compared to his lowest percentage ownership interest in L at any time during the testing period (20 percent following the sale to B).

(ii) Accordingly, although A and B jointly have increased their aggregate total ownership interest in L between January 2, 1988 and January 1, 1989 by only 25 percentage points (i.e., the total ownership interest in L held by A and B at all times is not less than a 75 percent interest), the total of their separate increases in the percentage stock ownership of L, compared to their respective lowest percentage ownership interests at any time during the testing period, is 55 percentage points. Thus, an ownership change occurs as a result of A's acquisition of L stock on January 1, 1989.

Planning to Avoid Code section 382. Parties acquiring a corporation with significant NOLs have a natural interest in exploring whether it is possible to plan around the limitations of Code section 382. As a practical matter, a creeping acquisition that occurs over time may avoid the Section 382 limitation so long as there is not a sufficiently large transfer of equity interest within any three-year period to constitute an ownership change.

In this regard, the acquiring parties may intentionally avoid acquiring sufficient stock interest so as to trigger an ownership change and the application of Code section 382. For example, if a corporation with substantial NOLs is being acquired by its senior management, the management might acquire an interest constituting less than 50 percent of the total stock within any three-year testing period so that the corporation can take advantage of the existing NOLs. In this type of situation, query whether the management team could also negotiate a phantom stock plan, characterized as compensation but having an economic value tied to the value of equity, that could serve as a mechanism to convey the desired "quasi-equity" interest in the corporation without triggering the application of Code section 382.

Be aware, however, that an acquisition that avoids the objective tests of Code section 382 can still be challenged by the IRS using the subjective intent tests under Code section 269. See the discussion of Code section 269 later in this chapter.

As a practical matter, parties interested in acquiring a loss corporation are usually seeking majority control immediately and are not interested in maintaining a minority position for at least three years in a company that, by definition, has been losing money.

SPECIAL RULES REGARDING OPTIONS

Code section 382 uses a mechanical mathematical test to measure changes in stock ownership. However, as every good lawyer knows, equity in a corporation can come in many forms. The IRS is empowered to issue regulations as may be necessary (1) to treat warrants, options, contracts to acquire stock, convertible debt interests, and other similar interests as stock and (2) to treat stock as not stock.[40] In addition, Code section 382 expressly states that, except as provided in regulations, an option to acquire stock shall be treated as exercised if that exercise results in an ownership change.[41]

In 1987, the IRS issued regulations to address options and similar interests.[42] These regulations are effective for testing dates prior to November 5, 1992.[43]

The pre-November 5, 1992, regulations provide that, solely for the purpose of determining whether there is an ownership change on any testing date, stock of the loss corporation that is subject to an option shall be treated as acquired on any such date, pursuant to an exercise of the option by its owner on that date, if such deemed exercise would result in an ownership change.[44] These regulations further provide that an option to acquire an option with respect to the stock of the loss corporation, and each one of a series of such options, is considered an option to acquire such stock.[45]

The pre-November 5, 1992, regulations provide that the following interests will be treated in the same manner as options: a warrant, a convertible debt instrument, an instrument other than debt that is convertible into stock, a put, a stock interest subject to risk of forfeiture, and a contract to acquire or sell stock.[46] If an option treated as exercised lapses unexercised or its owner irrevocably forfeits his or her right to acquire stock pursuant to the option, the option will be treated as if it had never been issued.[47]

Reg. § 1.382-4(d), effective for any testing date on or after November 5, 1992, takes an entirely different approach to treatment of options. As a general rule, an option will ***not*** be treated as being exercised until it actually has been exercised.[48] However, for purposes of determining whether an ownership change has occurred, an option will be treated as exercised on the date of its issuance or transfer if, on that date, the option satisfies the ownership test, the control test, or the income test.[49] As a general rule, an option that is treated as exercised on the date of its issuance or transfer will be treated as exercised on any subsequent testing date for purposes of determining whether an ownership change has occurred.[50]

Ownership Test. An option satisfies the ownership test if a principal purpose of the issuance, transfer, or structuring of the option (alone or in combination with other arrangements) is to avoid or ameliorate the impact of an ownership change of the loss corporation by providing the holder of the option, prior to its exercise or transfer, with a substantial portion of the attributes of ownership of the underlying stock.[51]

Control Test. An option satisfies the control test if a principal purpose of the issuance, transfer, or structuring of the option (alone or in combination with other arrangements) is to avoid or ameliorate the impact of an ownership change of the loss corporation and the holder of the option and any persons related to the option holder have, in the aggregate, a direct and indirect ownership interest in the loss corporation of more than 50 percent (determined as if the increase in such persons' percentage ownership interest that would result from the exercise of the option in question and any other options to acquire stock held by such persons, and any other intended increases in such persons' percentage ownership interest, actually occurred on the date the option was issued or transferred).[52]

Income Test. An option satisfies the income test if a principal purpose of the issuance, transfer, or structuring of the option (alone or in combination with other arrangements) is to avoid or ameliorate the impact of an ownership change of the loss corporation by facilitating the creation of income (including accelerating income or deferring deductions) or value (including unrealized built-in gains) prior to the exercise or transfer of the option.[53]

CODE SECTION 382—SPECIAL RULES FOR BUILT-IN GAINS AND LOSSES

Code section 382(h) provides special rules (1) to restrict the use of unrealized losses by the old loss corporation that existed on the change date and (2) to increase the loss limitation to take into account the recognition of unrealized gains that existed on the change date. In effect, Code section 382(h) provides a mechanism to "book" the built-in gains and losses of the old loss corporation on the change date, and take these built-in gains and losses into account under the overall limitation on NOL carryforwards to the extent such gains or losses are subsequently recognized during the "recognition period."

Net Unrealized Built-in Gain. If the old loss corporation has a net unrealized built-in gain, the Section 382 Limitation for any recognition period tax year is increased by the recognized built-in gains for such tax year.[54] The term "net unrealized built-in gain" means, with respect to any old loss corporation, the amount by which the fair market value of the assets of such corporation immediately before an ownership change is more than the aggregate adjusted basis of such assets at such time.[55] The "recognized built-in gain" means any gain recognized during the recognition period on the disposition of any asset to the extent the new corporation establishes that (1) such asset was held by the old loss corporation immediately before the change date and (2) such gain does not exceed the excess of (a) the fair market value of such asset on the change date over (b) the adjusted basis of such asset on such date.[56]

Net Unrealized Built-in Losses. If the old loss corporation has a net unrealized built-in loss, the recognized built-in loss for any recognition period tax year shall be subject to the Section 382 limitation in the same manner as if such loss were a pre-change loss.[57] The term "net unrealized built-in loss" means, with respect to any old loss corporation, the amount by which the fair market value of the assets of such corporation immediately before an ownership change is less than the aggregate adjusted basis of such assets at such time.[58] The term "recognized built-in loss" means any loss recognized during the recognition period on the disposition of any asset except to the extent the new loss corporation establishes that (1) such asset was not held by the old loss corporation immediately before the change date, or (2) such loss exceeds the excess of (a) the adjusted basis of such asset on the change date over (b) the fair market value of such asset on such date.[59]

The recognition period is the five-year period beginning on the change date.[60]

Code section 382(h) contains a significant threshold requirement. If the amount of the net unrealized built-in gain or loss is not greater than the lesser of (1) 15 percent of the fair-market value of the corporation's assets immediately before the ownership change, or (2) $10 million, the net unrealized built-in gain or loss is zero.[61] Cash, cash items, and marketable securities with a value not substantially different from tax basis are not taken into account in determining the fair market value of the corporation's assets.[62]

CODE SECTION 383—EXCESS CREDITS LIMITATION

The rules set forth in Code section 382 limit the amount of net operating losses that can be used to offset income after a change in ownership. However, a corporation can have other potentially valuable tax attributes besides net operating losses. Under Code section 383, the IRS has promulgated regulations that prescribe rules similar to those under Code section 382 that apply to the use of other tax attributes, such as capital losses and tax credits.

The "Section 383 credit limitation" for a post-change year is defined by the regulations as an amount equal to the excess of (1) the new loss corporation's regular tax liability for the post-change year over (2) the new loss corporation's regular tax liability for the post-change year computed by allowing as an additional deduction an amount equal to the unabsorbed Section 382 limitation for the year.[63] The basic purpose of the Code section 383 regulations is to take into account the fact that while a pre-change loss allowable under the Section 382 Limitation offsets taxable income, a rule affecting pre-change tax credits must take into account the fact that tax credits offset a dollar of tax liability rather than a dollar of taxable income. In effect, the Section 383 credit limitation is a mechanism for converting the Section 382 limitation into an equivalent limitation on credits.

The terms and nomenclature used in Code section 383 regulations track and generally have the same meaning as in Code section 382 and the regulations thereunder.[64]

The following examples from Reg. § 1.383-1(d)(3)(ii) demonstrate the operation of the Section 383 credit limitation:

Example (1). L is a calendar year taxpayer and has an ownership change on December 31, 1987. For 1988, L has taxable income of $300,000, a regular tax liability of $100,250 and tentative minimum tax of $90,000. L has no pre-change losses, but has a business credit carryforward from 1985 of $25,000, no portion of which is due to the regular percentage of the investment tax credit under section 46. L has a section 382 limitation for 1988 of $50,000. L's section 383 credit limitation is $19,500, i.e., an amount equal to the excess of L's regular tax liability ($100,250) over its regular tax liability calculated by allowing an additional deduction of $50,000. Pursuant to the limitation contained in section 38(c), however, L is entitled to use only $10,250 of its business credit carryforward in 1988. The unabsorbed portion of L's section 382 limitation (computed pursuant to [Reg. § 1.383-1(e)]) is carried forward under section 382(b)(2). The unused portion of L's business credit carryforward, $14,750, is carried forward to the extent provided in section 39.

Example (2). Assume the same facts as in *Example (1)*, except that L's tentative minimum tax is $70,000. L's use of its investment tax credit carryforward is no longer limited by section 38(c); however, pursuant to section 383 and [Reg. § 1.383-1], L is entitled to use only $19,500 of its business credit carryforward in 1988. The unused portion of L's business credit carryforward, $5,500, is carried forward to the extent provided in section 39. There is no unused section 382 limitation to be carried forward.

CODE SECTION 384—LIMITATIONS ON USE OF PRE-ACQUISITION LOSSES TO OFFSET BUILT-IN GAINS

Code section 384 is designed to be a mirror image of Code section 382. Code section 384 basically prohibits corporations with losses from acquiring corporations with unrecognized built-in gains and then using such gains to offset pre-acquisition losses. Just as Code section 382 is designed to limit trafficking in loss corporations, Code section 384 is designed to prevent the "reverse" situation where a loss corporation intentionally purchases a "gain corporation."

Code section 384(a) states that if a corporation acquires, directly (or through one or more other corporations), control of another corporation or if the assets of a corporation are acquired by another corporation in a Type "A," Type "C," or Type

"D" reorganization and either of such corporations is a "gain corporation," then income for any recognition period tax year (to the extent attributable to recognized built-in gains) shall not be offset by any pre-acquisition loss (other than a pre-acquisition loss of the gain corporation).

The term "gain corporation" means any corporation with a net unrealized built-in gain.[65]

The term "recognized built-in gain" means any gain recognized during the recognition period on the disposition of any asset except to the extent the gain corporation (or in the case of an applicable tax-free reorganization, the acquiring corporation) establishes that (1) such asset was not held by the gain corporation on the acquisition date or (2) such gain exceeds the excess (if any) of (a) the fair market value of such asset on the acquisition date, over (b) the adjusted basis of such asset on such date.[66]

The term "acquisition date" means the date on which the acquisition of control occurs or, in the case of a reorganization, the date of the transfer in the reorganization.[67]

The term "control" means ownership of stock in the corporation which meets the requirements of Code section 1504(a)(2)(i.e., stock possessing at least 80 percent of the total voting power of the corporation's stock and a value equal to at least 80 percent of the total value of the corporation's stock).[68]

Except as provided in regulations, the terms "net unrealized built-in gain," "net unrealized built-in loss," "recognized built-in loss," "recognition period," and "recognition period taxable year" have the same respective meanings as when used in Code section 382(h).[69]

CODE SECTION 269—TAX AVOIDANCE LIMITATION

Code section 269 and its predecessor provisions date back to 1943 and were the first attempt by Congress to limit trafficking in what are now known as loss corporations.

Unlike Code section 382, which uses objective tests to determine whether NOL carryovers will be limited, Code section 269 looks at subjective intent. In particular, Code section 269 can be applied upon a mere determination that the taxpayer who obtained the requisite degree of control had the prohibited state of mind. Code section 269 can be applied to disallow an NOL carryover even though the carryover is not disallowed under Code section 382.[70] In effect, Code sections 269 and 382 operate in a complementary fashion and require that a taxpayer pass both a subjective and an objective test in order to utilize fully NOLs of an acquired loss corporation.

Code section 269(a) gives the IRS authority to disallow any deduction, credit, or other allowance where (1) any person or persons acquire, directly or indirectly, control of a corporation, or any corporation acquires, directly or indirectly, property of another corporation not controlled, directly or indirectly, immediately before such acquisition by such acquiring corporation or its stockholders, the basis of which property in the hands of the acquiring corporation, is determined by reference to the basis in the hands of the transferor corporation, and (2) the principal purpose for which the acquisition was made is evasion or avoidance of federal income tax by securing the benefit of a deduction, credit, or other allowance that such person or corporation would not otherwise enjoy.

For purposes of this test, "control" means the ownership of stock possessing at least 50 percent of the total combined voting power of all classes of stock entitled to vote or at least 50 percent of the total value of shares of all classes of stock of the corporation.[71]

There are no attribution rules for determining stock ownership under Code section 269.

Reg. § 1.269-3(b)(1) provides the following example:

Example. Individual A acquires all of the stock of L Corporation which has been engaged in the business of operating retail drug stores. At the time of the acquisition, L Corporation has net operating loss carryovers aggregating $100,000 and its net worth is $100,000. After the acquisition, L Corporation continues to engage in the business of operating retail drug stores but the profits attributable to such business after the acquisition are not sufficient to absorb any substantial portion of the net operating loss carryovers. Shortly after the acquisition, individual A causes to be transferred to L Corporation the assets of a hardware business previously controlled by A which business produces profits sufficient to absorb a substantial portion of L Corporation's net operating loss carryovers. The transfer of the profitable business, which has the effect of using net operating loss carryovers to offset gains of a business unrelated to that which produced the losses, indicates that the principal purpose for which the acquisition of control was made is evasion or avoidance of Federal income tax.

CHAPTER ENDNOTES

1. The testing period, with certain exceptions, is the three-year period ending on the day of any owner shift involving a 5 percent shareholder or the day of any equity structure shift. IRC Sec. 382(i).
2. IRC Sec. 381(a).
3. *Id.*
4. IRC Sec. 382(a).
5. IRC Sec. 382(b)(1).
6. IRC Sec. 382(c).
7. IRC Sec. 172.
8. IRC Sec. 382(d)(2).
9. IRC Sec. 382(j).
10. IRC Sec. 382(e).
11. IRC Sec. 382(k)(5).
12. IRC Sec. 382(f)(1).
13. IRC Sec. 382(f)(2).
14. IRC Sec. 382(g)(1).
15. IRC Sec. 382(g)(3)(A).
16. IRC Sec. 382(g)(3)(B).
17. IRC Sec. 382(l)(3)(B).
18. *Id.*
19. *Id.*
20. IRC Sec. 382(k)(7).
21. IRC Sec. 382(g)(4)(A).
22. Reg. § 1.382-3(a)(1).
23. IRC Sec. 382(k)(6)(A).
24. IRC Sec. 382(k)(6)(C).
25. IRC Sec. 382(l)(3)(C).
26. IRC Sec. 382(i)(1).
27. IRC Sec. 382(i)(2).
28. IRC Sec. 382(i)(3).
29. Temp. Reg. § 1.382-2T(a)(1).
30. *Id.*
31. Temp. Reg. § 1.382-2T(c)(1).
32. *Id.*
33. *Id.*
34. *Id.*
35. IRC Sec. 382(k)(1).
36. IRC Sec. 382(k)(2).
37. IRC Sec. 382(k)(3).

38. *Id.*
39. Temp. Reg. § 1.382-2T(c)(3).
40. IRC Sec. 382(k)(6)(B).
41. IRC Sec. 382(l)(3)(A)(iv).
42. Temp. Reg. § 1.382-2T(h)(4).
43. Temp. Reg. § 1.382-2T(m)(4)(vi).
44. Temp. Reg. § 1.382-2T(h)(4)(i).
45. Temp. Reg. § 1.382-2T(h)(4)(iv).
46. Temp. Reg. § 1.382-2T(h)(4)(v).
47. Temp. Reg. § 1.382-2T(h)(4)(viii).
48. Reg. § 1.382-4(d)(1).
49. Reg. § 1.382-4(d)(2)(i).
50. Reg. § 1.382-4(d)(2)(ii).
51. Reg. § 1.382-4(d)(3).
52. Reg. § 1.382-4(d)(4)(B).
53. Reg. § 1.382-4(d)(5).
54. IRC Sec. 382(h)(1)(A)(i).
55. IRC Sec. 382(h)(3)(A)(i).
56. IRC Sec. 382(h)(2)(A).
57. IRC Sec. 382(h)(1)(B)(i).
58. IRC Sec. 382(h)(3)(A)(i).
59. IRC Sec. 382(h)(2)(B).
60. IRC Sec. 382(h)(7)(A).
61. IRC Sec. 382(h)(3)(B)(i).
62. IRC Sec. 382(h)(3)(B)(ii).
63. Reg. § 1.383-1(c)(6).
64. Reg. § 1.383-1(c)(1).
65. IRC Sec. 384(c)(4).
66. IRC Sec. 384(c)(1)(A).
67. IRC Sec. 384(c)(2).
68. IRC Sec. 384(c)(5).
69. IRC Sec. 384(c)(8).
70. Reg. § 1.269-6; Reg. § 1.269-7.
71. IRC Sec. 269(a).

SELLING THE BUSINESS TO YOURSELF: LIQUIDATION OF A CORPORATION OR PARTNERSHIP

CHAPTER 14

OVERVIEW

Many tax issues, some small and others not so small, arise on the liquidation of a business. If the business is a corporation, a liquidation is a sale or exchange event that triggers tax recognition.[1] In many cases, a liquidating corporation also has a "tail" of uncollected receivables and unpaidliabilities, which can create interesting and sometimes complicated challenges. Partnership entities, including LLCs, can generally liquidate without tax consequences, unless the liquidating distribution results in distributions of cash in excess of outside tax basis.[2]

A liquidation can be the best way—and sometimes the only way—for existing shareholders to realize value from a business when there is no obvious or identifiable third-party buyer. Even if there is a party interested in acquiring the ongoing business, the Acquirer may not want to purchase all the existing business assets. For example, one of the obvious sticking points in many negotiations is the value assigned to the existing accounts receivable (A/R). Knowing that the A/R is fully collectible, the Seller may want full face value. However, the Acquirer is not in a position to judge knowledgeably whether the A/R is collectible. A common solution is to leave the A/R in the hands of the Seller corporation, and for the Seller corporation to deal with collection and keep the proceeds.

Another common asset of a Selling Corporation in an asset sale is an installment obligation, including any earn-out arrangement, delivered by the Acquirer as part of the purchase price. As we will see below, distribution of installment obligations in the context of a corporate liquidation can have surprisingly complicated, and sometimes nasty, tax results.

Still another aspect of a liquidation is the orderly payment of any outstanding obligations that the Buyer declines to assume. Especially in the case of an asset acquisition, the Buyer is often reluctant to assume any liabilities, and at best will assume only those liabilities of a fixed and determinable amount. Providing for the orderly collection and liquidation of assets and the orderly payment of retained liabilities can be a surprisingly complicated and nuanced task.

TAXATION OF CORPORATE LIQUIDATIONS: COMPARING C AND S CORPORATIONS

A corporate liquidation not governed by Code section 332 triggers gain or loss at two levels. First, at the corporate level, Code section 336(a) treats a liquidating distribution as a sale or exchange transaction. Gain or loss is measured based on the fair market value (FMV) of the distributed assets. If the liquidating corporation is a C corporation, the gain is taxed at the corporate level (and any capital gain recognized under Code section 336(a) will be taxed at non-preferential corporate rates). If the liquidating entity is an S corporation, there is likewise gain at the corporate level, but other than possible "sting tax" liability under Code section 1374, the gain will pass through to the S shareholders under Code section 1366, will result in an increase in outside tax basis under Code section 1367, and then will trigger whatever consequences arise on distribution under Code section 1368. Generally there is only a single level of tax (or the equivalent of a single level of tax) in an S corporation liquidation.

The liquidating distribution of money and other property in exchange for stock triggers a second level of tax consequences at the shareholder level.[3] If the liquidating entity is a C corporation, the shareholders will each recognize gain or loss based on the difference between the fair market value of the distributed money and property and each shareholder's tax basis in the surrendered shares. Note that the shareholders' tax basis is not adjusted as a result of gain or loss recognized at the corporate level by the C corporation.

By contract, in an S corporation liquidation the shareholders' outside tax basis in their S corporation stock is adjusted based on the gain or loss recognized at the corporate level.[4] In turn, the S corporation shareholders will recognize gain or loss based on the difference between each shareholder's tax basis in the S corporation stock (as adjusted upward or down depending on the corporate-level recognition of gain or loss) and the fair market value of the money and other property distributed.

When a C corporation sells all or substantially all its assets, a question is when—or whether—to liquidate the corporation. In general, because of the step-up in tax basis on the death of a shareholder under Code section 1014, a viable strategy may be to keep the corporation alive, even though it is subject to the personal holding company (PHC) tax.

In the case of an S corporation, the challenge is deciding whether it is necessary to liquidate the corporation in the same year as the sale in order to avoid a mismatching of capital gain and loss.

Example 1: Shareholder A, the sole shareholder of an S corporation, inherited A's shares from A's father's estate. The S corporation has assets worth $5 million, and a tax basis in those assets at the corporate level of $1 million. At the time of A's father's death, the shares were valued at $4.5 million, and the tax basis was adjusted to $4.5 million under Code section 1014. If the S corporation sells its assets for $5 million, it recognizes $4 million of gain and this amount, in turn, will pass through to A as a positive adjustment to tax basis. This means that, following the sale of assets, the outside tax basis of A is now $8.5 million ($4.5 million of inherited tax basis + $4 million of gain resulting in outside tax basis pursuant to Code section 1367). If A liquidates the corporation in the same year as the sale, A will recognize a $3.5 million loss on the liquidation transaction ($5 million of assets received in exchange for shares with an adjusted tax basis of $8.5 million), which loss can be offset against the $4 million of gain recognized by the S corporation on the sale of assets, thereby reducing A's long-term capital gain (LTCG) for the year to $500,000 ($4 million of gain on the sale of assets minus $3.5 million loss on liquidation).

By contrast, if the S corporation is liquidated in the next tax year, A may have a tax disaster, namely, $4 million of LTCG subject to tax in the current year, and then a $3.5 million long-term capital loss (LTCL) in the following year that will be very difficult to use unless or until A recognizes capital gain from other sources.

GENERAL TREATMENT OF UNPAID LIABILITIES FOLLOWING A CORPORATE LIQUIDATION

Pursuant to Rev. Rul. 72-137,[5] the distribution of property to a liquidating trust constitutes a distribution of property to the shareholders in complete liquidation in exchange for their stock under Code section 331(a) because the shareholders are considered the owners of the liquidating trust. The ruling provides that the amount of the distribution to the trust is reduced by the amount of any ***known*** liabilities owed by the corporation but unpaid at the time of liquidation. Rev. Rul. 72-137 cites Rev. Rul. 59-228[6] for this proposition.

According to Rev. Rul. 72-137, if, in a subsequent year, the shareholders of the liquidating trust discharge a contingent liability of the liquidated corporation, such discharge will give rise to a capital loss in the year of discharge to the shareholders.[7]

In calculating the amount of gain or loss recognized by Target shareholders upon liquidation, the value of the assets distributed to the liquidating trust will be reduced by the amount of any known corporate liabilities that remain unpaid (and which are assumed by the liquidating trust). It is, therefore, imperative that all of the liabilities that are known be valued, if possible, to decrease the gain or increase the loss in the year of liquidation. This is especially important for an S corporation because any capital loss can be used to offset the amount of capital gain recognized by shareholders from the corporate-level asset sale. Any contingent liability paid by the liquidating trust in a subsequent year will give rise to a capital loss for the shareholders/beneficiaries of the liquidating trust in the year in which the contingent liability is discharged or otherwise paid.

The shareholders, through the liquidating trust, will not realize any income if the liquidating trust satisfies a known liability at the time of liquidation ***unless*** such liability is satisfied at less than face value or the liability exceeds the basis of any property used to satisfy the liability.[8]

TAX TREATMENT OF DEFERRED COMPENSATION ARRANGEMENTS

A common issue arises when the liquidating corporation has an unfunded deferred compensation obligation to a retired employee. In Rev. Rul. 59-228,[9] the IRS held that the assumption of pension liabilities by the stockholders of a liquidated corporation, to the extent of the present value thereof, reduced the actual amount received by the stockholders upon complete liquidation of the corporation, thus reducing the amount of gain or increasing the amount of loss otherwise determined to each stockholder in exchange for his or her stock under Code sections 331 and 1001. The ruling provides that any payments subsequently made by the former stockholders are not deductible from their gross income because they merely constitute payments in satisfaction of the pension obligations assumed. Finally, the ruling held that the corporation could not deduct the present value of the unpaid pensions on its final federal income tax return under either Code section 162 or 404.

Rev. Rul. 59-228 is both cryptic and somewhat superficial in its discussion of these issues. However, it is expressly cited in Rev. Rul. 72-137,[10] as well as in several private letter rulings on this issue, and remains valid authority. Note that this specific language used in Rev. Rul. 59-228 does not expressly use the term "present value" although this appears to be the meaning of the phrase "commuted (present) value."

Therefore, there appears to be a reasonable reporting position that the present value of the payments owed to a former employee (e.g., for the rest of his or her life) will reduce the amount of proceeds received by the shareholders in liquidation of the Target, but will *not* be deductible by the Target on its final federal income tax return.

A different kind of issue, and one that is hopefully well planned for, is the treatment of nonqualified deferred compensation that is required to be paid in the case of a complete liquidation. After the notorious Enron scandal, Congress enacted Code Section 409A to prevent similar tax avoidance schemes for deferred compensation. If a deferred payment falls under Section 409A, the adverse tax consequences include 1) current recognition of all deferred income, 2) interest on the deferred amounts for the deferral periods, and 3) a whopping penalty on the payee equal to 20 percent of the amount required to be included in income. The planning goal is to structure deferred compensation arrangements so they do not run afoul Code Section 409A. Significantly, payments of deferred compensation may be accelerated following a plan termination that occurs in connection with a corporate dissolution or bankruptcy. While the nuances of Code Section 409A are beyond the scope of this book, be aware that compensation payments triggered by sale or liquidation events should be carefully reviewed for Code Section 409A compliance issues.

TAXATION OF A LIQUIDATING TRUST

A liquidating corporation will typically have its remaining assets (i.e., those not otherwise directly distributed to the shareholders) distributed to a liquidating trust. Often, this is done so that a corporation can liquidate and trigger recognition of gain or losses in a specific year. For example, a liquidating trust may be created because a corporate liquidation must be completed by December 31 so that shareholders of an S corporation who recognized substantial taxable gains from sales of assets earlier in the year can recognize substantial capital losses to offset the capital gains.

A distribution to a liquidating trust that is used to hold the assets of a corporation pending the determination of the amount of liabilities and/or because some of the assets are not readily convertible into cash will be treated as a distribution to the shareholders in complete liquidation of the corporation.[11]

Reg. § 301.7701-4(d) defines liquidating trusts as follows:

> Certain organizations which are commonly known as liquidating trusts are treated as trusts for purposes of the [Code]. An organization will be considered a liquidating trust if it is organized for the primary purpose of liquidating and

> distributing the assets transferred to it, and if its activities are reasonably necessary to, and consistent with, the accomplishment of that purpose. A liquidating trust is treated as a trust for purposes of the [Code] because it is formed with the objective of liquidating particular assets and not as an organization having as its purpose the carrying on of a profit-making business which normally would be conducted through business organizations classified as corporations or partnerships. However, if the liquidation is unreasonably prolonged or if the liquidation's purpose becomes so obscured by business activities that the clear purpose of the liquidation can be said to be lost or abandoned, the status of the organization will no longer be that of a liquidating trust.

The IRS has issued Rev. Proc. 91-15,[12] as modified and amplified by Rev. Proc. 94-45[13] (dealing with revisions to the conditions for rulings on bankruptcy liquidating trusts), which specifies the conditions that must be present before the IRS will consider issuing an advance ruling concerning the classification of an entity as a liquidating trust. One should generally incorporate the relevant and required provisions of Rev. Proc. 91-15 into a liquidating trust.

A liquidating trust is generally treated as a grantor trust owned by its beneficiaries. A liquidating corporation's distributions to a liquidating trust for the benefit of the shareholders is treated as made directly to the shareholders followed by the shareholders contributing the assets received in liquidation to the trust for their own benefit. The shareholders are then considered to be owners of the trust under Code section 677 and the trust income is taxable to them each year.[14] Thus, the shareholders will be taxed on the income of the liquidating trust each year, regardless of whether they receive any distributions. However, one of the IRS requirements for ruling on liquidating trusts under Rev. Proc. 91-15[15] is that the shareholders receive at least annual distributions of the net income from a liquidating trust.

It appears that the reporting of income and expenses by the liquidating trust each year should be consistent with the general grantor trust rules under Code section 671 *et seq.*[16] Trust income that is taxable to the shareholders should not be reported on Form 1041. Instead, the amount of such income and the amount of any deductions and credits applicable thereto should be shown in a separate statement attached to Form 1041 filed by the liquidating trust each year with the IRS.[17] This statement should also be furnished to each of the individual beneficiaries/shareholders of the trust. The liquidating trust will have to apply for and obtain a separate federal tax identification number from the IRS. This ID number should be used on all liquidating trust bank accounts and other information statements, including the statement to be attached to Form 1041 and provided to the shareholders.

POST-SALE C CORPORATION STRATEGIES: THE PERSONAL HOLDING COMPANY ALTERNATIVE

Normally, a sale of a business by a C corporation is followed by a corporation liquidation so that the shareholders can enjoy the fruits of the sale. However, when a C corporation is owned by a single shareholder who is relatively elderly, an argument can be made that it is better ***not*** to liquidate the corporation. The strategy instead is to have the C corporation continue in existence, in order to avoid the second leg of the "double tax."

> ***Example 2:*** A C corporation sells assets with zero tax basis for $10 million and pays approximately $4 million in federal and state taxes. Assume the sole shareholder has zero basis in the shareholder's stock. If the corporation liquidates and distributes $6 million in cash, and the shareholder is in a state with a five-percent state tax on capital gains, the shareholder will pay roughly 20 percent, or $1.2 million, in additional taxes, leaving $4.8 million in cash. If the shareholder dies shortly thereafter, the shareholder has substantial other assets besides the proceeds from the corporate liquidation, and the shareholder's estate tax rate (federal and state) is 50 percent, $2.4 million would be left for the shareholder's heirs.
>
> By contrast, if after the sale the corporation remains in existence and the shareholder subsequently dies, the outside tax basis in the decedent's shares in the hands of the decedent's estate is increased to FMV, or $6 million.[18] In turn, the stock in the decedent's gross estate, assuming a 50-percent combined federal and state estate tax rate, would result in $3 million of additional estate tax, and leave $3 million for the shareholder's heirs.

This example intentionally was simplified to make the math easy to follow, but the point is that it often makes sense to keep a C corporation with low-basis stock in existence and not liquidate it. Instead, the strategy is to use Code section 1014 to step-up tax basis on death and thus eliminate the second level of income tax.

The main impediment to this strategy is the PHC tax. The PHC tax is a 15-percent penalty tax imposed on "undistributed personal holding company income" of a personal holding company.[19] The accumulated earnings (AE) tax under Code section 531 *et seq.* may come into play if for any reason the post-sale C corporation is not a PHC (e.g., because it has sufficient amounts of active income to "flunk" the 60-percent-of-AOGI test).

Comment: The AE tax imposed by Code section 531 does not apply to a PHC.[20] Application of the PHC tax is purely mechanical, i.e., no wrongful intent is required. A corporation is a personal holding company if two tests are met:[21]

- *Stock ownership test.* More than 50 percent of its stock by value is owned directly or indirectly at any time during the last half of the year by five or fewer individuals. (Elaborate ownership attribution rules apply; see Code section 544.)

- *Passive income test.* At least 60 percent of its adjusted ordinary gross income (AOGI) consists of PHC income. ("AOGI" is defined by Code section 543(b)(2) as, roughly, gross income less gains from asset sales, and using a special calculation for rental income.)

Personal holding company status can be avoided by making sure PHC income items do not exceed 60 percent of AOGI. Alternatively, the tax can be avoided by investing in tax-exempt investments or by paying sufficient dividends to eliminate undistributed PHC income (although this latter strategy is effectively the same as paying the PHC tax). "Undistributed PHC income" is defined in Code section 545 as, essentially, taxable income less regular federal tax for the year and a few other adjustments, and further reduced by dividends paid.

PHC income items are listed in Code section 543(a). The following is a simplified list:

- *Dividends, interest, royalties, and annuities.*

- *Rents.* Rents are generally PHC income. However, Congress created an exception for true leasing companies. Rents are not included in PHC income if "adjusted income from rents" is 50 percent or more of AOGI and the amount of dividends paid equals or exceeds the amount by which personal holding company income for the tax year exceeds 10 percent of "ordinary gross income."[22]

- *Software royalties.* The Code provides an exception for computer software royalties ("active business computer software royalties") similar to the rent exception for true leasing companies. The exception applies if the following four conditions are met:[23]

  1. The computer software royalties must be received by a corporation engaged in the active conduct of the trade or business of developing, manufacturing, or producing computer software.

  2. The software royalties constitute at least 50 percent of the corporation's ordinary gross income for the tax year.

  3. Business and research expenses relating to the business of developing, manufacturing, or producing computer software must equal or exceed 25 percent of the corporation's ordinary gross income for the tax year, or the average of such deductions for the five-tax-year period ending with the tax year must equal or exceed 25 percent of the corporation's average ordinary gross income for that period.

  4. Dividends must equal or exceed the excess of personal holding company income over 10 percent or ordinary gross income.

- *Payments for use of corporate property.* Such payments by a 25 percent or more shareholder are PHC income.[24] This is to discourage a shareholder from using the corporation to own and depreciate property such as a yacht, house, etc. used by the shareholder.

- *Income from personal service contracts.* It is PHC income when the payor can designate a 25-percent or more shareholder as the performer of contracted services.[25]

The PHC tax can potentially be avoided by electing S corporation status. However, an S corporation is subject to a rough equivalent to the PHC tax under Code section 1375. If an S corporation has accumulated earnings and profits at the close of the tax year and more than 25 percent of its gross receipts are passive investment income, the corporation will have to pay a tax equal to 35 percent of its excess passive income.[26] In addition, if an S corporation has accumulated earnings and profits (from prior C corporation years) at the close of each of three consecutive tax years and more than 25 percent of its gross receipts for each of those years is passive investment income, the corporation will lose its eligibility for S status.[27] As a practical matter, therefore, converting from C corporation status to S corporation status will avoid the PHC tax permanently only if the S corporation distributes all of its retained earnings and profits within the first three years after electing S status.

Comment: Distributing the E&P from C corporation years may be feasible in some cases but prohibitively expensive in others. Fortunately, the 15-percent tax rate on dividend income has made this cost significantly easier to bear. In lieu of a cash dividend, Reg. § 1.1368-1(f)(3) permits an S corporation to make a deemed dividend with the consent of all affected shareholders.

One can also reduce or avoid the PHC tax through investment strategies, including by investing in tax-exempt obligations, growth (nondividend) stocks, or other investments not generating current taxable income. In effect, if a corporation does not have current taxable income, it will not have a PHC tax.

Another PHC tax management strategy is to flunk the 60-percent test by putting active business income into the corporation. For example, a C corporation could use a small amount of its assets to purchase a "new" business that generates "good" income. Bear in mind that "good" income for the PHC tax is anything except the specific types of (generally passive) income listed in Code section 543. Any active business will suffice, and it does not have to be a profitable business—the 60-percent test is a gross-income test. Also, investing in a partnership may be sufficient for this purpose because the business of the partnership is the business of all its partners. Gross income allocated to a corporation as a partner in a partnership engaged in an active business may help the corporation avoid the PHC tax.[28]

TAX ISSUES ON LIQUIDATION OF AN S CORPORATION

As previously noted, it often makes sense to liquidate an S corporation in the same year that an asset sale occurs in order to utilize outside tax basis (and recognize capital loss). However, there can be circumstances when an S corporation does not want to liquidate, especially if there is an installment sale as part of the sale of assets. The concern is that a liquidation under such circumstances can cause S corporation shareholders to recognize part or all of the gain on the installment note at the time of distribution. The specific technical issue is that the provisions of Code sections 453(h) and 453B(h), which were intended to permit an S corporation to distribute installment notes on liquidation without immediate tax consequence, do not work when there is both cash and an installment note.

Example 3: An S corporation sells $10 million worth of assets (with zero tax basis) for $6 million in cash and a $4 million installment note, due and payable three years after closing. The $6 million of current gain passes through to the shareholders and increases their outside tax basis from zero to $6 million.[29] If the S corporation now liquidates, the $6 million of outside tax basis is allocated proportionately to the distributed assets, based on FMV. That means that there is a $6 million cash distribution, and only $3.6 million of tax basis allocated to the cash, causing a gain recognition of an additional $2.4 million, or a total of $8.4 million in the year of sale, even though only $6 million of cash is received! The "missing" $2.4 million of tax basis is allocated to the $4 million installment note. If the installment note is eventually paid in full, there is an additional $1.6 million in gain ($4 million reduced by $2.4 million of tax basis in the note). However, if the installment note is received as part of a contingent payment transaction with a maximum selling price of $10 million, and future contingencies triggering payment are not met, a disaster unfolds: Three years later the $2.4 million of tax basis would produce a $2.4 million capital loss that cannot be offset against the $8.4 million of gain recognized in the year of sale.

An obvious strategy is to keep the S corporation alive and distribute the $6 million as a cash distribution under Code section 1368, thus reducing the outside tax basis in the shares to zero and leaving the S corporation holding a $4 million installment note.

If the S corporation is a former C corporation with accumulated E&P, however, the problem is not yet solved. An S corporation with E&P from prior C corporation years is subject to two provisions that can cause problems if it no longer carries on an active trade or business: Code section 1375, which imposes a "sting tax" if more than 25 percent of income is from passive sources, and Code section 1362(d)(3), which can cause the entity to lose its S status if it has passive income in excess of 25 percent of its gross receipts for three consecutive years. Possible solutions include distributing the E&P as a dividend (using the Reg. § 1.1368-1(f)(3) procedure in lieu of an actual cash distribution) or managing the passive income level, using techniques similar to those used for managing the PHC tax.

A possible alternative solution is as follows: (1) distribute all cash and other assets of the S corporation pursuant to Code section 1368, thereby recovering and using outside tax basis as much as possible to avoid gain; (2) adopt a plan of liquidation and sell all remaining assets for an installment note (secured by a bank letter of credit if the risk of future payment is a concern); (3) distribute the installment note, taking advantage of the fact that no cash is being distributed by the liquidating S corporation and therefore no distortion or acceleration of gain now occurs under Code sections 453(h) and 453B(h).

Example 4: Assume the same facts as Example 3 but further assume the S corporation has $2 million of cash plus business assets worth $10 million, and that the shareholders have $2 million of outside basis in their S corporation shares.

1. The S corporation distributes $2 million of cash, which is received tax-free by the shareholders, pursuant to Code section 1368, reducing their outside tax basis to zero.

2. The S corporation adopts a plan of liquidation and then sells assets for a $10 million installment note, with $6 million due and payable shortly after the liquidation is completed, and the remaining $4 million due and payable (as before) in three years.

3. The S corporation liquidates and distributes its sole asset, the installment note, which does not trigger current tax under Code sections 453(h) and 453B(h) to either the shareholders or the distributing S corporation.

4. The shareholders receive a $6 million payment shortly thereafter which is treated as a payment for their stock (with adjustments that mimic or mirror an asset sale) under Code section 453(h).

CHAPTER ENDNOTES

1. IRC Sec. 336(a).
2. See IRC Sec. 731, discussed in Chapter 9.
3. IRC Secs. 331 and 1001.
4. IRC Secs. 336(a) and 1367.
5. 1972-1 CB 101.
6. 1959-2 CB 59.
7. Rev. Rul. 72-137 cites *F.D. Arrowsmith*, 344 US 6 (1952), 73 SCt 71. See also, *Estate of Sl J. Schbneider, et, al., v. Commissioner of Internal Revenue.* 855 F.2d 435 (1988) 62 A.F.T.R.2d 88-5587, 88-2 USTC P 9484.
8. See IRC Secs. 61(a)(3) and (12), 1001(a) and (b); Reg. §§ 1.61-12(a), 1.1001-2(a)(1); IRS Letter Ruling 8529048, 4-22-85, CCH IRS Letter Rulings Reports.
9. 1959-2 CB 59.
10. 1972-1 CB 101.
11. Rev. Rul. 72-137, 1972-1 CB 101. See also, Rev. Rul. 65-257, 1965-2 CB 89 (where, pursuant to a plan of complete liquidation, cash equal to the appraised value of stock owned by the shareholders is placed in escrow by the complete transfer of such cash to an independent party until there is a final determination of the value of the stock, the liquidating corporation will be considered to have distributed the cash in complete liquidation of the corporation); and Rev. Rul. 63-245, 1963-2 CB 144 (where the only unsold or uncollected asset of a corporation in the process of liquidation consists of a claim for refund of federal taxes, the corporation will be considered to have distributed all of its assets in complete liquidation if it is divested of such claim by a complete transfer of it to an independent trustee selected by the stockholder pursuant to the plan of liquidation approved by the stockholders.)
12. 1991-1 CB 484.
13. 1994-2 CB 684
14. These positions are supported by Rev. Rul. 80-150, 1980-1 C.B. 316; Rev. Rul. 75-379, 1975-2 C.B. 505, Rev. Rul. 72-137, 1972-1 CB 101; and IRS Letter Ruling 9603013, 10-18-95, CCH IRS Letter Rulings Reports.

15. 1991-1 CB 484.
16. Rev. Rul. 80-150, 1980-1 C.B. 316; Rev. Rul. 75-379, 1975-2 C.B. 505, Rev. Rul. 72-137, 1972-1 CB 101; and IRS Letter Ruling 9603013, 10-18-95, CCH IRS Letter Rulings Reports.
17. Reg. § 1.671-4(a).
18. IRC Sec. 1014.
19. IRC Sec. 541.
20. IRC Sec. 532(b)(1).
21. IRC Sec. 542(a).
22. IRC Secs. 543(a)(2) and 543(b)(3).
23. IRC Sec. 543(d).
24. IRC Sec. 543(a)(6).
25. IRC Sec. 543(a)(7).
26. IRC Sec. 1375(a).
27. IRC Sec. 1362(d)(3).
28. See, e.g., IRC Sec. 702(c).
29. IRC Sec. 1367.

SELLING THE BUSINESS TO THE BUSINESS: CORPORATION AND PARTNERSHIP REDEMPTIONS

CHAPTER 15

OVERVIEW

One of the most natural and obvious potential purchasers of a business interest is the business itself. A corporate (or partnership) redemption transaction is economically similar to a sale of a business interest to the remaining shareholders/ partners in the business. However, unique rules apply to redemption transactions, which make this a special area with distinctive tax planning implications.

Most of this chapter will focus on redemption of shares of stock by an issuing corporation. However, we also will deal with the distinctive rules under Subchapter K that apply to a redemption of a partnership interest.

In general, how a redemption of corporate stock is taxed depends on whether the transaction is treated as a sale or exchange (thus producing capital gain to the shareholder) or as a dividend distribution with respect to the stock (thus producing dividend income to the shareholder). Before the Jobs and Growth Tax Reconciliation Act of 2003 (P.L. 108-27), the difference between capital gains treatment and dividend treatment was huge—a maximum 20-percent federal tax rate on long-term capital gain (LTCG) versus a maximum 39.6 percent rate on dividend income. Today, however, both long-term capital gain and dividends are taxed at the same tax rate to individuals (currently a maximum of 20 percent). Therefore, the tax rate disparity (and the importance of tax planning) has diminished considerably for many individual shareholders. Nonetheless, there remain significant differences in the tax treatment of the two types of transactions—and, of course, there is the very real possibility that different tax rates on dividend income and capital gains will be enacted in the near future.

A "redemption" involves the acquisition by a corporation of its stock from a shareholder in exchange for corporate property. A transaction is a redemption whether the acquired stock has been cancelled, retired, or held as treasury stock.[1] The kind of "property" that can be transferred in a redemption transaction includes money, tangible and intangible assets, and even securities, but does not include stock (or rights to acquire such stock) from the distributing corporation.[2]

What distinguishes a redemption from a dividend is that the corporation accepts surrender of its own stock in exchange for the transfer of corporate property. Obviously, a pro-rata redemption of all the shares of existing shareholders, in proportion to their respective interests in the corporation, would be indistinguishable from a dividend distribution. Therefore, relatively sophisticated rules have been developed under Code section 302 to distinguish between a redemption and a dividend.

A redeeming corporation recognizes gain (but not loss) at the corporate level to the extent that it distributes corporate property with a fair market value in excess of its tax basis in the property.[3] This distribution will be treated like any other corporate disposition of property. For example, Code section 1231 property will be subject to the recapture rules under Code section 1245.

For shareholders, a distribution of corporate property in exchange for their stock will be characterized under Code section 302 as either a "distribution" or as a "redemption." If it is a redemption, then the transaction will be treated as a sale or exchange by the shareholder of his or her stock.[4] A shareholder will recognize capital gain (long-term capital gain if the stock has been held for more than one year) to the extent that the fair market value of the distributed property is in excess of the shareholder's tax basis in the shares. Whether a transaction qualifies as a redemption of stock, or as a dividend, depends on the amount of stock being redeemed and the proportionate interest held by other shareholders in the corporation, all of which is defined in Code section 302.

> *Note on Nomenclature:* Because terminology is important in tax law, be aware of the following distinctions. A "dividend" is a distribution by a corporation of its current or accumulated earnings and profits to its shareholders. No shares are surrendered by shareholders to their corporation in return for the distribution. A "redemption" is a distribution of property by a corporation to one or more shareholders in exchange for shares of stock that the shareholders own in the corporation making the distribution. A "liquidation" is a distribution by a corporation of its assets to creditors and shareholders in settlement of the corporation's affairs. A liquidation does not necessarily end a corporation's legal existence (that requires a dissolution).

DISTINGUISHING A DIVIDEND FROM A REDEMPTION—CODE SECTION 302

Distributions of property by a corporation to its shareholders with respect to its stock are governed by Code section 301 unless they are treated under Code section 302 as payments in exchange for stock. Under Code section 301, a distribution is characterized as a "dividend" to the extent that the corporation has earnings and profits and results in taxable income to a shareholder (currently at the preferential 20-percent tax rate for individuals).[5] The corporation distributing a dividend does not get a deduction for the distribution and must recognize capital gain and/or ordinary income at the corporate level to the extent that the distribution consists of property with the fair market value in excess of its tax basis.[6] The portion of a distribution that is not a dividend (because it is in excess of the corporation's current or accumulated earnings and profits (E&P) or because the corporation has no E&P) is received tax-free and reduces a shareholder's basis in stock (but not below zero). To the extent that a distribution not characterized as dividend exceeds the amount of a shareholder's adjusted basis in stock, it is treated as gain from a sale or exchange of property and will result in long-term capital gain if the stock has been held for more than one year.[7]

A corporate shareholder does not benefit from the preferential tax rate on dividends afforded to individual shareholders but can enjoy the benefits of the dividends-received deduction under Code section 243. Under current law, the dividends-received deduction ranges between 70 percent and 100 percent of the amount received as a dividend. The exact percentage depends on the nature of the corporation paying the dividends and the recipient's ownership interest in the payor. The dividends-received deduction is subject to various limitations described in Code section 246.

REDEMPTIONS TREATED AS SALES OR EXCHANGES

The Code defines the term "redemption" as follows:[8]

> [S]tock shall be treated as redeemed by a corporation if the corporation acquires its stock from a shareholder in exchange for property, whether or not the stock so acquired is cancelled, retired, or held as treasury stock.

Code section 302 provides rules for determining whether a redemption results in a sufficient reduction in the shareholder's stake in the corporation so that it is appropriate to characterize the transaction as a sale or exchange of stock rather than as a distribution with respect to the stock. If a corporation redeems its stock and Code section 302(b)(1), (2), (3), (4), or (5) applies, the redemption will be treated as a distribution in part or full payment in exchange for the stock.[9] Any other redemption will be treated as a distribution of property to which Code section 301 applies.[10]

Code section 302(b) provides five circumstances in which a redemption will be treated as a sale or exchange of stock:

1. If the redemption is not essentially equivalent to a dividend.[11]

2. If the redemption is substantially disproportionate with respect to the shareholder.[12]

3. If the redemption is in complete redemption of all the stock in the corporation owned by the shareholder.[13]

4. If the redemption is of stock held by a noncorporate shareholder in "partial liquidation" of the corporation making the distribution.[14]

5. If the redemption is of stock of a publicly offered regulated investment company and A) such redemption is upon the demand of the stockholder, and (B) such company issues only stock which is redeemable upon the demand of the stockholder.[15]

Comment: The second and third categories listed in Code section 302(b) are the most important because they are objective and can be mechanically and mathematically tested to assure that the transaction will qualify as a sale or exchange and not as a dividend. The first category is a subjective test that is available as a basis for argument, but it does not provide quantitative certainty. The fourth test applies only to partial liquidations, which are described briefly below, and generally apply in narrow circumstances. The fifth test is designed to ensure that capital gain treatment is available for shareholders redeeming their shareholdings in mutual funds.

Termination of Shareholder's Interest. Code section 302(b)(3), the "Termination of Interest Test," is probably the most commonly applied rule and is satisfied when all of the redeeming shareholder's stock is redeemed in exchange for property distributed by the corporation. The theory behind Code section 302(b)(3) is that a person who sells an entire interest in the corporation and has no continuing interest in the corporation should be given capital gains treatment, even if there are family members or other persons under the constructive ownership rules (described more fully below) that would otherwise cause the shareholder to be viewed as to having a continuing interest in the corporation. The family attribution rules provided by Code section 318(a) are not applied for purposes of determining whether the complete termination of interest test has been satisfied if *all* three of the following apply:[16]

1. Immediately after the distribution, the distributee has no interest in the corporation (including an interest as officer, director, or employee), other than an interest as a creditor.

2. The distributee does not acquire any such interest (other than stock acquired by bequest or inheritance) within ten years from the date of the distribution.

3. The distributee agrees to notify the IRS if the distributee acquires any prohibited interest within the ten-year period and retain necessary records.

Code section 302(b)(3) permits a family-owned corporation to purchase the stock of a senior member of the family and characterize that transaction as a sale or exchange even though other family members continue to own stock in the corporation.

Example 1: A father owns 75 percent of the stock of a corporation, and his daughter owns 25 percent. Upon his retirement, the father and the corporation agree that the corporation will redeem all of the father's stock for $1 million paid ratably over ten years. The father does not remain on the board of directors. Nor is he employed in any manner by the corporation after the redemption. This redemption would be considered a sale or exchange of the stock, under Code section 302(b)(3), even though the daughter owns all the remaining shares in the corporation. The $1 million payment obligation would be eligible for installment sale treatment described in Code section 453 and discussed in Chapter 10.

Substantially Disproportionate Redemption of Stock. Code section 302(b)(2) provides a second objective test, called the "Substantially Disproportionate Test," which attempts to measure whether there has been a meaningful mathematical reduction in the shareholder's interest in the corporation as a result of the distribution. To qualify as "substantially disproportionate," three objective requirements must be satisfied:

1. *Requirement 1.* After the redemption, the shareholder must own less than 50 percent of the total combined voting power of all classes of stock entitled to vote.

Comment: Because of the economic and legal benefits of corporate voting control, a person, for example, owning 95 percent of the stock of a corporation who redeems enough shares to reduce his or her interest to 65 percent has not suffered a significant diminution in corporate control. Although there has been substantial reduction in the percentage of stock held (from 95 percent to 65 percent), there has not been a real "economic" reduction in control of the corporation. Such a reduction does not occur until an interest has been reduced below the 50-percent level traditionally associated with corporate control.

---

2. *Requirement* 2. The ratio between the voting stock of the corporation owned by the shareholder immediately after the redemption and all the voting stock of the corporation at such time must be less than 80 percent of the ratio between the voting stock of the corporation owned by the shareholder immediately before the redemption and all voting stock of the corporation at such time.

Comment: Although the language is a little stilted, the intention of this second requirement is to ensure that a shareholder has reduced his or her interest in the corporation by a meaningful amount as a result of the redemption. The Code applies an 80-percent test. The shareholder's percentage ownership in the corporation's voting stock after redemption must be less than 80 percent of what it was before the redemption.

This second requirement is best illustrated by some actual mathematical examples.

Example 2: Corporation X has 400 shares of outstanding voting common stock. Shareholders A, B, C, and D own 100 shares each. Assume that Corporation X redeems 40 shares owned by A, 30 shares owned by B, 20 shares owned by C, and 10 shares owned by D. The analysis is as follows:

1. Interest in the corporation before the redemption:

A: 100 ÷ 400 or 25%.

B: 100 ÷ 400 or 25%.

C: 100 ÷ 400 or 25%.

D: 100 ÷ 400 or 25%.

2. Number of shares in the corporation after the redemption:

A: 100 – 40 = 60 shares.

B: 100 – 30 = 70 shares.

C: 100 – 20 = 80 shares.

D: 100 – 10 = 90 shares.

Corporation X: 400 shares – 100 shares = 300 shares outstanding following the redemption.

3. Percentage interest in Corporation X after the redemption:

A: 60 ÷ 300 = 20%.

B: 70 ÷ 300 = 23.33%.

C: 80 ÷ 300 = 26.67%.

D: 90 ÷ 300 = 30%.

The ratio of the interest in the corporation after the redemption divided by the ratio of the interest before the redemption is as follows:

A: 20% ÷ 25% = 80%.

B: 23.33 % ÷ 25% = 93.32%.

C: 26.67% ÷ 25% = 106.68%.

D: 30% ÷ 25% = 120%.

In this first example, *none* of the four ratios is less than 80 percent (A's ratio is exactly 80 percent). Therefore, none of these redemptions qualifies as a sale or exchange under Code section 302(b)(3).

Example 3: Assume the same facts as in Example 1 except that Corporation X does not redeem any of the shares owned by D. Following the redemption, Corporation X has 310 shares outstanding.

Under these facts, A's interest in Corporation X after the redemption is 60 ÷ 310 = 19.35%, B's interest is 70 ÷ 310 = 22.58%, and C's interest is 80 ÷ 310 = 25.81%. In this revised computation, A's interest in the corporation following the redemption is reduced to 19.35 percent. Therefore, the ratio between A's percentage interest in the corporation after the redemption and A's percentage interest before the redemption is now 77.4 percent (19.35% (25%). The redemption of 40 of A's shares qualifies as a sale or exchange under Code section 302(b)(2).

These examples illustrate that a shareholder needs to have not only a substantial reduction in absolute share ownership but also a substantial reduction in percentage interest in the corporation. In Example 2, even though Corporation X redeemed 40 of A's shares, A still did not meet the qualifying standard because of the reduction in the shares held by other shareholders.

The shareholder's ownership of the common stock of the corporation (whether voting or nonvoting) after and before the redemption must also meet the 80-percent requirement described under Requirement 2 above. If there is more than one class of common stock, the determination shall be made by reference to fair market value.

Comment: The purpose of this additional 80-percent test, applied to common stock ownership, is to act as a "backstop" to the rule measuring a reduction in voting stock. Basically, the implicit assumption of this substantially disproportionate test is that there is a meaningful reduction in the equity interest of an individual shareholder, measured *both* by a substantial reduction in voting control and a substantial reduction in common equity ownership. Note that both tests must be met and failure of either one results in the transaction not being characterized as a sale or exchange under Code section 302(b)(3) rules.

Not Essentially Equivalent to a Dividend Redemption. The "not essentially equivalent to a dividend" test is a subjective test based not on an absolute mathematical standard, but rather on whether, under all the facts and circumstances, the transaction is in the nature of a redemption. The most important guidance on this provision is *M.P. Davis*,[17] in which the Supreme Court held that to qualify under Code section 302(b)(1) a redemption must result in a "meaningful reduction in a shareholder's proportionate interest in the corporation." The Supreme Court held that the constructive ownership rules are relevant to the inquiry and that the business purpose for a redemption is not relevant in determining whether or not it was essentially equivalent to a dividend. Dividend equivalence depends upon the facts and circumstances of the case.[18] Obviously, this provision will apply, if at all, if there is a significant reduction in share ownership but not significant enough to meet the mathematical requirements of the previous two tests (under Code section 302(b)(2) and (3)).

For example, in Rev. Rul. 75-502,[19] a redemption that reduced a shareholder's voting interest from 57 percent to 50 percent was held to come within the ambit of Code section 302(b)(1) because the shareholder no longer had voting control (a single unrelated shareholder held the remaining 50 percent of the corporation's common stock). In Rev. Rul. 76-364,[20] a reduction from 27 percent to 22.27 percent was qualified as not essentially equivalent to a dividend because the shareholder no longer had the ability to control the corporation with one other shareholder.

Comment: Code section 302(b)(1) is not something that anyone "relies on" because it lacks the certainty and objectivity of the tests under Code section 302(b)(2) and (3).

Redemption from Noncorporate Shareholder in Partial Liquidation. Code section 302(b)(4) applies to partial liquidations, which are defined in Code section 302(e). Basically, a distribution is treated as a partial liquidation if (1) the distribution is not essentially equivalent to a dividend (determined at the corporate level rather than at the shareholder level) and (2) the distribution is pursuant to a plan and occurs within the tax year in which the plan is adopted or within the succeeding tax year.[21] Here, "not essentially equivalent to a dividend" has a different meaning than the subjective test of § 302(b)(1) and pro-rata redemptions are allowed.[22] In a partial liquidation, a distribution is not essentially equivalent to a dividend if it is (1) a distribution attributable to the distributing corporation's ceasing to conduct, or consists of the assets of, a qualified trade or business and (2) immediately after the distribution the distributing corporation is actively engaged in the conduct of a qualified trade or business.[23]

Comment: The exception contained in Code section 302(b)(4) is designed for rather specific circumstances where a corporation operating two active businesses liquidates one of the businesses and continues operating the second business.

Redemption of stock in a Regulated Investment Company. Code section 302(b)(5) was inserted as part of the RIC Modernization Act of 2010 and prevents a redemption by a Regulated Investment Company (a RIC or, more commonly, a mutual fund) from being characterized as a dividend if (1) the redemption is upon the demand of the stockholder, (2) the company issues only stock which is redeemable upon the demand of the stockholder, and (3) the stock is in a publicly offered regulated investment company (within the meaning of Code section 67(c)(2)(B)).[24]

CONSTRUCTIVE OWNERSHIP RULES

The constructive ownership of stock rules of Code section 318(a) are applied to determine the ownership of stock for purposes of ascertaining whether a redemption qualifies as a sale or exchange.[25] These constructive ownership rules prevent a redemption from qualifying as a sale or exchange when a person's economic stake in a corporation is reduced or eliminated but the person retains a continuing interest through family members or related entities.

There are four general types of attribution:

1. *Family attribution.* An individual is considered to own stock owned, directly or indirectly, by or for the individual's spouse, parents, children, and grandchildren (but not brothers and sisters).[26]

2. *Attribution from a partnership, estate, trust, or corporation.* Stock owned, directly or indirectly, by or for a partnership or estate is considered as owned proportionately by its partners or beneficiaries. Stock owned, directly or indirectly, by or for a trust is considered as owned by its beneficiaries in proportion to the actuarial interest of such beneficiaries in the trust. Stock owned, directly or indirectly, by or for any portion of a trust of which a person is considered the owner under the grantor trust rules is considered as owned by that person. If 50 percent of more in value of the stock in a corporation is owned, directly or indirectly, by or for any person, that person will be considered as owning the stock owned, directly or indirectly, by or for that corporation in that proportion that the value of the stock that the person owns bears to the value of all of the stock in that corporation.[27]

3. *Attribution to partnerships, estates, trusts, and corporations.* Stock owned, directly or indirectly, by or for a partner or a beneficiary of an estate is considered as owned by the partnership or estate. Stock owned, directly or indirectly, by or for a beneficiary of a trust is considered as owned by the trust unless the beneficiary's interest in the trust is a remote contingent interest. Stock owned, directly or indirectly, by or for a person who is considered the owner of any portion of a trust under the grantor trust rules is considered as owned by the trust. If 50 percent or more in value of the stock in a corporation is owned, directly or indirectly, by or for any person, the corporation will be considered as owning the stock owned, directly or indirectly, by or for that person.[28]

4. *Option attribution.* If any person has an option to acquire stock, the stock shall be considered as owned by that person.[29]

Comment: The Code section 318 attribution rules will not be dealt with in painful detail in this book, but it should be noted that attribution rules are often extremely complicated, especially when there are tangled family relationships, commonly owned corporations, and other factors that require a careful mathematical parsing of the attribution rules under Code section 318 in order to do the corresponding parsing of the mathematical redemption tests under Code section 302(b)(2). The following is an example designed to illustrate the sometimes Byzantine complexity of this exercise.

Example 4: Husband, wife, son, daughter, and grandson (son of the son) owned, respectively, 50, 40, 30, 20, and 10 shares of Corporation X. This is the amount of stock deemed to be held respectively by each of the individuals:

Husband: 150 shares (50 + 40 + 30 + 20 + 10)

Wife: 150 shares (50 + 40 + 30 + 20 + 10) Son: 130 shares (50 + 40 + 30 + 10) Daughter: 110 shares (50+40+20) Grandson: 40 shares (30+10)

Example 5: A and B are equal partners in a partnership, P. A and B also own 70 percent and 30 percent, respectively, of the stock of Corporation C. P and C are equal owners of Corporation X. The attribution of ownership in Corporation X to A, B, P, and C is as follows:

1. A has a 50-percent interest in P, which owns 50 percent of the stock of Corporation X, and A owns 70 percent of Corporation C, which owns 50 percent of the stock of Corporation X. Therefore, A is treated as owning (50% × 50%) + (70% × 50%) = 60% of the stock of Corporation X.

2. B owns 50 percent of P, which owns 50 percent of the stock of Corporation X (but has a 30-percent interest in Corporation C, which does not lead to attribution). Therefore, B is treated as owning 25 percent of the stock of Corporation X.

3. P has a 50-percent direct ownership interest in Corporation X and is attributed 70 percent of the 50 percent interest held by Corporation C in Corporation X because of attribution through shareholder A. Therefore, P is treated as owning 50% + (70% × 50%) = 85% of the stock of Corporation X.

4. Corporation C has a 50-percent direct ownership interest in Corporation X. Corporation C is treated as constructively owning the 25-percent interest in Corporation C that A constructively owns through P.

Therefore Corporation C is treated as owning 75 percent of the stock of Corporation X.

It is not unusual to apply the Constructive Ownership Rules at a sometimes brutal level of complexity to inter-related corporate and family holdings. This is especially true when one is attempting to qualify under the 80-percent reduction test of Code section 302(b)(2). However, for purposes of the termination of a shareholder's interest test under Code section 302(b)(3), the family attribution rules under Code section 318(a)(1) do not apply if certain criteria are met.

Code Section 302(c)(2). The family attribution rules of Code section 318(a)(1) will not be applied to a redemption of all of a shareholder's stock in a corporation if immediately after the distribution the distributee has no interest in the corporation (including an interest as officer, director, or employee), other than an interest as a creditor, the distributee does not acquire any such prohibited interest (other than stock acquired by bequest or inheritance) within ten years from the date of the distribution, and the distributee files an agreement to notify the IRS if any prohibited interest is acquired. The family attribution rules cannot be avoided if (1) any portion of the distributee's stock was acquired (directly or indirectly) within the prior ten-year period from a person whose stock ownership would (at the time of the distribution) be attributable to the distributee under Code section 318(a) or (2) any person owns (at the time of the distribution) stock whose ownership is attributable to the distributee under Code section 318(a) and that person acquired any stock in the corporation, directly or indirectly, from the distributee within the ten-year period ending on the date of the distribution, unless that stock so acquired is redeemed in the same transaction. The preceding sentence will not apply if the acquisition or disposition by the distributee did not have as one of its principal purposes the avoidance of federal income tax.[30]

TAX TREATMENT OF REDEEMING CORPORATION

Code section 311 applies to a transfer of property by a corporation in redemption of its stock, whether the redemption is treated as a sale or exchange under Code section 302(a) or as a distribution to which Code section 301 applies. Code section 311(b) requires recognition of gain (but, significantly, not recognition of loss) if a corporation distributes appreciated property in a redemption transaction.

Code section 304 provides special rules that apply to a redemption of stock through a related corporation. Because clever tax planners can sometimes accomplish indirectly that which would be blocked directly, Code section 304 provides that a purchase of stock by a controlled subsidiary or controlled related corporation may be treated as a redemption of the acquiring corporation's stock. If such a redemption does not qualify as a sale or exchange under Code section 302, it will be taxed under Code section 301.

TAX STRATEGIES IN C CORPORATION REDEMPTIONS

The historic goal in structuring a redemption was to make sure that it qualified as a sale or exchange and enjoyed capital gain treatment rather than dividend treatment. However, the benefit of this strategy was greatly reduced or even eliminated by the dramatic reduction in dividend tax rates provided by the Jobs and Growth Tax Reconciliation Act of 2003. Prior to that Act, dividends were taxed to individuals at a maximum rate of 39.5 percent, and capital gains were taxed at a maximum rate of 15 percent. Since that Act, both dividends and capital gains have been taxed to individuals at the same rate, currently 20 percent.[31]

If a distribution is characterized as a dividend, the entire amount will be treated as income to the recipient shareholder, unless or until all the earnings and profits of the corporation have been fully distributed. If a distribution is a redemption qualifying as a sale or exchange, only the amount in excess of the share-holder's basis in the redeemed shares will be taxed. Another important factor to consider is that capital gains can be used to offset unused capital losses, while dividends cannot. This can be important for people who have had very substantial market losses or other investment losses and do not have other assets with which to generate capital gain.

Comment: People who have sustained major capital losses in the stock market would naturally prefer capital gain to dividend income, even though both are taxed at the same rate, because capital losses can only be offset against capital gains, and capital losses that cannot be used before a taxpayer's death are forever lost.

A corporate shareholder may take advantage of the dividends received deduction under Code section 243, which is 100 percent of the amount received for dividends received from a fellow member of an affiliated group, 80 percent of the amount received if the corporate shareholder owns at least 20 percent of the stock (by vote and value) of the corporation paying the dividend, and 70 percent of the amount received for dividends received from any other corporation.[32] Corporations do not receive preferential capital gains tax treatment.[33] Therefore, a redeeming corporate shareholder will, in most cases, prefer to trigger a dividend rather than a sale or exchange.

REDEMPTIONS BY S CORPORATIONS

The same basic rules that apply to a C corporation stock redemption also apply to an S corporation. Thus, if a stock redemption qualifies for exchange treatment under Code section 302(b), the S shareholder recognizes gain or loss equal to the difference between the fair market value of the property received and the adjusted tax basis in the redeemed stock. By contrast, if the redemption does not qualify for exchange treatment, the distributions by the S corporation to the shareholder will be taxed under Code section 1368. If the S corporation has no accumulated earnings and profits (e.g., because it was never a C corporation), the distribution is first applied as a tax-free reduction of basis, and the excess is treated as capital gain.[34] If the S corporation has accumulated E&P, the distribution is generally treated first as a tax-free distribution from the accumulated adjustments account, then as a dividend to the extent of E&P, then as a tax-free distribution of basis, and finally as capital gain.[35]

If an S corporation in redemption distributes appreciated property then, whether the transaction is treated as a sale or a distribution, gain is recognized by the corporation under Code section 311(b) in an amount equal to the fair market value of the property transferred over its tax basis. Because it is an S corporation, such gain is distributed to the shareholders in proportion to their stock and increases their tax basis in their shares.[36] In the case of a redemption, such basis increase will reduce gain (or increase loss) on the sale of stock. If there is a redemption of the shares of one shareholder and not others, there will be a change in the percentage of shares owned by the shareholders and how they share items of income, gain, loss, deduction, and credit.[37] Curiously, the default rule for accounting under the S corporation rules is that all income and loss for the S corporation's tax year (generally the calendar year) is allocated on a per share per day basis, and not (as one would intuitively assume) based on an interim closing of the S corporation books. To accomplish the more logical and expected result, all shareholders need to make a joint election under Code section 1377(a)(2).

Example 6: X, an S corporation that has never been a C corporation, has 100 issued and outstanding shares of voting common stock, and Alexa owns 80 shares with a tax basis of $500,000 and for a holding period of more than one year. X redeems 40 of Alexa's shares for $1,000,000 in cash, leaving Alexa with 40 out of 60 outstanding shares. The transaction does not qualify as a redemption under Code section 302(b) because Alexa retains over 50% control of the corporation following the redemption, and so Alexa is treated as receiving a distribution under Code section 1368. Alexa receives the first $500,000 as return of tax basis, and the next $500,000 as long-term capital gain. Her basis in the remaining 40 shares is zero.

Example 7: Assume the same facts as Example 6, except that the corporation has 200 shares issued and outstanding, and Alexa holds 80. If X redeems 40 of Alexa's shares for $1,000,000 in cash, the transaction is a substantially disproportionate redemption under Code section 302(b)(2). This is because Alexa's ratio of both voting stock and common stock ownership immediately after the redemption (40/160 = 25%) compared to her ratio before the redemption (80/200 = 40%) is reduced to less than 80 percent (25%/40% = 62.5%). Therefore, Alexa is deemed to sell 40 shares (out of 80) for $1,000,000. Assuming her tax basis in those 40 shares is $250,000, Alexa recognizes gain of $750,000 on the transaction ($1,000,000 – $250,000), and her tax basis in the remaining 40 shares is $250,000.

Example 8: Assume the same facts as Example 6, except that instead of distributing cash to redeem Alexa's 40 shares the S corporation distributes appreciated securities with a tax basis of $500,000 and a fair market value of $1,000,000. Such distribution triggers taxable gain to the S corporation under Code section 311(b), in the amount of $500,000, which is distributed pro rata to shareholders under Code section 1366, and resulting in an increase in tax basis under Code section 1367. Alexa is allocated $200,000 of this gain amount (40% × $500,000), thereby increasing her tax basis in her 80 shares to $700,000 ($500,000 + $200,000). Upon the redemption of 40 of her shares, Alexa now has tax basis in those 40 shares of $350,000 and recognizes additional gain of $650,000 ($1,000,000 – $350,000). Thus, Alexa's total gain on the transaction is $850,000, and her tax basis in her remaining 40 shares is $350,000.

REDEMPTIONS BY PARTNERSHIPS

A distribution by a partnership is generally governed by the very favorable rules of Code section 731. Under those rules, no gain is recognized by a partner except to the extent that any money (for these purposes "money" includes marketable securities[38]) distributed exceeds the adjusted basis of such partner's interest in the partnership immediately before the distribution.[39] No gain or loss is recognized by the partnership on a distribution to a partner of property, including money.[40]

However, Code section 731(d) states that the rules in Code section 731 are expressly subject to the provisions of Code section 736 (relating to payments to a retiring partner or a deceased partner's successor in interest), Code section 751 (relating to unrealized receivables and inventory items), and Code section 737 (relating to recognition of pre-contribution gain in the case of certain distributions).

As discussed in Chapter 9, Code section 736 is an oddly worded section that applies specifically to transactions when a partner's entire interest is being redeemed by a partnership that intends to continue in business (including where the partner has died and the interest is being redeemed from the deceased partner's estate or other successor in interest). Code section 736 does not apply to distributions to a continuing partner,[41] nor does it apply to a liquidation of the entire partnership (as opposed to the redemption and liquidation of a single partner). Although the language of Code section 736 is complicated and arcane, it basically gives the partnership and its partners a reasonable amount of flexibility in determining the tax consequences of a redemption of a partnership interest.

Code section 736 treats payments in liquidation of a partner's interest as being either (1) payments for a partner's interest in partnership property, in which case Code section 736(b) directs that such payments be treated under the normal rules governing a distribution by a partnership (i.e., Code sections 731(a) and 751) or (2) payments governed by Code section 736(a), in which case they are treated as ordinary income, either as part of the distributive share of partnership income under Code section 736(a)(1) or as a "guaranteed payment" under Code section 736(a)(2).

Code section 736(b) arguably is the "general rule" even though, in the convoluted structure of Code section 736, it appears to be the exception. Code section 736(b)(1) covers payments made in liquidation of the interest of a retiring partner or a deceased partner. Such payments, to the extent that they are considered made in exchange for the partner's interest in partnership property, will generally result in capital gain to the redeemed partner. Code section 736(b)(2), however, will treat as ordinary income to the partner (and deductible by the partnership) the following types of payments:

- Payments made for unrealized receivables (as defined in Code section 751(c)) of the partnership.[42]

- Payments for the goodwill of the partnership, except to the extent that the partnership agreement provides for a payment with respect to goodwill.[43]

The special rules under Code section 736(b)(2) apply only if capital is not a material income-producing factor for the partnership and the retiring partner was a general partner of the partnership.[44] In other words, service partnerships have the right to decide whether to treat a payment for a general partner's interest in partnership unrealized receivables and goodwill as a distribution of partnership income or a guaranteed payment under Code section 736(a) or as a purchase of property (and not deductible by the partnership) under Code section 736(b).

Code section 736 allows a partnership and its partners (both the redeemed partner and the continuing partners) flexibility in structuring the tax consequences of a redemption. The partners have significant flexibility to decide what portion of a redemption payment or payments is attributable to partnership property under Code section 736(b) and what portion is paid out of the partnership's current income under Code section 736(a). If the redemption is implemented through a series of payments, the partners have flexibility in allocating each payment between Code section 736(a) and Code section 736(b).[45]

Perhaps most important, the partners can choose whether to treat a general partner's interest in the unrealized receivables and goodwill of a service partnership as ordinary income to the redeemed partner, and, in effect, deduct the payment at the partnership level as a Section 707(c) guaranteed payment, or whether to treat such a payment as a purchase of property, generally producing capital gain to the redeemed partner under Code section 731 while resulting in no deduction for the payment by the partnership. (The partnership can, however, make a Code section 754 election to adjust basis in partnership property under Code section 734(b).)

The following examples are derived from Reg. § 1.736-1(b)(7).

Example 9: Partnership ABC is a personal service partnership, and its balance sheet is as follows:

Assets

	Adjusted basis per books	*Market value*
Cash	$13,000	$13,000
Unrealized receivables	0	30,000
Capital and Section 1231 assets	20,000	23,000
Total	33,000	66,000

Liabilities and Capital

	Per books	*Value*
Liabilities	$ 3,000	$ 3,000
Capital:		
A	10,000	21,000
B	10,000	21,000
C	10,000	21,000
Total	33,000	66,000

Partner A retires from the partnership in accordance with an agreement whereby A's share of liabilities ($1,000) is assumed. In addition A is to receive $9,000 in the year of retirement plus $10,000 in each of the two succeeding years. Thus, the total that A receives for A's partnership interest is $30,000 ($29,000 in cash and $1,000 in liabilities assumed). Under the agreement terminating A's interest, the value of A's interest in Section 736(b) partnership property is $12,000 (one-third of $36,000, the sum of $13,000 cash and $23,000, the fair market value of capital and Section 1231 assets). A's share in unrealized receivables is not included in A's interest in partnership property described in Code section 736(b). Since the basis of A's interest is $11,000 ($10,000 plus $1,000, A's share of partnership liabilities), A will realize a capital gain of $1,000 ($12,000 minus $11,000) from the disposition of A's interest in partnership property. The remaining $18,000 ($30,000 minus $12,000) will constitute payments under Code section 736(a)(2) that are taxable to A as guaranteed payments under Code section 707(c). The payment for the first year is $10,000, consisting of $9,000 in cash, plus $1,000 in liability assumed.[46] Thus, unless the partners agree otherwise under Reg. § 1.736-1(b)(5)(iii), each annual payment of $10,000 will be allocated as follows: $6,000 (18,000/30,000 of $10,000) is a Section 736(a)(2) payment and $4,000 (12,000/30,000 of $10,000) is a payment for an interest in Section 736(b) partnership property. (The partnership may deduct the $6,000 guaranteed payment made to A in each of the three years.) The gain on the payments for partnership property will be determined under Code section 731, as provided in Reg. § 1.736-1(b)(6). A will treat only $4,000 of each payment as a distribution in a series in liquidation of A's entire interest and, under Code section 731, will have a capital gain of $1,000 when the last payment is made. However, if A so elects, as provided in Reg. § 1.736-1(b)(6), A may treat such gain as follows: Of each $4,000 payment attributable to A's interest in partnership property, $333 is capital gain (one-third of the total capital gain of $1,000), and $3,667 is a return of capital.

Example 10: Assume the same facts as in Example 9, except that the agreement between the partners provides for payments to A for three years of a percentage of annual income instead of a fixed amount. Unless the partners agree otherwise under Reg. § 1.736-1(b)(5)(iii), all payments received by A up to $12,000 shall be treated under Code section 736(b) as payments for A's interest in partnership property. A's gain of $1,000 will be taxed only after A has received A's full basis under Code section 731. Since the payments are not fixed in amount, the election provided in Reg. § 1.736-1(b)(6) is not available. Any payments in excess of $12,000 shall be treated as a distributive share of partnership income to A under Code section 736(a)(1).

Example 11: Assume the same facts as in Example 9, except that the partnership agreement provides that the payment for A's interest in partnership property shall include payment for A's interest in the goodwill of the partnership. At the time of A's retirement, the partners determine the value of partnership goodwill to be $9,000. The value of A's interest in partnership property described in Code section 736(b) is thus $15,000 (one-third of $45,000, the sum of $13,000 cash, plus $23,000, the value of capital and Section 1231 assets, plus $9,000 goodwill). From the disposition of A's interest in partnership property, A will realize a capital gain of $4,000 ($15,000, minus $11,000), the basis of A's interest. The remaining $15,000 ($30,000 minus $15,000) will constitute payments under Code section 736(a)(2) that are taxable to A as guaranteed payments under Code section 707(c).

Example 12: Assume the same facts as in Example 9 except that the capital and Section 1231 assets consist of an item of Section 1245 property (as defined in Code section 1245(a)(3)). Assume further that under Reg. § 1.751-1(c)(4) the Section 1245 property is an unrealized receivable to the extent of $2,000. Therefore, the value of A's interest in Section 736(b) partnership property is only $11,333 (one-third of $34,000, the sum of $13,000 cash and $21,000, the fair market value of Section 1245 property to the extent not an unrealized receivable). From the disposition of A's interest in partnership property, A will realize a capital gain of $333 ($11,333 minus $11,000, the basis of A's interest). The remaining $18,667 ($30,000 minus $11,333) will constitute payments under Code section 736(a)(2) that are taxable to A as guaranteed payments under Code section 707(c).

CHAPTER ENDNOTES

1. IRC Sec. 317(b).
2. IRC Sec. 317(a).
3. IRC Sec. 311(b).
4. IRC Sec. 302(a).
5. IRC Sec. 301(c).
6. IRC Sec. 311(b).
7. IRC Sec. 301(c).
8. IRC Sec. 317(b).
9. IRC Sec. 302(a).
10. IRC Sec. 302(d).
11. IRC Sec. 302(b)(1).
12. IRC Sec. 302(b)(2).

13. IRC Sec. 302 (b)(3).
14. IRC Sec. 302(b)(4).
15. IRC Sec. 302(b)(5).
16. IRC Sec. 302(c)(2).
17. *U.S. v. Davis*, 390 US 301, 90 S.Ct. 1041 (1970).
18. Reg. § 1.302-2(b).
19. 1975-2 CB 111.
20. 1976-2 CB 91.
21. IRC Sec. 302(e)(1).
22. IRC Sec. 302(e)(4).
23. IRC Sec. 302(e)(2).
24. IRC Sec. 302(b)(5).
25. IRC Sec. 302(c)(1).
26. IRC Sec. 318(a)(1).
27. IRC Sec. 318(a)(2).
28. IRC Sec. 318(a)(3).
29. IRC Sec. 318(a)(4).
30. IRC Sec. 302(c)(2)(B).
31. IRC Sec. 1(h)(11) provides that dividends are taxed as "net capital gain."
32. IRC Sec. 243(a)(1).
33. IRC Sec. 11.
34. IRC Sec. 1368(b).
35. IRC Sec. 1368(c).
36. See IRC Secs. 1366 and 1367.
37. IRC Sec. 1377(a).
38. IRC Section 731(c)(1)(A).
39. IRC Sec. 731(a)(1).
40. IRC Sec. 731(b).
41. Reg. § 1.736-1(a)(1)(i).
42. IRC Sec. 736(b)(2)(A).
43. IRC Sec. 736(b)(2)(B).
44. IRC Sec. 736(b)(3).
45. Reg. § 1.736-1(b)(5)(iii).
46. IRC Sec. 752(b).

SELLING THE BUSINESS TO CO-OWNERS: SHAREHOLDERS BUY-SELL AGREEMENTS

CHAPTER 16

OVERVIEW

Shareholders Agreements, often referred to as "Buy-Sell Agreements," are written agreements between some or all shareholders of a closely held corporation. A principal purpose of such agreements is to specify how shares of the corporation can be sold or transferred by the participating shareholders. Such agreements can also address a variety of other corporate and/or shareholder issues. Shareholders Agreements are also sometimes called Shareholder's Agreements, Shareholder Agreements, and Shareholders' Agreements. This book uses the term "Shareholders Agreements."

The objective of a Shareholders Agreement is to provide limitations, restrictions, and mechanisms for addressing a variety of business issues that, in the absence of such an agreement, would generally be handled in a different manner under corporate law. Note that in many cases the issues addressed in a Shareholders Agreement could be addressed in other corporate documents, such as the Articles of Organization or By-Laws. For example, it is not unusual to include in the Articles and/or By-Laws restrictions on transferability of shares. However, a Shareholders Agreement is often the most convenient document in which to set forth and implement a comprehensive strategy for the management of a closely held business by a limited number of shareholders.

A very interesting issue—and one on which there is not a lot of authority—is how to interpret the governing documents of a corporation when there are inconsistencies between or among the Articles of Organization, the By-Laws, and a Shareholders Agreement. For example, if the Articles of Organization contain a restriction on the transferability of shares, and the Shareholders Agreement (executed later in time) contains a different restriction, which should prevail? The author has posed this issue to various corporate attorneys over the years, and the responses have been surprisingly diverse. Some attorneys have viewed the Articles of Organization as the fundamental organizing document or the "constitution" of the corporation, and therefore have concluded that the provisions in the Articles should trump any contrary provisions, whether in the By-Laws or in the Shareholders Agreement. By contrast, other attorneys have argued that the Shareholders Agreement expresses a binding legal agreement among the shareholders to operate and govern the corporation in a specified manner. Therefore, it implicitly contains contractual obligations to amend the Articles of Organization to bring the Articles into conformity with the subsequent contractual agreement. This argument may find support in case law such as *Donahue v. Rodd Electrolyte Co. of New England, Inc.*,[1] decided under Massachusetts law, which generally holds that the shareholders of a closely held business have relationships among themselves that are equivalent to the fiduciary obligations among partners in a partnership (sometimes called the "*Donahue* Doctrine"). Because a partnership is a contractual undertaking among partners, this may tend to support the theory that a contractual agreement among the shareholders of a closely held corporation should be given the highest level of respect and effect.

Probably the single most important issue addressed in a Shareholders Agreement is the transferability (or the limitations on transferability) of shares in the corporation. As a general rule, closely held corporations are often in the nature of a "business partnership" among a small group of shareholders. Although the form of the entity is corporate in nature, the *Donahue Doctrine* validates the viewpoint that it is really in the nature of a partnership among partners. Accordingly, just as a partnership interest is generally not transferable to a new partner (in such a case, the existing partners would have to admit or accept the transferee into the partnership), it is likewise very common for the shareholders of a closely held company to limit the free transferability of the stock.

The basic premise of a transfer restriction is that shares should not be freely transferable to unacceptable outsiders. However, the exact structure of the transfer limitation varies greatly from one situation to the next. One of the most frequent arrangements is a mechanism for transferring the shares on the death of any shareholder. A common arrangement calls for all participating shareholders to own life insurance on each other's lives and be contractually obligated to buy the decedent's shares from the estate (or a related trust) when that shareholder dies. These arrangements involving life insurance as a funding source are discussed in greater detail below.

Restrictions on lifetime transfers are also very common, but here there is far more diversity among the arrangements. One typical arrangement is for the transferring shareholder to give a right of first refusal to the other shareholders. Such a right gives the other shareholders the opportunity to match a bona fide offer by an outside party. A variation on this theme is for the remaining shareholders to have a right to buy shares valued by a relatively conservative formula (e.g., book value). Although such formulas often produce relatively low valuations, the rationale is that a shareholder who is "quitting" the business should not be able to command a market or premium price for the shares. A variation on this approach is to pay a more realistic market price, but to pay it over a relatively long period of time (e.g., up to ten years). For reasons that are both practical and necessary, Shareholders Agreements typically have a bias in favor of the company and the shareholders that remain with the company and against any shareholders who wish to leave.

An interesting and important tax issue is whether the stock subject to a repurchase right should be purchased by the corporation or by the other shareholders. For tax reasons discussed more fully below, it is almost always better for the shareholders to purchase the stock because a cross-purchase acquisition results in valuable outside tax basis in the purchased shares. A redemption by the company causes the tax basis to "disappear" in the redeemed (now treasury) shares.

Although restrictions on share transfers is the single most important objective of a Shareholders Agreement, many other management and business issues can also be addressed in the agreement. These issues can include provisions designed to prevent inadvertent termination of S-corporation status, mandatory minimum distributions from an S corporation to cover tax liabilities of shareholders resulting from pass-through taxation of income, provisions addressing how to proceed in the event of a deadlock, and various other general governance agreements – such as agreeing that each shareholder has a right to elect one director to the Board of Directors.

SHARE TRANSFER RESTRICTIONS IN SHAREHOLDER AGREEMENTS

A typical Shareholders Agreement provides a mechanism by which one or more shareholders can transfer their shares, typically with different provisions addressing lifetime transfers and transfers after death. The benefits of establishing a specified transfer mechanism and purchase price for shares include the following:

1. It establishes both the price and the mechanism for liquidating stock held by the estate of a deceased shareholder.
2. It causes all shareholders to exercise the appropriate, specified mechanism to control future ownership interests in the business.
3. In many cases, it reduces the risk of potential disputes over future share valuation (although in some cases Shareholders Agreements are disputed or challenged themselves).

Benefits to Minority Shareholders. Shareholders Agreements can be particularly important for protecting the interests of minority shareholders in a closely held business. Since such shareholders lack control, a minority interest is often almost entirely illiquid, and can sometimes be close to worthless without a Shareholders Agreement. The Shareholders Agreement can also give minority owners significant rights that they would not otherwise have in the absence of such an agreement (e.g., the agreement may require that certain major transactions may only be approved by unanimous shareholder consent or by a supermajority of shareholders, in which case a minority shareholder can effectively block such transactions). Obviously, to the extent that the Shareholders Agreement provides a mechanism to liquidate minority interests, either by selling the shares to other shareholders or to the corporation, it may create a market and a pricing formula that is more favorable to the minority shareholders than an outright prohibition on transferability. Realistically, a minority stake in a closely held business (e.g., 10 percent of the voting shares) is likely to be sold to an outside party at a very steep discount. The Tax Court has sustained discounts for lack of marketability in the 40- or 50-percent range in recent years, and such steep discounts seem economically realistic, given the fact that such an investment is effectively "dead" money unless or until the majority shareholders decide to sell or liquidate the business. By contrast, a right of minority shareholders to transfer or sell their stock to the company or other shareholders, even if the pricing mechanism is relatively conservative (e.g., book value or a variation on book value), may end up providing a better price than could be received in a true arm's length transaction.

Structuring Alternatives – Diversity Is the Rule. The possible structuring arrangements under a Shareholders Agreement are as infinite as the number of business relationships and the differing interests of the respective parties. Typically, a Shareholders Agreement provides that a selling shareholder can – and, in many cases, must – offer the shares first to the corporation and/or the other shareholders before selling them to outside parties. Sometimes the arrangement is structured as a redemption that is mandatory. Alternatively, there may be a prohibition on any transfer of stock without the consent of the other shareholders. In more flexible cases, the corporation and/or other shareholders are given a right of first refusal; they may purchase the shares themselves or refuse, allowing a sale to outside parties. Depending on the nature of the arrangement, it is also common (and sometimes necessary) to have mechanisms for valuing the stock, such as establishing a price based on book value or on some other "objective" criteria.

Need to Explain an Agreement to Clients. Shareholders Agreements will often significantly restrict the ability of shareholders to transfer their stock. Therefore, it is critical to make clients aware of the importance and scope of these agreements. The Shareholders Agreement is often drafted by a single attorney. Because there are inherent conflicts of interest in representing multiple parties with potentially divergent interests, a waiver of potential conflicts of interest and a clear explanation of the purposes and role of the Shareholders Agreement is required. The best way to address this problem is to explain it carefully – both orally and in writing – so that clients are fully apprised of the consequences of executing such an agreement.

USING LIFE INSURANCE TO FUND BUY-OUTS ON DEATH; TAX-RELATED STRUCTURING CONSIDERATIONS

It is very common to use life insurance as the funding mechanism for a buy-out of closely-held stock upon the death of one of the shareholders. The arrangement can either call for the life insurance proceeds to be paid on death to the corporation, coupled with an obligation of the corporation to redeem the decedent's stock (and an obligation of the estate to tender the stock), or the life insurance can be paid to other shareholders who then have a "cross-purchase" obligation to purchase the stock from the estate. Prior to 1987, most closely held businesses in the US operated as C corporations and most structured their life insurance-funded buy-back agreements as corporate-owned life insurance coupled with a redemption arrangement. However, as a result of tax-law changes introduced by the Tax Reform Act of 1986, it is now far more common to structure life insurance arrangements such that the life insurance is owned outside the corporation, for the reasons described below.

Cross-Purchase Is Preferable. For tax reasons, it is almost always desirable to structure a buy-out on death funded by life insurance as a cross purchase transaction whenever possible. This is true both for C corporations and S corporations, although for different reasons.

In the case of a C corporation, the decisive factors are usually the alternative minimum tax (AMT) and tax basis issues. In general, life insurance proceeds on the death of an insured are "tax-free" to the recipient under Code section 101, and can thus be received by individual shareholders without tax cost or consequence. However, if the owner and beneficiary of a life insurance policy is a C corporation, the insurance proceeds will be considered "earnings" and will increase (often significantly, since life insurance is usually written for relatively large amounts) the corporation's adjusted current earnings (ACE).[2] In turn, 75 percent of the excess of ACE over alternative minimum taxable income (AMTI) is then included in the corporation's alternative minimum taxable income.[3]

Example 1: Branch Corporation, a C corporation, is owned 50 percent each by two brothers, and the corporation holds a $2 million life insurance policy on each brother, with the obligation to purchase the stock of the decedent for $2 million if either brother dies. In year 2006 one of the brothers dies. Assume Branch Corporation in that year is subject to the corporate AMT, and that before taking into account the life insurance proceeds, the corporation's ACE amount is exactly equal to its AMTI determined without regard to the ACE adjustment under Code section 56(g) and without regard to the AMT net operating loss (NOL) deduction. On that basis, the $2 million will be included in the ACE amount, and cause the ACE to exceed AMTI by $2 million. In turn, 75 percent of this excess, or $1.5 million, will be added to the AMTI for year 2006. Since we are assuming that the corporation was already subject to the AMT before taking into account the insurance adjustment, this will increase AMTI by $1,500,000 and, at the corporate AMT tax rate of 20 percent, would result in the corporation owing an additional $300,000 ($1,500,000 × 20%) of AMT tax in the current year.

Comment: For purposes of providing a simple-to-follow illustration, the above example assumes the corporation is already in the corporate AMT and that ACE exactly equals AMTI. In the real world, the corporate AMT is arguably less expansive and pervasive than the individual AMT and may not always be triggered (or at least not triggered as much), as this example implies.[4] Nonetheless, increasing the corporate AMTI by 75 percent of the life insurance proceeds will, in many cases, cause the C corporation to owe additional tax (i.e., to the extent the AMT calculation results in a tax liability greater than the regular tax for the tax year, the taxpayer pays the additional amount in that year, subject to a possible tax credit under Code section 53 applicable to future years). Note that since the $2 million of insurance proceeds is already earmarked for the redemption transaction, this additional tax liability will come out of the pocket of the C corporation, with the possibility of a tax credit under Code section 53 against regular tax liabilities in future years.

Note further that even if the AMT cost described above does not apply, e.g., because the corporation comes within the small corporation exemption under Code section 55(e), the cross-purchase structure is still the preferred alternative because of the increased tax basis a cross-purchase produces under Code section 1012.

Under a cross-purchase agreement, by contrast, the life insurance proceeds are paid to individual shareholders without adverse alternative minimum tax consequences for those individuals (Code section 56(g) applies only to C corporations). In addition, the cross-purchasers get a step-up in their tax basis in the purchased stock equal to the payment for the stock. As we will discuss below, this "outside" tax basis is not always of great use in a C corporation context because the benefit of the tax basis is locked up until the C corporation liquidates. However, it obviously makes sense to get the benefit of the tax basis because, in a corporate redemption transaction, the tax basis disappears into what becomes treasury stock. As we will discuss below, the extra tax basis can be especially valuable if the corporation is an S corporation.

S Corporation Tax Issues. The corporate alternative minimum tax problem under Code section 56(g) does not exist for life insurance proceeds paid to an S corporation, but there are tax basis issues and other problems that likewise make the cross-purchase structure preferable. First, life insurance proceeds, when paid to an S corporation, result in a positive adjustment (equal to the amount of the tax-exempt income) to the outside basis of the shareholders. Part of this tax basis adjustment will presumably be allocated to the decedent's shares now held by the estate. However, the tax basis in those shares was increased to fair market value at the date of death, pursuant to Code section 1014. Thus, the estate stock ends up with an "excess" of tax basis, which very likely will produce a large (and not-very-useful) capital loss to the estate. The capital loss will not be allocated to the surviving shareholders, who may be in a better position to utilize the tax basis. Such tax basis, by contrast, would inure to the benefit of the surviving shareholders under a cross-purchase agreement.

Example 2: Priam Prism Corporation, an S corporation, is owned 50-50 by two unrelated individuals, Alex and Ben. Priam Prism owns (and is the beneficiary of) two $1 million life insurance policies, one policy on the life of Alex and one on the life of Ben. Assume that Priam Prism, Alex, and Ben have entered into a binding Shareholders Agreement pursuant to which Alex and Ben agree that on the death of either of them the estate of the decedent will sell back the decedent's shares to Priam Prism in a redemption transaction for $1 million. Assume Ben predeceases Alex. On Ben's death, the tax basis of the shares in the hands of Ben's estate is increased to the fair market value of the shares, which, because of the binding Shareholders Agreement, is $1 million.[5] Therefore, Ben's estate holds the shares with a tax basis of $1 million. Some time later, the corporation receives $1 million of tax-free life insurance proceeds as the death benefit for the life insurance policy insuring Ben.

Assuming Ben's estate still owns the stock, this $1 million payment will result in a positive adjustment in that amount to the outside basis of the shareholders pursuant to Code section 1367(a)(1)(A). That adjustment could end up being allocated 50-50 between the shares held by Alex and the shares held by the estate of Ben (depending on timing and elections described below). This means that following the basis adjustment, the shares in the hands of the estate could now have a tax basis of $1.5 million ($1 million resulting from the basis step up on death, and another $500,000 for the receipt by the S corporation of the $1 million death benefit). However, Ben's estate will only be paid the contractual redemption price of $1 million. Hence, Ben's estate will recognize a $500,000 capital loss. Given that Ben's estate has recently had the tax basis in all its assets stepped up to fair market value, the estate is unlikely to have significant appreciated assets to generate an offsetting capital gain. This is *not* good tax planning!

The magnitude of the tax basis distortion in Example 2 depends in part on how the shareholders elect to be taxed under the S corporation basis adjustment and distribution rules. One possibility is that Alex and Ben's estate each are allocated 50 percent of the tax basis adjustment for all items that occur while Ben's estate still owns the stock. This would be the rule if Alex and Ben's estate were to file an election under Code section 1377(a)(2).

Alternatively, if Alex and Ben's estate are allocated S corporation income under the default per share, per day rule, the portion of the $1 million allocated to Ben's estate would depend on when in the tax year the redemption takes place. For example, if the redemption takes place on January 5 and the S corporation uses a calendar tax year, Ben's estate would be allocated only a small portion of the tax basis (representing a 50-percent interest in S corporation items for five days out of 365). On the other hand, if the proceeds are received on December 31, Ben's estate would be allocated 50 percent of all items over the entire year.

There are several theoretical ways to address the problem posed in Example 2 (other than the correct solution, which is a cross-purchase structure), but none of these other alternatives is particularly good. First, if it is possible to control when the insurance check is paid to a cash basis corporation, having it paid in early January would help to minimize (but would not completely eliminate) the tax basis distortion, assuming the parties use the "default" per share, per day distribution rule and redeem the estate stock early in the year. The problem, of course, is that there is no assurance that the shareholder will conveniently die at a time that makes this timing strategy possible.

The second alternative is to have the estate sell the stock to the corporation *before* the insurance proceeds arrive (e.g., by transferring the stock and taking back a promissory note from the corporation in the amount of $1 million). The problem with this strategy is that an executor may be reluctant to give up control over the stock (and *de facto* control over the company) until the insurance proceeds are in the hands of the company. After all, $1 million in cash may be enough of a temptation to cause the surviving shareholder, Alex, to reconsider his contractual commitments.

In general, Shareholders Agreements should expressly address the treatment of the decedent's shares while they are in the hands of the estate. For example, one must decide whether the ownership of the decedent's stock will be transferred on death to the corporation or shareholders, even though payment will not be made to the estate until sometime after the shareholder's death. Alternatively, if the shares are held for any length of time by the estate, provisions must be made to assure that the estate receives appropriate distributions to correspond to the taxable income allocated to it from ongoing activities of the S corporation. In drafting these provisions, one must also address carefully whether the interest held by the estate is a "second class of stock" that would potentially cost the corporation its eligibility to elect S status.

Related Income Tax Issues for Decedent's Estate. A related and complementary issue is determining how the estate should share in the income and other tax attributes of an S corporation during a particular year prior to a redemption (or, for that matter, a cross-purchase). Without going into the full details, it may be appropriate to make an election under Code section 1377(a)(2) to cut off the allocation of income from the S corporation to the estate effective on the date when the shares are redeemed. (In the absence of such an election, the entire annual income of an S corporation can be allocated on a per share, per day basis, which can create unfair distortions, especially if substantial income is earned by the S corporation after the estate stock has been redeemed.)

A variation on this timing strategy is to redeem the estate stock at the very beginning of a tax year (generally the calendar year for an S corporation) so that, even under the per share, per day rule that applies in the absence of an election under Code section 1377(a)(2), the estate has an extremely small share of any tax items for the applicable year. In other words, a redemption implemented on January 1 or January 2 minimizes any income allocation and basis distortions; however, for the control reasons noted above, an executor may be far more concerned about receiving the redemption payment than about successful income tax planning.

STRUCTURING CROSS-PURCHASE ARRANGEMENTS: ISSUES WITH TRUSTS AND INSURANCE PARTNERSHIPS

A cross-purchase arrangement neatly solves the vexing tax basis, AMT, and other problems resulting from a redemption structure. First, because the life insurance proceeds are paid (in almost all cases) to individual shareholders, there is no C corporation AMT issue. Second, in the case of an S corporation, the insurance proceeds do not go to the S corporation. Hence, tax basis distortion is avoided. Third, there is no "disappearing" tax basis. The surviving shareholder or shareholders enjoy a step-up in outside tax basis equal to the life insurance proceeds used to fund the cross-purchase. All these benefits occur easily and automatically as a consequence of the cross-purchase structure. The only major objection to this approach is a practical one: Each shareholder wants to make sure the other parties in fact use the life insurance proceeds as intended, and thus the parties may want the life insurance held in a trust or other holding mechanism to make sure the surviving shareholders perform their contractual commitments. However, trying to implement a cross-purchase with numerous shareholders – and trying to structure a common holding vehicle for life insurance policies – is not without its own set of problems and challenges.

Structuring Multiple Policy Cross-Purchase Arrangements. Although the tax benefits of a cross-purchase arrangement are straightforward, the actual implementation of the transaction can sometimes be surprisingly complicated and difficult. One reason is that the cross-purchase arrangement requires fragmentation of the insurance coverage into many smaller insurance policies if the number of shareholders is greater than two. For example, assume that there is a medical group of 10 doctors, each owning 10 percent of the practice, and the goal is to put into place a cross-purchase agreement among them. One simple strategy would be to have the corporation own 10 life insurance policies, one on each of the 10 doctors, and then redeem the shares when a doctor dies.

This would raise the AMT problems described above (assuming the physician practice is operated through a C corporation), or the possible tax basis distortions described above (if the corporation is an S corporation). However, for 10 doctors to implement a successful cross-purchase arrangement, each doctor would have to have an insurance policy on the life of each of the doctor's nine fellow shareholders. The formula for computing the number of life insurance policies required for n doctors is $n \times (n - 1)$. Because n in this case is 10, the total number of policies required is $10 \times (10 - 1) = 90$. This is not a realistic alternative.

The Problems with Holding Insurance in a Trust. One early proposed "solution" to this problem was to set up a trust holding a life insurance policy insuring each shareholder and to have the trust purchase the stock of the decedent shareholder. However, this raised issues and risks under the so-called "transfer-for-value" rule in Code section 101(a)(2) and the regulations. Under the transfer-for-value rule, whenever a life insurance policy is transferred "for value" the death benefit of the insurance ceases to be tax-free. The subsequent receipt of the insurance proceeds becomes taxable income for the owner of the policy.

The transfer-for-value rule does not apply to a transfer to the insured, to a partner of the insured, to a partnership in which the insured is a partner, or to a corporation in which the insured is a shareholder or officer.[6] However, the exceptions to the transfer-for-value rule do not explicitly or implicitly include transfers to or transactions with a trust. Therefore, the concern is that when a trust pays insurance proceeds to a decedent's estate in exchange for the purchase of the decedent's shares and other interests in the corporation, the decedent is effectively transferring or surrendering to the trust his or her undivided interest in the life insurance policies on the lives of the surviving shareholders. Each time a decedent's shares are purchased, a larger percentage of the insurance proceeds can potentially become taxable income to the beneficiaries and/or the trust under the transfer-for-value rules.

Use of a Partnership to Hold Life Insurance. Due to the exemption from the transfer-for-value rule granted to transactions between a partner and a partnership, the obvious planning solution was to use a partnership instead of a trust. In some early letter rulings, the IRS ruled favorably on partnerships set up to hold life insurance policies on the shareholders of corporations.[7] However, in Rev. Proc. 96-12,[8] the IRS announced that it would not ordinarily rule on whether the transfer of life insurance policies to a partnership, substantially all of the assets of which consists of insurance policies on the lives of the partners, is exempt from the transfer-for-value rule. This cast a shadow on life insurance partnerships because a no-ruling position indicates that the IRS has serious reservations about the issue and wishes to study the matter carefully. The key issue is whether or not the alleged partnership is engaged in the carrying on of a trade or business or whether it has been availed of only for investment purposes.

Subsequent to Rev. Proc. 96-12, the IRS issued a favorable ruling, in IRS Letter Ruling 9725007[9], on the transfer-for-value issue where the insurance policies held by the partnership represented less than one half of the partnership's total assets. Another ruling, IRS Letter Ruling 9843024,[10] also ruled that a partnership was eligible for the exception of the transfer-for-value rule. The ruling implied (but did not expressly state) that the partnership had substantial assets other than its life insurance policies. This latter ruling contained a caveat that no opinion was expressed with respect to whether the transfer-for-value rule would apply if the partnership disposed of all of its assets other than life insurance policies or if, at the time of the sale of the policies, the insured partner's interest in the partnership was below a certain unspecified percentage.

Note that the "check-the-box" regulations under Code section 7701, pursuant to which a taxpayer can generally elect to have a noncorporate entity such as an LLC treated as a partnership for tax purposes, do not appear to apply or be germane in this life insurance partnership analysis because the central focus of those regulations is the demarcation between corporate and partnership status, whereas the key issue in the transfer-for-value analysis is whether the partnership is engaged in a trade or business (and thus a "partnership" for tax purposes) or whether it is not engaged in a trade or business (and thus should be classified as a "trust" for tax purposes). One can argue that the check-the-box regulations represent a more fundamental policy that form should prevail over substance in all entity classifications issues, but to date this has not been the IRS's view as applied to this specific area of the law. Accordingly, the life insurance partnership remains under a cloud at the present time.

ALTERNATIVE STRUCTURES TO A CONVENTIONAL CROSS-PURCHASE ARRANGEMENT

Although a conventional cross-purchase arrangement, involving separate life insurance policies on each shareholder is very common, there are alternative structures for using life insurance that can meet the specific needs of a particular group of shareholders. For example, "first-to-die" insurance or "second-to-die" insurance may be appropriate in specific situations, and can be significantly less expensive than other forms of life insurance.

Example 3: Assume a corporation with two equal shareholders concludes that the most important issue is to obtain insurance proceeds on the death of the first shareholder to die. Therefore, instead of having two insurance policies to implement a cross-purchase arrangement, the company and/or the shareholders may be able to purchase a single first-to-die policy on the two shareholders. This will save considerably on the insurance premiums and may satisfactorily address the perceived needs of the parties.

"Horse Race" Arrangement. An interesting and intriguing Shareholders Agreement is what is sometimes called a "horse race" arrangement, where the two principal shareholders agree that each of them will address personal estate planning and insurance planning as a personal, private matter, and will not look to the shares in the company as a significant or major asset in the decedent's estate. In effect, they conclude that (1) on the death of one of them, the business in the hands of the survivor is severely harmed and has limited value, (2) the survivor faces a major business challenge and numerous stresses, which will be only more daunting if half the stock is now owned by the decedent's surviving spouse, (3) for economic incentive and other reasons, they agree that the survivor should be allowed to buy the business from the decedent's estate for a very low and reasonable price, and (4) the economic risks of dying early, allocated to each individual under this agreement, can be properly hedged by each shareholder individually through prudent estate planning (e.g., by implementing a life insurance strategy, such as putting adequate insurance into an irrevocable life insurance trust (ILIT)). The reason this is sometimes called a "horse race" arrangement is that, when the parties agree to set an intentionally low redemption or cross-purchase price, they do not know which of them will benefit by surviving the other, but both agree at the outset to the logic of the arrangement. The arrangement is not only "fair" – it is actually a smart estate plan because the insurance payoff on death does not go into the decedent's estate, but instead into an ILIT that can then be available for the benefit of a surviving spouse and passed without estate tax to the next generation of the family.

SELF-FUNDING STOCK PURCHASES FOR LIFETIME TRANSFERS AND ON DEATH

Life insurance is very popular for funding stock purchase obligations on death because death is often an unexpected event, and the cost of the life insurance – especially when the insured shareholders are younger – is relatively low compared to the death benefit. By contrast, when a Shareholders Agreement provides for purchase of shares other than on the death of a shareholder, such lifetime share transfers are usually funded from the resources of the business. Although some businesses will occasionally purchase disability policies to fund a buy-out in the event of a disability, this is far less common than the use of life insurance to fund purchases on death.

Self-Funding. It is not unusual for a Shareholders Agreement to call for either a mandatory purchase (relatively uncommon) or an optional right to purchase (e.g., a right of first refusal, which is very common) shares from a shareholder seeking to make a lifetime transfer. However, the problem and challenge with imposing restrictions on a lifetime transfer is that the company will have to be, directly or indirectly, the source of the funds to pay the acquisition price. This is typically dealt with by (1) stipulating a relatively modest purchase price and/or (2) allowing for payment over a relatively long period of time (e.g., ten years). In particular, a Shareholders Agreement will often provide that purchasing shareholders have at least one option that allows them to pay for shares over a period of years using the revenues of the business.

For example, the parties could give the remaining shareholders a right of first refusal to purchase shares on the same terms as a bona fide offer, but, in addition, permit them to pay an agreed price, equal to the value that would be payable to a shareholder on death, but with payment terms of 20 percent down and the rest payable over five or ten years (depending on the amount to be paid and the relative cash-generating potential of the related company or business). In addition to addressing certain issues under Code section 2703, discussed more fully below, the arrangement allows the shareholders to either match a bona fide offer or, if more favorable to their cash flow needs, to pay a stipulated amount over a period of years using funds generated by the business.

Uninsurable Shareholders. A common problem is that although stock purchase obligations on death are generally funded with life insurance, as shareholders age, it is not unusual to find that some shareholders become uninsurable. Meanwhile, the parties may have a mechanism in place that raises the purchase price for shares on the death of a shareholder above the amount that is covered by insurance. This "spread" between insurance proceeds and the amount payable to the estate of the decedent shareholder is also often subject to self-funding, typically over a period of time.

ADDITIONAL INCOME TAX ISSUES

As noted above, a cross-purchase arrangement has favorable income tax consequences to the purchaser because the purchaser gets a step up in tax basis equal to the purchase price. The Seller, meanwhile, should have long-term capital gain, assuming the shares have been held for more than one year, regardless of whether the transaction is a cross-purchase or a redemption. Although the current tax rate structure does not provide a rate differential between dividends and long-term capital gains, a selling party should at least be aware of the so-called "dividend trap" under Code section 302(b), which can potentially arise in a redemption transaction. Note that, with respect to lifetime transfers, capital gain treatment has historically been very important to the Seller because stock in a closely held business often has a very low tax basis, and the capital gain tax rate has generally been very attractive. The current equalization of capital gains and dividend tax rates for federal income tax purposes makes this issue less important than before—as long as the rates stay at equal levels and state taxes do not produce significant disparities. Even with equal tax rates, the parties generally want to make sure to avoid the dividend trap in order to utilize tax basis in stock and thereby reduce tax costs.

The Dividend Trap. A transaction structured as a redemption can nonetheless be characterized as a dividend in some circumstances, especially if the corporation is family owned and the transaction does not meet the applicable requirements of Code section 302. Because Code section 302 attributes stock of related persons to the Seller, a sale of some but not all of the family stock (including a sale by an estate) can be recategorized under certain circumstances as a dividend, with corresponding and potentially adverse income tax results (i.e., the entire amount of the cash proceeds would be treated as a fully taxable dividend, and the tax basis in the stock would provide no tax benefit). This situation is especially unfortunate if the stock being acquired from an estate has high tax basis because the tax basis is wasted through poor tax planning.

The "simple" way to avoid the Code section 302(b) dividend trap is to make sure that the Seller's entire interest in the stock is sold in the redemption transaction.[11] Note that Code section 303 allows for a partial redemption of stock held by an estate to help pay estate taxes and certain other death transfer costs. Under those specific circumstances, the transaction will be characterized as a sale or exchange even though it would normally fail to qualify under the normal Code section 302(b)(3) criteria.

Comment: Be aware that the tax treatment of a redemption of a partnership interest under Code section 736 is very different from the tax treatment of a purchase or redemption of shares from the estate of a decedent.

Life Insurance Premiums Are Not Deductible. Although it should be obvious, life insurance premiums paid by a company to implement a stock redemption arrangement are not deductible by the company.[12] This is not always understood by shareholders who do their own tax planning.

Code section 1244 Strategy. It has been suggested that to fund a small redemption, other shareholders could contribute cash to the corporation and receive Code section 1244 stock (rather than buy the stock directly from the selling shareholder). The corporation could then use the cash to redeem the departing shareholder's shares. The benefit of this strategy, if it works, is that any future losses with respect to the Section 1244 stock will be ordinary losses, rather than (less valuable) capital losses. However, because the maximum benefit allowable under Code section 1244 is $50,000 ($100,000 in the case of spouses filing a joint return), at best it is significant only in smaller transactions.

FREEZING THE VALUE OF STOCK FOR ESTATE TAX PURPOSES

A Shareholders Agreement is a rational mechanism by which unrelated shareholders in a closely held business can manage and order their relationships and conduct their business. However, when the shareholders are also members of a single family, a Shareholders Agreement can also potentially be used as an estate planning device to depress the value of shares for estate tax purposes on the death of a senior family member. A major part of estate planning in the 1980s involved so-called "corporate freeze" transactions, whereby the senior generation of a family-owned business would seek to "freeze" the value of their equity for estate tax purposes and transfer the future appreciation in value to their children and others through various techniques, ranging from recapitalizations (giving senior family members preferred stock and junior family members common stock) to creative uses of Shareholders Agreements among family members. In response to these taxpayer strategies, Congress in 1990 enacted Chapter 14, Code sections 2701-2704, with various limitations and anti-abuse rules. Code section

2703 addresses shareholder buy-sell agreements and provides a variety of rules concerning the ability of family members to set (and, inherently, restrict) the purchase price on death of stock in a family-owned business.

Shareholder Agreements among Unrelated Parties. Code section 2703 was designed to provide additional requirements, on top of those already imposed by case law and Reg. § 20.2031-2(h), before a value placed on shares by a Shareholders Agreement would be honored for estate tax purposes. The old (pre-October 9, 1990) rules were that an agreement would set the value of stock for estate tax purposes if the following requirements were satisfied:

1. The price was determinable under the agreement.
2. The estate was obligated to sell at the agreement price (a mere option to sell was not sufficient).
3. The decedent was prohibited from selling the stock during his or her lifetime at a price greater than the agreed-upon price on death.
4. The price set by the agreement was fair and adequate at the time the agreement was entered into.
5. The agreement had a valid business purpose and was not merely a tax avoidance device.

As will be discussed more fully below, these pre-October 9, 1990 case law standards continue to have significance in determining whether, for example, an agreement is a bona fide arrangement and not a testamentary device. Meanwhile, the regulatory standards for determining whether a Shareholders Agreement among unrelated parties will be respected as setting the value of stock for estate tax purposes are set forth in Reg. § 20.2031-2(h), which today reads as follows:

> *Securities subject to an option or contract to purchase.*—Another person may hold an option or a contract to purchase securities owned by a decedent at the time of his death. The effect, if any, that is given to the option or contract price in determining the value of the securities for estate tax purposes depends upon the circumstances of the particular case. Little weight will be accorded a price contained in an option or contract under which the decedent is free to dispose of the underlying securities at any price he chooses during his lifetime. Such is the effect, for example, of an agreement on the part of a shareholder to purchase whatever shares of stock the decedent may own at the time of his death. Even if the decedent is not free to dispose of the underlying securities at other than the option or contract price, such price will be disregarded in determining the value of the securities unless it is determined under the circumstances of the particular case that the agreement represents a bona fide business arrangement and not a device to pass the decedent's shares to the natural objects of his bounty for less than an adequate and full consideration in money or money's worth. See section 2703 and the regulations at § 25.2703 of this chapter for special rules involving options and agreements (including contracts to purchase) entered into (or substantially modified after) October 8, 1990.

Nature and Scope of Code section 2703. Code section 2703, enacted in 1990 as part of then-new Chapter 14, adds to and complicates these rules by adding the following three additional requirements:

1. It must be a bona fide business arrangement.
2. It must not be a device to transfer property to a deceased shareholder's family for less than full and adequate consideration in money or money's worth.
3. Its terms must be comparable to similar arrangements entered into by persons in an arm's-length transaction.

> ***Comment:*** Code section 2703 has, by regulation and legislative intent, been limited to agreements among related parties.[13] For Shareholders Agreements between and among unrelated parties, the traditional tests presumably remain the applicable standard.

There have been surprisingly few cases and rulings on Code section 2703, despite its obvious ongoing importance in estate planning. IRS letter rulings issued under Code section 2703 in recent years have generally focused on whether a particular transaction was a modification of a contract entered into prior to the enactment of that Code provision, which would put at risk the "grandfathering" of pre-enactment arrangements.

The first two requirements imposed by Code section 2703 were identified in the Senate Finance Committee Report as similar to those contained in the prior regulations and in case law such as *Saint Louis County Bank.*[14] The legislative history emphasizes that these two requirements are separate and distinct, and expressly notes that "[t]he mere showing that the agreement is a bona fide business arrangement would not give the agreement estate tax effect if other facts indicate that the agreement is a device to transfer property to members of the decedents [sic] family for less than full and adequate consideration."

The third requirement, that the terms of the agreement be comparable to similar arrangements entered into by persons in an arm's-length transaction, was identified in the legislative history as a new standard not found in prior law. The Senate Finance Committee Report indicates that this comparable-to-similar-arrangements standard "requires that the taxpayer show that the agreement was one that could have been obtained in an arm's length bargain. Such determination would entail consideration of such factors as the expected term of the agreement, the present value of the property, its expected value at the time of exercise, and the consideration offered for the option." The legislative history notes that the standard is not met simply by showing isolated comparables; it requires a demonstration of the general practice of unrelated parties, and anticipates that expert testimony would be appropriate evidence of such practice.

The regulations under Code section 2703 provide that an arrangement covered by that provision will be treated as comparable to similar arrangements entered into by persons in an arm's-length transaction if it is one that could have been obtained in a fair bargain among unrelated parties in the same business dealing with each other at arm's length.[15] An arrangement is considered a "fair bargain among unrelated parties under negotiated agreements in the same business" if the arrangement conforms with the general practice of unrelated parties under negotiated agreements in the same business. Factors identified by the regulations to make this determination generally track those previously identified in the legislative history and include the expected term of the agreement, the current fair market value of the property, anticipated changes in value during the term of the agreement, and the adequacy of any consideration given in exchange for the right granted.[16]

Evidence of general business practice is not met by showing isolated comparables.[17] If more than one valuation method commonly is used in a business, one of the recognized methods should be appropriate.[18]

The regulations address the fact that, technically, Code section 2703 does not limit its application to transactions among related persons. The regulations provide that a Shareholders Agreement is considered to meet each of the three requirements if more than 50 percent by value of the property subject to the agreement is owned directly or indirectly by individuals who are not members of the transferor's family or natural objects of the transferor's bounty.[19] Significantly, however, under this standard a Shareholders Agreement between two unrelated 50-50 shareholders is subject to scrutiny under Code section 2703. (See, however, cases such as *W.L Carpenter,*[20] where the Tax Court in a memorandum decision upheld the estate tax valuation of stock transferred under a Shareholders Agreement where there was no family relationship between the two unrelated shareholders and the court found that the business purpose of the arrangement was to enable surviving shareholders to keep the business operating.)

Structuring Shareholders Agreements under Code section 2703. Pre-1990 case law continues to provide some of the basic requirements for a price set by a Shareholders Agreement to be binding for estate tax purposes, including the following:

1. The agreement must fix a purchase price, whether a fixed dollar amount or a set formula, that is objectively determinable, and that price must be reasonable at the time when the agreement is entered into. Note that courts have, for estate tax purposes, upheld the validity of an agreement fixing a price if the value or formula was reasonable at the time the agreement was executed, even though the fair market value of the stock would have been much greater at death absent the agreement.[21] Note that case law has even upheld (albeit in an older case) the use of a "book value" formula for valuing stock.[22]

2. The fixed price must been binding upon the shareholder at all times during the shareholder's lifetime as well as at death. The shareholder cannot have a right to sell the stock at a higher price during his or her lifetime. The theory is that if the shareholder can sell the stock during his lifetime at a higher price, the Shareholders Agreement is effectively revocable and only becomes irrevocable on death. A restriction on price that applies during a shareholder's

lifetime but not at death does not fix the value of the stock in the deceased shareholder's gross estate.[23]

3. The estate must be contractually obligated to sell the stock at the price fixed by the Shareholders Agreement. This can be met either by an obligation or by a call right exercised by an option holder under the agreement.

4. The agreement must be a bona fide business arrangement and not a device to pass the decedent's property to the natural objects of the decedent's bounty for less than full and adequate consideration. This is derived from case law, but it also constitutes the first two prongs of the three-pronged test imposed by Code section 2703. Case law recognizes that continuity of family ownership and control is a legitimate and bona fide business purpose. However, a bona fide business arrangement can still be viewed as a "device" for passing wealth.

5. Arguably the most vexing issue is how to set a purchase price for shares that will not, in hind sight, be challenged by the IRS. Some parties agree to set or reset the purchase price by mutual agreement periodically (e.g., every three years). Other parties use a formula which can involve book value or a variation of book value (e.g., book value determined using the cash method of accounting or 80 percent of book value), or require an appraisal. Realistically, it is often both prudent and necessary to "fix" a purchase price at or near the life insurance death benefit payable by policies held by the parties to fund a cross-purchase of shares on the death of a shareholder. It is not unusual to have a price "fixed" by the insurance coverage.

Shareholders Agreements for Unrelated Persons. For shareholders who are not family members and not governed by Code section 2703, satisfying the historic requirements for a valid Shareholders Agreement generally means that the price at which stock must be sold at death must be fair and reasonable at the time the agreement is entered into. Shareholders also must be prevented from transferring their stock during their lifetime at a price that is greater than the mandatory price on death. Some agreements prohibit all forms of voluntary lifetime transfers. However, the more common restriction is the right of first refusal, which prohibits stockholders from accepting an outside offer without first offering the stock to the other parties at the agreement price. This type of restriction has been sustained by the courts.[24]

A "Fixed and Frozen" Purchase Price. One major issue (both for related and unrelated shareholders) is whether the parties can agree on a fixed price up-front that is reasonable at the time the agreement is entered into, and then leave that price unchanged despite subsequent growth in the value of the underlying company. Note that there is significant (pre-1990) case law indicating that so long as the agreement price represents full and adequate consideration for the stock interest at the time the agreement is made, this price will be given binding effect, even if there is a substantial discrepancy between the agreement price and the fair market value of the unrestricted interest on the date of death.[25]

The opposite question is whether the parties can reset the price periodically. The IRS in the past has argued that shareholders' ability to reset the price makes the price indeterminate and insufficient for estate tax purposes.[26] This IRS position has been justly criticized by commentators.[27]

INCIDENTS OF OWNERSHIP IN LIFE INSURANCE

An issue that can sometimes be a trap arises if a corporation has life insurance on the life of a shareholder and that shareholder has any "incidents of ownership" in the policy. In general, if an insured shareholder dies, the policy is payable to the corporation. The insured possessed no "incidents of ownership" and the proceeds are not includible in the insured's gross estate.[28] However, if the insured possessed at the time of death any incidents of ownership in the policy, the proceeds are includible in the insured's gross estate even though the corporation is named as the owner and beneficiary of the policy.[29] If the insured is a controlling shareholder (more than 50 percent of the combined voting power), then, to the extent that proceeds are payable other than to or for the benefit of the corporation, any incidents of ownership in the insurance held by the corporation as to the insurance will be attributed to the majority shareholder and can cause the amount of proceeds from the policy to be includible in the majority shareholder's gross estate.[30]

CHAPTER ENDNOTES

1. 367 Mass 578, 328 NE2d 505 (1975).
2. IRC Sec. 56(g)(1).
3. IRC Sec. 56(g).
4. For example, there is an exemption from the AMT for gross receipts over the prior three years. IRC Sec. 55(e)(1)(A), small corporations averaging less than $7.5 million.
5. IRC Sec. 1014; see IRC Sec. 2703.
6. IRC Sec. 101(a)(2).
7. See IRS Letter Ruling 9012063 (1989) IRS Letter Ruling 9042023.
8. 1996-1 CB 616, IRS Letter Ruling 9045004 (1990).
9. 3-18-97, CCH IRS Letter Rulings Reports.
10. 7-24-98, CCH IRS Letter Rulings Reports.
11. See IRC Sec. 302(b)(3).
12. IRC Sec. 264(a)(1).
13. Reg. § 25.2703-1(b)(3).
14. 674 F2d 1207 (1982).
15. Reg. § 25.2703-1(b)(4)(i).
16. Reg. § 25.2703-1(b)(4)(i).
17. Reg. § 25.2703-1(b)(4)(ii).
18. Reg. § 25.2703-1(b)(4)(ii).
19. Reg. § 25.2703-1(b)(3).
20. 64 TCM 1274 (1992).
21. See *F.H. Wilson v. F.C. Bowers*, 57 F2d 682(1932).
22. *T. Gore*, 224 F2d 892 (1955).
23. *Worcester County Trust Co.* 134 F2d 578 (1943). *L. Weil Estate*, 22 TC 1267 (1954).
24. See *H.A. May*, 194 F2d 396(1952).
25. *H.A. May, supra; C.F. Lomb*, 82 F2d 166(1936) *J.C. Hall Estate*, 92 TC 312 (1989).
26. See IRS Letter Ruling 8710004 (1986).
27. See Jerald David August, *Buy-Sell Agreements, Estate, Business, and Tax Considerations*, Chapter 4, 51st NYU Institute on Federal Taxation.
28. IRC Sec. 2042.
29. *Id.*
30. Reg. § 20.2042-1(c)(6).

COMPENSATION, CONSULTING, NONCOMPETE, AND GOODWILL

CHAPTER 17

OVERVIEW

In a business acquisition, the Acquirer almost always ends up paying some amount of money to individual owners/employees of the Target for personal services (compensation and consulting payments), for a covenant not-to-compete (noncompete payments), and, increasingly, for personal goodwill. These categories of payments are generally described in this book as "personal payments". In addition, an Acquirer may also make payments to an individual owner and/or employee of the Target for the use of property (e.g., to lease real estate used in connection with the Target business), to license patents or other intangible property owned by such individual, and for the use or license of other property rights. Such payments are referred to in this book as "parallel payments".

Both personal payments and parallel payments have twin objectives when paid in connection with an acquisition transaction: (1) they secure for the Acquirer the legal contractual benefit for which the payments are made (e.g., personal services, noncompete covenants, or the use of property), and (2) such payments often have more advantageous tax consequences to the Acquirer, to the Target owners, or both, compared with other payment allocations in the acquisition transaction.

The purpose of this chapter is to explore various tax issues that can arise when personal payments or parallel payments are used in connection with an acquisition transaction.

REASONABLE COMPENSATION

The Acquirer may want to benefit from the services of a Target employee, either by employing such person after the acquisition or by having such person act as a consultant. Payments for such services are deductible under Code section 162 by the payor so long as each payment constitutes "reasonable" compensation for the employment or consulting services being provided. Meanwhile, compensation payments, both reasonable and "unreasonable" are ordinary income to the recipient and are also subject to either social security and Medicare taxes (on wages) or the self-employment (SE) tax on consulting payments.

There are virtually no cases where the IRS has challenged the "reasonableness" of compensation when there has been a true arm's-length relationship between unrelated parties. The IRS is likely to challenge the reasonableness of compensation in two specific contexts:

1. When the payment is between a business entity and an owner or related party, and the payment of compensation has tax advantages.
2. When there is a business acquisition and the parties to the transaction save taxes by allocating a portion of the purchase price to employment agreements, consulting agreements, noncompete agreements, and other types of personal payments or parallel payments.

Comment: In the context of closely held C corporations, it is common for the corporation to "overpay" compensation as a technique to distribute corporate earnings to shareholder/employees and thus avoid (or reduce) the double taxation of C corporation profits. When used in this fashion, compensation payments reported as wages on Form W-2 turn the W-2 into a "synthetic K-1" (i.e., it largely accomplishes the equivalent of "pass-through" taxation, albeit subject to FICA or SE taxes that may or may not apply to K-1 income). By contrast, in the context of a closely held S corporation, there is a tendency to go in the opposite direction and make "unreasonably low" compensation payments so that more of the income is distributed to shareholders on Form K-1 and thus arguably free of FICA or SE taxes.[1]

The IRS has developed various guidelines for its audit agents to determine whether compensation is "reasonable". In general, when a compensatory or consulting transaction arises in the context of one of the "suspect" circumstances, the IRS tends to look at comparable salaries paid to persons in similar arm's-length arrangements. For example, the IRS will use various statistical studies showing the compensation paid to an executive of a distribution company, or a CEO of a software company, based on comparable criteria (e.g., companies within a certain range of gross revenues or sales).

The IRS has developed specific guidelines for employment contracts and covenants not-to-compete in connection with the acquisition of a company.[2]

Reasonable compensation comprises an interesting subset of IRS practice. It often depends not just on whether the payment amount is "reasonable" in exchange for the value of the services rendered but also, in a very practical sense, on whether the IRS can significantly increase the tax assessment by allocating the personal payment to something else. For example, in the context of an acquisition transaction, depending on the form and structure of the transaction, disallowed compensation might be (a) characterized as additional purchase price for the acquisition of stock (causing the purchase price to become "trapped" tax basis, i.e., nondeductible and nonamortizable tax basis in the stock); (b) viewed as additional purchase price allocated to goodwill in an asset purchase; or (c) treated as payment for a noncom-petition covenant and thus amortizable ratably over fifteen years under Code section 197.

Note that, even if compensation is determined to be reasonable, there are certain other limitations on the deductibility of executive compensation. For example, there is a $1 million limitation per year on compensation paid to a covered employee of a publicly held corporation.[3] No deduction is allowed for a payment (referred to as an "excess parachute payment") contingent on a change in ownership or effective control of a corporation or in the ownership of a substantial portion of the assets of a corporation.[4]

One of the more credible ways to justify compensation payments is to spread the payments among various persons in a manner other than pro rata in proportion to their stock of the Target. Needless to say, payments that are pro rata in proportion to stock ownership strongly infer that the payments are not for the services rendered by each individual, but rather relate to the shares being acquired.

Example 1: Assume Carter Landscaping Supplies, Inc. (Carter), a C corporation, produces $1 million of taxable income from its operations and, on the last day of the year, pays a $1 million bonus to Albert Shrubs, the President and sole shareholder of Carter. As reported, Carter would have no income for the year and would pay no federal income tax. Albert would report $1 million of compensation income. In effect, although the payments to Albert are subject to FICA taxes, the arrangement has substantially accomplished the pass-through of the corporate profits to Albert, who will pay tax at a single level on his Form 1040 return.

Example 2: Using facts from Example 1, assume the IRS audits Carter Landscaping Supplies, Inc.'s tax return, determines that $400,000 of the payment to Albert Shrubs is unreasonable, and disallows $400,000 of Carter's deduction. Carter will now have $400,000 of taxable income and, assuming a 40 percent effective federal and state tax rate, will owe $160,000 in tax. In addition, the IRS is likely to assert that Carter has made a distribution of $400,000 to Albert. The $400,000 will be treated as a dividend to Albert to the extent of Carter's earnings and profits. Note that in this example, Carter's E&P account will be reduced by federal and state taxes paid; hence, Carter's E&P for the current year will be $240,000 ($400,000 of taxable income minus $160,000 of taxes paid). Therefore, the amount of the dividend will be $240,000 (plus any portion of the distribution treated as made out of accumulated earnings and profits from prior years). To the extent that the $400,000 distribution to Albert exceeds Carter's current and accumulated earnings and profits, it will be treated as a return of tax basis to Albert. To the extent that the distribution exceeds Albert's tax basis in Carter shares, the excess will be treated as capital gain to Albert.[5]

The point is that the disallowance of part of a compensatory payment as "unreasonable" generates both substantial corporate level tax and significant tax at the shareholder level and can result in a significant increase in the aggregate tax collected by the IRS.

Example 3: Assume that Carter Landscaping Supplies, Inc. is an S corporation and that, instead of paying $1 million of compensation, it pays zero compensation and distributes $1 million on the K-1 to Albert Shrubs. This would allow Albert (and Carter) to avoid FICA tax (and SE tax) on the $1 million of income reported by Albert on his Form 1040. However, since Albert is actively involved in the management of the business, the compensation amount is implausibly low, and the IRS will likely adjust the compensation figure upward.[6]

Practice Point: FICA taxes are comprised of two components, 1) the OASDI component, which is 12.4 percent on taxable wages (half paid by the emplyee and half paid by the employer) up to an annually indexed maximum amount ($127,200 in 2017 and 2) the HI component, which is 2.9 percent on all taxable wages (again, half paid by the employee and half by the employer) up to $200,000 of wages (or up to $250,000 for married couples filing jointly), and increasing by 0.9 percent above the applicable threshold and paid only by the employee. Realistically, the IRS is aware that adjusting compensation from a ridiculously low level (and zero is as ridiculous as it gets) to an amount at or above the OASDI maximum produces approximately $19,300 of FICA tax. By contrast, amounts in excess of the OASDI maximum produce only a 2.9 percent adjustment (increasing above the threshold amount to a 3.8 percent adjustment), if recharacterized as compensation. Past experience suggests that the IRS views such a small amount of additional revenue as not worth the bother, and so tax practitioners routinely recommend that compensation levels of S corporation owner/employees be set at or above the OASDI maximum to forestall an IRS audit for unreasonably low compensation.

Example 4: C Corporation, owned by Mother, pays $200,000 in "compensation" to College-Aged Son, who performs minimal services. The IRS could disallow C Corp. a deduction for the $200,000 (thus giving C Corp. an additional $200,000 of taxable income) and treat the $200,000 distribution as a dividend to Mother and a gift of $200,000 from Mother to College-Aged Son. Alternatively, the IRS could treat the payment as unreasonable compensation and both (1) disallow the deduction at the corporation level (resulting in $200,000 of taxable income) and (2) treat the $200,000 as compensation to College-Aged Son. The IRS can challenge a compensation payment as unreasonable, but taxpayers generally cannot argue against the form of transaction reported by them.[7]

Factors Applied to Measure Reasonableness

The test of whether compensation payments are "reasonable" and thus deductible under Code section 162 is based on the facts and circumstances of the specific situation. The test of deductibility in the case of compensation payments is whether they are reasonable and are in fact payments purely for services.[8] Any amount paid in the form of compensation, but not in fact as the purchase price of services, is not deductible.[9] An ostensible salary paid by a corporation may be a distribution of a dividend on stock.[10] The form or method of fixing compensation is not decisive as to deductibility.[11] In any event the allowance for the compensation paid may not exceed what is reasonable under all the circumstances.[12] It is, in general, just to assume that reasonable and true compensation is only such amount as would ordinarily be paid for like services by like enterprises under like circumstances.[13] The circumstances to be taken into consideration are those existing at the date when the contract for services was made, not those existing at the date when the contract is questioned.[14] The court cases have made it clear that the "reasonableness" inquiry is always unique to the specific situation and thus every case of reasonable compensation must stand on its own facts and circumstances.[15]

The following is a brief list of factors that have been taken into account in determining whether compensation payments meet the "reasonable" requirement:

1. Reliance on prior cases is of limited value because each decision depends on the particular facts and circumstances.

2. Sudden increases in compensation will be scrutinized carefully, especially if there is no indication of an increase in duties. The IRS will look at prior years to determine the comparative "worth" of an individual. Sudden, large increases in salary disproportionate to dividends paid may be viewed as an attempt to distribute profits. Salary increases in direct proportion to shareholder holdings are also likely to draw a challenge.

3. The salary scale for employees generally may be used to measure the reasonableness of an officer's salary by comparison. Note also that the IRS will also look at compensatory data for the industry, and at similar industries, to determine if compensation is "reasonable".

4. Evidence of significant contribution to the success of a business or responsibility for the initial development of the business will be arguments in favor of reasonableness despite a higher than usual salary.

Necessity for Actual Performance of Services

Code section 162 permits deductions only for services "actually rendered". Total absence of services is generally a question only in closely held corporations. It is not necessary for services to be performed during the current year even though payment would push compensation to a higher than usual amount, as long as the obligation to pay can be verified. An accrual basis taxpayer may deduct the compensation in the year in which the obligation arose; this can be a trap if the corporation fails to make actual payment in a timely basis to a related party. Compensation for future services is not deductible in any case; pre-payments have to be deducted ratably over the period in which the services are rendered. Allocation of compensation may be required by Code section 482 if an employee performs services for more than one corporation; such allocation should be made on the basis of actual services performed and not on the basis of net income.

Compensation is sometimes paid in situations not involving direct performance of services. For example, when an employer continues an individual's salary while the individual is serving in the military or other civic duty (e.g., jury duty), the deduction will be allowed provided it is considered reasonable.

COVENANTS NOT TO COMPETE

Treatment by Payor

A covenant not-to-compete entered into in connection with an acquisition (directly or indirectly) of an interest in a trade or business (or a substantial portion thereof) is characterized as a Section 197 intangible. Therefore any payments attributable to such a covenant are capitalized and amortized ratably over the fifteen-year period beginning on the date on which such intangible is acquired.[16]

Tellingly, the legislative history (the House Ways and Means Committee Report) to the adoption of Code section 197 states that:

> As under present law, to the extent that the amount paid or incurred under a covenant not to compete (or other similar arrangement) represents additional consideration for the acquisition of stock in a corporation, such amount is not taken into account under this provision, but, instead, is to be included as part of the acquirer's basis in the stock.

Noncompete amounts determinable at the closing are capitalized and amortized over fifteen years by the payor. To the extent contingent noncompete payments are paid after the closing date, such payments are capitalized and amortized ratably over the remainder of the fifteen-year period. A portion of any deferred noncompete payments, whether fixed and determinable at closing or contingent, will be subject to recharacterization as interest or original issue discount under the applicable rules.

Example 5: Acquirer agrees to pay Target's sole shareholder, Erika Fine, noncompete payments in connection with a business acquisition totaling $1 million. This payment will be paid $600,000 at closing, and two installments of $200,000 each paid at the end of years two and three.

Based on these facts (and assuming the amounts allocated to the noncompete payments represent present fair market value and thus not subject to recharacterization as additional purchase price for other assets), where amounts chargeable to the capital account (i.e., capitalized and amortized under Code section 197) are payable on a deferred basis after the acquisition of the Section 197 intangible to which they relate, such payments are treated under the regulations as payable under a debt instrument given in consideration for the sale or exchange of the Section 197 intangible.[17] Thus, the purchase of the noncompete covenants by Acquirer will be treated as the equivalent of an installment note under the applicable rules of Code sections. 483 and 1274, and a portion of the deemed debt instrument will be treated as interest (or OID) payments by Acquirer, while the "principal" portion of the deemed debt instrument will be capitalized on the date of acquisition and then amortized ratably for the next fifteen years (180 months) under Code section 197.

Comment: The regulations under Code section 197 bring the hard mathematical rigor of the installment sale rules under Code section 453 and the unstated interest/OID rules of Code sections. 483 and 1274 to the acquisition of Section 197 intangibles. Since these rules apply to deferred payments made with respect to all the other assets in the transaction (see Chapter 10) this makes eminent sense. Note that to the extent there are contingent deferred payments for the purchase of any Section 197 intangibles, the regulations indicate that Reg. §§ 1.1275-4(c)(4) and 1.483-4(a) provide the relevant rules governing the extent to which contingent amounts payable under a debt instrument given in consideration for the sale or exchange of an amortizable Section 197 intangible are treated as payments of principal and the time at which the amount treated as principal is included in basis. To the extent relevant, Reg. § 1.461-1(a)(1) and (2) provide the rules governing the time at which other contingent amounts (i.e., not treated as payable under a debt instrument) are taken into account in determining the basis of an amortizable Section 197 intangible. The combined interaction of these rules is that a contingent deferred payment, upon satisfaction of the contingency and subsequent payment, will be characterized as partly a payment of principal and partly a payment of accrued interest. See the discussions in Chapter 10, generally, related to contingent payments. In turn, once the "principal" amount of the payment is fixed and determinable, the rules indicate that the amount will be added to amortizable basis in the applicable intangible asset and then amortized ratably over the remainder of the fifteen-year (180-month) amortization period.[18]

Treatment by Payee

The recipient of a noncompete payment treats such payment as ordinary income.[19] Note that noncompete payments are not subject to FICA or SE taxes.[20] Income will be recognized and reported based on the recipient's method of accounting (e.g., an individual payee on the cash method will report noncompete payments as received), even though such payments are capitalized and amortized over fifteen years by the payor.

The seminal authority on the modern treatment of noncompete payments by the recipient is set forth in Rev. Rul. 69-643, one of the most astonishingly short yet far-reaching revenue rulings ever issued by the IRS. The entire and full text of the revenue ruling is as follows:

> M, a domestic corporation, sold its plant, equipment, trade name, and good will to O, an unrelated domestic corporation. One of the conditions of the sale was an agreement by M's president, A, that he would not engage in a similar business in a stipulated area. A received money from O with respect to the above agreement.
>
> Held, the amount received by A in consideration of his agreement not to compete is ordinary income for him in the year of receipt.
>
> O.D. 668, C.B. 38, 93 (1920), is hereby superseded, since the position stated therein is set forth under the current statute and regulations in this Revenue Ruling.
>
> In C.C. *Hamlin Trust*,[21] the court stated:
>
> Where a covenant not to compete constitutes a nonseverable element of a transaction in which

> the owner of a going concern sells the property and transfers the good will of the business, the covenant is to be treated as a contributing element of the assets transferred and the entire revenue received is subject to tax on the basis of a capital gain. [Cites omitted]. But if a covenant not to compete can be segregated in order to be assured that a separate item has actually been dealt with, then so much as is received for the covenant is ordinary income rather than income from the sale of a capital asset.

Realistically, an individual shareholder/employee of a corporation, in a typical transaction involving the sale of a business, should have three sources of personal income: (1) payments for consulting or other services actually rendered on behalf of the buyer; (2) a payment for a covenant not-to-compete; and (3) a payment for personal intangible assets owned by the individual (such as customer contacts, relationships, personal good will, and other intangible property attributes). As the case law described above illustrates, there is a long and well-established tradition of treating noncompete payments as ordinary income. On the other hand, as evidenced by the *Martin Ice Cream* and *Norwalk* cases, it is increasingly clear that (1) individuals own important intangible assets; (2) the assets belong to the individual unless they have been transferred (via a noncompete agreement or other contractual arrangement) and not to the employer corporation or other employer business entity; and (3) oddly and ironically, the mechanism for transferring this personal goodwill must necessarily be a noncompete agreement with the Acquirer, raising the conundrum of how to distinguish a "purchase" of personal goodwill from a "noncompete" payment.

As the court in *Hamlin Trust*, in a far less sophisticated era in terms of intellectual property, nonetheless clearly noted, a covenant not-to-compete can easily constitute a "nonseverable element" of a sale of business assets. Thus, the *Hamlin Trust* case provides both the authority and the logic to assert that where a noncompete agreement is really a necessary element of transferring personal goodwill, no portion of the noncompete payment should be characterized as ordinary income. At the very least, recent authority, strongly supports the position that personal intangible property, and attributes in the nature of personal goodwill, should be viewed as assets of a capital nature belonging to the individual, not to the corporation, and as capital assets, not ordinary assets, upon disposition.

SALE OF PERSONAL GOODWILL—THE ARGUMENT FOR CAPITAL GAIN TREATMENT

There is a natural symbiotic relationship between the goodwill of an ongoing business and covenants not-to-compete given by the key employees of that business. Goodwill represents the ongoing value and earning power of a business and can often be sold for the capitalization of the anticipated future revenue stream. A covenant not-to-compete, meanwhile, is often a necessary component to assuring that those earnings are, in fact, transferred with the acquisition of the business, and are not diverted away by the Seller.

Case law has long recognized the intimate relationship between a covenant not-to-compete and a sale of business goodwill. Some cases have held that, when a covenant not-to-compete accompanies the sale of goodwill and is intended primarily to ensure the purchaser the benefits and enjoyment of the purchased goodwill, the items are not severable; the entire acquisition is treated as a sale of goodwill.[22] Other cases have held that when the covenant not-to-compete and a sale of goodwill are separate items and the agreement separately states consideration for each, the allocation made by the agreement is respected.[23]

The sale of goodwill results in capital gain for the Seller; a covenant not-to-compete produces ordinary income.[24] From the Acquirer's perspective, as a result of Code section 197, both the covenant not-to-compete and goodwill result in the same tax treatment (i.e., fifteen-year amortization).

When the Target is a partnership, the sale of goodwill in connection with an asset sale produces long-term capital gain (assuming the one-year holding period is met) for the Seller. Likewise, when a business is operated through an S corporation or an LLC and its business assets are sold, a payment for goodwill passes through to the individual owners as long-term capital gain. However, when a C corporation sells its business assets, including its goodwill, the amounts allocated to goodwill will be recognized at the C corporation level, without the benefit of a favorable capital gains tax rate and subject to the double tax regime of C corporation taxation.

An important question has always existed regarding whether, when an individual sells the assets of a C corporation and executes a noncompete agreement in connection with that transaction, some portion of the "noncompete payments" is actually in the nature of a sale of a capital asset belonging to the individual shareholder/employee. The U.S. Tax Court, in *Martin Ice Cream*,[25] held that in appropriate circumstances, a Target shareholder can claim long-term capital gain treatment for payments received from an Acquirer for personal goodwill sold in connection with the sale of assets by a C corporation.

In *Martin Ice Cream*, Father and Son owned the stock of Target in a ratio of 51 percent to 49 percent. Target had two businesses: 1) a wholesale premium ice cream distribution business, and 2) a retail distribution business, distributing ice cream to small stores. Father had been instrumental in building business #1 over the years. It was decided to sell business #1's intangible assets and customer list to the purchaser, which was Target's principal premium ice cream supplier. Father was allocated 100 percent of the proceeds from the sale of business #1, while Son kept business #2 and retained 100 percent of Target stock. The transaction was implemented through a split-off transaction whereby the assets of business #1 were dropped into a newly-formed subsidiary, and the assets of the subsidiary were spun off to Father in exchange for all of his Target stock. Shortly after the split-off, Father sold the stock of the former subsidiary (now owned solely by him) for $1.5 million.

The court held that the split-off transaction was a taxable distribution and not tax-free under Code section 355 because the newly-formed subsidiary was not engaged in an active business after the split-off transaction. Therefore, Target recognized gain on the distribution of the subsidiary assets (i.e., the assets used in business #1) to the father in redemption for the father's shares.

However, the most important aspect of the *Martin Ice Cream* case was the discussion about the sale of personal goodwill. It was determined that only $141,000 of the consideration paid was allocated to the value of the subsidiary stock. This was because Father's oral agreement with Acquirer, and Father's relationships with the owners and managers of the supermarkets to which Target distributed its products, all of which was part of the value of the business, could not be attributed to Target or the subsidiary corporation because Father had never entered into a covenant-not-to-compete with Target nor any other agreement (not even an employment agreement) by which Father's personal relationships and expertise became the property of the Target company. The Tax Court concluded: "This court has long recognized that the personal relationships of a shareholder/employee are not corporate assets when the employee has no employment contract with the corporation. Those personal assets are entirely distinct from the intangible corporate asset of goodwill."[26]

The *Martin Ice Cream* case was provocative authority at the time the decision was rendered, but arguably it accurately reflects the fact that personal relationships and goodwill generally belong to the individual absent some contractual agreement transferring those assets to a corporation or other legal entity.

Similarly, in the *Norwalk* case, involving liquidation of a C corporation formerly engaged in an accounting practice, the Tax Court held that the "goodwill" and "going concern value" of the practice belonged to the individual accountants, not to the corporation, for purposes of determining the amount of gain recognized under Code section 336(a).[27] The transaction in *Norwalk* involved the liquidation of an accounting firm where a group of certified public accountants had engaged in the practice of accounting through a C corporation, and wanted to convert their accounting practice to a limited liability corporation, through a liquidation of the corporation and a subsequent contribution of the corporate assets to the LLC. The IRS argued that the "goodwill" and "going concern value" of the accounting practice, including its clients and client base, belonged to the corporation rather than to the individual accountants, for purposes of determining the amount of gain recognized under Code section 336(a) upon the liquidation of the corporation. In that case, the IRS asserted that the corporation had made liquidating distributions of intangible assets as well as tangible assets to its shareholders, and that the liquidating distributions specifically included such intangible assets as its client base, client records, work papers, going concern value, and goodwill. The IRS asserted that the corporation recognized gain in the distribution of such assets under Code section 336(a).

The accountants, in their capacity as shareholders of the liquidating corporation, contested this position, arguing that because the accountant/shareholders had not entered into a noncompetition agreement with their corporation, nor made or entered into any other contractual obligations to transfer their personal goodwill to their corporation, the corporation could not be deemed to own the goodwill nor any customer-based intangibles with greater than nominal value. Rather, the taxpayers in *Norwalk* asserted that they, not the corporation, owned the goodwill, and therefore the corporation could not recognize gain on an alleged distribution of these intangible assets, because it did not own them.

The Tax Court ruled in favor of the taxpayers, stating, "There is no saleable good will where, as here, the business of a corporation is dependent upon its key employees, unless they enter into a covenant not to compete with the corporation or other agreement whereby their personal relationships with clients become property of the corporation." (Citing *Martin Ice Cream*). The Court in *Norwalk* rejected the expert opinions of IRS witnesses, which valued the good will, client list and other assets of the professional corporation based on the assumption that the ability of accountants/shareholders to compete with the professional corporation was restricted. Because the shareholders, not the corporation, were found to own the goodwill and customer-based intangible assets, there was no taxable distribution of these assets in the liquidation because they belonged to the taxpayers, not the corporation.

Similarly, in *Derby v. Commissioner*,[28] the Tax Court addressed a situation where individual physicians contributed their medical practices to a tax-exempt medical foundation, and claimed a charitable contribution deduction for their respective contributions. The Tax Court addressed the value the medical practices and, in doing so, addressed specifically the issue that the medical practices being contributed did not have covenants not to compete with the contributing physicians, and, therefore, the goodwill value of the medical practices was inherently inflated, since the physicians could at any time depart this erstwhile medical practice being contributed to the tax-exempt medical foundation, and go practice medicine on their own. The *Derby* case therefore adopts the same position as the *Norwalk* decision, namely, that the goodwill of a professional services business belongs to the professional, absent a covenant not to compete with the employer corporation.

See also *F.J. Longo*[29] where the court stated: "there is no salable goodwill where the business of the corporation is thus so dependent upon its personnel, unless these key employees enter into a covenant not to compete with the corporation." See also *S.H. Bryden*[30] where the court noted that a customer list "has very little value, if any, unless those individuals responsible for the accounts were under contract either to remain with the corporation or not to compete with it." Likewise, in *E.C. O'Rear*,[31] the court stated that "it is at least doubtful whether a professional man could sell or dispose of any good will which may attach to his practice, except perhaps by contracting to refrain from practicing."

Following the *Martin Ice Cream* and *Norwalk* decisions, taxpayers have taken, perhaps predictably, more creative positions regarding the "goodwill" used in their businesses, particularly in professional practices. In CCA 200305007,[32] the IRS addressed the situation where a taxpayer engaged in accounting practice attempted to treat royalties received from a corporate employer as royalty payments rather than wages. The IRS stated as follows:

> Taxpayer owns the accounting lists but the Taxpayer also performs accounting services for the accounting clients on the accounting lists. The payments received by the Taxpayer were not for selling the accounting lists to another entity to perform accounting services but instead were payments for the Taxpayer to perform accounting services. Whether the Taxpayer had sold the accounting lists to an entity controlled by the Taxpayer or not, the Taxpayer was still going to perform the accounting services for those clients on the accounting lists. Royalty payments are by definition passive and thus cannot include compensation for services rendered by the owner of the property.

Likewise, in *Charlotte's Office Boutique, Inc.*,[33] the court held that payments made by a corporation to its shareholder/employee were not "royalties" for use of intangible property, but rather were "wages" where the shareholder/employee performed substantial services.

TAX PLANNING FOR REASONABLE COMPENSATION

The following guidelines should be considered to help reduce the risk that compensation payments may be challenged as "unreasonable":

1. Formalize compensation decisions in writing.
2. Pay special attention to factors on which the IRS focuses:
    a. Comparable status of the individual in other industries.
    b. The individual's salary history.
    c. The individual's contribution to the company's success.
    d. The individual's specific duties and responsibilities.

3. Back up your decision with reports and investigations of comparable employees in other companies in the same industry if possible. The IRS loves to use statistical surveys showing industry standards because, by definition, half the salaries in the real world will be "above average".

4. Consider electing S corporation status. Because earnings flow through to shareholders, accumulated earnings and excessive compensation problems can be avoided by becoming an S corporation.

ACCUMULATED EARNINGS PROBLEMS

Reasonable compensation questions frequently coincide with closely held C corporations that have significant profits and may also be at risk for an assessment of the accumulated earnings (AE) tax.[34]

The AE tax[35] is a tax at the corporate level on C corporations that permit the earnings and profits to accumulate beyond the reasonably expected needs of the business. The purpose of the tax is to force the corporation to distribute its excessive retained earnings as dividends. Accordingly, if a corporation has excessive retained earnings and fails to distribute current earnings as a dividend, the AE tax is imposed at the corporate level at the dividend tax rate (currently 20 percent) on "accumulated taxable income".[36] Accumulated taxable income is taxable income with certain adjustments specified in Code section 535(b), and reduced by dividends paid and by the greater of (1) $250,000 ($150,000 for some personal service companies) or (2) amounts retained for reasonable business needs minus net capital gains.[37] The AE tax is in addition to any income taxes the corporation may have already paid on the taxable income, i.e., it is a second tax on a modified version of after-tax income. Significantly, the AE tax is imposed on the current year's taxable income, even though it is triggered by an excess accumulation of profits from prior years. Indeed, an important planning strategy for the AE tax exploits the fact that tax-exempt interest income is not "taxable income" and thus is not included in the calculation of accumulated taxable income.[38]

Be careful about using large salary increases to avoid the accumulated earnings tax. If the IRS recharacterizes the "salary" payments as unreasonable compensation, one could have the worst of all tax consequences:

1. The corporation would have additional income and owe additional income taxes.

2. The corporation could be potentially liable for the accumulated earnings tax.

3. The employee could be subject to income tax for the full amount received, some of which may be dividend income.

IRS "DOUBLE DIPPING" ON DISALLOWED COMPENSATION DEDUCTIONS

Although it is relatively unusual, when "unreasonable" compensation is paid, the IRS (and also the state taxing authority) may assert that the corporation should be denied a deduction for the portion deemed unreasonable (because Code section 162 only allows a deduction for "reasonable" compensation) but may then assert that the payment to the shareholder/employee should be treated as "compensation" subject both to income taxation at ordinary income tax rates *and* FICA taxes. In general, it is an axiom of tax law that a taxpayer is more or less stuck with the form of the transaction the taxpayer chooses in the first instance. Although the IRS has the right to challenge a taxpayer's characterization of a transaction, the taxpayer does not. When a taxpayer characterizes a payment as "compensation", the IRS can take the position that it may be "unreasonable" compensation, but it is nonetheless compensation. Such a position gives the IRS the best of all worlds and the taxpayer the worst of all nightmares. Although many assume that the IRS will treat disallowed unreasonable compensation as the equivalent of a corporate distribution, one should be cautious in drawing this conclusion. Because a dividend is no longer taxed at ordinary income rates, the IRS has every incentive to treat the payment as compensation to the recipient, rather than allowing it to be characterized as a dividend.

Example 6: RichCo, Inc., a highly profitable privately-owned C corporation, has an exceptional year and decides to pay Rich, its president and majority shareholder, a year-end bonus of $4 million on top of other (very high) compensation. The corporation has no history of year-end bonuses, and the payment has every indicia of trying to avoid double taxation of C corporation profits.

The IRS could disallow the $4 million payment as compensation and characterize it instead as a dividend to Rich. The effect of this recharacterization would be as follows.

If the payment were respected as a $4 million compensation payment to Rich, his combined federal, state, and social security tax on the bonus (using an assumed 43-percent combined tax rate) would be $1,720,000 ($4 million × 43%).

If the bonus payment were recharacterized as a dividend, the corporation would first pay a tax at the corporate level on an additional $4 million of income, which (using an assumed 40-percent combined federal and state tax rate) would be $1,600,000 ($4 million × 40%). The corporation would then be deemed to distribute a dividend to Rich. Since the corporation now has $1.6 million of tax liabilities at the corporate level, its E&P for this specific transaction would be adjusted downward to $2.4 million ($4 million of income minus taxes paid of $1.6 million). This $2.4 million will be added to the existing E&P from the corporation to determine whether the distribution of $4 million to Rich is solely a dividend, or some combination of dividend, return of capital, and/or capital gain.[39] Assuming that RichCo has more than $4 million in E&P, the $4 million payment shareholder, Rich, is taxed as a dividend, which, at an assumed 20-percent combined federal and state tax rate, results in an additional $800,000 ($4 million × 20%) of tax. Thus, the total tax bill for Rich and the corporation, instead of being $1,720,000 paid by Rich on compensation, is $2.4 million ($1.6 million paid by the corporation on income, and $800,000 paid by Rich on the dividend).

However, assume that instead of characterizing the payment to Rich as a dividend, the IRS characterizes it as "unreasonable" compensation. The corporation is once again disallowed the compensation deduction, resulting in $4 million of additional income and (at an assumed combined federal and state tax rate of 40 percent) an additional $1.6 million of corporate-level tax ($4 million × 40%). However, Rich is still deemed to receive a compensation payment, and so he still owns $1,720,000 of federal, state, and incremental social security tax. Thus, the total tax cost is now $3,320,000, which results in an effective combined tax (corporate and employee/shareholder tax liabilities combined) of 83 percent!

The conventional wisdom is that electing S status solves this unreasonable compensation problem, and it generally does—so long as the S corporation engages in under compensation rather than over compensation as a tax strategy. However, the author practices law in Massachusetts, which imposes a corporate level "sting" tax of 2.85 percent on the profits of large S corporations. The effect of this corporate-level tax is to approximately equalize by the effective Massachusetts tax rates on C corporation profits (taxed at eight percent) and large S corporation profits (taxed in 2016 at 5.1 percent at the shareholder level and 2.85 percent at the corporate level).

The author is aware of a case in the early 1990s, when the then 2.9-percent HI component of the SE and Social Security taxes was still capped at $125,000 of income, in which a large Massachusetts S corporation decided to avoid the then 4.5-percent (later reduced to 2.85 percent) S corporation sting tax by paying a $4 million bonus to the sole shareholder. This bonus, if allowed as reasonable compensation, would reduce corporate-level income by $4 million, without materially increasing the employee-shareholder's tax liabilities. (Since the HI component did to apply to this incremental income, W-2 income and K-1 income was taxed at the same effective rate.)

On audit by the state taxing authorities, the compensation deduction at the corporate level was disallowed as "unreasonable". The initial assumption was that the payment would be recharacterized as a distribution by the S corporation. (S corporations do not pay dividends, of course, since that is a term reserved for C corporation distributions from earnings and profits.) If recharacterized as a distribution, the S corporation would owe the corporate-level sting tax that the taxpayer was trying to avoid, but otherwise would not be worse off than if no planning had been done.

To the surprise of everyone (especially the architects of this too-clever strategy) the bonus payment was not recharacterized as an S corporation "distribution" but rather was "unreasonable" compensation. The effects were staggering. Instead of paying a single level of tax at the shareholder, together with what was then a 4.5-percent corporate level tax, the shareholder faced the following tax assessments:

1. $4 million of additional income at the S corporation level, subject to a 4.5-percent corporate-level tax ($4 million × 4.5% = $180,000).

2. $4 million of compensation at the shareholder level (unreasonable compensation is still compensation, and therefore taxable to the shareholder-employee—it is merely not deductible under Code section 162 by the corporate employer) ($4 million × 43% tax rate = $1,720,000).

3. Here is the kick in the teeth: The compensation payment to the shareholder-employee is not deductible, so in addition to paying the 4.5-percent corporate level tax, the S corporation has $4 million of taxable income that flows out to the shareholder on Form K-1. In effect, the shareholder is taxed twice on the same $4 million! ($4 million × 40% = $1,600,000).

Total tax bill: $180,000 + $1,720,000 + $1,600,000 = $3,500,000. On $4 million, that is an 87.5-percent effective combined tax rate.

Comment: It is just beginning to dawn on people, including at the IRS, that the reduced dividend rate makes it even more profitable to characterize a payment as "unreasonable" compensation (i.e., both as "compensation" and as a nondeductible payment) rather than recharacterize it as a dividend. Since IRS audits tend to be very good at identifying exactly the audit issues that are likely to generate revenue, do not be shocked if you see this position appear in IRS audits in future years.

CHAPTER ENDNOTES

1. *Yeagle Drywall Co.*, 82 TCM 814 (2001) (S corp. distributions to president/99-percent shareholder held wages subject to employment taxes).
2. See Industry Specialization Program (ISP) Coordinated Issue Papers, All Industries, Covenants Not to Compete (5/7/92), and Employment Contracts (5/7/92).
3. IRC Sec. 162(m).
4. IRC Sec. 280G.
5. IRC Sec. 301(c).
6. See *Yeagle Drywall Co.*, supra.
7. See *Summit Sheet Metal Co.*, 72 TCM 1606 (1996) supra.
8. Treas. Reg. § 1.162-7(a).
9. Treas. Reg. § 1.162-7(b)(1).
10. *Id.*
11. Treas. Reg. § 1.162-7(b)(2).
12. Treas. Reg. § 1.162-7(b)(3).
13. *Id.*
14. *Id.*
15. *Miller Manufacturing Co.*, 149 F2d 421 (CA4 1945).
16. IRC Sec. 197(d)(1)(E).
17. Treas. Reg. § 1.197-2(f)(3)(iv)(B)(2).
18. Treas. Reg. § 197-2(f)(1)(i).
19. See *C.C. Hamlin Trust*, 209 F2d 1969, Rev. Rul. 69-643, 1969-2 CB 10.
20. See *A.G. Furman, III*, 602 F. Supp. 444 (1978), aff'd. CA-4 (unpublished opinion), 767 F2d 911; *H.R. Barrett*, 58 TC 284 (1972).
21. 209 F2d 761 (1954)
22. See *Toledo Newspaper Company*, 2 TC 794 (1943).
23. *D.H. Ullman*, 264 F2d 305 (1959).
24. *Hamlin Trust*, (*supra*); Rev. Rul. 69-643, 1969-2 CB 10.
25. 110 TC 189 (1998).
26. *Id.* at 207.
27. 76 TCM 208 (1998).
28. 110 TC 189 (1998).
29. 27 TCM 1075, (1968) TC Memo. 1968-217.
30. 18 TCM 810, (1959).
31. 28 BTA 698 (1933). Aff'd, 80 F2d 473 (1935).
32. September 26, 2002.
33. 121 TC 89 (2003).
34. IRC Sec. 531 *et seq.*
35. IRC Secs. 531-537.
36. IRC Sec. 531.
37. IRC Sec. 535(a).
38. Rev. Rul. 70-497, 1970-2 CB 128.
39. See IRC Sec. 301 for the ordering rules on distributions from a C corporation.

SELLING THE BUSINESS TO EMPLOYEES: LEVERAGED BUYOUTS, ESOPs, AND OTHER ARRANGEMENTS

CHAPTER 18

OVERVIEW

Perhaps the most obvious potential purchaser for any business is a group comprised of existing employees of that business. Indeed, in many small businesses, an employee may be the only natural buyer of the going concern, since taking over a small business often requires a specialized knowledge of clients or customers that only an existing employee will possess. In larger companies, meanwhile, the employees, especially the senior management, are often knowledgeable and eager potential purchasers of a successful business that they, as a group, already run.

Existing employees bring a huge natural advantage to the bargaining table: Unlike almost any other buyer, they know the existing business intimately—perhaps even better than the owners. Employees rarely need a sales pitch on the positive aspects of the business. On the other hand, employees often lack the single most important attribute of an Acquirer: money. Employees, by the fact of being employees, have generally provided services for a salary and have not amassed the capital that comes as the natural reward for successful entrepreneurial endeavor.

The natural condition of employees as a potential Acquirer, therefore, is that the employees need a major source of financing. This financing usually comes from one of three sources:

1. The *Seller*, in the form of substantial installment sale financing, contingent payments, and other mechanisms that are designed to permit the business to earn the money to pay for itself over time.
2. An *outside financing source*, such as a bank or other lender, that is willing to provide financing for a leveraged buy-out in the expectation that the business will earn the money to pay off the financing.
3. An *employee stock ownership plan* (ESOP), which is actually a tax-subsidized version of the second alternative. An outside source provides financing for employees to purchase the business and then looks to the business to generate the money to pay for the acquisition.

The common characteristic of all three arrangements is that (1) the employees as a group do not have significant personal capital, and (2) they therefore look to cash flow from the business to service the acquisition debt.

Installment and contingent payment transactions financed by the Seller are explored in considerable detail in Chapter 10. A sale to an employee group is merely a relatively common version on that basic transaction. Sellers are often more inclined to enter an installment sale arrangement with existing employees than with others, partly out of a sense of loyalty (giving the long-term employees a chance to succeed), partly out of a sense of confidence (the Seller can be confident that the employees will be able to take over the business and run it successfully—after all, they already run it), and partly out of a sense of nostalgia (existing employees may provide a greater sense of continuity to a Seller's vision of the business than an outsider). The tax structuring issues arising in an installment sale are covered in Chapter 10.

The remainder of this chapter will focus on two other common methods of selling a business to its employees: (1) a leveraged buyout, or "LBO," and (2) an employee stock ownership plan (ESOP).

LEVERAGED BUYOUTS—SUMMARY STRUCTURING AND TAX ISSUES

A "leveraged buyout" (LBO) is often associated with the junk bond era of the 1980s when high-yield debt was used by various Acquirers, including management groups, to finance the acquisition of businesses ranging in size from the nobodies to the Nabiscos of the business world. The economic premise of an employee LBO is that employees can use borrowed capital to acquire a business that, following acquisition, will produce a sufficiently strong cash flow to service the debt. An LBO can be structured in a variety of ways, but whatever the transaction path, the ending point is generally the same: old shareholders have been bought out using predominantly borrowed funds (and possibly using a modest-to-moderate amount of equity provided either by employees and/or new equity investors), and employees (and possibly new equity investors) own all or substantially all of the business.

LBOs are often even more complicated than the usual business acquisition transaction. This is probably because, in addition to the usual two parties to the acquisition (Buyer and Seller), the lender plays an exaggeratedly important role in most LBOs because of the importance of the financing. This turns the transaction from a bilateral negotiation into more of a triangular negotiation, which never makes the deals easier, faster, or simpler to structure and close.

One common LBO structure is for the Target itself to borrow funds, have the employees (and possibly new equity investors) take a moderate position in the stock of the Target, and then have the Target use the financing proceeds to redeem a significant portion or all of the "old" Target shareholders, leaving the employee/investor group in control. A second alternative is for the employees (and possibly new equity investors) to form a new corporation, borrow funds from outside lenders, and then implement a reverse cash merger of the new corporation into the Target, with the Target as the survivor, but the old Target shareholders being paid out in cash. A third alternative is to form Newco (a new corporation) and use the outside financing to acquire the assets of the Target. There are a wide variety of other possible acquisition structures, but all these transactions end up in the same place, with old Target shareholders being bought out with funds largely borrowed from a third-party lender.

In an LBO, the transactional emphasis is on the "L," (i.e., the debt that creates leverage in the transaction). The Acquirer group (whether it is the employees, an outside investor group, or both) generally seeks to issue debt instruments (in order to acquire stock or other equity) and then use Target-generated cash flow to pay off principal plus interest (generally at a high-yield rate). These new debt securities can be issued to one of three obvious "lender" groups: (1) a third-party lender, in exchange for funds that the Acquirer can then use to purchase the Target; (2) the Target shareholders, in exchange for a sale or redemption of all or substantially all of their Target stock; or (3) the Target itself, in exchange for Target assets. The debt issuer can be either the Acquirer or the Target itself.

When the Seller funds the acquisition of the business, issuing debt instruments to the Seller for property can throw the transaction into the installment sale rules under Code section 453 and the OID/imputed interest rules under Code sections 1274 and 483.[1] However, depending on which party issues what kind or character of debt instrument and to whom, the transaction can be characterized as a taxable disposition of Target shares under Code section 1001, a redemption governed by Code section 302, or a dividend under Code section 301. The discussion in the remainder of this section assumes that the transaction is being financed by third-party lenders and is not an installment sale. See Chapter 10 for a discussion of seller-financed acquisitions.

LBOs by their nature tend to require substantial interest payments in the early years, and the Acquirer can generally use interest deductions to offset any taxable income generated by the Target business. (But see the relatively complex rules, discussed below, limiting deductibility of interest for certain kinds of acquisition debt.) Over time, however, as the debt payments include a growing amount of nondeductible principal repayments, the Acquirer often needs to do some combination of selling Target assets to pay down debt, and/or increasing both income and cash flow from retained Target assets, so that the remaining debt can be paid down and eventually off.

In general, Congress has looked askance at leveraged buyouts or other financial manias that have periodically swept the U.S. public stock markets, and has often reacted to perceived abuses with attempted legislative "cures." For example, in 1969, Congress enacted Code section 279 to disallow corporate deductions for interest in excess of $5 million per year on certain debts incurred to acquire the stock or at least two-thirds of the assets of another corporation. This legislation was in response to the conglomerate acquisition wave of the 1960s. In the late 1980s, in response to the advent of the junk bond market, Congress enacted various additional provisions, including limitations under Code section 163(e)(5) on the current deductibility of OID on certain acquisition debt, anti-stripping rules under Code section 163(j), expanded regulatory authority under Code section 385 to allow the IRS to bifurcate hybrid instruments that have debt and acquisition components, and a variety of other rather complex and, in the end, essentially fruitless efforts to regulate highly complex transactions by imposing highly complex rules. Code section 279, for example, tracks the financing techniques of the late 1960s relatively closely and was easily side-stepped by savvy tax planners during the LBO explosion of the 1980s.

However, because the LBO landscape is now littered with these anti-abuse provisions, structuring LBOs requires special care in order to avoid these often-arcane tax "landmines." A not-so-brief list of the tax issues that can come up in an LBO includes the following:

- Code section 279 can disallow interest deductions on certain forms of acquisition debt that are convertible into equity, or that are part of an investment unit that includes an option to acquire equity.

- Code section 163(e)(5) can apply to defer or disallow deductions for original issue discount on high-yield debt and on a "payment-in-kind" debt instrument.

- Code section 163(j) can cause interest deductions to be deferred on debt that is either held or guaranteed by a tax-exempt organization or by a foreign person related to the issuer.

- Code section 163(l) can disallow interest deductions on debt that is convertible into, or payable in, or by reference to, the value of equity of the issuer or a related party or, effective for debt instruments issued after October 3, 2004, equity held by the issuer or any related party in any other person.

- Code section 163(d) limits interest deductions for noncorporate investors who use the borrowed funds to purchase stock in a corporation to their net investment income for the tax year.

- The debt instrument itself may be subject to an assertion by the IRS that such security should be viewed as equity rather than as debt.[2] This could, for example, cause debt to be recharacterized as preferred stock, and in turn cause "interest" payments to be recharacterized as nondeductible dividends.

- If a debt instrument is given in exchange for the purchase property, the transaction will likely be an installment sale governed by Code section 453, and the instrument itself will be subject to the original issue discount rules under Code section 1274 and/or the imputed interest rules under Code section 483.

- Where the LBO transaction includes the issuance of preferred stock at a discount, there can be imputed dividends to stock recipients under Code section 305.

- Some existing shareholders of the Target (generally individuals) may be looking for capital gain on the acquisition transaction, while other shareholders (generally corporations) may prefer to receive payments as dividends.

- Another complicated area is whether common—but often large—expenses incurred in the acquisition transaction are currently deductible or are capitalizable under the principles enunciated in the ***INDOPCO*** case, described below.

Some of these issues are discussed in greater detail, below.

Code Section 279. This section prevents current interest deductions on certain relatively specific kinds of "corporate acquisition indebtedness," to the extent such interest exceeds an amount equal to (1) $5 million reduced by (2) interest paid or incurred during the year on debt that is issued to provide consideration, directly or indirectly, for an acquisition transaction but which is not corporate acquisition indebtedness. As noted above, Code section 279 was enacted in 1969 and is oriented toward certain "old fashioned" transaction structures that were common during the acquisition binge of the late 1960s, but no longer are prevalent. These Code section 279 rules are often arbitrary and would be more objectionable if they were not so easily avoided. As it stands, Code section 279 is almost purely a "trap for the unwary" rather than a meaningful limitation on the ability to implement leveraged buyouts. The full nuance of Code section 279 is beyond the scope of this book, but it will be noted that there are a variety of well-tested ways to avoid Code section 279, including the following: (1) have the Target issue the applicable debt to finance redemption of Target stock, and thereby avoid the definition of corporate acquisition indebtedness, which applies only to debt used for the "acquisition of ... stock in another corporation"; (2) issue an investment unit that consists of subordinated debt plus common stock of the Acquirer; (3) subordinate the acquisition debt only to secured debt; or (4) create a holding company for the Acquirer and issue debt to the holding company so that such debt is subordinated not by contractual agreement but by operation of the law.

Code Section 163(e)(5). This section was enacted in 1989 to address, once again in a painfully specific manner, an objectionable acquisition technique. This time, the perceived abuse was debt instruments that did not pay current interest but were issued with substantial OID, or which required or permitted the issuer to pay interest in the form of additional debt instruments. Basically, tax deductions in the form of OID were being generated without any cash currently changing hands. The solution was a combination of deferring and/or denying interest deductions to the issuer, even though the holder continues to report interest (OID) income as it accrues. Again, a detailed exploration of these complex rules is beyond the scope of this book, but basically they are another trap for the unwary, and so any LBO debt issued with OID or payable in payment-in-kind (PIK) instruments must be scrutinized carefully.

Code Section 163(j). Another provision, enacted in 1989 and expanded in 1993, is Code section 163(j), which limits a corporation's ability to deduct interest paid or accrued on debt issued to or guaranteed by a related tax-exempt organization or a foreign person. The perceived abuse was that leveraged debt was being used to created current deductions (including with OID) while the payee was not subject to U.S. income taxation. This was viewed as a mechanism for "stripping" earnings from the issuer. Code section 163(j) bars current interest deductions, but does permit disallowed interest deductions to be carried forward to future years. Again, the full flavor and nuance of Code section 163(j) is beyond the scope of this book, other than to warn parties structuring an LBO to consider its provisions carefully.

Code Section 163(d). This section limits the ability of a noncorporate borrower to deduct interest on money borrowed to acquire an investment. If an LBO is structured as a direct borrowing by individual investors who then use the borrowed funds to acquire Target stock (or to acquire Newco stock where Newco, in turn, either acquires or mergers into the Target) such debt will be subject to Code section 163(d). Generally, an individual can deduct investment interest expense on Schedule A of Form 1040, but only to the extent of the taxpayer's "net investment income" for each tax year. Any investment interest expense not deductible under these rules can be carried forward to and deducted in the next tax year, subject to the same limitation. For tax years after 1992, net investment income for this purpose does not include a taxpayer's long-term capital gains unless the taxpayer makes a special election to forego the favorable long-term capital gain tax rate on the portion of such gains that the taxpayer elects to treat as investment income in order to claim a current interest deduction under Code section 163(d). Qualified dividend income was also eligible for this same election opportunity for years 2003 through 2008, but not after 2008.

The effect of these Code section 163(d) rules is that individual participants in an LBO acquisition of a C corporation may not have enough investment income to deduct currently the interest expense attributable to the LBO debt. In a small transaction, an individual can possibly borrow money as "home equity indebtedness" under Code section 163(h)(3), but this is subject to, among other limitations, a $100,000 cap. In a management LBO, it does no good to argue that the debt is incurred in connection with the borrower's trade or business of being an employee because debt incurred in the trade or business of being an employee is expressly defined as nondeductible "personal interest" under Code section 163(h)(2)(A). When debt is incurred to acquire S corporation stock, the rules are a complicated and convoluted mess, but, pending future regulations, the current guidance is under IRS Notice 89-35,[3] which provides that individuals should apply a "look through" methodology such that the portion of the debt allocable to business assets of the S corporation will produce deductible "business" interest, while the portion allocable to investment-type assets of the S corporation will be subject to Code section 163(d) limitations. Realistically, most LBOs require (especially in the early years) that the taxable income of the Target be offset by interest expense deductions from servicing the LBO debt. Therefore, as a practical matter, LBOs will usually need to be structured to avoid Code section 163(d) limitations (e.g., by making a C corporation (including possibly the Target), rather than individual investors, the borrower of LBO financing).

Code Section 385. This code section was an exhortation by Congress to the IRS to issue regulatory guidance that could be used to determine whether a debt instrument is really "debt" or a form of disguised equity. This issue is a very interesting and complicated question. The distinction (when it can be made) is hugely important because interest payments with respect to debt are generally deductible by the payor under Code section 163 (subject, of course, to the complicated rules and traps described above) while payments with respect to equity will generally be treated as nondeductible distributions, most likely as dividends or so-called "preferred OID."[4] Meanwhile, on the other side of the transaction, interest payments received are generally taxable as ordinary income, while dividends received are either eligible for a favorable long-term-capital-gains tax rate (for individuals) or subject to the dividend exclusion rules under Code section 243 (for corporations).

The problem is that distinguishing debt from equity is often surprisingly difficult. In the early 1980s, the IRS tried valiantly to implement this direction from Congress, but three separate drafts of regulations under Code Section 385 proved to be both extremely complicated and frustratingly imprecise. As a result, the IRS finally withdrew the regulations before they ever took effect. From the early 1980s until 2016 (a period of over thirty years), the IRS was unwilling to venture back into this particular analytical swamp and did not try to provide any additional regulations on debt versus equity.

However, in early 2016, in response to the embarrassing trend of US corporations leaving the US and "inverting" to other (more tax friendly) jurisdictions,[5] the IRS took another stab at issuing regulations under Code section 385 to address debt versus equity issues.[6] Perhaps tellingly, the 2016 proposed regulations did not, in any manner, provide guidance on tackling the vexing and difficult question of how to distinguish debt from equity.[7] Instead, the IRS appears resigned to letting "inconsistent" case law drive the ongoing development of applicable "general federal tax principles"—namely, the factors to be applied in making the "uncertain and difficult" facts and circumstances analysis—which are briefly summarized in the preamble to the proposed regulations. Those principles, whatever they are, would continue to govern the debt/equity determination except to the extent overruled by the regulations.

At the moment, therefore, the guidance consists entirely of existing case law and IRS rulings.[8] Although the IRS has been reluctant to issue regulations clarifying this area, it has not been reluctant to litigate the debt versus equity issue in circumstances it judges appropriate. Not surprisingly, the IRS almost always argues that debt should be recharacterized as equity (and rarely the other way around) because disallowing interest deductions is usually the best way to produce significant tax revenues.[9]

Dividend versus Capital Gain. Selling individual shareholders naturally would like to recognize capital gain on the transaction, and therefore prefer a transaction that causes the old shareholders of the Target to be bought out either in a sale or exchange transaction governed by Code section 1001, or in a transaction that qualifies as a corporate redemption under Code section 302. A redemption in and of itself can qualify as a sale or exchange producing capital gain, but only if the old shareholders are redeemed in a transaction that meets the requirements of Code section 302, which is discussed in Chapter 15. On the other hand, because of the dividends received deduction, a corporate shareholder of the Target is likely to prefer dividends rather than capital gains because dividends are eligible for the dividend exclusion rules of Code section 243 while capital gains are taxed at ordinary corporate tax rates under Code section 11(b).

Capitalization or Deduction of Expenses—INDOPCO. Another significant tax issue is whether expenses incurred in an LBO transaction can be deducted currently or must be capitalized and amortized over a period of years. In *INDOPCO, Inc.*,[10] the U.S. Supreme Court ruled that expenses (such as legal fees, investment banking frees, and other expenses) incurred by a Target in connection with a "friendly" reverse subsidiary cash merger were nondeductible, capitalizable expenses because the transaction resulted in long-term benefits to the Target.

By contrast, in *Kroy (Europe) Limited*,[11] a corporation decided to "go private" through an LBO and borrowed $60.6 million from various sources to finance the LBO. To obtain these loans, Kroy paid certain loan fees which Kroy amortized and deducted as ordinary and necessary business expenses. The loan fees included an advisory fee of $1.2 million and a placement fee of $625,000, paid to a bank; a credit arrangement and facility fee of $1 million, paid to one of the lenders; a commitment fee, a closing fee and a bank agent fee, totaling $667,000, paid to a second lender; and $599,170 of reimbursement for legal and accounting fees to the lenders and advisors. On appeal from a judgment in favor of the IRS, the Ninth Circuit held that Code section 162(k), disallowing any amount paid by a corporation in connection with the redemption of its stock, did not apply to the loan fees paid to secure these loans, even though the loans were thereafter used as part of a plan to redeem the stock. The Ninth Circuit analyzed the "origin of the claim" test, from *F.W. Woodward*,[12] and agreed that while expenses having their "origin" in a stock redemption transaction are nondeductible, other expenses having origin in a separate and independent borrowing transaction remain deductible as ordinary and necessary business expenses under Code section 162(a).

ESOPS—OVERVIEW

One very specific mechanism for financing an LBO by employees is to establish an employee stock ownership plan (ESOP). An ESOP is, simultaneously: (1) a form of qualified retirement plan for employees under the provisions of the Employee Retirement Income Security Act of 1974 (ERISA), and under the provisions of the Internal Revenue Code that generally apply to qualified plans, Code section 401 *et seq.*; (2) a mechanism that allows employees to acquire securities of the employer on a tax-advantaged basis; (3) a creative and sometimes very effective tool of corporate financing; and (4) in the view of some, a potential anti-takeover defense.

An ESOP is a form of qualified retirement plan, called a stock bonus plan, that is permitted (and indeed generally required) to invest primarily in the employer's securities.[13] An ESOP invests most or all of its assets in employer securities, can borrow money (including from the employer), and can purchase employer's securities from related parties and existing shareholders in transactions that would normally be prohibited transactions under ERISA and the Code for other types of qualified plans. These flexible rules mean that, among other things, an ESOP can be used as a vehicle for tax-advantaged financing by the employer, as will be discussed more fully below.

An ESOP is expressly created to accept deductible pension contributions from the employer, is authorized to borrow additional funds from a lender (including the employer), and is allowed to use borrowed funds to purchase stock of the employer for the benefit of the employee-participants. The stock can be purchased either from the employer corporation or from existing shareholders in the corporation. The employer can contribute to the ESOP up to 25 percent of the eligible compensation paid to employees, and can even make additional deductible contributions above this level if the funds are used to pay interest of loans borrowed by the ESOP to purchase employer securities. Meanwhile, if the ESOP owns at least 30 percent of the employer stock, existing shareholders who sell employer stock to the ESOP are permitted to roll over the proceeds tax-free into other eligible investments, including stock of publicly traded companies.

Example: Tasty Popcorn Corporation forms an ESOP and guarantees a bank loan to the ESOP, the proceeds of which are used to purchase 30 percent or more of the outstanding common stock of Tasty Popcorn. Subsequent contributions by Tasty Popcorn to the ESOP are tax deductible (subject to certain limitations) if the contributed funds are then used to purchase Tasty Popcorn stock[14] or are used to pay interest or principal on the debt incurred by the ESOP to purchase the stock.[15] Since Tasty Popcorn Corporation can deduct its contributions to the ESOP, this allows Tasty Popcorn to service the debt financing (including principal payments) using pre-tax dollars. Although contributions by Tasty Popcorn to the ESOP are subject to limitations based on the eligible salary of covered employees (under the limits applicable to other retirement plans), Tasty Popcorn is allowed to make additional deductible contributions to the ESOP to pay interest on the debt (but not to pay principal). If Tasty Popcorn wants to distribute even more money to the ESOP, certain dividends paid on stock held by the ESOP are deductible by Tasty Popcorn.[16] Meanwhile, assuming the ESOP owns at least 30 percent of the Tasty Popcorn stock, selling Tasty Popcorn shareholders are permitted to roll over their capital gain realized on the sale of Tasty Popcorn stock into a relatively broad category of investments, including publicly traded stocks of domestic operating companies.[17]

LEGAL REQUIREMENTS TAX ATTRIBUTES OF AN ESOP

General Legal Requirements. An ESOP is, first of all, a form of qualified retirement plan that must meet numerous requirements imposed both by ERISA and by the Code. Some of these requirements are general requirements applicable to all qualified retirement plans, while others are specific rules and exceptions that permit the ESOP to make a concentrated, leveraged investment in employer securities that would be barred to most other forms of qualified retirement plan. This makes ESOPs a complicated and exception-ridden sub-category of an already complicated area of tax and labor law.

As an ERISA-qualified retirement plan, the ESOP is subject to the usual panoply of qualified plan restrictions, including nondiscrimination tests, limitations on deductions for employer contributions, and various other limitations. There are also specific distribution requirements, fiduciary obligations, and prohibited transaction rules. A full discussion of these technical ERISA and Code rules is beyond the scope of this book, but obviously compliance is a central part of any implementation of an ESOP transaction.

For businesses already familiar with other types of qualified retirement plans, such as profit sharing or 401(k) plans, ESOPs operate under the same basic set of rules regarding eligibility, investing, and nondiscrimination rules. A trust forms part of an ESOP, which is managed by ESOP trustees and run by a plan administrator selected by the employer. The employees have individual accounts under an ESOP, but, unlike profit sharing or 401(k) plans, these accounts are invested solely in employer stock. The plan can provide whether the employee will receive cash, or stock, as a retirement benefit. As discussed more fully below, employees must have the election to take employee stock in a retirement distribution. If such stock is not publicly traded, the employer corporation (not the ESOP) is required to give employees a put right to sell the stock back to the employer.

Described technically, an ESOP is a tax-qualified retirement plan that satisfies the requirements of Code sections 401(a) and 4975(e)(7). Under Code section 4975(e)(7), an ESOP is a defined contribution plan with the following characteristics:

1. It is a stock bonus plan qualified under Code section 401(a), or a combination of a stock bonus plan and money purchase plan, both of which are qualified under Code section 401(a).

2. It is designed to invest primarily in qualifying employer securities, as defined in Code section 409(l).

3. It provides plan participants with certain required "pass-through" voting rights, Code section 409(e).

4. It provides participants with both the right to elect to receive employer securities as a distribution from the plan (potentially attractive if the employer is publicly traded) and the right to elect to put the employer stock back to the employer (attractive if the employer stock is not publicly traded and not otherwise liquid), Code section 409(h).

5. It meets the benefit distribution requirements of Code section 409(o).

6. It meets various other requirements under Code sections 409 and 4975(e)(7), and the applicable federal regulations.

As a starting point, a trust forming part of an ESOP must "generally" meet the requirements of Code section 401(a) to be a qualified trust—although there are enough exceptions or special rules applicable only to ESOPs to make this "general" statement only vaguely accurate and not at all helpful. In addition to meeting these general rules, the ESOP must be a defined contribution plan and a qualified stock bonus plan, and must also meet the additional, specific ESOP requirements contained in Code section 4975(e). In the past (for plan years beginning before 2002), ESOPs were sometimes structured as a combination of a stock bonus plan and money purchase plan so that the contribution limit could be increased from 15 percent of eligible employee compensation under a stock bonus plan to 25 percent under a combined stock bonus/money purchase plan. However, changes to Code section 404(a)(3) in 2001 increased the deductible limit for a stock bonus plan to 25 percent and made it unnecessary to structure ESOPs as a combination of a stock bonus plan and money purchase plan.

An ESOP must invest primarily in "employer securities," defined in Code section 409(l) as common stock issued by the employer (or by a corporation that is a member of the same controlled group) that is readily tradable on an established securities market. If such common stock does not exist, "employer securities" means common stock issued by the employer (or by a corporation that is a member of the same controlled group) having a combination of voting power and dividend rights equal to or exceeding that class of common stock of the employer (or a corporation that is a member of the same controlled group) having the greatest voting power and the class of common stock of the employer (or a corporation that is a member of the same controlled group) having the greatest dividend rights. "Employer securities" also includes "noncallable" preferred stock if such stock is convertible at any time into the qualified common stock described above at a conversion price that (as of the date of acquisition by the ESOP) is reasonable. Preferred stock is treated as "noncallable" for this purpose if, after a call, there will be a reasonable opportunity for a conversion that meets the requirements of the preceding sentence.

Code section 409(e) imposes voting requirements that basically allow ESOP participants to vote the shares allocated to their respective accounts under the plan. If shares in an ESOP are not yet allocated (e.g., because such shares were acquired since the last allocation date, or acquired with loan proceeds and not yet released from the suspense account for allocation purposes), the fiduciaries may vote such shares, unless the plan provides otherwise.

Code section 409(h)(1) contains two requirements that are designed to give the participants the maximum economic benefit and maximum liquidity from ownership of employer stock. Under these rules, a participant entitled to a distribution from the plan (1) has the right to demand that his or her benefits be distributed in the form of employer securities, and (2) if the employer securities are not readily tradable on an established market, has a right to require that the employer (not the ESOP) repurchase the employer securities under a fair valuation formula. The purpose of these rules is to give participants the right to receive employer securities if that is desirable (e.g., if there is substantial appreciation potential in the stock and it is publicly traded) and also to provide a source of liquidity (the put right requiring the employer to buy the stock) if the stock is not publicly traded. As will be discussed more fully below, this put right means that the employer actually has to "pay for" its securities twice, the first time to fund the ESOP and the second time if and when the put right is exercised. As a practical matter, this double-payment obligation can place substantial strains on the liquidity of the employer corporation if put rights are exercised in substantial percentages close in time.

The ERISA and Code provisions generally prohibit loans between a qualified retirement plan and a "party in interest," but there is an exception to this general prohibition for ESOPs.[18] This exception permits the employer to loan the ESOP funds to acquire employer securities, and also facilitates back-to-back loans, whereby the employer borrows funds from a third-party lender (who considers the employer a safer lending risk) and re-loans the proceeds to the ESOP.

Overview of Tax Attributes of an ESOP. As a stock bonus plan, an ESOP is allowed to receive deductible contributions from the employer in annual amounts of up to 25 percent of the eligible employee compensation.[19] Code section 404(a) contains additional rules, specific to an ESOP, that apply if plan contributions are timely applied by the plan to the repayment of a loan incurred for the purpose of acquiring qualifying employer securities. First, notwithstanding Code section 404(a)(3) and (7), Code section 404(a)(9)(A) provides that the employer can deduct up to 25 percent of eligible employee compensation if such contributions are applied timely by the ESOP to repayment of principal on the applicable loan. Second, and even more importantly, the employer can deduct *all* contributions applied timely by the plan to the repayment of interest on the applicable loan.[20]

The practical effect of these rules, as discussed more fully below, is that an employer corporation can structure corporate financing through an ESOP and thereby make it possible to repay the debt, both principal and interest, on a fully deductible basis (subject to the 25-percent-of-compensation limitation on principal repayments). These rules do not apply to an S corporation.[21] Therefore, contributions to an S corporation ESOP are subject to the 25 percent of compensation deduction limit whether the contribution is used to pay principal, interest, or both.

> ***Comment:*** The interaction of Code section 404(a)(3) and 404(a)(9)(A) is curious, but it appears that the 404(a)(9)(A) rule is a special, independent rule that can be read as being *in addition* to the general limitation under Code section 404(a)(3). This suggests that an employer could make deductible contributions to another defined contribution plan, equal to 25 percent of eligible employee compensation, and then make additional deductible contributions to an ESOP of up to 25 percent of eligible employee compensation, so long as the contribution is applied to principal repayments on the ESOP loan, and unlimited additional deductible contributions, if applied to interest payments on the ESOP loan.[22]

Under Code section 404(k), the employer is also allowed a deduction for certain dividends paid on stock held by the ESOP. Such dividends are deductible if (1) paid in cash directly to plan participants or their beneficiaries, (2) paid to the plan but distributed in cash to plan participants or their beneficiaries within ninety days of the end of the plan year, (3) at the election of plan participants or their beneficiaries, payable as provided in (1) or (2) or paid to the plan and reinvested in qualifying employer securities, or (4) used to make payments on an ESOP loan, the proceeds of which were used to acquire the employer securities with respect to which the dividend is being paid. This dividend deduction is another mechanism for increasing the tax-deductible flow of funds from the employer to the ESOP. Under the regulations adopted in 2006, payments "to reacquire stock held by an ESOP, including reacquisition payments that are used to make benefit distributions to participants or beneficiaries," cannot be applicable dividends, even if the redemption proceeds are characterized as a dividend for tax purposes, because "treatment of those payments as applicable dividends would constitute, in substance, an avoidance or evasion on taxation..."[23] Note that, with the addition in 2004 of Code section 4975(f)(7), the Code now explicitly permits S corporation ESOPs to use S corporation distributions on both allocated and unallocated shares to make payments on an ESOP loan used to acquire qualifying employer securities, effective for all distributions made after December 31, 1997. Code section 1042 confers a very attractive tax benefit on shareholders of the employer by permitting any such shareholder (other than a C corporation) to avoid gain on the sale of the employer stock to the ESOP so long as the sale proceeds are reinvested in "qualified securities" within sixty days of the ESOP sale. Code section 1042 is discussed in greater detail below, but among the securities that can serve as "qualified replacement property" are securities of publicly traded domestic operating companies. Thus, the current owner or owners of the employer corporation can use the ESOP not only to create a buyer for their stock where none otherwise existed, but can also defer some or all of the gain on that sale while diversifying their investment from stock in a single privately owned company into a portfolio of publicly traded stocks of large corporations.

Historically, S corporations could not take advantage of the ESOP provisions, since for tax years beginning before 1998, an ESOP did not qualify as an eligible S corporation shareholder. However, today, thanks to changes in the law, S corporations can enjoy many, though not all, of the benefits of an ESOP. In particular, an S corporation cannot take advantage of (1) the special rules under Code section 404(a)(9) that permit deductibility of enhanced contributions[24] or (2) the deduction under Code section 404(k) for dividends paid to an ESOP with respect to employer securities[25] and S shareholders are denied the favorable nonrecognition or "rollover" provisions under Code section 1042 on selling employer stock.[26] On the other hand, income distributed by an S corporation to an ESOP holding its stock is inherently tax deferred because an ESOP itself is not subject to current tax. Moreover, changes in 2004 now permit distributions on S corporation stock held in an ESOP to be used to make payments toward ESOP loans used to finance the acquisition of such stock.[27] As a practical matter, therefore, S corporations are often viable candidates for implementation of an ESOP. Indeed, as discussed below, the IRS has become vigilant about what it considers abusive transactions involving S corporation ESOPs.

Code section 409(p), enacted in 2001, is an anti-abuse provision requiring that an ESOP holding S corporation stock must provide that no portion of the assets of the plan attributable to (or allocable in lieu of) such employer securities may, during a nonallocation year, accrue (or be allocated directly or indirectly under any plan of the employer meeting the requirements of Code section 401(a)) for the benefit of any disqualified person. Congress was concerned with two identified types of abuses. First, a highly paid professional could contribute his or her business to an S corporation and establish an ESOP to acquire all of its shares, and thereafter the S corporation could employ the professional as its sole employee and sole ESOP participant. The S corporation and the individual would not be subject to current federal income taxation, except to the extent that the individual received compensation from the S corporation or took distributions from the ESOP. Second, an S corporation owner might sell all his or her stock to an ESOP, but retain options to acquire additional shares representing, post-exercise, a 99 percent interest in the S corporation. The S corporation could operate for years on a tax-free basis, and in the future the owner would be able to take back 99 percent of the S corporation's tax-free growth.[28] As a practical matter, Congress has shown a willingness to permit S corporations to set up ESOPs, albeit with certain (largely appropriate) modifications and adjustments not required of C corporations. However, because the IRS is very aware that ESOPs present opportunities for clever and, in the IRS's view, improper avoidance or evasion of taxes, the IRS is using Code section 409(p) to attack various arrangements involving S corporations and ESOPs.[29]

PRACTICAL BUSINESS USES OF AN ESOP

As a form of qualified plan, an ESOP, among other things, is a way of providing employees with a retirement benefit. However, ESOPs are more frequently viewed as a complicated but sometimes intriguing financing tool for an employer corporation. As will be explored below, an ESOP can be used to finance the sale of the employer business to its employees, but it can also be used creatively in other, perhaps unexpected ways. For example, it can be used (1) to finance the spin-off of assets or a subsidiary to employees; (2) to raise capital by transferring existing third-party debt to an ESOP and having the ESOP assume the debt to "pay" for employer securities; and (3) in various, nonabusive transactions involving S corporations.

Retirement Plan. An ESOP is, of course, a qualified retirement plan. Money contributed to an ESOP is deductible currently by the employer but not currently taxable to a participating employee. Rather, an ESOP participant is taxed only when the participant receives a distribution from the plan. Thus, for example, an ESOP participant will be taxed upon receipt of a dividend paid on the employer's stock, if such dividend is distributed, but not on dividends retained by the ESOP and reinvested in employer stock. This asymmetry in timing between deductions by an employer and income recognition by an employee exists with all qualified retirement plans, but an ESOP is distinctive because a leveraged ESOP can be used by a corporation to finance acquisitions (including of its own stock) on an entirely pre-tax basis because amounts contributed to the ESOP and used to pay principal on the ESOP loan are the economic equivalent of being able to deduct both loan principal and interest payments.

Leveraging. Most ESOPs are leveraged (i.e., they borrow money to help finance the purchase of employer stock). A loan is sometimes made directly to the ESOP by a bank or other third-party lender, and in that case is often secured by a guarantee of the employer corporation, or by one or more of its shareholders because the only assets that the ESOP can pledge as collateral are the shares. More commonly, however, the financing is implemented through back-to-back loans. The ESOP will borrow money from the employer corporation (the "internal loan"), and the employer corporation, in turn, will fund this internal loan by borrowing from a bank or other third-party lender (the "external loan").

The terms of the internal loan and the external loan can be the same, but it is not necessary or even always appropriate for the terms of these two loans to be identical, and using different terms may meet financing objectives of the employer. For example, if the term of the external loan (the time period) is longer than the internal loan, the corporation will be accelerating its tax deductions faster than it pays off loan principal to the bank. Conversely, if the period of the internal loan is longer than the term of the external loan, the stock will be allocated to the employees at a slower pace. An issue to note is that the external loan requires actual payment of cash, whereas the internal loan is essentially an exchange of checks (and corresponding book entries) between the ESOP and the employer.

Generally, lenders strongly prefer to lend to the corporation, rather than the ESOP, because this avoids having to comply with the exempt loan requirements imposed by ERISA (e.g., the only collateral that the ESOP can provide is the employer securities, the loan must be a term loan, and the loan may be payable on demand only if the ESOP is in default).[30] By contrast, by using back-to-back loans, the outside lender and employer can agree on whatever terms they deem appropriate for the external loan (e.g., the lender can take more desirable collateral, such as the publicly traded securities purchased by the selling shareholder in the transaction and rolled over under Code section 1042), and then the internal loan from the employer to the ESOP can conform to the exempt loan requirements.

Self-Created Acquirer of the Business. For owners seeking to sell a closely held corporate business, an ESOP may be the only realistic or viable acquirer of that corporation. A second benefit (and the principal tax benefit) is that proceeds from stock sold to an ESOP, which would otherwise be subject to long-term capital gain, can be reinvested tax-free into various other investments, including publicly traded stock, as long as certain requirements are satisfied. See the discussion of Code section 1042, below. Obviously, use of an ESOP to liquidate the existing shareholders' investment and transfer ownership to employees is a central purpose of ESOPs, and a function an ESOP is well-suited to serve.

Refinance Corporate Debt. An ESOP can be used to refinance existing corporate debt and to repay that debt with what amounts to pre-tax dollars, thereby lowering the corporation's effective borrowing costs. In this type of refinancing strategy, the employer corporation issues shares of its stock to the ESOP, in an amount equal to the value of the outstanding debt, which debt is then assumed by the ESOP. This makes repayment of the debt tax-deductible (subject to the annual contribution limits of Code section 404(a)(9)). Instead of having the ESOP assume debt, of course, the ESOP and employer can transform the debt into a back-to-back loan by creating an internal loan (from employer to ESOP) that matches the external loan (from lender to employer). As a practical matter, this financing strategy takes advantage of the fact that an employer corporation can essentially "require" that an employee retirement plan invest in the employer corporation. In this strategy, the ESOP is not used to finance a transfer of ownership, but rather is used as a mechanism to implement a mandatory investment by employees in the business, thereby helping the corporation improve its balance sheet (with a consequential dilution of the existing shareholders' ownership).

Spin-offs and Mergers. ESOPs can be used to spin off a division of an existing company and form a new company owned by employees through the ESOP. The stock of the newly created spin-off company is sold to the ESOP, using outside financing or possibly installment debt, and the ESOP then uses pre-tax money to pay off the debt. Again, this strategy permits a corporation to "sell" a division of its business to employees and to use the ESOP as a de facto capital call on employees (or, in this specific example, former employees, who now own the spin-off company).

Succession Planning. An ESOP can be useful in succession planning for a closely held corporation. In particular, an acquisition of employer stock from an estate can be financed by the ESOP from a third-party lender and then repaid with pre-tax dollars. However, one should be aware that stock owned directly or indirectly by an estate is considered to be owned proportionally by its beneficiaries, and this attribution rule can potentially cause the stock purchase from the estate to be characterized as a dividend rather than as a sale or exchange, under Code sections 302 and 303, to surviving members of a decedent's family if those family members also own stock in the closely held family business.

Charitable Giving. There are various other techniques that can place an ESOP in the middle of sophisticated estate planning, such as in connection with charitable contributions, including transfers of employer stock to a charitable remainder trust.

WHEN AN ESOP DOES (AND DOES NOT) MAKE SENSE

An ESOP offers unique and often intriguing financial and tax benefits, especially to the current shareholders of the employer. The biggest benefit, of course, is that the selling shareholder can "invent" a buyer for the employer stock, and, depending on how the ESOP is implemented, can enjoy various forms of transition control coupled with the ultimate goal of liquidity. The biggest tax benefit conferred on the existing shareholders is the opportunity to avoid capital gain on the stock sale (assuming the ESOP purchases at least 30 percent of the outstanding employer stock) by reinvesting in qualified replacement property, including publicly traded stocks. Naturally, ownership looking to sell a business and having a hard time locating a serious purchaser will want to at least consider the ESOP alternative.

There are, however, various constraining or limiting factors that will determine whether an ESOP transaction can be structured successfully for a specific employer. The biggest constraining factor is that, in order for a leveraged ESOP to be able to afford a substantial ownership interest in a business (a 30 percent stake is the level at which Code section 1042 becomes available), the business must have a significant number of employees who are eligible to participate in the retirement plan. This is because amounts contributed to the ESOP on a deductible basis by the employer corporation (unless the amounts are used to pay interest on any debt incurred by the ESOP) are limited by the compensation of the employee participants. Simply put, an employer with only a small number of eligible employees will probably not be able to amortize the ESOP loan.

Another major constraining factor is the employer corporation's ability to generate sufficient cash flow to fund the requisite ESOP contributions. The fact that contributions are deductible (within the limits described above) means that the ESOP is being funded on a pre-tax basis, but even so there must be enough income and cash flow to finance these debt commitments while also meeting the ongoing financial needs of the business.

Although an ESOP offers obvious benefits to a selling shareholder, it is often less clear that employees are equally benefited. In particular, when an employer provides an ESOP for its employees, generally a significant portion, perhaps all, of an employee's retirement benefits is now directly tied to the value of the employer's stock. Since the employee's current job and financial future are already symbiotically related to the employer's success, it is not always considered appropriate to have such a concentration of risk and reward, even in cases where the employer is a viable business with good prospects of success. Obviously, an ESOP is suitable only for corporations that are expected to grow and prosper. Although the fiduciary requirements of ERISA are beyond the scope of this book, the viability of the transaction is a central element in determining whether an ESOP can be implemented.

The voting control of the employer corporation often ends up being exercised by and through the ESOP, which can be a good or bad thing, depending on which side of a vote an individual happens to be on. In general, the voting rights of the employer's stock held by the ESOP trust are passed through to the participants to the extent the shares have been allocated to their account.[31] However, when there are unallocated shares, voting rights can be exercised by the trustee of the ESOP trust. An ESOP trustee and/or participants with significant voting control can lead to obvious potential tensions or disputes regarding the long term objectives of the corporation.

Creating an ESOP requires a valuation of the employer corporation stock on the date that the stock is purchased by the ESOP. The valuation is done by a qualified independent appraiser. Note that, to the extent that shareholders in the corporation are making other, intra-family transfers or other gift tax sensitive transfers, this creates a "valuation" that may be inconsistent with intra-family transfer objectives.

MORE TECHNICAL DISCUSSION OF CERTAIN SPECIFIC TAX BENEFITS AND INCENTIVES FOR ESOPS

Code Section 1042. This provision allows the selling shareholder to elect to defer recognition of gain on a sale of "qualified securities" to an ESOP if the shareholder reinvests the proceeds in "qualified replacement property" within a specified "replacement period." A Code section 1042 election is available only if the ESOP owns, immediately after the sale in question, at least 30 percent of either (1) the shares of each class of outstanding stock in the corporation (other than certain nonvoting, nonconvertible preferred stock) which issued the qualified securities or (2) the total value of all outstanding stock of the corporation (other than nonvoting, nonconvertible preferred stock).[32] The shares being sold must have been held by the seller for at least three years prior to the time of the sale.[33] The election must be filed no later than the due date (including extensions) for the seller's tax return for the tax year in which the sale occurs.[34]

For purposes of Code section 1042, "qualified securities" means employer securities, as defined in Code section 409(l), that (1) are issued by a domestic C corporation that has no stock outstanding that is readily tradable on an established securities market, and (2) were not received by the taxpayer in (a) a distribution from a plan described in Code section 401(a), or (b) a transfer pursuant to an option or other right to acquire stock to which Code section 83, 422, or 423 applied.[35]

The term "replacement period" means the period that begins three months before the date on which the sale of qualified securities occurs and that ends twelve months after the date of such sale.[36]

The term "qualified replacement property" means any security issued by a domestic operating corporation that did not, for the tax year preceding the tax year in which the security was purchased, have passive investment income in excess of 25 percent of the gross receipts of the corporation for the preceding tax year.[37] The issuer of the replacement securities cannot be the same as the issuer of the qualified securities being replaced (or a member of the same controlled group of corporations).[38] A corporation is an "operating corporation" if more than 50 percent of its assets were, at the time the security was purchased or before the close of the replacement period, used in the active conduct of the trade or business.[39] Qualified replacement property is restricted to stocks and bonds in United States domestic operating companies and does not include investments in mutual funds, partnerships, or REITs.

Code Section 404(k). This IRS code section provides that an employer corporation (other than an S corporation) is allowed a deduction for any dividends paid on stock owned by an ESOP if, in accordance with the provisions of the plan, the dividend is paid in cash and is either paid directly to plan participants or paid to the plan and distributed in cash to the participants no later than ninety days after the close of the plan year in which the dividend is received. The deduction is allowable in the tax year in which the dividend is paid to, or distributed to, a participant.

Comment: This recognizes that in effect a dividend paid to an ESOP, followed by an immediate distribution from the ESOP to the employee, is a de facto form of compensation paid to employees, and therefore is deductible by the distributing corporation.

The employer corporation may also deduct dividends that are used by the ESOP to make payments on a loan incurred to purchase the employer shares on which the dividends are paid.[40] The deduction is allowed in the tax year of the corporation in which the dividends are used to make the loan payments.

Comment: Allowing the employer corporation not only to make contributions to the ESOP but also to deduct dividends paid on stock owned by the ESOP increases the amount of cash flow available to the ESOP, and thus the amount of the loan that can be financed by the ESOP. As a practical matter, this suggests that a form of convertible preferred stock providing a high dividend rate may be an attractive security purchase by an ESOP.[41]

For tax years beginning after 2001, an employer is allowed to deduct dividends that are, at the election of participants or their beneficiaries, reinvested in qualifying employer securities.[42]

The IRS can disallow deductions of dividends if it is determined the dividends constitute an evasion of tax.[43] The IRS position is that, in order to avoid disallowance under this provision, the dividends must be reasonable. There is some uncertainty as to whether the basis of "reasonableness" is determined on the basis of a reasonable compensation test or whether it should be based on a comparison to the dividends paid on comparable securities.

Under the regulations adopted in 2006, payments "to reacquire stock held by an ESOP, including reacquisition payments that are used to make benefit distributions to participants or beneficiaries," cannot be applicable dividends, even if the redemption proceeds are characterized as a dividend for tax purposes, because "treatment of those payments as applicable dividends would constitute, in substance, an avoidance or evasion on taxation…"[44] A deduction for this type of payment would be tax avoidance or tax evasion because it would allow a corporation to claim two deductions for the same economic cost: once for the value of the stock originally contributed to the ESOP and again for the amount paid to redeem the same stock. Contemporaneously adopted regulations provide that this type of payment is covered by section 162(k),[45] which generally states that no deduction otherwise allowable shall be allowed for any amount paid or incurred by a corporation in connection with the reacquisition of its stock.

SUMMARY AND HYPOTHETICAL EXAMPLES INVOLVING ESOP TRANSACTIONS

To recap the discussion, an ESOP transaction is suitable if a corporation has a relatively large employee base, the corporation's employees are willing to have their retirement plan invest in employer securities, and the corporation has sufficient cash flow to fund debt incurred to buy at least a 30 percent equity stake from the selling shareholder. The discussion below recaps the advantages and disadvantages to each of the major players in an ESOP transaction, and then explores various hypothetical examples illustrating the potential uses of an ESOP.

Issues for Selling Shareholder. If the corporation is a C corporation and the shareholder sells employer securities to an ESOP holding 30 percent or more of the required classes of employer stock, the shareholder can take advantage of Code section 1042 and defer tax on the gain by reinvesting the proceeds into qualified replacement property, including publicly traded stocks, within the applicable fifteen-month period. The shareholder is the party most clearly benefited from an ESOP sale because the shareholder creates a market for the shareholder's stock and diversifies the shareholder's portfolio.

Issues for the Employer Corporation. The employer can make deductible contributions to the ESOP up to a maximum annual contribution equal to 25 percent of the covered compensation of its employees. In addition, a C corporation can deduct interest payments for an ESOP loan used to acquire employer securities and can also deduct "reasonable" dividends that are paid in cash with respect to shares held in the ESOP, if used for specified purposes. The ESOP uses these plan contributions, plus the dividends, to repay the ESOP loan. As the ESOP repays the loan, the corresponding shares effectively purchased by this repayment are allocated to the employees' accounts.

Issues for Employees. The employees' principal tax advantage is receiving employer equity on a tax-deferred basis. The potential drawback is that there is a concentration of the employee's wealth and the employee's well-being—not only the ongoing employment relationship, but also the value of the stock. On the other hand, if the employer is successful, this is a good thing. A related issue is that the employee will eventually want to liquidate the ESOP account and receive cash, unless the stock of the employer has become publicly traded or otherwise highly liquid. If the employer stock is not readily tradable on an established market, the ESOP participants must be given a "put" right requiring the employer to repurchase the stock based on a fair valuation formula, determined by an independent appraiser pursuant to Code section 401(a)(28)(C).

As a practical matter, ESOP plans anticipate that nonpublicly traded stock will be redeemed when an employee retires. This is a not-inconsequential drawback to the extent that the employer corporation is being required to fund, from its current cash flow, not only the original acquisition of ESOP stock from the selling shareholder, but also the future redemption of all shares contributed to the ESOP. In effect, the same corporation must buy the exact same number of shares two times over the employment cycle of its workforce, first from the shareholder who sells to the ESOP and second from the ESOP.

S Corporations and ESOPs. Since 1998, S corporations have been permitted to adopt ESOP plans. However, S corporations are subject to significantly different rules designed to limit certain benefits of an ESOP to an S corporation. In particular, rollover treatment under Code section 1042 is not allowed if the corporation is an S corporation, and distributions to shareholders are not deductible. On the other hand, when stock of an S corporation is contributed to an ESOP, the income of the S corporation passes through to the ESOP, and in effect, the earnings of the corporation become exempt from federal (and in many cases, state) income tax. This seemingly too-good-to-be-true situation led some people to use (and in the IRS's viewpoint, abuse) the S corporation ESOP rules by effectively creating S corporations as tax-exempt entities! The S corporation ESOP transactions have drawn extremely close scrutiny from the IRS and are being viewed in many cases as abusive.[46]

Example 1—Sale of Shares to Leveraged ESOP by Sole Shareholder: Employer Corporation, a C corporation for federal income tax purposes, has 100 employees and operates a business that generates $10 million of gross revenue and $1 million of profits each year. John Runson, the sole shareholder of Employer, owns 100,000 shares of Employer common stock, the sole class of Employer stock issued and outstanding, and John wishes to sell 30 percent of the stock, or 30,000 shares, to an ESOP. Employer establishes an ESOP, and Employer concludes that it can financially afford to contribute $50,000 per month, or a total of $600,000 per year, to the ESOP as defined contributions on behalf of its employees. Such contribution amounts are within the applicable limits on maximum contributions imposed by Code sections 404(a)(3) and 404(a)(9).

A fair valuation of the Employer stock concludes that 30,000 shares, representing a 30 percent interest, have a value of $3 million. A bank is willing to loan $3 million to the ESOP so long as the loan is guaranteed by the corporation. The ESOP borrows the $3 million, at an interest rate of 8 percent per annum, and the ESOP purchases the 30,000 shares from John. Based on a projected monthly payment of $50,000, the ESOP will fully amortize the loan over seventy-seven monthly payments of $50,000 (the final fractional payment would be $43,966.66).

John, meanwhile, reinvests the $3 million of sales proceeds by purchasing within twelve months the stock of a diversified portfolio of publicly traded domestic operating companies. To meet the applicable requirements under Code section 1042, John must have held the Employer stock for at least three years, and the Employer stock must be a "qualified security," which it would be in this case because there is only one class of stock currently issued and outstanding. The purchaser of John's stock is required to be an ESOP (which it is) and must own 30 percent of the Employer stock after the sale (which it does). John must reinvest the proceeds in "qualified replacement property," which is required to be the stock of domestic (U.S.) C corporations that are also operating companies. To meet this requirement, John can pick a diversified portfolio of publicly traded companies.

Comment: This is a "classic" use of an ESOP to create liquidity in the employer shares for an existing shareholder who then avails himself or herself of the benefits of Code section 1042 and rolls over the entire proceeds into a diversified portfolio of publicly traded operating companies. The hypothetical indicates that the company has $10 million of gross revenue and $1 million of profits each year, and, as with all financial projections, the parties anticipate that the $1 million of profit will continue into the future. Employer Corporation (controlled by John Runson, its sole shareholder) decides to commit $600,000 out of the $1 million of profit to fund the ESOP. There appears to be enough money left over ($400,000 of profit) to fund the ongoing operations of Employer.

Note that contributing $600,000 each year to the ESOP provides a deduction for Employer that significantly reduces its corporate tax liability. If we assume a 40 percent combined federal/state tax rate, this reduces Employer taxes by $240,000, and leaves that much more available collectively to John and Employer. Note that John receives a $3 million "tax-free" payment for this 30 percent equity transfer, and still retains 70 percent of Employer. Meanwhile, the $600,000 is transferred to the ESOP and, in turn, is used to amortize the $3 million bank loan. Since the total amount required to amortize the loan will be approximately $3,843,966.66 (76 payments × $50,000, and a final payment of $43,966.66) this indicates that $843,966.66 goes toward interest payments and the balance goes to amortize principal.

Meanwhile, the 30,000 shares will be held by the ESOP in a suspended account and will be apportioned to the employees as the loan is paid off, generally in proportion to their respective compensation levels. Note that while the company is contributing a total of $600,000 per year to the ESOP, it will in fact be making defined contributions with respect to each of the 100 employees. Each of the employees will be assigned shares of stock as the loan principal is amortized. Thereafter, under the voting pass-through rules described above, each of the account holders will have the right to vote, according to their shares, on appropriate issues of corporate governance. Trustees will vote shares in the suspense account, subject to their fiduciary duties, while the loan is being amortized.

Example 2—Use of an ESOP as a Financing Vehicle to Acquire a Target Corporation: Same facts as Example 1, except that instead of purchasing Employer shares from John, Employer Corporation wishes to acquire assets from a Target corporation for $3 million. As a financing strategy, Employer sets up an ESOP, which in turn borrows $3 million from a bank with interest at a rate of 8 percent per annum, and then uses the $3 million to buy 30,000 newly issued shares of common stock from Employer Corporation.

(*Note:* Assume that $3 million is the fair value of these shares.) Employer, in turn, uses the $3 million to purchase the assets of Target. Employer guarantees the ESOP loan to the bank and then make annual contributions of $600,000 per year ($50,000 per month) to the ESOP until the bank loan is fully amortized.

Comment: The benefit of this financing strategy is that Employer Corporation is in effect financing the acquisition of the Target assets with debt payments that are fully deductible, not only as to the interest component but also as to the principal component. This means that the Employer can repay the principal on the ESOP loan (through deductible contributions) with $3 million of pre-tax income rather than having to finance the plan payments with after-tax revenue. Assuming Employer is in a combined 40 percent tax bracket, federal and state, Employer would need to earn $5 million of taxable income to end up with $3 million of net after-tax income to pay off the principal portion of a $3 million loan. (Interest on the $3 million loan, in the amount of $843,966.66, is being omitted from this analysis because such interest is deductible by Employer whether incurred directly (and thus deductible under Code section 163(a)) or whether deducted as a contribution to an ESOP under Code section 404(a)(9)(B).)

This simplified analysis demonstrates that the acquisition cost of purchasing Target assets is reduced to 60 percent ($3 million of current pre-tax income) compared to the amount of pre-tax income ($5 million) that would need to be earned absent the ESOP structure.

The trade-off for using an ESOP to finance the acquisition is that the ESOP now owns a

23 percent equity interest in the corporation (30,000 shares out of 130,000), resulting in dilution of earnings and equity to John, the current shareholder.

Example 3—Use of ESOP to Spin Off Unwanted Division to Employees: Same facts as Example 1, except that Employer Corporation has two lines of business and would like to sell off one of the lines, which it views as nonessential to its core business. The employees of the unwanted division are, understandably, worried about losing their jobs and would like to buy the division and continue to run it as a separate company. The division, if separated from Employer, is projected to generate $4 million of gross revenues and $300,000 of profits. The parties obtain a valuation that concludes that $3 million is a reasonable purchase price for the division. A proposed financing mechanism would be for Employer to contribute the line of unwanted business to a newly formed subsidiary, Newco, which, in turn, would create a leveraged ESOP. The ESOP would borrow from the bank $3 million, at 8 percent interest per annum, subject to a guaranty of Employer. The ESOP would then purchase all the stock of Newco from Employer for $3 million.

Comment: Once Newco is operational, it will make annual contributions on behalf of its employees to the ESOP to amortize the $3 million loan. Note, however, that as a result of dividing Employer into two smaller corporate entities, there will be fewer employees at Newco than there were at Employer, and therefore a lower maximum amount that can be contributed to the ESOP to help pay the loan principal.[47] For example, at 8 percent per annum, debt service on the loan is already $240,000 per year, and at the moment Newco's profit is just $300,000. Several things can happen, but almost necessarily one of them has to happen: Newco can increase its profitability, it can sell off assets to free up cash, it can seek outside investors to put in additional cash, or it can do some combination of all of these. Newco can contribute to the ESOP amounts up to 25 percent of the eligible compensation of its employees, which amount can be used to amortize loan principal,[48] and it can contribute any additional amount it wants to pay interest on the loan.[49] All these numbers and projections will be scrutinized carefully when the loan is negotiated with the bank, so there should be no surprises (at least as long as Newco performs as projected, but that is a whole different issue).

In summary, although there does not appear to be a lot of "wiggle" room in this particular financing, that is generally true of all leveraged financing. Ultimately, leveraged financing of an acquisition can be rather like chasing your tail: the loan can only be as large as the cash flow generated by the Target, but the stronger the cash flow is, the higher the asking price is likely to be, and hence the higher the acquisition loan. Obviously, there is an equilibrium point between and among all the parties to a transaction (otherwise no transactions would ever get done). In this circumstance, the Employer might, for example, reduce its selling price of the assets to Newco, or possibly keep a portion of the Newco stock and sell less than 100 percent to the ESOP. Employer could also include, as part of the Newco assets, a significant amount of cash or liquid investments that could be used to help pay down the debt. (This last suggestion is really just a variation on reducing the purchase price, but everyone likes to do a deal his or her own way, so Employer might actually decide to choose one approach over the other for business reasons (e.g., Employer might be willing to transfer accounts receivable and let Newco collect the money over time.))

Example 4—ESOP Where Employer Has Strong Cash Flow But Small Number of Employees: Same facts as Example 1, except that, while Employer has $1 million of income per year and strong cash flow, Employer has only 10 employees, and the maximum that can be funded under the 25 percent rule in Code section 404(a)(9)(A) is a total of $200,000. The ESOP borrows $3 million to buy 30,000 shares from John Runson, the sole shareholder. Since Employer has strong cash flow, Employer could also make additional contributions to the ESOP above the 25 percent limitation imposed under Code section 404(a)(9)(A) to make interest payments.[50] This means that the ESOP could apply up to $200,000 per year toward amortization of principal on the $3 million debt and that Employer could contribute the additional amount required to cover interest (approximately $240,000 in the first year, but decreasing over time as the principal amount decreases).

Note, however, that, because the ESOP cannot pay more toward principal than the maximum contribution under Code section 404(a)(9)(A), unless the bank is willing to accept slow amortization (which may be a possibility, especially if Employer represents a strong guarantee) or unless Employer increases its employment base significantly (hard to count on that), this factual situation represents a tight fit for an ESOP transaction.

Comment: This example illustrates that, even if Employer has the exact same profitability levels as in Example 1, the number of employees and their total eligible compensation can be a significant constraint on ESOP financing.

Example 5—Spin-Off and Sale of a Division Using a Leveraged ESOP Financed by Back-to-Back Loans: Same facts as Example 3, except that the bank is unwilling to lend to the ESOP, but is willing to lend to Employer. In this circumstance, Employer once again creates Newco as a wholly owned subsidiary, and forms an ESOP for Newco. Newco then borrows $3 million from the bank, guaranteed by Employer, and Newco then loans the $3 million to the ESOP on identical repayment terms. The ESOP uses the loan proceeds to purchase all outstanding Newco shares from Employer, and the shares are pledged as collateral for the ESOP's loan from Newco. Newco, going forward, makes deductible contributions to the ESOP of whatever amounts Newco would ultimately contribute to Newco under Example 3 (although the loan structure is back-to-back, the funding in the end should be identical). The ESOP would use the annual contributions from Newco to repay its debt to Newco, which in turn would use the payments from the ESOP to repay its debt to lender.

Comment: From the perspective of Newco, assuming the back-to-back loans are on identical terms, payments to Newco from the ESOP will exactly equal the amount of principal and interest owed by Newco to the lender. This means that Newco will once again be paying off the bank financing on a fully deductible basis. It will contribute to the ESOP on a deductible basis the exact amount of the debt service, will receive the payment back from the ESOP (with tax-free return of principal and taxable interest), and in turn will pay the outside lender nondeductible principal payments but deductible interest payments. Thus, the entire debt service amount is deductible.

For example, assume the debt service owed by Newco to the third-party lender requires an annual payment of $100,000, $40,000 of which is interest and $60,000 of which is principal. Newco contributes $100,000 to the ESOP as deductible contributions, and has a $100,000 deduction. Newco then receives a payment on its loan, $40,000 of which is interest income and $60,000 of which is tax-free return of principal. Newco then pays the $100,000 to the lender. $60,000 is nondeductible principal payment, and $40,000 is deductible interest. Newco ends up with a net deduction of $100,000 and a net payment to the lender of $100,000.

This illustrates that it does not matter whether the ESOP loan is a back-to-back loan or a direct loan by the bank to the ESOP: both the economic and tax results should be the same.

Example 6—ESOP and Charitable Giving: John Runson decides for family and financial estate planning reasons to contribute 20 percent of the stock in Employer Corporation to a charitable remainder trust, which will pay John and his wife an annuity for a specified period of time and then leave the remainder interest to a designated charity. Following the contribution of stock to the charitable remainder trust, an ESOP is established and purchases this 20 percent interest from the trust, after borrowing the funds from the bank. The sale creates a liquid market for the Employer shares and allows the sale to be financed on a pre-tax basis. Note that because the sale falls below the 30 percent threshold required by Code section 1042, there would be no available tax-free rollover of the proceeds; however, this is irrelevant in the case of a charitable remainder trust because the trust is already exempt from tax under Code section 501(c)(3).

Example 7—Charitable Contribution Followed by Sale to ESOP: In this transaction, the shareholder contributes stock in Employer to a charity, which promptly sells the stock for its fair market value (required by the ESOP rules) to an ESOP established by Employer. Assume the redemption price paid by the ESOP is $100,000 and the funds are provided to the ESOP by an Employer contribution. As a result of this transaction, the shareholder can claim a $100,000 charitable contribution deduction under Code section 170, the charity is able to liquidate the stock for cash, and Employer claims a $100,000 deduction for the cash contributed to the ESOP.

Comment: The transaction in Example 7 arguably provides a "double" deduction because both the corporation and the shareholder get the equivalent of a $100,000 deduction for the same $100,000 paid to the charity!

Example 8—Sale of C Corporation Stock to ESOP, Followed by S Election: Same facts as in Example 1, except that John Runson proposes to sell all his stock to the ESOP for $10 million. John borrows $10 million from the bank and loans the $10 million to Employer, which in turn loans it to the ESOP. The loan from John to the corporation is at the same interest rate and on the same payment terms as the loan from the bank (and the loan from the corporation to the ESOP).

The ESOP purchases 100 percent of John's stock for $10 million, and John uses the proceeds immediately to pay off the bank. Now, John has created a transaction economically similar to an installment sale of his stock to the ESOP, but it is technically a loan in a form of a promissory note from the corporation rather than from the ESOP. Assuming that John has substantial other sources of wealth, John can use any source of wealth to buy qualified replacement property (there are no tracing rules based on the source of funds) within the applicable twelve to fifteen month period under Code section 1042. John has thus diversified his investment portfolio tax-free and is now owed $10 million, plus interest, on his loan to Employer Corporation.

Employer and the ESOP participants now elect for Employer to be taxed as an S corporation after the sale. All income from the business activities of Employer are now exempt from federal and most state income taxes, and so the entire corporate tax flow can now be used to repay the back-to-back $10 million debt owed by the ESOP to Employer, or by Employer to John. Employer Corporation, of course, first makes contributions/distributions to the ESOP, which uses the contributions to pay its loan to Employer, which in turn uses the payments to pay its loan to John. As the ESOP debt owed to the corporation is paid off, the employees are allocated shares in the Employer stock.

Comment: An S corporation owned 100 percent by an ESOP is the equivalent of a tax-exempt organization. Both Code section 409(p) and Rev. Rul. 2004-4 look closely at transactions where S corporation ESOPs are being used aggressively, but the transaction described above is absolutely vanilla (John is totally cashed out, and we will assume the remaining shareholders are unrelated to John, so that there is no potential for abuse).

Example 9—S Corporation Distributes Shares to Employee: Corporation X, a calendar year S corporation, maintains Plan Y, an ESOP. Y holds 100 shares of X stock that it purchased on January 1, 2001, for $10,000 with employer contributions. Y's pro rata share of X's income for X's 2001 tax year is $1,000 (comprised entirely of nonseparately computed income of $10 per share), which Y properly reports on Form 5500, Annual Return/Report of Employee Benefit Plan. X makes no distributions to its shareholders during 2001.

A, an individual who is a U.S. citizen, is an employee of X and a participant in Y. Y holds five shares of X stock for the benefit of A from January 1 to December 31, 2001. On December 31, 2001, Y distributes the five shares of X stock to A, subject to A's right to require X to repurchase the shares under a fair valuation formula in accordance with Code section 409(h). On that date, the fair market value of the five shares is $580.

Stock of an S corporation held by an ESOP is subject to the same basis adjustments under Code section 1367(a) as stock held by any other S corporation shareholder. Accordingly, Y must increase its basis in X stock under Code section 1367(a)(1) for the items of income described in Code section 1366(a)(1). Specifically, Y's pro rata share of X's nonseparately computed income for X's 2001 taxable year increases the basis of each share of X stock held by Y by $10. Therefore, the basis of each of the five shares of X stock held by Y for the benefit of A is increased by $10 from $100 to $110.

Code section 402(e)(4)(B) provides that, for purposes of Code sections 402(a) and 72, in the case of any lump-sum distribution that includes securities of the employer corporation, there is excluded from gross income the net unrealized appreciation attributable to that part of the distribution that consists of securities of the employer corporation. Under Code section 402(e)(4) and Reg. § 1.402(a)-1(b)(2), the amount of net unrealized appreciation in the X stock is $30, the excess of the market value of the stock at the time of distribution ($580) over Y's adjusted basis in the stock ($550). Unless A rolls the distributed stock over into an eligible retirement plan in accordance with the rules of Code section 402(c), A will have $550 of ordinary income as a result of the distribution.[51]

CHAPTER ENDNOTES

1. See Chapter 10.
2. See IRC Sec. 385.
3. 1989-1 CB 675.
4. See IRC Sec. 305.
5. See "Building the New Berlin Wall: Treasury's Anti-Inversion Regulations," by Joseph B. Darby III, Business Entities, (a WGL publication) May/June 2016, pp. 20-27.
6. Prop. Reg. §§ 1.385-1 through 1.385-4; REG-108060-15, 81 Fed. Reg. 20,911 (Apr. 4, 2016).
7. On April 20, 2017 the Trump Administration signalled that it intended to review the anti-inversion regulations issued in 2016, most likely with the intention of rescinding or withdrawing them.
8. See Rev. Rul. 68-54, 1968-1 CB 69; Rev. Rul. 73-122, 1973-1 CB 66.
9. See, e.g., Kloppenberg & Co., 51 TCM 1607, Dec. 43,219(M), TC Memo. 1986-325.
10. S.Ct. 503 US 79, 112 S.Ct. 1039 (1992).
11. 27 F3d 367(1994).
12. S.Ct. 397 US 572, 90 S.Ct. 1302 (1970).
13. IRC Sec. 4975(e)(7).
14. IRC Sec. 404(a)(3).
15. IRC Sec. 404(a)(9).
16. IRC Sec. 404(k).
17. IRC Sec. 1042.
18. ERISA Sec. 408(b)(3) and IRC Sec. 4975(d)(3).
19. IRC Sec. 404(a)(3).
20. IRC Sec. 409(a)(9)(B).
21. IRC Sec. 404(a)(9)(C).
22. See IRS Letter Ruling 200436015, June 9, 2004.
23. Reg. § 1.404(k)-3 Q&A 1.
24. See IRC Sec. 404(a)(9)(C).
25. See IRC Sec. 404(k)(1).
26. See IRC Sec. 1042(c)(1)(A).
27. IRC Sec. 4975(f)(7).
28. See H.R. Rep. No. 51, 107th Cong., 1st Sess., Part 1, at p. 100 (2001).
29. See, e.g., Rev. Rul. 2004-4, 2004-1 CB 406.
30. ERISA Sec. 408(b)(3); 29 USC §1108(b)(3) CFR Sec. 2550.408b-3.
31. See IRC Sec. 409(e).
32. IRC Sec. 1042(b)(2).
33. IRC Sec. 1042(b)(4).
34. IRC Sec. 1042(c)(6).
35. IRC Sec. 1042(c)(1).
36. IRC Sec. 1042(c)(3).
37. IRC Sec. 1042(c)(4)(A)(i).
38. IRC Sec. 1042(c)(4)(A)(ii).
39. IRC Sec. 1042(c)(4)(B).
40. IRC Sec. 404(k).
41. See IRS Letter Ruling 9522041, March 6, 1995 (deduction allowed for dividends paid on preferred stock to an ESOP, where the dividend is a percentage of the issuing corporation's year-end pre-tax income).
42. IRC Sec. 404(k)(2)(A)(iii).
43. IRC Sec. 404(k)(5)(A).
44. Reg. § 1.404(k)-3 Q&A 1.
45. Prop. Reg. § 1.162(k)-1(a).
46. See Rev. Rul. 2004-4, 2004-1 CB 406.
47. IRC Sec. 404(a)(9)(A).
48. See IRC Sec. 404(a)(9)(A).
49. IRC Sec. 409(a)(9)(B).
50. IRC Sec. 404(a)(9)(B).
51. See Rev. Rul. 2003-27, 2003-1 CB 597.

TAX DEFERRAL/ REDUCTION BENEFITS UNDER CODE SECTIONS 1031, 1033, 1044, 1045, AND 1202

CHAPTER 19

OVERVIEW

A disposition of a business, whether through a sale of its assets or a sale of its equity, is typically treated for federal income tax purposes as a taxable sale or exchange of the applicable property, governed by Code section 1001. However, there are numerous exceptions to this rule. Among the ones discussed thus far in this book are the following:

1. Transactions that come within the nonrecognition provisions of Code section 368 (if the transaction qualifies as a "reorganization").

2. Tax-free business formation transactions under Code sections 351 or 721.

3. A qualifying reinvestment upon a sale of employer stock to an ESOP under Code section 1042.

4. Transactions that are treated as a taxable transaction but with a different tax character (e.g., a sale of stock that is recharacterized as a dividend under Code section 302 or a stock sale that is recharacterized as an asset sale because of an election under Code section 338).

In addition, Sellers can take advantage of other Code provisions that, if applicable to a transfer of a business or its assets, either cause the transaction not to be taxable currently, or cause it to be taxable at a more favorable rate. These provisions include the following:

1. Code section 1031, which permits nonrecognition of gain on a "like-kind" exchange of business assets.

2. Code section 1033, which permits nonrecognition on a replacement of involuntarily converted assets (e.g., assets taken by eminent domain power or assets destroyed by fire, flood, etc.).

3. Code section 1045, which permits a noncorporate shareholder who acquired through direct investment "qualified small business stock" (stock in a domestic C corporation with no more than $50 million in aggregate gross assets at the time of the investment) to defer gain on sale of such stock if it has been held more than six months and if the amount realized on the sale is reinvested in other qualified small business stock within sixty days.

4. Code section 1202, which provides for a partial exclusion of gain on sales of "qualified small business stock" held by noncorporate taxpayers for more than five years.

5. Code section 1044, which permits a tax-free rollover of gain on the sale of publicly traded securities (subject to an annual limitation of $50,000 and a $500,000 lifetime limitation for individuals, and an annual limitation of $250,000 and $1 million lifetime limitation for C corporations) if the amount realized on such sale is reinvested in a "specialized small business investment company."

Each of these provisions is discussed more fully below.

CODE SECTION 1031— LIKE-KIND EXCHANGES OF BUSINESS ASSETS

Overview. Code section 1031 is one of the most commonly exploited nonrecognition provisions in the Code. Indeed, each year U.S. taxpayers avoid billions of dollars of tax liability through the legitimate use of this Code provision. The large majority of like-kind exchange transactions involve exchanges of real estate, but a significant and perhaps growing number of exchange transactions involve nonrealty business assets, including property ranging from airplanes to radio stations to fleets of vehicles. This section will review the general rules for implementing a like-kind exchange under Code section 1031, and then discuss the rules specific to an exchange of assets used in a trade or business (as distinct from the more common exchange of real estate interests).

Code section 1031(a)(1) is a remarkably concise provision, and reads as follows:

> No gain or loss shall be recognized on the exchange of property held for productive use in a trade or business or for investment if such property is exchanged solely for property of like kind which is to be held either for productive use in a trade or business or for investment.

Almost every word or phrase in this sentence has important legal implications that will be discussed in greater detail below.

Comment: Like-kind exchange treatment is mandatory for transactions that meet the requirements of Code section 1031. This becomes important when a taxpayer would actually like to treat an exchange of real property as a recognition event (e.g., because the real property has a built-in loss). In a loss situation, it is often desirable to structure the transaction so that it fails to qualify for nonrecognition treatment under Code section 1031.

Code section 1031 can apply to either or both parties in an exchange transaction. Note that one party can be eligible for Code section 1031 treatment even though the other is not. For example, in a deferred like-kind exchange the accommodation party frequently is not eligible for Code section 1031 treatment because the accommodation party does not meet the "held" requirement, discussed below.

A related-party rule provides that if the taxpayer directly or indirectly exchanges property with a related party in a Code section 1031 exchange, and within two years either the related party or the taxpayer disposes of the new property, the original exchange will not qualify for nonrecognition under Code section 1031.[1] Certain types of dispositions, such as dispositions due to death, involuntary conversion, or not made for a tax avoidance purpose, are excepted from this rule.[2]

"Held for Productive Use in a Trade or Business or for Investment" There are two aspects to the "held" requirement (1) that property be "held," and (2) that property be held for "productive use in a trade or business or for investment."

The "held" requirement means that property is not eligible for Code section 1031 treatment if it is acquired solely to facilitate an exchange or otherwise is acquired for immediate transfer in a second transaction.[3] In substance, the IRS takes the position there is an implicit time period for which the property must be held.

A frequent situation where this "held" issue comes up is if property is held in a pass-through entity, such as a trust or a partnership, and the parties wish to break up their co-ownership by acquiring other property through the mechanism of a Section 1031 exchange. For example, the partners may wish to distribute partnership property to themselves as co-owners and then do a like-kind exchange whereby one former partner acquires a new property in exchange for his or her former interest in the partnership asset. However, because of the "held" requirement, such a "drop and swap" transaction is risky unless the partnership asset is distributed sufficiently far in advance so that the former partners can establish that they "held" the property individually prior to the second step of the transaction. Case law on these multi-step transactions tends to be quite favorable to taxpayers, but the very existence of a body of case law shows that the IRS has in the past been ready to litigate this issue.[4]

The second element is that property must be held "for productive use in a trade or business or for investment." The phrase "held for productive use in a trade or business..." is not defined in the Code or the regulations.

In the absence of any other guidance, it is probably reasonable to assume that this phrase has the same or similar meaning to the phrase "property used in the trade or business" for purposes of Code sections 167 and 1231. Applying these rules, personal property, such as a residence, or property held as inventory, will not qualify under this language, even if the property received in exchange is "like kind." One significant point is that the determination of whether property is held for investment or for use in a business often depends on a taxpayer's motives at the time a transaction occurs.

For example, a former residence can be converted to investment property, and vice versa, based on the use and intentions of the owner. A practical rule of thumb is to have at least one tax return showing that the real property is held for a qualifying use (e.g., by claiming depreciation) before you attempt to claim like-kind exchange treatment. One year of investment or business use would be the absolute minimum, and would probably be subject to close scrutiny and possible challenge by the IRS; three to four years of holding the property for an eligible purpose would be a much safer fact pattern.

"Like-Kind" Property Defined. By far the biggest constraint on implementing an exchange of non-real estate business assets is the requirement that the exchanged assets be of "like kind." The term "like kind" refers to the "nature or character of the property, and not its grade or quality."[5] One kind or class of property may not be exchanged for property of a different kind or class.[6]

As a practical matter, like-kind exchanges of real estate assets are usually much easier to implement than exchanges of non-real estate assets. Under the regulations, all real estate is like kind to all other real estate.[7] Thus, improved real estate used in a trade or business can be exchanged under Code section 1031 for unimproved land to be held for investment. A lease of real property with a remaining term of thirty years is considered "like kind" to a fee interest in real estate.[8] Shorter leaseholds are like kind to equivalent leaseholds.[9] An undivided interest as tenant in common in a parcel of real property can be exchanged for sole ownership of another parcel of real property.[10] Foreign real property and U.S. real property are not "like kind" for purposes of Section 1031.[11]

Personal property held for the requisite purposes may also be exchanged tax free under Code section 1031. However, exchanges of personal (non-real estate) property require a more careful matching of kind and class, which is not required of real estate. Note that although Code section 1031 can apply to an exchange of business assets, it will not apply to an exchange of equity. This is because Code section 1031(a)(2) expressly excludes from like-kind exchange treatment any exchange of "stock, bonds, or notes... other securities or evidence of indebtedness or interest... interests in a partnership ... certificates of trust or beneficial interests, or ... choses in action."

Determining Whether Business Assets are of "Like Kind". It is clear that a taxpayer can use Code section 1031 to implement a tax-free exchange of tangible personal property for other tangible personal property. An exchange of a truck used in a trade or business for a new truck to be used in a trade or business, or an automobile used in a trade or business for a new automobile to be used in the trade or business, constitutes a like-kind exchange.[12] Over the years, like-kind exchanges have encompassed everything from exchanges of major league[13] baseball contracts[14] to exchanges of forty-nine steer calves aged seven to eleven months for registered Aberdeen-Angus cattle.[15] The IRS, for example, has ruled that sports utility vehicles and passenger automobiles are like-kind property[16] based on the conclusion that the differences between an automobile and an SUV do not rise to the level of a difference in nature or character but are merely differences in grade or quality. However, the IRS reached an opposite conclusion in ruling that a light duty truck is not of like kind to an automobile because the vehicle is different in nature and character.[17] The IRS has held that gold bullion held for investment and silver bullion held for investment are not property of like kind.[18]

Regulatory Guidance on Whether Depreciable Tangible Personal Property is Like Kind. Reg. § 1.1031(a)-2 provides a variety of rules for determining whether an exchange of personal property is considered to be either of "like kind" or of "like class." The regulation states that personal properties of a "like class" are considered to be of a "like kind" for Code section 1031 purposes.[19] In addition, an exchange of like-kind property qualifies for nonrecognition whether or not such properties are of like class. In determining whether exchanged properties are of like kind, no inference is to be drawn from the fact that the properties are not of a like class.[20]

This far-from-intuitive discussion about "like kind" and "like class" is further explained and applied to depreciable tangible personal property by a classification system implemented in the regulations. The regulations provide for and define 13 General Asset Classes,[21] which are based in the asset classes originally defined in Rev. Proc. 87-56,[22] and also define Product Classes, which are based on the six-digit product classes defined under the North American Industry Classification System (NAICS).[23] These two classification systems are described in more detail below. Depreciable tangible personal property is of like class to other depreciable tangible personal property (and therefore "like kind") if they are either within the same General Asset Class or within the same Product Class.[24] A single property may not be classified within more than one General Asset Class or within more than one Product Class.[25] In addition, property classified within any General Asset Class may not be classified within a Product Class.[26] A property's General Asset Class or Product Class is determined as of the date of the exchange.[27]

Reg. § 1031(a)-2(b)(2) provides for 13 General Asset Classes, which again are based on the classes set forth in Rev. Proc. 87-56. These include the following: office furniture, fixtures, and equipment (asset class 00.11); information systems (computers and peripheral equipment) (asset class 00.12); data handling equipment, except computers (asset class 00.13); airplanes (airframes and engines), except those used in commercial or contract carrying of passengers or freight, and all helicopters (airframes and engines) (asset class 00.21); automobiles and taxis (asset class 00.22); buses (asset class 00.23); light general purpose trucks (asset class 00.241); heavy general purpose trucks (asset class 00.242); railroad cars and locomotives, except those owned by railroad transportation companies (asset class 00.25); tractor units for use over-the-road (asset class 00.26); trailers and trailer-mounted containers (asset class 00.27); vessels, barges, tugs, and similar water-transportation equipment, except those used in marine construction (asset class 00.28); and industrial steam and electric generation and/or distribution systems (asset class 00.4).

The regulations also define Product Classes, which consist of tangible personal property that is described in a six-digit product class within Sections 31, 32, and 33 of the North American Industry Classification System (NAICS) set forth in the Office of Management and Budgets' North American Industry Classification System (2002), as periodically updated ("the NAICS Manual").[28] Any six-digit Product Class ending in the number "9" (a miscellaneous category) is not considered a Product Class, and therefore property in such category cannot be considered of "like class" based on the NAICS Manual. However, the property may still be shown to be of like kind to other property.[29] Property that is listed in more than one Product Class is treated as listed in any one of those Product Classes.[30]

Reg. § 1.1031(a)-2(b)(7) provides the following examples to illustrate these rules:

Example 1. Taxpayer A transfers a personal computer (asset class 00.12) to B in exchange for a printer (asset class 00.12). With respect to A, the properties exchanged are within the same General Asset Class and therefore are of a like class.

Example 2. Taxpayer C transfers an airplane (asset class 00.21) to D in exchange for a heavy general purpose truck (asset class 00.242). The properties exchanged are not of a like class because they are within different General Asset Classes. Because each of the properties is within a General Asset Class, the properties may not be classified within a Product Class. The airplane and heavy general purpose truck are also not of a like kind. Therefore, the exchange does not qualify for nonrecognition of gain or loss under section 1031.

Example 3. Taxpayer E transfers a grader to F in exchange for a scraper. Neither property is within any of the general asset classes. However, both properties are within the same product class (NAICS code 333120). The grader and scraper are of a like class and deemed to be of a like kind for purposes of section 1031.

Example 4. Taxpayer G transfers a personal computer (asset class 00.12), an airplane (asset class 00.21) and a sanding machine (NAICS code 333210), to H in exchange for a printer (asset class 00.12), a heavy general purpose truck (asset class 00.242) and a lathe (NAICS code 333210). The personal computer and the printer are of a like class because they are within the same general asset class. The sanding machine and the lathe are of a like class because they are within the same product class (although neither property is within any of the general asset classes). The airplane and the heavy general purpose truck are neither within the same general asset class nor within the same product class, and are not of a like kind.

Intangible Property and Nondepreciable Personal Property. Intangible personal property and nondepreciable personal property can also be eligible for Code section 1031 exchange treatment.[31] However, a determination of what is and is not of "like kind" is often even more uncertain and complex than with tangible property. Under the regulations, intangible personal property is not divided into "classes," both because of the variety of such kinds of property and the lack of a readily available classification system. Instead, the regulations state that the like-kind test "depends on the nature or character of the rights involved (e.g., a patent or a copyright) and also on the nature or character of the underlying property to which the intangible personal property relates."[32]

The regulations take the very broad and encompassing view that goodwill and going concern value of a business are never like kind to the goodwill and going concern value of another business.[33] *Note:* It is not clear that this regulatory prohibition on exchanging goodwill and going concern is within the regulatory authority of the IRS. The ambiguity is especially pronounced since many of the assets that the IRS does recognize as exchangeable, namely trademarks, trade names, and other similar assets, often have substantial goodwill or going concern value.

The following examples from the regulations illustrate these rules:[34]

Example (1). Taxpayer K exchanges a copyright on a novel for a copyright on a different novel. The properties exchanged are of a like kind.

Example (2). Taxpayer J exchanges a copyright on a novel for a copyright on a song. The properties exchanged are not of a like kind.

In TAM 200035005,[35] the IRS issued a surprisingly broad ruling on an exchange of radio licenses for a television license. The taxpayer proposed to transfer radio stations, including FCC radio licenses involving AM and FM frequencies, located in three different cities, in exchange for a television station, including the FCC television license, based in a fourth (separate) city. The ruling request focused solely on the exchange of the radio licenses for the television license, although the ruling did suggest in passing that the taxpayer's position was that the tangible property exchanged was in the same SIC product class. The IRS stated that the determination of whether the licenses were of like kind depended on (1) the nature or character of the rights involved; and (2) the nature or character of the underlying property to which the intangible personal property relates. Applying this two-prong test, the IRS concluded that the rights conferred under FCC licenses, whether for radio or television, were identical in most respects, and that the differences do not change the nature or character of the rights granted in the licenses, but are merely differences in grade or quality. The IRS further concluded that the "underlying property" referred to in the regulations in this case comprised the "electromagnetic spectrum" under which radio and television licenses operate. The IRS concluded that the property was like kind even though radio and television are assigned different specific frequencies on the electromagnetic spectrum. Television requires a much broader bandwidth than an audio broadcast, and a radio licensee cannot use its frequency to broadcast television, nor can a television frequency broadcast radio. However, the IRS concluded that these differences are not differences "in nature and character" but are merely differences "in grade or quality."

Given the rather specific standards for determining what constitutes a like-kind asset, it would be logical and certainly conservative to evaluate an exchange of business assets for other business assets on an asset-by-asset basis.[36] However, the IRS in the past has sometimes taken a much broader approach to business exchanges. In Rev. Rul. 85-135,[37] the IRS determined that the taxpayers, exchanging two television stations, recognized no gain or loss on the exchange, and gave no indication that the taxpayers had to or should have analyzed the exchange on an asset-by-asset basis. The IRS took a similarly broad approach in certain subsequent private letter rulings, but these were thereafter revoked. In Rev. Rul. 89-121,[38] the IRS ruled that the exchange of assets in a business for assets of a similar business may not be treated as an exchange of a single property without an analysis of the assets being exchanged. This rule supposedly "clarified" Rev. Rul. 85-135.

In TAM 200602034,[39] the IRS confirmed its position that an exchange of businesses must be analyzed on an asset-by-asset basis, citing Rev. Rul. 89-121, and provided guidance on how it intends to apply its two-part analysis for whether intangible property (and nondepreciable personal property) is "like kind," i.e., (1) the character of the rights involved and (2) the nature of character of the underlying property to which the intangible personal property relates. In TAM 200602034, the taxpayer entered into four distinct transactions involving the transfer and acquisition of tangible and intangible business assets. The taxpayer claimed like-kind exchange treatment for the intangible assets, but did not claim like-kind exchange treatment with respect to any of the tangible assets. The exchanged intangible assets included (1) patents, (2) trademarks and trade names, (3) designs and drawings, (4) software, and (5) trade secrets and know-how. The IRS noted that when personal property is concerned, the IRS standards for determining whether property is "like kind" have been stricter than for real property, and that such policy had withstood judicial scrutiny, citing *California Federal Life Ins. Co.*[40] The IRS then stated that in the case of exchanges of intangible property, the standards are even more rigorous than for tangible property. Turning to the intangible property before it, the IRS analyzed the assets as follows:

- For patents, the IRS concluded that the first prong of its test was satisfied, and, in applying the second prong, looked at whether the property to be made under the respective patents would be within the same General Asset Class or same Product Class, or would otherwise be like kind.

- For trademarks and tradenames, the IRS held that they are closely related to (or part of) goodwill or going concern value and thus could not qualify as "like kind."

- For "unregistered intellectual property" (including designs and drawings, software, and trade secrets), the IRS was fairly liberal in concluding that such assets generally satisfy the first prong of its test, and therefore, like patents, focused on whether the specific underlying properties to which the unregistered intangibles related are within the same General Asset Class or same Product Class.

- The exchanges included certain "foreign intangibles" and the IRS ruled that Code section 1031(h)(2) applies to both tangible and intangible personal property, and held that property used predominantly in the United States is not like kind with property used predominantly outside the United States. The IRS concluded that "use" takes place where intangible assets are "enjoyed" and not whether they are owned or managed.

- The IRS also noted certain deficiencies in the identification of replacement properties, and ruled that no proper identification occurred except as to the replacement property received within the identification period.

Comment: Although the IRS "talks tough" about applying a narrow standard to intangible property, TAM 200602034 provides substantially more guidance than existed previously concerning the possibilities (and perils) of exchanging intangible business assets for other intangible business assets. Overall, this is likely to encourage rather than discourage efforts to structure like-kind exchanges of business assets.

See also the like-kind exchange rules under Reg. § 1.1060–1(b)(8).

"Exchange" Requirement. The "exchange" requirement is simultaneously a necessary and an exceedingly awkward element of Code section 1031. The exchange requirement has always been part of the statutory scheme laid out in Code section 1031 and its predecessor provisions, and today it continues to be a required element to enjoying nonrecognition benefits. However, one can argue rather compellingly that the regulations enacted in 1991 (discussed more fully below) and subsequent IRS rulings and procedures have transformed the "exchange" requirement into a mere formality that is all form and no substance, and that today the requirement is simply a vestige from the past. Nonetheless, the "exchange" element remains a basic requirement and often a major hurdle in structuring a transaction to qualify for the nonrecognition benefits of Code section 1031.

The exchange requirement is conceptually straightforward if only two parties are involved. However, in the real world it is difficult to locate and match up two parties willing to enter into a true bi-lateral exchange transaction, and so exchanges were notably difficult to implement prior to 1991. In that year, the "Starker Regulations" gave a formal blessing to the use of a "qualified intermediary," who is a party paid a fee by the taxpayer to facilitate an exchange. A taxpayer can hire a qualified intermediary, find a purchaser ("buyer") of the taxpayer's property (the "relinquished property"), sell the relinquished property through the qualified intermediary to the buyer, and use the proceeds from that sale to purchase like-kind property (the "replacement property") through the qualified intermediary from a separate, unrelated party ("seller"). These regulations also approved (and gave substantial guidance on how to implement) a deferred exchange, whereby the qualified intermediary sells the relinquished property to the buyer, and then holds the proceeds for a period of up to 180 days while the taxpayer identifies (within forty-five days) and then enters into a purchase contract for the replacement property, which property is then acquired by the qualified intermediary and transferred to the taxpayer, all within the applicable 180-day period.

Qualified Intermediary Requirements. Reg. § 1.1031(k)-1(g)(4) provides that a "qualified intermediary" can serve as a facilitator in a like-kind exchange transaction without causing the original transferor to be deemed to have actual or constructive receipt of money. A qualified intermediary is a person who (1) is not the taxpayer or a "disqualified person" and (2) acts to facilitate the deferred exchange by entering into a written agreement with the taxpayer for the exchange of properties pursuant to which such person acquires the relinquished property from the taxpayer (either on its own behalf or as the agent of any party to the transaction), transfers the relinquished property, acquires the replacement property (either on its own behalf or as the agent of any party to the transaction), and transfers the replacement property to the taxpayer.[41]

Deferred Like-Kind Exchanges. In *T.J. Starker*,[42] the court approved a five-year deferral in completion of a Section 1031 transaction, which led to statutory changes enacted in 1984 that are embodied in Code section 1031(a)(3). The "Statutory Starker" rules require that the parties to the exchange must identify the replacement property within forty-five days of a transfer and close the exchange within 180 days of the first transfer or the filing date of the transferor's return, whichever is earlier. These rules, in turn, were given elaborate definition and practical implementation through the 1991 regulations.

A "Reverse Starker" exchange, in which the taxpayer receives replacement property before he or she transfers the relinquished property, is now also permitted under a "safe harbor" promulgated by the IRS in Rev. Proc. 2000-37.[43] Also called a "parking lot transaction," the taxpayer can acquire a replacement property in advance and "park" the property with an "exchange accommodation titleholder" (EAT) until the taxpayer is ready to implement a conventional "forward exchange" using a qualified intermediary (QI). The QI, which is permitted to be the EAT or is otherwise usually related to the EAT, is assigned the purchase and sale agreement for the relinquished property, transfers that property to the buyer, and then transfers the "parked" replacement property in completion of the exchange. Rev. Proc. 2000-37 generally looks to the regulations governing deferred exchanges to provide similar rules for parking transactions (e.g., with respect to identification and other mechanical rules and procedures).

Identification and Receipt Requirements. The regulations specify the manner for identifying replacement property. It must be identified in a written document signed by the taxpayer and hand-delivered, mailed, telecopied, or otherwise sent before the end of the identification period (forty-five days from the date of the original transfer) to a person involved in the exchange other than the taxpayer or a disqualified person (as defined in Reg. § 1.1031(k)-1(k)).[44] An identification made in a written agreement signed by all parties thereto before the end of the identification period will be treated as meeting the identification requirements.[45] Notwithstanding the identification requirements described above, if replacement property is received by the taxpayer before the end of the identification period, the property in all events will be treated as identified before the end of such period.[46]

Replacement property is identified only if it is unambiguously described in the written document or agreement.[47] Real property generally is unambiguously described if it is described by a legal description or street address or distinguishable name (such as "Empire State Building").[48]

The regulations provide important flexibility by allowing taxpayers to identify more than one property as replacement property. Regardless of the number of relinquished properties transferred by the taxpayer as part of the exchange, the maximum number of replacement properties the taxpayer may identify is (1) three properties without regard to the fair market value of the properties (the "Three-Property Rule"), or (2) any number of properties as long as their aggregate fair market value (on a gross basis—i.e., without regard to liabilities which encumber the property) as of the end of the identification period does not exceed 200 percent of the aggregate fair market value of all the relinquished properties as of the date the relinquished properties were transferred by the taxpayer (the "200-Percent Rule").[49]

If, as of the end of the identification period, the taxpayer has identified more properties than permitted by the Three-Property Rule or the 200-Percent Rule, the taxpayer is treated as if no replacement property had been identified.[50] However, the identification requirements will be deemed satisfied with respect to (1) any property received by the taxpayer before the end of the identification period, and (2) any replacement property identified before the end of the identification period and received before the end of the exchange period, but only if the taxpayer receives before the end of the exchange period identified replacement property constituting at least 95 percent of the aggregate fair market value of all identified replacement properties.[51]

An identification of property may be revoked at any time before the end of the identification period if the revocation is made in a written document signed by the taxpayer and delivered, in the same manner as required for the original identification notice, to the person to whom the original identification notice was sent.[52]

Receipt of "Identified Replacement Property". Once property is identified, the taxpayer will be deemed to have received the identified property if (1) the taxpayer receives it before the end of the exchange period, and (2) it is "substantially the same property" as identified.[53] The regulations do not define "substantially," but Example 4 in Reg. § 1.1031(k)-1(d)(2) indicates an informal "75 percent" test. Thus, if taxpayer B identifies real property P, consisting of two acres of unimproved land with the fair market value of $250,000, and later receives one and one-half acres of property P for an assumed transactional value of $187,500, and the portion received does not differ from the basic nature or character of P as a whole, B is considered to have received substantially the same property as identified. (*Note:* This is a simplification of a more complicated fact pattern.)

Special Rules for Identification and Receipt of Property to Be Produced. The regulations confirm that it is possible to have a Code section 1031 transaction where the replacement property is not yet in existence at the time it is "identified" as replacement property.[54]

Property to be produced is subject to the same identification requirements as other types of property. For example, if the identified replacement property consists of real property where improvements are to be constructed, the identification requirements can be satisfied by providing a legal description of the underlying land and as much detail as practicable at the time the identification is made regarding construction of the improvements.[55] In turn, whether there is receipt of the "identified replacement property" is determined by whether the taxpayer has received substantially the same "property" described at the time of the identification, allowing for variations due to usual or typical production changes.[56] However, if substantial changes are made in the property to be produced, the replacement property received will not be considered to be substantially the same property as identified.[57]

The 180-day rule continues to apply to this type of transaction, so the property must be received within the 180-day period whether or not it is completed. Any additional production occurring with respect to the replacement property after the property is received by the taxpayer will not be treated as receipt of property of a like kind.[58]

Boot Rules—Receipt of Money or Other Property. Reg. § 1.1031(k)-1(f) and (g) provides general rules about actual or constructive receipt. The regulations basically indicate that if a taxpayer does not comply with the safe harbors, the constructive-receipt doctrine remains a substantial problem.

Meaning of "boot." Code section 1031 allows the taxpayer to avoid recognition of gain only if the like-kind property is exchanged "solely" for property of a like kind. It is virtually impossible in the real world to find a parcel of real estate exactly equal in value to the parcel that one is transferring. Accordingly, there is almost always an adjustment between the parties in the form of cash, other property and/ or assumption of debt. In general, the receipt of any nonqualifying property, whether cash or other property, and including specifically the income imputed to a taxpayer as a result of the net assumption of indebtedness by the other party in exchange, is called "boot" and results in taxable income or gain being recognized by the transferor in the exchange transaction, up to the lesser of the total gain or the full amount of the boot. It should be emphasized, however, that even when "boot" is received, the remaining portion of the gain in excess of the boot amount will be eligible for Code section 1031 treatment.

Amount of boot. Boot rules are mechanical to apply but complex. As noted above, boot causes recognition of gain in an amount equal to the *lesser* of (1) the full amount of gain realized in the exchange, or (2) the amount of the boot.

Types of boot. Boot is a colloquial term used to describe the cash and other nonqualifying property received in addition to qualifying property in a Section 1031 exchange. The amount of boot is equal to the sum of the money plus the fair market value of the other nonqualifying property received in the exchange.[59]

Consideration received in the form of an assumption of liabilities (or a transfer subject to a liability) is to be treated as "other property or money" for the purposes of Code section 1031(b).[60] Where, on an exchange described in Code section 1031(b), each party to the exchange either assumes a liability of the other party or acquires property subject to a liability, then, in determining the amount of "other property or money" for purposes of Code section 1031(b), consideration given in the form of an assumption of liabilities (or a receipt of property subject to a liability) shall be offset against consideration received in the form of an assumption of liabilities (or a transfer subject to a liability).[61]

Consideration given in the form of cash or other property is netted against consideration received in the form of an assumption of liability or a transfer of property subject to a liability; however, consideration received in the form of cash or other property is not netted against consideration given in the form of an assumption of liability or a receipt of properties subject to a liability.[62]

Examples of boot rules. Examples of boot rules are shown below.

Example 1: Chad Kauffman, in a transaction qualifying under Section 1031, transfers property with a fair market value of $200,000, a tax basis of zero, and subject to a liability of $100,000 to Marisa Kane in exchange for property with a fair market value of $150,000 and subject to a liability of $50,000. Since the transaction resulted in a net reduction of $50,000 in the amount of liabilities either assumed by Chad or to which Chad's property was subject, Chad is deemed to have received boot to the extent of such reduction in net liabilities. Therefore, Chad will recognize gain on the transaction equal to the lesser of (1) the total gain realized by Chad on the transaction or (2) the amount of boot ($50,000).[63] Since the gain realized on the transaction is $200,000 (fair market value of $200,000 over tax basis of zero) the amount of gain currently recognized by Chad on the exchange transaction under these rules is $50,000.

Meanwhile, on the other side of the transaction, Marisa has also engaged in a like-kind exchange. However, Marisa has experienced a net increase in indebtedness (from $50,000 to $100,000) and so she is deemed not to receive any other property in this transaction under the liability netting rules.[64]

Example 2: Barbara Caudle, in a like-kind exchange transaction qualifying under Section 1031, transfers property with a fair market value of $300,000, a tax basis of zero, and subject to a liability of $200,000 plus cash of $50,000 and securities worth $50,000 to Wendy Talbott in exchange for property with a fair market value of $250,000, a tax basis of $100,000, and subject to a liability of $50,000.

Barbara has received boot in the amount of $50,000 determined as follows: indebtedness relieved of $200,000 is treated as money received, minus money deemed paid in the form of indebtedness on replacement property ($50,000) and minus cash and securities given ($100,000). Barbara will therefore recognize gain equal to the lesser of the gain realized on the transaction or the boot. Since the gain realized (fair market value of $300,000 minus tax basis of zero equals $300,000 of realized gain) is greater than the boot ($50,000), the amount of gain is the lesser of these two amounts, or $50,000.

Wendy, meanwhile, has received boot in the amount of $100,000, in the form of the cash and securities received by Wendy from Barbara. Note that although Wendy has taken on an additional $150,000 of indebtedness in the exchange, the $100,000 of consideration received by Wendy in the form of cash or other property cannot be netted against consideration given in the form of an assumption of liability or a receipt of properties subject to a liability.[65] Wendy will recognize the lesser of gain realized (fair market value of $250,000 minus tax basis of $100,000, or $150,000) or the boot ($100,000), and so the gain recognized by Wendy is $100,000.

Observation: If Barbara had instead used $100,000 of Barbara's assets to pay down the liability on Barbara's property before the exchange, so that a property with a fair market value of $300,000 and subject to a liability of (after paydown) $100,000, were being exchanged for a property with a value of $250,000 and subject to a liability of $50,000, Barbara would still have $50,000 of "boot" on the transaction (because of a reduction in net liabilities from $100,000 to $50,000). However, Wendy would now receive no boot on the transaction, since Wendy would be increasing liabilities from $50,000 to $100,000. Moreover, immediately following this transaction, Wendy could refinance the newly acquired property, increasing the debt to $200,000, and effectively take out the $100,000 in cash, but now it would be tax-free!

Example 3: Evan Stone, in a like-kind exchange transaction qualifying under Section 1031, transfers property with a fair market value of $350,000, tax basis of $100,000, and subject to a liability of $150,000 to Kevin Syzdek in exchange for property with a fair market value of $300,000, tax basis of $150,000, and subject to a liability of $200,000 plus cash in the amount of $100,000.

Evan has received boot in the amount of $100,000: a deemed cash payment of $150,000 for the indebtedness to which the transferred property was subject, which amount is offset by indebtedness of $200,000 on the acquired property; however, Evan will have $100,000 of boot as a result of the cash received. Again, this illustrates that although a taxpayer may net boot given in the form of indebtedness against boot received in the form of indebtedness, the taxpayer may not net boot given in the form of indebtedness against boot received in the form of cash or other property. Evan's realized gain on the transaction is $250,000 (fair market value of the property of $350,000 over tax basis of $100,000) and the boot amount is $100,000, so Evan will recognize the lesser of these two amounts.[66]

Kevin, meanwhile, has not received any boot under the applicable rules. Kevin has been deemed to receive consideration of $200,000 (the liabilities to which the transferred property was subject), and has been deemed to give consideration of $150,000 (liabilities to which the replacement property received by Kevin is subject) and has paid an additional $100,000 in cash, which can also be used to offset consideration received in the form of liabilities assumed. As this example illustrates, cash given by Kevin can offset consideration received in the form of liabilities assumed for boot netting purposes, but the converse is not true, i.e., consideration given by Evan in the form of liabilities assumed by Evan cannot be used to offset cash boot received by Evan.

Capital gain treatment of boot. Where boot is received by a party in a transaction otherwise qualifying under Code section 1031, the taxpayer typically recognizes capital gain. This is because, by definition, an asset qualifying under Code section 1031, must be used by the taxpayer in a trade or business or held for investment, and thus must necessarily be a capital asset (or a Code section 1231 asset) in the hands of the exchangor. However, it is possible to realize a recapture of depreciation under Code section 1245 or Code section 1250 in a Section 1031 exchange, in which case the recognition of boot can result in recognition, in whole or in part, of ordinary income or unrecaptured Section 1250 gain. Also, an investment tax credit must be recaptured on a disposition of the investment property. This recapture rule encompasses dispositions pursuant to tax-free exchanges.

Basis and Depreciation in Replacement Property. The basis of property received in an exchange qualifying under Section 1031 is the basis of the property surrendered, decreased by the amount of money received, and then increased by any gain or decreased by any loss recognized on the exchange.[67] The basis of the property received is also increased by the amount of brokerage commissions paid by the taxpayer.[68]

Depreciation. The IRS takes the position that property received in a Section 1031 exchange is depreciated under MACRS (current Code section 168) even if the relinquished property was depreciated under the more favorable ACRS.[69]

CODE SECTION 1033—INVOLUNTARY CONVERSIONS

Code section 1033 is a nonrecognition provision similar to Code section 1031 that is intended to mitigate the otherwise-harsh tax consequences that would occur when property (including business property) is subject to an "involuntary conversion." In general, when property is subject to destruction, theft, or taking by eminent domain, the "conversion" of the property is not only an economic reversal but also a taxable event! In particular, if a taxpayer receives a condemnation award or insurance payment for the value (or approximating the value) of converted property, then, absent the provisions of Code section 1033, the receipt of such proceeds would be treated as a sale or exchange of the converted property and could trigger taxable gain, thus compounding the economic disaster with an echoing tax disaster. The likelihood that proceeds will exceed significantly the tax basis of an asset is especially pronounced with depreciable real estate (since value often goes up even as tax basis goes down), but could happen generally to any common appreciating asset used in a business.

To ameliorate this harsh result, Code section 1033 provides that "if property (as a result of its destruction in whole or in part, theft, seizure, or requisition or condemnation or threat or imminence thereof) is compulsorily or involuntarily converted" no gain will be recognized if the converted property is timely replaced with property "similar or related in service or use" within applicable time periods, and so long as certain requirements are met.

> ***Comment:*** Obviously, an "involuntary conversion" of property by its nature is not part of a planned disposition of business assets. However, once an involuntary conversion occurs, the exercise of replacing the converted property is often similar to an acquisition of business assets—with complexity, unpredictability, and time limitations thrown in for good measure.

Under Code section 1033, a taxpayer who realizes gain on an involuntary conversion can elect to defer all or a portion of such gain (and in some circumstances is required to defer such gain) if the taxpayer acquires property "similar or related in use" and certain timing and other requirements are met.

An "involuntary conversion" includes the destruction of property in whole or in part, the theft of property, the seizure of property, the requisition or condemnation of property, or the threat or imminence of requisition or condemnation of property, or a conversion into similar property, into money, or into dissimilar property.[70]

If there is an involuntary conversion of property directly into other property similar or related in use, the nonrecognition provisions of Code section 1033 are mandatory, even if the taxpayer would prefer otherwise.[71] By contrast, if property is involuntarily converted into money (which is usually the case) or property not similar or related in use, gain on the conversion is recognized; but then, if the taxpayer acquires timely other property "similar or related in service or use" (or a controlling interest in a corporation holding such property), the taxpayer can elect not to recognize all or a portion of such gain.[72] Code section 1033 applies only with respect to gains, and losses from involuntary conversions are recognized or not recognized without regard to that section.[73]

The "similar or related in service or use" standard for qualifying replacement property under Code section 1033 is a significantly narrower and more stringent category of comparison than the "like kind" standard used under Code section 1031. For example, in a case where rental real estate was destroyed by fire and a replacement building on the same land was used for "private offices," the Tax Court held that the replacement property did not qualify as "similar or related in service or use," since a mere showing that both old property and new property are general business properties is insufficient where functionally the new building was not similar to or related in use to the old building.[74] On the other hand, in a case involving two unimproved parcels of industrial property of different sizes, the Tax Court observed that no two parcels of real estate can be similar in all respects, and concluded that the replacement parcel met the "similar" test because it was of similar class and location, being industrial property in the same city adjacent to the same public services and labor markets.[75]

Code section 1033 does adopt the "like-kind" test as its standard for qualifying replacement property where there is an eminent domain-type taking of real property. In particular, Code 1033(g)(1) provides that "if real property held for productive use in trade or business or for investment is (as the result of its seizure, requisition, or condemnation, or threat or imminence thereof) compulsorily or involuntarily converted, property of a like kind to be held either for productive use in trade or business or for investment shall be treated as property similar or related in service or use to the property so converted."

Although the "similar" test under Code section 1033 generally requires a more stringent similarity than the "like kind" test under Code section 1031, there can be specific circumstances where the Section 1033 standard may actually be broader. For example, a replacement building on land already owned by the taxpayer can qualify as property similar or related in use but cannot qualify as like-kind property.

The replacement period under Code section 1033 generally runs from the earlier of the date of the involuntary conversion, or the date condemnation was first threatened or became imminent,[76] and continues until two years after the close of the first tax year in which any gain from the conversion is realized.[77] Code section 1033(g)(4) extends this Section 1033 replacement period from "two years" to "three years" in the case of condemnation or threat of condemnation of real property held for productive use in a trade of business or for investment.

Comment: The Code section 1033 replacement period, though dramatically longer than the 180-day deferred exchange period allowed for like-kind exchanges, is still often not long enough. For example, it is not unusual in a condemnation case for the taking party (some branch of government) to offer a "low ball" condemnation award, forcing the taxpayer to litigate for a larger award, and such cases can go on for years. Fortunately, a taxpayer can apply to the IRS for an extension of the replacement period.[78] Be aware, however, that the extension application must be submitted before the end of the applicable two-year (or three-year) period.[79] The IRS does have authority to waive a late application if the taxpayer can show to the satisfaction of the IRS: (1) reasonable cause for his failure to file the application within that period and (2) the late application was made within a reasonable time after the expiration of that period.[80] Although the IRS is generally liberal in granting extensions, a prudent taxpayer may nonetheless decide to reinvest any proceeds received within the required replacement period, even if more are expected to be recovered eventually.

CODE SECTION 1045—ELECTION TO NOT RECOGNIZE GAIN ON SALE OF QUALIFIED SMALL BUSINESS STOCK (QSBS)

Code section 1045, added to the Code by the Taxpayer Relief Act of 1997, generally provides that an eligible taxpayer (an individual or a pass-through entity, but not a C corporation) may elect not to recognize capital gain from the sale of "qualified small business stock" (stock issued to the taxpayer as a result of a direct investment in a C corporation that had less than $50 million of capital at the time of the investment) provided that the qualified small business stock (QSBS) being sold has been held for more than six months and provided the taxpayer purchases other QSBS within the sixty-day period beginning on the date of the sale.

Comment: The specific requirements of Code section 1045 are highly technical and require careful analysis. In general, this Code provision is both cumbersome in its language and awkward in its cross references to other complicated Code provisions. The following is a more detailed look at the various requirements.

Eligible Taxpayers. An eligible taxpayer is defined as any taxpayer "other than a corporation."[81] Notwithstanding this language, Code section 1045 in fact bars only a C corporation stockholder from utilizing these provisions; it treats an S corporation as a pass-through entity eligible for the benefits of Code section 1045. See Code section 1045(b)(5), which incorporates by reference certain rules of Code section 1202, including 1202(g)(4), which includes S corporations among the eligible taxpayers.

QSBS—Acquisition Requirements. The taxpayer must hold "qualified small business stock," which has the meaning given such term by Code section 1202(c).[82] First, the stock must be issued after August 10, 1993. Second, the stock must be acquired in a qualifying manner, which generally means acquired by the taxpayer at its original issue, either directly or through an underwriter, in exchange for money or other property (but not stock) or as compensation for services provided to the issuing corporation, other than services performed as an underwriter for the stock.[83] Third, the issuing corporation must meet the issuer requirements, discussed below.

QSBS—Acquisition through Options. There are special rules for stock acquired through the exercise of options. Stock acquired through an option exercise is treated as acquired at original issue, and thus meets that part of the QSBS definition. (*Note:* The stock option apparently must still be acquired from the issuing company and must be for money or property, or received as compensation for services.) However, a potential concern is that, when stock is acquired on an option exercise, the determination of whether the C corporation issuer meets the gross assets test (discussed below), is made at the time of the exercise or conversion, and the holding period of the stock for purposes of the six-month requirement of Code section 1045 also begins at that time.

QSBS—Issuer Requirements. In order for its stock to be QSBS, the issuing corporation must, at the date of its issuance of the applicable shares of stock, be a "qualified small business," which in turn has the following requirements:

1. The company in question must be a domestic (U.S.) C corporation.[84]
2. The corporation's gross assets cannot exceed certain limitations.[85]
3. The corporation must comply with any reporting requirements imposed by the IRS.[86]
4. During substantially all of the taxpayer's holding period of the stock, the corporation must have been a C corporation that met the active business requirements of Code section 1202(e), and was an "eligible corporation."[87]

The term "eligible corporation" includes all domestic C corporations other than a DISC or former DISC, a corporation that directly or indirectly uses the Code section 936 possessions credit, a RIC, REIT or REMIC, or a cooperative.[88]

QSBS—Gross Assets Limitation. The most significant concern is normally whether the issuing corporation satisfied the gross assets limitation, set forth at Code section 1202(d)(1)(B), at the time that stock was issued (or on the date the taxpayer exercised his or her options to acquire the related shares of stock). The requirements to meet the gross assets limitation are as follows:[89]

1. At all times after August 10, 1993, and before it issues the stock, the corporation must have aggregate gross assets (as defined below) that do not exceed $50 million.
2. Immediately after it issues the stock, the corporation must have aggregate gross assets that do not exceed $50 million. For this purpose, amounts received in the issuance are taken into account.

For purposes of these rules, "aggregate gross assets" means the sum of the cash and the aggregate adjusted bases of other property held by the corporation.[90] The adjusted basis of any property contributed to the corporation, and of any property whose basis is determined in whole or in part by reference to the adjusted basis of property so contributed, is determined by treating the basis of the contributed property immediately after the contribution as equal to its fair market value at that time.[91]

Comment: When stock options are issued, the taxpayer must measure both the six-month holding date and the corporation must meet the gross asset test based on the time the options were exercised, not when the options were first issued. The gross asset test is based on cash plus tax basis in corporate property, and it is a pretty large company that exceeds this limitation. Most publicly traded companies probably were not likely to exceed this level before completing an IPO.

Comment: If the issuing corporation satisfies these gross asset tests immediately after the issuance of stock to the taxpayer (including immediately after the exercise of a stock option), the stock remains QSBS (assuming all the other requirements are met) even if the issuing corporation subsequently goes over the $50 million gross asset level. Once a corporation exceeds this $50 million level, however, it can never issue QSBS again, even if it later dips below the $50 million level.[92]

QSBS—Active Business Requirement. There is also an active business requirement, which means at least 80 percent of the issuing corporation's assets must be used in the active conduct of one or more qualified trades or businesses.[93] A "qualified trade or business" is any trade or business other than:

1. One involving the performance of services in the fields of health, law, engineering, architecture, accounting, actuarial science, performing arts, consulting, athletics, financial services, or brokerage services.[94]
2. One where the principal asset of the trade or business is the reputation or skill of one or more of its employees.[95]
3. Any banking, insurance, financing, leasing, investing, or similar businesses.[96]
4. Any farming business, including the business of raising or harvesting trees.[97]

5. Any business involving the production or extraction of products of a character for which a depletion deduction is allowable.[98]

6. Any business of operating a hotel, motel, restaurant, or similar business.[99]

QSBS Must Be Held at Least Six Months. The stock must be held for at least six months to qualify for nonrecognition treatment.[100] However, a problem with option stock is that the holding period (and, probably more importantly, the gross asset test) does not start (and is not measured) until the option is exercised.[101]

Capital Asset Requirement. The QSBS must be a capital asset in the hands of the taxpayer. Note that Code section 1045(a) talks about nonrecognition of gain and expressly excludes from eligibility a sale that produces ordinary income. Therefore, technically, it would appear that ISO stock must be held for the two-year/one-year periods under Code section 422 in order to be eligible for Code section 1045, and that any disqualifying disposition of the ISO stock (e.g., a sale after stock has been held for six months, but before the two-year/one-year requirements have been met) would not be eligible for Section 1045.

Sale of QSBS. There must be a "sale" of the QSBS.[102] There are complicated issues about whether an "exchange" (receiving back property other than money) also qualifies,[103] but a sale for cash is clearly a qualifying sale.

Replacement Purchase of QSBS in Sixty Days. The replacement purchase must be a purchase of QSBS and must occur within the sixty-day period beginning on the date of the sale.[104] Since sixty days can be a remarkably short period of time, it is important to note when the period starts and when it ends. The language suggests that the day of the sale is day one of the sixty-day period (i.e., a sale on April 1 must be followed by repurchase no later than May 30, and not May 31). Exactly which date is the "sale" date is sometimes confusing if one sells through a public market or exchange such as the NASDAQ, because of the difference between the transaction date and the settlement date. There does not appear to be a clear answer as to which is the "sale" date for Code section 1045 purposes, but one should definitely take a conservative approach, if possible.

Since the replacement stock must be purchased at original issue from the C corporation, the "purchase date" is likely to be very clear, based on the issue date on the records of the corporation.

"Purchase" of Replacement QSBS. A "purchase" of stock occurs if the unadjusted basis of the stock, determined without taking into account the basis reduction rules under Code section 1045, is the cost of the stock.[105]

Comment: This generally suggests that one could potentially implement an installment purchase of the replacement stock (i.e., enter into a binding purchase transaction, but make some or all of the deferred payments after the end of the sixty-day period).

Another issue is that one must purchase the replacement stock within the sixty-day window starting on the day of the sale (i.e., one cannot make a replacement purchase before the original QSBS is sold). However, it appears that one does not have to trace funds, and therefore can use any money available to purchase the replacement stock, and specifically does not have to use the exact "proceeds" of the first sale to implement the replacement purchase.

There is no requirement that the replacement stock be the stock of only one corporation, and it appears that one can buy multiple stocks, so long as the stock of each corporation meets the requirements to be QSBS.

Holding Period and Basis Rules. The tax basis of the replacement stock is generally the purchase price, reduced (in the order acquired) by the amount of the gain deferred under Code section 1045.[106]

Comment: Although the basis rule is a little convoluted, it appears to mean that one can buy one lot of replacement stock, and end up with zero basis in that stock, and then buy a second lot of replacement stock and end up with high basis (or at least higher basis). A possible strategy would be to have low basis and high basis replacement stock, and be able to sell the high basis stock (at little or no taxable gain) in the future. This would be a strange basis rule, but a logical reading of the basis rules suggests it might be a possibility.

Comment: This potential strategy is moot if there is little or no basis in the QSBS being sold.

The holding rules allow the taxpayer to tack the holding period of the QSBS onto the holding period of the replacement stock.[107] Note that, if the taxpayer engages in sequential QSBS rollover transactions, the holding period tacking rule does not apply to help meet a new (second) six-month holding requirement for Code section 1045.[108]

Making a Code Section 1045 Election. A taxpayer must make a valid election to rollover the gain from the sale of qualified small business stock. The election must be made by the due date (including extensions) for filing the income tax return for the tax year in which the stock is sold.[109]

The election is made by (1) reporting the entire gain from the sale of QSBS on Schedule D of the return in accordance with the instructions for Schedule D; (2) writing "Section 1045 rollover" directly below the line on which the gain is reported; and (3) entering the amount of the gain deferred under Code section 1045 on the same line as the gain is reported under clause (2) above, and entering it as a loss, in accordance with the instructions for Schedule D.[110]

Once a valid election is filed, it can only be revoked with the consent of the IRS.[111]

CODE SECTION 1202—EXCLUSION OF GAIN ON SALE OF QUALIFIED SMALL BUSINESS STOCK

A provision closely related to Code section 1045, and which may provide a valuable planning alternative to many taxpayers, is Code section 1202. Section 1202(a) provides that a taxpayer other than a C corporation can exclude from gross income at least 50 percent, and up to 100 percent, of the gain recognized on the sale or exchange of qualified small business stock (QSBS), subject to certain caps described below, so long as the QSBS has been held for more than five years.[112] However, be aware from the outset that "Section 1202 gain" from the sale of QSBS is taxed at a special tax rate of 28 percent, and so to the extent that Code section 1202 rules do not exclude gain it is taxed at a rate significantly higher than the current long-term capital gains tax rate. As with Code Section 1045, the class of shareholders eligible to enjoy the benefits of Code Section 1202 includes individuals and pass-through entities, but C corporations are not eligible.

The percentage of gain excluded from gross income on the sale of QSBS varies depending on when the QSBS was first acquired by the taxpayer. Under Section 1202(a)(1), 50 percent of the gain on disposition is excluded if the QSBS was acquired before February 18, 2009. The American Recovery and Reinvestment Tax Act of 2009 raised the Section 1202 exclusion percentage from 50 percent to 75 percent for QSBS acquired after February 17, 2009 but before September 27, 2010. The Small Business Jobs Act of 2010 then amended Section 1202 to exclude 100 percent of the gain from the sale or exchange of QSBS acquired between September 27, 2010 and January 1, 2011. Then, in 2015, the Protecting Americans from Tax Hikes Act ("PATH Act") made permanent the exclusion of 100 percent of the gain from disposition of QSBS acquired after September 27, 2010 and held for more than five years.

The exclusion of gain under Code Section 1202 from the sale of QSBS is not unlimited, and is subject to a cap determined at the individual shareholder level. If a taxpayer has eligible QSBS gain for the taxable year, there is a cumulative cap on the aggregate amount of QSBS gain that may be excluded, which cap is applied for all dispositions of QSBS issued by a specific corporation (i.e., the cap applies for each corporation in which a taxpayer makes a qualifying investment, but does not prevent the taxpayer from enjoying the benefits of Code Section 1202 for investments in a second or third qualifying corporation). The cap on excluded gain applied for each taxable year is limited to the greater of—

(A) $10,000,000 reduced by the aggregate amount of eligible gain taken into account under Section 1202(a) for prior taxable years and attributable to dispositions of stock issued by the applicable corporation, or

(B) 10 times the aggregate adjusted bases of qualified small business stock issued by such corporation and disposed of by the taxpayer during the taxable year.

For purposes of subparagraph (B), the adjusted basis of any stock is determined without regard to any addition to basis after the date on which such stock was originally issued. In the case of married individuals filing separate returns, the limitation is applied to each return with $5 million substituted for $10 million.

QSBS is defined in exactly the same manner for both Section 1045 and Section 1202. (Code section 1045(b)(1) adopts the definition of QSBS by reference to Code section 1202(c).) Additional benefits are available if the QSBS was issued prior to February 17, 2009 by a corporation that conducted business in empowerment zones; in such cases, the Code section 1202 exclusion is increased from 50 percent to 60 percent, but only with respect to any gain recognized before January 1, 2019.[113] The higher 60 percent exclusion is subject to certain additional limitations and restrictions. The special empowerment zone rules do not apply for QSBS stock issued after February 17, 2009, but these rules remain relevant for QSBS stock issued prior to that date (until January 1, 2019 when it expires).

Practical Problems with Using Code Section 1202 Effectively. The practical problem with Code section 1202 for many years was that subsequent changes in tax rates for long-term capital gains after 1993 and prior to 2010 made Section 1202 largely irrelevant, and in some cases perversely harmful, to a seller of QSBS. Section 1202 was enacted as part of the Revenue Reconciliation Act of 1993 at a time when the maximum capital gains tax rate for individuals was 28 percent. During that initial period, the QSBS provisions represented a true 50 percent (or 60 percent) reduction in the tax liabilities on sale of QSBS, and thus was a considerable tax incentive.

Over the ensuing years, however, the capital gains tax rate for individuals was reduced to a maximum rate that was as low as 15 percent (and even lower in the case of lower-income taxpayers),[114] while "Section 1202 gain" (i.e., the total gain on sale of QSBS minus the amounted excluded under Code section 1202) continued to be subject to a maximum tax rate of 28 percent.[115] This means that the effective tax rate on a sale of QSBS, assuming a 50 percent exclusion, was effectively 14 percent for taxpayers in the maximum bracket (a 28-percent tax rate on the remaining 50 percent of total gain after applying the 50 percent exclusion). Meanwhile, assuming the QSBS was a capital asset in the hands of the taxpayer (very likely, unless the holder was a securities dealer) and has been held for the long-term capital gains period of more than one year (thus satisfying Code section 1212 requirements), then the maximum tax rate on a sale of such stock was at most only 15 percent! This already miniscule spread was often reduced even further if the alternative minimum tax came into play for the selling shareholder. Even worse, for certain taxpayers in lower tax brackets, the tax rates on long-term capital gain in that era could be as low as zero percent and so, perversely, the application of the Section 1202 exclusion coupled with the 28 percent rate would actually result in a ***higher*** effective tax rate than would otherwise apply if the stock were not QSBS! Needless to say, QSBS was hardly the incentive in those years that it was intended to be when first enacted in 1993.

The PATH Act, enacted in 2015, has ameliorated – but not entirely eliminated – some of the dysfunctional aspects of Code Section 1202 for QSBS acquired after September 27, 2010 and held for more than five years by excluding 100 percent of the gain from disposition of QSBS, up to the greater of $10 million or ten times the taxpayer's basis in the stock.[116] The PATH Act also eliminated the AMT preference associated with excluded gain on a sale of QSBS. With the new 100 percent exclusion, and with no excluded 1202 gain added back for AMT purposes, the QSBS stock has become an important and meaningful incentive for investors in qualifying small businesses.

> ***Important Planning Note:*** Unlike the provisions of Code section 1045, the provisions of Code section 1202 are ***not*** elective. Therefore, a qualifying sale of QSBS shares will be subject to these provisions even if it produces a less favorable tax result. Note that prior to the changes introduced by the PATH Act, taxpayers who were penalized by the application of Code section 1202 were advised to consider ways to avoid this absurd result by planning in advance to avoid the technical requirements of this provision (e.g., by selling the applicable shares before meeting the required five-year holding period).
>
> These perverse incentives and outcomes have been significantly reduced, at least prospectively, by the changes enacted effective September 27, 2010. Note, however, that shares of QSBS stock issued prior to February 17, 2009 are only eligible for a 50 percent exclusion from gain, while the remaining portion of gain will be taxed at the "Section 1202 gain" tax rate, which continues to be 28 percent. In effect, the reduction in capital gains tax rate for taxpayers who would otherwise be in the 20 percent bracket is only 6 percent. Moreover, if the investment has been highly successful, such that the $10 million/Ten-times-tax-basis limitation on exclusion comes into play, a taxpayer can still potentially be worst off under Code Section 1202 than if the stock was merely characterized as a capital asset subject to "normal" capital gain tax rates.

There are various technical requirements under Code section 1202, including rules for determining when the five-year holding period commences, and certain tacking rules (e.g., QSBS stock received by a partner from a partnership includes the holding period in the hands of the partnership). The general rules governing Section 1202 and QSBS are addressed and explained in the preceding section, in connection with Code Section 1045.

Interaction between Code Sections 1045 and 1202. Code sections 1045 and 1202 both offer special tax advantages to holders of "qualified small business stock," and the two provisions share in common a variety of rules.[117] Almost amazingly, there is no language in either Code section addressing whether a taxpayer can enjoy the benefits of both provisions with respect to the same sale of QSBS stock, and if so, how the provisions should be coordinated. However, since neither provision expressly excludes the application of the other to the same transaction, arguably both can and should apply to a transaction in the appropriate circumstances. This, in turn, leads to a question of how and in what order to apply the applicable gain exclusion and gain recognition rules.

Example 4: Jennifer Darby has held for more than five years 1,000 shares of QSBS in a C corporation called Technology Co, which shares she acquired in 2002 for an investment (and a tax basis) of $5,000. Jennifer sells her Technology Co stock in 2017 for $1,005,000, thus recognizing a net long-term capital gain (before the application of Code sections 1045 and 1202) of $1 million. Within sixty days of her sale of the Technology Co stock, she reinvests $605,000 of the sale proceeds into QSBS shares of another C corporation, Biology Co, and Jennifer elects the deferral benefits of Code section 1045 with respect to her reinvestment.

Comment: First of all, Code section 1202 is not elective, and so, absent her election under Code section 1045, Jennifer would be required to exclude 50 percent of her ($1 million) gain under Code section 1202 and then subject the remaining gain, or $500,000, to tax at a maximum 28-percent tax rate (plus, if applicable, a 3.8 percent net investment income tax), thus resulting in $159,000 of federal tax on the gain ($500,000 times 31.8 percent), which is the equivalent of a 15.9 percent tax rate on the entire gain. Note that Jennifer will be subject to this Code section 1202 tax regime even if she would otherwise be better off under the long-term capital gains tax regime (e.g., because the long-term capital gains rate applicable to Jennifer under Code section 1(h) is below the 15.9 percent effective tax rate under Section 1202 in the year of sale). For example, if Jennifer recognizes only $50,000 of long-term capital gain by selling less of the QSBS stock in 2017, her tax rate on LTCG could be significantly less than a 15.9 percent effective rate.

Since Jennifer elected to apply the provisions of Code section 1045 to her $600,000 investment in the QSBS stock of Biology Co, the question is how to apply, simultaneously, Code sections 1045 and 1202. One possibility is that Code section 1045 applies first, to exclude recognition of $600,000 of gain, and then Code section 1202 applies to the remaining gain, which is then taxed in the manner described above, i.e., 50 percent of the remaining $400,000 of gain, or $200,000, is excluded under Code section 1202, and the remaining 50 percent, or $200,000, is subject to tax at a 31.8-percent tax rate, resulting in $63,600 of federal tax.

An alternative theory—and even more beneficial to the taxpayer—would be to apply the exclusion from gross income under Code section 1202 first, and then apply Code section 1045. Thus, Jennifer could arguably exclude 50 percent of her gain, or $500,000, from gross income, and then further rollover the balance of the gain (and more, since she reinvests $605,000) under Code section 1045. Since Jennifer purchases more than $500,000 of replacement QSBS stock, this computational approach would arguably eliminate *any* gain in the current year and reduce her current tax liability to zero. Although the relatively recent 100 percent exclusion for QSBS stock acquired after September 27, 2010 makes Code section 1202 a very attractive benefit, the cap on that benefit (the lesser of $10 million or ten times the tax basis in the stock) means that the timing of the application of Section 1045 continues to be highly relevant.

Although there is no clear answer to this ordering question under either Code section 1045 or Code section 1202, the best answer may lie in the interaction of Code section 1(h)(4) and 1(h)(7), which state that "Section 1202 gain" is, in essence, the 50 percent (or in some cases 40 percent) of gross income not excluded under

Code section 1202, and that such Section 1202 gain is taxed at a 28-percent tax rate (plus the 3.8 percent NIIT). This may suggest that (1) since Code section 1045 determines whether or not gain is recognized, such determination should be made first, and (2) once the recognized gain amount is determined, one should then apply the applicable (ranging from 50 percent to 100 percent) exclusion under Code section 1202 to the gain recognized, and then subject the remainder (the "Section 1202 gain") to a 28-percent tax rate (plus, if applicable, the 3.8 percent NIIT).

However, in the absence of any authority or IRS guidance, any of the three alternative interpretations noted above (i.e., that only one section or the other applies; or that both apply, and Code section 1045 applies first; or that both apply and Code section 1202 applies first) might be considered at least a plausible reporting position.

CODE SECTION 1044

Code section 1044, similar in some respects to Code section 1045, provides that a taxpayer may elect to exclude from current recognition the amount of capital gain (but not ordinary income) that would otherwise be recognized upon a sale of publicly traded securities by reinvesting the sales proceeds in any common stock or a partnership interest in a "specialized small business investment company" (SS-BIC) within the sixty-day period beginning on the day the publicly traded securities are sold.[118] This provision is available to individuals (with a $50,000 annual and a $500,000 lifetime limitation on the aggregate amount of excluded gain) and to C corporations (with a $250,000 annual and a $1 million lifetime limitation on excluded gain).[119] The provision is not available to partnerships, S corporations, trusts, or estates.[120] To the extent that the gain is excluded, the taxpayer takes a tax basis in the SSBIC that is reduced by the amount of gain not recognized as a result of the election.[121]

Code section 1044 is another of the rather quixotic investment incentives created by the Revenue Reconciliation Act of 1993. The purpose was to encourage capitalization of SSBICs, which are partnerships or corporations licensed by the Small Business Administration under Section 301(d) of the Small Business Investment Act of 1958 (as in effect on May 13, 1993). SSBICs are organized to stimulate and supplement the flow of private equity capital and loans to small businesses.

On the one hand, Code section 1044 is extremely broad in terms of the types of securities sales that are potentially eligible for nonrecognition: It can apply to gain on the sale of any publicly traded securities. However, this broad scope is narrowed considerably on the replacement leg of the transaction because Code section 1044 places low limits on the rollover amount and very significant limitations on the scope of eligible reinvestment securities. As with Code section 1045, the deferral does not apply if the gain on the sale of the publicly traded securities is treated as ordinary income.[122] If a successful rollover is accomplished, the tax basis in the replacement stock is reduced by the gain not recognized.[123]

Comment: Although Code section 1044 is one of the few mechanisms that can be used to shelter and defer gain on sales of publicly traded securities, the annual dollar limitations are so low and the replacement investments are so limited that, unless a taxpayer desires to establish and operate an SSBIC, it is probably not a mainstream planning alternative.

CHAPTER ENDNOTES

1. IRC Sec. 1031(f)(1).
2. IRC Sec. 1031(f)(2).
3. See Rev. Rul. 75-292, 1975-2 CB 333 (ruling that property acquired in a Section 1031 transaction and immediately contributed to a corporation under IRC Sec. 351 is not held for a qualified purpose).
4. See *B.B. Maloney*, 93 TC 89, Dec. 4 5,863 (1989) (investment property held by corporation was exchanged for other investment property and then the corporation distributed the replacement property in a IRC Sec. 333 liquidation held: the first transaction was a IRC Sec. 1031 exchange notwithstanding the subsequent liquidation); see also *N.J. Magneson*, 81 TC 767, Dec. 40,557 (1983), *aff'd*, 753 F2d 1490 (1985) (investment property exchanged for 10 percent individual interest in second property that, under pre-arranged plan, was then contributed to a partnership for a general partnership interest consisting of a 10 percent capital interest and a 9 percent interest in a net profits and losses; second property satisfied "held" requirement; court suggested different result might apply if second property were immediately contributed for a limited partnership interest or stock in a corporation instead of general partnership interest).
5. Reg. § 1.1031(a)-1(b).
6. *Id.*
7. *Id.*
8. *Id.*
9. Rev. Rul. 76-301, 1976-2 CB 241.

10. Rev. Rul. 79-44, 1979-1 CB 265; Rev. Rul. 73-476, 1973-2 CB 300.
11. IRC Sec. 1031(h)(1).
12. Reg. § 1.1031(a)-1(c).
13. Rev. Rul. 67-380, 1967-2 CB 291.
14. *C.H. Wylie*, DC, 281 F.Supp. 80 (1968).
15. IRS Letter Ruling 200450005, August 30, 2004.
16. See IRS Letter Ruling 200240049, July 1, 2002.
17. Rev. Rul. 82-166, 1982-2 CB 190.
18. Reg. § 1.1031-2(a).
19. *Id.*
20. *Id.*
21. Reg. §1.1031(a)-2(b)(2).
22. 1987-2 CB 674.
23. Reg. § 1.1031(a)-2(b)(3).
24. Reg. § 1.1031(a)-2(b)(1).
25. *Id.*
26. Id.
27. *Id.*
28. Reg. § 1.1031(a)-2(b)(3).
29. See Reg. § 1.1031(a)-2(b)(1).
30. Reg. § 1.1031(a)-2(b)(3).
31. Reg. § 1.1031(a)-2(c)(1).
32. Reg. § 1031(a)-2(c)(1).
33. Reg. § 1.1031(a)-2(c)(2).
34. Reg. § 1.1031(a)-2(c)(3).
35. May 11, 2000.
36. See, e.g., Reg. § 1.1031(a)-2(b)(7), Example 4.
37. 1985-2 CB 181.
38. 1989-2 CB 203.107, Dec. 37,624 (1981).
39. Jan. 13, 2006.
40. 680 F2d 85 (1976).
41. Reg. § 1.1031(k)-1(g)(4).
42. 602 F2d 1341(1979).
43. 2000-2 CB 308.
44. Reg. § 1.1031(k)-1(c)(2).
45. Reg. § 1.1031(k)-1(c)(2).
46. Reg. § 1.1031(k)-1(c)(1).
47. Reg. § 1.1031(k)-1(c)(3).
48. Reg. § 1.1031(k)-1(c)(3).
49. Reg. § 1.1031(k)-1(c)(4).
50. Reg. § 1.1031(k)-1(c)(4)(ii).
51. Reg. § 1.1031(k)-1(c)(4)(ii).
52. Reg. § 1.1031(k)-1(c)(6).
53. Reg. § 1.1031(k)-1(d).
54. Reg. § 1.1031(k)-1(e).
55. Reg. § 1.1031(k)-1(e)(2).
56. Reg. § 1.1031(k)-1(e)(3)(i).
57. *Id.*
58. Reg. § 1.1031(k)-1(e)(4).
59. Reg. § 1.1031(b)-1(a).
60. Reg. § 1.1031(b)-1(c).
61. Reg. § 1.1031(b)-1(c).
62. See Reg. § 1.1031(d)-2, Example 2.
63. See Reg. § 1.1031(b)-1(a).
64. See Reg. § 1.1031(d)-2, Example 2.
65. *Id.*
66. Reg. § 1.1031(b)-1(a).
67. IRC Sec. 1031(d).
68. Rev. Rul. 72-456, 1972-2 CB 468.
69. IRS Letter Ruling 8929047, April 25, 1989.
70. Reg. § 1.1033(a)-1(a).
71. Reg. § 1.1033(a)-1(a).
72. IRC Sec. 1033(a)(2)(a); Reg. § 1.1033(a)-1(a).
73. Reg. § 1.1033(a)-1(a).
74. *Lynchburg National Bank & Trust Co.*, 20 TC 670, 208 F2d 757(1954).
75. *Columbus Die, Tool & Machine Co.*, 11 TCM 1053, Dec. 19,268(M) (1952).
76. IRC Sec. 1033(a)(2)(B).
77. IRC Sec. 1033(a)(2)(B)(i).
78. IRC Sec. 1033(a)(2)(B)(ii).
79. Reg. § 1.1033(a)-2(c)(3).
80. Reg. § 1.1033(a)-2(c)(3)(i) and (ii).
81. IRC Sec. 1045(a).
82. IRC Sec. 1045(b)(1).
83. IRC Sec. 1202(c)(1)(B).
84. IRC Sec. 1202(d)(1).
85. IRC Sec. 1202(d)(1)(A) and (B).
86. IRC Sec. 1202(d)(1)(C).
87. IRC Secs. 1202(c)(2) and (e)(1)(B).
88. IRC Sec. 1202(e)(4).
89. IRC Sec. 1202(d)(1)(A) and (B).
90. IRC Sec. 1202(d)(2)(A).
91. IRC Sec. 1202(d)(2)(B).
92. House Ways and Means Committee Report on Section 13113 of the Revenue Reconciliation Act of 1993.
93. IRC Sec. 1202(e)(1)(A).
94. IRC Sec. 1202(e)(3)(A).
95. IRC Sec. 1202(e)(3)(A).
96. IRC Sec. 1202(e)(3)(B).
97. IRC Sec. 1202(e)(3)(C).
98. IRC Sec. 1202(e)(3)(D).
99. IRC Sec. 1202(e)(3)(E).
100. IRC Sec. 1045(a).
101. H. Rept. No. 103-111 (P.L. 103-66), p. 603.
102. IRC Sec. 1045(a).
103. IRC Sec. 1045(a) does not include an "exchange" as a transaction eligible for rollover, although the Conference Report and the "Bluebook" issued by the Joint Committee Staff both indicate an eligible shareholder can rollover gain from a "sale or exchange." See Conf. Rept. No. 105-220 (P.L. 105-34), p. 385.

104. IRC Sec. 1045(a)(1).
105. IRC Sec. 1045(b)(2).
106. IRC Sec. 1045(b)(3).
107. IRC Sec. 1223(13).
108. IRC Sec. 1045(b)(4)(A).
109. Rev. Proc. 98-48, 1998-2 CB 367, § 3.01.
110. See Rev. Proc. 98-48, 1998-2 CB 367, § 3.02(1).
111. Rev. Proc. 98-48, 1998-2 CB 367, § 3.04.
112. IRC Sec. 1202(a).
113. IRC Sec. 1202(a)(2).
114. IRC Sec. 1(h)(1)(B), (C), and (D) for tax years prior to 2013.
115. IRC Secs. 1(h)(7) and 1(h)(4)(A)(ii).
116. IRC Sec. 1202(h)(1)(B).
117. IRC Sec. 1045(b)(5), for example, imports into IRC Sec. 1045 the provisions of subsections (f), (g), (h), (i), (j), and (k) of IRC Sec. 1202.
118. IRC Sec. 1044(a).
119. IRC Sec. 1044(b).
120. IRC Sec. 1044(c)(4).
121. IRC Sec. 1044(d).
122. IRC Sec. 1044(a).
123. IRC Sec. 1044(d).

SPECIAL TAX ISSUES WHEN BUYING AND SELLING INTELLECTUAL PROPERTY

CHAPTER 20

OVERVIEW

Intellectual property plays an increasingly important role in the creation of economic wealth. This is true throughout the world, but especially in the United States. Since 1980, when inflation reached a cyclical peak in the United States and other countries, the real price of many forms of tangible property, from the prices of metals and commodities to the prices of computers, have dropped dramatically in real terms. Modern economic experience suggests that virtually all forms of tangible property, whether basic materials or manufactured products, tend to be produced with increasing efficiency and with long-term reductions in real costs.

Meanwhile, intellectual content (whether scientific, engineering, mathematical, software, trademark, trade name, trade dress, trade secrets, or patent) has grown dramatically in value and importance, and has contributed not only economic value but also enrichment and betterment to daily life. For example, an important innovation in the last twenty years—at least in the humble opinion of this author—is the creation of extremely warm, durable, and comfortable fabrics known as synthetic fleeces, such as the product called Polartec. In turn, a clothing designer may develop a well-regarded brand name, and may as part of that brand create a faddishly popular line of clothing made principally from a synthetic fleece product. The resulting item of apparel combines the technology of the fabric, the design content of the designer, and the brand-name and marketing value of the label. When these and other forms of intellectual content are brought together, apparel ceases to be mere clothing (one of the three necessities of life) and becomes fashion (which, in the opinion of the author's daughters, is also a necessity of life).

Not surprisingly, a large and growing portion of the value in most businesses today resides in the intellectual property. After all, an Acquirer can (and in fact often does) move a newly acquired business to a new location, replace existing tangible property (from machinery to computers) with new substitutes, and reduce and/or replace unskilled members of the work force. What makes the Target business appealing to the Acquirer is the assets that cannot be easily acquired and replaced, which usually means the intellectual content of the Target's products and services, from patents and trademarks, to trade secret processes, to the trained and skilled workforce in place. Much of the value (and purchase price) in a modern acquisition is allocated to these intangible assets. In turn, these intangible assets often have unusual and distinctive tax characteristics, which will be explored in this chapter.

This chapter addresses tax issues in buying and selling certain common and important intangible business assets, including the following:

1. Patents.
2. Trade names, trademarks, and franchise rights.
3. Copyrights.
4. Software.
5. Trade secrets.
6. Contracts.

GENERAL TAX ATTRIBUTES OF BUYING, CREATING, USING, AND SELLING INTELLECTUAL PROPERTY

Intellectual property by its nature raises distinctive tax issues, and these in turn are further complicated by some provisions of the Code that are uniquely applicable to certain categories of intellectual property.

Deduction v. Capitalization. When money is expended by an individual or business to create intellectual property, the initial question is whether the expenditure is deductible on a current basis under Code section 162 or capitalizable under Code section 263. Code section 162 allows a current deduction for "all the ordinary and necessary expenses paid or incurred during the taxable year in carrying on any trade or business. . . "In contrast, Code section 263 prohibits the deduction of "[a]ny amount paid out for new buildings or for permanent improvements or betterments made to increase the value of any property or estate." The U.S. Supreme Court has stated that in distinguishing a current business expense from a capitalizable expense, "decisive distinctions are those of degree and not of kind."[1] Indeed, in a famous opinion written by Justice Cardozo, the Supreme Court said, "The standard set up by the statute is not a rule of law; rather a way of life. Life in all of its fullness must supply the answer to the riddle."[2] Therefore, the distinction between a currently deductible expense and a capitalized expense turns on specific facts and circumstances.

A major case defining the capitalization requirement is *INDOPCO, Inc.*[3] In that case, the Supreme Court held that over $2.7 million in legal fees and investment banking fees incurred in the course of a friendly takeover of one corporation by another were required to be capitalized under Code section 263 and were not deductible under Code section 162. Significantly, the Supreme Court in *INDOPCO* said, "Deductions are exceptions to the norm of capitalization."[4] The Court held that the determination of whether certain expenditures were deductible or capitalizable "envisions an inquiry into the duration and extent of the benefits realized by the taxpayer."[5] The *INDOPCO* decision indicated that a taxpayer's enjoyment of economic benefits beyond the year in which the expenditure is incurred was important in determining whether the appropriate tax treatment was deduction or capitalization. On the other hand, the decision, despite its bias in favor of capitalization, recognized that an expense was not automatically capitalizable just because it would produce a future benefit.

> *Comment:* ***INDOPCO*** is a landmark U.S. Supreme Court decision that, reduced to its essentials, merely says that it is not easy to distinguish a deductible expense from a capitalizable one. The IRS has issued several subsequent rulings that attempt to explain, define, and in some cases expand the ***INDOPCO*** decision.[6] However, as a practical matter, ***INDOPCO*** remains, at best, an exhortation, rather than a bright line test, for how to distinguish deductible expenses from capitalizable expenses.

A related capitalization issue arises under the "UNICAP" rules of Code section 263A. This provision relates specifically to capitalization of the costs attributable to property produced or acquired by the taxpayer for resale. Briefly, these provisions require that businesses capitalize into the cost of inventory not only the direct cost of producing or acquiring the property, but also the property's share of indirect costs. The underlying rationale of the statute is to provide a consistent, uniform, and comprehensive set of rules for the treatment of inventory. Because it deals with the purchase, creation, and/or sale of tangible property, Code section 263A does not, on its face, seem to apply to intangible or intellectual property assets. However, because intellectual property is often converted into and sold in a final tangible form—films, CDs, video tapes, and books are examples of intellectual property reduced to a tangible medium—intellectual property is often subject to the UNICAP rules.

Code section 263A(b) provides that the definition of "tangible personal property" includes "a film, sound recording, video tape, book, or similar property." Reg. § 1.263A-2(a)(2)(ii) defines "similar property" as "intellectual or creative property for which, as costs are incurred in producing the property, it is intended (or is reasonably likely) that any tangible medium in which the property is embodied will be mass distributed by the creator or any one or more third parties in a form that is not substantially altered. However, any intellectual or creative property that is embodied in a tangible medium that is mass distributed merely incident to the distribution of a principal product or good of the creator is not other similar property for these purposes."

On the other hand, Code section 263A(h) created an exception for certain expenses incurred by an individual engaged in the trade or business of being a writer, photographer, or artist. Basically, individuals engaged in these activities are allowed to deduct expenses that would otherwise be capitalizable under the requirements of Code section 263A. This exemption was enacted in 1988 in order to allow writers, photographers, and artists to be able to deduct the ongoing expenses of their occupations, rather than being forced to capitalize them on a product by product or project by project basis. Code section 263A(h) allows eligible individuals to deduct a "qualified creative expense," which is defined to include any expense paid or incurred by an individual in the trade or business of being a writer, photographer, or artist which would be deductible but for Code section 263A.

By contrast, the regulations under Code section 263A describe the costs of producing a book as an example of capitalizable expenses, including costs that might be considered the production of an intangible asset. For example, regulations specify that capitalizable costs include those incurred by the author in researching, preparing, and writing the book.[7] Regulations further provide that capitalizable production costs include pre-publication expenditures, such as payments to authors, as well as the cost of editing, compiling, illustrating, designing, and developing books.[8] The costs of producing a book also include the costs of producing the underlying manuscript, obtaining the copyright, or any license rights.[9] In addition, there are separately capitalizable costs related the printing and binding that reduces a book into a tangible medium.[10]

Deductions for Creating Intellectual Property under Code Section 162 v. Code Section 174. Because intellectual property is typically created by the mental endeavors of individuals, one frequent characteristic of intellectual property is that the costs associated with these efforts (notably the employment cost of salary, benefits, and similar expenses) are often eligible for immediate deduction, either under Code section 162 as ordinary and necessary business expenses or under Code section 174 as research and experimental expenses. Research expenditures also may be eligible for a research credit under Code section 41.

Intellectual property creation costs frequently qualify as research expenses under Code sections 174 and 41. Code section 174 provides a current deduction for certain types of "research or experimental expenditures" made in connection with the taxpayer's trade or business. Code section 41, meanwhile, permits a tax credit for increases in research expenditures from one year to the next. A taxpayer can take advantage of both Code section 174 deductibility and the Code section 41 tax credit with respect to the same research expenditures, subject only to the limitation of Code section 280C, which generally requires that Code section 174 deductions be reduced, on a dollar-for-dollar basis, for the tax credit permitted under Code section 41. Note, however, that because the criteria for a deduction under Code section 174 and a credit under Code section 41 are significantly different, expenses may qualify under one provision but not the other.

Code section 174 is a substantial reward and incentive for conducting qualifying research because it allows research into the creation of new assets to be deducted immediately, instead of capitalized and amortized. Obviously, deducting expenses is better than capitalizing them, even if the capital asset is placed in service immediately. Code section 174 is even more beneficial when expenditures are incurred with respect to an asset that is in the process of creation, and may not be placed in service for many years.

Code section 174 is available even if the taxpayer is not yet engaged in a trade or business, so long as the expense is incurred "in connection with" a trade or business.[11] As a result, a startup business can deduct research expenses under Code section 174, even if it has not yet begun to engage in the "carrying on of a trade or business" within the meaning of Code section 162. Code section 174 does require that the taxpayer have a realistic prospect of entering into a trade or business and case law indicates that the taxpayer must engage in a trade or business sometime in the future.[12]

The Code section 174 requirement that research expenditures be incurred in connection with a trade or business prevents Code section 174 from being used by parties who merely invest or fund the research of a third party. In the 1980s, there were many so-called "R&D Partnerships," which were investment partnerships set up to fund research and development into a particular science or technology. The partnership agreed, as part of the relationship, to lease or license the rights to all the research by the developing party. Typically, an R&D Partnership would provide the funding to a corporation to develop its technology and would attempt to deduct all the expenses currently and then enjoy through licensing agreements the fruits of the research. However, numerous court cases held that the partnership in question was not sufficiently engaged in a trade or business to meet the requirements of Code section 174.[13] Although most of the R&D Partnerships were denied the benefits of Code section 174, in *W.V. Scoggins*,[14] the court of appeals concluded that the R&D Partnership in that case was eligible to claim deductions under Code section 174. In that case, partners in the R&D Partnership possessed the technical expertise and financial ability to conduct or create a business using the technology developed under the development agreement. Also, the license granted in that case was not exclusive, and the licensee was under no obligation to market the technology. Also significant in the court's mind was the fact that the research cost was $500,000 while the option to acquire the technology on the part of the licensee was $5 million.

Code section 174 is limited to research and experimental expenditures, and does not apply to expenses incurred in "development." To be currently deductible under Code section 174, the expenses must "represent research and development costs in the experimental or laboratory sense."[15] In addition, the amount of any expenditure must be reasonable under the circumstances.[16] The regulations provide additional gloss to the definition of "research expenditure" by proposing and applying the "uncertainty" standard. Under this standard, "[e]xpenditures represent research and development costs in the experimental or laboratory sense if they are for activities intended to discover information that would eliminate uncertainty concerning the development or improvement of a product. Uncertainty exists if the information available to the taxpayer does not establish the capability or method for developing or improving the product or the appropriate design of the product. Whether expenditures qualify as research or experimental expenditures depends on the nature of the activity to which the expenditures relate, not the nature of the product or improvement being developed or the level of technological advancement the product or improvement represents."[17]

Conversely, the regulations also define certain expenses that are not within the scope of "research." For example, the regulations explicitly state that the expenditures incurred for "research in connection with literary, historical or similar projects" do not fall within the definition of Code section 174 expenditures.[18] Also excluded are the costs of development of a product. For example, ordinary testing or inspection of materials for purposes of quality control, efficiency surveys, management studies, consumer surveys, advertising, or promotions do not qualify as R&D expenditures.[19] The regulations tend to be skeptical about permitting a deduction under Code section 174 where the expenditure results in the creation or improvement of tangible personal property or real property. Reg. § 1.174-2(b)(4) indicates that "expenditures in connection with the acquisition or production of depreciable property to be used in the taxpayer's trade or business are limited to amounts expended for research or experimentation. For the purpose of the preceding sentence, amounts expended for research or experimentation do not include the costs of the component materials of the depreciable property, the costs of labor or other elements involved in its construction and installation, or costs attributable to the acquisition or improvement of the property."

> ***Example 1:*** A taxpayer undertakes to develop a new machine for use in his business. He expends $30,000 on the project, of which $10,000 represents the actual cost of the material, labor, etc., to construct the machine and $20,000 represents research costs that are not attributable to the machine itself. Under Code section 174(a), the taxpayer would be permitted to deduct the $20,000 as expenses not chargeable to capital account. The $10,000 must be treated as a capitalized expense with respect to the asset (the machine).[20]

Transfers of Intellectual Property—Code Sections 1235, 1253, 1221, and 1231. The sale or transfer of intellectual property often triggers the application of specific code provisions covering specific categories of intellectual assets. For example, Code section 1235 is a special, favorable provision granting long-term capital gain treatment on the sale of patents by certain individuals (generally inventors). Code section 1253 is a far less favorable provision that governs the sale of trademarks, trade names, and franchises and often limits or bars capital gain treatment. The sale of a copyright by its creator is generally excluded from capital gain treatment by Code section 1221(a)(3) and thus will generally cause gain on the sale to be characterized as ordinary income. However, the sale of the exact same asset by someone other than the creator (e.g., by a purchaser of the copyright) is likely to be governed by Code section 1221 or Code section 1231 and, if held for more than one year, is likely to generate long-term capital gain.

Each of these provisions, as it relates to a specific form of intellectual property, is discussed more fully in the applicable discussion of each category of intellectual property below.

Taxation of Asset Acquisitions—Code Section 197. The acquisition of business assets causes all intangible property (including intellectual property plus various forms of goodwill and similar assets) to come within the application of Code section 197, which requires amortization of the purchase price on a straight-line basis over fifteen years. This is discussed in greater detail below, and also in Chapter 11.

TAXATION OF PATENTS

Overview of U.S. Patent Law. The U.S. Constitution grants Congress the power to enact laws that "promote the progress of science and useful arts, by securing for limited times to authors and inventors the exclusive right to their respective writings and discoveries."[21] Pursuant to this power, the U.S. Congress has enacted a series of patent laws, starting with the Patent Act of 1790, and continuing today with the laws found at 35 USC § 101 *et seq*. Under present law, the U.S. Patent and Trademark Office (USPTO) is authorized to issue patents.

There are three types of patents: utility patents, plant patents, and design patents. A utility patent is the kind of patent that most often comes to mind because it is for inventions of a scientific nature. Plant patents are similar to utility patents in most respects, with the notable exception that they are granted specifically to producers of new asexually reproduced plants. Design patents, by contrast, protect only that which is purely ornamental in a design and are unavailable to protect any functional aspect of that design. Design patents provide an alternative to copyright protection for original ornamental design elements of products. The "patents" discussed in this book are generally utility patents (and plant patents) rather than design patents.

Patents grant inventors the exclusive right to make, use, or sell their inventions for a period of twenty years (fourteen years for design patents).[22] The term of a patent begins on the date on which the patent issues and ends twenty years from the date on which the patent application was filed in the United States. At the present time, there is an enormous backlog of patent applications, especially in sophisticated areas of technology. Therefore, setting the end of the term at twenty years from the date that the patent is filed can actually result in a shorter period of exclusivity than under prior law, which provided for a term of seventeen years from the date of issue.

Five requirements of a utility patent. To obtain a utility patent, five basic requirements must be satisfied:

1. The invention must constitute patentable subject matter.[23]
2. The invention must demonstrate utility.[24]
3. The invention must represent novelty.[25]
4. The invention must be non-obvious.[26]
5. The invention must be described with a sufficient and enabling written description.[27]

Patentable subject matter. The requirement of patentable subject matter is set forth in 35 USC § 101, which states as follows:

> Whoever invents or discovers any new and useful process, machine, manufacture, or composition of matter, or any new or useful improvement thereof, may obtain a patent therefor, subject to the conditions and requirements of this title.

In general, only processes, machines, articles of manufacture or compositions of matter are considered patentable subject matter. On the one hand, the Supreme Court has concluded that Congress wanted the patent laws to be interpreted broadly.[28] On the other hand, patentable subject matter does not include scientific principles,[29] natural phenomena,[30] or abstract ideas.[31]

Utility requirement. Assuming the invention in question constitutes patentable subject matter, there are four other requirements that must be demonstrated, namely utility, novelty, non-obviousness, and an appropriate written description. The utility requirement is set forth in USC § 101, as follows:

> Whoever invents. . . any. . . useful process, machine, manufacture, or composition of matter. . . may obtain a patent. . .

A "useful" invention is one that provides some benefit to humanity. The U.S. Supreme Court has arguably imposed a relatively high standard for utility. In *Brenner v. Manson*,[32] for example, an inventor filed a patent application on a new process for making a steroid compound that did not have any demonstrable use. The Supreme Court, in disallowing the patent claim, held that the compound must have "substantial utility" before a patent could be issued, and found that the patent application did not disclose any use for the chemical compound produced by the process. The Supreme Court stated that a patent is "not a reward for the search, but compensation for successful conclusion." The Supreme Court specifically rejected the argument that the new process would be useful as a step in promoting further research on useful processes and compounds.

Novelty requirement. The third requirement is novelty, which is intended to make sure that a patent is not granted on a technology that already exists in the public domain. The novelty requirement is pieced together from several provisions contained in 35 USC § 102.

Novelty has a number of complicated facets under patent law. Often, the novelty requirement focuses on whether there has been a public awareness of the invention being claimed, including a disclosure (inadvertent or otherwise) by the erstwhile inventor. U.S. law permits an inventor to disclose a new idea or process in a publication before filing a patent application, so long as the application is filed within one year of publication. By contrast, in most other jurisdictions any prior publication will bar a patent application.

Non-obviousness requirement. The fourth requirement is lack of obviousness. The U.S. Supreme Court has held that even new and useful inventions may not be patentable if there are only obvious differences between that invention and the prior art.[33] In determining obviousness, the court must determine the scope and content of the prior art, the differences between the pertinent prior art and the invention, and the ordinary level of skill in the pertinent art.[34]

In general, the concept of "prior art" is a complicated topic and is not amenable to easy summaries. Prior art includes existing patents, prior publications, and anything in public use or on sale in the United States. Time restrictions apply to each of these items.[35]

Written description requirement. The written description requirement is set forth in 35 USC § 112, which states as follows:

> The specification shall contain a written description of the invention, and of the manner and process of making and using it, in such full, clear, concise, and exact terms as to enable any persons skilled in the art to which it pertains, or with which it is most nearly connected, to make and use the same, and shall set forth the best mode contemplated by the inventor of carrying out his invention.

The USPTO and court cases have generally interpreted this written description requirement as having three distinct components:

1. There must be a written description of the invention.
2. There must be "enablement," which is basically a description of how to make and use the invention.
3. There must be a disclosure of the "best mode" of practicing the invention.[36]

If a patent application does not satisfy all three of these requirements, such failure is grounds for rejection.

Although there was some uncertainty about whether the written description requirement was a true and separate requirement under patent law, the Federal Circuit Court of Appeals made it clear that a separate written description was a distinct and necessary requirement, in the case of *Vas-Cath, Inc. v. Mahurkar*.[37]

The written description requirement is intended to inform those skilled in the art that the patent applicant was in full possession of the invention at the time the patent application was filed.[38] In turn, the requirement ensures that the claimed patent is fully disclosed to the public so that others can develop improvements on the invention and can use the invention after the patent expires. The Federal Circuit, the successor to the Court of Customs and Patents Appeals (CCPA), has held that, to meet the written description requirement, an inventor must precisely describe an invention by "words, structures, figures, diagrams, formulas, etc., that fully set forth the claimed invention."[39] The basic test is always whether the disclosure conveys to those skilled in the art that the applicant had possession of the subject matter claimed.[40]

Design Patents. A design patent is a specific category of patent that protects the "design" of an article of manufacture. Generally, a utility patent protects the way an article of manufacture is used and works, while a design patent protects the way an article looks. Both design and utility patents may be obtained on the same article of manufacture if the requisite level of "invention" exists both in its utility and in its ornamental appearance. Thus, utility and design patents afford legally separate and distinct forms of protection – although the utility and ornamentality of an article are not always easy to separate.

A "design" means the visual ornamental characteristics embodied in, or applied to, an article of manufacture. A design that is dictated primarily or entirely by the function of the article lacks ornamentality and does not qualify for a design patent. For example, if an article does not have a unique or distinctive shape or appearance that is unrelated to the function being performed, then the design lacks the required ornamentality.

Furthermore, subject matter that could be considered offensive to any race, religion, sex, ethnic group, or nationality is not proper subject matter for a design patent application.[41]

To obtain a design patent protection, the following specific requirements must be satisfied:

1. The design must be an *article of manufacture*.[42]
2. The design musts demonstrate *originality*.[43]
3. The design must be *ornamental*.[44] The design must have novelty.[45]
4. The design must be *non-obvious*.[46]
5. The design must be *adequately described*.[47]

Article of Manufacture requirement. A design patent requires that the design be for "an article of manufacture."[48] This mean a tangible human-made object. For example, a computer generated icon by itself cannot receive design patent protection; however, the icon appearing in a computer display can.[49]

Originality requirement. For a design to be patentable it must be "original." For example, a design that simulates a well-known or naturally occurring object or person is not original as required by the statute.[50]

Novelty requirement. A design must be "new" which includes meeting the novelty requirement applicable to a utility patent. However, the novelty of a design patent is related to the ornamentation, and the standard is that is must be distinguishable to an "average observer".

Non-Obviousness requirement. The non-obviousness requirement for utility patents also applies to design patents. The determination, however, is different in that the standard for design patents is whether it would be non-obvious to a designer of ordinary skill, whereas the standard for utility patents is whether is it non-obvious to a the person of ordinary skill in the art.[51] Obviousness is a test of the overall article, not each design element.[52]

Ornamentality requirement. To be patentable, a design must be primarily ornamental. In determining whether a design is primarily functional or primarily ornamental the claimed design is viewed in its entirety, for the ultimate question is not the functional or decorative aspect of each separate feature, but the overall appearance of the article, in determining whether the claimed design is dictated by the utilitarian purpose of the article.[53] For a design to be ornamental, it must be created for the purpose of ornamenting.[54]

Adequate description requirement. The specification, which typically includes a drawing and in some cases a required model, should demonstrate the unique design aspects for which the applicant is seeking design patent protection.

Taxation of Patents. Patents are subject to a variety of uniquely taxpayer-friendly rules under the Code. Indeed, as will be explored in detail below, patents enjoy markedly more favorable tax treatment than other common forms of intellectual property. The costs of creating a patent can generally be deducted immediately under Code section 174—specifically the costs of obtaining the patent, including attorney's fees expended in making and perfecting a patent application.[55] For most other intellectual property, by contrast, the creation costs are more likely to be required to be capitalized. Moreover, on a subsequent sale of the patent, these Code section 174 deductions, unlike depreciation or amortization deductions, are not subject to recapture.[56] To the extent a taxpayer has tax basis in a self-created or separately acquired patent, the IRS permits a favorable amortization rule called the "income forecast method," described more fully below.

On sale, an individual patent inventor and certain individual financial backers (collectively called "holders") can enjoy the uniquely favorable provisions under Code section 1235 that allow long-term capital gain (LTCG) treatment even if the patent would not otherwise qualify (e.g., because the patent has not been held for more than one year or because the patent would be considered "inventory" in the hands of the inventor (because the inventor is a professional inventor in the trade or business of inventing)). Notably, Code section 1235 is complementary to Code sections 1221 and 1231.

Thus, any patent owner can potentially enjoy long-term capital gains treatment on a sale of a patent under Code sections 1221 or 1231, even if Code section 1235 is inapplicable.

These rules and their practical significance are discussed more fully below.

Tax Issues on Creation of a Patent. At the election of the taxpayer, "research or experimental expenditures" incurred in connection with such taxpayer's trade or business can be taken as a current deduction[57] or capitalized and amortized over a period of not less than sixty months, beginning with the month in which the taxpayer first realizes benefits from such expenditures.[58] The term "research or experimental expenditures" is further defined in regulations that attempt to distinguish between eligible and non-eligible expenses by applying the so-called "uncertainty test," namely that eligible research is "intended to discover information that would eliminate uncertainty concerning the development or improvement of a product." Although the "uncertainty test" produces less-than-certain guidance in many areas of business endeavor, these regulations are almost uniquely clear that the costs of developing patentable inventions do in fact fall within the scope of Code section 174. In particular, the regulations define the term "research or experimental expenditures" such that it "includes the costs of obtaining a patent, such as attorneys' fees expended in making and perfecting a patent application."[59] Therefore, as a practical matter, virtually all of the costs of obtaining a patent or developing a patentable product or process should qualify as "research or experimental expenditures" under Code section 174.

In addition, expenses of developing a patent may also constitute "qualified research expenditures" that can be used in determining the research credit available under Code section 41. Code section 41 permits a credit against federal income tax equal to 20 percent of qualified research expenses for a particular tax year in excess of a base amount. Note that the definition of "qualified research expenses" for purposes of Code section 41 is significantly narrower than the definition of "research or experimental expenditures" under Code section 174. Therefore, expenses may qualify for the deduction but not for the credit. The Code section 41 credit is available only if qualified research expenses exceed the applicable threshold. As a practical matter, the Code section 41 credit is generally available only if a business is either a startup entity (in which case the base amount is set to produce intentionally high available credits) or, if the business is older than ten years, only if the business is generally increasing its "research and experimentation" expenditures over the average of prior years.

Although it is anticipated that most or all expenses of creating a patent will be deductible or amortizable under Code section 174, to the extent any portion of the expenses do not so qualify, the expenses will be capitalized and amortizable under Code section 167.[60] The Code section 167 regulations specifically identify patents and copyrights as examples of intangible assets that can be depreciated because the useful life of the property can be reasonably estimated.[61] A patent can be depreciated under Code section 167 using the straight line method over its remaining useful life.[62] However, the more common method is the so-called "income forecast method," recommended by the IRS in Rev. Rul. 79-285.[63] Under this method, tax basis in a patent is recovered over the period that a taxpayer reasonably expects to derive income from the exploitation of the patent, in proportion to the projected income. The income forecast method involves projecting the income from a patent over a particular period, and then prorating deduction of the tax basis in proportion to the anticipated income over that period.

Tax Issues on Acquisition of a Patent. If a taxpayer acquires a patent by purchase rather than by self-creation, the first question is whether it is a "separately acquired asset" or whether it was "acquired in a transaction (or series of related transactions) involving the acquisition of assets constituting a trade business or substantial portion thereof."[64] Separately acquired patents are expressly excluded from the definition of "section 197 intangible" by Code section 197(e)(4)(C) and instead are depreciated under Code section 167 and, as discussed above, generally will be depreciated based on the income forecast method. By contrast, patents acquired in an acquisition of assets constituting a trade or business (or substantial portion thereof) are Code section 197 intangibles, and therefore are amortizable ratably over a fifteen-year period.[65]

Given that the income forecast method is often dramatically more favorable in permitting recovery of tax basis compared to fifteen-year amortization, there will be at least some thought given to whether a patent can be "separately" acquired. Note, by comparison, that the acquisition of a trademark, even if it is the sole asset being acquired, is treated as the acquisition of a "trade or business" and is always governed by Code section 197 (as are any other assets acquired with such trademark).[66] An interesting (and not insignificant) question may be whether a particular patent, even if it is the only asset acquired, by its nature constitutes a trade or business (e.g., because at the time of the acquisition the patented product is already marketed and popular).[67]

Any patent acquired as part of an asset acquisition of a business and thus governed by Code section 197 will be subject to fifteen-year amortization. This rule applies even if the patent has less than fifteen years before it expires. The portion of the purchase price allocated to the patent in the asset acquisition will be determined using the residual method under Code section 1060 (see Chapter 3) based on the fair market values of the acquired assets, with a residual allocation to goodwill. The basic policy underlying Code section 197 is that all intangible assets acquired in an asset acquisition (other than those expressly excluded under Code section 197(e)) will be subject to fifteen-year amortization, thereby eliminating (or at least greatly reducing) the wrangling over basis allocation and fair market value that existed prior to the enactment of Code section 197. Significantly, Code section 197(f)(1) contains an important and far-reaching anti-abuse provision that, in order to prevent taxpayers from significantly shortening the applicable fifteen-year amortization period, prohibits the claiming of losses on a disposition or abandonment (for worthlessness) of an intangible subject to Code section 197, and instead requires reallocation of the remaining tax basis to the remaining intangible assets.

Example 2: Corporation C purchases the assets of a business for $6 million. The assets include a patent, tangible manufacturing machinery used to manufacture a patented product, and goodwill. The patent has four years left before it expires. The parties allocate $1.5 million to the patent, $1.5 million to the tangible property, and $3 million to the goodwill. The tangible property is depreciated under Code section 167 as five-year property, and the patent and goodwill are amortized under Code section 197. Four years after the acquisition, the patent expires, at which time the remaining tax basis in the intangible assets is as follows: $1,100,000 in the patent ($1,500,000 × 11/15), and $2,200,000 in the goodwill ($3,000,000 × 11/15). Under Code section 197(f)(1), the expiration of the patent causes Corporation C to realize a loss of $1.1 million, but under Code section 197(f)(1) this loss is not recognized. Instead, the unused tax basis in the patent (i.e., the $1.1 million) is reallocated solely to the goodwill (and not to the tangible assets). The goodwill now has an adjusted tax basis of $3,300,000 ($2,200,000 + $1,100,000), and this will be amortized over the remaining eleven years of the amortization period.

Tax Issues on Selling a Patent. The generic tax-planning goal is to enjoy long-term capital gains on the sale or disposition of a patent. There are three possible Code provisions that could provide favorable LTCG treatment: (1) Code section 1235, available to individual inventors and certain early-stage individual financial backers; (2) Code section 1221, applicable to capital assets; and (3) Code section 1231, applicable to "property used in the trade or business, of a character which is subject to the allowance for depreciation provided in Code section 167, held for more than one year."

Code Section 1235. Code section 1235(a) states in relevant part:

> A transfer (other than by gift, inheritance, or devise) of property consisting of all substantial rights to a patent, or an undivided interest therein which includes a part of all such rights, by any holder shall be considered the sale or exchange of a capital asset held for more than one year. . ..

This Code provision was specifically enacted to eliminate what was sometimes a complicated historical distinction between professional and amateur inventors under prior law. In its present form, Code section 1235 applies to certain individual taxpayers, defined as "holders," and applies such that a qualifying transfer of a patent by a holder will be eligible for long-term capital gains treatment, even if the patent has been held for less than one year and/or even if the patent would otherwise be considered "inventory" in the hands of a professional inventor. To enjoy the favorable benefits of Code section 1235, the transaction must meet all of the following criteria:

1. The transferor seeking the benefits of Code section 1235 must qualify as a "holder" (which generally means an individual creator plus certain individual financial backers who acquire for money an interest in the invention before it is reduced to practice).

2. The property being transferred must be a "patent."

3. There must be a qualifying "transfer" to an eligible purchaser.

4. Such transfer must include "all substantial rights" in the patent or "an undivided interest" in all substantial rights.

Holder Requirement. Code section 1235 is only available to a "holder," which is defined as "(1) any individual whose efforts created such property, or (2) any other individual who has acquired his interest in such property in exchange for consideration in money or money's worth paid to such creator prior to actual reduction to practice of the invention covered by the patent, if such individual is neither (A) the employer of such creator, nor (B) related to such creator."[68]

There are a number of important factors to note about this definition of "holder." First, "holder" is narrowly defined to include only an "individual" creator or an "individual" that acquired an interest from the creator "prior to actual reduction to practice of the invention. . . "[69] This means that corporations, including S corporations, can never be a "holder" for purposes of Code section 1235. A partnership likewise cannot be a "holder," but the regulations provide that an individual partner may qualify as a holder with respect to his or her share of a patent held by a partnership.[70] Similarly, if the inventor is a member of a partnership composed only of individuals and the inventor uses partnership property to develop an invention with the understanding that the patent will become partnership property, each individual member of the partnership is considered a holder.[71] This favorable rule applies to individual partners even if other partners are corporations (but does not, of course, apply to the corporations themselves).[72]

The definition of holder further bars from coverage any person that is either the creator's employer or any person related to the creator.[73] As discussed below, related to the "transfer" requirement, Code section 1235 does not generally offer its generous benefits either to employees (if they are "hired to invent") or to employers (under any circumstances), even though a huge portion of patentable inventions today are developed by paid researchers working for businesses. Code section 1235 does, however, apply to inventors who are established to be independent contractors and are paid to transfer the rights in their own patents.[74] Code section 1235 is, in effect, a sentimental homage to the individual inventor working in the basement—a circumstance far more descriptive of the 19th century than the 21st.

Code section 1235 also excludes from the definition of holder all persons "related" to the creator, and defines relatedness broadly by lowering the normal related-party tests under Code sections 267(b) and 707(b) from "more than 50 percent" to "25 percent or more," just to make sure the related-party exclusion is broadly defined.[75] There are actually two technically distinct related-party prohibitions in Code section 1235. First, a party related to the creator can never become a "holder" under Code section 1235(b)(2) through being an early investor or financial backer of the creator. (A related party can, of course, be a holder by virtue of being a co-inventor.) Second, even if an individual is unquestionably a "holder," Code section 1235 does not apply if the patent is transferred to a related party.[76] The legislative history makes it clear that this prohibition was intended to prevent "possible abuses arising from the sale of patents within essentially the same economic group."[77]

Patent Requirement. The second fundamental requirement under Code section 1235 is that there must be a transfer of a "patent." Significantly, Code section 1235 does not define the term "patent," but the regulations offer a remarkably broad and expansive definition of that term. Reg. § 1.1235-2(a) states as follows:

> The term "patent" means a patent granted under the provisions of title 35 of the United States Code, or any foreign patent granting rights generally similar to those under a United States patent. It is not necessary that the patent or patent application for the invention be in existence if the requirements of Code section 1235 are otherwise met.

The case law confirms that Code section 1235 is available to any "patentable product" or "patentable invention", including design patents.[78] Code section 1235 does not require that a patent be issued or a patent application even filed.[79] As a practical matter, however, it is unlikely that a taxpayer will claim the benefits of Code section 1235 without submitting a patent application at some point in time—if only upon audit by the IRS! Realistically, patents can take years to prosecute, and it is unlikely that an IRS audit agent will try to make an independent determination about whether a patent application constitutes a "patentable" invention. However, claiming that a product is "patentable" without even attempting to obtain a patent would invite close scrutiny and a substantial likelihood of disallowance on audit.

Transfer Requirement. A third requirement is that there must be a "transfer (other than by gift, inheritance, or devise)"[80] of the patent to an eligible party. First of all, donative or family transfers, by gift, inheritance or devise, are expressly excluded from eligible transfers. Furthermore, since the transfer must entail all substantial rights (as discussed below) it will necessarily be in the nature of a sale or exchange, whether structured as an assignment of the patent or a license of the applicable rights. Note, however, that a precise reading of Code section 1235(a) indicates that a "transfer" does not, technically, need to be a sale or exchange in order to qualify for the benefits of that Code section; rather, the syllogism is the opposite, namely, a qualifying transfer of all substantial rights "shall be considered the sale or exchange of a capital asset held for more than one year. . . ." This precise technical distinction does not appear to make any difference in the practical application of the provision.

The transfer requirement usually comes up as an important issue in two specific circumstances: (1) if the inventor is an employee or independent contractor who is "hired to invent" and transfers the patent to the employer/contracting party pursuant to that contractual engagement or (2) the transfer is to a person related to the creator of the patent.

When the inventor is an employee, the regulations take the position that Code section 1235 should not be available to turn W-2 wages into long-term capital gain. The regulations state: "Payments received by an employee as compensation for services rendered as an employee under an employment contract requiring the employee to transfer to the employer the rights to any invention by such employee are not attributable to a transfer to which Code section 1235 applies."[81] The basic argument is that an employee in such circumstances has pre-assigned all patent rights to the employer as a condition of employment, and hence does not have any rights to "transfer." However, this "hired to invent" rule does not apply if the employee is not being paid a salary or contractual compensation to invent on behalf of the employer/payer. The regulations acknowledge that the issue is ultimately a question of fact, and case law demonstrates that, based on specific facts, the courts are sometimes willing to treat an employee as making an eligible "transfer."[82] However, most litigated cases have gone in the IRS's favor on this issue.[83]

In the case of a transfer to a related person, Code section 1235(d) bars such transfer from being eligible for capital gains treatment under Code section 1235. The legislative history indicates that Congress enacted the provision because it was concerned about tax-favored transfers that stayed within the same economic group. Note that because Code section 1235(d) lowers the related party tests under Code sections 267 and 707 from "more than 50 percent" to "25 percent or more," Code section 1235(d) has a nasty tendency to capture or cover transactions that no one considers to be "related party" transactions. This provision should be regarded as a dangerous trap for the unwary. Any transaction intending to come within Code section 1235 should consider carefully potential Code section 1235(d) problems.

All Substantial Rights. A fourth requirement is that a transfer must consist of "all substantial rights to a patent, or an undivided interest therein which includes a part of all such rights.. . ." The regulations provide that "all substantial rights" means "all rights (whether or not then held by the grantor) which are of value at the time the rights to the patent (or an undivided interest therein) are transferred."[84] The "all substantial rights" requirement means, as a practical matter, that many of the logical ways of exploiting, separating, and licensing patent rights are not covered by Code section 1235.

The regulations indicate that there is not a transfer of "all substantial rights" if a patent is licensed to cover only a limited geographic area that is less than the entire country of issuance, is limited in duration to a period less than the remaining life of the patent, is limited to a specified field of use, or grants less than all inventions or claims that exist and have value at the time of the grant.[85] Likewise, the retention of a right to terminate the transfer at will is retention of a substantial right.[86] Rights that may or may not be substantial retained rights, depending on the circumstances, include retaining the right to prohibit any sublicensing or sub-assignment of the patent and the failure to convey the right to use or sell the patent property. Note that virtually all of these examples represent common licensing schemes, and thus would cause such a license or transfer to be ineligible for the benefits of Code section 1235.

As a practical matter, parties attempting to qualify under Code section 1235 must structure the transfer to make it absolutely clear that the transferee is receiving all substantial rights and that the transferor will retain only those rights expressly approved and permitted under the regulations (e.g., retention of legal title for the purpose of securing performance or payment by the transferee in a transaction involving transfer of an exclusive license to manufacture, use, and sell for the life of the patent, or retention of a security interest).[87]

Code Sections 1221/1231. Even if the transaction does not come within the scope of Code section 1235, a transfer of a patent can result in long-term capital gain if the patent is either a capital asset in the hands of the transferor[88] or is property used in the trade or business of the transferor, subject to the allowance for depreciation provided in Code section 167, and held for more than one year.[89]

As an initial observation, the tax character of a patent in the hands of its inventor may not be entirely clear, which is why Code section 1235 was enacted in the first place. If a patent is viewed as "inventory" in the hands of the inventor, it will fall into the matching exceptions contained in Code sections 1221(a)(1) and 1231(b)(1)(A) and not be eligible for long-term capital gain treatment. However, this would probably arise only in the case of a "professional inventor"; in all other cases the patent is likely to be either a Code section 1221 asset or a Code section 1231 asset.

Note that because all expenses in creating a patent usually are expensed under Code section 174, discussed above, a patent may have zero depreciable basis in the hands of the creator. The argument can be made that in such case that the patent is not "subject to the allowance for depreciation" and, thus, must be a Code section 1221 asset rather than a Code section 1231 asset. The author's view is that a patent otherwise used in a trade or business should be a Code section 1231 asset, even if it has zero depreciable basis, on the theory that it is still a depreciable asset (subject to the allowance for depreciation) and merely has zero tax basis. In the end, this distinction usually does not matter because in either case gain on the sale of the patent will be long term capital gain so long the patent is held for more than one year.

In the case of a patent acquired by a business from the creator, the tax characterization is usually clear because in almost every case the patent is likely to be acquired as an asset to be used in a trade or business, and thus governed by Code section 1231. Of course, it is not impossible to conceive of an investor who acquires a patent as an "investment asset," not for the purpose of licensing the patent (which would constitute using the patent in the trade or business of licensing) but rather for the purpose of having the patent appreciate in value and then selling it. However, such a situation is for the most part of theoretical interest only because a patent purchaser usually has a strong interest in recovering its tax basis in the patent through depreciation or amortization deductions, and thus will almost certainly treat it as a Code section 1231 asset. In all events, whether governed by Code section 1221 or Code section 1231, the patent purchaser can enjoy subsequent long-term capital gain treatment so long as the patent right is held for more than one year before it is resold.

License as a "Sale". As the preceding discussion demonstrates, whether a patent is self-created or acquired by purchase, so long as the patent is not inventory and so long as it has been held for more than one year it will be eligible for LTCG treatment, either under Code section 1221 or 1231, upon the occurrence of a "sale or exchange." Because patent rights are often transferred through the mechanism of a license, an important initial question is whether the transfer of rights is structured as a "sale" or a "license"—and whether, even if it is structured as a license, it constitutes a "sale" for tax purposes. A "sale or exchange" is required in order for the transferor to enjoy LTCG treatment under Code section 1222(3) or 1231(a)(3)(A), while a license that is not a sale or exchange for tax purposes will generate ordinary income to the licensor.[90]

Whether a transfer constitutes a sale or a license is determined by all the facts and circumstances. In general, a sale of a patent occurs when a patent owner transfers the exclusive right to make, use, or sell a patented article, or an undivided interest in all three rights.[91] Obviously, a license that grants to the licensee all substantial rights in and to the patent would be treated as a sale eligible for LTCG treatment even under the far more restrictive rules of Code section 1235. In general, the case law determining whether a transaction is a sale of a patent or a license of patent rights is both voluminous and complex, but it is clear that an exclusive license of less than all rights in a patent can sometimes qualify as a "sale." In particular, a license granting the licensee exclusive geographical rights or field-of-use rights under a patent has been held to be a sale.[92] Thus, case law supports the fragmentation of patents into geographic regions and fields of use, and permits a patent holder to treat such licenses as a "sale" of such rights, so long as the transferee has the exclusive right to make, use, and sell the patented article within the applicable region or field.[93]

As an alternative strategy, fragmenting the patent by licensing an undivided interest in all patent rights can also qualify as a "sale."[94] Note that the sale of an undivided interest in all rights is even expressly within the scope of Code section 1235. This will suggest to the mathematically inclined that a patent holder could, theoretically, sell an infinite number of undivided interests. However, as a practical matter, the greater the number of such licensing transactions, the more likely a court may be to review the arrangement as a license rather than a sale of rights. Nonetheless, both the exclusive licensing of important patent rights, and the non-exclusive licensing of an undivided interest in all patent rights, can each potentially qualify as a "sale" producing the desired LTCG treatment.

TAXATION OF TRADEMARKS AND TRADE NAMES

Overview of Trademark Law. Trade names, trademarks, and similar intellectual property rights embody the special recognition value and market power that a business, its name, and its trade dress obtain over a period of years and decades of business marketing and advertising. In particular, common law has long recognized the principle that a competitor cannot improperly expropriate the goodwill of an existing business by using a similar or confusing name that causes the public to confuse or be unable to distinguish one business from the other. These common law concepts have been embodied in federal law in the Lanham Act.[95] Note that, unlike patent and copyright law, the federal trademark law does not generally preempt state laws providing trademark protection. There is federal and state law defining both the nature of the rights and the legal mechanisms for protecting these rights.

The Lanham Act defines the term "trademark" to include "any work, name, symbol, or device, or any combination thereof (1) used by a person, or (2) which a person has a bona fide intention to use in commerce and applies to register on the principal register established [under the Act], to identify and distinguish his or her goods, including a unique product, from those manufactured and sold by others and to indicate the source of the goods, even if that source is unknown."[96]

In order to qualify for protection, the trademark must meet three requirements: (1) designation, (2) distinctiveness, and (3) actual use or intent to use.

Designation. The designation requirement basically addresses the mechanism or medium for expressing the trademark. Permitted designations include numbers, letters, slogans, pictures, symbols, characters, sounds, graphic design, product, and packaging, among many others.

Distinctiveness. This is the most important element of a trademark because to be both valuable and protectable a trademark needs to distinguish the protected goods from all others.

Intent to use. Trademarks under common law can only be created by actual use. The Lanham Act permits a registration of trademarks, but requires that a registrant must have a bona fide intent to use the mark, and must then proceed to use the mark in order to enjoy priority running from the filing date.

Creation and Acquisition of a Trademark. A trademark is a Code section 197 intangible, and thus subject to fifteen-year amortization.[97] However, unlike patents, copyrights, and many other forms of intellectual property, a trademark does not come under any of the "separately acquired" exceptions under Code section 197(e), and thus is amortized over fifteen-years even if it is the sole asset being acquired. According to the legislative history to Code section 197, the acquisition of a franchise, trademark, or trade name *by itself* is the acquisition of a trade or business.[98] Thus, acquisition of a trademark automatically makes all other intangible assets acquired with it into Code section 197 intangibles. See Chapter 11.

Sale of a Trademark—Code Section 1253. Trademarks and trade names, like patents, have their own special Code section, in this case Code section 1253. However, whereas Code section 1235 gives very favorable treatment to individual inventors (generally giving capital gain treatment to a qualifying holder, even if a one-year holding period is not satisfied and even if the holder is a professional inventor), Code section 1253 embodies two basic policies, and both are generally adverse to taxpayers.

First, Code section 1253(a) provides a rule that even if the transfer of a trademark or trade name otherwise qualifies as a sale or exchange of a capital asset (i.e., even if the transaction meets the necessary requirements under Code section 1231 to generate long-term capital gain on sale) such favorable treatment is barred if the transferor retains a "significant interest" in the transferred trade name or trademark. In turn, a "significant interest" is both defined broadly and left in a relatively open-ended status, with the Code providing a list of six specific examples of retained interests that are expressly identified as "not exclusive," meaning that there are other situations that may also constitute the retention of a "significant interest." Among the six examples in Code section 1253(b)(2) is if the Seller will receive a contingent payment, based on productivity or use, that is "substantial" in relation to the total amount of payments.[99]

Basically, a simple and reasonably accurate way to summarize the policies embodied in Code section 1253(a) and (b) is that the Code will permit long-term capital gain treatment for a sale of a trademark only if it is a "vanilla" transaction where all rights in the trademark are transferred by the transferor, no significant rights are retained, and the payment arrangement does not have the look and feel of a license (i.e., the sales price is a fixed amount, or a substantially fixed amount, and is not substantially contingent upon the use, productivity, or other exploitation of the trademark or trade name).

Note that Code section 1253(a) applies its narrowing effects only after one does the initial analysis of whether the transaction in question would generate long-term capital gain. In particular, if a trademark is licensed in a transaction that qualifies as a license for tax purposes, payments received by the transferor will be royalties, characterized as ordinary income, and will not trigger capital gain. Likewise, even if the trademark is transferred in a sale or exchange transaction, the asset in question must qualify for long-term capital gain treatment under Code section 1231. Note that a trademark is inherently an asset used in a trade or business, and thus should qualify as a sale or exchange of a capital asset under Code section 1231 so long as the trademark has been in existence for at least one year (the one-year holding requirement).

The second narrowing function of Code section 1253 is found in the last two subsections, Code section 1253(c) and (d). Code section 1253(c) indicates that even if a transfer qualifies as a sale or exchange the portion of payments received by the transferor that are contingent on productivity or use of the trademark will be treated as ordinary income. This provision reflects the view that a transfer of a trademark, when the payment is based on its contingent value in the hands of the transferee, has the look and feel of a license, and therefore the transferor must treat all of the payments structured in this fashion as ordinary income, even if the transfer otherwise qualifies as a sale or exchange.

Code section 1253(d), meanwhile, does allow a transferee to treat "contingent serial payments" as deductible immediately under Code section 162, rather than capitalizable under Code section 197. However, as a practical matter this favorable rule is, in fact, quite narrowly construed, because the transferee can enjoy the benefits of this rule only if the payments are made at a fixed rate or under a fixed formula that applies consistently over the entire term of the agreement. Moreover, in the case of a sale (as opposed to a license) of a trademark, the term of the agreement is considered perpetual, and therefore Code section 1253(d) is realistically not available in a normal sale transaction because the Buyer will rarely be willing to give the Seller a perpetual fixed right to enjoy a return on the transfer.

Code section 1253, when originally enacted, was directed at franchisers, who in the period before the enactment of this provision generally treated a sale of franchise rights as a capital gain transaction, and at franchisees, who were treating their payments to the franchisers as immediately deductible payments under Code section 162. Code section 1253 therefore contains provisions that were clearly designed to address and prevent franchisers from enjoying capital gains treatment on the transfer of a franchise interest or right. However, the provision applies to *all* transfers of trade name and trademark rights, and therefore throws out a lot of babies as well as a lot of bath water. In particular, Code section 1253(a) takes the view that even if a transaction is a "sale" under normal federal income tax rules, it will still be denied capital gain treatment if there is significant retained right on the part of the transferor. Obviously, a franchiser retains a variety of rights, such as the right to control quality, control appearance, and other factors that would be picked up by this rule. However, note that among the expressly listed retained rights that are considered "significant" under Code section 1253(b), and thus trigger an application of Code section 1253(a), is any contingent payment arrangement based on production or use where the contingent payment amounts are "substantial" in relationship to the total amount of payments.[100] In effect, Code section 1253 bars favorable LTCG treatment to a true sale transaction if the means of payment is economically similar to what is usually considered a licensing type of arrangement, namely royalty payments based on productivity or use.

The other policy imbedded in Code section 1253 is the view that contingent payment amounts ought to be viewed as royalties, even if they arise in a transaction that is otherwise a sale or exchange. Note that Code section 1253(c) matters only if the underlying transaction is first characterized as a sale (meaning that the transaction comes within Code section 1231, is not barred from sale or exchange treatment by Code section 1253(a), and is not otherwise considered a license) and that provision then characterizes any contingent payments received by the transferor as ordinary income, even if the overall transaction itself (meaning the fixed payments) is eligible for long-term capital gain treatment.

Meanwhile, on the other side of the ledger, the transferee making the contingent payments is subject to a much more stringent rule concerning whether these payments will be permitted to be deducted currently as paid. Basically, contingent payments will be deductible under Code section 162 by the payor only if they meet the rather mechanical and mathematical formula of being serial payments (meaning based on a fixed formula or fixed amount for the entire period of the term of the agreement). Any contingent payments that do not fall within this relatively strict requirement are treated as additional purchase price payments and will be capitalized and amortized under Code section 197, based on when in time the payments are made. This is, in short, a very adverse, back-loading rule. Note also that to the extent contingent payments and/or fixed payments are viewed as an installment sale of the trademark from the transferor to the transferee, a portion of the total payments may be characterized as original issue discount (OID), and should be accounted for under the OID rules and not under Code section 197. See Chapter 10.

COMPARISON OF TAX RULES APPLICABLE TO PATENTS AND TRADEMARKS

This section provides a brief comparison of the tax treatment accorded patents compared to the tax treatment accorded trademarks for the purpose of illuminating how each of the relevant Code provisions works, and to underscore the fact that patents are generally favored under the tax law, while trademarks are generally disfavored.

Creation. The creator of a patent can generally deduct all expenses under Code section 174 and may also be eligible to claim a research credit under Code section 41. Code section 174 applies if the expenses are incurred "in connection" with a trade or business, which is a lesser standard than "carrying on" a trade or business under Code section 162. Thus, a patent does not even need to be created in the carrying on of a trade or business, as long as there is an intention to eventually go into the business.

Trademarks, by contrast, are always governed by Code section 197. Therefore, all expenses related to the creation of a trademark are subject to fifteen-year amortization from the date that the trademark is first placed in service.

Capital Gain on Transfer. On the transfer of a patent, Code section 1235 broadens the fundamental circumstances in which a transferor can enjoy long-term capital gain treatment. Briefly, a patent can always potentially qualify as either a Code section 1221 capital asset or as a Code Sec 1231 asset used in the conduct of a trade or business. In addition, Code section 1235 provides favorable long-term capital gains treatment to a narrow class of individuals (i.e., the patent inventor or an individual funding the inventor) by eliminating both the exclusion for "inventory" and the one-year holding requirement that would otherwise apply under both Code section 1221 and Code section 1231.

By contrast, Code section 1253 first requires that the trademark be eligible for capital gain treatment under Code section 1231, and narrows eligibility by stating that even if the transaction would otherwise be a sale it will not enjoy long-term capital gain treatment if there is retention of any significant interest by the transferor in the trademark after the transfer. In addition, even if the transaction clears the hurdles of Code section 1253(a) and (b), any payments to the transferor that are contingent in nature are re-characterized by Code section 1253(c) as ordinary income rather than capital gain, simply because the mechanism chosen for determining the payment amount is contingent on productivity and use, which is viewed with disfavor under Code section 1253.

Tax Consequences to Purchaser. On the purchaser's side, a patent that is separately acquired is not governed by Code section 197, but rather is governed by Code section 167. Moreover, the IRS has strongly suggested that the income forecast method may be the best way to depreciate a patent. Thus, the cost of acquiring a patent can often be depreciated over a relatively short period of time that corresponds to the expected useful life of the patent.

By contrast, a trademark acquisition is always governed by Code section 197, causes all other intangible assets acquired in connection with the trademark also to be governed by Code section 197, and requires amortization over fifteen years. Moreover, except in the case of contingent serial payments, any contingent payments made with respect to the trademark are added to the amortizable basis and amortized over the remainder of the fifteen-year amortization period otherwise applicable under Code section 197. This has the effect of substantially back-loading the tax benefit of such payments. Code section 1253(d) does contain, for contingent serial payments, a right to deduct them under Code section 162 if they meet the relatively strict mechanical and mathematical tests required by that provision.

COPYRIGHTS

Overview of Copyright Law. A copyright is a federally protected right, mentioned in the U.S. Constitution, and, as embodied in the Copyright Act of 1976, is currently codified at 17 USC §§ 101–810. A copyright grants the copyright holder the exclusive right to reproduce, distribute, publicly perform, display, and create derivative works from the original work of authorship. The protection extends to "original works of authorship fixed in any tangible medium of expression."[101] Copyright protection does not extend to ideas, procedures, processes, systems, methods of operation, concepts, principles, or discoveries.[102] (This latter category of creative endeavors is protected, if at all, by patent law, trade secret law, or trademark law.) Copyright protection is granted to the original author (or authors) of a work. The copyright law expressly creates an exception for "work made for hire," which applies when an employee prepares a work as part of the employee's employment or a work is specially ordered for use as a contribution to a collective work, an audiovisual work, a translation, or compilation and the parties expressly agree in writing that the work will be considered a work made for hire. The copyright protection lasts, for a work created by an individual author, for the life of the author plus 70 years.[103] The copyright term for anonymous works, pseudonymous works, and works made for hire is 95 years from the year of first publication, or 120 years from the date of creation, whichever expires first.[104]

Expenses of Creating a Copyright. As with all intellectual property, a taxpayer spending money to create a business asset would naturally like to deduct those expenses as rapidly as possible. The question is whether the expenditures to create a copyright are governed by the principles of Code section 263 (generally requiring capitalization when the benefits of an expenditure will extend beyond the tax year), whether the expenditures are required to be capitalized under Code section 263A (generally providing capitalization rules for the creation of inventory), or whether the expenditures can be deducted currently under one of the available code provisions, particularly Code section 162 (ordinary and necessary business expenses incurred in the carrying on of a trade or business), Code section 212 (expenses incurred for the production or collection of income), Code section 174 (research expenses), or Code section 263A(h) (discussed below), which permits writers, photographers, and artists to deduct expenses currently that would otherwise be subject to capitalization under Code section 263A.

Under Code section 263A, taxpayers who produce tangible personal property as part of a trade or business must capitalize all direct and indirect expenditures incurred to create that property.[105] Significantly, the definition of tangible personal property includes "a film, sound recording, video tape, book, or similar property."[106] If the taxpayer's expenses fall within this Code provision, all direct material and direct labor costs and indirect costs are required to be capitalized, and these capitalized expenses, in turn, will generally be depreciated using the interesting and curious "income forecast method" described in Code section 167(g) and applicable to the categories of property described in Code section 263A(b)(1).[107]

In response to enormous complaints about the effects of these UNICAP rules on individual writers and artists, an exception was created for "qualified creative expenses" under Code section 263A(h). The exception states that certain expenses incurred by an individual engaged in the trade or business of being a writer, photographer, or artist are exempt from the capitalization requirements if these expenses would be deductible but for Code section 263A.[108] The purpose of this provision was to exempt freelance writers, photographers, and artists from the burdens of the UNICAP rules because income from their creative activities might not be received for many years. There are two things to note about this exception:

1. It applies only to individuals in the trades or businesses of being a "free-lance" (meaning self-employed) writer, photographer, or artist. Thus, anyone who is not a self-employed individual, or who is not active within the three recognized fields, cannot take advantage of this exception.

2. The exception provides merely that Code section 263A will not apply to require the capitalization of any qualified creative expense. A taxpayer must still determine whether a qualified creative expense is subject to capitalization under Code section 263 or whether it is deductible currently under one of the other provisions noted above.

The legislative history, for example, notes that attorneys and consultants can produce a written product over a period of years and receive payment after the product is completed, and the uniform capitalization rules do not apply to the costs incurred to produce such a written report. In effect, Code section 263A(h) puts writers, photographers, and artists on the same accounting method as attorneys or consultants by allowing them to expense such things as overhead and operational costs, compensation costs, and similar expenses but still calls for capitalization of expenditures (e.g., for office equipment) that would normally be capitalized under the normal accounting rules for other service providers.

Prior to the enactment of Code section 263A(h) in 1988, the IRS provided some relief from the burdens of the UNICAP rules. Under IRS Notice 88-62, these rules remain available even after the enactment of Code section 263A(h). In that notice, the IRS permits certain writers, photographers, and artists to defer expenditures that would otherwise be subject to the UNICAP rules and amortize such costs over a three-year period, with an amortization deduction equal to 50 percent of the "qualified creative costs" in the first year and 25 percent in each of the next two years.

Comment: Notice 88-62 provides favorable treatment to a broader category of expenses than Code section 263A(h) but is still limited to self-employed individuals in the specified fields of endeavor.

The Code from time to time provides for special rules applicable to certain (favored) industries. For example, Code section 181 was added to the Code in 2004 to encourage domestic film production. This Section applied to any "qualified film or television production, and any qualified live theatrical production, as an expense which is not chargeable to capital account." Section 181 provided for a 100 percent deduction of the costs of "any qualified film or television production, and any qualified live theatrical production," up to a cap of the first $15 million aggregate production costs, with a higher aggregate cap of $20 million available if production occurs in certain low-income or distressed areas. The choice of whether to claim Code section 181 deductions or use the income forecast method of depreciation recovery, was at the election of the taxpayer. Although Code section 181 has been renewed continuously – and sometimes retroactively – over the years since 2004, it has lapsed for 2017. Congress may still revive it, even retroactively, at some point in the future.

Ordinary and Necessary Business Expenses v. Hobby Losses. Even assuming that expenses are "qualified creative expenses," another significant tax hurdle is whether the expenses are incurred in the carrying on of a trade or business. Many of the activities covered by copyright law are notoriously fun and popular, from writing to painting to creating movies, and so the IRS will look at whether the activity rises to the level of a trade or business. Code section 183 applies to limit losses to the income from the "hobby" activity unless the taxpayer entered into the activity with the objective of making a profit. The criteria for "profit motive" under Code section 183 is more than a little convoluted since the regulations recognize that the ultimate test is the subjective intent of the taxpayer, but this subjective test is subject to an analysis made "by reference to objective standards" whether the taxpayer truly entered into the activity with the objective of making a profit.[109] Among other things, Code section 183 provides a rebuttable presumption that an activity is conducted for profit if in any three of the previous five consecutive years, the gross income derived from the activity exceeds the deductions attributable to the activity.[110]

A related consequence of receiving business income is the obligation to pay not only income tax but also self-employment tax. The independent, self-employed artist must keep records of business and non-business income, including any part- or full-time work, separate and documented.

Sale of Copyright Property by Creator. A sale of copyrighted property is subject to uniquely adverse treatment under the Code. Code section 1221(a)(3) provides that a copyright in the hands of a taxpayer whose personal efforts created such property is expressly excluded from the definition of a capital asset, and a corresponding exclusion exists under Code section 1231(b)(1)(C). Therefore, a copyright is an ordinary asset in the hands of its individual creator. This treatment of a copyright is in marked contrast to the very favorable treatment of a patent in the hands of a patent creator[111] and even in contrast to the requirements for obtaining capital gain treatment with respect to a trademark under Code section 1253.

As is so often the case in the area of intellectual property, there is a different, more favorable rule for a certain politically influential group – in this case the song writers. Thanks to an impressive lobbying effort in by the Nashville Songwriters' Association International, Code section 1221(b)(3) currently provides that a taxpayer may elect that the exclusions from capital asset classification found in Code section 1221(a)(1) and 1221(a)(3) do not apply to "musical compositions or copyrights in musical works sold or exchanged by a taxpayer described in subsection (a)(3)". In short, songwriters can enjoy capital gains treatment on the sale of their songs, while authors must recognize ordinary income on the sale of their books. This strikes the author of this treatise and palpably unfair.[112]

Capitalization by Buyer. The correct method for depreciating a purchased copyright depends on whether the copyright is a separately acquired asset, or is acquired in connection with the acquisition of assets constituting a trade or business or a substantial portion thereof. If a copyright is separately acquired, the basis in the asset equals its cost under Code section 1012, and the cost can be depreciated under Code section 167(g).[113] As with patents, the IRS has generally encouraged the depreciation of copyrights using the income forecast method, over the periods during which the taxpayer usually derives income from the copyright.[114]

By contrast, a copyright acquired in connection with the acquisition of assets constituting a trade or business is a "Section 197 intangible."[115] Therefore, copyrights acquired in connection with the acquisition of a trade or business will be capitalized and amortized on a straight-line method over fifteen years under Code section 197.[116] Note that fifteen-year amortization applies regardless of the useful life, or remaining statutory period, of the copyright protection. As is true with all Code section 197 assets, any time there is a periodic contingent payment paid or incurred after the tax year in which the copyright is acquired the purchaser much capitalize and amortize these contingent payments over the remaining years in the amortization period. The regulations under Code section 197 generally provide that with respect to both fixed and contingent payments paid for the right to use a Code section 197 intangible, the payments are treated as payments under a debt instrument issued in exchange for the property under Code sections 483 and 1275.[117] These regulations generally provide that the installment sale/OID rules will apply in determining when amounts treated as payments of principal are to be capitalized and amortized. See Chapter 10.

Comment: The application of the income forecast method was modified by the enactment of Code section 167(g) in 1996. That provision limits the application of the income forecast method to specific categories of assets, including motion picture films and video tapes, sound recordings, copyrights, books, patents, and other property specified by regulation. The applicable regulations, in turn, extend the income forecast method to depreciation of the theatrical productions and any other property designated by the IRS. The regulations provide a variety of rules for determining how the forecast method of income is to be interpreted and applied.[118]

Sale of Copyright by Party Other Than Creator. A copyright in the hands of a purchaser will generally be property described in Code section 1231 (i.e., property used in connection with the conduct of a trade or business and subject to the allowance for depreciation) if held the requisite one year. Significantly, a copyright protects, in a broad way, a number of very specific, distinct interests, including the right to reproduce the underlying work, the right to prepare derivative works, the right to distribute copies to the public by sale, rental, and lease, the right to perform the work, and the right to display the work publicly. The general rule is that a "sale" of a copyright or an interest in a copyright occurs whenever the holder transfers "the exclusive right to exploit the copyright work in a medium of publication throughout the life of the copyright."[119] Rev. Rul. 60-226 reversed the IRS's early position that a copyright constitutes a single unit of property and instead recognized that, as with the sale of a patent, one can divide the copyright into a number of discrete property rights, and it will be considered a "sale" as long as there is a transfer of the exclusive right to exploit the copyrighted work in a medium of publication throughout the life of the copyright. Rev. Rul. 60-226 also clarified that the mechanism of payment does not determine whether there is a sale or a license (i.e., the transfer of the applicable rights is considered a sale, even if some or all of the future payments are contingent on performance or use of the transferred property).

Assuming that Code section 1231 is applicable and that the Seller is transferring the exclusive right to exploit the copyrighted work in a medium of publication throughout the life of the copyright, the transfer will be subject to the general rules of Code section 1231, namely that the gain on the sale will be subject to depreciation recapture under Code section 1245 and then will be eligible for long-term capital gain treatment so long as the asset has been held for more than one year. However, the exact character of a copyright in the hands of a purchaser can be a complicated and intellectually intriguing issue. Many copyrights, for example, are exploited through licensing rights to customers, and the question is whether the copyright will be excluded from Code section 1231 property because it is property "primarily held by the taxpayer for sale to customers in the ordinary course of his or her trade or business."[120]

The specific question is whether the copyrighted work is being held primarily for sale or whether it is being held for lease. In Rev. Rul. 62-141, the IRS addressed the issue in connection with the production of television films, movie films, and tapes. In that particular ruling, the taxpayers produced and leased television and move films and tapes but, after the initial showings, sold the assets. The IRS concluded that the fact that the films were leased for a period of time prior to sale would not prevent them from being considered held "primarily" for sale to customers within the meaning of Code section 1231(b)(1)(B). Realistically this is a complicated and nuanced analysis because the copyright itself is subject to license or sale separate and apart from the underlying tangible property produced in connection with its exploitation (e.g., the films in Rev. Rul. 62-141).

Sale v. License. Another significant issue is whether a transfer of a copyright interest is a sale or a license. Note that, in general, it is very common to transfer the rights under a copyright via an exclusive license, rather than by sale or assignment of the copyright itself. The IRS has recognized that a sale of a copyright or an interest in a copyright will arise whenever the holder transfers "exclusive right to exploit the copyrighted work in a medium of publication throughout the entire life of the copyright."[121] Thus, the question is not the mechanical or technical structure of the transaction, but whether there has been a transfer of (1) exclusive right in a specified medium of publication and (2) a transfer throughout the life of the copyright. Conversely, a license will arise whenever the transfer of interest has a non-exclusive right or a term shorter than the full life of the copyright.

In contrast to other major categories of intellectual property, where often the single biggest tax planning issue is to structure of transfer of rights as a "sale" that results in LTCG for an individual transferor, a copyright transfer by the person whose personal efforts created such property will generate ordinary income even if the transaction is unquestionably a "sale." This is because a copyright in the hands of the individual creator is excluded both from capital asset status by Code section 1221(a)(3) and from capital gain treatment as a business asset by Code section 1231(b)(1)(C). By contrast, an unrelated party that purchases a copyright from its creator in a sale will presumably use the copyright in a trade or business as Code section 1231 property (unless it is held strictly for investment as a capital asset under Code section 1221, which is unlikely), and will be able to depreciate or amortize the asset, either under Code section 167, if it is separately acquired, or under Code section 197, if it is acquired in connection with the assets of a trade or business or a substantial portion thereof.[122] In turn, a subsequent sale of the copyright by a purchaser, assuming the asset has been held for more than one year, should generate long-term capital gain, subject to the recapture under Code section 1245 of any previously claimed depreciation/amortization deductions.[123]

Comment: The distinction between the sale and license of a copyright is of singularly little importance in most cases, because (1) most copyright transactions involve the creator, e.g., licensing or selling to a publisher in exchange for royalty payments, and (2) the resulting income is ordinary whether the transaction is characterized a sale or a license. However, as will be explored in the next section, dealing with software, a high-stakes tax issue can arise if software (or any other copyrighted asset) is created, not by the "personal efforts" of one individual, but rather by the collective efforts of numerous employees working for an S corporation or LLC and assigning all rights to the employer entity. In such case, a substantial argument can be made that the employer is not a taxpayer "whose personal efforts created such property," and thus the employer can characterize the copyright asset as either a capital asset of Code section 1231 property, and claim long-term capital gain treatment or all or a portion of any subsequent sale.

When a copyright transaction is viewed as a license rather than a sale, the royalty income received by the licensor is taxed as ordinary income.[124] Advance royalty payments are included in gross income for the year that the payments are received, regardless of the period covered or the method of accounting used.[125]

Comment: Proposed Reg. § 1.61-8(b) would give the IRS authority to issue rules that allow taxpayers to defer recognition of advance payments under circumstances specified by the IRS. The apparent objective of the IRS is to mitigate some of the harsh consequences of these timing rules.

To the extent that license payments are ordinary income to the licensor, they are typically deductible by the licensee under Code section 162. Conversely, to the extent that the transfer of a copyright is treated as a "sale," the acquirer of those rights, even if the acquisition is in the form of a license, would be deemed to be making capitalizable payments. As noted above, the rules for determining whether these payments are principal versus interest, and when the principal payments can be capitalized and recovered through amortization and depreciation, are generally governed under the rules of Code sections 483 and 1274 (addressing debt instruments issued in connection with the acquisition of property).

COMPUTER SOFTWARE

Computer Software as Intellectual Property. The operational nature of computer software is familiar to everyone, but its legal nature is remarkably complex. In general, intellectual property is intimately related to the legal mechanisms used to protect it from competition by others. In the case of copyrights, patents, and trademarks, federal and/or state law provide a form of legal monopoly that provides uniqueness and value to the intellectual property falling within those categories. Trade secret protection, meanwhile, is the fourth major mechanism for protecting valuable intellectual property rights from competition, and the protection works well when the nature of the intellectual property is such that it is used within the business privately and does not need to be disclosed in a meaningful way to the public.

The legal conundrum with computer software for many years was the fact that software does not easily fall within any of the four conventional mechanisms for legally protecting intellectual property. All software programs are a form of expression that naturally comes within the scope of copyright protection, but the problem is that copyright protection is not adequate because any capable software programmer can "rewrite" a software program using different words, symbols, and expressions and accomplish the same functionality. Obviously, it is the functionality, not the mode of expression, that makes software valuable. Likewise, some aspects of the computer program may have sufficient novelty and inventiveness to qualify for patent protection, but this is both unusual and, ultimately, is not an adequate protection even if a patent is granted because a patent necessarily must be published and, once published, talented software writers may have the ability to "reverse engineer" the software to accomplish the desired functionality, while avoiding patent infringement.

By process of elimination, the best way to protect proprietary software turned out to be trade secret law because licensors could prohibit licensees from reading, copying, and/or reverse engineering computer software under explicit language in a license agreement. However, as personal computers grew in popularity, and as software began to be mass marketed, it became unrealistic to negotiate a license agreement with each and every purchaser of software, and so "shrink-wrap" and "click-wrap" licenses were developed in a legal effort to preserve trade secret protection while allowing the mass marketing of desirable software at affordable prices. As late as the early to mid-1990s, it was considered "doubtful" whether shrink-wrap agreements were enforceable. However, a series of cases upheld the validity of shrink wrap or click wrap licenses,[126] and so trade secret law and related contract protection remain the principal legal means of protecting the intellectual property embodied in a software program.

Computer Software under the Code. Like many other categories of intellectual property, "computer software" first became a defined term in the Internal Revenue Code when Code section 197 was adopted in 1993. Code section 197(e)(3)(B) defines "computer software" to mean "any program designed to cause a computer to perform a desired function. Such term shall not include any database or similar item used unless the database or item is in the public domain and is incidental to the operation of otherwise qualifying computer software." In Rev. Proc. 2000-50, a more recent revenue procedure that provides guidelines on the treatment of the costs of computer software, the definition of "computer software" is significantly more elaborate and is defined as follows:

> Any program or routine (that is, any sequence of machine-readable code) that is designed to cause a computer to perform a desired function or set of functions, and the documentation required to describe and maintain that program or routine. It includes all forms and media in which the software is contained, whether written, magnetic, or otherwise. Computer programs of all classes, for example, operating systems, executive systems, monitors, compilers and translators, assembly routines, and utility programs as well as application programs, are included. Computer software also includes any incidental and ancillary rights that are necessary to effect the acquisition of the title to, the ownership of, or the right to use the computer software, and that are used

only in connection with that specific computer software. Computer software does not include any data or information base described in [Reg.] section 1.197-2(b)(4) (for example, data files, customer lists, or client files) unless the data base or item is in the public domain and is incidental to a computer program. Nor does it include any cost of procedures that are external to the computer's operation.

Tax Treatment of Expenses for Self-Created Software. Self-created computer software is excluded from the definition of Code section 197 intangible assets.[127] All or a portion of these costs in developing self-created software may be currently deductible under Code section 174 as research or experimental expenditures. Alternatively, as an administrative rule, all software expenditures, even those that do not qualify as research or experimental under Code section 174, may be deducted currently under a method of accounting provided in Rev. Proc. 2000-50, subject to the consistency rules of that revenue procedure. Taxpayers can also decide to capitalize the cost and amortize the cost over the three-year period provided in Code section 167(f). The legislative history to Code section 197 indicates that self-created intangible assets includes software produced by the taxpayer or by another person under a contract entered into prior to the production of the intangible asset.[128] Thus, software developed under contract with an independent contractor, to be owned by the taxpayer, will be treated as "created" by the taxpayer.[129]

A creator of computer software would ideally like to deduct as much of the creator's costs immediately, preferably under Code section 174 (and thus avoid recapture issues under Code section 1245 later).[130] Since most or all of a software program's value will result in the realization of benefits beyond the current tax year, expenses that for whatever reason cannot be deducted as "research" under Code section 174 (or under Rev. Proc. 2000-50) would logically be subject to capitalization under Code section 263. However, assuming the software is then used in the carrying on of a trade or business, even if expenses are required to be capitalized, this is not as adverse a result as it would be for most other assets because the depreciation of computer software is now accorded favorable treatment under Code section 167(f), which permits amortization of software over a thirty-six-month period.

There is a long and complicated history about whether and what software development costs constitute research or experimental expenditures for the purposes of Code section 174. In Rev. Proc. 69-21 (predecessor to Rev. Proc. 2000-50), the IRS provided a liberal interpretation of how to apply Code section 174. Basically, the IRS stated that it would not dispute a taxpayer's treatment of software development costs provided that the costs were: (1) consistently treated as current expenses and deducted in full in a manner similar to that required by Code section 174(a)(1) or (2) consistently treated as capital expenditures and regularly recovered through amortization deductions in a manner similar to that required under Code section 174(b) over a period of five years from the date the development of the software was completed. In effect, the taxpayer could either identify the portion of the software development costs that would be viewed as experimental or research under Code section 174, or the taxpayer could avail himself or herself of the broader scope of Rev. Proc. 69-21, which applied rules analogous to those under Code section 174, but did not require that the software development costs satisfy the "uncertainty test" of Reg. § 1.174-2(a)(1). Instead, Rev. Proc. 69-21, which was updated and reissued in Rev. Proc. 2000-50, allowed all costs incurred in developing computer software to be deducted currently, or else capitalized and amortized over five years.

The 1993 enactment of Code section 167(f), which allows amortization of computer software costs over a thirty-six-month period, has somewhat reduced the importance of Rev. Proc. 69-21, and later Rev. Proc. 2000-50. Note, however, that it is still beneficial to claim deductions under Code section 174 because such deductions are not subsequently recaptured as ordinary income under Code section 1245 if there is a future sale or exchange of the software.[131] On the other hand, it should be noted that because in most cases computer software is developed and is licensed to many customers, the "sale" alternative ultimately may be less valuable or less important than, say, in the case of a patent.

Tax Treatment of Costs to Acquire Software—Code Section 197. This code provision has relatively detailed and nuanced rules that apply to acquisitions of computer software. In general, most software is not subject to the provisions of Code section 197. Code section 197(e)(3) specifically excludes the following:

1. *Off-the-shelf computer software.* Code section 197(e)(3)(A)(i) excludes software that: (1) is readily available for purchase by the general public, (2) is subject to a non-exclusive license, and (3) has not been substantially modified. Such software can be depreciated on

a straight-line basis of thirty-six months under Code section 167(f), and this is true even though the off-the-shelf software is acquired in connection with the acquisition of assets constituting a trade or business.

2. *Separately acquired computer software.* Code section 197(e)(3)(A)(ii) excludes from the definition of Code section 197 intangibles all separately acquired software (i.e., software not acquired in a transaction involving the acquisition of assets constituting a trade or business or a substantial portion thereof). Software falling within this exclusion can generally be depreciated over thirty-six months under Code section 167(f).

3. *Bundled software.* There is a special rule for so-called "bundled software," which is software that is acquired as a nonseparately stated item in the acquisition of a computer itself. The regulations specifically exclude bundled software from the definition of a Code section 197 intangible, although the language is subtle, and merely indicates that Code section 197 does not apply to any amount "taken into account in determining the cost of property that is not a Code section 197 intangible."[132] Bundled software is treated as part of the cost of the hardware, and so the costs are capitalized under Code section 263 and depreciated under Code sections 167/168 (generally over five years).

4. *Leased or licensed software.* The regulations under Code section 197 expressly provide that Code section 197 is applicable to a lease or license of a Code section 197 intangible.[133] The basic view is that acquiring software by lease or license, rather than by purchase, should not permit an asset acquirer to avoid the fifteen-year amortization rules under Code section 197. However, there are a several pragmatic and sensible rules for implementing this provision. First, where a software lease or license calls for periodic payments over the term of the contract, the legislative history to Code section 197 indicates payments should not be subject to that provision and instead should be taken into account and deducted under the payor's method of accounting.[134] Second, if leased or license software is excluded from the application of Code section 197 because it comes within one of the three categories described above, it should likewise not come within Code section 197 simply because it is leased or licensed, and the regulations confirm this result.[135] To the extent software is acquired in connection with an acquisition of assets constituting a trade or business or a substantial portion thereof, payments allocable to such software will be subject to Code section 197.

License v. Sale of Software Assets. Because computer software is exploited and transferred in commerce in exceptionally diverse ways, care and attention must be given to whether a transfer of rights should be considered a "sale" or something other than a sale (i.e., a license, lease, etc.). Note that even if a transferee acquires the exclusive right to use software, this still may not constitute a sale because "all rights" in computer software would include the right to produce and modify the software as well. Note also that a not-uncommon method of transferring software rights is through a "lease." The difference between a license and a lease is that a license typically is a perpetual right to use the computer software, while a lease is a permission of limited duration (e.g., leasing a computer and the related software for a period of three years to use in a business).

For reasons inherent in the nature of computer software and its economic exploitation, it is often a complicated exercise to decide whether a transfer of rights is a sale or a license. For example, a vendor of off-the-shelf software typically gives the purchaser all rights to use the software in its current form but does not give the purchaser the right to re-license, modify, resell, or otherwise use the software other than in its current form for the purchaser's own use. A rule of thumb in determining whether a sale or license has arisen is whether the source code has been transferred along with the object code. Because income from the sale of software potentially can be taxed (subject to Code section 1221(a)(3) as capital gain, while income from a license is taxed as ordinary income, the stakes are often substantial.

The regulations under Code section 861 have attempted to address the sale versus license question in connection with computer software sold or licensed to sources outside the United States.[136] The regulations use a copyright as the appropriate initial property analogy and distinguish between transfers of "copyright rights" and transfers of "copyrighted articles.[137] The determination whether a transfer of a copyright right is a sale or exchange of property is made on the basis of whether, taking into account all facts and circumstances (and applying the principles of Code sections 1222 and 1235), there has been a transfer of all substantial rights in the copyright.[138] A transaction that does not constitute a sale or exchange because not all substantial rights have been transferred will be classified as a license.[139] The determination whether a transfer of a copyrighted article is a sale or exchange is made on the basis of whether, taking into account all facts and circumstances, the benefits and burdens of ownership have been transferred.[140] A transaction that does not constitute a sale or exchange because insufficient benefits and burdens of ownership of the copyrighted article have been transferred will be classified as a lease.[141]

Tax Issues on Disposition of Computer Software by Creator. When software is being sold by its creator, one of the interesting and complicated twists is to define the legal character of the property being sold. In particular, a self-created software asset may be protected by copyright, patent, both, or neither. The characterization matters because the sale of a copyright by a taxpayer whose personal efforts created the copyrighted property is excluded from the definition of capital asset,[142] and likewise from Code section 1231 property,[143] and therefore will generate ordinary income. On the other hand, if the software is viewed as in the nature of a patent, Code section 1235 provides very favorable capital gains treatment.

There is a surprisingly sparse amount of legal authority on the issue of how to characterize computer software when it is sold by its creator. In *D.D. Levy*,[144] the U.S. Tax Court considered the proper characterization of gain recognized in the sale of computer software created by the taxpayer and concluded that the eligibility of software for protection under the copyright law brought the sale within the exclusion of Code section 1221(a)(3) and that therefore the sale generated ordinary income to the selling taxpayer. The Tax Court's conclusion that because software is in theory a form of written expression, and therefore a software program is eligible for copyright protection, may make some sense in the case of an individual software writer who writes a software program because the analogy to an author of a book is at least apt. However, the reality is that, whereas copyright offers substantial protection to the author of a book, it offers virtually no protection to the author of a software program because the value of software is not in the nominal form of expression. (Any good software writer can rewrite a program using different terms so that it copies none of the expression and all of the content.) At most, the *Levy* case should be viewed as a rule applicable only to individuals whose personal efforts created the software.

By contrast if there is a sale of software by a corporation that paid its employees to "create" software, the better position appears to be that a subsequent sale of software by the corporation is not governed by Code section 1221(a)(3). The key provision, Code section 1221(a)(3)(A), excludes from capital asset treatment "a copyright, a literary, musical, or artistic composition, a letter or memorandum, or similar property, held by—(A) a taxpayer whose *personal efforts* created such property. . . ." [emphasis added]. Thus, the issue turns on whether a corporation can ever be a taxpayer whose "personal efforts" created the software. In Rev. Rul. 55-706,[145] the IRS addressed this question in the case of a corporation's sale of old films that it had produced. The IRS ruled:

> The property created by these corporations is not considered to be created by the personal efforts of a taxpayer where all of the costs and expenses are paid for by the corporation at the current going rate for the services rendered. The production of each of the films in the instant case involved a multiplicity of skills and abilities, the combined efforts of numerous individuals of various backgrounds and trades, and the use of substantial amounts of capital. Thus, no single individual may be said to have created by his personal efforts the films in question or a property in the films.

Based on this reasoning, the IRS ruled that the films were not held for sale in the ordinary course of business, were not created by the personal efforts of the corporation, and therefore were capital assets. Rev. Rul. 62-141[146] superseded Rev. Rul. 55-706 with respect to sales made on or after August 27, 1962.

The IRS, in the 1965 case *Desilu Prods., Inc.*,[147] apparently did not argue, and the court did not discuss, the application of Code section 1221(3) (predecessor to Code section 1221(a)(3)) to "work for hire" creations. In *Desilu*, the corporation produced television films and sold some of those films on March 6, 1962, to CBS. The IRS contended that the taxpayer had recognized ordinary income on the sale of the films under Code section 1221(1) (predecessor to Code section 1221(a)(1)) as property held for sale to customers in the ordinary course of a trade or business. The Tax Court rejected this argument and allowed the taxpayer capital gain. No reason is mentioned in the opinion for the failure of the IRS to argue Code section 1221(3) (predecessor to Code section 1221(a)(3)). The most plausible conclusion to be drawn is that the IRS conceded that Code section 1221(3) did not apply.

Some ambiguity was injected into this area by the case of *Chronicle Publishing Co.*[148] In that case, the Tax Court rejected the taxpayer's contention that Code section 1221(a)(3) can never apply to a corporation. The case involved the contribution of a newspaper clippings library created by a corporate taxpayer. The taxpayer argued that Code section 1221(a)(3) does not apply to a corporation. It rested its argument on the fact that the legislative history to the section and its predecessor speak only of "individuals" and does not mention a corporation as falling within the "taxpayer" category. The court conceded that the objective of those statutory provisions was to ensure that individuals who sold or exchanged the product of their personal efforts should realize ordinary income and not capital gain, and conceded that corporations cannot be the creators of property described in Code section 1221(a)(3)(A). However, property described in Code section 1221(a)(3)(B) and (C) is not so limited. Therefore, the court concluded letters, memoranda, and similar property produced by corporations or other business entities may be included within the scope of Code section 1221(a)(3). Therefore, the author believes that if the *Chronicle Publishing* case is carefully read and interpreted, it in fact supports the conclusion that a corporation is not subject to Code section 1221(a)(3)(A).

Note also that there is a relatively good argument that if software is subject to patent protection the asset should be categorized as a patent rather than a copyright and therefore eligible for favorable LTCG treatment on the sale.[149] However, even if this construction is correct, this last rule is of rather specific and limited value because few software programs are patented.

Disposition of Software by Someone Other Than Creator. A less complicated set of rules applies when computer software is purchased by an Acquirer, used in a trade or business, and subsequently resold. As explained above, software may be subject to depreciation under Code section 167(f) or amortization under Code section 197. In either case, the property, assuming it is being used in the trade or business, will be Code section 1231 property. Note that Code section 197(f)(7) states that "any amortizable section 197 intangible shall be treated as property which is of a character subject to the allowance for depreciation provided in section 167." This means that whether it is depreciated under Code section 167 or amortized under Code section 197, the asset will be subject to Code section 1231. A sale of software governed by Code section 1231 will have the usual consequences on disposition, namely recapture of ordinary income under Code section 1245 (including recapture of any amortization deductions claimed under Code section 197) and long term capital gain treatment for gain in excess of the recapture amounts so long as the asset has been held for more than one year.

A disposition by license or lease is a very common way to exploit a software program and produces what are called "royalty" payments (in the case of a license) or "rental" payments (in the case of a lease). As with other forms of intellectual property, if a software license transfers all rights in and to the software, then the license can qualify as a "sale." By contrast, if the license only transfers certain rights and the licensor retains rights such as the right to modify the software, the transaction is not a sale.

Note that with respect to patents it is clear that a transfer of an undivided interest in all patent rights is a sale that can produce long-term capital gain, both under Code section 1235 and under Code sections 1221 and 1231. However, because as a practical matter it would be awkward to grant a software license giving the licensee an undivided interest in all rights (e.g., rights to modify, use the associated trade name and trademark, etc.), this issue is not likely to come up very often in the real world of software licensing.

TRADE SECRETS

Trade Secrets as Intellectual Property. The legal protection provided to an owner of a "trade secret" was recognized under English and American common law and is relatively old,[150] but its modern genesis and importance really began in the 1970s, with the advent of the software industry and the birth of the modern era of intellectual property.

Unlike copyright, patent or (since 1946) trademark law, trade secrets have historically been protected under state law rather than federal law.[151] Trade secrets have been defined since 1939 in the First Restatement Torts, Section 757, as:

> any formula, pattern, device or compilation of information which is used one's business, which gives him an opportunity to obtain an advantage over competitors who did not know or use it . . . it differs from other secret information in a business . . . and that it is not simply information as to single or femoral events in the conduct of the business . . . a trade secret is a process or device for continuous use in the

operation of the business. Generally it relates to the production of goods, as, for example, a machine or formula for the production of an article.

The Uniform Trade Secret Act (USTA) was introduced in the 1980s, and since then 48 states have enacted statues based on this model act. The UTSA provided its own definition of a trade secret, expanding somewhat the Restatement's definition.[152]

Trade secret protection surged in importance in the 1970s as software companies struggled to find an adequate way to protect the enormous time and effort invested in the creation of their products. The problem was that none of the well-established forms of legal protection for intellectual property–patents, copyrights, or trademarks–provided any meaningful protection to software. Software products only occasionally qualified for patent protection, because software is written and created in a deliberate, mechanical and predictable way, and so software generally will not meet the novelty and non-obvious requirements of patent law. Trademark law likewise offered scant protection: The trademark or trade name of a software product was not what made the software intrinsically valuable and certainly did protect software from pirating.

Copyright law at first seemed to offer the greatest promise of protection for newly created software products. After all, software programs are "written" in a software "language," and so the protection provided to the copyright interest in a software program was initially intriguing. However, practical experience soon made it clear that copyright protects the mode of expression but not the underlying ideas expressed in a writing – which is where the value lies in a software program. For example, if a software program uses the algorithm "if A then B, otherwise C," this algorithm is not infringed under copyright law by the algorithm "if not X, then Z, otherwise Y" even though they are logically identical. In short, the ability extract the algorithms embedded in a software product, and then replicate it easily with language that was non-infringing in a copyright sense, meant that almost anyone could reverse engineer or rewrite a competitor's software without violating the copyright statute (assuming they could access the software code without making an actual "copy").

Almost by necessity, software companies (and their legal advisors) turned to trade secret law as the best available alternative for protecting software from use by competitors. All trade secret protection is ultimately derived from contractual covenants between the party owning the protected trade secret, and another party that has or seeks access to it. Obviously, if one person knows a "secret" and never divulges the secret, it remains, intrinsically, a secret. The dramatic expansion in trade secret law occurred thanks to the recognition by courts that when a party violates a contractual obligation not to disclose information, this contractual breach does not thereby put the property in the public domain, and thus, in effect, the rights in the trade secret can be protected from use by other parties – including another party that is wholly innocent of wrong-doing but who learns of the information solely as a result of the improper disclosure.[153] Whether a business can "put the genie back in the bottle" as a practical matter, of course, is a different issue, but at least in principle a trade secret improperly disclosed can be legally "undisclosed" or perhaps "re-secreted" and its use by others barred.

Interestingly, as trade secret protection established itself as the best method of protecting intellectual property in the software industry, it soon became apparent to technology and "know-how" companies that trade secret protection was arguably superior even to the benefits of patent protection. In particular, protecting know-how as a trade secret – if it could be protected, which was often a big "if" – provided an indefinite or even permanent form of protection against competition. A patent, by contrast, is a government granted monopoly that (a) lasts for a maximum of twenty (20) years from filing, (b) entails significant legal and other costs both to pursue a patent application and then, if one is granted, to protect it from infringement, and (c) requires as a condition of the patent monopoly a public disclosure, which means that any party, after twenty years, can practice freely the technology in question, guided by the patent holder's description. For this reason trade secret protection has come to be known as the "poor man's patent."

Courts have generally treated trade secrets, know-how, and similar sounding categories of intellectual property as one and the same for both tax and general legal purposes, and this is probably correct. The key factor is whether a party takes meaningful and consistent steps to keep the valuable information proprietary and "secret," including with non-disclosure agreements signed by employees, consultants and anyone else given access to the proprietary information.

Tax Aspects of Creating Know-How. As with all business-related expenditures, the initial question is whether the expenditure is deductible, including under Code section 162, or whether it is capitalizable, including under Code sections 263 or 263A. However, because trade secrets are often similar to patents, expenditures to create know-how may also be eligible for deductibility under Code section 174, as research and experimental expenditures. As discussed in Paragraph 2011.01 above, Code section 174 has a more relaxed standard of deductibility than Code section 162 because it only requires that the expense be incurred "in connection with" as opposed to "in the carrying on of" a trade or business. As a practical matter, this means that a taxpayer can deduct R&E expenditures under Code section 174 during the "start up" phase prior to actually entering into the carrying on of a trade or business.[154]

By contrast, expenditures that do not come within the scope of Code section 174, if incurred by a start up business before it becomes engaged in the carrying on of a trade or business, must be capitalized as part of the start up costs and amortized over fifteen (15) years under Code section 195. Once again, while a taxpayer can deduct expenses under Code section 174 prior to entering into a business, the taxpayer must have both an intention and a realistic prospect of entering into a trade or business involving the technology under development.[155]

Trade secrets, like patents and copyrights, can qualify as "self-created" intellectual property that is automatically excluded from the definition of Code section 197, and thus eligible for depreciation under Code section 167. See Code section 197(c)(2), which contains the exception for self-created intangible assets, including know-how. However, unlike patents and copyrights, the capitalized expenses incurred to create trade secrets and knowhow are not eligible to be depreciated under the income forecast method in Code section 167(g).[156]

This can create an interesting and sometimes problematical trap. If self-created intangibles are not governed by Code section 197 because of Code section 197(c)(2), and instead are governed by Code section 167, the intangible will be depreciable *only* if it possesses a reasonably determinable useful life.[157] In some cases, it may be possible to determine a useful life for a trade secret, although the viability of such an argument varies widely depending upon the nature of the "know how" and the intellectual property in question. A legitimate concern is that the "trade secret" may have an indefinite useful life – that, after all, is pretty much why businesses are interested in using trade secret protection in the first place.

Interestingly, expenses may be eligible for deduction under Code section 174, (or capitalized and amortized over sixty (60) months under Code section 174(b)), but if the expenditures do not qualify under either Code section 174 or Code section 162 as currently deductible, and are not subject to the allowance of depreciation under Code section 167 (because the property does not have an ascertainable useful life) there may be no mechanism for amortizing the capitalizable costs of a trade secret. Thus, unlike almost any other category of self-created intellectual property, trade secrets have the risk of having permanently non-recoverable capitalized expenditures, precisely because they have the potential to have a permanent or indefinite period of value.

A related issue arises when a taxpayer pays a third-party under contract to create property that is or will be owned by the taxpayer under the contractual arrangement. It is often important to structure the contractual relationship so that it meets the requirements of Code section 174. Code section 174 generally allows the taxpayer to currently deduct payments made to another party to conduct research and development on the taxpayer's behalf.[158] Note that the exclusion from Code section 197 for self-created property includes property (such as trade secrets or know-how) actually created by another third-party person under a contract with the taxpayer.[159]

To meet the requirements under Code section 174, the contract research must be undertaken at the taxpayers order and at the taxpayer's risk, so that the asset is treated as "self-created" for purposes of Code section 197. The regulations under Code section 197 state in relevant part as follows:[160]

> (ii) Created by the taxpayer – (A) Defined. A section 197 intangible is created by the taxpayer to the extent the taxpayer makes payments or otherwise incurs costs for its creation, production, development, or improvement, whether the actual work is performed by the taxpayer or by another person under a contract with the taxpayer entered into before the contracted creation, production, development, or improvement occurs. For example, a technological process developed specifically for a taxpayer under an arrangement with another person pursuant to which the taxpayer retains all rights to the process is created by the taxpayer.

As noted in the preceding discussion, expenses capitalized to know-how under Code section 167 can be depreciated over an applicable useful life so long as the useful life is reasonably ascertainable, because the property is self-created and not includable under Code section 197(c)(2). Unfortunately, the entire point of a trade secret is to keep the value of the secret for an indefinite perhaps even a quasi-permanent period of time. For example, the formula of Coca-Cola – a trade secret since the 1880s and going strong – serves as a paradigm to illustrate how a trade secret can have enduring and seemly perpetual value. This is one of the areas where Code section 197 does not rescue capitalizable expenditures from their pre-1993 treatment.

Sale of Trade Secrets and Know-How by the Creator. From a tax perspective, the key analytical question is usually not whether a type of intellectual property should called a "trade secret," a form of "know-how," or given some other label, but rather, upon the transfer of the relevant information, whether the transaction should be properly characterized as a "sale" or "exchange" of property, or whether it should be characterized as the performance of services.[161]

A classic example of this conundrum of "service" versus "property" is the creation of a map. A person could be hired to create a map, and the services inherent in the creation of the map might be viewed as the rendering of personal services for the payor. However, once a map is created, it becomes a separate form of property (with both tangible and intangible characteristics, if it is a map in printed form), and the services previously rendered have been transformed into "property".

As with other forms of intellectual property, "know how" is derived from the fertility of the human imagination, and so at some point in time personal efforts will be the central contribution to the creation of the know-how or trade secret in question. That is to say, even if the trade secret, know-how or similar intellectual property exists as separate and identifiable form of "property," it is often necessary to have the related services of an individual who can provide instruction and impart the information comprising the trade secret. Distinguishing between intellectual property and the rendering of personal services to educate people regarding the intellectual property is often described (rather cleverly) as the distinction between "know-how" and "show-how." Trying to discern whether a form of trade secret is know-how or show-how–whether it is a transfer of property or services–is often a complex and solipsistic exercise.

To no one's surprise, the IRS typically likes to call something a service rather than a transfer of property – the better both to assert a right to tax the transaction and to impose an ordinary income tax rate. See, for example, the IRS position in Rev. Rul. 64-56, which indicates, among other things, that the mere fact that secret information can be recorded on paper or some other physical medium of expression is not, by itself, an indication that the information is property.

In contrast to patents (Code section 1235), trademarks (Code section 1253), and copyrights (Code section 1221(a)(3)), self-created trade secrets do not have a special code provision governing the sale or exchange of the property rights. It should be noted at the outset that self-created trade secrets and related know-how will very often have zero basis, similar to the situation of a patent, because the costs incurred in creating the trade secrets are often currently deductible under Code section 174. Moreover, deductions taken under Code section 174(a) for R&E expenditures are not subject to recapture as ordinary income on the subsequent sale of the related technology.[162]

Whether the tax basis in a trade secret is zero or whether the tax basis is a capitalized amount that is either not depreciable or has not yet been fully depreciated, a sale of the trade secret will result in recognition of gain (and possibly recapture income under Code section 1245 if the trade secret has been depreciated under Code section 167).

Generally speaking, a trade secret by its nature will be property used in a trade or business, and therefore, upon a sale, the trade secret will be excluded from the definition of a capital asset under Code section 1221(a)(2), and will be includable in the category of property described in Code section 1231, so long as the trade secret has been held for more than one year.

Again, note that Code section 1245 will likely apply if the costs of creating a trade secret have been subject to depreciation under Code section 167. However, as noted above, trade secrets, more than most other forms of intellectual property, are likely to not have a readily ascertainable life and are likely to not be subject to depreciation under Code section 167.

As always, if a sale transaction occurs between related parties, and the property in question is depreciable property in the hands of the transferee (which will almost always be the case where there is a sale of a trade secret, since the trade secret will generally be amortizable under Code section 197), Code section 1239 will treat the gain recognized by the seller as ordinary income for tax purposes.

Acquisition and Subsequent Use of Trade Secret Assets

An acquirer of trade secrets in a transaction that qualifies as a sale or exchange under Code section 1001 will have a tax basis equal to the acquisition costs. This "cost basis" principle is derived from Code section 1012.In contrast to a self-created trade secret, an acquirer will treat trade secrets as a Code section 197 intangible, pursuant to Code section 197(d)(1)(C)(iii). This provision includes "know-how" as well as various other trade secret type descriptions, such as "formula", "process", "design", "pattern", "format", or "other similar item."

Therefore, even though an acquired trade secret and know-how may very well have the very same definite useful life as it would have in the hands of a creator, it is now eligible for amortization of a period of fifteen (15) years. Again, the entire purpose of Code section 197 was to simplify the treatment of intangible property by eliminating factual controversies over the useful life of such assets, while also eliminating and potential incentive that a taxpayer might have to allocate purchase price between and among the intangible assets acquired in connection with the acquisition of a trade or business.

Although the term "trade secret" does not appear anywhere in Code section 197(d)(1), this otherwise highly redundant provision seems to touch on all the kinds of property interests that would normally be associated with trade secrets. One might observe that a trade secret is simply a kind of intangible property that happens to be subject to protection by its owner, including contractual non-disclosure covenants with third parties.

Like other forms of property, a trade secret or know-how can be "sold" not only by an assignment of property, but also through an exclusive perpetual license. A transfer of the exclusive right to use a trade secret or know-how for a period less than the estimated useful life of the asset simply results in a license and not a sale. See Rev. Rul. 64-56. The IRS's ruling position in Rev. Rul. 64-56 is that the "all substantial rights" test is satisfied only if there is an exclusive perpetual right to use the know-how in question.

An interesting exception that is particularly germane to trade secrets is contained in Code section 197(e)(4)(D), which provides a modified version of the "separately acquired rule". In particular, it provides that a Code section 197 intangible asset need not include any separately acquired contract right if such right either (i) has a fixed duration of less than fifteen years, or (ii) is fixed to an amount and the cost is properly recoverable over a method similar to the unit reduction method.

The legislative history to Code section 197 provides the following example, related to a license of know-how, to illustrate the provision:

> [A]ssume company A enters into a license with company B to use certain know how developed by B. In addition, assume that the license is for five (5) years, and that the license cannot be renewed by A except on terms that are fully available to A's competitors and that the price paid by A will reflect the arm's length price that a third party would pay A for the license immediately after renewal. Finally, assume that the license does not constitute a substantial portion of a trade or business and is not entered into as part of a transaction (or a series of related transactions) that constitute the acquisition of a trade or business or substantial portion thereof. It is anticipated that in these circumstances the regulations will provide the license is not a Section 197 intangible because of its fixed duration.

In fact, the regulations under Code section 167 address this example, and conclude that the cost of the license paid by A will be amortizable over the five-year life of the contract.[163] In general, the regulations under Code section 167 provide the methods to be used by taxpayers to amortize the costs of rights that are excluded by Code section 197(e)(4)(D). The foregoing rule applied to licensing arrangements involving trade secrets that have a fixed duration of less than fifteen (15) years. If the licensing arrangement is equal or greater to fifteen (15) years, the asset will be considered a 197 intangible and amortized ratably over the fifteen (15) year period.

As discussed in Chapter 2, to the extent that payments to purchase a license for greater than fifteen (15) years, such payments will be treated as capitalizable expenditures that are contingent in nature and will be capitalized and amortized ratably over the remaining months of the fifteen (15) year amortization period beginning in the month the amount is paid or incurred.[164]

Disposition of a Trade Secrets by Taxpayer Following Purchase. A trade secret acquired by purchase will generally be used in a trade or business and thus governed by Code section 1231, assuming it has been held for more than one year. In particular, it is an asset that is subject to the allowance for depreciation, by virtue of the language contained in Code section 197(f)(7), indicating that an amortizable Code section 197 intangible is treated as property subject to the allowance for depreciation under Code section 167.

Under Code section 1231, the subsequent sale of such an asset held for more than one year will generate, firs, recapture under Code section 1245, to the extent prior amortization, and then, second, long-term capital gain on any excess.

Comment: It is not impossible to imagine a situation where a trade secret or know-how is acquired by someone as an investment asset, and not as property to be used in connection with a trade or business. Unlike a patent, which has a naturally deteriorating value because of its legal expiration date, a trade secret may have indefinite value. This is not likely by any stretch of the imagination, but it is at least more plausible than the possibility of someone investing and holding a patent as a Code section 1221 capital asset.

If there is a sale of the trade secret between related parties, and the property is depreciable in the hands of the purchaser, then Code section 1239 will characterize the gain recognized by the seller as ordinary income.

Note that a license of a trade secret or know-how for a period of less than fifteen (15) years, is excluded from the definition of Code section 197 intangible by Code section 197(e)(4)(E). Such assets are not amortizable under Code section 197, but may be amortizable under the provisions of Code section 167 and the applicable regulations discussed above. As such, these assets are likely to be assets used in a trade or business (i.e., Code section 1231 property) and thus subject to the usual rules of recapture, to the extent of prior depreciation under Code section 1245, and then long term capital gain treatment under Code section 1231 (or ordinary income treatment in the case of a sale to a related party under Code section 1239).

CONTRACT RIGHTS AND CONTRACT-BASED INTANGIBLES

Overview of Contract Rights and Contract-Based Intangibles. Samuel Goldwyn once famously declared, "An oral contract isn't worth the paper it's written on."

However, the truth is that contract rights (sometimes even those oral agreements so witheringly disparaged by Mr. Goldwyn) can be very valuable assets to a business. Indeed, in some cases contract rights define the essence of the business itself.

Take, for example, one of my favorite for-profit organizations, the Boston Red Sox Baseball Team, which, in addition to inspiring fanatical fandom, is a pretty valuable business enterprise (estimated by Forbes to be worth $2.7 billion in April 2017). The Boston Red Sox Baseball Team, when the business is distilled down to its essence, owns little more than a few bats and balls, and a whole lot of very valuable contracts.[165]

First of all, it is important to note that the Red Sox do not actually "own" any of their players. (Ownership of human beings, as you may recall, is prohibited by the 13th Amendment.) What the team does own is contract rights for the exclusive baseball-playing services of its players for a specified number of years, as well as a contractual franchise right to participate in 162 regular season games as part of Major League Baseball, and a whole bevy of other contracts that involve the granting of television rights, radio rights, ticket licenses, T-shirt licenses, parking concessions, food concessions, Boston Red Sox baseball hat manufacturing rights, and a whole panoply of other valuable property rights and contractual undertakings.

The point is that contract rights can be highly valuable business assets, and indeed in some cases may be the principal assets, of the business. At the same time, a contract is a complicated and nuanced type of property right, especially when one tries to classify it within the rather hidebound and traditional "property" categories provided by the Internal Revenue Code. Sorting through the distinctive tax characteristics of contract rights will be the interesting and challenging exercise for the final section of this chapter.

Tax Issues on Creation of Contract Rights. Contracts and the related rights and obligations are typically "created" by negotiations between a business and another party. Interestingly, while a negotiation conducted between the president of a company and another business entity may result in the creation of a valuable intangible asset, few businesses think that the salary paid to the president, or the other expenses incurred in connection with the negotiation, should be "capitalized" into the resulting asset.

In fact, under the INDOPCO case and other authority addressing the capitalization of costs into the creation or acquisition of assets, one can make a rather plausible argument that perhaps these costs *should* be capitalized into the contract as an "asset" created by the business. In fact, in the case of government licenses – a special category of contract with distinctive treatment under Code section 197 – the IRS has successfully asserted that the costs of obtaining a license or government permit should be capitalized into the permit rather than deducted.[166] Nonetheless, in the case of a non-government contract, many businesses (and their tax advisors) are likely to take the position that the salary paid to the president is deductible as an ordinary and necessary business expense under Code section 162.

If expenses related to the creation of a non-government contract are in fact capitalized, it is likely to be a classified as type of "self-created" intangible and thus excluded from the scope of Code section 197 by Code section 197(c)(2), and instead capitalized and (if it has a reasonable ascertainable useful life, which most contracts do) depreciated under Code section 167. Note that the categories of "Section 197 intangibles" excluded from "amortizable Section 197 intangible" if self-created include workforce in place including its composition and terms and conditions (contractual or otherwise) of its employment;[167] any customer-based intangible,[168]and any supplier-based intangible,[169] all of which are generally created by or embodied in common commercial business contracts.

However, Code section 197(c)(2) conspicuously does NOT carve out from the scope of Code section 197 "any license, permit, or other right granted by a governmental unit or an agency or instrumentality thereof. . ."[170], and therefore the expenses for obtaining a government license or permit should be capitalized and amortized on a straight-line basis over fifteen years under Code section 197.[171]

Sale of Self-Created Contract Rights – Valuation of Contract Rights. A sale of self-created contract rights often triggers unusual—or worse, unpredictable—tax consequences. Indeed, both the IRS rulings and case law in this area are (to be kind) notably inconsistent in trying to determine whether the sale of a self-created contract right generates ordinary income or capital gain. Therefore, the purpose of this section is to "explain the unexplainable," *i.e.*, to review the disparate case law and then offer a coherent theory for how a sale of contract rights "should" be treated for federal income tax purposes.

One challenging issue to address at the outset is the fact that while contract rights are often clearly valuable, the specific value of the assets may not be clear at all. For example, assume that Corporation T, which manufactures and sells sophisticated medical devises, is acquired by Corporation A, and that among T's assets are various long-term maintenance contracts with T's customers calling for fixed annual payments of $100,000 per year in exchange for agreeing to maintain sophisticated equipment in working order. The cost to T (and now A) of providing the required maintenance services is expected to be, on average, $60,000 per contract per year.

What is the value of each such contract? One view—which is wrong—is that each contract is worth $40,000 per year, *i.e.*, the spread between average income and average expense. In fact, the maintenance provider must support a staff of trained people, must incur general overhead and administrative expenses, and must be rewarded for bearing the risks of the business—*i.e.*, no one is going to "pay" $40,000 for a $100,000 contract and expect to make "zero" profit. In fact, if the party providing maintenance services can easily sell other maintenance service contracts to other customers for the "going rate" of $100,000, then the value of this particular $100,000 contract is actually "zero"—*i.e.*, a rational services provider would not pay anything for a contract that the services provider can simply obtain directly with other customers on the same terms.

Arguably, an appropriate analogy for how to measure gain on the sale of a contract right is to look at how one measures gain on the sale or disposition of a bond. A bond is an investment asset whereby the purchaser pays a fixed amount (typically but not always the face amount of the bond) and receives from the bond issuer a promise to repay the principal with interest at specified times. Interest accrues at a specified rate (fixed or variable) and is often payable on a quarterly or annual basis, with the principal often due at the end of the stated term.

The "value" of a long-term bond, *e.g.*, a thirty-year U.S. Treasury bond, goes up and down based on the interest rate payable on that particular bond compared to prevailing market interest rates. For example, if a long-term bond is issued with a fixed annual interest rate of 8 percent, and market interest rate on similar U.S. instruments subsequently drops to 6 percent, there will be a corresponding increase in the value of the bond. Conversely, if prevailing interest rates go up, the value of the bond will go down.

A bond is treated as a capital asset and, if the bond is held for more than one year, the sale (after adjusting for accrued but unpaid interest) produces long-term capital gain or loss.[172]

Now, applying these same principles to contract rights, assume that A, an individual, enters into a contract, for a period of ten years, to mow the local high school football field for contract price of $10 an hour. Assume that the contract calls for the grass to be mowed once per week and allows for eight hours of services, or $80, per mowing.

Obviously, if A actually mows the football field, the $80 for that particular week will be ordinary income received by A for services rendered. However, if A has the right to assign the mowing contract and in fact sells the contract to an unrelated party, the analogy to a bond becomes apparent. In particular, if $10 an hour happens to be a good hourly rate in the labor market where the football field is located, a person might be willing to pay $5 per week for the right to "net" $75. In effect, the contract purchaser is willing to work for $75 per day, and thus willing to pay $5 for the opportunity to earn $80.

This mowing contract is in the nature of a contractual "property" right, and so if the contract is held for more than one year and then sold at a profit (because of fluctuations in the market price of labor) this accretion of value is clearly analogous to the market fluctuations in interest rates that have a corresponding effect on the value of a bond.

The point missed by many commentators (including many courts) is that a purchaser of the mowing contract will not pay the equivalent of $80 per week for the right to mow the football field (*i.e.*, nobody will work for free). Rather, the "value" in any contract is simply the disparity between the contract price for goods or services embodied in the contract and the current "market" price at which the purchaser of that contract is willing to provide such goods and services. Thus, if a hypothetical purchaser will pay $5 to acquire the mowing contract (because $75 is now the "right" price for the required labor), the contract seller receives a $5 premium. This is no different (or very little different) than the situation where the owner of a bond paying 8 percent later sells it to a purchaser who is satisfied with a 6 percent return, while the bond seller pockets the profit. On the other hand, if $80 a day is the going rate for the mowing services, then the value of the contract is zero because any person could directly arrange to mow the football field at that rate. No sensible person would pay a premium for a contract when the person could obtain directly in the marketplace a contract at the same terms.

Taxation on Sale of Self-Created Contractual Rights. The preceding discussion, drawing an analogy between the fluctuating values of contract rights and bonds, can be a somewhat useful (though far from perfect) tool for analyzing the correct income tax treatment on the sale of a contract right.

In particular, if the contract in question is in the nature of "property,"[173] has been held for more than one year,[174] and constitutes either a "capital asset," within the meaning of Code section 1221,[175] or "property used in the trade or business"[176] within the meaning of Code section 1231, the sale of such contract arguably "should" generate long-term capital gain. Depending on the nature of the contract, of course, the price paid by a purchaser may be similar to the "premium" paid to A in the preceding discussion for the mowing contract, in which case treating such premium as "capital gain" would be consistent with general policy principles upon which the capital gains tax preference is based.[177]

The problem is that "contract rights" covers too broad and diverse a landscape of economic rights and relationships to draw simple conclusions. In *Comm. v. Ferrer*,[178] the Second Circuit candidly acknowledged the difficulties of applying consistent or even coherent rules in this complicated area of tax law, when it began its opinion with the following—rather startling—introduction:

> This controversy concerns the tax status of certain payments received by Jose Ferrer with respect to the motion picture "Moulin Rouge" portraying the career of Henri de Toulouse-Lautrec. The difficulties Mr. Ferrer must have had in fitting himself into the shape of the artist can hardly have been greater than ours in determining whether the transaction here at issue fits the rubric "gain from the sale or exchange of a capital asset. . ." or constitutes ordinary income, as the Commissioner contends.[179]

In *Ferrer*, the taxpayer had three property rights under contract: (1) a lease to produce the play; (2) a power to prevent the sale of movie, radio and television rights; and (3) a right to receive a percentage of the movie proceeds. After an extended, almost painfully detailed analysis, the court found that the first two rights were "capital assets" that produced capital gain on sale, while the third produced ordinary income. In reaching these fine distinctions, the Court observed: "In all these cases [in which a capital asset was found to exist] the taxpayer had something more than an opportunity, afforded by contract, to obtain periodic receipts of income, by dealing with another. . .or by rendering services. . .or by virtue of ownership of a larger estate. . . . We are painfully aware of the deficiencies of any such attempt to define the wavering line even in this limited area, but it is the best we can do."[180]

One major cause of analytical confusion in this area is that most contracts being sold produce a kind of income that, if received by the contract holder, would clearly be ordinary income. This frequently leads courts to treat a sale of the underlying contract as a mere acceleration of ordinary income (in effect, an assignment of income) and thus to characterize the resulting gain on sale as ordinary in nature. In *Comm. v. PG Lake, Inc.*,[181] the U.S. Supreme Court, in holding that proceeds from the transfer of mineral payments were ordinary income rather than capital gain, stated, "The substance of what was received was the present value of income which the recipient would otherwise obtain in the future. In short, consideration was paid for the right to receive future income, not for an increase in the value of the income-producing property."[182] This rule is sometimes referred to as the "substitute for ordinary income doctrine."[183]

To generate capital gain on sale, a contract must be viewed either as a "capital asset" under Code section 1221 or as an "asset used in the conduct of a trade or business" under Code section 1231. In order to qualify under either of these Code provisions, the contract being sold must first of all constitute "property." Although Code section 1221 on its face appears to give broad meaning to this term,[184] the U.S. Supreme Court has found it "evident that not everything which can be called property in the ordinary sense and which is outside the statutory exclusions [of section 1221] qualifies as a capital asset;" rather, the term "capital asset" "is to be construed narrowly in accordance with the purpose of Congress to afford capital-gains treatment only in situations typically involving the realization of appreciation in value accrued over a substantial period of time. . ."[185]

In *Guggenheim v. Commissioner*[186] (involving a sale of syndicated interests in a racehorse), the Tax Court noted, "Simply because the property transferred will produce ordinary income, and such income is a major factor in determining the value of the property, does not necessarily mean that the amount received for the property is essentially a lump-sum substitute for ordinary income."[187] In *Guggenheim*, the court focused on whether substantial investment risks involved in holding the asset that was the source of the income were transferred.[188]

In *U.S. v. Dresser Industries*,[189] involving the transfer of the "exclusive" right to exploit a patent, the court distinguished between proceeds from "the present sale of the future right to earn income [capital gain] and the present sale of the future right to earned income [ordinary income]."[190]

In *Estate of Shea*,[191] the court held that the transfer by the taxpayers' S corporation to a third party of a shipping charter, a contract to provide cargo space on the corporation's ships, was a sale of "property" under Code section 1231, resulting in capital gain. The corporation had originally acquired the shipping charter along with the ship to which it was subject, later substituted a different ship, and eventually sold the charter as a separate asset. In its holding, the court stressed that the shipping charter was not a contract to perform personal services, that the taxpayer had been required to capitalize the acquisition cost of the charter, and that the value of the charter was primarily determined by its rate as compared to prevailing market rates. Thus, the court observed, the difference between the amount paid for the charter and the amount received upon disposition represented appreciation in value over time, due purely to the action of market forces. This, according to the court, was precisely the type of profit for which capital gain treatment was intended, citing *Gillette*.[192]

Estate of Shea is exactly consistent with the discussion of the hypothetical grass-mowing contract discussed above. However, courts often seem to lose sight of the forest for the trees when personal services are involved. For example, in *Harry M. Flower*,[193] a contractual right to receive income upon the performance of personal services was held to be an ordinary asset generating ordinary income on sale. In *Flower*, the taxpayer held, through his corporation, a sales franchise right to sell products on an exclusive basis in a specified territory, and, after disagreements with the franchisor, agreed to terminate the contract in exchange for payments.

The court in *Flower* began by noting that "[T]he Court of Appeals of the Fifth Circuit, to which an appeal of this case would normally lie, has seemingly not been entirely consistent in its approach to this issue under somewhat similar factual circumstances. . ."[194] Nonetheless, the court concluded that the "prevailing opinion. . .recognizes the legal principle that consideration received for the transfer of a contract right to receive income for the performance of personal services is taxable as ordinary income."[195] Almost amazingly, the court in *Flower* ignored the goodwill built up by the taxpayer in the territory over the years, including a contractual obligation to spend 50 percent of the net commission each year on promoting the sale of products of the franchisor. The *Flower* decision was probably influenced by the fact that the taxpayer in question received a "termination" payment that may have looked and felt to the court like an informal severance arrangement. Put another way, the decision would be much harder to justify if the contract had been sold to an unrelated third party, who then had to perform the sales services under the contract.

In summary, the courts continue to struggle with the factual complexities of sale-of-contract cases, and have a particularly difficult time separating the concepts of "the present sale of the future right to earn income [capital gain] and the present sale of the future right to earned income [ordinary income]."[196]

The good news is that, in many cases, taxpayers will have a reasonable reporting position that a sale of contract rights "should" generate capital gain. Logic is on the taxpayer's side, even if the law (as yet) is not quite so clear cut.

Tax Treatment of Purchased Contact Rights in Hands of Purchaser. Thanks to the advent of Code section 197, enacted in 1993,[197] the tax treatment of contract rights purchased in connection with the acquisition of a business are clearer than in the case of "self-created" contract rights. In general, the contract rights commonly used in a trade or business, including those related to workforce in place,[198] customer-based intangibles,[199] and supplier-based intangibles,[200] clearly come within the scope and definition of "Section 197 intangibles" and thus on purchase are subject to amortization on a straight line over fifteen years, along with all the other amortizable Code section 197 intangibles acquired as part of the transaction.

Note that, under the applicable rules of Code section 197, a contract right acquired in connection with an acquisition of assets constituting a trade or business or a substantial interest therein becomes part of the lump-sum amount capitalized and amortized under Code section 197, and a subsequent termination or expiration of the contract does not trigger a loss or an accelerated write off attributable to the contract. Rather, all amounts capitalized into the acquisition of Code section 197 intangibles in the applicable transaction are amortized over fifteen years unless and until ALL the relevant assets are written off or disposed of by the acquirer.[201] Thus, for example, if an asset acquisition of a business includes the assignment of a customer contract (a customer-based intangible) with three years remaining on the contract, the portion of the purchase price allocable to that contract will be recovered by the purchaser ratably over fifteen years, even though the asset may terminate in three years.

An interesting question is whether a different, and possibly shorter, amortization or depreciation period is available if the contract is question is "separately acquired" within the meaning of Code section 197(e)(4). Under Code section 197(e), the term "section 197 intangible" does not include certain enumerated categories, and Code section 197(e)(4), carving out certain "separately acquired" assets (meaning assets not acquired in a transaction (or series of related transactions) involving the acquisition of assets constituting a trade business or substantial portion thereof).

The list of "separately acquired" assets includes three potential exceptions relevant to this discussion. The first exception, under Code section 197(e)(4)(B), is for "any right to receive tangible property or services under a contract or granted by a governmental unit or agency or instrumentality thereof".[202] The remaining two exceptions, under Code section 197(e)(4)(D), provide that "to the extent provided in regulations, any right under a contract (or granted by a governmental unit or an agency or instrumentality thereof) if such right (i) has a fixed duration of less than fifteen (15) years, or (ii) is fixed as to amount and, without regard to this section, would be recoverable under a method similar to the unit-of-production method."

Regarding the first exception, the Code section 197 regulations state, somewhat amazingly, that "Any right that is described in [Code Section 197(e)(4)(B)] is not treated as a Code section 197 intangible even though the right is also described in Code Section 197(d)(1)(D) and paragraph (b)(8) of this section (relating to certain governmental licenses, permits, and other rights) and even though the right fails to meet one or more of the requirements of paragraph (c)(13) of this section (relating to certain rights of fixed duration or amount)."[203] In effect, this type of government contract is completely carved out of Code section 197, even if it seems to fall into other categories such as Code section 197(d)(1)(D), and instead depreciated under Code section 167 in accordance with principles set forth in the regulations under Code section 167.[204]

The two exceptions under Code section 197(e)(4)(D) are, if anything, even more obtuse and complicated than the first carve out. These two exceptions apply both to governmental and non-governmental contact rights, and arise in two contexts, (i) contracts with a fixed duration of less than fifteen (15) years or (ii) contracts fixed as to amount and, without regard to this section, would be recoverable under a method similar to the unit-of-production method.

With respect to the first exception under Code section 197(e)(4)(D), the legislative history to Code section 197 provides the following example:[205]

> [A]ssume that a taxpayer acquires from another person a favorable contract right of such person to receive a specified amount of raw materials each month for the next three years (which is the remaining life of the contract) and that the right to receive such raw materials is not acquired as part of the acquisition of assets that constitute a trade or business or a substantial portion thereof (i.e., such contract right is not a Code section 197 intangible). It is anticipated that the taxpayer may be required to amortize the cost of acquiring the contract right ratably over the three-year remaining life of the contract.

With respect to the second exception under Code section 197(e)(4)(D), the legislative history to Code section 197 provides the following example:

> [I]f the favorable contract right is to receive a specified amount of raw material during an unspecified period, it is anticipated that the taxpayer may be required to amortize the cost of acquiring the contract right by multiplying such cost by a fraction, the numerator of which is the amount of raw materials received under the contract during any taxable year and the denominator of which is the total amount of raw materials to be received under the contract.[206]

Where the contract right includes extension or renewal rights that are likely to be exercised, the regulations provide as follows:

> [T]he duration of a right under a contract (or granted by a governmental unit) includes any renewal period if, based on all of the facts and circumstances in existence at any time during the taxable year in which the right is acquired, the facts clearly indicate a reasonable expectancy of renewal.[207]

Tax Treatment on Sale of Purchased Contract Rights. Contract rights acquired by purchase from another party that are then subject to amortization under Code section 197 (or, if one of the Code section 197(e)(4) exceptions applies, under Code section 167) and are held for more than one year will clearly be property described in Code section 1231(b). In turn, the sale such a contract, as Code section 1231(b) property, to a subsequent purchaser (e.g., in an acquisition of the business by a new acquirer) will trigger the usual and familiar consequences. Thus, if the contract (as Code section 1231(b) property) is sold at a loss (i.e., for less than its remaining tax basis) there will be recognition of an ordinary loss by the seller. Meanwhile, if the contract is sold for more than its remaining tax basis, there will first be recognition of Code section 1245 recapture income (to the extent of prior depreciation of the Code section 197 intangible) and then long-term capital gain (if the cóntact, as Code section 1231(b) property, is sold for more than its original purchase price).

THE CHART

For purposes of this last section of Chapter 20, I will briefly slip into the first person pronoun to provide a personal explanation of the goals and objectives that I am trying to accomplish in this chapter.

This chapter examines the U.S. federal income tax issues that arise in what might be called the "lifecycle" of intellectual property. The lifecycle is comprised of six (6) distinct stages in the creation, exploitation, and transfer of intellectual property. Each of these six stages is a column in The Chart set forth below.

I first developed The Chart – it is not a stretch to say that I "invented it" – in the fall of 2003, while teaching a course entitled "Taxation of Intellectual Property" at the Boston University School of Law in the Graduate Tax Program.

I was teaching the IP tax course that fall for the first time, and, after a couple of weeks, it became clear that the substantive material was incredibly detailed and confusing to the students. The nadir occurred in the third week, when I tried to parse the very detailed and anomalous set of rules that comprise Code section 197. By the end of the two-hour class, the students had the goggle-eyed look of the totally bewildered. Meanwhile, at the front of the room, I stood before a blackboard covered in the usual tax hieroglyphics, aware that I had explained the material accurately, but at the same time had explained it in a way that might as well have been inaccurate, or in a foreign tongue, because the students clearly did not understand anything that I just put on the board, and therefore were not going to retain it. It had been a detailed, technically precise, and time-consuming exercise in futility.

Over the next week, I obsessed about presenting the material better, in a way that quantified and reduced the material into "bite-sized" pieces or components that students could understand and assimilate in a successful manner. After playing around with a variety of pedagogical strategies and ideas, I came up with The Chart.

The Chart has six columns, comprised of the sequential steps in the life of Intellectual Property: (1) the *creation* of intellectual property by its *creator*, (2) the *use* of the property by its *creator*, (3) the *sale* of the property by its *creator*, (4) the *purchase* of the property by someone who is *not the creator*, (5) the *use* of the acquired property by the person who is *not the creator*, and (6) the subsequent *sale* of the property by someone who is *not the creator*.

Obviously, the transactional sequence could continue beyond six steps, with a second or third acquirer, but, the beauty of The Chart is that, once you get to step six and move on to step seven (*i.e.*, the purchase of the property by a new party also not the creator) the tax consequences loop back to step four, and so there is an endless open loop in steps four, five and six, returning to step four with each next acquirer.

On the vertical index, I put each of the following important categories of intellectual property: (1) patents, (2) trademarks, (3) copyrights, (4) trade secrets, (5) software, (6) contract rights, (7) goodwill, and (8) non-compete agreements.

The Chart, therefore, is a grid, with six elements on the horizontal index and the eight elements on the vertical index, therefore creating a total of 48 "boxes." Each box contains the number or numbers that corresponded with the Code provisions that generally governed the tax treatment of that particular type of intellectual property in that particular step in the property's life cycle.

The following is a complete version of The Chart, which will be referenced repeatedly throughout the remainder of the book. Do yourself a favor and bend this page right now.

The Chart

TYPES OF INTELLECTUAL PROPERTY	EVENTS TRIGGERING TAX CONSEQUENCES					
	Creation of Intellectual Property	*Use of Property by Creator*	*Sale of Property by Creator*	*Purchase of Property by Non-Creator*	*Use of Purchased Property by Non-Creator*	*Sale of Purchased Property by Non-Creator*
Patents	Code §174 and §263	N/A or Code §167(g)	Code §1235 Code §1231 Code §1221	Code §1001/§1012	Code §167(g)/§197	Code §1221/§1231
Trademarks	Code §162/§263	Code §197	Code §1253 Code §1231	Code §1001/§1012	Code §197	Code §1253 and §1231
Copyrights	Code §263A/§263A(h) (if (h) applies, then §162/§263)	N/A or Code §167(g)	Code §1221(a)(3)	Code §1001/§1012	Code §167(g)/§197	Code §1221/§1231
Trade Secrets (Confidential Information)	Code §174/§162/§263	N/A or Code § 167	Code §1221/§1231	Code §1001/§1012	Code §197	Code §1221/§1231
Software	Code §174 (Rev. Proc. 2000-50)/§263	N/A or Code §167(f)	Code §1221(a)(3)/ §1231	Code §1001/§1012	Code §167(f)/§197	Code §1221/§1231
Contractual Rights	Code §162/§263	N/A or Code §167	Code §61/1231	Code §1001/§1012	Code §167/§197	Code §61/§1231
Goodwill	Code §162/§263	N/A or Code §167	Code §1231	Code §1001/§1012	Code §197	Code §1231
Covenant Not to Compete	Code §162/§263	N/A or Code §167	Code §1231	Code §1001/§1012	Code §167/§197	Code §1231

From the very first week I used it, the students in the BU Graduate Tax Program loved The Chart. It organizes complex and difficult sets of rules into a simple "road map" for how to analyze and evaluate the tax treatment of intellectual property in most, or all, common business contexts. Some students have referred to it, cheerfully and unashamedly, as the "cheat sheet" because it distills volumes of sophisticated and arcane information into a simple, memory-jogging format.

Interestingly, and perhaps even tellingly, The Chart by itself is not all that useful to the uninitiated. Reading this book will largely explain and provide the background information necessary to understand and use the shorthand that is embodied by each Code section reference within each specific box on The Chart. For example, Chapter 11 of this Book examines, in detail, Code section 197, which is perhaps the single most important provision with respect to intellectual property in the entire Internal Revenue Code. It is a complex provision, with notably nuanced differentiations between and among different types of intellectual property. The Chart helps – in fact, it makes it almost too easy. The Chart identifies that Code section 197 only rarely applies to self-created intangibles – just one box in column 2 – but appears in every box in column 5, because all Code Section 197 intangibles are subject to fifteen-year straight-line amortization when the assets of a business are purchased. However, column 5 also makes clear that some (but not all) purchased intellectual property can be subject to the more favor depreciation rules under Code section 167 if the property is "separately acquired".

In column 3 of the Chart, there is often a special provision of the Internal Revenue Code that applies to a sale of intellectual property by the creator of that property. For patents, there are the unique provisions of Code section 1235; for trademarks, there are the unique provisions of Code section 1253; for copyrights, there are the unique provisions in Code section 1221(a)(3); for trade secrets, there are the general provisions of Code section 1231 and 1221; for software, there is the unique question about whether it is governed by Code section 1221(a)(3) or by Code section 1231; for contract rights, the law is so murky and confounded that the real question is whether the sale of the property is governed by Code sections 1221/1231 or whether it should be characterized as ordinary income under Code section 61; and for goodwill, there is, well, one of the most complicated and litigated issues in modern U.S. income tax history, and this continues to be so, even though Code section 197 was supposed to "put an end" to disputes over this issue.

In short, there is a lot of detail and nuance to the taxation of intellectual property, but the Chart may sometimes be a useful the road map on how to get to a particular destination.

CHAPTER ENDNOTES

1. *T.H. Welch*, S.Ct., 3 USTC ¶ 1164, 290 US 111, 114, 54 S.Ct. 8 (1933).
2. *T.H. Welch*, S.Ct., 3 USTC ¶ 1164, 290 US at 115.
3. 503 US 79, 112 S.Ct. 1039(1992).
4. *INDOPCO, Inc.*, 503 US 79, 84, 112 S.Ct. 1039 (1992).
5. *INDOPCO, Inc.*, 503 US 79, 88, 112 S.Ct. 1039 (1992).
6. See Rev. Rul. 95-32, 1995-1 CB 8 (permitting a utility to deduct current expenditures incurred in implementing energy conservation and load management programs); Rev. Rul. 94-77, 1994-2 CB 19 (permitting an employer to deduct currently the cost of severance payments to former employees); Rev. Rul. 2001-4, 2001-1 CB 295 (allowing the deduction of certain costs for the maintenance of airplanes where the maintenance did not add to the airplane's value or prolong its useful life); Rev. Rul. 2000-4, 2000-1 CB 331 (allowing taxpayers to deduct currently the cost of obtaining, maintaining, and renewing ISO 9000 certification, based on an analogy to advertising, training, and similar expenditures incurred in operating the business; the IRS specifically ruled that any future benefits derived from ISO 9000 would be "incidental").
7. Reg. § 1.263A-2(a)(2)(ii).
8. Reg. § 1.263A-2(a)(2)(ii)(1).
9. *Id.*
10. See Reg. § 1.263A-2(a)(2)(ii)(A)(1).
11. IRC Sec. 174(a)(1).
12. See, e.g., *H.J. Green*, 83 TC 667, Dec. 41,596 (1984).
13. See *J.R. Harris*, 16 F3d 75 (1994); *P.D. Martyr*, 60 TCM 1115, Dec. 46,949(M), TC Memo. 1990-558; *R.E. Kantor*, CA-9, 93-2 USTC ¶ 50,433, 998 F2d 1514.
14. 46 F3d 950 (1995).
15. Reg. §1.174-2(a)(1).
16. IRC Sec. 174(e).
17. Reg. § 1.174-2(a)(1).
18. Reg. § 1.174-2(a)(3)(vii).
19. Reg. § 1.174-2(a)(3)(i)-(v).
20. See Reg. § 1.174-2(b)(4).
21. U.S. Constitution, Article I, §8, clause 8.
22. 35 USC § 154.
23. 35 USC § 101.
24. 35 USC § 101.
25. 35 USC § 102.
26. 35 USC § 103.

27. 35 USC § 112.
28. *Diamond v. Chakrabarty*, 447 US 303, 308 (1980). ("Congress intended statutory subject matter to 'include anything under the sun that is made by man.'" 447 U.S. at 309, quoting Committee Reports accompanying the Patent Act of 1952).
29. See *O'Reilly v. Morrisey*, 56 US 62 (1854) (attempt to patent electromagnetism).
30. *Funk Brothers Seed Company v. Kalo Inoculant Company*, 333 US 127 (1948) (attempt to patent mixture of naturally occurring strains of bacteria). But see *Association for Molecular Pathology*, 133 S.Ct. 2107 (2013). (Synthetically changed natural phenomena, also called complementary DNA (cDNA) can be patented.)
31. See generally *Chakrabarty*, 447 US at 309.
32. 383 US 519 (1966).
33. *Graham v. John Deere Company*, 383 US 1 (1966).
34. *Id.*, 383 US at 17.
35. 35 USC § 102.
36. See *Amgen, Inc. v. Chugai Pharmaceutical Company*, 927 F2d 1200, 1210 (Federal Circuit 1991).
37. 935 F2d 1555, 1563 (Federal Circuit 1991).
38. *Lockwood v. American Airlines*, 107 F.3d 1565, 1572 (Federal Circuit 1997).
39. *Lockwood v. American Airlines*, 107 F.3d 1565 (1997).
40. *Vas-Cath*, 935 F2d at 1564.
41. 35 U.S.C. 171 and 37 CFR § 1.3.
42. 35 U.S.C. §171.
43. Id.
44. Id.
45. 35 U.S.C. §171, §102.
46. 35 U.S.C. §103.
47. 35 U.S.C. §111-114.
48. 35 U.S.C. §171.
49. *In re Hruby*, 373 F.2d 997 (C.C.P.A. 1967).
50. https://www.uspto.gov/patents-getting-started/patent-basics/types-patent-applications/design-patent-application-guide#differ.
51. *Graham v. John Deer*, 383 U.S. 1 (1966).
52. *Jack Schwartz Shoes, Inc. v. Skechers U.S.A., Inc.*, 233 F. Supp. 2d 512, 538 (S.D.N.Y. 2002).
53. *L.A. Gear, Inc. v. Thom McAn Shoe Co.*, 988 F.2d 1117, 1123 (Fed. Cir. 1993).
54. *In re Carletti*, 328 F.2d 1020, 1022, 140 USPQ 653, 654 (CCPA 1964).
55. Reg. § 1.174-2(a)(1).
56. Rev. Rul. 85-186, 1985-2 CB 84 (research costs previously deducted under IRC Sec. 174 not subject to recapture on later sale of resulting technology).
57. IRC Sec. 174(a).
58. IRC Sec. 174(b).
59. Reg. § 1.174-2(a)(1).
60. Reg. § 1.167(a)-6(a).
61. See Reg. § 1.167(a)-3.
62. See Reg. § 1.167(a)-6.
63. 1979-2 CB 91.
64. IRC Sec. 197(e)(4).
65. IRC Sec. 197(d)(1)(C)(iii).
66. Reg. § 1.197-2(e)(2).
67. See Reg. § 1.197-2(e)(1).
68. IRC Sec. 1235(b).
69. IRC Sec. 1235(b).
70. See Reg. § 1.1235-2(d)(2).
71. See Reg. § 1.1235-2(d)(2).
72. *Id.*
73. IRC Sec. 1235(b)(2)(A) and (B).
74. *C.W. Gilson*, 48 TCM 922, Dec. 41,437(M), TC Memo. 1984-447.
75. IRC Sec. 1235(d).
76. IRC Sec. 1235(d).
77. S. Rep. No. 1622, 83d Cong., 2d Sess. 441 (1954).
78. *C.W. Gilson*, 48 TCM 922, Dec. 41,437(M), TC Memo. 1984-447.
79. *Id.*
80. IRC Sec. 1235(a).
81. Reg. § 1.1235-1(c)(2).
82. See, e.g., *T.H. McClain*, 40 TC 841, Dec. 26,252 (1963), acq. (holding payments to an employee qualified under IRC Sec. 1235, even though the employee had previously executed an assignment of inventions agreement, because the employer intended and agreed to share the benefits of the patent with the employee).
83. See, e.g., *H.S. Lehman*, CA-2, 88-1 USTC ¶ 9107, 835 F2d 431.
84. Reg. § 1.1235-2(b)(1).
85. Reg. § 1.1235-2(b)(1)(i)-(iv).
86. Reg. § 1.1235-2(b)(4).
87. See Reg. § 1.1235-2(b)(2).
88. IRC Sec. 1221.
89. IRC Sec. 1231. See Rev. Rul. 69-482, 1969-2 CB 164.
90. *E.C. Myers*, 6 TC 258, Dec. 14,992 (1946).
91. *National Bread Wrapping Machine Co.*, 30 TC 550, Dec. 23,027 (1958).
92. *V.A. Marco*, 25 TC 544, Dec. 21,388 (1955), acq. (license of the exclusive rights to make, use, and sell a patented invention in the geographic region comprised of the United States west of the Mississippi River); *W.S. Rouverol*, 42 TC 186, Dec. 26,748 (1964, nonacq. (license of exclusive rights to make, use, and sell patented transmission was divided into exclusive rights in multiple fields of use).
93. *Cubic Corp., v. United States.*, 72-1 USTC ¶ 9165 (SD Cal. 1971), *aff'd* 541 F.2d 829 (unpubl.), (9th Cir. 1974), *cert. denied*, 419 U.S. 900, 95 S.Ct. 183, 42 L.Ed.2d 146 (1974); *See also PPG Industries, Inc. v. Commissioner*, 55 TC 928 (1970).
94. *A.G. Eickmeyer*, 86-2 USTC ¶ 9623, 10 Cls. Ct. 598 (citing a commentator suggesting that a one-thousandth undivided interest could qualify).
95. 15 USC § 1051 *et seq.*
96. 15 USC § 1127.
97. IRC Sec. 197(d)(1)(F).
98. H.R. Rep. No. 213, 103rd Cong., 1st Sess. 678 (1993); see Reg. § 1.197-2(e)(2).
99. IRC Sec. 1253(b)(2)(F).
100. IRC Sec. 1253(b)(2)(F).

101. 17 USC §102(a).
102. 17 USC §102(b).
103. 17 USC §320(a).
104. 17 USC § 302(c).
105. IRC Sec. 263A(b)(1).
106. IRC Sec. 263A(b).
107. IRC Sec. 263A(a)(2); see IRC Sec. 167(g)(6),
108. IRC Sec. 263A(h)(2).
109. Reg. § 1.183-2(a).
110. IRC Sec. 183(d).
111. IRC Sec. 1235.
112. For the full story behind NSAI's successful lobbying efforts, see Joseph B. Darby III, "Thank God I'm a Country Boy," Practical US/Domestic Tax Strategies, World Trade Executive, Inc., Vol. 8, No. 2, February 2008.
113. See IRC Sec. 197(e)(4)(C).
114. See Rev. Rul. 79-285, 1979-2 CB 91.
115. IRC Sec. 197(d)(1)(C)(iii).
116. IRC Sec. 197(e)(4).
117. See Reg. §§ 1.197-2(f)(2)(iii) and (3)(iv)(B). See, for example, Reg. § 1.197-2(k) example 9.
118. See Prop. Reg. § 1.167(n)-3.
119. Rev. Rul. 60-226, 1960-1 CB 26, 27.
120. See IRC Sec. 1231(b)(1)(B).
121. Rev. Rul. 60-226; see also Rev. Rul. 54-409, 1954-2 CB 174.
122. IRC Sec. 197(e)(4)(C) and (d)(1)(C)(iii).
123. IRC Sec. 197(f)(7) treats amortization deductions under IRC Sec. 197 as the equivalent of depreciation deductions under IRC Sec. 167, and in turn causes amortization to be subject to the IRC Sec. 1245 recapture rules.
124. See *Irving Berlin Music Corp.*, 487 F2d 540, (1973).
125. See Reg. § 1.61-8.
126. See *ProCD v. Zeidenberg*, 86 F3d 1447 (7th Cir. 1996), rev'g, 908 F.Supp. 640 (W.D. Wis. 1996).
127. IRC Sec. 197(c)(2).
128. H.R. Rept. No. 213, 103d Cong., 1st Sess. 684 (1993); see Reg. § 1.197-2(d)(2)(ii)(A).
129. See IRS Letter Ruling 200236028 (Sept. 6, 2002).
130. See Rev. Rul. 85-186, 1985-2 CB 84 (research costs previously deducted under IRC Sec. 174 not subject to recapture on later sale of resulting technology).
131. Rev. Rul. 85-186, 1985-2 CB 84; note that it is not arguably clear whether expenses deducted under Rev. Proc. 200-50, which is based on the "principles" of IRC Sec. 174, also would be excluded from recapture but the treatment should be the same.
132. Reg. § 1.197-2(g)(7).
133. Reg. § 1.197-2(B)(11).
134. H.R. Rep. No. 213, 103d Cong., 1st Sess. 680 (1993); Reg. § 1.197-2(a)(3) (IRC Sec. 197 does not apply to amounts that are not chargeable to capital account).
135. Reg. § 1.197-2(b)(11) and (c)(4).
136. Reg. § 1.861-18.
137. *Id.*
138. Reg. § 1.861-18(f)(1).
139. *Id.*
140. Reg. § 1.861-18(f)(2).
141. Reg. § 1.861-18(f)(2).
142. IRC Sec. 1221(a)(3).
143. IRC Sec. 1231(b)(1)(C).
144. 64 TCM 534, Dec. 48,432(M), TC Memo. 1992-471 (1992).
145. 1955-2 CB 300.
146. 1962-2 CB 182.
147. 24 TCM 1695, Dec. 27,640(M), TC Memo. 1965-307.
148. 97 TC 445, Dec. 47,711 (1991), *recons. denied*, 63 TCM 1899, Dec. 47,952(M), TC Memo. 1992-45.
149. See Reg. § 1.1221-1(c)(1), which the author believes should be interpreted as setting forth a general rule ("'similar property' includes . . . any other property eligible for copyright protection") and an exception ("does not include a patent or an invention").
150. An early US case upholding trade secret protection is *Vickery v. Welch*, 36 Mass. (19 Pick.) 523, 527 (1837) (recognizing the valuable right to maintain the "art or secret manner of making chocolate").
151. The Economic Espionage Act of 1996 added a certain element of federal legal protection that may be useful in protection trade secrets, especially in cases where state protections are inadequate. See Ernie Linek, A Brief History of Trade Secret Law, Part 2, Bio Process International 2(10):20-26 (November 2004).
152. The Restatement requires that the secret must have been continually used in business in order for protection to apply, whereas the UTSA can apply to secrets which have not yet been used in business.
153. See *Dorel Juvenile Group, Inc. v. DiMartinis*, 495 F.3d 500, 504 (7th Cir. 2007) ("a court may grant an injunction that would stretch beyond the public release of trade secret information in order to prevent a wrongdoer from gaining the advantage of a head start"); Winston Research Corp. v. Minnesota Mining & Mfg. Co., 350 F.2d 134, 144 (9th Cir. 1965) (upheld District Court's grant of limited two year injunction against using trade secret by competitor following improper public disclosure).
154. See *Snow v. Commissioner*, 416 US 500 (1974).
155. See, *e.g.*, *H.J.* Green, 83 TC 667, Dec. 41,596 (1984).
156. See Rev. Rul. 60-358 (1960).
157. See Reg. § 1.167(a)-3.
158. Reg. §174-2(a)(8).
159. See Prop. Reg. § 1.197-2(d)(2).
160. Reg. § 1.197-2.
161. See Rev. Rul. 64-56, 1964-1 CB 133. See also Rev. Rul. 71-564 1971-2 CB 179.
162. Rev. Rul. 85-186 1985-2 CB 84.
163. Reg. § 1.167(a)-14(c)(2)(ii).
164. See Reg. § 1.197-2(f)(2).
165. The legal entity that owns the Boston Red Sox, Fenway Sports Group, LLC, also happens to owns Fenway Park, the iconic home field of the team, and numerous other valuable assets; but many major league baseball teams rent the facility used for home games, and so the core assets of a professional sports "team" as a business are almost entirely contractual, with some trademark

and copyright assets added to the mix (the latter assets being exploited primarily through licensing contracts).

166. See, *e.g.*, *Chandler Trailer Convoy, Inc.*, TC Memo 1973-285, 32 TCM 1372 holding that $25,201.14 spent by petitioner to obtain an ICC nationwide certification was not a deductible business expense under Section 162 but rather a (nondeductible) capital expenditure under IRC Sec. 263.

167. IRC Sec. 197(d)(1)(C)(i).

168. IRC Sec. 197(d)(1)(C)(iv).

169. IRC Sec. 197(d)(1)(C)(v).

170. IRC Sec. 197(d)(1)(D), which is not excluded under IRC Sec. 197(c)(2).

171. Presumably, this distinction between non-government and government contracts arises in part because non-government contracts commonly have a fixed period (albeit sometimes subject to renewal or extension) while a government license or permission (e.g., a liquor license or restaurant license) tends to be perpetual. IRC Sec. 197(d)(1)(D) thus reverses the outcome in Chandler Trailer Convoy, footnoted earlier, in which capitalized costs were non-deductible because the applicable government certification did not have a definite or ascertainable life.

172. Bonds held for investment, like other assets held for investment, do not fall within any of the eight "excluded" categories under IRC Sec. 1221(a), and so they are capital assets.

173. See TAM 200049009 (12/11/2000), examining the meaning of "property."

174. A requirement for long-term capital gain treatment under both IRC Secs. 1222(3) and 1231(b)(1).

175. IRC Sec. 1221 defines all property as being a "capital asset" unless it comes within one of the eight specific exclusions contained in section 1221(a)(1)-(8). One of the most important is the exclusion under 1221(a)(2), for property used in a trade or business and subject to the allowance for depreciation.

176. The term "property used in the trade or business" means property used in the trade or business, of a character which is subject to the allowance for depreciation provided in IRC Sec. 167, held for more than one year and which is not (A) inventory, (B) property held for sale to customers, (C) a copyright or similar "ordinary income" property as defined in IRC Sec. 1221(a)(3), or (D) a publication of the United States Government. See IRC Sec. 1231(b)(1).

177. See the discussion in *James E. Foy*, 84 TC 50 (1985).

178. 304 F.2d 125 (2nd Cir., 1962).

179. 304 F.2d at 130-131.

180. *Ferrer* is just one of many cases in which a court has resorted to the Solomonic wisdom by deciding to "cut the baby in half" *i.e.*, by finding that some contract rights are capital in nature while others are ordinary. See, *e.g.*, *Bisbee-Baldwin Corp. v. Tomlinson*, 320 F.2d 929 (5th Cir. 1963), where it was held that mortgage servicing contracts were a capital asset, but ordinary income treatment applied to the portion of the contract rights that gave the contract owner the right to receive service fees for the remaining years of the underlying mortgage loans. Such bifurcated treatment, of course, merely adds to the sense of confusion in this area.

181. 1 AFTR 2d 1394, 356 U.S. 260 (1958).

182. 1 AFTR 2d at 1397.

183. See also *U.S. v. Maginnis*, 356 F.3d 1179 (9th Cir., 2004) where the court determined that the lump sum payment received by the taxpayer for the sale of his remaining lottery prize winnings was ordinary income and not gain from the sale of a capital asset.

184. See generally the discussion of "property" in TAM 200049009.

185. *Commissioner v. Gillette Motor Co.*, 364 U.S. 130, 134 (1960). In *Gillette*, the court concluded that compensation for temporary seizure of business facilities is ordinary income.

186. 46 TC 559 (1966), acq. 1967-2 CB 2.

187. 46 TC at 569.

188. *Id.*

189. 324 F.2d 56 (5th Cir. 1963).

190. 324 F.2d at 59 [Emphasis in original].

191. 57 TC 15 (1971).

192. 57 TC at 24-25.

193. 61 TC 140 (1973).

194. 61 TC at 148.

195. *Id.*

196. *U.S. v. Dresser Industries*, 324 F.2d at 59 [Emphasis in original.]

197. See the discussion of IRC Sec. 197 and its history in Chapter 11.

198. IRC Sec. 197(d)(1)(C)(i).

199. IRC Sec. 197(d)(1)(C)(iv).

200. IRC Sec. 197(d)(1)(C)(v).

201. See the relevant discussion in Chapter 11.

202. IRC Section 197(e)(4)(B)

203. Reg. § 1.197-2(c)(6)

204. See Reg. § 1.167(a)-14(c)(1)

205. H.R. Rep. No. 213, 103d Cong., 1st Sess. 681 (1993). This example is substantively embodied in Reg. § 1.167(a)-14(c)(1)(ii) and § 1.167(a)-14(c)(2).

206. H.R. Rep. No. 213, 103d Cong., 1st Sess. 681 (1993). This example is substantively embodied in Reg. § 1.167(a)-14(c)(1)(i).

207. Reg. § 1.167(a)-14(c)(3).

INCOME TAX TABLES

APPENDIX A

TAX YEARS BEGINNING IN 2014 AND BEYOND

The American Taxpayer Relief Act of 2012 (ATRA) made the income tax brackets put into place under the Economic Growth and Tax Relief Reconciliation Act (EGTRRA) permanent and added a new top tax bracket for certain high income taxpayers. The permanence of the ATRA provisions eliminated much of the uncertainty faced by taxpayers in previous years.

Under ATRA, for tax years beginning after 2012, individual income tax rates are set at 10 percent, 15 percent, 25 percent, 28 percent, 33 percent, 35 percent and 39.6 percent.

Below are the 2016 and 2017 income tax rate brackets.

Individual 2017 Tax Rates

Taxable Income				
Tax Rate	**Single**	**Married Filing Jointly**	**Married Filing Separately**	**Head of Household**
10%	$0 to $9,325	$0 to $18,650	$0 to $9,325	$0 to $13,350
15%	$9,325–$37,950	$18,650–$75,900	$9,225–$37,950	$13,350–$50,800
25%	$37,950–$91,900	$75,900–$153,100	$37,950–$76,550	$50,800–$131,200
28%	$91,900–$191,650	$153,100–$233,350	$76,550–$116,675	$131,200–$212,500
33%	$191,650–$416,700	$233,350–$416,750	$116,675–$208,350	$212,500–$416,700
35%	$416,700–$418,400	$416,700–$470,700	$208,350–$235,350	$416,700–$444,550
39.6%	Over $418,400	Over $470,700	Over $235,350	Over $444,550

Estates and Trusts 2017 Tax Rates

Taxable Income	
Tax Rate	
15%	$0 to $2,550
25%	$2,550–$6,000
28%	$6,000–$9,150
33%	$9,150–$12,500
39.6%	Over $12,500

Individual 2016 Tax Rates

	Taxable Income			
Tax Rate	**Single**	**Married Filing Jointly**	**Married Filing Separately**	**Head of Household**
10%	$0 to $9,275	$0 to $18,550	$0 to $9,275	$0 to $13,250
15%	$9,275–$37,650	$18,550–$75,300	$9,275–$37,650	$13,250–$50,400
25%	$37,650–$91,150	$75,300–$151,900	$37,650–$75,950	$50,400–$130,150
28%	$91,150–$190,150	$151,900–$231,450	$75,950–$115,725	$130,150–$210,800
33%	$190,150–$413,350	$231,450–$413,350	$115,725–$206,675	$210,800–$413,350
35%	$413,350–$415,050	$413,350–$466,950	$206,675–$233,475	$413,350–$441,000
39.6%	Over $415,050	Over $466,950	Over $233,475	Over $441,000

Estates and Trusts 2016 Tax Rates

Taxable Income	
Tax Rate	
15%	$0 to $2,550
25%	$2,550–$5,950
28%	$5,950–$9,050
33%	$9,050–$12,400
39.6%	Over $12,400

2014 AND 2015 TAX YEARS

Below are the 2014 and 2015 income tax rate brackets.

Individual 2015 Tax Rates

	Taxable Income			
Tax Rate	**Single**	**Married Filing Jointly**	**Married Filing Separately**	**Head of Household**
10%	$0 to $9,225	$0 to $18,450	$0 to $9,225	$0 to $13,150
15%	$9,925–$37,450	$18,450–$74,900	$9,225–$37,450	$13,150–$50,200
25%	$37,450–$90,750	$74,900–$151,200	$37,450–$75,600	$50,200–$129,600
28%	$90,750–$189,300	$151,200–$230,450	$75,600–$115,225	$129,600–$209,850
33%	$189,300–$411,500	$230,450–$411,500	$115,225–$205,750	$209,850–$411,500
35%	$411,500–$413,200	$411,500–$464,850	$205,750–$232,425	$411,500–$439,000
39.6%	Over $413,200	Over $464,850	Over $232,425	Over $439,000

2014 Tax Rates

Tax Rate	Single	Married Filing Jointly	Married Filing Separate	Head of Household
10%	$0–$9,075	$0–$18,150	$0–$9,075	$0–$12,950
15%	$9,075–$36,900	$18,150–$73,800	$9,075–$36,900	$12,950–$49,400
25%	$36,900–$89,350	$73,800–$148,850	$36,900–$74,425	$49,400–$127,550
28%	$89,350–$186,350	$148,850–$226,850	$74,425–$113,425	$127,550–$206,600
33%	$186,350–$405,100	$226,850–$405,100	$113,425–$202,500	$206,600–$405,100
35%	$405,100–$406,750	$405,100–457,600	$202,550–$228,800	$405,100–$432,200
39.6%	$406,750 and up	$457,600 and up	$228,800 and up	$432,200 and up

CORPORATIONS†

(Tax Years Beginning in 2013[1])

Taxable Income			
From	**To**	**The tax is:**	**Of the amount over:**
$0	$50,000	15%	N/A
$50,001	$75,000	$7,500 + 25%	$50,000
$75,001	$100,000	$13,750 + 34%	$75,000
$100,001	$335,000	$22,250 + 39%	$100,000
$335,001	$10,000,000	$113,900 + 34%	$335,000
$10,000,001	$15,000,000	$3,400,000 + 35%	$10,000,000
$15,000,001	$18,333,333	$5,150,000 + 38%	$15,000,000
Over	$18,333,333	35%	

† Personal Service Corporations are taxed at a flat rate of 35%.
[1] IRS Publication 542.

AMT EXEMPTION AMOUNTS, RATES AND PHASE-OUTS

APPENDIX B

AMT Exemption Amounts				
Year	Married Filing Jointly	Single Filers	Married Filing Separate	Estates and Trusts
2017	$84,500	$54,300	$42,250	$24,100
2016	$83,800	$53,900	$41,900	$23,900
2015	$83,400	$53,600	$41,700	$23,800
2014	$82,100	$52,800	$41,050	$23,500
2013	$80,800	$51,900	$40,400	$23,100
2012	$78,750	$50,600	$39,375	$22,500

	Excess Taxable Income Rate of 28% (AMTI)		AMT Phase-out Income Level			
Year	Married Filing Separate	All Other Filers	Single	Married Filing Jointly	Married Filing Separate	Estates and Trusts
2017	$93,900	$187,800	$120,700	$160,900	$80,450	$80,450
2016	$93,150	$186,300	$119,700	$159,700	$79,450	$79,450
2015	$92,700	$185,400	$119,200	$158,900	$79,450	$79,450
2014	$91,250	$182,500	$117,300	$156,500	$78,250	$78,250
2013	$89,750	$179,500	$115,400	$153,900	$76,950	$76,950
2012	$87,500	$175,000	$112,500	$150,000	$75,000	$75,000

CASE TABLE

INDEX

A

B

C

Q

R

U

V

W